# The Mind of Gladstone

# The Mind of Gladstone

## Religion, Homer, and Politics

D. W. BEBBINGTON

OXFORD
UNIVERSITY PRESS

*This book has been printed digitally and produced in a standard specification
in order to ensure its continuing availability*

# OXFORD

UNIVERSITY PRESS

Great Clarendon Street, Oxford OX2 6DP

Oxford University Press is a department of the University of Oxford.
It furthers the University's objective of excellence in research, scholarship,
and education by publishing worldwide in

Oxford New York

Auckland Cape Town Dar es Salaam Hong Kong Karachi
Kuala Lumpur Madrid Melbourne Mexico City Nairobi
New Delhi Shanghai Taipei Toronto
With offices in
Argentina Austria Brazil Chile Czech Republic France Greece
Guatemala Hungary Italy Japan South Korea Poland Portugal
Singapore Switzerland Thailand Turkey Ukraine Vietnam

ISBN 0-19-926765-0

*To the* WARDEN AND STAFF,

*past and present,*

*of* ST DEINIOL'S LIBRARY, HAWARDEN,

*in appreciation*

# Preface

WILLIAM EWART GLADSTONE is a figure of world historical importance because of his achievement as a statesman. He successfully reorganized the taxation of the first modern industrial nation; he suggested far-ranging solutions to the perennial problems of the relationship between Britain and Ireland; he led the Liberal party to victory in three general elections, and after another, despite not having been leader during the election, he was propelled into office because no other premier was conceivable. He was an MP for over sixty years; he was among the greatest of political orators; and he remains the only person to have become Prime Minister after the age of 80. He embodied the spirit of the Victorian House of Commons. Yet this book is not about his political life, concentrating instead on aspects of his intellectual career. It deals with his ideas rather than with his ambitions, manoeuvres, or policies. That task is far easier than it would have been in the past thanks to the publication, completed in 1994, of the statesman's diaries. Recording Gladstone's daily reading, the diaries provide a guide to his assimilation of opinions from elsewhere. They allow the development of Gladstone's views to be traced with far more confidence than before. They show how the mind of the statesman evolved.

The mental world of Gladstone is eminently worth exploring. He wrote copiously, corresponding with many of his contemporaries as well as issuing a plethora of books, pamphlets, and articles. He touched on most aspects of the thinking of the age, but, like most thinkers worth studying, concentrated his efforts in particular fields. As somebody who originally intended ordination in the Church of England, Gladstone was perennially fascinated by questions of religion. He followed the theological debates of the day with unceasing vigilance, often contributing to them himself. As a product of a rigorous classical education, he maintained a lifelong commitment to the study of antiquity. The poet Homer, standing at the beginnings of recorded history, was long the subject of his researches. In the political field, he necessarily often focused on pressing issues of policy, but he also reflected at length on deeper-seated subjects. Whether in private memoranda or in public speeches, he explored issues of political thought, both as a Conservative at the opening of his career and as a Liberal during its flowering. So the central themes of this book are three: religion, Homer, and politics. One of its aims is to show that they were not isolated from each other, but rather intertwined.

It is a pleasure to acknowledge the help of many people and institutions with the project that over many years has given rise to this volume. At the start the late

Colin Matthew encouraged me to take up the enterprise, subsequently offering guidance with unfailing generosity. Sir William Gladstone, the great-grandson of the Prime Minister, kindly gave me access to the books kept in the Temple of Peace, Gladstone's study at Hawarden Castle. They are quoted here by permission of Sir William's son, Charles Gladstone. Sir William's late brother, Peter Gladstone, allowed me to see the family papers at Fasque in Kincardineshire. I am grateful to Pusey House, Oxford, for permission to quote from the Pusey and Scott Papers and to other libraries and archives for the use of their holdings. In particular I want to express my appreciation of the provision for the study of Gladstone at his own foundation, St Deiniol's Library, Hawarden. The wardens, librarians, and other staff, together with the staff of the Flintshire County Record Office, have made it a great pleasure to read the statesman's books and papers there. Peter Francis, the present warden, was good enough to arrange a visiting scholarship. The dedication expresses a little of my debt to the institution. The British Academy awarded me a grant to permit the purchase of a section of the Gladstone Papers at the British Library; it also supported some of my travel expenses, as did the Carnegie Trust for the Universities of Scotland and the Arts Faculty of the University of Stirling. I am very pleased to acknowledge this essential aid.

Several friends have given advice, help with sources, and constructive criticism, sometimes at considerable trouble to themselves: Eugenio Biagini, Ruth Clayton, Peter Erb, Jane Garnett, Emma Macleod, Jim McMillan, Colin Nicolson, Mark Nixon, Alison Peden, and Mike Rapport. Their generosity with their time is much appreciated, though they bear no responsibility for the finished product. Listeners to various papers based on parts of the project have refined it by asking pertinent questions. Members of my course on Gladstone Studies at the University of Stirling over the years often contributed more than they knew, and one of them, Christine Hayter, deserves special thanks for putting her notes on Gladstone's speeches at my disposal. Margaret Hendry, formerly Departmental Assistant in the Department of History, gave her services once more by skilfully typing the text. My wife Eileen and my daughter Anne have visited Gladstonian sites, attended Gladstonian occasions, and pursued Gladstonian themes with forbearance as well as dedication. To them, as ever, I am extremely grateful.

*D W B*

June 2003

# Contents

# Abbreviations

The following abbreviations are used in the notes:

| | |
|---|---|
| *Autobiographica* | *The Prime Ministers' Papers: W. E. Gladstone: 1. Autobiographica*, ed. John Brooke and Mary Sorensen (London, 1971) |
| *CPR* | W. E. Gladstone, *Church Principles considered in their Results* (London, 1840) |
| *D* | *The Gladstone Diaries*, ed. M. R. D. Foot and H. C. G. Matthew, 14 vols. (Oxford, 1968–94) |
| *Gleanings* | W. E. Gladstone, *Gleanings of Past Years, 1843–79*, 7 vols. (London, 1879) |
| GGM | Glynne–Gladstone Manuscripts, Flintshire Record Office, Hawarden |
| GP | Gladstone Papers, British Library, London |
| HSM | Hope-Scott Manuscripts, National Library of Scotland, Edinburgh |
| *IRHS* | W. E. Gladstone, *The Impregnable Rock of Holy Scripture*, revised and enlarged edn. (London, 1890) |
| *JM* | W. E. Gladstone, *Juventus Mundi: The Gods and Men of the Heroic Age* (London, 1869) |
| *Landmarks* | W. E. Gladstone, *Landmarks of Homeric Study* (London, 1890) |
| *Later Gleanings* | W. E. Gladstone, *Later Gleanings* (London, 1897) |
| Lathbury | *Correspondence on Church and Religion of William Ewart Gladstone*, ed. D. C. Lathbury, 2 vols. (London, 1910) |
| Matthew | H. C. G. Matthew, *Gladstone, 1809–1898* (Oxford, 1997) |
| Morley | John Morley, *The Life of William Ewart Gladstone*, 3 vols. (London, 1903) |
| S & P | W. E. Gladstone, 'Speeches and Pamphlets', St Deiniol's Library, Hawarden |
| *SHHA* | W. E. Gladstone, *Studies on Homer and the Homeric Age*, 3 vols (Oxford, 1858) |
| *SRC* | W. E. Gladstone, *The State in its Relations with the Church* (London, 1838) |
| *SRC*, 4th | W. E. Gladstone, *The State in its Relations with the Church*, 4th edn., 2 vols. (London, 1841) |
| *Studies Subsidiary* | W. E. Gladstone, *Studies Subsidiary to the Works of Bishop Butler* (Oxford, 1896) |
| *T* | *The Times* |
| *WJB* | W. E. Gladstone (ed.), *The Works of Joseph Butler, D.C.L.*, 2 vols. (Oxford, 1896) |

# 1

# Introduction

'GENERALLY SPEAKING', declared the preacher in St Paul's Cathedral on Easter Day 1870, '. . . men who write books are unpractical.' The preacher was Henry Parry Liddon, a leading Anglo-Catholic churchman who in the following month was to be installed as a canon of the cathedral. But, he went on, when 'a literary statesman' with applied skills of government does arise, 'it is reasonable to combine the book with the policy of . . . the minister, on the grounds that both are products of a single mind'.[1] The exceptional figure Liddon had in view must surely have been William Ewart Gladstone, then in office as Prime Minister for the first time. Both men were graduates of Christ Church, Oxford, though Liddon was the younger by twenty years. While Gladstone served as MP for the University of Oxford, the churchman was one of his most ardent supporters. When, in 1865, the statesman delivered a lecture on the place of ancient Greece in the providential order as Lord Rector of the University of Edinburgh, Liddon was full of enthusiasm for (as he wrote to a friend) the 'wonderful Rectorial address' showing such a grasp of 'a subject lying altogether apart from the field of his daily work'.[2] In the year before the sermon at St Paul's, Gladstone had published *Juventus Mundi*, the second of his works on Homer. The book was probably in Liddon's mind when, as a canon-elect of the cathedral on Gladstone's own nomination, the churchman expressed his admiration for the ability to unite literary composition with practical statesmanship. Liddon surmised that in these circumstances the writings would sometimes recall the statesman, that 'the public policy of the country will now and then be more intelligible when placed in the light of the known peculiarities of the author'.[3] It is the contention of this book that Liddon was correct. Gladstone's literary output was not just a significant intellectual achievement in its own right but also had a bearing on the central role he played in British politics.

It was a commonplace among Gladstone's contemporaries, especially his supporters, that he took great delight in the life of the mind. According to an anonymous admirer in 1890, he was 'devoted as ardently to scholarship as to

---

[1] H. P. Liddon, *Forty Sermons on Various Subjects preached in the Cathedral Church of St. Paul, London* (London, 1886), p. 10.
[2] J. O. Johnston, *Life and Letters of Henry Parry Liddon, D.D., D.C.L., LL. D.* (London, 1904), pp. 98–9, 91, 99.  [3] Liddon, *Forty Sermons*, p. 11.

politics'.[4] Just after the statesman's death in 1898, his son-in-law Edward Wickham, Dean of Lincoln, went further, claiming that politics gave him no pleasure. 'His heart', Wickham wrote, 'was more in his books and in the questions of theology and philosophy which stirred him deeply.'[5] Certainly Gladstone loved published works. Books, Gladstone declared in a much quoted eulogy, 'are the voices of the dead. They are a main instrument of communication with the vast procession of the other world.'[6] In his early years he was one of the band of men who founded the London Library; in his closing years he created another library, later known as St Deiniol's, in his home parish of Hawarden, with his own collection of 27,000 books as its core.[7] The statesman was himself a prolific author, publishing some two-dozen titles (over and above political speeches) together with a plethora of articles. When in opposition during his later career he would turn out an article virtually every month for the *Contemporary Review*, the *Nineteenth Century*, or the *North American Review*. The writing covered questions of politics, religion, philosophy, literature, and classical studies while touching on related themes in history, science, anthropology, and other fields. It was the verdict of John Morley, Gladstone's first biographer, that he was not a 'great born man of letters like Gibbon, Macaulay, Carlyle'.[8] Yet in his day Gladstone enjoyed an enviable degree of recognition for his standing as a writer. When, in 1883, the *Pall Mall Gazette* asked just over 500 people to specify their choice of the ablest living authors for an imaginary English Academy, Gladstone came as high as thirteenth in virtue of his *Studies on Homer and the Homeric Age* (1858). He stood well below the top four who each received more than 400 votes—Tennyson, Ruskin, Matthew Arnold, and Browning—but, with 107 votes himself, he ranked ahead of W. E. H. Lecky (95), F. W. Farrar (78), J. R. Seeley (62), and Leslie Stephen (55). The result, claimed the newspaper, was 'a fair gauge of literary fame'.[9] Gladstone attained a measure of celebrity in his own day as a scholar.

Yet his writing was far from immune to criticism. Even a contributor to a memorial volume published in the year after Gladstone's death felt bound to concede that he was no master of English prose. Unlike his magnificent speeches, which were brought to life by his personality, Gladstone's writing, the author admitted, was inadequately polished, his sentences ungainly and his meaning obscure.[10] The statesman lacked a natural fluency. While working on one of his earliest books, Gladstone himself reported to his brother-in-law that he went through his labour 'not by a genuine elasticity of spirit but by a plodding

---

[4] 'Mr. Gladstone and the Classics', *Mr. Gladstone in Scotland* (Edinburgh, [1890]), p. 35.

[5] E. C. Wickham, 'Mr. Gladstone as seen from Near at Hand', *Good Words* (July 1898), p. 482.

[6] W. E. Gladstone, 'On Books and the Housing of Them', *Nineteenth Century*, 27 (1890), p. 386.

[7] F. W. Ratcliffe, 'Mr Gladstone, the Librarian, and St Deiniol's Library, Hawarden', in P. J. Jagger (ed.), *Gladstone, Politics and Religion* (London, 1985), pp. 51–2; P. J. Jagger, 'Gladstone and his Library', in id. (ed.), *Gladstone* (London, 1998).

[8] Morley, 1, p. 195.          [9] Cutting from the *Pall Mall Gazette*, 26 Nov. 1883, GGM 1635.

[10] William Tuckwell, 'Mr. Gladstone as a Critic', in Sir Wemyss Reid (ed.), *The Life of William Ewart Gladstone* (London, 1899), p. 469.

movement'.[11] His style, according to one review in the 1870s, was 'diffuse and laboured', a censure that Gladstone took to heart by underlining it.[12] He had little or no style at all, remarked another review of the same period, though he seemed to manage without one. 'Sometimes we have a sentence so long and involved that nothing but a passionate intensity of meaning and a profuse vocabulary could have avoided a disastrous collapse.'[13] The quality of Gladstone's analysis received almost as much condemnation as the pattern of his prose. Like Newman, thought the novelist Mary Ward, Gladstone lacked a critical sense of evidence.[14] The statesman showed the same characteristics, it was said in 1876, in his writing as in his politics: a 'readiness to make sweeping deductions from narrow premises', a 'headstrong and impetuous view of the moment', and an 'unwillingness to believe that any "reasonable mind" can differ from him'.[15] But the sharpest critic was Gladstone's opponent in two controversies towards the end of his career, the scientist T. H. Huxley. Gladstone brought to the discussion of questions in letters or science, according to Huxley, the methods of the politician, 'rhetorical artifices', 'mere dexterity in putting together cleverly ambiguous phrases', and 'the great art of offensive misrepresentation'.[16] Even when allowance has been made for *odium theologicum* and political partisanship, many of these charges stick. It had become second nature for Gladstone to construct passages containing their own potential for spin. The result can be illustrated from a sentence in his book *The Impregnable Rock of Holy Scripture* (1890). 'But this', he wrote, 'I have no doubt is due in part to an enemy very far more powerful than what is called the higher criticism.'[17] On the one hand, the phrases 'I have no doubt' and 'very far' are emphatic, adding authority to the statement; on the other, the words 'in part' and 'what is called' are qualifications, allowing for future modification. The result was built-in complexity. Gladstone's habitual verbal juggling detracted alike from the clarity of his prose and from the power of his argument.

Nevertheless Gladstone's intellectual approach had many conspicuous strengths. They arose not from genius, according to a journalist covering his earlier career, but much more from excellent education and sustained study.[18] His family, as well as his school, encouraged him to nurture a natural inclination towards verbal combat. The consequence, as a political subordinate put it, was that his mind was 'like the steam-hammer, which can either crack nuts, or mould masses of stubborn iron'.[19] A delicate capacity for fine distinctions coexisted with a titanic ability to demolish opponents. Yet, as he justly remarked in correspondence, he had learned to probe the source of differences in human opinions and

---

[11] W. E. Gladstone to Lord Lyttelton, 9 Dec. 1840, GGM 35.

[12] Cutting from the *Globe*, 10 Mar. 1876, p. 6, GGM 1640.

[13] Cutting from the *Athenaeum*, 22 Feb. 1879, p. 241, GGM 1642.

[14] [Mary A.] Ward, *A Writer's Recollections* (London, 1918), p. 239.

[15] Cutting from unidentified source, 18 Mar. 1876, GGM 1640.

[16] T. H. Huxley, 'Illustrations of Mr. Gladstone's Controversial Method', *Nineteenth Century*, 29 (1891), p. 465.    [17] *IRHS*, p. ix.

[18] James Grant, in A. F. Robbins, *The Early Public Life of W. E. Gladstone* (New York, 1894), p. 394.

[19] S[amuel] Laing, *Problems of the Future and Essays* (London, 1889), p. 300.

so had come to take a sympathetic interest in views very different from his own. Although a dogmatist, he was not liable to hard thoughts or hard words about others in speculative matters.[20] 'Even when you differ most', he adjured himself in a private memorandum of 1882, 'be ever eager to learn . . .'[21] His extraordinary volume of reading reveals how fully he took his own advice. He devoured books old and new, congenial and uncongenial, weighty and slight. Daily diary entries record the reading of some 21,000 titles,[22] and that tally is by no means comprehensive because from other evidence it is clear that he absorbed many items that are not recorded. It was rare, even when Gladstone was premier, for a day not to include a bloc of general reading. The range extended far beyond the English language, entailing explorations of Italian (in which he delighted and from which he translated whole volumes) and French (which accounted for nearly 7 per cent of the items listed in the diaries). Although the number of books recorded as read in German was smaller (235 as against some 1,200 in French),[23] its mastery was a crucial accomplishment since it was the language of advanced scholarship in many theological and classical fields. Thus in 1847 Gladstone asked his brother-in-law to obtain for him seven German works relating to Homer from the London Library, and he was still wading through theological tomes in the language over forty years later.[24] Although (as we shall see) Gladstone often had a sharply defined polemical purpose in his scholarly endeavours, he also possessed a catholicity of intellect that delighted in new information on whatever theme. There was therefore a sense in which he showed a remarkably open mind.

Yet there is no doubt that certain authors exercised a disproportionate sway over his intellectual formation. John Morley, Gladstone's first biographer, records that he used to refer to his four 'doctors': Aristotle, Augustine, Dante, and Butler.[25] Aristotle's ethical texts formed the core of the syllabus that Gladstone had studied at Oxford. The Greek philosopher supplied him with a whole array of intellectual tools that he subsequently deployed to analyse politics, theology, and even his feelings for women other than his wife.[26] The opinion of Aristotle could still be cited as settling an issue in Gladstone's last published book of 1896.[27] Next there was Augustine. The greatest of the fathers of the Western Church inspired the dogmatic content of Gladstone's mature religious faith. During the 1830s Gladstone put himself through a sustained examination of Augustine's writings in the original Latin, and, impressed by the theologian's intellect as well as by his emphases, the statesman never subsequently deviated from the substance of

---

[20]  W. E. Gladstone to Harriet Grote, 29 Apr. 1874 (copy), GP 44443, f. 182v.

[21]  GP 44766, f. 49 (7 Apr. 1882).                                      [22]  *D*, 14, p. xi.

[23]  Christiane d'Haussy, 'Gladstone, France and his French Contemporaries', in Peter Francis (ed.), *The Gladstone Umbrella* (Hawarden, Flintshire, 2001), p. 118.

[24]  W. E. Gladstone to Lord Lyttelton, 22 Jan. 1847, GGM 35. W. E. Gladstone to Lord Acton, 7 June 1888; 21 Mar. [sc. 4 Mar.] 1890; 4 Aug. 1891 (copies), GP 44094, ff. 32v, 78–8v, 176.

[25]  Morley, 1, p. 207.

[26]  The last is evident ('myself in regard to you') in his unguarded correspondence with the coquettish Mrs Laura Thistlethwayte: W. E. Gladstone to Laura Thistlethwayte, 21 Oct. 1869, in *D*, 8, p. 566.

[27]  *Studies Subsidiary*, p. 4.

Augustine's teaching.[28] Another Christian writer, but this time a creative artist, was the third doctor. Gladstone became fascinated by the poetry of Dante, and especially his *Paradiso*, from the 1830s onwards, delighting in the mediaeval Florentine's use of language as well as his spiritual vision. The poet, a partisan of the empire against the papacy, confirmed the Catholic, but not Roman Catholic, allegiance of the statesman.[29] Finally there was Bishop Butler. Gladstone encountered the writings of Butler at Oxford, but his enthusiasm for their study was rekindled in the 1840s. Thereafter the statesman regarded the eighteenth-century bishop's apologetic for revealed religion as a model of reasoning technique as well as a decisive vindication of Christian belief. In conversation during the 1890s he would see no force in objections to Butler's case and, as his final publishing enterprise, edited the bishop's works, adding a set of essays defending and applying his subject's line of thought.[30] There were other authors for whom Gladstone professed an almost lifelong devotion—Edmund Burke in politics, for example, or William Palmer in religion—but it was to these four that he constantly turned for stimulus and orientation. Authors from Greek and Latin antiquity, the Christian middle ages, and the Georgian Church of England gave him a thorough grounding in the historical experience of western civilization.

Gladstone once remarked that 'it is but rarely that we can trace the influence exercised by particular books upon particular minds through the medium of actual record'.[31] The statesman himself must stand as one of the most striking exceptions to his own generalization. His diary entries, continuous from 1825 to 1894, allow the student of his mind to identify when, and sometimes to what extent, he read specific works, though rarely specific passages. The annotations by the editors, Michael Foot and Colin Matthew, provide invaluable guidance in identifying the titles, and the index of Gladstone's reading, printed in the final volume of the published diaries, supplies a means of access to individual entries.[32] Beyond the diaries, however, are the actual books that Gladstone read, most of them preserved at St Deiniol's Library or, in a few cases, at his home, Hawarden Castle. The statesman habitually added marginal notes during his reading and compiled an index to specially significant passages at the end of each volume. The symbols used in the marginalia have been more or less understood for some time, and their value has been demonstrated by John Powell.[33] In 2001 Ruth Clayton published Gladstone's own key to the symbols that she had discovered in one of the books at St Deiniol's. It included 'ma' (the Italian for 'but') for reservation, '+'

[28] *Autobiographica*, p. 142.
[29] Owen Chadwick, 'Young Gladstone and Italy', *Journal of Ecclesiastical History*, 30 (1979), repr. in P. J. Jagger (ed.), *Gladstone, Politics and Religion* (London, 1985).
[30] Asa Briggs (ed.), *Gladstone's Boswell: Late Victorian Conversations by L. A. Tollemache and Other Documents* (Brighton, 1984), pp. 41–2, 142–3. *WJB*; *Studies Subsidiary*.
[31] *Studies Subsidiary*, p. 132.
[32] Occasional errors and omissions in the published diaries and index have been recorded in the footnotes of this book whenever they have been noticed.
[33] John Powell, 'Small Marks and Instinctual Responses: A Study in the Uses of Gladstone's Marginalia', *Nineteenth-Century Prose*, 19 (n.d.).

for approbation, 'x' for disapprobation, and 'xx' or even 'xxx' for special disapprobation.[34] The symbols make us aware of Gladstone's initial reactions, revealing something of his anterior state of mind as well as of his view of fresh opinions. Although only a small proportion of the annotations in the Hawarden collections has been examined for the current book, in a few cases they have proved highly revealing. There is almost endless scope for future study of Gladstone's mind within the library he founded at Hawarden.

The books, however, do not exhaust the sources for the statesman's intellectual evolution. As he read a volume, Gladstone would sometimes take detailed notes on the contents, almost page by page. This practice, begun at school and university, was much more common in the early part of Gladstone's career, when he had sufficient time for the task and wished to lay the foundations of his thinking. Most of these manuscripts survive in the Gladstone Papers at the British Library. Although they chiefly contain the marrow of the books, they also include personal reflections. 'Also NB connection of mild manners & light diet', he noted down when first carefully scrutinising the *Iliad* in 1846. 'But beware', he added, 'of rash inferences therefrom.'[35] These analyses of texts are supplemented by essays, some of them lengthy, and brief memoranda, some of them printed in the later volumes of the diaries. Such manuscripts beam a shaft of light into Gladstone's mind: because they were intended for his eyes alone, they capture his authentic convictions. They form, for example, the prime source for his early political thought. Another category of manuscript in the British Library consists of the sermons preached by Gladstone in his capacity as head of household from the 1830s to the 1860s. Although conditioned by the (supposed) spiritual needs of the hearers, they lay bare the speaker's religious assumptions and sometimes his social and psychological premises too. Never previously used, they turn out to reveal the most deep-seated shift in his convictions during the 1850s and 1860s. The body of private manuscript material in the British Library, neglected in comparison with the correspondence that is also there, supplies much of the raw material for the present study. Its relative abundance for the earlier stages of Gladstone's career explains how it is possible to give detailed coverage to the era when his thought was undergoing its most rapid evolution. It also allows the statesman to be evaluated not by what he said in public but by what he thought in private.

There are, however, additional bodies of primary sources over and above Gladstone's published output. Gladstone's vast correspondence (when in office he could dispatch more than 20,000 letters a year) contains a good deal of material relevant to the statesman's intellectual development. Most useful, perhaps, is the exchange of letters in his later years with the polymath Lord Acton, some of which has appeared in print.[36] In Gladstone's earlier years there was an equivalent openness on theological topics with Robert Hope-Scott and Henry Manning,

[34] Ruth Clayton, 'W. E. Gladstone: An Annotation Key', *Notes and Queries*, 246 (2001).

[35] GP 44736, f. 57v (on XIII.5, 6).

[36] J. N. Figgis and R. V. Laurence (eds), *Selections from the Correspondence of the First Lord Acton*, 1 (London, 1917).

whose correspondence with Gladstone, edited by Peter Erb, is about to be published. The Gladstone Papers usually contain the letters Gladstone received rather than those he sent, though copies of important out-letters were sometimes made (as in the Acton correspondence) and occasionally his letters were returned to Gladstone (as in the Manning correspondence). A few other archive collections, including Hope-Scott's and Edward Pusey's, include significant letters written by Gladstone that are not preserved at the British Library. By far the most important cache of manuscripts outside the Gladstone Papers, however, is the collection of Glynne–Gladstone Manuscripts at the Flintshire Record Office, housed in the rectory at Hawarden where Gladstone's brother-in-law Henry Glynne once lived. The family papers are mostly assembled here. They include the most illuminating correspondence on classical themes, the letters sent to another of Gladstone's brothers-in-law, Lord Lyttelton. Here, too, are Gladstone's dossiers of reviews of his own works, some of them with revealing annotations. The statesman's speeches, the finest output of all, have not been ignored for this study, for, as Chapter 9 shows, they constitute by far the best source for the nature of Gladstonian Liberalism as defined by its author. There is nevertheless a wealth of manuscript material, probably unparalleled in quantity for any other major public figure of any land in any century, that lies behind the published output. The approach taken here is to allow Gladstone's personal musings and exchanges of thought with his closest circle to illuminate the man of action. The aim, as it were, is to study Gladstone from the inside out.

He was an independent thinker from an early age, but not from a very early age. There is evidence for the future statesman's opinions while he was still in the sixth form at Eton in a magazine he edited during 1827, *The Eton Miscellany*. Amidst the forced humour and schoolboy self-mockery there are indications of the man that was to be. His concluding words, for example, mount to a high religious seriousness in thanking the Almighty for his blessings.[37] His friends had supposed, when the miscellany began, that he would be able to contribute nothing but Methodist hymns.[38] There is also, however, a candid avowal of ambition, though veiled in an ironical mode, together with a recognition that ambition could best be fulfilled in parliament.[39] Gladstone's political views were still in flux. On the one hand a Whiggish friend, Arthur, the son of the historian Henry Hallam, could taunt him with displaying a 'Cavalier spirit' and devotion to Charles I, king and martyr, but on the other Gladstone claimed to be 'no party man' and in 1826 expressed doubts about the plans of the Tory administration.[40] His chief fixed point was allegiance to George Canning, his father's patron and

---

[37] 'Bartholomew Bouverie', *Eton Miscellany*, 2 (1827), pp. 263–4.
[38] A. H. Hallam to W. W. Farr [17 July 1827], in Jack Kolb (ed.), *The Letters of Arthur Henry Hallam* (Columbus, Ohio, 1981), p. 155.
[39] *Eton Miscellany*, 2, pp. 146, 109.
[40] A. H. Hallam to W. E. Gladstone [31 Dec. 1826]; Hallam to Gladstone [8 Jan. 1827], [13 Aug. 1827]; Hallam to W. W. Farr [20 Sept. 1826], [28 September 1826], in Kolb (ed.), *Letters of Hallam*, pp. 108, 109, 115–16, 164, 81, 87.

Prime Minister briefly in 1827: 'Distant from all extremes—firm in principle, and conciliatory in action—the friend of Improvement, and the enemy of Innovation ...'[41] Canning inspired a plastic liberal Toryism capable of being moulded into almost any shape. On cultural issues Gladstone expressed respect for Homer, though (unlike in later years) doubting whether he was the real or sole author of the *Iliad*; he airily dismissed Aristotle, Plato, and Cicero as the authors of 'vague and futile systems' in a way that would later have horrified him; and he reached the conventional judgement that Newton, Shakespeare, and Milton were unrivalled in the history of the world.[42] Literature, with the encouragement of Hallam, was a major preoccupation, though Gladstone never felt he thoroughly understood or appreciated a poem until he had discussed it with his friend.[43] To the end of his days Gladstone recalled Hallam's moral character and mental powers with deferential admiration.[44] While at Eton the young Gladstone was already preoccupied with religion, politics, and broader cultural questions, but, not surprisingly, he had attained few settled convictions of his own. It was only after leaving school that he developed a personal standpoint. For that reason the study of his mind that follows begins with his undergraduate career at Oxford from 1828 to 1831.

The literary interests kindled at school, however, never deserted him. He toyed with writing English verse and contributed reviews of novels to the monthlies until late in life. He read the latest fiction, often judging it severely. Thus he condemned Elizabeth Gaskell's *Cranford* as 'actionless' and pronounced George Eliot's novels to be lacking in harmony because absurd people married one another.[45] His warmest appreciation was reserved for Sir Walter Scott, whose only fault, he claimed, had been to write too much. Scott possessed the 'power of reviving antiquity' and an ability to draw character that ranked him third in world literature, behind only Homer and Shakespeare.[46] Gladstone enthused over Scott's *Woodstock* while at school and in 1895 was still eulogizing 'the immortal works of Sir Walter Scott'.[47] The Scottish novelist, as we shall see, exercised sufficient sway over Gladstone's imagination to affect his analysis of Homer.[48] No other literary figure—apart from Homer himself together with Dante—achieved a comparable feat in influencing his deeper convictions. In modern poetry Gladstone placed Wordsworth firmly below Tennyson,[49] on whom he wrote a eulogistic article in the *Quarterly Review*. The statesman very reasonably isolated for special praise Tennyson's gift of drawing on nature for illustrations, but also admired his feeling for beauty, harmony, motion, light, and colour as well as his

---

[41] *Eton Miscellany*, 2, p. 64.                                    [42] Ibid., pp. 7, 57, 62.

[43] [W. E. Gladstone] to Henry Hallam, 12 Apr. 1834, in *Remains in Verse and Prose of Arthur Henry Hallam* (London, 1863), p. xxxiv.

[44] W. E. Gladstone, *Arthur Henry Hallam* (Boston, Mass., 1898), pp. 7–10.

[45] *D*, 7 Oct. 1856; Briggs (ed.), *Gladstone's Boswell*, p. 47.

[46] Speech at Hawarden, 3 Feb. 1868, in cutting from *Chester Courant*, in 'Speeches and Writings', St Deiniol's Library, Hawarden.

[47] A. H. Hallam to J. M. Gaskell, 23 Aug. 1826, in Kolb (ed.), *Letters of Hallam*, p. 68. *T*, 16 Apr. 1895, p. 10.        [48] See Ch. 6, pp. 150–1.        [49] Briggs (ed.), *Gladstone's Boswell*, p. 125.

mastery of language. If Tennyson could maintain the level of 'Guinevere' for the entire cycle of *The Idylls of the King*, Gladstone wrote on its appearance in 1859, the work as a whole would be 'by far the greatest poetical creation, that, whether in our own or in foreign poetry, the nineteenth century has produced'. Tennyson, however, was not a seminal force in Gladstone's world of ideas. The contemporary poet's standards are judged by reference to Homer and Dante, the true arbiters of taste. In terms of values, *The Idylls* were 'national', 'Christian', 'human', and 'universal'—qualities that Gladstone looked for in Tennyson because other sources had taught him to prize them.[50] It is true that the statesman's continuing fascination with literature did more than satisfy his capacity for flights of fancy since he warmed to its intellectual content when, but only when, it harmonized with his existing way of thinking. He would have had no time for Tennyson, as he had little for Milton, if the poet had espoused principles contrary to those Gladstone professed. Even Tennyson, however, like all other modern imaginative writers other than Scott, exercised virtually no creative role in his thought. Although Homer and Dante were in an exceptional category, generally literature was a mirror rather than a motor of his mind. It therefore receives only incidental attention in these pages.

The same is true of many other facets of Gladstone's mental world. His massive three-volume *Studies on Homer* reveals an engaging intellectual curiosity: anthropology and etymology are central to volume 1; the second volume concentrates on mythology; the third deals, among other topics, with geography, aesthetics, and colour theory. As fellow-guests discovered at dinner parties, Gladstone was a ready speaker on almost any subject. Yet his conversation tended to concentrate on how the themes were handled by Homer or how they impinged on his other central concerns. Marcia Pointon has shown how Gladstone's artistic taste was far from random but instead was moulded by his religion and his love for Dante.[51] Likewise in music, an interest he shared with his wife Catherine, Gladstone was most attracted by compositions for the liturgy. His taste was formed by the reinvigoration of Anglican worship in the wake of the Oxford movement.[52] Gladstone monitored the spread of choral singing in parish churches, insisting that every syllable should be as plainly audible as if the words were spoken.[53] He held strong opinions on the subject because the welfare of true religion was at stake. Similarly on questions of education, his principal preoccupations were with how changes would impinge on the Church of England or else with how much attention was being paid to Homer, Butler, and the Italian language. Other issues that, like education, became subjects for legislation took up a great deal of his reading time. Railways, protective tariffs, and Irish land tenure necessarily became the focus of his attention for protracted periods. Yet these topics, and even the political economy that underlay his attitude to each of them, are not the theme of what

[50] W. E. Gladstone, 'Tennyson' [1859], *Gleanings*, 2, pp. 171, 174, 153.

[51] Marcia Pointon, 'Gladstone as Art Patron and Collector', *Victorian Studies*, 19 (1975).

[52] See Ch. 4, p. 82.      [53] GP 44776, ff. 16–20 (7 Jan. 1894), in *D*.

follows here. The subjects examined in this book are those on which he lavished as much leisure time as he could spare from public life, the ones that conditioned his stance towards art, music, education, or political economy. The areas for consideration here are the fields of study that clustered round his fundamental values.

These subjects are essentially three: political theory, theology, and classical studies. Each branched out into a variety of related disciplines, and Gladstone would sometimes pursue these adjacent studies with single-minded rigour, but these three alone remained the core of his intellectual concerns. To awed observers he might appear superbly informed on almost any issue, but he realized that, in the nineteenth century, mental resources had to be carefully husbanded. Leibniz in the seventeenth century, he once observed, had been the last man of encyclopedic learning; now was the day of specialism.[54] Naturally he spent time in examining the foundations of his own profession, the issues raised in political theory. Early in his career he devoted painstaking study to authors ancient and modern who discussed public affairs from a philosophical standpoint. He even wrote a book, *The State in its Relations with the Church*, which was conceived as a contribution to political science. Although in later years he was more cautious about addressing similar theoretical topics in print, he continued to take notes and reflect on them. His public speeches contain far more than is usually noticed of an abstract nature. But the statesman never lost the conviction that nearly drove him from Oxford into the Christian ministry, the belief that eternal issues were ultimately far more important than temporal affairs. His second work, though he was well embarked on a career in politics, was on *Church Principles considered in their Results* (1840); a plethora of theological articles followed; and he devoted a great deal of energy during his last three decades to defending Christian orthodoxy against hostile assailants. The study of divinity was ever a favourite pastime. Yet, like many another Victorian gentleman, the statesman also spent vacant hours translating classical verse; and he published two volumes of the results, one jointly with Lord Lyttelton. From the 1850s onwards, however, his classical scholarship concentrated on the earliest of Greek poets, Homer. Gladstone devoted five separate books and over two-dozen articles to Homeric studies. The statesman's stance could therefore be summed up by a former subordinate as 'ecclesiastically-minded and Homerically-minded'.[55] Politics, theology, and the classics formed the trio of his intellectual priorities.

Gladstone's thought has not received the attention it deserves. Biographers (with some exceptions) have usually concentrated on the statesman's public career, relegating his ideas to the margins unless they demonstrably impinged on his policies. This remains true, for example, of Roy Jenkins's admirable recent study of a politician by a politician.[56] In one sense the biographers are right: in a

[54] Gladstone, 'On Books', p. 386.
[55] S[amuel] Laing, *Modern Science and Modern Thought* (London, 1886), p. 322.
[56] Roy Jenkins, *Gladstone* (London, 1995).

world-historical perspective what Gladstone did as Prime Minister matters more than what he thought of Homer. Yet the ideas of so scholarly a man warrant examination in their own right; and the suggestion of Liddon that there is an affinity between his writings and his politics is pre-eminently worthy of investigation. The neglect of Gladstone's mind, however, has been by no means total. Sidney Checkland has touched on the young man's intellectual development down to 1851 in the context of his family history.[57] Peter Jagger has examined his earliest religious evolution and Perry Butler has pursued the task over a longer period, shedding light on the germination of Gladstone's first two books.[58] Richard Helmstadter has helpfully discussed *The State in its Relations with the Church* and Agatha Ramm has analysed Gladstone's early Aristotelian cast of mind.[59] In another article Agatha Ramm has vindicated Gladstone's right to be treated as a man of letters.[60] The statesman's Homeric studies have been scrutinized by Hugh Lloyd-Jones and Frank M. Turner.[61] Deryck Schreuder has written a synoptic essay on Gladstone's religion and his politics, while Boyd Hilton, in two stimulating accounts, has proposed a specific relationship between the two that the present book will aim to evaluate.[62] Most telling, however, is the treatment of the statesman's ideas by Colin Matthew, the editor of *The Gladstone Diaries*. Because he explored the manuscript sources as well as the diaries far more thoroughly than any previous scholar, Matthew was able to offer a more rounded picture of Gladstone's worldview.[63] Yet in his study of the man and statesman, even Matthew was not concentrating on the thinker. Much remains to be done in uncovering the structure and development of Gladstone's ideas.

A beginning is made in this book. Far more could be achieved in the elucidation of almost any aspect of Gladstone's thought, and, now that the published diaries are available, it is to be expected that study of the statesman's cultural significance will flourish as never before. For the time being, however, this volume tries to establish some preliminary parameters. It is offered not as an intellectual biography, which would be a far more massive undertaking, but as a

[57] S. G. Checkland, *The Gladstones: A Family Biography, 1764–1851* (Cambridge, 1971).

[58] P. J. Jagger, *Gladstone: The Making of a Christian Politician: The Personal Religious Life and Development of William Ewart Gladstone, 1809–1832* (Allison Park, Penn., 1991); Perry Butler, *Gladstone: Church, State and Tractarianism: A Study of his Religious Ideas and Attitudes, 1809–1859* (Oxford, 1982).

[59] R. J. Helmstadter, 'Conscience and Politics: Gladstone's First Book', in B. L. Kinzer (ed.), *The Gladstonian Turn of Mind: Essays presented to J. B. Conacher* (Toronto, 1985); Agatha Ramm, 'Gladstone's Religion', *Historical Journal*, 28 (1985).

[60] Agatha Ramm, 'Gladstone as Man of Letters', *Nineteenth-Century Prose*, 17 (1989–90).

[61] Hugh Lloyd-Jones, 'Gladstone on Homer', *Times Literary Supplement*, 3 Jan. 1975, pp. 15–17, repr. in Lloyd-Jones, *Blood for the Ghosts* (London, 1982); F. M. Turner, *The Greek Heritage in Victorian Britain* (New Haven, Conn., 1981), 159–70, 236–44.

[62] D. M. Schreuder, 'Gladstone and the Conscience of the State', in P. T. Marsh (ed.), *The Conscience of the Victorian State* (Hassocks, Sussex, 1979); Boyd Hilton, 'Gladstone's Theological Politics', in Michael Bentley and John Stevenson (eds), *High and Low Politics in Modern Britain* (Oxford, 1981); Boyd Hilton, *The Age of Atonement: The Influence of Evangelicalism on Social and Economic Thought, 1785–1865* (Oxford, 1988), ch. 9.

[63] The introductions to the diary volumes were consolidated, with minor revisions, in Matthew.

case-study in the evolution of Gladstone's thinking, though one that concentrates on what was most important to the statesman himself. In Chapter 2 there is an analysis of Gladstone's early political thought that examines not only the content but also the sources of his highly intellectual version of Conservatism. Chapters 3 to 5 turn to the statesman's theology. They scrutinize how he left behind his early evangelicalism, transferring his allegiance to a personal form of Orthodox High Churchmanship before moving on again into Tractarianism. Subsequently, without repudiating his High Churchmanship, he continued his pilgrimage in a Broad Church direction. Chapters 6 and 7 explore another field, Gladstone's study of Homer, his chief scholarly preoccupation in later life. There is discussion of the reasons for his engagement with the Greek poet before an analysis of how his views on what he called Homerology changed over time. Then, in Chapter 8, there is an examination of Gladstone's part in the debates surrounding the Victorian crisis of faith. The coverage returns in Chapter 9 to political thought with a dissection of the type of Liberalism that Gladstone purveyed as leader of the party. There the broader significance of his religious and classical studies for public affairs comes more fully to light. Pivotal concepts derived from these sources turn out to have become organizing principles of the Liberal message he brought to the masses. Gladstonian Liberalism, as a body of ideas, was profoundly indebted to the classical texts and ecclesiastical concerns on which Gladstone lavished so much of his time; and it was rooted in the particular understanding of the human condition that Gladstone took from his theological and Homeric investigations. The resulting amalgam enjoyed enormous appeal in Gladstone's own day, but also had affinities with much of the progressive political thinking of the earlier twentieth century. Gladstone's mind shows him to have been a man who drew deeply from the wells of western civilisation and then passed on an influential set of political ideals to the future.

# 2

# The Foundations of Gladstonian Conservatism

ON TUESDAY 17 May 1831 the young Gladstone, then in his final year as an undergraduate at Christ Church, addressed the Oxford Union Society for three-quarters of an hour. The Reform Bill was the all-absorbing question of the moment, the central issue of the current general election. Gladstone passionately denounced the bill, ensuring the triumph of the anti-reforming cause in the debate. It was, according to one of his hearers, 'the most splendid speech, out and out, that was ever heard in our Society'.[1] Gladstone's draft for the occasion survives and, though no doubt he did not adhere slavishly to the text, it indicates the opinions that so electrified his audience. He condemned the press, 'which I do not hesitate to call diabolical', for stirring up popular feeling; he called on the peers to 'stand upon the lofty ground of the Constitution' and resist so revolutionary a measure. He appealed to the tradition of Pitt, Burke, Windham, Perceval, and Canning; and he warned against destroying the existing balance of constitutional forces. But his speech was not merely an echo of the rhetoric unleashed against reform during the parliamentary election. Its power lay in the invocation of theoretical premises for the practical case. The principle of government, he contended, was subordination.

Human *will* [he went on] therefore has nothing whatever to do with the foundation of government—it can never establish nor overthrow its legitimacy—divine will alone is its ground—and as to human opinion, it is only valuable and deserving of regard in exact proportion as it is calculated, from the virtue and ability of those who hold it, to embody and develope [*sic*] those eternal laws which alone are the source of authority, and which alone propose to us the objects of true and legitimate obedience.[2]

Here is a broad assault on contemporary assertions about the will of the people, a claim that power should be wielded only by a qualified elite and a summons to conform to the dictates of natural law. Gladstone was laying ideological foundations for continued resistance to reform. It is little wonder that this speech won him the patronage of the most stalwart of reactionaries, the Duke of Newcastle, and consequently an entrée to the House of Commons.

[1] Charles Wordsworth, *Annals of My Early Life, 1806–1846* (London, 1891), p. 85.
[2] GP 44721, ff. 23–34 (n.d.), quoted at ff. 25, 27v, 24v.

Yet Gladstone was not naturally intransigent. His youthful politics had been shaped by George Canning, the name standing last in the list of authorities to whom he appealed in the Oxford debate. He had prepared for the occasion by reading up Canning's speeches against reform and his notes contain a series of quotations from the same statesman supporting the existing limited monarchy of the United Kingdom.[3] Canning, Gladstone was to admit in the 1860s, had misled him into resistance to reform.[4] Although the statesman had died in 1827, only three months after achieving the premiership, he remained the young man's political hero. Gladstone's father, the merchant John Gladstone, had installed Canning as MP for Liverpool in 1812 and William enjoyed personal contact with him. Even though John Gladstone's enthusiasm for Canning had waned after 1822, when he abandoned Liverpool and became Foreign Secretary, William persisted in idolizing the statesman. On Canning's death William eulogized him in the Eton literary magazine and went on pilgrimage to his hero's tomb in Westminster Abbey.[5] If on parliamentary reform the statesman stood with the opponents of change, in general Canning was no reactionary. He was recognized during the 1820s, in fact, as the leader of the more enlightened section of Lord Liverpool's cabinet. His foreign policy was directed not to the maintenance of the existing order but towards national self-determination in Greece and South America. Although his stance differed less from that of his predecessor Lord Castlereagh than has sometimes been supposed, circumstances allowed his overseas measures to take on a distinctly liberal tinge. Likewise he favoured the relaxation of the corn laws and the introduction of Catholic emancipation.[6] The prevailing influence over Gladstone's earliest politics was therefore—with the single exception of parliamentary reform—a definitely progressive version of Toryism.

At Oxford, however, Gladstone began the quest for political axioms that he could make his own. The 'business of the true statesman', he planned to declare in the peroration of his anti-reforming diatribe at the Union, 'is to look to the *principles* established by God for the wellbeing of the nations and with those principles to live or die'.[7] Religion, youthful idealism, the classical curriculum, and a temperamental desire to penetrate to the heart of things alike drove him to establish the intellectual groundwork for questions of policy. He was by nature, if not a political philosopher, then a political theorist. He ransacked likely sources for guidance. Thus, for instance, in September 1831 he read *The Principles of Moral Philosophy investigated and applied to the Constitution of Civil Society* (1789), by the evangelical clergyman Thomas Gisborne. Perhaps, he hoped, a work grounding politics in ethics and religion might yield gems of wisdom, but he was disappointed. The book, written by the father of a Whig MP, turned out to teach that

---

[3] *D*, 16 May 1831. GP 44721, ff. 38–9 (n.d.).                                    [4] Morley, 1, p. 70.
[5] S. G. Checkland, *The Gladstones: A Family Biography, 1764–1851* (Cambridge, 1971), p. 159. Morley, 1, p. 39.
[6] Wendy Hinde, *George Canning* (London, 1973); Peter Dixon, *Canning: Politician and Statesman* (London, 1976).                                    [7] GP 44721, f. 34v.

the foundation of civil government lay in the consent of the governed, and so was pronounced 'wishy washy'.[8] Such deference to the popular will held no attractions for an opponent of parliamentary reform. What was needed was some way of relating the detail of politics to 'the great *purpose of our being*'.[9] During his years at Oxford from 1828 to 1831 and over the ensuing decade, while serving in parliament, Gladstone set about the task of exploring the field for himself. Intensive reading, careful note-taking, and the arduous composition of dissertations— usually for nobody but himself—enabled him to formulate a coherent understanding of society and politics. The memoranda and essays survive in the Gladstone Papers, and so it is possible to reconstruct the political theory with which the young man set out on his parliamentary career. It reveals the basis for such confident statements as the Oxford Union denunciation of reform.


I


Exactly a week after the Union speech, while planning a university petition against the Reform Bill, Gladstone began a paper 'On the principle of Government'. Its first part was delivered to his small circle of friends at the Essay Society on Saturday 28 May 1831; the second part, on the grounds of political obedience, was written between 31 May and 6 June.[10] This document deserves to be recognized as the fullest statement of Gladstone's political thought—strictly defined—not only during his undergraduate years but also in his whole period as a Conservative. Indeed there is no composition from any point in his career that matches this essay as a sustained exposition of the ideas underlying his political position. In many respects, furthermore, Gladstone adhered to the premises outlined here until the end of his days. The continuity is symbolized by the maxim of Lord Bacon with which the paper opens: 'civil knowledge is conversant about a subject which of all others is most immersed in matter, and hardliest reduced to axiom.'[11] Gladstone was to quote the same dictum frequently; and it recurs in his *Studies Subsidiary to the Works of Bishop Butler*, published only two years before his death.[12] Throughout his long life he was aware of the difficulty of achieving what he here attempted, the setting out of the basic axioms on which his public life was predicated. Because it represents his earliest exercise in systematic political thought, and also because many of its ideas were to be strangely persistent, the essay 'On the principle of Government' is worthy of close analysis.

'In the first place', he writes, 'let it be laid down, that a state of graduated subordination is the natural law of humanity.'[13] The word 'graduated' has been inserted in the manuscript after its original composition, no doubt to make the stark principle more palatable. But graduation, the notion that there are many

[8] GP 44812, f. 195v (n.d.). *D*, 5 Sept. 1831.  [9] GP 44820, f. 61 (n.d.: 1833?).
[10] GP 44721, ff. 1–17 ('1830 or 31' in later hand by Gladstone). *D*, 25 May–6 June 1831.
[11] GP 44721, f. 3.      [12] *Studies Subsidiary*, p. 6.      [13] GP 44721, f. 4.

degrees of power, is not part of Gladstone's essential case. Rather he is eager to assert the 'law of subordination' against its detractors, the egalitarian school. William Godwin, whose *Enquiry concerning Political Justice* (1793) was an exposition of advanced Whig levelling ideas, might have been in Gladstone's mind, and he does treat Godwin as an antagonist in a later manuscript of 1831, but the reference to those 'who look upon universal equality as the state to be desired' is deliberately comprehensive.[14] Egalitarianism, so much the ideological fruit of the French Revolution, was to remain as hateful to Gladstone as it was to Thomas Malthus, whose entire theory was originally designed as a rebuttal of Godwin.[15] There is no sign, however, of any direct Malthusian influence over Gladstone's mind, either at this stage or later. Rather, his source is, in the first place, the broad tradition associated with the theme of the Great Chain of Being. He argues that the principle of subordination may be inferred from 'the analogy of the universe'. The whole cosmos, 'infinitely divisible into parts from its ruler downwards', is organized so that each part is dependent on the part above it in the structure, and so ultimately dependent on the Almighty.[16] Why, he asks, should human society be any different? The rejection of equality as an ideal is rooted in an ancient vision of a ranked world order.

Gladstone, however, goes on to provide a second, and to his mind, more conclusive, rationale for the natural inequality of humanity. Egalitarians, he concludes, 'found their notions of the origin of government in the corruption of man's nature which renders coercion necessary'.[17] The entrusting of power to the rulers, on this view, is a remedy for the sinfulness of human beings after the Fall as, for example, in Augustine's *City of God*. To a limited extent Gladstone, though he had not yet read Augustine, agrees.[18] Law, what the young politician calls 'positive coercion', exists in the contemporary fallen world in order to restrain evil human inclinations. Nobody doubts, he claims, that there is a need for government in the present state of humanity. But government is essential for the welfare of society whether or not mankind is fallen. In the original human condition before the Fall there must have been what he calls 'negative coercion'. The state of innocence was a state of probation in which will was exercised; will had to be disciplined and so restrained. 'To some hands therefore duly authorised the power of maintaining and proportioning these restraints must have been committed—or, to vary the form of the proposition, government must have been divinely ordained.' The need for government went back to the garden of Eden. It was a gift of God to human beings in their ideal state, not merely a curb for the consequences of their sin. 'Some then are to rule, others to obey.'[19] If the reasoning possessed an antique flavour, the lesson for potentially revolutionary times was uncompromising.

---

[14] GP 44721, f. 16. The diaries do not indicate whether he read Godwin, the reference to whom is in 'Essay in the Schools', GP 44812, f. 64v (16 Nov. 1831).

[15] T. R. Malthus, *An Essay on the Principle of Population* (London, 1798), esp. ch. 10.

[16] GP 44721, f. 4.                                                                                    [17] Ibid., f. 16.

[18] There is no reference to *The City of God* in the diaries until 11 October 1835.

[19] GP 44721, ff. 2, 4.

The same conclusion could be reached by a different route. Gladstone specu-
lates as much about 'the ultimate state of man' as about 'the original state of man'.
Like many other early nineteenth-century thinkers, he seems to envisage a future
millennial state on earth in which human beings enjoy a carefree existence under
the immediate authority of the Almighty.[20] Coercion, whether positive or negative, will be superfluous because people will be activated by what Gladstone calls
'self government'. Good habits will have so developed that human beings will
spontaneously fulfil the divine purposes. There will be (here Gladstone quotes
Coleridge) 'the highest form of freedom' in which the will of individuals will be
totally reconciled with the commandments of God. In this idyllic state 'the causes
of our moral derangement are removed', the Fall is reversed:

we shall return again to a close analogy with the spirit and harmony of those combinations
whereof the universe is composed—each family under its head—each nation under its
King, supreme in matters both temporal and spiritual—no desire of power on the one
hand except as subject, derived from and dependent upon the national head—and on the
other no cravings of lust nor excesses of tyranny or violence, but a simple and sincere desire
to administer the resources of the state in such a manner as shall best conduce to the
general good . . . [21]

Gladstone readily concedes that this utopian vision is 'only airy speculation', but
asserts that different estimates of the eventual goal of history sharply divide political thinkers. Here he is entirely right. For the egalitarians behind the French
Revolution such as Condorcet or Volney, the ideal society would do away with the
authority of one person over another, but for Gladstone and other traditionalists
political subordination would be an enduring feature of the ideal society. Analysis
of the eventual future as much as of the remotest past showed that government
was not a temporary palliative but a correlate of essential human nature. The
imposition of order from above was not an evil to be minimized but a good to be
respected.

Conversely freedom from restraint was not to be sought for its own sake. Some
would object in the name of liberty, Gladstone suggests, to the entire notion of
coercion by government, but 'freedom relatively to us is by no means an absolute
and necessary good'. Freedom is a morally neutral idea, capable of being used for
good or evil. All depended on the purpose: in the hands of a bad man, the freedom to act would be misused. Restraint was therefore undesirable only when it
prevented obedience to the universal rules of right conduct laid down by the
Almighty. When it obstructed the wicked in their ways it was necessary for the
public welfare. So it was right that freedom, the capacity for self-government,
should be abridged in the name of the moral law. It was 'the prevailing error of all
times, and particularly of the present ones, that men are looking at the power of
self-government as intrinsically a good'. Whigs, radicals, and reformers were
committing precisely that error. Concerning self-government, enlarging liberty

---

[20] J. F. C. Harrison, *The Second Coming: Popular Millenarianism, 1780–1850* (London, 1979).
[21] GP 44721, ff. 2, 4, 16.

was an unsafe rule in the circumstances of 1831: 'as a guide in framing or modify-
ing a Constitution, the right principle seems to me to be, not to give as much
political liberty to the subjects as can be conceded compatibly with the maintenance of public order, but as little.'[22] By the time he was Liberal leader, such sentiments about liberty were the youthful follies that Gladstone most regretted; but
the anti-reformer of 1831 held a reasoned view of the subject, not merely a prejudice. Freedom, he believed, should not be pursued as an end in itself.

It was certainly wrong, in Gladstone's view, to advocate greater freedom on the
ground that the people desired it. The popular sovereignty associated with the
French Revolution was anathema to him. Although he probably did not read *The
Social Contract* until August of the same year (he inserted in the manuscript 'On
the principle of Government', no doubt at this time, a quotation from the
book),[23] the case of such writers as Rousseau that power belongs to the people
seemed to Gladstone the epitome of political falsehood. Authority, he supposed,
descended from heaven; it did not arise from the people. Gladstone treats the
notion that the will of the people forms the basis for political obligation as the
antithesis of his own theory of legitimacy. Even if the popular will had originally
constituted the government, he argues, it would not necessarily follow that it
should direct the government in the present. If, *a fortiori*, the popular will had not
founded the government, it had no moral right to direct it. As a matter of fact, it
was not the case that the people, claiming sovereignty, had set up the institutions
of state: 'it is historically untrue', he points out, 'that existing governments
emanated from popular will.'[24] The appeal to history seemed to settle the question. The mass of the people had no intrinsic authority. In his antagonism to
popular sovereignty Gladstone was aligning himself with such French reactionaries as Joseph de Maistre, whose main writings, however, exercised no influence
over him because they were not published until long afterwards, and for whose
papal absolutism he was to show no sympathy whatsoever.[25] Nevertheless, as
much as de Maistre, Gladstone felt himself to be defending the God-given
European order whose foundations had been rocked by the French Revolution.

One of Gladstone's methods, however, was to suggest that the idea of popular
sovereignty was alien to England. Even the Whig tradition had repudiated it. What
was the doctrine of the architects of the Glorious Revolution of 1688? They held that
the people had bound themselves to their rulers by an original compact. While
reserving to themselves the rights and liberties of the subjects, they had entrusted
authority to others. Magna Carta and other bulwarks of the people's liberties were
conceived as cases of return to the first scheme of government, not as new assertions

---

[22] GP 44721, ff. 6, 8, 16.
[23] *D*, 13 Aug. 1831. GP 44721, f. 4v. The insertion, which is actually an approving reference to
Rousseau's high views of the family, is made in a different ink.                    [24] GP 44721, ff. 11, 14.
[25] W. E. Gladstone, 'Catholic Interests in the Nineteenth Century', *Quarterly Review*, 92 (1852),
p. 151. Of de Maistre's works, Gladstone records having read only *Du Pape* (1819), an expression of
extreme ultramontanism: *D*, 23 Mar. 1845. For de Maistre, see Jack Lively, *The Works of Joseph de
Maistre* (London, 1965).

of the popular will. Ignoring the implication that the people must originally have enjoyed the sovereignty they had conferred on their rulers, Gladstone held that 'those truly great and admirable men, the Whigs of eighty eight', had given no sanction whatever to the supposition that power flowed from the people. 'They held that under this compact the King was to be regarded as the fountain of authority and as possessing this office altogether independently of any variations in the inclinations of the subjects.' Their rule was non-resistance to the monarch in ordinary circumstances; only when he infringed the compact could measures be taken against him. Such were the views, for instance, of Sir Joseph Jekyll when opening the case against Dr Sacheverell, the high Tory champion of unqualified non-resistance, at his impeachment in 1710. Gladstone, the veteran of many a debate on the politics of this period at Eton (where contemporary issues were banned), was scoring a telling point. The heroes of many of the reformers of 1831 gave no comfort to the radical opinions now being hatched. Although, as Gladstone is careful to remark, he dissented from '*a part* of the theory' himself, he admired 'its general tone ... and the practice and policy' built on it by the early Whigs.[26] The contractarian position they espoused had no place for popular will as the foundation of the constitution.

Yet the idea of an original compact—or social contract—held no appeal for Gladstone. For almost a century, since David Hume, it had been criticized as a sham. Many, Gladstone observes with typical moderation, 'have doubted and I think with justice its literal correctness'. William Paley's exposure of the weakness of contractarianism had specially impressed him. Gladstone lists five stock objections: the theory was historically false, and if it was replied that it was a convenient fiction, then its authority was fictitious too; it was absurd to suppose those without experience of government dictating its conditions; there could be no implied contract where there was no liberty to refuse the terms; there was no scope for amendment of the constitution; and the people might depose their prince on the slightest transgression. But Gladstone wishes to dig deeper. The idea of a contract depended on the presupposition that the body of the people originally agreed to follow the will of the majority. Why should the right of government lie in the majority? Wisdom did not lie in majorities: 'the fruits of Lord Burleigh's meditations would be very different in kind & degree from those which one or twenty times Mr Such-a-ones would produce.' Majorities, furthermore, are guided by their whims. 'Particularly, considering that the inclinations of the majority of men are swayed by passions ... there is ... a *presumptive* argument established, that upon any question where time has not yet given reason full scope and sway, the majority will be in the wrong ...'[27] Gladstone shared fully in the received opinion of his day that democracy was a synonym for mob rule. William Mitford, with the social catastrophe of revolutionary France in mind, had so depicted the Athenian democratic experiment.[28] Human beings en masse were not fitted to wield power.

---

[26] GP 44721, ff. 11–12.   [27] Ibid., ff. 12–13.
[28] M. L. Clarke, *Greek Studies in England, 1700–1830* (Cambridge, 1945), p. 108. Gladstone, according to the diaries, had read Mitford thoroughly between 2 December 1828 and 20 February 1829.

The original principle of government was not a contract, Gladstone contends, but 'subjection to paternal and patriarchal authority'. Rulers were in a strong sense the fathers of their people. This notion, to Gladstone, was 'historically obvious'. What he meant was that each individual is born into a state as well as into a family, and just as he owes natural obligations to his parents, so he owes them to the political authorities. 'Each man came into the world and practical life of the world under a heavy debt, in extent such as he could not estimate and in kind such as he could not pay ... Hence each successive man has *found* a government and his first duty has been to submit to it.' The government provides benefits that are similar, but on a larger scale, to those supplied by the family: protection from external danger and a secure environment in which to grow up. The relationship of the child to the state is equivalent to its relationship to its parents. There can be no calculation of the extent of the resulting obligation. 'We cannot', declares Gladstone, 'make a valuation of the favours we have received, and mete out a certain quantum of reciprocal benefit and then say we are free.'[29] On the contrary, gratitude spurs the dutiful child to an awareness of infinite obligation. The model of the bond between parent and child remained the sanction of modern governments. Although he considered his theory up-to-date in its application, Gladstone's views were strongly reminiscent of Sir Robert Filmer's *Patriarcha* (1680), originally a pre-Civil War manuscript tract in defence of absolute monarchy but then the target of John Locke's *Two Treatises of Government* (1690). For Gladstone, as for Filmer, kings held paternal rights and responsibilities, just like Adam and the patriarchs, and subjects occupied the rank of children. There does not seem to have been direct influence, for there is no record of Gladstone reading *Patriarcha*, nor even *Two Treatises*, though he later encountered Filmer in the pages of Algernon Sidney's *Discourses concerning Government* (1698) and referred to him in his own work, *The State in its Relations with the Church* (1841 edn.).[30] Nevertheless, as Harry Dickinson and J. C. D. Clark have argued, Filmerite notions remained much more pervasive in the eighteenth century than has usually been thought.[31] Gladstone, it is clear, was the inheritor of a long-standing tradition in arguing for patriarchalism.

In the light of his affinity with Filmer, it is perhaps not surprising to find Gladstone taking a high view of regal power. He actually states his preference, in the abstract, for absolutism. 'Unrestricted monarchy', he writes, 'I should conceive to be the government best suited to man in his perfect state because the most efficacious ...' He is referring to the 'ultimate state' of humanity, where God's will is done on earth, but he recognizes that in the present fallen human condition there is the danger of the crown becoming tyrannical. The existence of human depravity meant that modifications to the ideal of unfettered monarchy were necessary. There must be 'checks and balances' within the state. The various

---

[29] GP 44721, f. 14.          [30] GP 44729, f. 19 (1 Sept. 1840). *SRC*, 4th, 1, p. 113.
[31] H. T. Dickinson, *Liberty and Property: Political Ideology in Eighteenth-Century Britain* (London, 1977), ch. 1; J. C. D. Clark, *English Society, 1688–1832* (Cambridge, 1985), esp. pp. 257–8.

political forces of the realm should resolve their differences at a single point, 'as in the British House of Commons'; and 'the *interests* of all classes of the community' should find full expression. These principles, which later in his careeer Gladstone was to develop, were at this stage treated as mere details of the constitution. Its essence lay in the crown, to which Gladstone professed a strong attachment. He avowed 'determined hostility to the theories of that school of politicians who consider monarchy as a kind of curse inflicted on mankind'.[32] The devotion to the throne that was to cause him such anguish when its occupant showed little appreciation of his services was more than a sentiment. Gladstone's monarchism was deeply rooted in his earliest political theory.

If, despite the similarities to such diverse writers as Malthus, de Maistre, and Filmer, they were not the determinants of Gladstone's viewpoint, what were the main sources of this earliest phase of his political thought? One was undoubtedly Edmund Burke. It was natural for a disciple of Canning such as Gladstone to turn for inspiration to Burke, the ideological father of the strand in the Pittite tradition that Canning represented. On 25 May 1831, a day when he 'wrote a good deal on "Principle of Government"', Gladstone also recorded in his diary that he read 'Canning & Burke'. The text by Burke in question was *An Appeal from the New to the Old Whigs* (1791), a defence of the consistency of his stance on the French Revolution with the Whig tradition. Gladstone moved on, while still composing his essay on government, to Burke's powerful onslaught on the people's right to choose their rulers, *Reflections on the Revolution in France* (1790).[33] As Gladstone recalled in retrospect, his fear of the Reform Bill became associated with Burke's anti-revolutionary teaching.[34] The downgrading of liberty, the critique of contractarianism, and the insistence that the subject of political analysis must be nothing but 'man in civil society'[35] all chimed in with Gladstone's preoccupations. He inserted in his manuscript a quotation from Burke to the effect that government as well as liberty is good, incorporated the statesman's opinion that a minority would not be bound by a majority decision in framing a contract, and cited his pregnant phrase 'the corporate mind' of a nation.[36] Most important, Gladstone appropriated Burke's argument that the events of 1688 did not represent a case of the governed choosing their governors but, on the contrary, vindicated the principle of hereditary succession to the throne.[37] The 'fathers of the British Revolution', Gladstone wrote, 'did not consider themselves as having made an independent choice of a sovereign, but as having installed into a rightfully inherited office the nearest of the royal blood which was not disqualified by the impediment of Catholicism'.[38] It was an argument that entered deep into Gladstone's consciousness, emerging again as a commonplace book entry of the early 1830s.[39] The reading of *Reflections* was not the reason why Gladstone

[32] GP 44721, ff. 15–16, 17, 16.    [33] *D*, 25, 23 May, 1 June 1831.    [34] Morley, 1, p. 70.
[35] Edmund Burke, *Reflections on the Revolution in France*, ed. C. C. O'Brien (Harmondsworth, 1968), p. 150.    [36] GP 44721, ff. 6v, 13, 14.    [37] Burke, *Reflections*, pp. 99–110.
[38] GP 44721, f. 15.    [39] GP 44820, f. 98 (n.d.).

opposed reform, or even why he took so uncompromising a line, for he had argued his case in the Union Society debate before he took up Burke's writings. But the Whig statesman did provide additional ways of expounding the young man's respect for the ancient constitution, ways that, once adopted, remained integral to Gladstone's manner of thinking.

A second, and more substantial, source for Gladstone's political theory was the Bible. An undergraduate notebook survives, undated but perhaps from the year of the Oxford Union speech, in which Gladstone has arranged scripture passages according to topic. There is coverage of the ecclesiastical power of kings and of the purposes of government, but most relevant is Romans 13: 1: 'Let every soul be subject unto the higher powers. For there is no power but of God: the powers that be are ordained of God.' The passage appears in the section on the power of kings and submission.[40] This verse, as so often in Christian history, was the starting point for the reflections of a devout young man on proper political arrangements. It was in his mind as he discussed the Glorious Revolution. The leaders of the revolution, he argues, were in a different position from the subjects of an absolute monarch addressed by the apostles because, as parliamentarians, they formed part of the machinery of government. They could not be censured for infringing the principle of non-resistance by subjects to the crown. Yet 'they retained the whole substance of the Scripture doctrine in declaring that the doctrine of passive obedience alone was to be held under all ordinary governments in all ordinary times'. They respected the homilies of the Church of England that endorsed non-resistance, showing an 'undeviating regard to the laws and will of the Almighty'. 'How wide', Gladstone exclaims, 'was the contrast between the temper and principles of these philosophic statesmen, and those of our own times!'[41] Gladstone shared the seventeenth-century conviction that the monarchy was hedged about, if not with divinity, then with divine authority.

The Bible, however, taught something more. There was the assurance expressed in the Psalms and elsewhere that 'the Lord reigneth' (Ps. 93: 1). This was the root of the doctrine of providence that Gladstone wholeheartedly embraced for the whole of his life.[42] So he believed that when a lawful change of government, such as that of 1688, took place, 'men are indeed the instruments by whose intervention it is effected but not the source from whence it derives its sanction'. Events were the unfolding of the will of God. To Gladstone as much as to the great providentialist theologians of the past such as Augustine or Bossuet the developing historical process threw up regimes whose existence was part of the divine purpose. Whatever the change of government, however, the Almighty had planned that human beings should be integrated in a continuing ordering of society: 'all moral and all other social relations are so evidently fixed for us by the hand of Providence independent of human will.' Gladstone is referring here to the

---

[40] GP 44816B, ff. 222–22v (n.d.: 1831?).                    [41] GP 44721, f. 12.

[42] Boyd Hilton, *The Age of Atonement: The Influence of Evangelicalism on Social and Economic Thought, 1785–1865* (Oxford, 1988), pp. 345–6.

unchosen responsibilities of individuals to their parents and, by extension, to their rulers. The 'original obligation' is an expression of 'the Divine will'.[43] Whatever the government, the placing of each human being in society created the moral imperative to obedience. The duty of submission to the powers that be seemed to result from the rule of providence over human affairs.

A third, and certainly the preponderant, source for 'On the principle of Government' was Aristotle.[44] The ancient Greek philosopher's *Nicomachean Ethics* is quoted four times. Aristotle constituted the core of Gladstone's formal curriculum and during May 1831 he was studying the *Ethics* almost daily. On the day he began the essay on government he also 'wrote a good deal on Ethics'.[45] Nearly a fortnight earlier he had commenced a large notebook on Aristotle with a laudatory essay on the philosopher's analytical method.[46] Gladstone falls naturally into Aristotelian categories in his analysis of government. Thus a will '*perfectly bad*' is contrasted with one 'perfectly good'; he employs Aristotle's characteristic teleology in writing of 'the end', or goal, as determining the nature of an entity; and he even uses the philosopher's own technical terms when declaring that freedom is 'a *dynamis* of contingent quality and application, determined to good or evil according to its *telos*'—meaning that it is decided by its end.[47] Aristotelian ideas inevitably enter the substance as well as the language of Gladstone's case. He argues, for example, that rule should be restricted to those with 'the requisite qualification'.[48] He is reflecting the teaching of Aristotle that justice can be administered only by those possessing 'a state of mind which disposes them to perform just actions, and behave in a just manner, and desire what is just'.[49] It is the Aristotelian background that makes Gladstone able to announce confidently the axiom that 'the *right* to govern' lies only where 'the *capacity* to govern is also to be found'.[50] Although this contention is said to be part of 'the order of Providence', it is derived primarily from Aristotle's understanding of what it is to be human. Gladstone is insistent that his analysis is concerned with human nature in itself, what Aristotle took for his subject-matter, rather than with fallen human nature, the theme of most of the Bible. For that reason the Aristotelian dimension of Gladstone's thought takes priority over the biblical element.

Yet the two are not treated as distinct, for Gladstone has tried to produce a synthesis of the Aristotelian and the biblical accounts of the human condition. He writes of 'the natural & providential law of our being', treating the two adjectives as overlapping if not synonymous. The natural is what Aristotle describes; the providential is what the Bible reveals. There is no hint of a discrepancy in

---

[43] GP 44721, ff. 15, 14, 15.
[44] Cf. Agatha Ramm, 'Gladstone's Religion', *Historical Journal*, 28 (1985).
[45] D, 24 May 1831.                    [46] D, 12 May 1831. GP 44814, ff. 2–5 (1831).
[47] GP 44721, ff. 8, 4, 6; *dynamis* and *telos* appear in Greek characters in the original.
[48] Ibid., f. 17.
[49] *The Ethics of Aristotle*, trans. J. A. K. Thomson (Harmondsworth, 1955), p. 139.
[50] GP 44721, f. 13.

Gladstone's discussion, for he was standing in a tradition of Christianized Aristotelianism that had melded them together over the centuries. He constantly appeals to what is natural, in the manner of Aristotle, but refers it to the intentions of the Almighty. For Gladstone, the foundation of government is 'the original circumstances of human nature'. Human beings should exercise 'right reason' to perceive the 'eternal laws which alone are the source of authority'.[51] This was the customary language of those who, since the time of Aquinas, had honoured the natural law as the true guide to political arrangements. The tradition upholding natural law, with roots in Aristotle but more in Cicero, had been thoroughly integrated in European Christian thought. One of Gladstone's essays in his Aristotelian notebook discusses the existence of a *physikon dikaion*, a natural law. The idea of virtue, he considers, may not be entirely uniform over space and time, but the degree of diversity is so small as to make it reasonable to hold that there is a universal standard of morality, a *physikon dikaion*.[52] Allegiance to natural law created an affinity with Burke at the level of premises as well as prescriptions. The extent to which Burke participated in the natural law tradition has been considerably debated,[53] but there can be no doubt that his talk of earthly political arrangements reflecting the eternal order is at least rooted in that way of thinking. So the package of Burke, the Bible, and Aristotle, all associated with natural law, pointed Gladstone in a single direction, towards the exposition of a political doctrine based on the structure of the cosmos.

The synthesis is evident in the rationale for subordination supplied in Gladstone's manuscript. Burke wrote about 'civil social man and no other'; the Book of Genesis declared that it was 'not good that the man should be alone'; and Aristotle famously taught that man was a 'political animal', a creature designed for living in a *polis* or city-state.[54] Each authority treated human beings as necessarily part of a community. So did Gladstone: 'the principle of association', he explains, is a more fundamental reason for subordination than human corruption, because 'it lies deeper in our nature and belongs to its original and underanged constitution'. The inference seemed clear: 'where there is association there must be government.' Subjection to rulers was inevitable for the ordering of the society to which, of necessity, each human being belonged. 'Civil government is then not a matter of option but of nature. I am not morally free to choose whether I will live in society or retire to the woods . . .' Individuals have to discharge their social relations in the place where they have been brought up from infancy. This, Gladstone explains, is by the dispensation of providence. It was the doctrine alike of Burke, scripture, and Aristotle. These three influences ensured that the foundations of Gladstone's political thought were laid in a holistic understanding of society. Like his other contemporaries, the romantic

---

[51] GP 44721, f. 14, 15, 13, 24v.                    [52] GP 44814, ff. 16–22.

[53] Charles Parkin, *The Moral Basis of Burke's Political Thought* (Cambridge, 1956), represents the case in favour, and Paul Lucas, 'On Edmund Burke's Doctrine of Prescription; Or an Appeal from the New to the Old Lawyers', *Historical Journal*, 11 (1968), the case against.

[54] Burke, *Reflections*, p. 150; Genesis 2: 18; Aristotle, *The Politics*, trans. T. A. Sinclair (Harmondsworth, 1962), p. 28.

poets in England or Hegel in Germany, Gladstone's political starting point was the social nature of human existence. His preoccupation, what he defined as 'the end' of government, was 'the wellbeing of the whole'.[55] 'On the Principle of Government' shows that Gladstone, even before the opening of his political career, exalted the role of community in human life.

The essay on government, however, is not exhaustive as a statement of Gladstone's initial position. In particular there is no allusion to the utilitarian school in the essay, but elsewhere in his undergraduate papers the utilitarians loom large. In the notes for the Union debate, for instance, he makes a sally against the utilitarians, charging them with endangering the stability of the state through having 'no idea of any except pecuniary injury'.[56] Historians have rightly modified earlier exaggerations of the political influence of utilitarianism,[57] but in the early 1830s its intellectual standing was high. For anybody with a speculative turn of mind it was essential to come to terms with the body of opinion that took as its slogan 'the greatest happiness of the greatest number'. Gladstone mentions its arch-theorist Jeremy Bentham, but not until a detached note of around 1835, and then only very briefly.[58] The diary contains no record of Gladstone having read Bentham, but he encountered many of the characteristic teachings of the school in William Paley's *Principles of Moral and Political Philosophy* (1785). Gladstone spent a month in the summer vacation of 1830 concentrating on Paley's work.[59] He locates the writer as an opponent of the moral sense school which held that some faculty of making moral judgements, usually called conscience, is innate in human beings. For Paley a right action, since it is whatever maximizes happiness, is learned by experience. Hence the standard of right and wrong is not fixed. Gladstone will have none of this, arguing that variability in the approval of virtue, far from showing that morality is not innate, might equally be supposed to undermine Paley's own principle that the rightness of actions is governed by expediency. Furthermore it is a mistake, Gladstone believes, to hold, with the utilitarian writer, that the propriety of an action can be assessed by its effects. Paley, according to Gladstone, 'overlooked what he might have learned ... from Aristotle: that essential requirement to *moral* action, that sole ingredient which renders action *moral*, the motive on which it proceeds'.[60] Gladstone is insisting on what would now be called a non-natural theory of ethics, the contention that morality cannot be reduced to non-moral categories. He was formulating a set of root-and-branch objections to utilitarianism.

---

[55] GP 44721, ff. 4, 5, 4.  [56] Ibid., f. 24.

[57] William Thomas, *The Philosophical Radicals: Nine Studies in Theory and Practice* (Oxford, 1979).

[58] GP 44725, f. 283v ('35 or 6?' in later hand by Gladstone).

[59] *D*, 11 Aug.–11 Sept. 1830. 'Paley's Moral Philosophy', GP 44812, ff. 173v–88 (n.d.). Gladstone had not read the book at Eton: the entries in the catalogue of 'Gladstone's Reading' in volume 14 of the diaries suggesting that he had done so during 1827 are mistaken, for they refer (as the entry for 2 December makes explicit) to Paley's *View of the Evidences of Christianity* (1794). On Paley's moral philosophy, see M. L. Clarke, *Paley: Evidences for the Man* (London, 1974), and D. L. LeMahieu, *The Mind of William Paley: A Philosopher and his Age* (Lincoln, Nebr., 1976).

[60] GP 44812, ff. 174v, 175v, 180.

The strongest reason for his reaction against Paley was religious. The utilitarian theorist stated that we do not know the quantity of virtue necessary to salvation. 'This', Gladstone exclaims, 'is the most fatal proposition I have seen in the whole book ... The truth is that salvation by faith in the blood of Christ as the touchstone of qualification for heaven, is most unhappily & unaccountably, here altogether overlooked.' The young evangelical was horrified that an archdeacon should give vent to an unscriptural assertion of salvation by works. It put him on guard against the rest of Paley's teaching. Soon he was diagnosing the identification of happiness with goodness as the fundamental theological mistake. The Almighty, it was true, willed the happiness of his creatures, but only on condition that they repented of their sins. Paley's 'wretched system' placed the achievement of the human will for happiness above the fulfilment of the will of God. That error was the fruit of 'the perverted inclinations of our own hearts, which desired pleasure and not God'. Utilitarianism, by making the self-interested desire for happiness the criterion of ethics, gave intellectual expression to the rebelliousness of fallen humanity.

Who can bear to be told that he loves his parents and his brethren for his own advantage? That the mother whose eyes dwell lovingly on her infant

> "That comfort him by night and day,
> That light his little life away"—

and whose bowels are ever yearning for his bliss, does it for her own advantage?

The principles of natural affection, on the contrary, were planted in the human heart by God, so that utilitarianism must be repudiated as an 'attempt to enshrine Pleasure in the temple of Love'.[61] The extravagant language, with its sentimental attachment to family thrown into the scales against the archdeacon, bears witness to the strength of Gladstone's aversion. Paley seems to have triggered a deep-seated disgust for the whole utilitarian system.

The effect is visible in one of Gladstone's examination papers in the Schools at the end of his Oxford career. He was required to write an extended essay on the following subject: 'It is the doctrine of Aristotle that no man's virtue is perfect, so long as he requires any effort of self-denial. Explain this position, as it is inculcated in his theory, and in contrast with the "apathy" of the Stoical system: and deduce consequences from it as to the principle of conscience, how far it is factitious or innate.'[62] This 'very fine but very difficult subject' was a surprise for Gladstone, since he had been expecting a question on Roman history, but he wrote hard on it from 10 a.m. to 3 p.m.[63] On the same evening, despite the prospect of six hours in the Schools the following day, he recorded a detailed abstract of his answer. Although he claimed to have no idea how well he had done, the essay is a brilliantly structured tour de force which provides a window into his overall thinking at that point. Aristotle is vindicated, and then the Stoics assessed. Gladstone shows sympathy for them as the

---

[61] GP 44812, ff. 176v, 177v, 179v.     [62] Ibid., f. 63v.     [63] *D*, 16 Nov. 1831.

founders of the natural law tradition, but he contends that they were wrong in that 'they extirpated affection as well as passion' and in that they rejected 'the *notion of discipline*'. Both natural affection and self-discipline rated highly in Gladstone's mind. When he moves on to consider conscience, he rejects the utilitarian supposition that the standard of morality is the consequences of an action for the agent, identifying this position with Epicurus, Godwin, and Paley. Here was an unholy trinity: the ancient philosopher who made pleasure his lodestar; the opponent of Burke who treated the popular will as infallible; and the representative of utilitarianism who irresponsibly elevated pleasure and the human will together. The utilitarians were hedonists, making government as well as society rest on human self-interest. Their teaching, as Gladstone puts it in a separate memorandum, embodied the 'selfishness of human nature'.[64] These were the people who, in Gladstone's day, were yoking the intellectual errors of the Epicureans with the political subversiveness of Burke's opponents. The self-interest that they championed was not merely a mistaken foundation for ethics. It also operated, in Gladstone's estimation, as a solvent of the bonds of society. Utilitarianism was the greatest of threats to the values of the community.

## II

Gladstone graduated from Oxford at the end of 1831 with a coherent body of political thought—anti-egalitarian, anti-popular, and anti-utilitarian; traditional, patriarchal, and holistic. During the remainder of the 1830s, while sitting as a Tory MP, he was to elaborate, but barely to alter, the structure that he had forged out of Burke, scripture, and Aristotle. One supplementary element was added only eighteen months after he went down from Oxford, when a former undergraduate friend asked him to outline a speech for delivery at the Union against the proposition 'That Hereditary Aristocracy is an Evil'.[65] Gladstone set out systematically ideas that he had no doubt long entertained but that, as a new parliamentary protégé of the Duke of Newcastle, he now felt particularly bound to assert. Hereditary rule and primogeniture, he begins, are recognized in scripture.

> Next I say, that human equality, which we sometimes hear spoken of, is not only a monster, but is far more a monster than any <u>inequality</u> whatsoever: because whereas inequality of human condition <u>may</u> be excessive because out of proportion to desert, and therefore faulty, that on the other hand equality of human condition <u>must</u> be out of proportion to desert and therefore faulty.[66]

It is a very Gladstonian debating point. Should there be, he goes on, instead of an aristocracy, a meritocracy in which political power is entrusted only to proved capacity? No, because the transmission of honour and power down the generations

---

[64] GP 44812, ff. 63v–64v, 198v.
[65] S. C. Denison to W. E. Gladstone, 9 Apr. 1833, GP 44353, f. 118.
[66] 'That an hereditary aristocracy is an evil. Negative', GP 44722, ff. 194–200v (11 Apr. 1833), quoted at f. 195v.

is as reasonable as the transmission of property; and because ability is likely to recur in the son of a power-holder. In a mixed government such as Britain, there needs to be a third element to balance the monarchy and the populace; and a hereditary monarchy requires the buttress of a hereditary aristocracy. But Gladstone, as he showed elsewhere, was aware of the risks of an aristocracy—luxury, idleness, and pride.[67] The elite must never become an exclusive caste, avoiding the twin perils of undue approximation to the moneymaking classes (which would be demeaning to the great landlords) or an impassable barrier between the two (which would make the landed another race). Nevertheless the aristocracy of England—at least down to 1830—had served as an effective check on the monarchy and the papacy, and it still functioned satisfactorily.[68] It was a typical battery of arguments, founded squarely on the inegalitarian case that Gladstone had generated during the reform crisis. An idealistic vision of the landed elite was to remain an enduring feature of his thinking.

Practical experience of public life, even of government, during the 1830s changed neither Gladstone's fundamental opinions nor his way of expressing them. In April 1835, as Under-Secretary of State for the Colonies, he composed a memorandum intended for his chief, Lord Aberdeen, on the need for the education of ex-slaves in the West Indies to be conducted on Anglican lines. He delved down to 'the great principles of Government', contending that there were essentially two conflicting theories. One regarded the public authorities as the creatures of the popular will.

The other theory imports that Government has in it something of a paternal character and obligation: that it has not usually as matter of fact derived its authority from expressions of the collective will of the people, or from any substantial consent of individuals: that as an institution it is natural and not conventional or arbitrary, and in that sense divine and not human . . .

Government is 'paternal', 'natural', 'divine': here are the features of the theory of 1831. A popular element checks the potential for tyranny or abuse, Gladstone goes on, but that does not affect the title of 'the powers that be' which are based on the 'most urgent wants of our nature' and which are 'ordained of God'. Aristotle once more blends with the apostle Paul. A paternal regime could possibly be a republic, but is more naturally a monarchy. And government tries to recruit an elite consisting of 'the virtue and vigour of the national mind' who are best equipped to rule.[69] There is remarkable continuity in this policy document with the theoretical case developed in the private paper 'On the principle of Government'. Gladstone had seen no reason to shift his ground.

During the early 1830s the young politician toyed with the scheme of composing a book that would draw his theories together. Even before he sat his final Oxford examinations, he confided to his diary the idea 'of gathering during the

---

[67] GP 44725, f. 35 (10 Nov. 1835).                    [68] GP 44722, ff. 199v–200v.
[69] 'West Indian Education', GP 44724, ff. 4–36 (7 Apr. 1835), quoted at ff. 23, 23v, 23v–4, 26v.

progress of my life, notes & materials for a work embracing three divisions—Morals—Politics—Education'.[70] John Morley calls this 'a curious entry',[71] and yet the project shaped Gladstone's intellectual activities over the next four years. He filled notebooks, wrote brief memoranda, and pursued a steady programme of reading in the fields that had claimed his allegiance at university. He drew up more than one outline for what he called 'a scientific treatise of morals'. The various systems of ethics were classified and reclassified. Thomas Hobbes, Jonathan Edwards, and William Warburton were to be considered, though without much apparent enthusiasm. Ralph Cudworth, the seventeenth-century Cambridge Platonist, and Joseph Butler, the eighteenth-century bishop who was to retain Gladstone's admiration into old age, were evidently approved for their defence of 'immutable morality'.[72] Paley was once more yoked with the Epicureans as their opponent. A section was to be headed 'Happiness: why not treated of',[73] and we know the answer from what Gladstone had fulminated against the utilitarians as an undergraduate. 'In truth', he remarked, 'we find the solution of *all* these mysteries in the Bible',[74] but the problem was that the Bible did not lay out its principles systematically. On the other hand Aristotle did, and his influence is apparent in the intended discussion of the doctrine of a mean and the insistence that the science of morals is mainly concerned with 'the *end* of human action'.[75] Ethics, Gladstone remarked, had now become 'the master-science, having rightfully supplanted that supremacy which was accorded . . . by the ancients to the science of politics or social relations'.[76] During the phase of the early 1830s questions of moral theory loomed largest in his mind.

In the autumn of 1835, however, the relative weighting of ethics and politics was reversed. Perhaps impelled by his spell in office earlier in the year, Gladstone set himself a stiff course of reading in order to establish the principles on which the politician should act. Aristotle's *Politics* was complemented by Sir William Blackstone's *Commentaries on the Laws of England* (1765–9) and Alexis de Tocqueville's newly published *Democracy in America* (1835). Blackstone, whose pages he had already studied during the summer of 1832, was now examined closely for his classic exposition of the legal system.[77] The *Commentaries*, containing the substance of Blackstone's lectures as the first Vinerian Professor of English Law at Oxford, carried the unique authority of Gladstone's own university. They also appealed to him because, as Bentham had noted with disgust, they grounded the English constitutional balance in the qualities of the Almighty.[78] De Tocqueville added to Blackstone's account of a polity in which authority descended from above the counterpoint of a profound analysis of a state in which authority ascended from below. 'The people', wrote the Frenchman, 'reign over the American political world as God rules over the universe.'[79] Gladstone judged

---

[70] *D*, 3 Oct. 1831.     [71] Morley, 1, p. 76.     [72] GP 44820, ff. 3–5, quoted at ff. 5, 3.
[73] Ibid., f. 6 (3 Nov. 1833).     [74] Ibid., f. 4.     [75] Ibid., ff. 2v (n.d.), 12 (n.d.).
[76] Ibid., f. 8 (4 Mar. 1832).     [77] *D*, 27 Aug.–10 Sept. 1832, 15 Sept. 1835–11 Jan. 1836.
[78] William Blackstone, *Commentaries on the Laws of England*, 8th edn., 4 vols. (Oxford, 1778), 1, pp. 48–52. Jeremy Bentham, *A Fragment on Government*, ed. Wilfrid Harrison (Oxford, 1948), p. 58.
[79] Alexis de Tocqueville, *Democracy in America*, ed. J. P. Mayer and Max Lerner (New York, 1966), p. 53.

*Democracy in America* to be 'a most able book—and most beautifully arranged'.[80] Aristotle's *Politics*, however, made at least as powerful an impression. Book IV, chapter 12, on adapting constitutional arrangements to social conditions, particularly struck Gladstone, leading him to write a detailed discussion of the text.[81] 'But at all times', Gladstone read, 'a legislator ought to endeavour to attach the middle section of the population firmly to the constitution.' The task that Aristotle laid down was precisely the mission of Peelite Conservatism. 'It is a mistake made by many,' the philosopher went on, 'even by those seeking to make an aristocratic constitution, not only to give too great preponderance to the rich, but to cheat the people.'[82] Here was a lesson that Gladstone took to heart, ever seeking to stabilize the aristocratic order by concessions to the people. The *Politics*, he concluded, was 'a book of immense value for all governors and public men'.[83]

This bloc of reading stimulated Gladstone into writing a revealing cluster of papers on political theory in November and December 1835. A week after completing de Tocqueville in early November he jotted down a set of notes for a treatise on government of his own. The influence of the Frenchman's work on America is apparent in the space given to the treatment of the legislative, executive, and judicial branches separately, though there is also consideration of how far the three overlap. But how, Gladstone asked, could this analysis be applied to the British constitution? He begins by pointing out that the king functions legislatively by summoning parliament and giving to bills the force of law, but the writer soon reaches an impassable obstacle that prevents further progress. 'It is necessary to remember', he tells himself, 'that we may easily in comparison construct a balance of the mere instruments of government, if the elements of which the nation is formed be uniform and few as in America.' In the democracy of the United States, power rested with the bulk of the population, who were subsistence farmers. In Britain, however, power was not only wielded by numbers but also claimed by right of birth, virtue, intellect, property, and prescription. There were too many components in the political system for the checks against injustice of the American arrangements to operate. Yet it could not be assumed that in an aristocratic country the rulers would perform their duty wisely. 'Mere responsibility can never be effective without the aid of opinion.'[84] Gladstone was beginning to see in public opinion, a factor that de Tocqueville held to be the directing power in France as well as the United States,[85] the grand check on government in Britain. It was an idea that was to figure prominently in his later thinking.[86]

The same manuscript sketch of a treatise on government begins with a classification of the various possible grounds of political obligation.[87] It recurs in almost identical form in a paper on 'Prevalent theories of Government' composed

[80] *D*, 3 Nov. 1835. Cf. GP 44724, ff. 181–6 (4 Nov. 1835).

[81] GP 44724, ff. 207–8 (n.d.).

[82] Aristotle, *Politics*, pp. 175–6.

[83] *D*, 20 Nov. 1835.

[84] GP 44725, ff. 31–5 (10 Nov. 1835), quoted at ff. 34, 35.

[85] de Tocqueville, *Democracy in America*, pp. 112–13.

[86] See Ch. 6, p. 153.

[87] GP 44725, f. 31.

in the following month.[88] Hobbes is summarily dismissed as not worthy of detailed consideration. The idea of the absolute divine right of kings is treated with respect, but rejected because rulers, like the ruled, have no liberty to give free rein to their preferences. Henry VIII, for example, should not have declared the succession by will, for that system, as opposed to the received hereditary principle, does not (as Gladstone puts it) have the 'uniformity and perspicuity' that would mark out a divine law. The theory of an original contract, as upheld by Hooker, Locke, the Whigs of 1688, and Burke (no doubt insofar as he concurs with the Whigs of 1688), is unsustainable for the same reasons that Gladstone had maintained in 1831. Rousseau's version of contractarianism, which entrusted sovereignty to the ruling power without opportunity of recall, is identified with the practice of America but not fully evaluated before the manuscript breaks off. Two other schemes were to have been rejected: the notion of delegation, which seems to mean representation; and Paley's system of general expediency. The 'truest form of theory upon the subject', however, 'was that of a natural, and therefore divine, obligation: of what we believe, under pagan modifications, the principles are contained in the Politics of Aristotle: as they are distinctly owned in the commentaries of Blackstone'.[89] Gladstone's fresh reading had not challenged the premises of his thinking, but rather had deepened the convictions already formed during the reform crisis.

Two further papers from the same batch show Gladstone wrestling with the issue of how far that theoretical standpoint could be modified in the policy decisions of real life. One paper, which does not develop its case very far, nevertheless pointed to the problem. What was the seat of authority in political affairs? Unlike ethics, with its necessary deference to scripture, the practice of politics lacked an undisputed court of appeal. An ideal constitution could be deduced from the will of God expressed mediately (in nature) or immediately (in scripture), but the young Peelite recognized that, because of human imperfection, the ideal would sometimes need to be modified.[90] In what way, then, should changes be made by the government in order to ward off the risk of the collapse of the state? This issue was addressed in a further paper, 'Of concession', written on 30 November while Gladstone was nearing the end of the first volume of Sir Archibald Alison's *History of Europe during the French Revolution* (1833). Alongside Louis XVI, the instance of Charles I was in his mind. The traditional Tory case was that both kings made mischief by yielding to popular clamour; Whigs held that both did too little too late. Each side, according to Gladstone, overlooked 'the main determining consideration, the inherent reasonableness of the concession itself'. Thus

---

[88] Ibid., ff. 190–205. The MS is undated and is not (*pace* Matthew, p. 35) continuous with the paper on 'The true position of Will in Government' that follows in the Gladstone Papers and is dated 16 December 1835. It is nevertheless part of the batch of writing recorded in the diaries for the period 8–19 December 1835.                                                                                                  [89] Ibid., f. 190.

[90] Ibid., ff. 140–8. This MS is undated but attributed by the diaries to both 28 November 1835 (where it is wrongly described as being in GP 44724) and 11 December 1835. All that can be said firmly is that it comes from the same body of writing.

Charles I should have acted on principle, conceding what could properly be offered at an earlier point, but going no further than accepting triennial parliaments. Monarchy and church establishment were the non-negotiable 'vital and organic principles of the Constitution' in Gladstone's own day. In other areas where matters of principle were not at stake there was scope for giving ground, but never if they were extorted through fear since then they would be taken as 'part-payment of a debt'. Concessions not made out of principle would excite suspicion that they would be revoked. If possible popular clamour should be anticipated, but whether or not it existed the lodestar was this: 'To concede when right is good: and to concede liberally when we concede at all.'[91] Here, already formulated, was the ideology that was to guide Peel to repeal the corn laws. It was not left, as has usually been supposed, to the administration of 1841 for Gladstone to imbibe these maxims from his leader. Experience of serving under Peel early in 1835 blended with reading and reflection to make the young politician conscious and articulate on the issue of practicality before the year was out. Already Gladstone, though a principled Tory, was a mild and malleable one.

The combination of conviction and flexibility recurs in two related manuscripts from the same creative phase: 'Of the law of Social obligation' and 'The true position of Will in Government'. The first sets out once more to explore the rationale for obedience to government. The idea that the law carries authority only when it can be enforced, a notion associated with versions of legal positivism, is first dismissed on the ground that it has never been admitted that obedience to laws is optional. Law possesses its own moral authority. Nevertheless, Gladstone points out, human law is never to override divine law. The exceptional case cannot be foreseen, the only legitimate generalization being that such cases of conscience are rare. It is better not to discuss these instances because, if canvassed, they might activate the human bias towards disobedience. Silence on the exceptions has the sanction of both scripture and the leaders of the Glorious Revolution.[92] But who is to decide when a possible case for repudiating a human law arises? In an earlier essay on this subject, written probably a couple of years before, Gladstone had declared that in these circumstances each person is 'as a responsible & moral being, by virtue of these properties, constituted the judge'.[93] The individual, though never allowed to withstand a law except by reference to the divine will, possesses the duty of deciding when he may properly resist. By 1835, however, Gladstone had abandoned that position with its overtone of inalienable human rights. Instead he now urges that society is the proper judge of the applicability of the principle of obligation. He had moved even further towards a political theory shorn of individualism. His main assertion, furthermore, is uncompromising, as the underlining is no doubt meant to indicate:

---

[91] GP 44725, ff. 184–9 (n.d.), quoted at ff. 185, 187, 188v, 189v. *D*, 13 Nov.–16 Dec. 1835. Cf. GP 44725, ff. 103–8 (1–16 Dec. 1835).

[92] Ibid., ff. 150–83 and 207–16. The first is undated, but the second, which appears to follow on from it, is dated 16 Dec. 1835.        [93] GP 44820, ff. 58–60 (n.d.: 1833?), quoted at f. 59.

'unless it be a sin to obey, it is a sin to resist.'[94] Despite his deference to the Whigs of 1688, Gladstone is not far from the non-resistance principles of their Jacobite opponents.

The same paper goes beneath the problematic of political obligation to the foundation on which it rests: the issue of social obligation. In subsequently reviewing the document, Gladstone noticed that part discusses not the ground for obedience but the more basic question, 'is it optional morally to be or not to be members of a society'.[95] With Blackstone, he held that once society was taken as a given, government necessarily followed for its preservation.[96] So the basic issue was to establish the prior responsibility of each person to the larger whole. Here there is continuity with the earlier paper. 'The foundation of the claims of society', he had written a couple of years before, 'is this: that he [the individual] is already a debtor: a debtor from his birth upwards: & to an extent which he is not competent either to estimate or to repay.'[97] The doctrine in 1835 is identical. 'We are then,' he says, 'before we are conscious of it, receivers of benefit from human society, as we are from our parents.'[98] The reason for the consistency is also made plain. Gladstone appeals explicitly to Aristotle as the source for the idea that society is natural, not optional, and that social obligations are unavoidable, not voluntary. The Greek philosopher still set the parameters for Gladstone's thought as much as in 1833 or 1831. But there was now an added explanation of why we cannot escape, as he puts it, from 'the social principle, into the region of individualism'.[99] We are born, he argues, into the church involuntarily; secular society operates on the analogy of the Christian commonwealth; therefore society is naturally not arbitrarily formed. It is a curious argument, since its conclusion is intended to be universal but its premise is restricted to Christendom, yet it is a further significant symptom of Gladstone's intellectual development. His ecclesiastical views, as we shall see, had become more robust, and so they were now reinforcing the anti-individualist thrust of Gladstone's general theory.[100] The aim of those who frame or modify constitutions is, he concludes, 'to cause the nearest possible approximation of *political right*, to *absolute right*'.[101] The Hegelian idiom is appropriate for a scholar who was becoming ever more deeply committed to a holistic way of thinking.

Nevertheless Gladstone's confidence about the natural and divine sanction for society as well as government has to be balanced by a growing awareness of the role of the people. Although much weaker than the theme of descending authority, there is an element of ascending authority in Gladstone's theory. The people certainly do not constitute the arbiter of government: even in America, Gladstone points out, it is only at election time that the will of the majority prevails. But a renewed reading of Locke's *Essay concerning Human Understanding* (1690), also undertaken in December 1835, was drawing him towards a higher valuation of the

[94] GP 44725, f. 154.　　　[95] Ibid., f. 156v.　　　[96] Blackstone, *Commentaries*, 1, p. 48.

[97] GP 44820, f. 58.　　　[98] GP 44725, f. 162.　　　[99] Ibid., f. 173.

[100] See Ch. 3, pp. 48, 61.　　　[101] GP 44725, f. 182.

human will, so long as it remained the servant of the deliberative faculty. He inferred that 'the popular will . . . must be recognised as a component part of the state'.[102] It should be only secondary; it should rarely find its way into the laws; and it must never subvert the founding principle of government. Yet the wishes of the population had to be taken into account alongside higher determinants: 'the office of government, is not to carry out all the principles, nor all the sanctions, of the Divine Law, but it is limited by the natural consideration of practicability: it is to use men rather than coerce them, and must in many things permit, though it need never encourage, the agency of illegitimate motives.'[103] Those in power could not stamp an ideal imprint on society. Instead their aim must be to accommodate the social currents within the body politic so as to keep the show on the road. Here was the view that a decade later, in the Maynooth affair, was to induce Gladstone to compromise his vision of a state committed to upholding truth.[104] Already in 1835 the combination of his immense reading and his small experience of public affairs had induced him find a place for expediency in his strategic thinking. Gladstone was prepared to set aside utopianism for the sake of effective government.

Another paper, though a brief one, that may belong to the autumn of 1835 adds a further piece to the jigsaw of Gladstone's early political thought. Headed 'Love of country', it asserts, against the cosmopolitanism of the early eighteenth-century Tory Lord Bolingbroke, the importance of patriotism in the divine economy.[105] Gladstone's boyish partisanship for his own land had been elevated, no doubt partly by absorbing Burke's defence of the British constitution, into an abstract principle by 1833. 'Nations are *naturally* designed', he wrote in a commonplace book; 'their separation is of the constitution of the human race.' Madame de Staël's preface to *De L'Alllemagne* (1813) is cited as the source, but the theory has taken on the characteristic neo-natural law tone of Gladstone's thinking. The distinction between nations 'springs spontaneously and necessarily out of the laws and conditions of our nature'; it therefore bears the marks of design; and so the designer's purposes for them must be fulfilled.[106] Nevertheless the idea, as Gladstone developed it, also partook of the historicist trend that was revolutionizing European thought. Peoples, he came to hold, evolve their own distinctive character through their history. 'If we see a nation tearing up and casting away its ancient traditions,' he wrote in a detached memorandum of 1839, 'even though in their character they tell of its intellectual infancy, we feel that it is like a man disowning the simple and pure recollections of his boyhood.'[107] And just as a whole nation should cherish its past, so an individual should love his native land. That the Highlander clung to his rocks rather than emigrating to the American prairies was good for him—hard labour educated his character—and

---

[102] GP 44725, f. 215; 'of' is repeated in the original.          [103] Ibid.          [104] See Ch. 5, 107–8.
[105] GP 44725 ff. 292–6. The paper is undated and the heading is pencilled in a later hand. For Gladstone's subsequent treatment of nationhood, see Chs. 3, 7, and 9, pp. 60–1, 198, 206 and 274–8.
[106] GP 44803, ff. 20 (19 June [1833]), 18 (10 May [1833]).          [107] GP 44728, f. 328 (21 Nov. 1839).

for society, which depended on 'local and partial attachments' for its preservation.[108] Loyalties cannot be calculated. Any human being must be rooted in the soil of his own land.

Loyalty was one of the many lessons Gladstone had learned from ancient texts. Many commentators, and supremely Colin Matthew, have recognized that Gladstone was eclectic in his debt to classical authors.[109] The Oxford Schools essay, for example, shows a nodding acquaintance with the Epicureans and a fuller grasp of the Stoics.[110] During the autumn of 1836 he spent further time on Stoicism, reading a whole series of Cicero's writings.[111] These texts must have reinforced Gladstone's conviction that the universe was governed by natural law and certainly confirmed (against the utilitarians) the distinction between pain and evil.[112] Plato, whom he had examined in detail at an earlier stage, was evidently also a shaping influence. Between August 1832 and October 1833 Gladstone scrutinized the text of the *Republic*, noting certain sections with a bearing on religious truth or political practice. One passage buttressed his antagonism to 'the modern doctrine of extending political privileges to as many as possible, for their own sake'. Book VIII was 'very pungent' on democracy; it also vividly portrayed the career of a demagogue.[113] Having explored Plato's main political text so thoroughly, Gladstone went on in the following year to examine Aristotle's equivalent. Between August 1834 and November 1835 he absorbed the *Politics*. He mused on various implications, remarking, for instance, that 'the principal influence of law arises from its fixedness'.[114] To the ideas already imbibed from Aristotle's ethics the young politician now added a range of practical guidelines about their application to public life. A variety of classical authors, the core of his college curriculum, remained the bedrock of Gladstone's reading in the years after going down from Oxford.

His eclecticism does not mean, however, that Gladstone paid equal attention to the various ancient sources. In particular it would probably be a mistake to follow Colin Matthew in attributing as much weight to Plato as to Aristotle in his formation. At Oxford, it is true, Gladstone had been specially impressed by Plato's vision of the world. In 1829 and 1830 Gladstone twice read to the Essay Society a paper contending that 'the system of Plato was more practical, as well as more exalted, than that of Aristotle'. There could be no doubt, he argued, that Plato's thought was grander, and in his own day Plato supplied motives for good behaviour that were absent from the works of Aristotle. But, by contrast with the ardent Platonist and future theologian F. D. Maurice, who after hearing the paper endorsed Plato's teaching that 'taking in the truth ipso facto benefits the mind', Gladstone conceded that Aristotle's 'wonderful power of systematising and classifying' added greatly to his practical value. He concluded that 'while Plato

---

[108] GP 44725, f. 293v.    [109] Matthew, pp. 33–6.    [110] GP 44812, ff. 63v–4v.
[111] GP 44726, ff. 132–3, 149–50, 245–8, 249–54, 269–73, 292–4.    [112] Ibid., f. 230 (9 Nov. 1836).
[113] 'Notes on Plato's Republic', GP 44722, ff. 27–50, quoted at f. 50v.
[114] 'Aristotelis Politica', GP 44723, ff. 120–95, quoted at ff. 130–1.

certainly supplied what was most urgently required *then*, Aristotle *perhaps* ministers more suitably to the uses of modern times'.[115] This tentative undergraduate
evaluation made in 1829 hardened into conviction during Gladstone's detailed
work on Aristotle in preparation for Schools. Aristotle was the ancient author
with most contemporary application. The philosopher's analytical power made
him 'far more calculated to be useful in a Christian country' because there 'are
many supposed *motives* already supplied'.[116] Gladstone's considered estimate of
the two philosophers is evident from a paper apparently composed in 1835. Plato
contained 'thoughts exquisitely beautiful' but Aristotle had enunciated 'many
noble truths'.[117] For Gladstone beauty was not truth. Plato might have aesthetic
appeal, but Aristotle was a far more valuable tutor.

The Aristotelian understanding of the good life underlay Gladstone's enduring
hostility to the utilitarians. For Aristotle, life was the pursuit of virtue; for the utilitarians it was an exercise in self-interest. Gladstone maintained an onslaught on
Paley and his school, already begun at Oxford, in his subsequent memoranda.
'Utilitarianism', he wrote on 19 November 1836, 'deceives itself more than any
other philosophy . . .'[118] The consequences of acts, he suggested in another note,
are too evanescent to pin down, so that it is nonsense to suppose, with the
Benthamites, that their relative weight can be calculated.[119] Utility could not be
treated as the ruling principle of human action because it ignored the whole question of purpose. 'The question is', he wrote in 1835, 'useful for *what*?'[120] Gladstone
did not dismiss every aspect of utilitarian teaching. He was prepared to admit—a
large concession—that the rightness of an action depends on its results as well as
on its intention.[121] He was even willing to treat utility as a criterion for the validity of an action so long as it was construed as referring to the will of God.[122] But
that meant altering its standard formula. 'The utilitarian principle', he wrote,
'calls for correction at the very outset. It should not be the greatest happiness of
the greatest number but the greatest virtue.'[123] Repeatedly the young politician
returns to the theme that goodness is distinct from happiness, pleasure, or enjoyment. It is folly, he declares in a later manuscript, to urge human beings to grasp
enjoyment with the assurance that they will gain virtue—'as if virtue were drawn
after her with a cart rope'.[124] Virtue should be sought for its own sake, or rather
for the sake of its Creator. Gladstone was as hostile to utilitarianism as any of his
romantically inclined contemporaries, sharing with Carlyle and Newman a
distaste for its coolly analytical temper. It was a position he also held in common
with Disraeli, whose *Vindication of the English Constitution* (1835) criticized the

[115] GP 44719, ff. 113–22 (11 Dec. 1829), quoted at ff. 115, 124, 120. On Maurice's Platonism, see David
Newsome, *Two Classes of Men: Platonism and English Romantic Thought* (London, 1964).

[116] GP 44719, f. 120.

[117] 'Special influences of Christianity on conduct', GP 44725, f. 23. This undated paper refers to
Alison's *History of Europe*, which Gladstone read in Nov./Dec. 1835.

[118] GP 44726, f. 244 (19 Nov. 1836).       [119] GP 44820, f. 55 (n.d.).       [120] GP 44725, f. 283.

[121] Ibid., f. 283v.                                                 [122] GP 44820, f. 112 (22 Feb. 1834).

[123] GP 44725, f. 290 ('1835' by Gladstone in later hand).

[124] 'Mediation', GP 44728, ff. 175–92 (n.d. but probably, on the evidence of the diary, 5 Sept. 1847).

arbitrariness of the utilitarian position.[125] For each of these men the principle of utility was a misleading will-o'-the-wisp.

Gladstone's aversion to the utilitarian school had originally been formed with the assistance of Bishop Butler. The eighteenth-century philosopher had given him the confidence, while still at Oxford, to develop his critique of Paley. It was partly Butler's moral theory, expounded in his *Fifteen Sermons Preached at the Rolls Chapel* (1726), that swayed Gladstone. Although long afterwards he recorded having been dismayed by Butler's high estimate of human nature that seemed to ignore the consequences of the Fall,[126] the young politician gradually came to terms with this position, treating Butler's account as being, like Aristotle's, a description of the ideal rather than an account of the actual human condition.[127] Gladstone also shows signs of having accepted Butler's teaching in the *Rolls Sermons* that conscience is supreme in the constitution of the human mind, refer- ring to it in 1836 as '*de jure* the governing faculty'.[128] But the book by Butler that was to prove even more important in Gladstone's formation was his *Analogy of Religion* (1736). Its tight-knit apologetic argument in defence of Christian revela- tion so impressed Gladstone with its cogency that, apparently by 1833, he was already projecting the edition of Butler's work that he was eventually to publish in 1896. Later in the 1830s he actually wrote an outline of the edition that incor- porated notes and extended essays, very much along the lines of the publication sixty years afterwards.[129] It was from the *Analogy* that Gladstone drew the central argument against Paley that the Almighty designs goodness, not happiness, for his creatures.[130] Although Butler was subsequently to become even more of a mentor, already in the 1830s Gladstone was using the bishop's thought as a reservoir of creative ideas.

Gladstone's rejection of utilitarianism with the aid of Butler was associated with a broader dislike for what he called the 'mechanical philosophy', the general approach of the Enlightenment. Drawing on Coleridge, Gladstone distinguished between 'the pure reason, and the imagination of man', which was suited for a higher grasp of truth as a whole, and 'the understanding', which contented itself with examining 'a multitude of objects'.[131] The 'Spirit of the age' was preoccupied with the latter at the expense of the former.[132] Gladstone thought both capacities to be essential, but saw the role of the understanding as inferior to that of the reason. The understanding merely assembled particular facts by induction, but the reason deduced general principles from higher axioms. Induction was more suited to the study of the physical world than to the scrutiny of human behaviour, where

[125] John Vincent, *Disraeli* (Oxford, 1990), pp. 18–20.
[126] 'Early Religious Opinions' (26 July 1894), *Autobiographica*, pp. 140–1.
[127] GP 44821 D, f. 39 (n.d.); 44726, f. 232v (11 Nov. 1836).
[128] GP 44726, f. 215 (11 Oct. 1836). Cf. f. 143 (5 Sept. 1836).
[129] GP 44815 E, f. 1v (n.d.: 1833?); 44821 D, f. 53v (n.d.); 'On Bishop Butler', 44725, ff. 236–9 ('Before 1840?' by Gladstone in later hand).　　[130] GP 44812, f. 177v.
[131] GP 44723, ff. 407–10 ('Bef. 35' by Gladstone in later hand), quoted at f. 409.
[132] GP 44815 F, f. 3v (n.d.).

'experimental facts' were more open to debate. Where politics was concerned, science had the overriding task of making deductions 'from the nature of man, and the will of God'. It should point out, in relation to an organized political body, 'in what actual state it ought to be—how progress is to be made towards that state—and together with these of course there will be the consideration of the present condition which it is proposed to modify'. Because the first two looked to the future, only the third branch of enquiry would be governed by the ordinary principles of induction.[133] Gladstone was more concerned with how humanity ought to be than how it actually was, despising the rising empirical sciences that occupied themselves exclusively with investigation of the existing state of affairs. Political economy in particular became a bugbear. Despite his admiration for Thomas Chalmers, the Scottish churchman who had propounded a religious version of the science,[134] Gladstone regularly deprecated political economy in his private memoranda. It was given too much attention for a field of enquiry concerned merely with 'material objects'; political economy flourished while the higher science of politics, 'affecting the spiritual and mental character of individuals', was neglected; and the dreary science looked at human beings as machines rather than as characters to be modified.[135] It dwelt solely on the mundane level of empirical investigation. Like John Stuart Mill, whose *System of Logic* was to appear in 1843, Gladstone was preoccupied with the question of method, albeit at a much less rigorous level; but unlike Mill, he was convinced that the deduction of permanent principles took precedence over the induction of transient facts. Gladstone believed that truth, like authority, derived ultimately from a heavenly source.

The young politician's overall position can be illustrated by contrast with that of George Grote.[136] The spirit of political economy was embodied in Grote: he was a prosperous banker, a close friend of John Stuart Mill, a disciple of Mill's Benthamite father James and, from 1832, radical MP for the City of London. His earliest publication, in 1821, had been an attack on the assumption of Whigs and Tories alike that parliament should represent the various interest groups in British society. Grote complained that this arrangement meant that the community at large, which on utilitarian premises consisted of nothing but the individuals of whom it was composed, was subjected to the pursuit of sectional aims, particularly by the landed class. The banker was deeply hostile to all secondary associations intermediate between the state and the individual, much in the manner of Rousseau, because they prevented individuals from expressing their private interests.[137] Only the secret ballot, Grote's political panacea, could provide

[133] GP 44724, f. 71 (n.d.).

[134] S. J. Brown, 'Gladstone, Chalmers and the Disruption of the Church of Scotland', in David Bebbington and Roger Swift (eds.), *Gladstone Centenary Essays* (Liverpool, 2000).

[135] GP 44815 F, f. 3v; 44723, f. 408; 44724, f. 70v.

[136] The contrast is developed in D. W. Bebbington, 'Gladstone and Grote', in P. J. Jagger (ed.), *Gladstone* (London, 1998).

[137] George Grote, 'Essentials of Parliamentary Reform', in Alexander Bain (ed.), *The Minor Works of George Grote* (London, 1875), pp. 27–33.

a remedy. If each elector was able to cast his vote without fear of social pressures, especially from his landlord, then the will of the majority in the political nation would prevail. Grote's convictions were at every point the antithesis of Gladstone's: utilitarian, anti-aristocratic, and exalting the popular will. It was the secret ballot, however, that drew Gladstone's explicit attention. In 1838, when Grote was about to propose the ballot in the Commons for the fifth time, Gladstone read a pamphlet on the subject by S. C. Denison, the old Christ Church friend for whom he had drafted a Union speech in defence of the aristocracy, and composed a brief memorandum setting out the case against the innovation.[138] The ballot, Gladstone claimed, was designed to extinguish legitimate influence on voting, to snap the bonds between inferior and superior, to treat human beings as isolated units rather than as members of a larger social body. Representation in the House of Commons would be founded on the chaotic assertion of self-interest rather than on 'the expression of the *interests* of all classes of the community'.[139] Gladstone's hostility to Grote's views was so deep-seated as later to shape his Homeric studies.[140] The banker was at root an advocate of individualism, but Gladstone was a champion of broader groups. Resistance to philosophical radicalism was one of the forces that drove the evolution of the young politician's early political thought.

### III

The overall theory that Gladstone developed was deeply conservative. It asserted the obligation of each to each, but especially of the inferior to the superior. It bore the marks of its origins in the crisis over parliamentary reform in 1831. Fear that revolution might be round the corner meant that Gladstone interpreted the Pittite tradition less in the generous spirit of Canning—whose opposition to reform he nevertheless maintained—than in the alarmist style of Burke. The ideals of the French Revolution must be repudiated. Although Gladstone might have seen some merit in fraternity as a surrogate for the community spirit of the ancient city-state, he was dismissive of liberty as well as of equality. In his repudiation of liberty as an estimable value he actually stood to the right of Burke. Meanwhile his rejection of equality made him a stalwart defender of the landed classes. And at the apex of the political order he championed was the crown. He was as committed to a paternalist view of kingship as Sir Robert Filmer in the seventeenth century. Although Gladstone did not hold that monarchy was the inevitable outcome of his underlying principles, he did believe that it was 'the scheme of gov$^t$ most nearly analogous to the Divine gov$^t$ & most appropriate to human nature'.[141] Certainly he was convinced that the defence of the crown must

---

[138] GP 44728, f. 26 (13 Feb. 1838); S. C. Denison, *Is the Ballot a Mistake?* (London, 1838); D, 10–13 Feb. 1838.       [139] GP 44721, f. 17.       [140] See Ch. 6, pp. 146–7, 149–50, 151–3.
[141] GP 44729, f. 17 (29 Aug. 1840).

be a grand aim of the Conservative party in the 1830s. Moreover he continued to believe that the *ancien régime* of before 1832 was superior to the reformed constitutional system. His sublime vision of a church endorsed by the state, as we shall see, was another throwback to an earlier age.[142] As many commentators have appreciated, Gladstone believed that the ideal political pattern lay in the past. If he was not technically a reactionary, because he did not actively seek to return to an earlier state of affairs, his theoretical preferences lay in that direction.

Consequently his closest intellectual alignment was with the 'orthodox Anglican political theology' of the later eighteenth century, which, as J. C. D. Clark has insisted, survived into the nineteenth.[143] Drawing inspiration from the Jacobite non-jurors' ideal of passive obedience, it nevertheless endorsed the house of Hanover, surrounding its members with an aura of sacral kingship. Power came not from the people, insisted the High Churchman William Jones in a sermon of 1778 on 'The Benefits of Civil Obedience', but from above. Liberty was a false ideal, for human beings properly belonged to a social body that existed for the good of all.[144] Bishop Horne, whose works were edited by Jones, and Horne's contemporary on the episcopal bench Samuel Horsley, occupied a substantially similar position, though with a rather higher regard for liberty.[145] Gladstone shared their overwhelming desire to root policies deeply in the Christian tradition. If his Aristotelianism was more prominent than theirs, it merely served to reinforce the conviction that submission to parents and governors was equally natural. Although there is no sign that Gladstone directly absorbed the political doctrines of Jones, Horne, and Horsley, theirs was the High Church version of political theory for which he had a natural affinity.[146] In due course he did examine the ideas of their non-juring predecessors. At a later stage in his career he identified the idea that there is 'nothing between the Crown and the Divine Ordinance' as 'the theory of the Non-jurors as it affects the State'.[147] Gladstone had upheld this opinion in his theory of descending authority, but when he first carefully evaluated the thought of the non-jurors, in 1841, he decided that their doctrine of non-resistance could not be maintained in the modern world. Submission was now due not to an arbitrary ruler but to a constitutional monarch who governed according to law. Consequently it was 'to law we are to submit'.[148] Gladstone had a great deal in common with those who opposed the Glorious

---

[142] See Ch. 3, pp. 54–67.                              [143] Clark, *English Society*, pp. 216–35.
[144] William Jones, 'The Benefits of Civil Obedience', *The Theological, Philosophical and Miscellaneous Works of the Rev. William Jones, M.A., F.R.S.*, 12 vols. (London, 1801), 6, pp. 155, 158–9, 163–5.
[145] George Horne, 'Submission to Government' [1789], in William Jones (ed.), *The Works of the Late Reverend George Horne, D.D.*, 4 vols. (London, 1831), 4, p. 231; F. C. Mather, *High Church Prophet: Bishop Samuel Horsley (1733–1806) and the Caroline Tradition in the Later Georgian Church* (Oxford, 1992), pp. 227, 229–30.
[146] On the High Church political tradition, see P. B. Nockles, *The Oxford Movement in Context: Anglican High Churchmanship, 1760–1857* (Cambridge, 1994), ch. 1.
[147] W. E. Gladstone, 'Remarks on the Royal Supremacy' [1850], *Gleanings*, 5, p. 222.
[148] GP 44727, ff. 112–14v (27 July 1841), quoted at f. 113v. Gladstone was reading Robert Nelson's *Life* (1713) of the non-juror George Bull: *D*, 19, 25 July, 1 Aug. 1841.

Revolution for conscience's sake, but he never endorsed their extreme rigidity. For all his doctrinaire tendencies, he was disinclined to translate an exalted religious view of the state, whether Jacobite non-juring or Hanoverian High Church, into an intransigent political position.

That is because, already in the 1830s, his constitutional theory had a liberal dimension. His advocacy of the rights of the crown, for example, was not extreme but what he called 'moderate monarchism'. In a memorandum of 1837 he repudiated the charge that under Henry VIII he would have been an absolutist by claiming that he upheld 'a mixed and tempered government' in which any element under threat had to be defended.[149] As early as 1832 he argued that the English Tories occupied a middle position (no doubt Aristotle's praise for the mean was in his mind) between traditionalists and liberals in continental despotisms: 'the *same man* might be highly conservative in England, and yet a friend to great ameliorations in Austria.'[150] As though to vindicate his own progressive credentials, Gladstone has left an outline for a speech, apparently at Newark following the 1832 election, containing the headings 'Retrenchment—Reform—Peace'.[151] These liberal instincts, as we have seen, were consolidated on a firm theoretical basis following Gladstone's first taste of office under Peel in 1834–5. From Aristotle he drew the notion of attaching the middle classes to an aristocratic order; from de Tocqueville he acquired a recognition of the centrality of opinion in the modern state. The ideal polity would therefore need to make concessions to the popular will, though they must be principled and timely. Even the value of the popular element had become integrated in his theory. Which of the principles that governed the two parties, he asked in 1836, self-government or obedience, was best suited for human nature? He made the remarkable admission that the choice was probably one of temperament, depending 'heavily upon perceptions and persuasions incapable of analysis'. Revealed truth seemed to confirm Gladstone's decision that self-government was less necessary than obedience, and yet 'the two together as the active and the passive principle form the harmony of our nature'.[152] Thus right did not lie wholly with a descending theory of authority nor with the rationale of the Conservative party. Even before the appearance of his utopian political treatise on *The State in its Relations with the Church* (1838), Gladstone had incorporated open-mindedness into his system. He believed on principle that, however ideal states might be, they must change with the times and allow the people a share in power. Only a slight shift in the balance between self-government and obedience would suffice, at a theoretical level, to alter his political allegiance. Already the intellectual path was remarkably clear towards Liberalism.

Gladstone's political theory in the 1830s therefore displayed much of the complexity, even convolution, for which he was to become known in later years. Yet it rested on firm intellectual foundations. On the one hand, the Christian

---

[149] GP 44727, ff. 52–52v (17 May 1837).
[151] GP 44821 D, f. 66v (n.d.).
[150] GP 44815 A, ff. 51v, 51 (22 Oct. 1832).
[152] GP 44726, ff. 21–2 (23 Feb. 1836).

tradition taught respect for law and government; on the other, Aristotle recommended the pursuit of virtue. Morley quipped that at this stage in his career Gladstone, like the medievals, had greater faith in things because Aristotle said them than because they are true.[153] Gladstone himself would have recognized no such antithesis. For him Aristotle and the Bible spoke with one voice, and they were true. It was, however, a particular assumption of the philosopher, though one shared with nearly all writers of antiquity, that left the most indelible mark on the mind of the young politician. Classical sources were virtually unanimous that human beings belonged in communities. Aristotle, as the politician noted, argued that the *polis* was the highest form of *koinonia* (community).[154] The communitarian ideal, realized in the city-state, was the classical principle that exercised most fascination over Gladstone. He was far from considering it outdated by modern developments. The transport revolution, he contended, meant that the nation was now as closely integrated as a city in ancient times.[155] Hence the nation could still seek to realize the conditions of the tightly knit *polis* of antiquity. Gladstone realized that there were ineradicable interest groups within the community, potentially at odds with each other, but the remedy was that each individual must pursue the common good rather than any private interest. Plato, as Gladstone recorded, taught that we are to seek the welfare of the whole, not a part.[156] Against Paley, Grote, and the utilitarians, Gladstone was insistent that human beings are not rational egoists, constantly seeking personal advantage. The utilitarian case was erected on the premises of individualism, but Gladstone's was based on the belief that groups of human beings are more than the individuals of which they are composed. 'The mass', he wrote in a detached note of 1833, 'has a character distinct from the aggregate formed by addition together of the characters of the parts.'[157] Gladstone was holistic in all his theorizing. It was axiomatic that the social bodies into which people are born, whether families or nations, have profound claims upon their members. Gladstone's early Conservatism rested on the convictions of antiquity about human solidarity.

---

[153] Morley, 1, p. 201.          [154] GP 44723, f. 120.          [155] GP 44820, f. 90 (n.d.).
[156] GP 44722, f. 50v.          [157] GP 44815 F, f. 5 (14 Nov. [1833]).

# 3

# The Emergence of Church Principles

DURING THE early years of his parliamentary career Gladstone devoted a high proportion of his energies to religious affairs. Alongside his political concerns, as he recalled late in life, 'in an irregular way I gave much time to theology'.[1] He read widely, he wrote profuse private memoranda, and he published two substantial works on ecclesiastical topics. Yet Gladstone's theological evolution is not entirely clear in the secondary literature. According to G. W. E. Russell, writing in the year after the statesman's death, Gladstone built Catholic doctrine on evangelical foundations. There was no denial of the evangelical opinions in which he had been brought up, but merely the addition of further convictions representing a higher churchmanship.[2] Peter Jagger has adopted a similar view, contending that Gladstone moved to a 'Catholic-Evangelical' position.[3] Perry Butler treats Gladstone's Catholicism, largely superseding his evangelicalism but in some tension with his growing political Liberalism, as the ideological stance that he gradually assumed.[4] Boyd Hilton, however, argues for the persistence, despite modification, of evangelical themes in the politician's mind.[5] There is no unanimity on the matter. What will be explored in this chapter, therefore, is the direction and extent of the change in Gladstone's religious thought down to around 1841. It will first consider the evolution of his churchmanship, then turn to the exposition of his views in *The State in its Relations with the Church* (1838), and finally examine the position avowed in his *Church Principles considered in their Results* (1840). The aim is to establish the theoretical basis of Gladstone's attitude to ecclesiastical questions.

---

[1] *Autobiographica*, p. 146 (GP 44791, ff. 1–19).

[2] G. W. E. Russell, *Mr. Gladstone's Religious Development* (London, 1899), p. 17.

[3] P. J. Jagger, *Gladstone: The Making of a Christian Politician: The Personal Religious Life and Development of William Ewart Gladstone, 1809–1832* (Allison Park, Penn., 1991), p. 263.

[4] Perry Butler, *Gladstone: Church, State and Tractarianism: A Study of his Religious Ideas and Attitudes, 1809–1859* (Oxford, 1982), p. 234.

[5] Boyd Hilton, *The Age of Atonement: The Influence of Evangelicalism on Social and Economic Thought, 1795–1865* (Oxford, 1988), ch. 9. The doctrinal persistence of evangelicalism is asserted more strongly in Hilton's earlier essay 'Gladstone's Theological Politics', in Michael Bentley and John Stevenson (eds.), *High and Low Politics in Modern Britain* (Oxford, 1983), p. 31.

I

Gladstone's pilgrimage had begun from an evangelical position. His father, though a patron of evangelical causes in the Church of England, did not have a carefully articulated personal creed, but his mother, the shaping religious influence in the home, nourished what Gladstone recalled as a 'warm piety'.[6] Although in later life he remembered no conversion experience, his mother wrote to a friend when the boy was about 9 that she believed her son William had been 'truly converted to God'.[7] At Eton he found the sermons of Hugh Blair, the great exemplar of enlightened preaching in the Church of Scotland, totally inadequate. 'Not enough of them on Gospel', William noted in his diary in September 1826.[8] When, early in 1827, William was confirmed, his older sister Anne, who was also his godmother, admonished him in a full flood of evangelical rhetoric:

May you indeed be enabled to renounce all that you have promised & may you have instead, that 'Spiritual Mind which is life & peace,' & oh! my beloved William, the more we see of this world—or the nearer we may seem to approach Another, how unspeakably important do the years of youth appear; in <u>time</u>, we must reap the fruit of the seed then sown . . .[9]

Far from resenting such guidance, the 17-year-old recorded this as a 'long & most excellent & pious Letter from my Beloved Sister—unworthy am I of such an one'.[10] William became closely attached to Anne and, partly through her influence, absorbed the evangelical temper of the times.[11]

In retrospect Gladstone saw evangelicalism as individualistic. Its characteristic call for souls to make a personal surrender to Christ, he believed, inhibited any appreciation of ecclesiology. 'I had been brought up [he wrote in the 1890s] with no notion of the Church as the church or body of Christ. Not only was there no visibility, but there was not even any collectivity in my conception of outward religion and religious observances.'[12] The evangelical movement in the Church of England characteristically maintained a distinction between the visible church, the variety of organizations consisting of outwardly religious people, and the invisible church, the scattered ranks of true Christian believers. The former, which included the Church of England as an institution, embraced a multitude of the unconverted; only the latter, whose members were known solely to the Almighty, enjoyed any meaning in the plan of salvation. Accordingly church

---

[6] *Autobiographica*, p. 149 (GP 44790, ff. 156–65).

[7] Russell, *Gladstone's Religious Development*, p. 7.          [8] *D*, 24 Sept. 1826.

[9] Anne M. Gladstone to W. E. Gladstone, 7 Feb. 1827, GGM 541.

[10] *D*, 11 Feb. 1827.

[11] On Gladstone's early religious influences, see S. G. Checkland, *The Gladstones: A Family Biography, 1764–1851* (Cambridge, 1971), ch. 1; Jagger, *Gladstone*; David Bebbington, *William Ewart Gladstone: Faith and Politics in Victorian Britain* (Grand Rapids, Mich., 1993), ch. 2. M. J. Lynch, 'Was Gladstone a Tractarian? W. E. Gladstone and the Oxford Movement, 1833–45', *Journal of Religious History*, 8 (1975), exaggerates the extent of Gladstone's Tractarian allegiance before 1845.

[12] *Autobiographica*, p. 149.

structures, ecclesiastical government, and all that pertained to them were valued only to the extent that they promoted the interests of the gospel. The Church of England possessed no intrinsic theological significance.[13] These were the assumptions that Gladstone recalled from his boyhood. The contrast between the visible professing church and the invisible authentic church was a theme, for instance, in Joseph Milner's *History of the Church of Christ* (1794–1809), 'the only one on the domestic shelves'.[14] At 15, in a letter to his father, William might draw a contrast between the neglect by individuals of the duty to repent and the recognition of its importance by the 'Christian Church . . . the church collectively' in the liturgy,[15] but he saw no role for the Church of England as a teacher. Truth, he believed, in typical evangelical fashion, could be drawn directly from the Bible.[16] The tradition in which he was brought up was distinctly Low Church.

Accordingly Gladstone attributed little efficacy to the sacraments. He had been trained, he recalled in 1864, to believe that they were 'no more than signs'.[17] Evangelicals held in particular that the baptism of infants was merely a symbol of the salvation that was to be received through personal faith in maturer years. They therefore found the Prayer Book declaration that newly baptized infants are regenerated difficult to fit into their theological scheme. For them the standard view was that regeneration, or new birth, took place at conversion. In 1812, however, Richard Mant, later a bishop in the Church of Ireland, published his Bampton Lectures of the previous year denouncing evangelicals as disloyal churchmen.[18] How could they use the liturgy and yet repudiate baptismal regeneration? High Churchmen such as Mant believed that it was dangerous heresy to deny that the sacrament of baptism itself effected the new birth. He provoked a variety of evangelical replies, and the debate rumbled on for many years. Gladstone began to take an interest in the question in 1828. While staying in Edinburgh he encountered Edward Craig, the champion of the evangelical side in the baptismal debate in the Scottish Episcopal Church. Gladstone absorbed the polemics in the exchange, read more about the issue, and by August 1828, before he went up to Oxford, had decided that the truth probably lay not in Craig's view but with the High Church interpretation. 'And if', the prospective undergraduate wrote in an astonishing fourteen-page disquisition on the subject sent to his younger sister Helen, 'in the life and writings of the Apostles, we hear of no new birth except that in Baptism, by what authority shall we venture to add a doctrine of our own to the pure scheme framed by Christ?'[19] Yet the issue was by no means entirely settled, for he still, he told Helen, had other books to explore. The debate

[13] G. F. A. Best, 'The Evangelicals and the Established Church in the Early Nineteenth Century', *Journal of Theological Studies*, NS 10 (1959).

[14] *Autobiographica*, p. 140. Gladstone, however, does not record having read Milner until 1834. By then he felt reservations: 'I cannot think all the sentiments of the Introdn appropriate' (*D*, 17 Aug. 1834).

[15] W. E. Gladstone to John Gladstone, 18 Sep. 1825, GGM, quoted by Jagger, *Gladstone*, p. 62.

[16] *Autobiographica*, p. 142.                    [17] GP 44719, f. 125 (20 Oct. 1864).

[18] Richard Mant, *An Appeal to the Gospel* (Oxford, 1812).

[19] W. E. Gladstone to Helen J. Gladstone, 24 Aug. 1828, GGM 751. The issue is discussed in Butler, *Gladstone*, pp. 22–3; Jagger, *Gladstone*, pp. 139–42; and Bebbington, *Gladstone*, pp. 31–2, 34–5.

seemed crucial for Gladstone's future because at precisely this time, probably because of a suggestion from Craig, he was considering a career as a clergyman. Should he intend to preach conversion, with the more zealous evangelicals, or should he teach, with traditional High Churchman, that the new birth had taken place at baptism?[20] The issue was eventually laid to rest by thorough study of Richard Hooker's *Laws of Ecclesiastical Polity* (1594–7) over the summer of 1829. On his birthday at the end of the year he recorded his conclusion that 'we are regenerate by Baptism & Baptism alone'.[21] It was the first decisive break with the religious assumptions of his youth.

The next development took place in Gladstone's attitude to conversion, an evangelical shibboleth. It was a subject that called for thorough examination once he had adopted baptismal regeneration. If baptism rather than conversion was associated with the new birth, then what was the nature of conversion? Gladstone set out his answer in a paper headed 'The Doctrine of Conversion' composed in January 1830.[22] Although for some the experience could be momentous, it was not, as the Wesleyans maintained, 'the work of a moment'. Rather it lasted 'the whole of our earthly existence', or even beyond, reaching its consummation in the hereafter. In a narrower sense, however, conversion was a critical point in the middle of the process of replacing evil habits with good ones, a point when 'a man passes from the goats to the sheep'. No human being, whether the person concerned or an observer, could ascertain when that stage had been reached. A few who were made regenerate in baptism might have continued in a state of grace ever since and so need no turning, but almost all, if they were ever to enter the kingdom of God, required conversion. Gladstone borrowed his definition of the process from Richard Mant's Bampton Lectures. Conversion entailed conviction of sin of a 'rational' kind (to distinguish it from the evangelical variety), sincere penitence, purposes of amendment, and a real change of heart and life. Mant's standpoint was clearest in his other prescription: 'a regular and diligent employment of all the appointed means of grace.'[23] Orthodox High Churchmen such as Mant insisted on loyal conformity to the Church of England. Gladstone, who had read through the bishop's Bampton Lectures on recent Sundays,[24] was beginning to identify with a new point of view. Although evangelicalism was still putting issues such as conversion on his theological agenda, he was now adopting a solution along the lines of one of its leading opponents.

Gladstone's habit of introspection on matters of everyday life, itself partly the fruit of an evangelical upbringing, was preparing the ground for further theological evolution. He was upset at being upstaged by an undergraduate acquaintance whose wit and humour gained the applause of their circle. Meanwhile, 'some

---

[20] GP 44719, f. 235 (n.d.).                                   [21] *D*, 12 July–10 Oct., 29 Dec. 1829.
[22] GP 44719, ff. 216–23 (n.d.). *D*, 10, 11 Jan. 1830. The paper is helpfully discussed in H. C. G. Matthew, 'Gladstone, Evangelicalism and "The Engagement"', in Jane Garnett and Colin Matthew (eds.), *Revival and Religion Since 1700: Essays for John Walsh* (London, 1993), pp. 114–16.
[23] GP 44719, ff. 222, 217, 218, 220v. Mant, *Appeal to the Gospel*, 2nd edn. (Oxford, 1812), p. 391.
[24] *D*, 25 Oct.–20 Dec. 1829.

humble and unpretending yet solid and elevated mind, ever contemplating his associates as rational and responsible beings, and anxious, deeply anxious for their very highest interests, is voted dull & reserved, if not ill-tempered & morose . . .'. The distancing by the use of the third person does not mask the personal pain Gladstone was feeling. As in later life, he was so profoundly earnest as to lack commonplace affability. The remedy, he decided, was not to surrender one jot or tittle of principle. The popular rival, however, was an egotist, 'as full of self as an egg is full of meat', pandering to his audience for the sake of gratification (it is hard to banish thoughts of Gladstone's subsequent view of Disraeli). Hence the avenue to warmer social acceptance was clear: 'To divest self of selfishness: to have both mind, eyes and ears open to the mental requisitions or personal wants of others: to seek not the appearance mainly but the reality, of an interest in their welfare.' Gladstone would aim to be concerned—and to be seen to be concerned—even for the trivial plans and feelings of his friends.[25] Genuine, but evident, altruism was the panacea for his social ineptitude. The rather stilted technique, which reports of Gladstone's behaviour suggest he tried to pursue for the rest of his life, seems to have been the result of a deep sense of personal inadequacy. This aspect of Gladstone's self-consciousness needs to be added to Travis L. Crosby's recent psychological interpretation of the man. The cultivation of a deserved reputation for interest in others might perhaps be classified, following Crosby's analysis, as a coping strategy for dealing with stress, but in any case its deliberate formulation deserves recognition.[26] Gladstone was pinning high hopes on inhibiting selfishness.

The theme of the repression of self was readily fitted into his religious scheme. Indeed, it had no doubt been there since childhood, derived from the elementary moral instruction of the home. The 'main matter', he told himself in his birthday self-evaluation at the end of 1829, is 'to eradicate the love of self, & substitute the love of God throughout'.[27] The idea was amplified in a detached note of about the same time. The moral principle of selfishness was innate and yet must be eradicated. 'I do not say [he went on] that the love of self directs <u>every</u> action in the unbeliever or nominal Christian: nor that the love of God directs every action in the real Christian: but that in the opposite cases respectively, these opposite states are the states to which they are more or less rapidly tending.'[28] Selfishness was diagnosed as the essence of sin; sanctification was its steady replacement by the love of God. Here was the theological grounding of the detestation of Paley and the utilitarians, as discussed in the last chapter, for identifying morality with self-interest.[29] Consequently Gladstone saw altruism, with its attendant advantages for mixing in society, as a cardinal injunction of the Almighty. The avoidance of self-interest is still, at this stage, perceived as an individual struggle, but it would

[25] GP 44719, ff. 206–8 (n.d.).
[26] T. L. Crosby, *The Two Mr Gladstones: A Study in Psychology and History* (New Haven, Conn., 1997), pp. 5–9. Crosby gives little space to Gladstone's formation, allocating less than two pages (pp. 18–20) to his time at Oxford. [27] *D*, 29 Dec. 1829.
[28] GP 44719, f. 213. [29] See Ch. 2, p. 25–7.

soon be put in another context. What better way of neutralizing selfishness than appreciating the claims of the Christian community? The identification of the love of self as the grand foe of the soul naturally prepared the way for a fuller appreciation of the doctrine of the church.

That development took place after Gladstone had left Oxford, while he was undertaking a continental tour during the spring of 1832. In Rome he was impressed by the magnificence of St Peter's and yearned for a stronger bond with those at worship. The sense of alienation from Roman Catholics, he noted in his diary, meant nothing 'when we live gaily and blindly in the life of self', but when we are consciously struggling against sin it is painful that we lack 'those sympathies, which thus uniting man to man, make us present as it were a single front to the enemy'.[30] Preoccupied with selfishness, Gladstone now saw its remedy as human solidarity in the institutional church. He was on the brink of a great discovery. On Sunday 13 May at Naples, while recovering from seasickness, he read through some obscurer portions of the Anglican Prayer Book. He gained fresh glimpses, according to his diary, 'of the nature of a Church, and of our duties as members of it, which involve an idea very much higher & more important than I had previously had any conception of'.[31] He later looked back to this event as an epoch in his life; and John Morley, followed by other commentators, has recognized that his estimate was correct.[32] The Church of England, Gladstone perceived, was a branch of the church universal, possessing an absolute claim on his loyalties. He could no longer be satisfied with the idea of an invisible church current among evangelicals. Instead of the view that 'the Church consists only of those who vitally believe in Christ',[33] he adopted the conviction that all in its outward communion are fully members of the church. The church must be a visible institution, for only if it had an outward expression could it be real. Gladstone had grasped the basics of High Churchmanship.

A further stage in his theological evolution was the adoption of the doctrine of apostolic succession. On Gladstone's return from Rome, he began to wrestle with the question of whether the authority of the apostles to govern the church had been transmitted down the centuries to the bishops of his own day.[34] In old age Gladstone believed that it was in correspondence with Benjamin Harrison, an Oxford friend who was to become Archdeacon of Maidstone, that 'the notion of succession in the sacred ministry . . . dawned upon my mind'.[35] The correspondence took place in the autumn of 1833, when Harrison sent him the first two *Tracts for the Times*, propaganda from the Oxford movement that was launching its revitalization of High Churchmanship.[36] 'Exalt our Holy Fathers the Bishops', Gladstone read in Newman's first tract, 'as the Representatives of

[30] *D*, 31 Mar. 1832.                                                          [31] *D*, 13 May 1832.
[32] *Autobiographica*, pp. 142–3, 150–1. Morley, 1, pp. 87–8.
[33] GP 44722, f. 154 (n.d., but watermarked 1832).
[34] GP 44719, ff. 191–3 (n.d.). The visits to Rome and Naples are noted on f. 193v.
[35] *Autobiographica*, p. 151.
[36] Benjamin Harrison to W. E. Gladstone, 10 Nov. 1833, GP 44204, f. 12.

the Apostles . . .'[37] Early the following year, while visiting Oxford, the young politician absorbed a recent ordination sermon by G. W. Doane, Bishop of New Jersey in the American Episcopal Church, that seems to have swayed him deeply. It was 'admirable', he recorded in his diary; the 'whole excellent', he commented in his notes on the sermon.[38] It asserted baptismal regeneration and went on to ground ministerial authority in the apostolic succession. No doubt Gladstone discussed the sermon with Benjamin Harrison, whom he frequently met during his fortnight in Oxford, and perhaps also with Newman and Pusey, whom he also saw.[39] On his last day there he spent time with Harrison and read the twenty-fourth *Tract for the Times*, 'The Scripture View of the Apostolic Commission'.[40] Later in the year he was assuring Harrison that the argument in the doctrine's favour carried 'irresistible force'.[41] By the end of his life Gladstone was eager to play down the influence over him of the Oxford movement and of the *Tracts* in particular, but it seems clear that in this instance both the place and the writings were shaping factors.[42] Harrison was significant, though probably more face-to-face in Oxford than by letter, but an American bishop seems likely to have been most decisive in crystallizing Gladstone's acceptance of apostolic succession. It was the final step in consolidating his transition from evangelicalism to a form of High Churchmanship.

Rising churchmanship held implications for religious experience. Although devotional fervour had once been associated with High Churchmen, it had been played down by most of the representatives of the tradition in the early nineteenth century. The restraint of those who most respected the forms of the Church of England now contrasted with the freedom of the evangelicals in speaking of their interior lives.[43] Some of the sermons delivered by Orthodox High Churchmen that Gladstone heard at Oxford must have deprecated expressions of spiritual feeling as fanatical. In a notebook entry, probably of 1833, he tried to reconcile his evangelical inheritance with the High Church critique. The 'popular creed' of the evangelicals, he wrote, 'constantly appeals, without circumlocution or reserve or limit, to the most inward and retired and subtle feelings of the human heart'. They were in the habit of putting direct questions to only slight acquaintances about their religious state. Partly in reaction, he went on, others were arguing that Christian experience was no more than a fiction. That, he contended, it was not: experience was the internal dimension of the formation of habits that Aristotle had taught him to be essential for progress in virtue. Gladstone therefore set down guidelines for dealing with the subject. First, there should be no glib use of

[37] 'Thoughts on the Ministerial Commission respectfully addressed to the Clergy', p. 4, in *Tracts for the Times*, 1, new edn. (London, 1838). This was almost certainly one of 'Newman's & Keble's papers on the Church' that Gladstone read before Harrison sent copies (*D*, 27 Oct. 1833).

[38] *D*, 44815 F, f. 2v (n.d.). *D*, 19 Jan. 1834. Gladstone read two other pieces by Doane while in Oxford (*D*, 23, 29 Jan. 1834).                                         [39] *D*, 29, 30 Jan. 1834.

[40] *D*, 2 Feb. 1834.                 [41] Benjamin Harrison to W. E. Gladstone, 27 Oct. 1834, GP 44204, f. 52.

[42] Butler, *Gladstone*, pp. 51–2, 168–9, has noted the role of the *Tracts*.

[43] P. B. Nockles, *The Oxford Movement in Context: Anglican High Churchmanship, 1760–1857* (Cambridge, 1994), pp. 190–8.

'phrases heedlessly and indolently caught up from the mouth of others'. Secondly, there must be no attempt to 'distinguish emotions so delicately harmonised and blended' by specifying details of what could only be fairly described in general terms. And thirdly, all should beware of 'casting pearls before swine' by bringing such themes before those who gave no thought to them. Instead, in harmony with the more objective teaching of the Orthodox High Churchmen, the careless should be challenged by basic Christian truths that appealed to fear, hope, and gratitude.[44] Gladstone remained convinced of the importance of the interior life, but was becoming more cautious about putting his sense of the numinous into words.

One aspect of religious experience was particularly contested. Evangelicals in general held that authentic faith brought with it the assurance of salvation. Unless there was a personal awareness of acceptance by Christ, an individual's conversion was in doubt.[45] To other churchmen, of whatever camp, the claim seemed presumptuous nonsense. Mant, for instance, contended that assurance of eternal salvation was not the privilege of a true Christian.[46] Gladstone wrestled with the issue, feeling already by early 1834 that 'categorical certainty' was not to be expected on so momentous a question.[47] He set out his views more systematically in the spring of 1835 in a paper headed 'Considerations upon Christian experience'.[48] If in human love, he reasoned, most feelings were hidden (he had started his unsuccessful courtship of Caroline Farquhar), it was more so with love for God. Yet religious experience was something to be cherished, as it was by Coleridge in his *Aids to Reflection* (1825).[49] Gladstone was almost certainly confirmed in this conclusion by the *Remains* (1834–7) of the Irish lay theologian Alexander Knox, which he recorded reading in parallel with writing this document. Although Knox was from the High Church tradition, he, like Coleridge, valued the articulation of spiritual feelings; for, as Gladstone recorded approvingly in his comments on Knox, he taught 'vital religion'.[50] Augustine, however, declared in the *Confessions*, which Gladstone had read in the previous year, that nobody could be certain of avoiding mortal sin.[51] Assurance, Gladstone went on, could come only from special inspiration, which was a rare occurrence: it could certainly not be regarded as a necessary condition of salvation. So all that could properly be expected was something short of absolute certainty. We must make do with probable evidence, but, as Bishop Butler taught, that is sufficient ground for binding us to act—in this case as Christians. Producing suitable behaviour was the best way to grow in assurance.[52] Gladstone was diverging further from his

---

[44] GP 44820, ff. 47–8 (n.d.).

[45] D. W. Bebbington, *Evangelicalism in Modern Britain: A History from the 1730s to the 1980s* (London, 1988), pp. 6–7, 42–50.     [46] Mant, *Appeal to the Gospel*, sermon VIII.

[47] GP 44815 F, f. 36 (24 Jan. [1834]).

[48] GP 44724, ff. 54–67 (dated 17 Apr. 1835, but begun 8 Mar.).     [49] Ibid., ff. 55v–8.

[50] GP 44724, f. 73 (24 May 1835). Cf. *D*, 15 Mar.–24 May 1835.

[51] GP 44724, ff. 63, 60. Cf. *D*, 31 Aug.–26 Nov. 1834.

[52] GP 44724, ff. 59v, 60v, 62. Bishop Butler is not named, but, as Perry Butler notes, the teaching is his: Butler, *Gladstone*, p. 52.

evangelical background. Although he continued to value religious experience, he was now willing to side with Orthodox High Churchmen, Augustine, and Butler in dismissing high-blown claims about assurance of salvation.

There is a similar turning away from his earlier religious heritage in Gladstone's attitude to private judgement. How far did an individual possess the right to reach a personal interpretation of religious truth? According to contemporary Protestant polemic, private judgement was one of the greatest conditions, and equally one of the greatest benefits, of the Reformation. As Gladstone gradually elaborated his churchmanship, however, it became axiomatic that the Catholic creed was what a Christian should believe. In a paper on 'The Rule of Faith', composed in September 1836, Gladstone contended that the authority of the church circumscribed each person's liberty of judgement.[53] There was good reason why the individual should defer to ecclesiastical wisdom. All needed the guidance of others who were more prayerful or learned than themselves; the church existed to instruct; and the clergy were to be accepted as the ambassadors of Christ.[54] Gladstone, however, had not entirely abandoned the legitimacy of private judgement. The Church of England urged its members 'to bring into the service of God all the faculties of their minds'.[55] That position contrasted with the claim of the Roman Catholic Church to infallibility that extinguished the duty to seek out truth. Whereas an Anglican believed the Catholic creed by 'voluntary and responsible agency', the Roman view was that its reception was a 'mechanical or involuntary act'.[56] Passive intellectual submission formed no part of Gladstone's faith. The individual must think through the faith, as he had done, in order to reach the common mind of Christendom. So he was simultaneously insistent that the church had a duty to teach the truth and that each person had to embrace it personally. He was a firm upholder of what in 1842 he called 'the consent and witness of the Catholic Church', believing that it is 'highly irrational and presumptuous in the individual to prefer his own construction to hers'.[57] Although Gladstone was careful to avoid moving too far towards the Roman position as he understood it, he had left another facet of evangelical individualism far behind.

A further question thrown up by evangelical belief was the debate between free will and predestination. The general trend among Anglican evangelicals during the earlier nineteenth century was to shed the more distinctive Calvinistic features of their creed such as predestination. When he was an undergraduate, however, Gladstone had encountered the hearers of Henry Bulteel, the curate-in-charge of St Ebbe's Church, whose extreme Calvinistic views induced him to leave the Church of England in 1831. For a time Gladstone was attracted by their zeal until he decided that it 'appears to outstrip discretion'.[58] Nevertheless the

---

[53] GP 44726, ff. 155–74 (23 Sept. 1836).     [54] Ibid., ff. 161v–5.     [55] Ibid., f. 160.
[56] Ibid., ff. 84v–5 (24 July 1836).     [57] *Autobiographica*, p. 243.
[58] Memorandum, Mar. 1829, Lathbury, 1, p. 4. On Bulteel, see T. C. F. Stunt, 'John Henry Newman and the Evangelicals', *Journal of Ecclesiastical History*, 21 (1970).

issue continued to preoccupy him as he struggled towards a personally satisfying formulation of his faith. In the early 1830s he supposed, like many moderate evangelicals, that salvation must be a result of some metaphysical reconciliation of divine sovereignty and human agency that the mind cannot fathom.[59] In December 1835, however, he tried to settle the issue in an extended paper on 'The Predestinarian question'. At the end, very tentatively, he ventured to suggest a fresh solution to the conundrum: 'the Divine wisdom and mercy may be governed by the capabilities which are seen to lie in the structure of character.'[60] Predestination, that is to say, might be a function of God's foreknowledge of the moral response of each individual to his grace. This solution, which was similar to the formulation of Newman, whose *Parochial Sermons* Gladstone had started to read,[61] may nevertheless have developed separately in Gladstone's thinking. By making predestination dependent on human behaviour, he was taking a major step towards, in effect, adopting the free will position. His mind travelled further in the same direction. In September 1839 he carefully investigated perhaps the ablest defence of the Calvinistic position, *The Freedom of the Will* (1754) by the American Congregationalist Jonathan Edwards, who held that the determinism entailed by predestination was compatible with human liberty. Gladstone was not impressed. 'He flatly contradicts real necessitarianism', the politician commented, 'and leaves a sham necessitarianism.'[62] Human beings, Gladstone believed, enjoyed a higher form of liberty than Edwards allowed. Only if they were seen as responsible moral agents, capable of the holy living to which High Churchmen aspired, could any theory now find favour with Gladstone, and on that score Edwards's view of freedom was defective. By 1845 the politician was dismissing necessitarianism as a mere 'jangle of words'.[63] He had embraced a high view of freedom in the philosophical field long before he accepted it in the political arena.

In parallel with his evolution on predestination, Gladstone was remodelling his understanding of justification by faith. In the Calvinistic tradition there was a horror of confusing faith, which made people initially acceptable to God, with works, which subsequently made them advance in holiness. Faith brought justification; only afterwards did works lead to sanctification. Already by Christmas Day 1832 Gladstone was willing to concede that the distinction between justification and sanctification was unreal on the ground that faith and holiness grow up together in the human soul.[64] But Gladstone still shared with evangelicals the reason for their contention that the two stood apart: an insistence that salvation was a free gift of God, not something merited by human achievement. In 1836 the study of the evangelical Joseph Milner's *History of the Church of Christ* confirmed his conviction that in the early church justification was a matter of being

---

[59] GP 44815 A, ff. 33–4 (18 Oct. [1832?]); 44821 C, f. 7 (18 May [1834]).
[60] GP 44725, ff. 112–22 (13 Dec. 1835), quoted at f. 120v.          [61] *D*, 23, 30 Aug. 1835.
[62] GP 44728, ff. 279–303 (10–30 Sept. 1839), quoted at f. 287.
[63] GP 44731, ff. 57–60 (25 Aug. 1845).          [64] GP 44815 A, f. 48 (25 Dec. 1832).

accounted righteous rather than a question of possessing actual righteousness.[65] Converts, that is to say, were acceptable to God because of the merits of Christ, not their own. Milner points out that this was the characteristic case of the Reformers in their controversy with Catholic divines in the sixteenth century. So the politician's acceptance of Milner's case was a verdict in favour of Protestantism. Gladstone showed his continuing alignment with the Reformers in the following year by his reactions to the third volume of Newman's *Parochial Sermons* (1836). The leader of the Oxford movement was consciously diverging in a Catholic direction from the evangelical view of salvation. In the sixth sermon, on 'Faith and Obedience', for example, Newman contends that the two states of mind are one. Gladstone dissents sharply, inserting in his copy the words: 'but obedience presupposes faith.'[66] The confusion of the two, Gladstone believed, would lead to the supposition that justification was grounded in obedience, a meritorious quality, and so to the overthrow of the understanding he shared with Milner. Faith, the politician held, was nothing but a perception of the intellect and so contained no merit whatsoever.[67] Newman was propounding a view that Gladstone was disposed to reject entirely.

The debate nevertheless demanded further research. Newman was deeply influenced by the early church fathers; Milner also acknowledged their importance, and especially that of Augustine. The question at issue between them could be settled by an appeal to the authority of the greatest of the Latin fathers. So in the autumn of 1837 Gladstone launched into the study of nine of Augustine's treatises, all in the original Latin. He began, on 5 September, with the bishop's polemic against the Pelagians in which he denounces the opinion that divine mercy can be merited.[68] Bolstered by the authority of Augustine, Gladstone returned to writing about the doctrine of justification by faith later in the month. He lays down again that faith is 'an intellectual act', not, as Newman had declared, 'a spiritual disposition'.[69] Salvation is not granted in response to indications of holiness in a human life. That principle alone, he believed, could guarantee that justification was attributed to Christ alone. When, in the following year, Newman published his *Lectures on Justification*, Gladstone took them up with the comment, 'I tremble'.[70] Well he might, for in the book Newman developed an elaborate critique of the Protestant position still maintained by the politician. But Gladstone was by no means satisfied with the statement recently issued on the subject by the evangelical camp, G. S. Faber's *Primitive Doctrine of Justification* (1837).[71] It was, he wrote, 'a hard and dry skeleton of theology' to insist, as Faber

---

[65] D, 14 Aug.–12 Oct. 1836. GP 44726, ff. 201–3 (7 Oct. 1836). Cf. J. D. Walsh, 'Joseph Milner's Evangelical Church History', *Journal of Ecclesiastical History*, 10 (1959).

[66] J. H. Newman, *Parochial Sermons*, 3 (London, 1836), p. 86, Hawarden Castle.

[67] GP 44727, f. 101 (8 Aug. 1837).

[68] Ibid., ff. 124–5 (5 Sept.–24 Oct. 1837). Gladstone does not record the reading of this work in his diary, possibly because he was examining it in small snatches in order to crystallize his own views.

[69] 'On the nature and position of the doctrine of Justification by Faith', GP 44727, ff. 178–92, quoted at f. 180.          [70] D, 15 Apr. 1838.

[71] D, 22 Apr.–20 May 1838. Cf. Nockles, *Oxford Movement in Context*, pp. 261–4.

did, that justification precedes sanctification. The Book of Homilies of the
Church of England taught that love and other graces were present before justification even though they flowed from sanctifying grace.[72] Gladstone saw justification and sanctification as too interwoven for him to identify with the evangelical
view, and yet, as he told Henry Manning in 1841, he was profoundly apprehensive
about 'Oxford opinions' on the subject. 'I cannot tell', he wrote, 'in Newman's
book what the thing really is for which he is arguing: I dread beyond measure, I
confess to you, the doctrine of human <u>desert</u>, come in what form it may.'[73] Any
suspicion that the favour of God could be earned was to be rigorously excluded.
Unlike Newman, Gladstone was not drawn towards Rome by his reformulation
of the doctrine of justification. He had moved away from the evangelical position
on this as on other controverted issues, but the reading of Augustine, whose writings Gladstone cherished ever afterwards, restrained him from going beyond what
he considered the middle way of the Church of England.


II


While Gladstone's views on points of doctrine were still developing, he published
his first book. As the title of *The State in its Relations with the Church* (1838)
suggests, the treatise was an effort to relate his political thinking to his ecclesiology. It was not, however, a strictly theological work. John Keble, the Tractarian
leader, complained in a review that the book neglected the traditional biblical case
for the obligation of the state to maintain an established church.[74] Gladstone,
though giving more attention to the scriptural arguments for the establishment of
religion in the greatly expanded fourth edition of 1841, self-consciously avoided
writing as though he were a clergyman, an authorized teacher of doctrine. Instead,
as he told his friend Henry Manning, he wrote the work 'from a politician's point
of view'.[75] The book emerged from Gladstone's involvement in the constant
debates of the 1830s over establishment. Yet the subject preoccupied him because
of his newly discovered and passionately felt allegiance to the visible Church of
England. On 27 January 1833, two days before first attending the House of
Commons as a member, he jotted down in a commonplace book his understand-
ing of the rationale for his career. 'We love the <u>state</u>', he wrote, 'for the sake of the
Church … The highest light in which the State can be contemplated is as the
handmaid of the Church.'[76] The state, Gladstone believed, had a responsibility to
maintain the Christian truth professed by the Church of England. Even in Ireland,
where little more than 10 per cent of the population adhered to the Anglican

[72] GP 44728, f. 62 (20 Apr. 1838).

[73] W. E. Gladstone to H. E. Manning, 22 Apr. 1841, Lathbury, 1, pp. 235–6.

[74] [John Keble], 'Gladstone—The State in its Relations with the Church', *British Critic and
Quarterly Theological Review*, 26 (1839), p. 372.

[75] W. E. Gladstone to H. E. Manning, 14 May 1838, GP 44247, f. 49.

[76] GP 44815A, f. 10 (27 Jan. 1833).

established church, an obligation rested on the civil authorities to support the ecclesiastical settlement. The United Church of England and Ireland deserved the unqualified backing of parliament. It was a question, as Gladstone wrote in a paper of 1834, of the 'conscience of the Legislature'.[77] Through his book he was to become known as the champion of the view that the state had an exclusive duty towards Anglicanism.

Gladstone's papers reveal the extent to which his distinctive theory of the church–state nexus was rooted in the broader political thought discussed in the previous chapter. One argument was based on the existence of the state as a social body. Because this collective entity possessed opportunities to advance the religious interests of its component individuals, it had an obligation to do so. Since we call ourselves Christians, he contended, we have Christian obligations. 'And that which is binding upon us all individually, we cannot get rid of collectively.'[78] The duty to uphold the church flowed from the corporate existence of the nation. A second line of reasoning was founded on the patriarchal dimension of Gladstone's thought. The idea of a state religion, he declares, is an implication of 'the paternal view of government'.[79] In a long memorandum of 1835 intended for Lord Aberdeen as Colonial Secretary, Gladstone sets out this case in relation to the practical issue of what religious teaching should be authorized for schools in the West Indies. It might appear sensible to help all varieties of religion, as the Whig policy of concurrent endowment assumed. But an indiscriminate policy of assistance to all would endorse the pernicious idea that authority flows upward from the popular will. The state would be reduced to acting as a mere servant of the people, distributing benefits in accordance with the wishes of its masters. The contrasting parental notion of the state upheld the view that authority flows downward from the Almighty. The government would point its charges to the truth, 'dealing with subjects in some measure as a father dealing with Children'.[80] The Conservatives, as defenders of the higher view, should ensure that education in the West Indies was solidly Anglican. It is clear that Gladstone's theory of the established church was intimately connected with his fundamental convictions about the nature of political society.

The outline of a treatise on church–state relations appears in one of Gladstone's notebooks for 1835, the same period when he was composing his chief dissertations on political theory. The propositions form the core of what was to emerge as *The State in its Relations with the Church*:

That government is not an optional but a natural institution.
That governments are human agencies: rational: collective: and of functions sufficiently influential for good or evil to render them responsible to God.
If they have a moral being, they must also have a religious profession.
That where there is unity of government, there must be unity of this religious profession.

---

[77] 'Irish Church Property', GP 44723, ff. 106–15 (9, 24, and 28 June 1834), quoted at f. 109v.
[78] GP 44803 H, f. 19 (n.d.)          [79] GP 44821 B, ff. 20–35 (4 May 1834), quoted at f. 33.
[80] 'West Indian Education', GP 44724, ff. 4–36 (7 Apr. 1835), quoted at f. 25.

That this unity need not rigorously apply to circumstantials, even of importance, but of substance.

That it would be absolutely broken were the same government of the same kingdom to maintain & profess in one part of it a form of Christianity which anathematised that which it maintains in the other.[81]

It was a chain of reasoning that bound together Aristotelian premises with application to Ireland, taking in on the way the central argument that government should avow a religion on behalf of its subjects. All that remained for the book to appear was some stimulus. That came in the spring of 1838 when Thomas Chalmers, the leader of the evangelicals in the Church of Scotland, appeared in London to plead on behalf of the principle of establishment as it applied equally north and south of the border. Chalmers's claim that it did not matter which church was established so long as it was Protestant irritated Gladstone, calling into question his belief in the uniqueness of the Anglican mission.[82] Accordingly the politician was spurred into composing a work that combined the establishment principle with sound church principles. *The State*, as we may call it, was the result.

Gladstone wrote the book at lightning speed during July 1838. Although he drew on the advice of his friend James Hope, an ecclesiastically minded lawyer, who even suggested the word 'Relations' for the title,[83] it is clear that *The State* was the product of Gladstone's own mind. A primary practical aim was the defence of the Church of Ireland. Although the church could not be vindicated on the ground of numbers, Gladstone argues, that consideration did not 'change the nature of truth': if the establishment of the church was the duty of government, its status remained undisturbed by questions of arithmetic.[84] The maintenance of the Church of Scotland as a parallel establishment was allowable both because the Almighty had bestowed his blessing on its work and because a constitutional obligation to retain Presbyterianism was entrenched in the Act of Union of 1707.[85] The Scottish Church deserved government support alongside the Church of England in the colonies, but abroad there must be a scrupulous avoidance of assisting other faiths, especially Roman Catholicism, because that policy was an 'active participation in evil'.[86] Gladstone was declaring war on the Whig principle of concurrent endowment. These practical implications flowed from the fundamental doctrine

---

[81] GP 44821 D, f. 54v (n.d.). No other entries in this notebook appear to date from after the autumn of 1835.

[82] S. J. Brown, 'Gladstone, Chalmers and the Church of Scotland', in David Bebbington and Roger Swift (eds.), *Gladstone Centenary Essays* (Liverpool, 2000).

[83] J. R. Hope to W. E. Gladstone, 27 July 1838, GP44214, f. 23v, in Robert Ornsby, *Memories of James Robert Hope-Scott*, 2 vols. (London, 1884), 1, p. 146.

[84] *SRC*, p. 79. The first, second (1839), and third (1839) editions of *The State* are almost identical, the second doing little more by way of modification than adding a table of contents and an extra line on the first page, and the third issuing a minimally corrected text. The fourth edition (1841), however, was published in two volumes, each of which is longer than the first edition. There are tables in the fourth edition setting out the location of the passages retained from the third edition (*SRC*, 4th, 1, pp. xi–xl). In these notes the first edition is meant unless otherwise indicated.

[85] Ibid., pp. 241–7.          [86] Ibid., p. 278.

that 'in national societies of men generally the governing body should, in its capacity as such, profess and maintain a religion according to its conscience'. Gladstone asserted the principle on the ground, derived from his burning sense of personal responsibility, that individual governors had the duty to advance the faith, but also argued his distinctive case for 'national personality'.[87] The nation had a corporate duty to profess the faith. Gladstone's subject, he explained to Manning, was 'the law of conscience written on the heart of the State' together with 'the gradual and growing relaxations of that law'.[88] The politician aspired to expound the law and to limit the relaxations.

The book begins with a review of previous theories of church and state. William Warburton's still influential work, *The Alliance between Church and State* (1736), contended that it was convenient for the two institutions to support each other on grounds of mutual self-interest. Gladstone dismisses this case because it leads the state to choose for its partner the largest religious society.[89] 'Fatal admission—for Ireland!', he remarked in his private notes on Warburton.[90] William Paley's apologia for religious establishments was even more brashly utilitarian, and so Gladstone rejects it for its 'false ethical principles'.[91] He treats Thomas Chalmers's recent lectures with much greater respect, praising his 'profuse and brilliant eloquence' and echoing his arguments against exclusively voluntary support for religion in the body of his text.[92] Chalmers, however, since he lacked any appreciation of 'the divine constitution of the visible church', failed to provide any criterion by which government could select the correct religious community to endorse.[93] The absence of a distinct ecclesiology is also Gladstone's objection to Richard Hooker's classic statement of church–state relations from the end of the sixteenth century. Gladstone claims that Hooker shares his own premise of the corporate personality of the state, but disagrees with his view that church and state are names for different aspects of the single commonwealth of England. Gladstone's church principles dictated that the two must be recognized as sharply different or else the autonomy of the church might be imperilled by the state. Hooker, according to Gladstone, did exaggerate the legitimate role of the crown in ecclesiastical affairs.[94] Although aligning himself more with Chalmers, and especially with Hooker, than with Warburton or Paley, Gladstone makes it plain that he is striking out on a path different from any of theirs.

Gladstone shows much closer agreement with the only other view that he evaluates, that of Coleridge in his essay *On the Constitution of the Church and State* (1830). In this late work the Lake poet adopted his favourite German philosophical manner, parading much abstraction and esoteric learning, in order to set the relations of church and state in a fresh light. The state, he argued, required a 'National Church' so that its ministers could teach civility, 'all the qualities essential to a citizen'. It was 'a blessed accident' that the Christianity of the Catholic

---

[87] Ibid., p. 26.  
[88] W. E. Gladstone to H. E. Manning, 17 May 1838, GP 44247, f. 51v.  
[89] *SRC*, p. 13.  
[90] GP 44728, f. 126 (9 July 1838).  
[91] *SRC*, p. 14.  
[92] Ibid., pp. 19, 41, 43, 57.  
[93] Ibid., p. 21.  
[94] Ibid., pp. 10–11. Cf. pp. 67, 204.

Church existed to give content to the National Church.[95] Gladstone annotated his copy of the book, probably when he read it in October 1837.[96] In his own work Gladstone praises Coleridge's argument as 'beautiful and profound'. Although he dissents from the poet's analysis of the social estates of the realm, Gladstone concludes that his 'masterly sketch' contains 'substantial truth'. The politician alludes to Coleridge's remark about the identity of the National Church with the Christian Church being 'a happy accident', a slight misquotation that is surely a sign of familiarity.[97] Gladstone subsequently quotes Coleridge favourably, twice uses his phrase 'the national estate of religion' [98] and deploys this concept in the overall case of *The State in its Relations with the Church*. The public authorities, Gladstone contends, have a natural obligation to support this national estate whether or not it is the actual Church of England. Alec Vidler, Colin Matthew, and the editor of Coleridge's *Church and State* are right to recognize the sway of the poet-philosopher over the politician.[99] Standing in the German idealist tradition, Coleridge injects something of its characteristic visionary understanding of the nation into Gladstone's approach.

Coleridge, however, most attracted Gladstone because of the premises from which he argued. The poet shared the holistic assumption of classical writers that a people must be seen as a unity, a view that Gladstone had derived direct from antiquity. *The State* shows clear signs of indebtedness to Plato and Aristotle. In his book Gladstone refers three times to Plato, though, since none adds a point of substance to the argument, the extent of the direct influence of the philosopher over the work should not be exaggerated.[100] Neither of Plato's political works, the *Republic* nor the *Laws*, is cited in the first edition—though the *Republic* does appear in the pages of the fourth.[101] Aristotle, however, contributes more to the work. In an essay on Gladstone's book, Richard Helmstadter, while rightly warning against emphasizing its Aristotelianism to the exclusion of other influences, nevertheless estimates highly its debt to the Greek philosopher.[102] Aristotle is quoted (though only twice) in order to buttress significant points. The remark in the *Politics* that while the state 'started as a means of securing life itself, it is now in a position to secure the good life' is deployed to vindicate the claim that 'national organization is evidently of divine appointment'.[103] The *Politics* is also cited in order to reject 'the very low theory of government' propounded by

---

[95] S. T. Coleridge, *On the Constitution of the Church and State*, ed. John Colmer, *The Collected Works of Samuel Taylor Coleridge*, 10 (London, 1976), pp. 54–5.

[96] *D*, 29–31 Oct. 1837. Matthew, p. 39.  [97] *SRC*, pp. 17, 19, 18.

[98] Ibid., pp. 61–2, 37, 107.

[99] A. R. Vidler, *The Orb and the Cross: A Normative Study in the Relations of Church and State with Reference to Gladstone's Early Writings* (London, 1945), p. 27 n. Matthew, pp. 38–9. Coleridge, *Church and State*, ed. Colmer, pp. lxii–lxv.

[100] *SRC*, pp. 31, 109, 324.  [101] *SRC*, 4th, 1, p. 139.

[102] R. J. Helmstadter, 'Conscience and Politics: Gladstone's First Book', in B. L. Kinzer (ed.), *The Gladstonian Turn of Mind: Essays Presented to J. B. Conacher* (Toronto, 1985), pp. 15–17.

[103] Aristotle, *The Politics*, bk. 1, ch. 2, trans. T. A. Sinclair (Harmondsworth, 1962), p. 28 (Gladstone quotes the original Greek). *SRC*, p. 50.

Warburton.[104] Aristotle, because of his exaltation of the *polis* (shared, of course, with Plato), is aligned in Gladstone's thinking with a high view of the state. That is no accident, for the politician's whole cast of mind, as we have seen, was permeated by Aristotelianism. John Keble, in reviewing *The State*, observed that the writer was inclined to give his readers more credit for thoughtfulness than they were likely to possess. 'In this', he continued, 'as in some other respects he reminds us sometimes of Aristotle's manner in the Ethics.'[105] Although the *Ethics* is not cited in the first edition (it is in the fourth),[106] the book was foundational, as we have seen, to the political theory of which Gladstone's ideas on church and state were an outgrowth. *The State* is very much the work of a classical scholar.

The extent to which the book is rooted in Gladstone's broader political thought is not immediately evident in the first edition. In the substantial revision for the fourth edition, as we shall see, that was to change, but the original text does not obtrude its basic principles. It is true that there is citation of several of Gladstone's other favourite authors. Blackstone and de Tocqueville both appear,[107] and Burke is deployed at a pivotal point in the argument. The Irish politician's observation that the right to rule 'essentially resides in talent and virtue' is used to show that governors possess the personal qualifications to propagate religion.[108] Elsewhere Gladstone cites Burke's doctrine that an established religion 'consecrates the commonwealth and all that officiate in it'.[109] The sustained defence of a church establishment as 'the first of our prejudices' in Burke's *Reflections on the Revolution in France* had left its mark on Gladstone's thinking.[110] The widespread esteem for Burke as a wise defender of English liberties made him a safe court of appeal that would not alienate readers. But in general Gladstone, in his typical debating mode, tries to avoid elaborating assumptions with which his audience might disagree. Crucially he claims that it is not necessary 'here to enter into any detail upon the formal origin of political power'.[111] The sympathetic reviewer in the *Quarterly Review*, the Oxford High Churchman William Sewell, pointed out the omission and felt bound to make it good.[112] Gladstone, however, wanted to argue that, whether government derived its authority from God or from the people, the result was the same—an obligation on governors to support the national religion. To that extent he was deliberately sidestepping contentious issues in political philosophy.

Nevertheless Gladstone cannot wholly suppress his personal convictions. Even at the point where he wants to claim that a democratic government should maintain a church establishment, he refers to popular sovereignty as a 'fiction'.[113] The

---

[104] *SRC*, p. 50, citing Aristotle, *Politics*, bk. 3, ch. 5.
[105] [Keble], 'Gladstone on Church and State', p. 362.  [106] *SRC*, 4th, 1, p. 142.
[107] *SRC*, pp. 122, 232.  [108] Ibid., p. 53.  [109] Ibid., p. 316.
[110] Edmund Burke, *Reflections on the Revolution in France*, ed. C. C. O'Brien (Harmondsworth, 1968), p. 188.  [111] *SRC*, p. 37.
[112] [William Sewell], 'Gladstone on Church and State', *Quarterly Review*, 65 (1839), p. 107. Sewell visited Gladstone at Hawarden in December 1840, impressing him favourably. *D*, 17, 18, Dec. 1840.
[113] *SRC*, p. 37.

antithesis between ascending and descending theories of authority that he had sketched in his memorandum for Lord Aberdeen in 1835 runs through the book. According to the theory of popular sovereignty, authority rises from the mass of the people to their rulers. The effect, Gladstone says, is to 'degrade the character of government to that of a machine, leaving as the function of those who are engaged in it, simply to ascertain and to obey a popular will, like the index of a clock worked by a pendulum'.[114] By contrast Gladstone asserts what he calls 'paternal principles'.[115] All power in the universe, he asserts, is 'the property of God, the king of that universe'.[116] In the state, which, as much as the church, is ordained by God, government wields the delegated power of the Almighty over its charges. 'The rulers of nations', he writes, 'are as the heads of families.'[117] They possess patriarchal responsibilities to promote the welfare of those under their care. Gladstone cannot avoid taking for granted that this is the case in Britain. 'Because', he writes, '. . . the government stands with us in a paternal relation to the people, and is bound in all things to consider not merely their existing tastes, but the capabilities and ways of their improvement . . .'[118] The corresponding duty of the subject is submission. The Christian religion, Gladstone contends, 'inculcates absolute obedience to all law not sinful'.[119] The theory of church and state that he propounded in 1838 was a branch of the high-flying Tory paternalism that he had been developing over recent years.

The defence of establishment was also associated with another thread in Gladstone's early political thought, the idea of nationality. Colin Matthew points out the salience in *The State* of the concept of 'religious nationality', the character stamped on a whole people by its creed, and relates it to the sense of nationhood in Thomas Arnold's *Principles of Church Reform* (1833).[120] It also paralleled the thought of the Germans who influenced Arnold, and who, in the wake of Herder, were stressing the role of the nation in the divine purposes.[121] Gladstone, like many of his contemporaries, was being caught up in the broad sweep of European intellectual development. The idea of nationhood was central to his argument in two respects. In the first place, one of the justifications for the establishment of religion was the notion of corporate personality. He argues that there is 'a real and not merely suppositious personality of nations, which entails likewise its own religious responsibilities'.[122] Nations were entities over and above the individuals who composed them. National honour and good faith were generally recognized; why not national duty to God? In the second place, Gladstone wants to show the fitness of the Church of England to be established because of its perpetuity. He therefore insists on its continuity through the sixteenth century. In England the Reformation was not a change of creed but the repudiation of a foreign usurper of the church's headship, the pope. It was a struggle between 'this island of the free' and an 'Italian priest'. The English Reformation was therefore 'eminently

---

[114] *SRC*, p. 282.     [115] Ibid., p. 33.     [116] Ibid.     [117] Ibid., p. 50.     [118] Ibid., p. 83.
[119] Ibid., p. 60.                                                    [120] Matthew, p. 38.
[121] Duncan Forbes, *The Liberal Anglican Idea of History* (Cambridge, 1952).     [122] *SRC*, p. 37.

and specially national', an exercise, in fact, in nation-building.[123] The people of England, freed from an alien despotism, became (as Gladstone's contemporary the German historian Ranke would have put it) immediate to God, with no pretended earthly authority claiming jurisdiction over them. The resulting identification of the Church of England with the nation, Gladstone claims, brought the benefit that individuals, aware of being part of a larger whole, had their self-will repressed.[124] At the same time the division of Christianity into national bodies was the best way to ensure its universal spread.[125] Keble thought that Gladstone's book displayed an 'excess of our Church's nationality' that might be labelled 'a sort of *ultra-Anglican* spirit'.[126] It was an expression of the author's full participation in the trend of the times away from eighteenth-century cosmopolitanism towards a more strongly felt patriotism. At the same time it was a symptom of his communitarianism. The nation, it seemed to Gladstone at the time, was the broadest natural community that could exist on the face of the earth. It therefore figured prominently in his theory.

Equally Gladstone's personal ecclesiology looms large in *The State*. Augustine, his preferred guide on church questions, is cited four times. On one occasion, in an epigraph to a chapter, Augustine is quoted as commending the Catholic discipline that had been passed down from Christ through the apostles.[127] Gladstone's characteristic conviction that the church, as a corporate body, effectively inhibits selfishness appears more than once. 'The abhorrence of mere individual will as such', he writes, belongs to 'the Catholic church.'[128] And Gladstone's church principles enter the core of the whole case for the union of church and state. Why, he asks, should the state select the Church of England in particular for the privilege of recognition? The church, Gladstone answers, produces good moral results, especially good subjects; and her claim to possess the truth is presented as having divine authority.[129] These reasons, however, would be alleged by partisans of other religious bodies. The inducement held out by the Church of England but by no other Protestant body (Gladstone leaves the Roman Catholic Church out of account, a weakness in the argument he later recognized)[130] is its guarantee of permanence. The state needs to establish a church which offers assurance that it will not lapse after a little while into some other form of organization. Quakerism would be preferable to Socinianism because of its acceptance of the Bible; Congregationalism would be better than both because of its use of the sacraments; Presbyterianism would again be superior because of its confession of faith; and the English church would be best of all because of its additional guarantee in the form of the succession of clergy who had received all these good things from the beginning.[131] Thus the apostolic succession played a pivotal role in the central argument of the book. It was one of the convictions that Gladstone was soon to expound further, but it was equally a premise of *The State*.

---

[123] Ibid., p. 190.  [124] Ibid., pp. 107–8.  [125] Ibid., p. 298.
[126] [Keble], 'Gladstone on Church and State', p. 390.
[127] *SRC*, p. 126. See also pp. 49, 141, 302.  [128] Ibid., p. 104. Cf. p. 59.
[129] Ibid., pp. 57–62, 65–6.  [130] GP 44728, ff. 210–11 (8 Feb. 1839).  [131] *SRC*, p. 64.

Opinion was divided about the merits of the case that Gladstone made out in his book. *The Times* gave it several notices, moving from early warm commendation to later stern condemnation on the ground that it was allegedly tainted by Tractarianism. The 'baddish' coverage there, Gladstone learned, was the responsibility of a Presbyterian. The evangelical *Christian Observer* echoed *The Times*, and Chalmers lamented Gladstone's teaching.[132] Thomas Arnold liked half of the book, no doubt the corporatism but not the ecclesiasticism.[133] Gladstone waited in vain for the verdict of his senior political colleagues, finding to his discomfiture that Sir Robert Peel, Lord Stanley, and Sir James Graham did not even mention the complimentary copies he had sent them.[134] Bishop Blomfield, by contrast, a High Churchman with whom the author co-operated in church projects, wrote to him saying, according to Gladstone, 'everything I could wish'.[135] At Oxford the work was reportedly approved, while John Keble, for the Tractarians, reviewed it sympathetically but also critically in a way that Gladstone admired.[136] The warmest reception of all came from Germans. Baron Bunsen, soon to be Prussian minister in London, enthused over the contents: 'his Church is my Church,' he told Thomas Arnold, 'that is, the Divine consciousness of the State.'[137] Bunsen sent a copy to his crown prince, from 1840 to be King Frederick William IV, who had it translated into German. Gladstone reported to Henry Manning as early as 2 February 1839 that he had received 'another Prussian testimony in my favour'.[138] Germans were more accustomed to abstract discussions of public questions in Gladstone's manner, and theirs was the heartland of the romantic idealization of the state. Their appreciation of the book was therefore less surprising than it might seem.

The most celebrated response to *The State in its Relations with the Church*, however, came from T. B. Macaulay. The Whig politician, who at this stage in his career rarely took on polemical reviews,[139] saw the opportunity for a devastating critique in the *Edinburgh Review*. Gladstone heard in February 1839 that Macaulay was 'holding forth with much force on the subject' and intended to write 'in very decided hostility'.[140] The critic duly censured the book with pungent irony. 'It is the measure', he wrote, 'of what a man can do to be left behind by the world. It is the strenuous effort of a very vigorous mind to keep as far in the rear of the general progress as possible.'[141] Macaulay met Gladstone's argument head on,

[132] W. E. Gladstone to H. E. Manning, 2, 23 Feb. 1839, GP 44247, ff. 58v, 59v, 61v.

[133] Thomas Arnold to F. C. Blackstone, 25 Feb. 1839, in A. P. Stanley, *The Life and Correspondence of Thomas Arnold, D.D.*, 2nd edn., 2 vols. (London, 1844), 2, p. 148.                    [134] *D*, 9 Feb. 1839.

[135] W. E. Gladstone to H. E. Manning, 2 Feb. 1839, GP 44247, f. 58v.

[136] W. E. Gladstone to H. E. Manning, 23 Feb. 1839, GP 44247, f. 61v. W. E. Gladstone to J. R. Hope, 6 Nov. 1839, HSM 3672, f. 46.

[137] C. C. J. von Bunsen to Thomas Arnold, 4th Sunday in Advent 1838, in Frances Baroness Bunsen, *Memoirs of Baron Bunsen*, 2 vols. (London, 1869), 1, p. 304.

[138] W. E. Gladstone to H. E. Manning, 23 Feb. 1839, 2 Feb. 1839, GP 44247, ff. 61v, 58v–59.

[139] O. D. Edwards, *Macaulay* (London, 1988), p. 27.

[140] W. E. Gladstone to H. E. Manning, 23 Feb. 1839, GP 44247, f. 61v.

[141] [Macaulay], 'Church and State', p. 256.

contending that governments were not fitted to advance religion, rejecting Gladstone's version of church principles as untenable, and elaborating his own alternative theory of church and state. It was inconsistent, Macaulay held, to endorse the constitutional position of the Church of Ireland while repudiating the need for a church establishment in India, where his own experience of administration gave him telling authority. But the two most powerful sections of the article concentrated on drawing out the logical implications of Gladstone's theory. The author's broad principle that human associations must uphold a religion led, Macaulay urged, to absurd conclusions. 'Every stage-coach company ought, therefore, in its collective capacity, to profess some one faith,— to have its articles, and its public worship, and its tests.'[142] Macaulay made merry entirely legitimately, since Gladstone's words, extensively quoted, undoubtedly bore the meaning the reviewer assigned to them. The author had been unguarded in his generalizations. And Gladstone's reasoning, Macaulay held, should properly lead to a policy of persecution. If the government held paternal responsibilities, it must punish upholders of heresies that imperilled the salvation of the souls under its care. Gladstone's reasons for refraining from persecution were ill-judged, and he did, in any case, recommend the exclusion of non-members of the established church from civil office. 'But why stop here?', asks Macaulay delightedly. 'Why not roast dissenters at slow fires?'[143] Gladstone wrote immediately to correct his opponent's impression that he favoured the renewal of the Test Act, repealed in 1828, that had in theory disqualified non-Anglicans from a role in local government,[144] but he could not so easily dismiss the force of Macaulay's case about the religious obligations of corporate groups. It was a formidable onslaught.

Macaulay's case was very much in Gladstone's mind when he came to revise the book for the fourth edition. Although the new version, which appeared in 1841, was hugely extended into two volumes, the principles of the argument remained unchanged. But Macaulay's allegation that, on Gladstone's premises, all human associations must profess a religion had to be met. It was essential to lay down criteria for determining which collectivities are fundamental and so worthy of sacralizing. Gladstone supplies the criteria, as he had not in the original version. Such human associations have to be general, so that nobody is outside one, and permanent. They are natural, 'because they do not imply ... the antecedent consent of the individual', they are unlimited in purpose, 'so that no one can be the judge of his own duties in them', and they are moral, because they are concerned with 'the growth and formation of character'.[145] The criteria clearly reflect the Aristotelian assumptions about unavoidable social obligations on which Gladstone had built the structure of his political thought.[146] They duly yielded 'two forms of human association, and two only': the family and the

---

[142] Ibid., p. 239.  [143] Ibid., p. 248.
[144] W. E. Gladstone to T. B. Macaulay, 10 Apr. 1839, in W. E. Gladstone, 'A Chapter of Autobiography', *Gleanings*, 7, pp. 106–7.  [145] *SRC*, 4th, 1, pp. 72–3.  [146] Cf. above, p. 24, 33.

state.[147] Few (though he could name James Mill as an exception)[148] would deny the corporate religious responsibilities of the family. Gladstone was simply contending for their equivalent in the state. The other types of combination such as stage-coach companies listed by 'a mind of redundant opulence' (Macaulay is never named) do not have the same characteristics. 'Their functions are limited: their personality is little more than mechanical . . . [they] do not . . . contemplate moral results.'[149] There is a scale of types of human organization, and only those at the top have an obligation to profess a religion— even though other bodies may do so, and Gladstone is able to cite the Rhymney Mining Company and the Birmingham Railway Company as each building a church for its workers.[150] Although the absence of corporate homage to religion was always to be regretted, the outright duty rested only on the family and the state. Gladstone felt that he had made good the fatal defect in the argument of the earlier editions.

In order to establish his case, however, he also has to lay bare his most cherished theoretical assumptions. The original version of *The State* took for granted the importance of associations in general, but now Gladstone spends fully twenty pages setting out the most deep-seated of his political convictions, that human beings are social. He begins with a highly abstract point. The universe, as Plato, Cicero, and Virgil testify, is marked by 'oneness of life and action', but its unity was disrupted by the Fall. The result was the pervasiveness of sin in the form of the assertion of individual self-will. The divine remedy, apart from the redemption, was to ordain various expressions of *koinonia*, 'a common life', as 'the grand counteractor of the disorganising agency of the law of self-worship'.[151] The 'sense of a general brotherhood' decayed over time, but the 'law of mutual association' was nevertheless acknowledged as essential by Aristotle.[152] The common life, wherever it is established, entails 'an actual surrender of the individual will'.[153] It is embodied in the state and the family, and equally it 'is tabernacled in the fellowship of the Catholic Church, the communion of saints'.[154] The spirit of community was under attack in Gladstone's day from the 'tendency to detach social relations from the control of the affections' and to allow them to be governed by law or economy alone.[155] It was true, however, that the social principle could be abused because it enlarged human power, increased the liability of an individual to be influenced by others, and impaired moral responsibility.[156] That was why it needed to be regulated by the profession of a collective religion. Yet in general the 'joint, or common life' was a power for good, appointed by the Almighty for counteracting the evil impulses of humanity.[157] The whole passage is a paean of praise for social life as against the individualism of a Jeremy Bentham or James Mill. Gladstone's communitarianism emerges much more powerfully in the fourth edition of *The State* than it had done before.

---

[147] *SRC*, 4th, 1, p. 72.  [148] Ibid., p. 90.  [149] Ibid., pp. 95, 97.  [150] Ibid., p. 102 n.
[151] Ibid., p. 50.  [152] Ibid., pp. 53, 54.  [153] Ibid., p. 55.  [154] Ibid., p. 59.
[155] Ibid., p. 58.    [156] Ibid., p. 62.    [157] Ibid., p. 63

It finds expression in a remarkably high doctrine of the state. Gladstone uses the term not merely of the public authorities but equally of the nation politically organized.[158] He can write of nation and state interchangeably, but does also distinguish them by defining the state (rather imprecisely) as 'constituents of the active power' of national life.[159] The fourth edition differs from the earlier ones in allocating much greater space to an exposition of the role of the state. In the earlier editions the argument for establishment is based first on the religious responsibilities of individual members of government and only subsequently on the implications of the moral personality of the state.[160] In the fourth edition the case is mounted primarily on the consideration of the nature of the state while the argument from the duties of individual governors occupies little space and is professedly 'secondary'.[161] The reversal of priorities represents not a change of conviction but an enhancement of Gladstone's confidence in the dignity of the state. The fourth edition multiplies the exalted attributes of the state, which is now, unlike in the first, spelt with a capital 'S'. It is 'directly the parent, and the object, of some of the noblest feelings which belong to our nature'; 'it asserts the most absolute . . . claims upon all within its pale'; and it 'forges the chain of order as a sacred thing, by attaching its extremity to the eternal throne'.[162] The only minimizing of its role, as in the first edition, is by comparison with the church. The state must never, in Gladstone's view, supplant the church as 'the fountain of morality', the policy of Thomas Arnold and many of Gladstone's Whig opponents. With the single exception of the church, the state was the acme of social organization. Its functions, declares Gladstone, have 'real grandeur'.[163] The fourth edition presents a sustained eulogy of the potential of the state.

The idealization of the state reveals the affinity of Gladstone's theory with contemporary German political philosophy. This feature no doubt goes a long way towards explaining the warm reception of his book in Germany. Occasionally Gladstone drops a German word in the text of the fourth edition that betrays a fresh influence from that quarter. He refers to the interests or forces in the state, 'in the German phrase *momente*'; and to the encouragement of 'the *kunstleben*, the art-life'.[164] He writes approvingly of public patronage of the arts in 'other and perhaps more imaginative nations', a sympathy that he was subsequently to show in his active support while at the Board of Trade for the government-sponsored School of Design.[165] The state, he claims, has the prerogative, according to its own discretion, of giving 'cultivation and improvement' to its members.[166] It was a main instrument of the 'culture' of the individual.[167] The word 'culture' did not yet have the overtones of higher art and literature that it was later to acquire, and in Gladstone's usage means primarily moral development, the 'perfecting' of the

---

[158] Ibid., p.78.   [159] Ibid., pp. 46, 76, 77.   [160] *SRC*, pp. 26–40.
[161] *SRC*, 4th, 1, pp. 127–33.   [162] Ibid., pp. 84, 81, 82.
[163] Ibid., pp. 79, 80. Cf. Richard Brent, *Liberal Anglican Politics: Whiggery, Religion and Reform, 1830–1841* (Oxford, 1987), ch. 4.   [164] *SRC*, 4th, 1, pp. 78, 308.
[165] Ibid., p. 308. Cf. Quentin Bell, *The Schools of Design* (London, 1963), pp. 92–6, 144–8.
[166] *SRC*, 4th, 1, 81.   [167] Ibid., p. 84.

individual.[168] But that idea has German affinities. John Stuart Mill, in the same decade, was consolidating a view of humanity that took from German sources a parallel notion of self-development.[169] What, then, was the German influence playing on Gladstone? Part of it was no doubt mediated through Coleridge, who points to the need for 'cultivation',[170] but Gladstone was also examining German works himself. While completing the revision of *The State*, he read the newly published *Die Kirchenverfassung nach Lehre und Recht der Protestanten* by the conservative Lutheran jurist F. J. Stahl, and inserted several references to it in his own book. The citations, however, concern points of detail and it is unlikely that a work appearing so late in the preparation of the fourth edition would mould its contents.[171] A more likely candidate, as Peter Erb suggests, is Richard Rothe, a romantically inclined Lutheran theologian from Wittenberg whose *Die Anfänge der christlichen Kirche* (1837) Gladstone read on Baron Bunsen's recommendation in 1839. The book was quoted several times in Gladstone's *Church Principles*, and, though never cited, it may have left its mark on the revised version of *The State*.[172] Rothe describes not only the origins of the church but also the functions of the state. Gladstone was wary of the erastian thrust of the theologian's teaching,[173] but he seems to have been more favourably impressed with his high doctrine of the state. 'The state's goal', Gladstone marked with approval in his copy, 'embraces the totality of the moral goal.'[174] Perhaps Rothe's work reinforced Gladstone's already exalted understanding of the state.

Whatever the German sources, however, the doctrine set out in the fourth edition of *The State* shows an unexpected similarity with the ideas of *The Philosophy of Right* (1821) by the much more celebrated German thinker, G. W. F. Hegel. There is no evidence, either now or later, of Gladstone reading Hegel, and the politician took exception to the Hegelian elements in Rothe.[175] Yet Hegel's notion of the state being the march of God in the world, often seen as the apogee of German *étatisme*, finds distinct echoes in Gladstone. The state, he says, represents on an earthly scale 'the principles of the Divine nature, inclusively of the power to assert them'. It is 'the only general minister of Divine government, treading unequally in its steps'. Gladstone draws the same distinction as Hegel between 'the State in its idea', to which these lofty attributes are attached, and its existence in 'a particular country or constitution', which can do no more than

---

[168] Raymond Williams, *Culture and Society, 1780–1850* (Harmondsworth, 1961). *SRC*, 4th, 1, p. 84.

[169] John Stuart Mill, *On Liberty*, ed. Stefan Collini (Cambridge, 1989), p. xvii.

[170] Coleridge, *Church and State*, ed. Colmer, p. 42.

[171] *D*, 10–21 Nov. 1840. *SRC*, 4th, 2, pp. 20, 31, 85, 89, 159. On Stahl, see Nicholas Hope, *German and Scandinavian Protestantism, 1700 to 1918* (Oxford, 1995), pp. 383–4, 464.

[172] *D*, 11 Oct.–18 Nov. 1839. W. E. Gladstone to J. R. Hope, 6 Nov. 1839, HSM 3672, f. 47.

[173] W. E. Gladstone, 'The Theses of Erastus and the Scottish Church Establishments' [1844], *Gleanings*, 3, p. 22.

[174] Richard Rothe, *Die Anfänge der christlicher Kirche* (Wittenberg, 1837), p. 20, St Deiniol's Library, Hawarden, cited by P. C. Erb, 'Gladstone and German Liberal Catholicism', *Recusant History*, 23 (1997), p. 454, n. 26.

[175] 'Stahl's Kirchenverfassung', GP 44729, f. 61 (20 Nov. 1840). Cf. Erb, 'Gladstone and German Liberal Catholicism', p. 454, n. 26.

resemble the ideal.[176] As in Hegel, the state is 'centralised and represented in the person of the sovereign', and it is defined as 'that comprehensive and overreaching form of the natural life which includes and harmonises all its other forms'.[177] The family is one of the primary modes of human association incorporated within it, just as in *The Philosophy of Right*; and Hegel's notion of civil society, the apparatus of corporations and police necessary in commercial society, is represented by the 'inferior combinations' that Gladstone identifies, by contrast with Macaulay, as fundamentally different in function from the state.[178] Gladstone does not assign the inferior activities of human beings, economic and legal, exclusively to the province of these lesser organizations, for they fall within the 'lower purposes' of the state.[179] But he does draw a contrast between 'dealing with men as animals and machines' and 'the cultivation of their higher nature' that Hegel would have appreciated.[180] Although there is no trace of the Hegelian dialectic in Gladstone, there is a remarkable degree of parallelism between the two thinkers. It must arise from their addressing the same problem at a similar time. How, asked Hegel, do we achieve the conditions of the *polis* in a modern society?[181] Gladstone took the same ideals of the classical philosophers as his fundamental given, criticizing the individualistic tendencies of the early nineteenth century from the standpoint of antiquity. Although Gladstone was no Hegelian, he produced similar answers to the great German political philosopher because he was asking the same question about the nature of community in the modern world.

### III

While writing *The State in its Relations with the Church* in the summer of 1838, Gladstone received from his friend James Hope a copy of a newly published work, William Palmer's *Treatise on the Church of Christ*.[182] Taking its two weighty volumes with him on a holiday trip up the Rhine, Gladstone absorbed in a German setting its elaborate vindication of the exclusive claims of the Church of England.[183] As he wrote many years later, the book 'took hold upon me'.[184] Its treatment of many of his central preoccupations such as the relation of private judgement to the teaching of the church drew his admiration. Palmer set out views common among traditional High Churchmen, but in systematic fashion, with great learning and with polemical trenchancy. Objections to the case for the authority of the Church of England are spelt out and met one by one. The book harmonized with Gladstone's still deepening allegiance to the church. In 1835, for instance, he had written unconcernedly in a manuscript that '[o]ur own Church has seceded from her ancient mother', but in July 1838, on reviewing the paper, he

---

[176] *SRC*, 4th, 1, p. 85.  [177] Ibid., pp. 78, 84.  [178] Ibid., p. 96.
[179] Ibid., p. 87.  [180] Ibid., pp. 101–2.
[181] On Hegel, see G. W. F. Hegel, *The Philosophy of Right*, ed. A. W. Wood (Cambridge, 1991).
[182] James Hope to W. E. Gladstone, 28 July 1838, GP 44214, f. 24.
[183] D, 16 Aug–2 Sept. 1838.  [184] *Autobiographica*, p. 152.

insisted tartly that 'it has not'.[185] Palmer's book confirmed his belief that it was the Church of Rome, not the Church of England, that was in schism.[186] The *Treatise* gave Gladstone, as he recalled at the end of his life, 'the clear, definite and strong conception of the Church which through all the storm and strain of a most critical period has proved for me entirely adequate to every emergency and saved me from all vacillation'.[187] In the 1880s Gladstone supported a scheme for issuing a new edition of the book.[188] It articulated, with much more theological expertise than he could marshal, the ecclesiology that he shared with the old High Church tradition.

Nevertheless Gladstone expressed reservations, even on his first reading, about aspects of Palmer's case. He did not accept, for example, the theologian's denial that truth of doctrine was a distinguishing note of the church. Palmer was conscious of the frequent existence of error within the true church, but Gladstone was more eager—'within certain limits', he characteristically adds—to see orthodoxy as an ecclesiastical hallmark.[189] That objection to the argument of the *Treatise*, however, was the only one to suggest stronger claims for the church. His other points all tend to dilute the case made out by Palmer. Gladstone wanted to draw a sharper distinction between the teaching authority of scripture and the claims of tradition so as to ensure the supremacy of scripture. Palmer, too, wished to see tradition as merely subordinate to scripture, but Gladstone felt that their relative status should be guaranteed more effectively. He believed, against Palmer, that it was legitimate to hold some doctrines to be 'fundamental' while others, including the visibility of the church itself, were not.[190] He rejected the theologian's claim that the universal church cannot err.[191] And he repudiated the suggestion that the magistrate should enforce ecclesiastical decrees. All these qualifications tended to decrease the authority of the church. Gladstone's most significant reservations, however, were over the exclusivity of the church. He disagreed with Palmer's contentions that 'there <u>cannot</u> be two separate communions in the same place, both holding the essence of the Church of Christ' and that 'under <u>no</u> circumstances ought a member of the Church to join in any of the religious acts of separatists'.[192] Palmer was wrong to maintain that members of the sects were in the same condition as the heathen because, Gladstone pointed out, 'we see the same fruits of holiness in them that we see in holy members of the visible Church'.[193] Gladstone's familiarity with the Presbyterians around his Scottish home at Fasque had convinced him that salvation must be available beyond the bounds of Episcopalianism. Half-a-century later he still believed that the chief blot on the *Treatise* was its 'severity and rigour towards Presbyterianism and Nonconformity'.[194] There was a liberality in Gladstone's ecclesiology that Palmer

---

[185] GP 44724, f. 20v (7 April 1835).

[186] William Palmer, *A Treatise on the Church of Christ*, 2 vols., 3rd edn. (London, 1842), 1, pp. 337–52.

[187] *Autobiographica*, p. 152.

[188] W. E. Gladstone to J. J. I. von Döllinger, 1 Sept. 1882, Lathbury, 2, p. 321. GP 44769, ff. 77–9 (17 Apr. 1885).                    [189] GP 44728, f. 136 (19 Aug. 1838). Palmer, *Treatise*, 1, pp. 82–98.

[190] GP 44728, ff. 136–6v.          [191] Ibid., f. 139 (20 Aug. 1838).          [192] Ibid., f. 136.

[193] Ibid., f. 138v.                                        [194] GP 44769, f. 77.

could not match. Even when Gladstone was crystallizing an exalted churchmanship, he avoided pressing the position to an extreme.

Two years after assimilating Palmer, in the autumn of 1840, Gladstone published his own statement of ecclesiology. *Church Principles considered in their Results* is a massive work of 528 pages, not counting three appendices, two of them substantial. The influence of Palmer is evident, for example, in the technique of raising and meeting objections to the main case, and, like the *Treatise*, Gladstone's book is, as he recalled, 'a work of very sanguine Anglicanism'.[195] Because Gladstone shared with Palmer the conviction that only the clergy should teach with authority, he explains that he writes not as a 'commissioned instructor' but merely as a 'private person'.[196] In writing of church principles, his method is not 'the scientific process whereby these principles are deduced and proved from Holy Scripture'.[197] Rather, as a layman, he is examining, as the title of the book proclaims, their results. If the subject of ecclesiastical theory were divided into three, he told Henry Manning, then rector of Lavington in Sussex, his province was not the theological dimension but the remaining aspects of the ethical and the practical.[198] He could not entirely avoid theological exposition, and so he conscientiously submitted the manuscript to Manning for his clerical seal of approval.[199] Yet Gladstone wished to concentrate on the other two areas. The 'ethical tendencies' of church principles were 'their bearing ... upon the formation of human character'.[200] By illuminating their nurturing influence over the Christian life he might hope to create a favourable disposition towards them. Their practical consequences for 'the religious interests and feelings of the day in our own country' constituted the other topic. This was the division of his theme for which Gladstone claimed most novelty. He was attempting to demonstrate that church principles 'involve no painful consequences, introduce no real causes of division, deny to no man his spiritual privileges'.[201] A Catholic understanding of the Church of England was justified by its effects.

*Church Principles* can best be appreciated by examining in turn the various other ecclesiastical positions discussed in the book—the rationalist, the evangelical, and the Tractarian—before turning to the author's case for his own standpoint. The heyday of rationalism, Gladstone believed, had been in the eighteenth century. He heaps contempt on the latitudinarianism of the Georgian church. The 'cold theology of the last century' had consisted of a set of 'trivial, feeble, and depreciated notions' that allowed ecclesiastical institutions 'to slumber and decay'.[202] The church was regarded as 'little more than a religious club', dependent on the state for its authority as well as its temporalities.[203] Elsewhere he summed up the state of affairs as 'Hoadlyism', the prevalence of the time-serving attitudes of Benjamin Hoadly, the early eighteenth-century bishop who was a 'fatally notorious advocate of low doctrine'.[204] Such views, though declining in

[195] *CPR*, pp. 147–57. *Autobiographica*, p. 145.   [196] *CPR*, p. 34.   [197] Ibid., p. 30.
[198] W. E. Gladstone to H. E. Manning, 31 Aug. 1840, GP 44247, f. 88.   [199] *D*, 16 Aug. 1840.
[200] *CPR*, p. 31.   [201] Ibid., p. 32   [202] Ibid., pp. 27, 34, 13.   [203] Ibid., p. 99.
[204] Ibid., p. 249.

the church, had by no means disappeared, for a century later they were still buttressed by 'the spirit of the age'.[205] The root of the malaise, Gladstone contends, was the rationalism to which he devotes a whole chapter. 'Now rationalism', he explains, 'is commonly ... taken to be the reduction of Christian *doctrine* to the standard and measure of the human understanding.'[206] The underlying problem was that the understanding was warped by the effects of the Fall on each human being. It was inadequate simply to preach orthodox doctrine, for it would be unprofitable to the hearers. Hence 'there must in every case be an action upon the man independent of the understanding'.[207] The affections, which were capable of taking the will of God as their object, must be the avenue towards transforming human nature. Gladstone's analysis was typical of the romantic reaction against the legacy of the Enlightenment, the substance of the case (though not the abstract prose that was its vehicle) often reflecting Newman. He differed, however, in one crucial respect, for, unlike Newman, he was careful to guard against any depreciation of the proper use of the mental faculties. His argument, he declares, did not imply 'the impotence of the understanding' in religion.[208] He is opposing not the use but the abuse of the mind. The enthronement of reason was not the way to attain Christian truth.

Evangelicalism is much more favourably treated than rationalism. While scrupulously avoiding naming the movement, Gladstone praises the revival of 'personal religion' by 'the Romaines, the Newtons, the Scotts, the Cecils'.[209] If evangelicals were sometimes marked by intemperance in controversy and excessive appeal to inward experience, if they might hold low views of the sacraments and deny the apostolic succession, they were not properly blameworthy.[210] The fault lay with the previous lethargy in the church. 'As Lazarus at his resurrection came forth bound in his grave clothes', so the movement bore marks of the state from which it was emerging.[211] Now, however, evangelicals needed to recognize that Catholic convictions were 'the natural and effective complement' to their teaching, and so to 'explore an old way, not to survey for a new one'.[212] In particular they should abandon their exclusive reliance on preaching. Although evangelicals considered themselves the foes of the exaltation of reason, their concentration on propagating orthodox doctrine itself betrayed 'an imperfectly developed form of rationalism'.[213] They must grasp that it is the appointed role of the sacraments to kindle faith in the affections and go on to embrace church principles in their fulness. On reading Gladstone's book, F. D. Maurice fairly summarized the case against the evangelicals as, 'Press your opinions to their results and they become rationalistic'. It was an ingenious argument, he commented, but it was 'fitter for the courts than for a theological controversy'.[214] Gladstone, however, was doing more than scoring debating points. He was retracing the steps

---

[205] *CPR*, p.. 36.    [206] Ibid., p. 37.    [207] Ibid., p.46.    [208] Ibid., p. 52. Cf. Ch. 4, p. 100 n. 194.
[209] Ibid., p. 471.           [210] Ibid., pp. 20–1, 26, 165, 193.                    [211] Ibid., p. 19.
[212] Ibid., 471, 25.                                                            [213] Ibid., p. 38.
[214] F. D. Maurice to Archdeacon J. C. Hare, 28 Dec. 1840, in Frederick Maurice (ed.), *The Life of Frederick Denison Maurice*, 2 vols., 2nd edn. (London, 1884), 1, p. 302.

of his own pilgrimage over the previous decade, the growing recognition of the inadequacy of his youthful evangelicalism and its gradual supersession by an acknowledgement of the doctrines of the church, the ministry, and the sacraments. A large part of the purpose of his book was to invite other evangelicals to take the same path.

Among the Tractarians were men such as Benjamin Harrison or Newman himself who had done precisely that. Gladstone refers appreciatively in a footnote to Newman's *Prophetical Office of the Church* (1837),[215] but his stance towards Tractarianism is distinctly ambiguous. On the one hand he rejoices in its advocacy of the high claims of the Church of England, but on the other he expresses dismay about the evolution of opinion at Oxford. He was alarmed by the Romanizing tendencies that had come to light with the publication of Hurrell Froude's *Remains* in 1838. Holders of church principles, he admits, may 'be inclined to judge too harshly of mere Protestantism' or give undiscriminating 'praise of this or that portion of Roman Catholic institutions'.[216] Although Gladstone saw a right estimate of the church as the best barrier against secessions to Rome, noting that no proponent of the specific claims of the Church of England had ever become a Roman Catholic convert, his private anxieties about Newman's teaching on human merit, though not expressed in the book, must have sharpened his fears for the future.[217] What most disturbed Gladstone, however, was the rise of partisanship at Oxford. The Tractarians seemed to have formed a coterie to propagate their views, whereas Gladstone wished to carry the whole church into an era of fresh convictions. 'Church principle', he had written to Hope earlier in the year, 'utterly rejects the notion of party or combination standing between the individual and the Church.'[218] In his book Gladstone therefore insists that it is 'the greatest possible error to suppose that the teaching of these doctrines in the present day is peculiar to certain pious and learned individuals in the University of Oxford'.[219] A thirty-page appendix is devoted to quotations from a variety of quarters upholding the doctrines of church authority and apostolic succession. All are from non-Tractarian sources, and many are from the opponents of the Oxford movement. There are evangelicals, including Daniel Wilson, Bishop of Calcutta; there is R. D. Hampden, a liberal *bête noire* of the Tractarians; and there is Richard Bagot, Bishop of Oxford, whose 1838 charge criticizing the Tractarians is cited.[220] The reviewer of *Church Principles* in the *Edinburgh Review*, a Congregationalist, supposed that the book was an apologia for the Oxford movement.[221] He could hardly have been more mistaken. Gladstone goes out of his way to dissociate himself from the Tractarians in what amounts to a declaration of intellectual independence.

---

[215] *CPR*, p. 329 n.  [216] Ibid., p. 390.  [217] Ibid., pp. 390–2. Cf. above, pp. 53–4.
[218] W. E. Gladstone to James Hope, 13 Feb. 1840, HSP 3672, f. 58, Lathbury, 1, p. 223.
[219] *CPR*, p. 320.  [220] Ibid., pp. 535, 552–3, 550–1.
[221] [Henry Rogers], 'Puseyism, or the Oxford Tractarian School', *Edinburgh Review*, 77 (1843), pp. 501–62.

His own position is supported by only occasional appeals to theological authorities. He draws an epigraph from the Lutheran theologian Richard Rothe, but (as in *The State*) the quotation, together with several subsequent allusions to Rothe, tends to confirm rather than shape his argument.[222] These references were, in fact, late additions to the manuscript chapter, which originally existed as separate papers before being assembled for incorporation in the book.[223] Augustine, who supplies two epigraphs and a large number of quotations, is a more substantive influence.[224] Anglicans are deployed sparingly. There are allusions to John Jewel, Richard Hooker, and even Benjamin Hoadly,[225] but representatives of the High Church tradition barely put in an appearance. William Laud, John Bramhall, and William Sherlock are mentioned, and there is a citation of the non-juror Charles Leslie, one of Manning's favourite authors, but only for an incidental point.[226] Gladstone is trying to appear not as the spokesman of a particular point of view within the church but as a loyal son of the Church of England as a whole. In that capacity he expounds what he regards as the leading church principles: the visible church, the sacraments, and the apostolic succession. The true church, he argues against the evangelicals, is not an invisible phenomenon but a historical reality. He writes lyrically of 'this magnificent conception of a power incorporated upon earth, capable of resistance to all the enemies of Divine Truth with the certainty of ultimate victory'.[227] The church administers baptism, where regeneration takes place, and the eucharist, which conveys the body and blood of Christ in 'a real though not a carnal' way.[228] Her authority is guaranteed by the divine commission transmitted down the ages in her ministry. And the Church of England, rooted in antiquity and continuous through the Reformation, possesses full Catholic rights: 'she is at this day the same institution, through which the Gospel was originally preached to the English nation.'[229] Despite the lack of appeal to its representatives, Gladstone was substantially aligned with the old High Church tradition venerated by Palmer that long preceded the Oxford movement.

Yet the book defends that position from a highly distinctive standpoint. The premises of Gladstone's ecclesiastical theory are the same as those of his political theory. F. D. Maurice was struck by the Aristotelianism of *Church Principles*.[230] For Gladstone to describe his approach as 'ethical' was to echo the *Nicomachean Ethics*. The influence of Aristotle is also detectable in phrases

---

[222] *CPR*, pp. 85, 90, 101, 102, 216 n., 234, 237, 240, 360. W. E. Gladstone to J. R. Hope, 6 Nov. 1839, HSM 3672, f. 47. The debt is estimated higher by Erb, 'Gladstone and German Liberal Catholicism', p. 454, n. 26.

[223] *D*, 11 Oct. 1839. Cf. GP 44728, ff. 307–11 (Oct.–11 Nov. 1839). W. E. Gladstone to J. R. Hope, 24 Oct. 1839, HSM 3672, ff. 444–5.

[224] *CPR*, pp. 85, 158, 35, 81, 116–17, 152 n., 163–4, 172, 174, 208, 328, 336, 507.

[225] Ibid., pp. 193; 172, 173, 227, 229; 232, 244, 249.

[226] Ibid., pp. 420, 107, 170. W. E. Gladstone to H. E. Manning, 14 May 1838, GP 44247, f. 48v.

[227] *CPR*, p. 116.      [228] Ibid., p. 161.      [229] Ibid., p. 313.

[230] F. D. Maurice to Archdeacon J. C. Hare, 28 Dec. 1840, in Maurice (ed.), *Maurice*, 1, p. 302.

about the correspondence of the principles he is commending with 'the necessities and the capabilities of human nature'.[231] The Aristotelian approach leads
Gladstone to assume community and government to be as natural in the church
as they are in the state. He draws an explicit parallel between the church and civil
society, contending that the principles of combination and subjection in both
reflect the will of the Creator.[232] There is, he concedes in his treatment of apostolic succession, a difference between ecclesiastical and secular authority. The
continuity of its rulers, he argues, is what preserves the identity of the church,
whereas a nation maintains its continuity independently of its rulers.[233] Yet the
parallel is reinforced with the consideration, bolstered by an appeal to Burke, that
ecclesiastical power, no less than civil power, is best transmitted by inheritance
rather than by acquisition.[234] The family, furthermore, is treated as the model for
the church as much as for the state. Human beings are born into families and so
enter on 'the most complex reciprocal offices' that last throughout life.[235] Because
they are brought into the church through baptism before they can exercise any
power of choice, its members have similar mutual obligations. The church is like
the family, 'a bond of union, independent of and superior to the will of the
persons composing it'.[236] It has moral effects similar to those of the family: it
'tends to depress and absorb the idea of self', enlarging love and increasing
sympathy.[237] Gladstone's treatment of the sacraments also bears witness to the
prominence of communitarian themes. They are valuable, he argues, because 'in
them Christian brotherhood is entirely realised and represented'.[238] His ecclesiology has no need to rest on prior statements of the case by representatives of the
High Church tradition because it is rooted in his own social theory.

The book is also distinctive because Gladstone was concerned, as he had told
James Hope, to present church principles in a 'conciliatory' manner'.[239] Two
years later Manning, in a book dedicated to Gladstone, was to follow Palmer in
asserting, albeit in qualified form, the maxim *extra ecclesiam nulla salus*.[240]
Gladstone, however, would have no truck with the repudiation of those outside
the Church of England. The principles he advocated, he stresses, 'exclude no true
lover of Christ from the true Church of Christ'.[241] He ungrudgingly concedes the
lower claims of Dissenters for their churches because their lives produce the fruits
of righteousness. 'When the fact of holiness is established', he lays down, 'the
inference of grace is certain . . .'[242] Furthermore, while the Church of England
could not drop some of its tenets for the sake of wooing back Dissenters in the
manner urged by Thomas Arnold, Gladstone contends that she must desire to
include the greatest possible number of seekers of the truth. She must realize 'the
true Christian principle of comprehension at its *maximum*'.[243] The Church of
England, in fact, could become the centre of unity for divided Christendom. It

---

[231] *CPR*, p. 31.     [232] Ibid., p. 90.     [233] Ibid., pp. 216–17.     [234] Ibid., pp. 263–4.
[235] Ibid., p. 91.     [236] Ibid., p. 98.     [237] Ibid., p. 123.     [238] Ibid., p. 173.
[239] W. E. Gladstone to James Hope, 24 Oct. 1839, HSM 3672, f. 45.
[240] H. E. Manning, *The Unity of the Church* (London, 1842), p. 382.
[241] *CPR*, p. 411.     [242] Ibid., p. 415.     [243] Ibid., p. 499.

bridged the gulf between Protestant and Catholic and also had affinities with the churches of the east. Gladstone recognized that most national sections of the Roman Catholic Church would not join in a movement towards unity, yet he hoped that 'singly some one or more might lead the way in breaking from the heavy fetters which Trent has imposed upon them'.[244] A renewed Gallican impulse in France, or more likely some equivalent in a German state, might induce a national religious community to follow the English example of repudiating papal dominion while retaining Catholic identity. So on the Roman as well as on the Protestant flank there might be scope for ecumenical initiatives. Gladstone's hopes, however chimerical, were deeply felt and were to last his whole lifetime. They illustrate the extent to which, at the same time as asserting a high doctrine of the Church of England, he was eager for overtures towards other Christian bodies. *Church Principles* is remarkable for what Gladstone described to Manning in the following year as 'genuine elasticity in the principles of Catholic Communion'.[245]

## IV

The book reveals the extent to which Gladstone had altered his religious opinions over the previous dozen or so years. He had shifted from a straightforward evangelical position in his youth to a species of High Churchmanship. Although *Church Principles* was so irenical in tone, it did venture criticisms of the inadequacies of evangelical thinking. Later in the same decade E. B. Pusey, the continuing mentor of the Oxford movement, contended that the only weakness of the evangelicals lay in what they lacked: 'What religious persons among the so-called "Evangelical" portion of the Church, hold *positively*, that is, their faith, is true. They, then, who have received the fuller teaching of the primitive and undivided Church, have not to call upon them to lay aside anything which they believe, but to propose a fuller belief to them.'[246] Had Gladstone followed the path marked out by Pusey of simply building Catholic doctrine on evangelical foundations? There is a measure of truth in G. W. E. Russell's view that Gladstone's theological development followed exactly that pattern, an evolution entailing no denial of early opinions but merely an addition of further convictions.[247] Gladstone possessed little grasp of any doctrine of the church, ministry, or sacraments before Catholic principles moved in to fill the vacuum. Furthermore, his continuing insistence that salvation depends not on human merit but on divine grace represented a reaffirmation of his evangelical inheritance. Yet the private papers reveal a fuller and rather different picture. On a whole range of doctrines—baptism,

[244] *CPR*, p. 510.
[245] W. E. Gladstone to H. E. Manning, 22 Apr. 1841, GP 44247, p. 92v, Lathbury, 1, p. 235.
[246] E. B. Pusey, *Sermons during the Season from Advent to Whitsuntide*, 2nd edn. (Oxford, 1848), p. ii.
[247] Russell, *Gladstone's Religious Development*, p. 17.

conversion, assurance, private judgement, free will, and justification—Gladstone became, as we have seen, highly critical of the standard evangelical position. He consciously reacted against what in 1842 he called 'the intrusion of secondary or even of untrue notions' into the deposit of faith by evangelicals.[248] Gladstone repudiated much of what was uniquely evangelical as well as adding to it. It is true, as Boyd Hilton has observed, that he clung to the central doctrines of moderate evangelicals, but these were the dogmas of Augustinian orthodoxy which they shared with High Churchmen. It is not accurate to see him, with Hilton, as maintaining what was distinctively evangelical for the rest of his life.[249] Any interpretation of Gladstone's intellectual development must take account of the rejections as well as the reaffirmations of the 1830s.

What form of High Churchmanship did he attain by around 1841? After that date, as the next chapter will show, there was to be a change in the trajectory of Gladstone's theological convictions, but Perry Butler has rightly argued that Tractarianism was initially far less significant for his pilgrimage than earlier styles of High Churchmanship.[250] The reception of the doctrine of apostolic succession, it now appears, was something of an exception, because Gladstone adopted it under the immediate influence of Oxford. Nevertheless, despite an attraction to Newman's writings, he found the drift of Tractarianism troubling. The explanation is partly the tendency of Newman to toy with human merit before the Almighty, but the growing Tractarian sympathies for Rome and the strong sense of partisanship at Oxford also roused the politician's anxiety. Gladstone was much happier with the insistence of the old Orthodox High Churchmen that the whole Church of England, as a corporate body with fixed articles of faith, inherited the truth of God. Gladstone's ecclesiology was essentially that of Palmer and therefore that of the Orthodox tradition. Yet he had several reservations about details in Palmer; he would not follow recent representatives of the tradition in their distaste for spiritual experience; and, above all, he rejected the exclusiveness of Orthodox claims. In an age of growing tension between the Church of England and Dissent, Gladstone wanted a sympathetic approach to those outside the Anglican fold. There was a liberality about Gladstone's church principles that paralleled the broad-minded elements in his political theory. His version of High Churchmanship was therefore his own: militantly Anglican but generous to outsiders, hostile to rationalizers but otherwise non-partisan within the church.

Nor was Gladstone's ecclesiastical thought divorced from his thinking about politics. He wished to insist that the Church of England, bearing a divine commission that guaranteed its permanence, was the proper partner for the state. He might have been expected to draw on the High Church tradition of political thought that grounded the obligation to maintain an established church in the Old Testament, but that case, as Keble complained, did not attract him.[251] Rather he found inspiration in Coleridge, discovering, with the poet-philosopher, justification for the

---

[248] *Autobiographica*, p. 243.
[250] Butler, *Gladstone*.
[249] Hilton, 'Gladstone's Theological Politics', esp. p. 31.
[251] [Keble], 'Gladstone on Church and State', pp. 365–6.

establishment in the needs of the nation as a community. Gladstone's insistence on the corporate obligations of an organic state aligned him with contemporary German thinking and even, in some respects, with its culmination in Hegel. But Gladstone's ideal of state–church relations was not merely an elaboration of Coleridge's Germanic principles, for it rested on the holistic premise that he had learned from antiquity. Plato, Aristotle, and Augustine assumed the *polis* as the basis of social organization, and it was to Aristotelian teaching that Gladstone turned when he needed to defend the special status of the state and the family against Macaulay. If the social solidarity of the state was real rather than fictional, then it was as obliged to uphold the truth as any individual. There was a profounder sense, furthermore, in which there was a bond between Gladstone's thinking about the church and the state. The church, as much as the state, was a corporate entity. A visible church, with structures and rulers, was central to the faith, an antidote to selfish individualism. 'Community', Gladstone wrote in a memorandum that may date from 1834, 'is the very essence of the Church of Christ.'[252] His ecclesiastical thought, like his political thought, was based on communitarian principles.

---

[252] GP 44821 D, f. 16 (n.d.).

# 4

# The Religion of the Incarnation

RELIGIOUS AFFAIRS continued to preoccupy Gladstone during the 1840s. Despite sustaining parliamentary duties and holding office in Conservative ministries, twice with cabinet rank, the politician found time for a multitude of projects to advance the Christian faith. He erected a chapel on his father's estate at Fasque in Kincardineshire.[1] In collaboration with his friend James Hope, he founded a public school and theological seminary at Glenalmond in Perthshire with the ambitious object of turning Scotland into an Episcopalian country.[2] He supported the Colonial Bishoprics Fund, serving as an active treasurer from its inception in 1841 while it set about establishing a succession of sees in the expanding empire.[3] In this decade Gladstone was particularly close to Hope and Henry Manning, sharing with them his enthusiasms and disappointments. David Newsome has shown how the circle of close friends around Manning elaborated their hopes for an Anglican resurgence in these years.[4] Gladstone participated fully in their plans, zealously promoting the apostolic role of the Church of England in the life of the nation. As a result he was drawn beyond the version of church principles that he had elaborated in 1840. Then he had taken pains to dissociate himself from the Oxford movement, but in subsequent years he changed his mind. D. C. Lathbury rightly points to an alteration in Gladstone's attitude towards the Oxford movement at this time, though he unduly narrows the development to the year 1844.[5] Tractarianism moulded his piety in a fresh way, leading him towards a new theological principle that was to prove a formative element in the evolution of his broader thinking. Gladstone's acceptance of Tractarian teaching is the subject of this chapter.

I

From 1841 onwards the movement at Oxford was on the defensive. In that year John Henry Newman published *Tract XC*, confirming Protestant fears that he had

---

[1] S. G. Checkland, *The Gladstones: A Family Biography, 1764–1851* (Cambridge, 1971), pp. 342–3, 360.
[2] Robert Ornsby, *Memoirs of James Robert Hope-Scott*, 2 vols. (London, 1884), 1, pp. 206–13, 242–5, 274–82.
[3] W. F. France, *The Oversea Episcopate: Centenary History of the Colonial Bishoprics Fund, 1841–1941* (Westminster, 1941), pp. 11–12: W. E. Gladstone, 'Ecclesiastical State of the Colonies', *Quarterly Review*, 75 (1844).    [4] David Newsome, *The Parting of Friends* (London, 1966).    [5] Lathbury, 1, p. 293.

moved far in a Roman Catholic direction, and in the following year he withdrew from active leadership of the movement to the seclusion of Littlemore, a village that was part of his parish but well outside the city. After a fiercely fought contest in which Gladstone played a full part, Isaac Williams lost the election to the Oxford chair of poetry on the grounds of his authorship of one of the *Tracts*. The university authorities, determined to root out all expressions of crypto-Romanism, took up proceedings in 1843 against a sermon of Pusey's on the eucharist. Gladstone was now convinced that the true interests of the Church of England were under assault at the university. He wrote to Pusey for the first time since 1836 to express his regret that the Vice-chancellor should be acting against 'one whose feelings have ever been kept so much in harmony as yours with the actual Church of England'.[6] The politician went into print with an article on the 'Present Aspect of the Church', protesting against the militant Protestant hounding of anyone tinctured with Tractarianism and calling for the authorities to tolerate even immoderation among the more advanced disciples of the 'Oxonian divines'. With an eye on Newman in ominous self-imposed exile at Littlemore, however, Gladstone also argued that members of the Church of England had an 'absolute duty . . . to abide where they are'.[7] Secession to Rome would endanger all the gains made by Catholic teaching within the church. When, in the following year, W. G. Ward published his *Ideal of a Christian Church*, arguing, while still an Anglican, that the Church of Rome was the embodiment of the ideal he described, Gladstone wrote another article as a rebuttal; yet he also went out of his way to oppose Ward's condemnation by the University of Oxford.[8] Like Hope and Manning, the politician had come to see the cause championed at Oxford by Pusey as the best hope of the Church of England.

It is not surprising, therefore, that Gladstone was a regular attender at the chief London outpost of Tractarianism. The family's place of worship in the capital changed from St James, Piccadilly, to St Martin-in-the-Fields in January 1841, but Gladstone himself had a preference from April of the same year for Margaret Chapel—what was later to be rebuilt by William Butterfield as All Saints, Margaret Street.[9] The chapel was turned by Frederick Oakeley, before his departure to Rome in 1845, into an exemplar of dignified worship. On Easter Day 1844 Gladstone attended there both morning and evening, recording the services as 'most edifying and beautiful'; a Saturday act of worship in the following year 'composed me'.[10] The singing, he recalled towards the end of his life, was 'the heartiest and warmest I ever heard'.[11] What attracted him most was 'a reality of earnest concurrence in the work of holy worship'.[12] Daily churchgoing with

---

W. E. Gladstone to E. B. Pusey, 30 June 1843, Liddon Bound Volumes [hereafter LBV] 46/3, Pusey House Library, Oxford.

W. E. Gladstone, 'Present Aspect of the Church' [1843], *Gleanings*, 5, pp. 38, 72, 71.

W. E. Gladstone, 'Ward's Ideal of a Christian Church' [1844], *Gleanings*, 5.

*D*, 31 Jan., 4 Apr. 1841.                                        [10]  *D*, 7 Apr. 1844, 8 Feb. 1845.

W. E. Gladstone to W. A. Whitworth, 3 Sept. 1893, Lathbury, 1, p. 409.

*D*, 10 Apr. 1842.

weekly communion became Gladstone's ideal. Attendance on weekdays, except during vacations at Hawarden,[13] was usually impossible, though Gladstone tried to be in church on saint's days and in Lent. He could normally manage a eucharist every Sunday while he was in London, but not elsewhere,[14] and sometimes went to an early celebration so that on those days he clocked up three church services.[15] Worship, however, was not confined to church, for Gladstone insisted on leading his family and servants in daily prayers in their home. He cannibalized the Prayer Book to provide all the necessary elements of a weekday service—confession, Lord's Prayer, petition, intercession, thanksgiving, and benediction. Gladstone published the result in 1845 as *A Manual of Prayers from the Liturgy*, apparently at the suggestion of his father.[16] He was careful, however, to seek approval and correction of details from his diocesan Bishop Blomfield, because all was to be done under proper ecclesiastical authority.[17] The aim, he explained in the preface, was to bring family devotion 'into harmony with the temper and system of the Church'. Private judgement should be minimized in worship as much as in theology. Domestic prayers should aspire to be 'an image, though a broken and partial image', of the daily service in church that formed the acme of Catholic devotion.[18]

Another dimension of Tractarian piety that Gladstone aspired to cultivate was fasting. It was, he explained in 1847, a precept of the gospel to engage in 'voluntary restraint of lawful bodily enjoyments'.[19] He had considered the practice as long before as the late 1820s and had concluded by 1832 that its disuse was a scandal,[20] but it was only in the 1840s that he seriously took up the task. The purposes, he told his household in an address on the eve of the public fast in 1847, were to bring the body into subjection, to aid devotion, to quicken the sense of dependence on God for food, to increase sympathy for the poor, to encourage temperance, and to symbolize repentance.[21] The Church of England taught that there should be fasting on all Fridays except Christmas Day and on the forty days of Lent except Sundays.[22] Gladstone found it difficult to follow the first counsel. 'My Fridays', he noted in his diary in 1847, 'are still unmarked by their proper observance.'[23] The diaries also record his annual struggles in Lent. In 1840 he maintained his abstinence 'feebly: only till dinner & that with an exception'.[24] In 1842 Passion Week was 'but ill kept'.[25] In the following year he broke off because of the demands of night work in parliament.[26] Repeatedly pressures of public business and physical weakness made him sigh over his inadequate attainments. In 1847, free from office, he again attempted fasting and this time managed to lose

[13] e.g. *D*, 25 Dec. 1843—9 Jan. 1844.

[14] MS Lambeth 2758, Lambeth Palace Library, London, quoted by H. C. G. Matthew, 'Gladstone, Evangelicalism and "The Engagement" ', in Jane Garnett and Colin Matthew (eds.), *Revival and Religion Since 1700: Essays for John Walsh* (London, 1993), p. 121.   [15] e.g. *D*, 11 Jan. 1846.

[16] *D*, 22 Dec. 1844.   [17] *D*, 1, 2 Mar. 1845.

[18] [W. E. Gladstone], *A Manual of Prayers from the Liturgy arranged for Family Use* (London, 1845), pp. iv, v.   [19] 'Fasting', GP 44780, ff. 185–8v (21 Mar. 1847), quoted at f. 185.

[20] GP 44803B, ff. 18–19 (*c*.1828), 44722, f. 55 (14 Oct. 1832).

[21] 'The Public Fast', GP 44780, ff. 189–92v (23 Mar. 1847), at ff. 190v–2.   [22] GP 44780, f. 188.

[23] *D*, 12 Nov. 1847.   [24] *D*, 15 Apr. 1840.   [25] *D*, 22 Mar. 1842.   [26] *D*, 15 Apr. 1843.

three-and-a-half pounds' weight in three days.[27] He gave no dinner parties during Lent, he told Manning, but he did not make an absolute rule of refusing invitations.[28] On the last three days of the season he stepped up his efforts, so that, as he recorded on Easter Eve, he had 'kept the fast except liquid and a mouthful yesterday'.[29] That year seems to have been the apogee of his ascetic practice, for from the following autumn his attempts at abstinence were checked by ill health.[30] Fasting, however, was for a while a demanding spiritual discipline. It was of a piece with the arduous devotional temper of Pusey, whose translation of *A Guide for passing Lent holily* (1844) by the early eighteenth-century French divine J. B. E. Avrillon he studied during the season in 1845.[31] Gladstone's severe demands of himself marked him out as a Puseyite.

A further venture, this time guided by John Keble, shows the extent to which Gladstone identified in these years with the Anglo-Catholic vanguard. It was 'The Engagement', a small and secret group of well-to-do laymen who undertook to live by a rule and meet for annual consultation on St Barnabas's Day in Margaret Chapel. Colin Matthew has described the organization and pointed out the significant proportion of its members later associated with Gladstone in government.[32] Here it suffices to indicate the significance of the enterprise for the politician. For one thing, it fulfilled one of Gladstone's long-standing ambitions. In 1838 he had sketched a scheme for a 'Third Order', a body of men remaining in the world but undertaking a quasi-monastic common life.[33] A few years later he again, though much less elaborately, outlined a rule for such an organization.[34] Gladstone joined the Engagement itself in 1845, promising to perform regular charitable work, attend daily service (if possible), keep fasts, offer special prayers, restrict sleep and recreation, give alms, consider confession, and meet for consultation.[35] He aspired to greater consecration by following in the footsteps of St Barnabas, the patron of the Engagement. Barnabas, he believed, was one of the 'Christian heroes and saints of a peculiar excellence whose whole life is elevated to a higher tone of sanctity by a more immediate & entire devotion to the glory of God'.[36] His enthusiasm for the Engagement, however, was soon to wear thin. A year later he wrote to the co-ordinator, T. D. Acland, to complain that the whole project was too diffuse. Members knew each other very little or not at all, and so could not exercise mutual pastoral care. Gladstone's proposal that, as a remedy, the organization should be divided into sections does not seem to have been taken up, his participation faded, and the Engagement dissolved in 1852. The statesman, characteristically, was unhappy with a body so dependent on 'individual will'.[37] He

---

[27] *D*, 20 Feb. 1847.          [28] W. E. Gladstone to H. E. Manning, 9 Mar. 1847, Lathbury, 2, p. 276.

[29] *D*, 3 Apr. 1847.                    [30] *D*, 11 June 1848.                    [31] *D*, 24 Feb.–23 Mar. 1845.

[32] Matthew, 'Gladstone, Evangelicalism and "The Engagement" '.

[33] GP 44728, ff. 28–30 (9 Mar. 1838), Lathbury, 2, pp. 433–7.

[34] GP 44732, ff. 142–3 (n.d., but paper watermarked 1842).

[35] Undated memorandum of *c*.1846 by Gladstone in Lambeth MSS, in *D*, 23 Feb. 1845 n.

[36] 'St Barnabas Day', GP 44780, ff. 256–9v (11 June 1848), quoted at f. 258v.

[37] W. E. Gladstone to T. D. Acland, 10 June 1849, MS Eng. lett. d.89, f. 25, Bodleian Library, Oxford, quoted in Matthew, 'Gladstone, Evangelicalism and "The Engagement" ', p. 122.

wanted it, on the contrary, to exhibit something of the solidarity of the cloister. The Engagement, in a sense, was insufficiently based on Catholic principles to satisfy Gladstone.

The politician was an eager participant in the growing cultural ambience surrounding Tractarianism. The 1840s was the decade when ecclesiology, the study and improvement of ancient churches, took off in England.[38] Into this movement Gladstone entered with a zest that has rarely been recognized. In 1843 he noted 'the altered and altering architecture and arrangements of our churches' as a striking symptom of the Catholic advance in the Church of England.[39] Accompanying his brother-in-law, Sir Stephen Glynne, perhaps the most assiduous student of parish churches of his generation, in 1841 Gladstone actually attended a meeting of the Cambridge Camden Society that existed to further the restoration of the ecclesiastical heritage of England to its medieval grandeur.[40] Gladstone read the society's periodical, *The Ecclesiologist*, took a fascinated interest in fonts, pews, and all the other details of ecclesiastical decoration, and evaluated buildings according to the society's criteria. Thus Haughton, in Nottinghamshire, had a 'very curious & interesting' chancel interior, and the church was 'nice' but 'spoiled of course'.[41] He was reflecting the Camden Society's confident judgement that the Georgian age had neglected or ruined most parish churches. Hence there was a pressing need for their restoration. Gladstone read *An Apology for the Revival of Christian Architecture in England* (1843) by A. W. N. Pugin, the greatest church architect of the day, and visited his 'new Romish Church in Southwark'.[42] He made a point of seeing part of a new window raised at Westminster Abbey, 'this glorious pile'.[43] And, supremely, he conceived and planned a whole new Episcopal church on his father's estate at Fasque in Kincardineshire. Although William was sometimes prevented from giving the scheme his full attention, he supervised the design of the east window and commissioned the organ.[44] He had 'an excited but a happy day' when St Andrew's was opened in 1846.[45] The enterprise at Fasque was not merely a way in which the frustrated clergyman could indulge his religious tastes. Rather it was part and parcel of the ecclesiological preoccupations that gave expression to his developing theological stance.

Gladstone's cultural interests ranged widely at this period, but they were bound together by a common thread. Each was related to his Tractarian commitment. In the field of literature, for instance, in 1844 he reviewed a religious novel in the second issue of the *English Review*, a periodical launched to promote Catholic interests in the Church of England. Although Gladstone felt that the characters in *Ellen Middleton* were unamiable, he judged Lady Georgiana Fullerton, its author, to be what was all too rare, 'the true preacher in the guise of

---

[38] J. F. White, *The Cambridge Movement: The Ecclesiologists and the Gothic Revival* (Cambridge, 1962).    [39] Gladstone, 'Present Aspect of the Church', p. 18.    [40] *D*, 22 Nov. 1841.
[41] *D*, 27 June 1841.    [42] *D*, 22 Sept. 1843, 13 July 1843.    [43] *D*, 24 Mar. 1843, 5 Dec. 1841.
[44] Dean E. B. Ramsay to Sir John Gladstone, 25 May 1846, F 2/6 Bundle 6, Gladstone of Fasque Papers, Fasque, Kincardineshire.    [45] *D*, 18 Oct. 1846.

a novelist, as well as with the vestments of the female sex'.[46] Three years later Gladstone reviewed another work by a lady novelist, Elizabeth Harris's *From Oxford to Rome*, chronicling the experience of a clergyman and his sister who had transferred their allegiance to the Roman Catholic Church. It provided him with a vehicle for discussing and deploring the spate of secessions from the Church of England.[47] But it was not only the literature associated with the Tractarian impulse that drew Gladstone's attention. After his marriage in 1839, his wife Catherine encouraged him to pursue musical interests. What recurs strikingly in Gladstone's diary is attendance at concerts of 'ancient music', the pre-classical tradition so often bound up with Christian liturgy.[48] In 1846 he thought a composition by Palestrina 'the most beautiful piece I had ever heard, & one of the most religious'.[49] He attended a meeting of the Motett Society that existed to reprint old church music, took up chanting himself, and had the household practise psalms ready for Sunday worship in the manner recommended by the *English Review*.[50] He even, with Catherine's help, composed a couple of anthems himself.[51] When Gladstone's first son William was less than a year old, the infant was carried off to Westminster Abbey for the choral service: 'his love of music', Gladstone noted in his diary, 'will I hope afford the means of making some solemn impressions early & pleasurable.'[52] The child grew up to become a serious composer of church music, which is testimony to the power of early nurture—but also to the ethos his father inhabited when the boy was small.

Associated with Gladstone's delight in ecclesiastical music was a particular taste in fine art. Again it was a preference for the distinctively Christian compositions of long ago. 'Art and religion', wrote Gladstone as early as 1838, 'were wedded down to the time of Raphael's first manner of painting, in such a way that it was the first object of Art to be the exponent of religion, and no admixture interfering with that object had place.'[53] Gladstone was, in a sense, a pre-Raphaelite before the Pre-Raphaelite Brotherhood was formed. The absence of perspective in what was then called 'primitive art', the painting of the thirteenth and fourteenth centuries, was actually a recommendation to the politician because it enabled its exponents to give unqualified prominence to their subjects from sacred story. In Italy he had discovered the school of Giotto, possessing what he called 'spirituality', that is purity of design combined with simplicity of mood.[54] A grand aim was to revive such qualities in the harshness of industrial Britain. In 1842, following a conversation with Stephen Glynne and a local

---

[46] W. E. Gladstone, 'Ellen Middleton, a Tale; by Lady Georgiana Fullerton', *English Review*, 1 (1844), p. 336.          [47] W. E. Gladstone, 'From Oxford to Rome', *Quarterly Review*, 81 (1847).

[48] *D*, 25 Mar. 1840, 24 Mar., 24 May 1841, 2 May 1842, 29 Mar. 1843, 2 Apr. 1845.

[49] *D*, 30 Apr. 1846.

[50] *D*, 6 Dec. 1841, 22 Dec. 1844, 4 Jan. 1845. 'Church Music', *English Review*, 5 (1846), p. 186. On the revival of traditional church music in the 1840s, see Nicholas Temperley, *The Music of the English Parish Church*, 2 vols. (Cambridge, 1979), 1, ch. 8.          [51] *D*, 24 Oct. 1844.          [52] *D*, 3 June 1841.

[53] GP 44728, f. 118 (1 July 1838).

[54] Marcia Pointon, 'W. E. Gladstone as Art Patron and Collector', *Victorian Studies*, 19 (1975), pp. 77–83.

gentleman, he sketched a plan for 'The British Institute of Christian Art'. Consisting of clergymen as well as artists, and under the authority of the bishops, it was to promote the application of art to the service of religion.[55] Although this scheme came to nothing, Gladstone, through individual and sometimes through public patronage, was able to commission works of art that suited his taste. His favourite artist was William Dyce, a Scottish Episcopalian who was also active in reviving choral music through the Motett Society. Gladstone was to promote Dyce's interests in various ways before, in 1863, asking for a portrait of Dante's Beatrice with one of his own rescued prostitutes as a model.[56] The resulting painting is the epitome of the purity and simplicity Gladstone most admired in art, made all the more poignant by our knowledge of the history of the sitter. Fine art, in Gladstone's view, should be designed to achieve a religious end. That is why he most appreciated, and most wanted to be imitated, the visual art of the age of faith.

Gladstone habitually praised the thirteenth century in particular because it moulded the mind of Dante. The politician naturally associated Dante with Italy, a land which, ever since 1832, had enlarged his mental horizons and where, in 1839, he made his proposal of marriage to Catherine Glynne. There were several other reasons why the politician ranged the Florentine poet among his 'four doctors' alongside Aristotle, Augustine, and Butler. One was that Gladstone postulated an affinity between Dante and Aristotle: like the philosopher, the poet possessed 'an understanding edged for analysis'.[57] In a political essay of 1835 Gladstone cited Dante's *Inferno* for its high estimate of Aristotle.[58] He could have drawn on over 300 allusions to the philosopher in Dante's writings: only the Latin Bible is quoted or mentioned more often. For Dante, Aristotle is 'the Master', 'the Philosopher', the decisive authority on virtually every question.[59] A second reason is that Gladstone associated Dante with Augustine as well. Augustine, he wrote, was 'one of Dante's teachers'.[60] Like Augustine, or equally like Thomas à Kempis, the poet displayed 'a spirit of childlike and ecstatic devotion'.[61] But a third explanation is by far the most important. As Sir Owen Chadwick has shown, Gladstone's fascination with Dante sprang from the commendation of the poet Arthur Hallam.[62] Gladstone's precocious school friend had enthused over Dante, and especially the 'peculiar sweetness and tenderness' of the *Paradiso* and *Vita Nuova*, while they were together at Eton. After Hallam's death at the age of only 22, Gladstone canonized his literary opinions, particularly in relation to 'his

---

[55] GP 44730, ff. 198–9 ([9] Sept. 1842). *D*, 3 Sept. 1842.

[56] Marcia Pointon, *William Dyce, 1806–1864: A Critical Biography* (Oxford, 1979), pp. 165–6.

[57] *CPR*, p. 10.

[58] 'Of the law of Social obligation', GP 44725, f. 171 (8 Dec. 1835?).

[59] Edward Moore, *Studies in Dante*, 1st ser. (Oxford, 1896), pp. 4, 92.

[60] W. E. Gladstone, 'Lord John Russell's Translation of Dante's "Francesca da Rimini" ', *English Review*, 1 (1844), p. 173.        [61] *CPR*, p. 10.

[62] Owen Chadwick, 'Young Gladstone and Italy', *Journal of Ecclesiastical History*, 30 (1979), repr. in P. J. Jagger (ed.), *Gladstone, Politics and Religion* (London, 1985), pp. 73–4.

favourite Dante'. Hallam had defended Dante against the view of Gabriele Rossetti, father of Dante Gabriel Rossetti and an Italian liberal refugee, that the great Florentine's *Divine Comedy* was an elaborate polemic against the Roman Catholic Church. On the contrary, Hallam had averred, 'The spirit of Catholic Christianity breathes in every line'.[63] Looking at Dante with Hallam's eyes, Gladstone discerned in his verse a purity, a religiosity, 'a strength of sublime intuition' that he found inspiring.[64] The politician was participating in a general awakening, shared for instance by Carlyle and Ruskin, of a preference for the *Paradiso*, a section of Dante's *Divine Comedy* shaped by his love for Beatrice, over the other sections, the *Inferno* and the *Purgatorio*, which had attracted more appreciation down to the 1830s.[65] The *Inferno* might be more perfect in its kind, admitted Gladstone, but its kind was lower. The *Paradiso* was ultimately superior because of its subject, the joys of heaven.[66] Gladstone appreciated in Dante, and especially in the *Paradiso*, a supremely spiritual vision.

Dante was therefore qualified to be a wise instructor. Gladstone refers to him as 'that master-poet and rare Christian philosopher'.[67] Dante wrote as a Catholic, but, because of his partisanship for the medieval empire against the papacy of his day, not as devotee of Rome. Gladstone is therefore particularly happy to bow to his teaching. He repeatedly quotes or alludes to the poet in the course of his published essays, often to thrust home a lesson.[68] We cannot treat of Dante, he noted in a memorandum, probably of 1846, without entering theology.[69] 'Intense must have been his spiritual exercises,' he wrote in another, 'wonderful his progress, large his share in the fulfilment of the promise that the Spirit shall take of the things of the Redeemer and shall show them to those that are his.' Consequently *The Divine Comedy* should be valued less as a work of art than as a text bearing religious authority. The reader must associate himself with the mind of the poet: 'Let Dante be to him what Beatrice was to Dante.'[70] When, in 1844, Lord John Russell published a translation of the Francesca da Rimini episode from the *Inferno*, Gladstone discussed it in the *English Review*. After offering some faint praise, Gladstone observes that Russell appeared not to have given the continuous study to Dante which, of all authors, the poet demanded.[71] The Whig leader, as a liberal Anglican, did not have the requisite feeling for the text. Those who did appreciate Dante, by contrast, earned Gladstone's approval. The young Tractarian A. P. Forbes, for example, had a conversation with him on the poet in

---

[63] [W. E. Gladstone] to Henry Hallam, 12 Apr. 1834, in [Henry Hallam (ed.)], *Remains in Verse and Prose of Arthur Henry Hallam* (London, 1863), pp. xxxv, xxxvi, 288.          [64] *CPR*, p. 10.

[65] Steve Ellis, *Dante and English Poetry: Shelley to T. S. Eliot* (Cambridge, 1983), ch. 4.

[66] GP 44731, ff. 138–40 (n.d., 1846?).

[67] Gladstone, 'Lord John Russell's Translation', p. 164.

[68] W. E. Gladstone, 'Blanco White' [1845], 'Giacomo Leopardi' [1850], 'Tennyson' [1859], 'Macaulay' [1876], *Gleanings*, 2, pp. 18, 31, 60; 89, 91, 94, 128; 135, 138, 153, 174, 175; 279.

[69] GP 44731, f. 134 (n.d.). This and other memoranda that follow were probably written on 25 Sept. and 27 Oct. 1846 (cf. *Diaries*).          [70] GP 44731, f. 135v.

[71] Gladstone, 'Lord John Russell's Translation', pp. 166–7.

October 1846. Gladstone recorded that he particularly liked the clergyman, and soon afterwards successfully recommended him as Bishop of Brechin.[72] One's attitude to Dante seemed a sure touchstone of character. Although in 1861 Gladstone issued translations of three passages from Dante, his only other publication on the poet was a speculative article, composed as late as 1892, on whether Dante studied at Oxford.[73] It was a rather contrived attempt to bring together two of the chief loves of Gladstone's life, his university and his favourite Christian poet. Dante epitomized the Catholic culture that Gladstone relished during the 1840s.

II

Gladstone's High Churchmanship therefore took on a definitely Tractarian hue in that decade, transforming his mind as well as his taste. The most illuminating evidence for Gladstone's religious thinking during this period comes from a set of his manuscript sermons. Although he published several articles and continued to write private memoranda, the clearest evidence of his personal convictions on many themes comes from these addresses that were delivered to his household on Sunday evenings. The three volumes of sermons in the Gladstone Papers have been noticed, but they have not previously been examined.[74] There are as many as 179 complete sermons together with some thirty additional outlines or fragments, a remarkably substantial collection of homiletic material for any layman to have composed. Each complete sermon normally consists of eight half-pages of text, the other half-pages originally being left blank for subsequent alterations and insertions. Although there is an isolated early item from 1834, the continuous series runs from 1840, when Gladstone as a newly married man was setting up his London household at 11 Carlton House Gardens, until 1866. None survives from after that date—and if others had been written, they would almost certainly have been kept. The political pressures of the next few years were no doubt too acute to permit sermon preparation, and subsequently at Hawarden there was the parish church to attend. In the quarter-century when he was preaching, Gladstone normally delivered addresses only when in London, though he did speak from notes when abroad.[75] In one of the earliest sermons, on the 'Duties of Masters and Servants', he explained his understanding of the task: 'It is the duty of those who are placed at the head of a house, to see that God is reverently worshipped therein by all its inmates: to collect them for prayer: to lead them to

---

[72] *D*, 26 Oct. 1846. Rowan Strong, *Alexander Forbes of Brechin: The First Tractarian Bishop* (Oxford, 1995), pp. 47–8.

[73] Lord Lyttleton and W. E. Gladstone, *Translations*, 2nd edn. (London, 1863), pp. 154–65. W. E. Gladstone, 'Did Dante study at Oxford?', *Nineteenth Century*, 31 (1892). On Gladstone and Dante, see also Alison Milbank, *Dante and the Victorians* (Manchester, 1998), pp. 172–4.

[74] GP 44779–81. Matthew, p. 54. Butler, *Gladstone*, p. 159.

[75] GP 44781, f. 29 (8 Dec. 1850). *D*, 8 Dec. 1850.

an acquaintance with God's Holy Word.'[76] If heads of families failed in these responsibilities, he added, they put their own souls in great peril. A self-composed sermon, however, was not de rigueur every Sunday. Although that seems to have been Gladstone's original aim, he was unable to write one as early as June 1840, in the aftermath of his wife's first confinement, and so instead he read a published sermon, perhaps surprisingly by Thomas Arnold.[77] Newman and Pusey, his friend Henry Manning, and the incumbent of Margaret Chapel, Frederick Oakeley, were among the others whose sermons were similarly pressed into service.[78] The norm, however, was for Gladstone to act as preacher in his own right. The clergyman manqué found a pulpit in his own home.

The text was almost invariably taken from one of the lessons appointed for the day in the Book of Common Prayer. The Prayer Book shaped the worship in other ways, inducing Gladstone, for example, to quote and expound its collects.[79] He set great store by observing the church year. 'Would that our clergy', he exclaimed in his diary after visiting Westminster Abbey on the Sunday before Christmas in 1841, 'would preach more on the season.'[80] The recurrence of 'seasons of penitence & seasons of thanksgiving', he insisted in one of his own sermons, was no 'empty form'.[81] Accordingly in the sermons he dwelt on themes appropriate to Lent, Easter, Ascensiontide, and so on. There is often precise exegesis of the chosen passage. When preaching on 'Wherefore let him that thinketh he standeth take heed lest he fall', for example, he notes the context being a discussion by the apostle Paul of the sins of the Israelites and so goes through a catalogue of their wrongdoings as a basis for self-examination.[82] He expounds the apostle Paul's metaphor of running a race phrase by phrase; and he gives a particularly close reading of the parable of Dives and Lazarus.[83] Despite these signs of careful preparation, Gladstone was stern in self-criticism of his efforts: 'improper in arrangement & development', 'not properly jointed', and, simply, 'too hard' were some of the verdicts.[84] A couple of sermons prepared in advance were marked 'not read', perhaps because of dissatisfaction with their contents.[85] Many were modified or abbreviated in later delivery. It was Gladstone's custom to repeat a sermon on the appropriate occasion in subsequent years, usually after a gap, though at

---

[76] 'Duties of Masters and Servants', GP 44779, ff. 26–9v (22 Mar. 1840), quoted at ff. 29–9v.

[77] *D*, 28 June 1840.

[78] *D*, 24 Mar. 1842, 21 Feb. 1841, 23 Oct. 1842, 2 Aug. 1840.

[79] 'Reading Scripture', GP 44779, ff. 14–17v (1 Mar. 1840), at f. 16 'Fourth Sunday after Easter', GP 44779, ff. 223–6v (24 Apr. 1842), at ff. 222v–5v. 'Sunday after Ascension Day', GP 44779, ff. 234–8v (8 May 1842), at f. 236. 'Whitsunday', GP 44779, ff. 239–45v (15 May 1842), at f. 239.

[80] *D*, 19 Dec. 1841.          [81] 'Season of Lent', GP 44780, ff. 85–8v (25 Feb. 1844), quoted at f. 85v.

[82] GP 44779, ff. 141–4v (8 Aug. 1841), on 1 Cor. 10: 12.

[83] 'Septuagesima', GP 44779, ff. 193–7v (first read 17 Jan. 1845, but according to *Diaries* written on 23 Jan. 1842), on 1 Cor. 9: 24. 'First Sunday after Trinity', GP 44780, ff. 210–14v (read 8 June 1847, but according to the diaries written two days before), on Luke 16: 19–31.

[84] 'Fourth Sunday after Easter', GP 44779, 222–8v (24 Apr. 1842), at f. 222. *D*, 15 Oct. 1843. 'The just shall live by his faith', GP 44781, ff. 17–21v (18 Nov. 1849), at f. 17.

[85] 'Twenty-First Sunday after Trinity', GP 44779, ff. 280–4v (written 23 Oct. 1842). 'God the All seeing', GP 44779, ff. 304–8v (written 4 and 11 Dec. 1842).

least one was delivered in three successive years, on the Fourth Sunday after Trinity.[86] Addresses composed in 1840 and 1841 were still being repeated in 1866. Their themes tend to be timeless: the basic Christian doctrines or the standard Christian duties. Yet, because they are not documents for public consumption, they do go far towards revealing Gladstone's real theological position. Whereas he had to be guarded in the religious controversies of the time, such as that over the Jerusalem bishopric in 1841,[87] before his own household he could pour out his authentic feelings.

In many of the sermons the practical application is a warning against some form of human irresponsibility. The servants were admonished more than once to avoid waste. The man who, as Chancellor of the Exchequer, was to instruct civil servants to make sparing use of paper-clips naturally saw in the baskets carried round to collect scraps after the feeding of the four thousand the lesson that 'waste is a sin against God'.[88] Likewise there was to be a stewardship of time. In a New Year sermon for 1844 on 'the precious gift of time', Gladstone warned against consuming it 'in listless vacancy' and in the following year proceeded to practise what he preached by noting each day in his diary the total number of hours that were spent in sleep, meals, and recreation.[89] Sleep, he had observed in an earlier address, 'blunts & deadens the faculties of the soul'; eating, he declared in another, was not merely to please the palate.[90] The tongue must equally be disciplined. 'To conceal the truth', he assured the household in 1842, 'from those to whom it might be told is as truly a sin, as to impose upon them by falsehood.'[91] In order to avoid censoriousness, too, there must be forbearance. It was proper to issue a rebuke, declared Gladstone, but only in the course of fulfilling a duty.[92] Insult, conversely, was to be taken without resentment; and, through the example of Christ, his followers would be able to bear the trials of life such as false accusation.[93] In a letter to his wife of 1844 Gladstone explained the underlying principle as being a process of 'checking, repressing, quelling the inclination of the will to act with reference to self as a centre'.[94] The old theme of selfishness as the core of sin frequently appears in the sermons. Its remedy, a stern self-discipline, remained a constant feature of Gladstone's practical religion.

In writing to his wife in 1844 Gladstone describes the second obligation towards one's human will as 'to cherish, exercise, and expand its new and heavenly power of acting according to the will of God'.[95] Accordingly regular devotion is another prominent element in the teaching of the sermons. A certain intimacy with God is urged in an address on 'Prayer' of 1841:

---

[86] 'Fourth Sunday after Trinity', GP 44780, ff. 52–5v (2 July 1843).

[87] R. W. Greaves, 'The Jerusalem Bishopric, 1841', *English Historical Review*, 64 (1949).

[88] 'Seventh Sunday after Trinity', GP 44781, ff. 39–43v (9 Apr. 1852), quoted at f. 42v, on Mark 8: 1–9. Cf. GP 44779, f. 29v.

[89] 'New Year', GP 44780, ff. 77–80v (14 Jan. 1844), quoted at ff. 77, 77v. *D*, 24 Feb.–23 Aug. 1845.

[90] GP 44779, f. 24v; f. 50 (10 May 1840).        [91] GP 44779, ff. 271–4v (2 Oct. 1842), at f. 272.

[92] 'Fourth Sunday after Trinity', GP 44780, ff. 223–6v (4 July 1847), at f. 224.

[93] GP 44780, f. 176. 'Membership', GP 44779, ff. 82–5v (31 Jan. 1841), at f. 84.

[94] W. E. Gladstone to Catherine Gladstone, 21 Jan. 1844, Morley, 1, p. 216.        [95] Ibid.

A child tells his father & mother what he likes & dislikes, what he wants, what he fears, what has happened to him; & asks of them the aid which they may be able to give him . . . And therefore it would be strange indeed if the children of God . . . did not freely and constantly make known their state both within & without, the good & the evil that befal [*sic*] them, the doubts, the fears the sorrows & the sins of which they are conscious, to the Eternal Father Who alone is always able, always willing, always desirous, effectually to help them.[96]

This passage comes close to the heartbeat of Gladstone's personal religion. In another of the sermons, like Augustine in the *Confessions*, Gladstone bursts into a spontaneous invocation of God, pleading for his truth and his love.[97] In a later detached note he urges on himself the cultivation of ejaculatory prayer.[98] The servants are exhorted to 'Perseverance in Prayer', as though it were more a duty than a delight, in a sermon with that title, and another admits that devotion does not always lift the spirit: 'the idea of joy in connection with religion is of all others the hardest honestly to realise.'[99] Yet elsewhere there is a more than intellectual appreciation of God as love, 'the essence of His being'.[100] There is also a significant alteration, in a sermon of 1845 revised only a fortnight after its composition, of a reference to the Holy Spirit from 'itself' to 'Himself'.[101] If in an orthodox Christian the original word suggests a certain lack of spiritual sensitivity, the amendment reveals a fundamental reverence. The exercise of preaching allowed Gladstone to bare not only his mind but also his soul.

The sermons were naturally a vehicle for the inculcation of church principles. 'The Church of God', he told his household of 1841, 'is as truly a part of revelation as the written word of God'.[102] The doctrine of the church, after all, was prominent in the Bible and the Apostles' Creed. In a sermon of 1844 Gladstone contrived to bring out the teaching that the church was one, holy, and Catholic. His text was John 10: 16, 'And other sheep I have, which are not of this fold: them also must I bring, and they shall hear my voice: and there shall be one fold, and one shepherd.' He expounded the phrase about 'other sheep' as meaning that the church was to be Catholic in the sense of universal; because the sheep 'hear my voice', they are obedient to the shepherd and therefore holy; and 'one fold' spoke for itself of unity.[103] On other occasions Gladstone strained a passage even more to highlight the place of the church in the divine economy. The Holy Spirit, according to John 16: 8–11, was to reprove the world of sin, righteousness, and judgement. Righteousness, Gladstone explained, here meant the church, which was to be righteous herself and the teacher and mother of righteousness.[104] Such

---

[96] 'Prayer', GP44779, ff. 102–5v (21 Mar. 1841), quoted at f. 102v.

[97] 'Thirteenth Sunday after Trinity', GP 44780, ff. 121–4v (12 Jan. 1845), at f. 121.

[98] GP 44746, ff. 42–2v (12 Oct. 1856).

[99] 'Perseverance in Prayer', GP 44780, ff. 22–5v (12 Mar. 1843). 'Easter Eve', GP 44781, ff. 48–51v (18 Apr. 1852), quoted at f. 48.

[100] 'First Sunday after Trinity', GP 44779, 127–32v (13 Jan. 1841), quoted at f. 130v.

[101] 'Confirmation', GP 44780, ff. 150–3v (13 Apr. 1845), quoted at f. 151v. *D*, 27 Apr. 1845.

[102] GP 44779, ff. 151–4v (3 Oct. 1841), quoted at f. 153.

[103] 'Second Sunday after Easter', GP 44780, ff. 105–8v (21 Apr. 1844), quoted at ff. 105v–7v.

[104] 'Fourth Sunday after Easter', GP 44780, ff. 202–5v (2 May 1847), at f. 203.

tortured exegesis betrayed a passionate desire to enforce an ecclesiastical consciousness on his hearers. It was in harmony with the purpose of Manning's book *The Unity of the Church* (1842), which was dedicated to Gladstone. 'This union of Christians in one body', wrote the politician in a sermon composed on the day he finished Manning's work, 'is no fiction and not even a figure alone: but a substance and a reality for Christians who are such indeed ...'[105] The bonding of believers with Christ as head of the church entailed a solidarity with all others who enjoyed the same relationship. It created a form of 'Christian equality' that, while not superseding the ranking of secular society, did introduce the principle that people were to be valued for their spiritual gifts.[106] That was the foundation of 'the law of Christian brotherhood'[107] and the rationale for Gladstone's addressing his servants in these sermons as 'brethren'.[108] Catholic Christianity entailed real ties of fellowship that transcended any barrier of status.

In the sermons Gladstone habitually criticized from his new standpoint the evangelicalism that he had once professed. Perhaps he believed that there were currents of evangelical sentiment below stairs that needed to be turned into proper ecclesiastical channels. On one occasion in 1848 he censured those who declared that their hearts trusted in Christ, arguing that there was a difference 'between a barren, a verbal, an imagined reliance on Him, and that living faith which is rooted in penitential sorrow & which worketh by love'.[109] Gladstone was careful, however, to insist, both in public and in private, on the affinities between the evangelical movement and the church revival. Their essential points, he contended in 'Present Aspect of the Church', were held in common.[110] Although, he noted in a memorandum of 1843, what he called the spirit of Puritanism was wrong to maintain the principle of private judgement, the Puritan movement, by which he meant evangelicalism, could coexist with Catholicism in the Church of England. It could even, no doubt by the vividness of its spiritual sense, prevent 'that Catholicism which is genuine from degenerating into what is spurious'.[111] Gladstone also spoke in his household sermons of 'conversion'[112] and imparted something like an evangelistic appeal into some of their perorations.[113] Yet, without naming evangelicalism, he frequently pointed to deficiencies in the movement. Against its biblicism, for example, he declared that 'God did not give the Christian religion to mankind in the form of the Scriptures', but in the form of

---

[105] 'Nineteenth Sunday after Trinity', GP 44779, ff. 271–4v (2 Oct. 1842), quoted at f. 274v.
[106] 'Christian Equality', GP 44779, ff. 90–3v ([14] Feb. 1841). 'SS Philip and James', GP 44780, ff. 198–201v (2 May 1847), quoted at f. 201v.
[107] 'Sexagesima', GP 44781, ff. 73–6v (19 Feb. 1854), quoted at f. 76v.
[108] e.g. 'The Conscience', GP 44780, ff. 117–20v (22 [sc. 24] Nov. 1844), quoted at f. 118v.
[109] 'Parable of the Talents', GP 44780, ff. 276–9v (17 Dec. 1848), quoted at f. 278v.
[110] Gladstone, 'Present Aspect', pp. 11–12, 75.　　　　[111] GP 44733, ff. 150v–1 (12 Dec. 1843).
[112] e.g. 'New Year', GP 44780, ff. 77–80v (14 Jan. 1844), quoted at f. 79v; 'Holy Eucharist', GP 44780, ff. 248–51 (19 Mar. 1848), quoted at f. 250.
[113] e.g. 'Way of Salvation', GP 44779, ff. 56–60v (24 May 1840), at f. 57v; 'Second Sunday in Advent', GP 44780, ff. 73–6v (10 Dec. 1843), at f. 76v.

Christ and his apostles.[114] He explained that fasting and the observance of the church year were not, as evangelicals supposed, empty rituals that led away from Christ.[115] The rising apocalyptic strain among them was dismissed as 'a state of inflamed imagination'.[116] There might be 'talk of total corruption, of a free salvation, a glorious gospel, an assurance of pardon and the adoption of sons', but such evangelical jargon was hopelessly shallow.[117] It was no substitute for the passionate Tractarian quest for holiness.

That was the main thrust of Gladstone's critique of evangelicalism. Conversion or repentance was not, as evangelicals often claimed, the work of a moment:

There are those who think that the whole repentance necessary for a Christian is comprised in a single act of the will—that they have only to say to God, with sincerity, that they are sorry for the sins that they have committed—& that then no more remains than for them to enter upon all the joys, or so to speak upon all the luxuries of religion. Alas, they know not the subtlety of Satan . . .[118]

Because sin was more deeply ingrained than they supposed, the process of struggling against it had only just begun. The defectiveness of the teaching of evangelicals about repentance, according to Gladstone, was aggravated by their understanding of justification by faith. They saw faith, he claimed, in the sense of verbal assent as the avenue to all spiritual blessings and so exalted it above love, 'the very copy and impress of the image of God'. Works were downgraded to mere evidence of the reality of faith, whereas they should properly be the embodiment of holiness.[119] The evangelical position on assurance, with which Gladstone had wrestled in the 1830s, posed a further problem. 'It is not always possible or good', he roundly declared in a sermon of 1840, 'for men to be distinctly assured of their own spiritual state.'[120] The evangelical idea that every believer should expect assurance of salvation could actually operate as an obstacle to salvation. It could create a delusory presumption that no spiritual efforts were called for, so that the lulled conscience neglected the struggle against sin upon whose outcome salvation in reality depended. The evangelicals seemed to cut away the ground for the intense moral conflict, aided by the Almighty, that was near the heart of Tractarian spirituality.

The consequence for Gladstone's thought was a relative playing down of a central feature of the theology of the evangelicals , the doctrine of the cross. In his earlier years, as an inheritance from his evangelical upbringing, the politician had made this theme his own. In a memorandum on the scope of theology, probably jotted down in 1834, he awarded pride of place to the atonement: 'The great

---

[114] 'Twelfth Sunday after Trinity', GP 44779, ff. 275–9v (9 Oct. 1842), quoted at f. 275v.

[115] 'Fasting', GP 44780, at f. 186v; 'Season of Lent', GP 44780, ff. 85–8v (25 Feb. 1844), at f. 85v.

[116] 'Sixth Sunday after Epiphany', GP 44780, ff. 219–22v (20 June 1847), quoted at f. 222.

[117] 'St John the Baptist's Day', GP 44780, ff. 227–30v (9 [sc. 8] and 11 Aug. 1847), quoted at f. 228v.

[118] 'Public Worship', GP 44780, ff. 1–4v (22 Jan. 1843), quoted at f. 3.

[119] 'The just shall live by his faith', GP 44781, ff. 17v–18.

[120] 'The Resurrection (II)', GP 44779, ff. 38–41v (26 Apr. 1840), quoted at f. 39v. Cf. Ch. 3, pp. 50–1.

central truth of religion as it touches mankind, is, the crucifixion: not in its physical, but in its moral character. From it will be found to radiate every pencil of that halo of glory which fixedly attracts & detains the gaze of the Christian pilgrim.'[121] Occasional remarks from the 1840s single out the atonement in a similar vein: the sufferings of Christ, according to a sermon of 1842, form the motive for our charity; and in a memorandum of 1847 Christ's cross is said to be 'the source of all our light'.[122] But this exaltation of the cross is not the prevailing note of Gladstone's writing in these years. The reasoning behind the change is set out in a passionate sermon for St John the Baptist's Day composed in August 1847. The discourse takes the saint, 'that austere majestic preacher', as 'a standing protest against sin'.[123] The 'private crisis' described by Colin Matthew, involving sexual temptation relieved by the rescue of prostitutes, appears to have been at one of its periodic peaks, and Gladstone's sister Helen, whose fate often troubled her brother's conscience, seemed at death's door.[124] Accordingly his acute sense of inward wickedness colours his words. He laments how, 'in these days of relaxed religion', some—he means evangelicals—'appropriate redemption before they have in any degree measured the height and depth of their guilt'. One cause was their fear that dwelling on sins and their present remedy would marginalize the sacrifice of Christ.

But also [he continues] it is to be feared that too often the desire to maintain a supreme regard to the ransom paid for our souls by the Lord and to exclude all idea of our own merit is either only a name, or though a reality is used by Satan as a blind by which he hinders us from thoroughly examining our corruptions and coming to know how hideous they are.[125]

The doctrinal preoccupations of the evangelicals made them trifle with sin, the greatest of crimes. The atonement, in Gladstone's eyes, must on no account become a pretext for moral complacency.

When Gladstone does dwell on the doctrine of the cross, his emphasis is different from that of the evangelicals. They treated it as the divine method of bringing forgiveness to a sinful world, a means of pardon for past wrongdoing to any believer. That Gladstone does not deny; but he adds a fresh element to his *theologia crucis*. In a Good Friday sermon of 1840 on 'And they crucified him', Gladstone draws a distinction between Christ as sin offering and as thank offering:

Firstly as a sin offering He underwent shame & pain, that he might put away all our guilt from before the face of the Father & Eternal Judge: Secondly as a thank offering or eucharistic sacrifice, he surrenders His own Will into the hands of His Father: he quelled all the less noble movements of the flesh which in Him as in us naturally shrunk & recoiled from pain.[126]

---

[121] GP 44820, f. 112v (n.d., but f. 112 is dated 23 Feb. 1834).
[122] 'Quinquagesima Sunday', GP 44779, ff. 198–202v ([6 Feb.] 1842), quoted at f. 202; GP 44736, f. 355 ('Xm. 47' in pencil).      [123] 'St John the Baptist's Day', GP 44780, f. 230.
[124] Matthew, ch. 4. *D*, 6 Aug. 1847.
[125] 'St John the Baptist's Day', GP 44780, ff. 227v–8v. 'height' is spelt 'heighth' in the MS.
[126] 'And they crucified him', GP 44779, ff. 30–3v (17 Apr. 1840), quoted at f. 32.

The first aspect of the work of Christ corresponds to the evangelical understanding of the cross as expiatory; the second, with its allusion to eucharistic sacrifice, is the idea more familiar to Tractarians that power for moral transformation flows from the cross. Because Christ was obedient to the point of death, human beings can come to share in his perfect submission to the will of the Almighty. The expiatory role of Christ is not imitable; but believers, as Gladstone goes on to insist, must mortify their sinful tendencies in emulation of his second, transformative, role. The same twofold understanding of the cross, expressed in varying formulae, is apparent in many of Gladstone's sermons: Christ is both the priest of the atonement and the example of obedience; his work encompassed both expiation and 'actual deliverance from sin and death'; pardoning and sanctifying power alike flow from the cross.[127] In an address of 1847 Gladstone draws the same contrast, this time distinguishing between the work without us (pardon) and the work within us (renewal).[128] He was echoing the words of Manning in a recently read volume of sermons in which his friend describes the language of God's love as 'two-fold, both without and within'.[129] In a similar way Pusey spoke of the doctrine of the cross as twofold, the cross borne *for* us by Christ and then the cross borne *by* us ourselves.[130] Like his mentors, Gladstone stresses the second element rather than the first. Atonement, in a sense, could be taken for granted: the rooting out of actual sin, the process evangelicals seemed to ignore, had to be highlighted. Gladstone reinterpreted the cross in the light of the Tractarian summons to holy living.

There is even a tendency to downgrade entirely the significance of the crucifixion within the Christian scheme of things. The resurrection, Gladstone argues in several addresses, can be unduly eclipsed by an evangelical preoccupation with the cross:

> Now it sometimes happens that men have a perceptible sense of interest in the Crucifixion of Christ, who look upon His resurrection as an event of comparatively little importance: an interest founded on that peculiar form of selfishness which feeds itself with the hope, the vain and delusive hope, that the death of Christ will avail for the pardon of our sins without our renouncing sin in its substance . . . On this account we are more apt to be moved with some sort of concern in the death of Christ which procures deliverance from punishment, than in the resurrection of Christ, which represents our deliverance from the sins that had merited such punishment . . .[131]

Here the escape from everyday sin that elsewhere is often identified as the second effect of the cross is attributed instead to the resurrection, which in consequence

---

[127] 'The Holy Eucharist', GP 44780, ff. 130–3v (16 Mar. 1845), at f. 130; 'First Sunday after Easter', GP 44780, ff. 138–41v (23 Mar 1845), quoted at f. 140; 'Quinquagesima', GP 44781, ff. 1–4v (25 Feb. 1849), at f. 3.                [128] 'Fifteenth Sunday after Trinity', GP 44780, ff. 231–4v (24 Oct. 1847), at f. 233v.

[129] H. E. Manning, *Sermons*, 4 vols. (London, 1842–50), 3, p. 225. *D*, 25 July–17 Oct. 1847. Manning, however, attributes only the work without to the passion, while the work within is referred to the Spirit of love.

[130] *Plain Sermons by Contributors to the 'Tracts for the Times'*, 10 vols. (London, 1839–48), 3, p. 5.

[131] 'The Resurrection', GP 44779, ff. 34–7v (19 Apr. 1840), quoted at f. 34.

is highly valued. Likewise in an Easter sermon of 1848 the life-giving power of Christ is referred to his resurrection as well as to his death. It was wrong, Gladstone insists, to linger over the crucifixion, for in the early church the resurrection was regarded as 'the crowning and capital event of our Lord's whole work for us'.[132] Not only did Gladstone sometimes give the priority to the resurrection: he also broadened the idea of the work of Christ, located by evangelicals in the cross alone, to cover a longer period. Throughout his life, Gladstone claimed in 1849, Christ was offering obedience to his Father, a process only consummated on the cross.[133] 'His true sacrifice', he declared in 1846, 'was the unseen conflict & rending of the soul, whereof even the visible breaking of His body & outpouring of His blood were but as emblems . . .'[134] The crucifixion must be seen in its setting, as one episode, albeit a pivotal one, within the redemptive achievement of the Saviour. The phase of Gladstone's thought when the atonement was the core of his theology had been left far behind.

What had become central, in its place, was the twin axis of eucharist and incarnation. The holy communion service had been the subject of Gladstone's first household sermon in 1834, when he had contented himself with specifying the requisites for attendance as self-examination, faith, and charity.[135] There was nothing, other than the inclusion of the doctrine of baptismal regeneration, to distinguish the contents from evangelical sermons of the period. Already, however, he held that those who come in penitence and faith make 'a true and real communion of the body and blood of Christ', a phrase that implied a higher sense of what was conveyed than some evangelicals would have admitted.[136] By 1837 he was more specific, adding significant capital letters: 'I assume that the faithful in the Lord's Supper does truly partake of the Body and Blood of the Lord. Whether they be in the recipient only or also first in the thing received: whether the manner of their presence be or be not capable of definition: there can surely be no doubt of the fact, at least the Church doubts not thereof.'[137] The first issue, of whether the sacramental elements became the body and blood of Christ only when received, had long divided Anglican divines.[138] By the writing of *Church Principles* in 1840, Gladstone was implying the inadequacy of such a receptionist view by positing 'an intrinsic virtue' in the sacraments.[139] He certainly held that the eucharist was more than 'a bare Memorial', repudiating any 'weaker and lower doctrine' than that Christ is truly conveyed there.[140] In an address of 1841 he described the bread and wine as 'spiritually but truly the body and blood of Christ'.[141] He regularly insisted, however, that there should be no disputing about

---

[132] 'Easter Tuesday', GP 44780, ff. 252–5v (23 Apr. 1848), quoted at f. 253.

[133] GP 44781, ff. 13–16v (17 June 1849), at ff. 14v, 15.

[134] 'Palm Sunday', GP 44780, f. 173 (5 Apr. 1846).

[135] 'Requisites for attending the Holy Sacrament of the Lord's Supper', GP 44779, ff. 1–9 (1834).

[136] GP 44722, f.306 (n.d.: 1833?).           [137] GP 44727, f. 50 (14 May 1837).

[138] C. W. Dugmore, *Eucharistic Doctrine in England from Hooker to Waterland* (London, 1942).

[139] *CPR*, pp. 161–9, quoted at p. 163.

[140] GP 44732, f. 205 (27 Aug. 1843). 'The Holy Eucharist', GP 44780, f. 131.

[141] 'Thank-offering', GP 44779, ff. 163–6v (24 Oct. 1841), quoted at f. 166.

how that mysterious development took place.[142] Gladstone's position therefore accorded closely with that of Pusey, in the university sermon of 1843 for which he was censured, who taught there the doctrine of the real presence without speculating on its mode. Perhaps it was the statement of the same view by William Palmer in his *Origines Liturgicae* (1832) and his *Treatise on the Church* (1838) that most swayed Gladstone.[143] In any case, Gladstone had moved by the 1840s to a much higher eucharistic doctrine.

In that decade he inevitably pondered the Roman Catholic understanding of the sacrament. We know, he reflected in a memorandum of 1842, that the eucharist is a mystery, but we do not know whether, as Roman Catholics argue, it is a miracle suspending the laws of nature.[144] By 1845 he had determined the issue: the bread and wine remained what they were before consecration. That was to repudiate transubstantiation. It was a matter of trusting the senses with which the Almighty had endowed human beings: the elements 'continue to give us all the evidences of their being true Bread & Wine & it is our duty to believe those reasonable evidences'.[145] Nor was the Lutheran notion of consubstantiation, which depended on a similar groundless metaphysic, an acceptable alternative.[146] The spiritual presence of Christ in the elements was different in mode from what could be perceived with the eyes. There was, in Gladstone's view, a weighty corollary. The Roman Church, by encouraging the veneration of the consecrated host, allowed 'worship to be paid to the visible elements'. This was nothing but 'a fraud upon the senses' and so 'deeply to be deplored'.[147] Gladstone had concluded categorically that there was no suspension of the laws of nature. Many years later he summed up his attitude in a letter to his son Stephen, who was intending ordination. 'I am a firm believer', he wrote, 'in the words of our Lord, therefore in the "objective Presence". But it is the presence of a spiritual body (see the phrase of St. Paul in 1 Cor. xv.), therefore not according to the laws of a natural body.'[148] The central truth about the eucharist was the real presence of Christ, but Roman Catholics were mistaken about the mode.

In the earlier 1840s Gladstone was wary of the idea of eucharistic sacrifice as well as of the doctrine of transubstantiation. The representation of the sacrament as a sacrifice seemed bound up with Roman Catholic abuses such as the encouragement of attendance at mass without reception.[149] Palmer, in his *Origines Liturgicae*, had rejected the notion that the consecrated elements are offered in

---

[142] e.g. 'Holy Eucharist', GP 44780, f. 131.

[143] Dugmore, *Eucharistic Doctrine*, pp. 37–40. Alf Härdelin, *The Tractarian Understanding of the Eucharist* (Uppsala, 1965), pp. 140, 128. *D*, 17 Mar., 5 May 1833, 5 July 1840 (for Gladstone's reading *Origines Liturgicae*). [144] GP 44730, f. 197 (5 Sept. 1842).

[145] 'Holy Eucharist', GP 44736, f. 231 (21 Feb. 1847).

[146] 'H[oly] Euch[arist]',GP 44736, f. 239v (n.d., but probably 2 May 1847, when diary records a MS on the subject).

[147] 'Holy Eucharist', GP 44780, ff. 248–51 (19 Mar. 1848), quoted at f. 251.

[148] W. E. Gladstone to S. E. Gladstone, 15 Sept. 1868, Lathbury, 2, p. 180.

[149] 'H.E. sacrif.', GP 44737, f. 140 (18 January 1849).

sacrifice to God, and in 1844 Gladstone was still content to share his view.[150] Pusey, however, had moved forward in *Tract LXXXI* (1837) to claim, on patristic authority, that the bread and wine, after consecration, are indeed offered to God. He guarded himself by denying that this was an act of expiation, which might have threatened the uniqueness of the work of Christ, and by instead claiming, with the early fathers, that it was a 'commemorative sacrifice'.[151] In an article of 1845 Gladstone echoed Pusey's phrase, showing that he had come to align himself with the Oxford divine.[152] Two years later Gladstone, in a paper on his understanding of the sacrament, affirmed that the priest 'offers the Body and Blood of the Lord, sacrificed for us'.[153] The act, he added in a further paper of 1849, was not expiatory, for Christ expiates no more.[154] But, like Pusey in a publication of 1851, Gladstone identified the earthly sacrifice of the priest with the heavenly work of Christ. Through the sacrament the faithful 'partake in the act which the great High Priest performs continually there still offering Himself to the Father on our behalf, for our salvation'.[155] It was an idea that Gladstone repeated in his sermons.[156] The communion service gave access to the very courts of heaven, enabling sinful human beings to be identified with the exalted Christ. The eucharist had become clothed with immense imaginative significance.

The sacrament was therefore the focus of Christian worship. 'As God and as man', Gladstone told his household in 1846, Christ 'is present in the blessed Eucharist after a manner more intimate [and] more immediate than any in which He has been pleased to reveal Himself as present elsewhere . . .'[157] There are ample signs of the importance of the communion service to the politician. From 1841 onwards he put together a booklet of private devotions, the 'Secreta Eucharistica', to aid his spiritual recollection.[158] After a two-month trip to Germany in 1845 during which he had perforce never received the sacrament, he recorded in his diary 'the joy of Holy Communion'.[159] In one of his household addresses he actually apostrophizes the 'Sacrament of God'.[160] 'And as your feet pass outwards from the frequent Eucharist', he advises himself in 1844, 'let the sense of that wonderful Communion grow more solemn as the act grows less rare: and every time reflect while you retire, another chain bound upon my soul, another oath, heard in heaven and in hell: Oh perjured a thousand fold if now thou leave thy God.'[161] In the sermons he reprimands the servants for absence from the service, urges greater frequency of attendance, and censures indifference to the sacrament in the starkest terms: 'he that neglects the Eucharist', he says, 'neglects the

---

[150] GP 44734, f. 285 (8 December 1844).

[151] Härdelin, *Tractarian Understanding of the Eucharist*, pp. 199, 204, 208.

[152] W. E. Gladstone, 'Scotch Ecclesiastical Affairs', *Quarterly Review*, 77 (1845), p. 247.

[153] GP 44736, f. 232 (21 Feb. 1847).     [154] GP 44737, f. 141v.     [155] GP 44736, f. 232.

[156] 'Holy Eucharist', GP 44780, f. 251v. The passage expounding the eucharistic sacrifice is inserted. 'Thurs. bef. Easter', GP 44781, ff. 97–100v (5 Apr. 1855), f. 97.

[157] 'Eighth Day of the Month', GP 44780, ff. 163–6v (15 Feb. 1846), quoted at f. 166v.

[158] D, 25 Apr. 1841. GP 44831, Lathbury, 2, pp. 421–7.     [159] D, 7 Dec. 1845.

[160] 'Holy Eucharist', GP 44780, f. 251v.     [161] GP 44734, f. 133 (23 June 1844).

Saviour: he that rejects the Eucharist rejects the Saviour.'[162] The topic is dragged
in where its appearance is most unexpected. In a sermon on 'The Lord is at hand'
for the Fourth Sunday in Advent, for example, when one might expect anticipa-
tion of the second coming, the nearness of the Lord is explained as a consequence
of his dwelling in the faithful by his body and blood.[163] For Gladstone, as for most
Tractarians, the holy communion is evidently the most sublime religious experience, a visual embodiment of the faith. As he put it in 1848, 'it sums up in a
manner the whole of Christianity'.[164]

The importance of the eucharist, however, was largely a result of its intimate
connection with the doctrine of the incarnation. The prominence in Gladstone's
mind, at least during his middle years, of the motif of God assuming human
nature would hardly be evident without the sermons, but it emerges strongly in
that neglected source. In two sermons for Trinity Sunday composed in 1840 and
1841 he turns from the topic for the day to the incarnation on the ground that the
Trinitarian controversy depended on the question of Christ's divinity. Christ,
Gladstone declares in one of them, as God and man, restored humanity to God.[165]
The doctrine of 'the twofold nature of Christ', he contends in the other, is

> the bridge which spans across that gulph of separation which sin interposed between our
> God & us: because He is a man we are capable of being incorporated into Him; because He
> is also God, and manhood in Him is inseparably attached to Godhead we by becoming
> partakers of His manhood are made also partakers of the influences & power of his
> Godhead, & we regain the nature which Adam lost.[166]

The saving power of the incarnation meant that it was intensely practical: it
provided for us, Gladstone assured his household a year later, a 'new and holy
human nature'. We were to become partakers of Christ through his ordinances,
Gladstone explains, but in this sermon of 1842 the politician does not yet isolate
the holy communion as the chief means of incorporation into Christ.[167] That lofty
goal was achieved, according to a roughly contemporary memorandum, by the
word as well as the sacraments, but again the eucharistic dimension is not developed.[168] By the delivery of a sermon of 1845 on 'The Holy Eucharist', however, the
connection between the sacrament and the incarnation is firmly in place.
Gladstone now attributes the power of redemption and renovation that elsewhere
he had associated with the atonement or the resurrection to the incarnation. The
'human nature which He assumed for our sakes is to be the very means, the ordinary means, and yet one step further the only means whereby we can be relieved

[162] 'The Holy Communion', GP 44780, ff. 142–5v (9 April 1846), at f. 143; 'Eighth Day of the Month',
GP 44780, f. 166v; 'Palm Sunday', GP 44780, ff. 171–4v (5 Apr. 1846), at f. 174; 'Holy Eucharist', GP
44780, quoted at f. 133v.
    [163] 'Public Humiliation', GP 44779, ff. 179–84v (19 Dec. 1841), at f. 179.
    [164] 'Holy Eucharist', GP 44780, f. 248.
    [165] 'Trinity Sunday', GP 44779, ff. 66–9v (14 June 1840), at f. 69.
    [166] 'Trinity Sunday', GP 44779, ff. 123–6v (6 June 1841), quoted at ff. 126–6v.
    [167] 'Second Sunday after Trinity', GP 44779, ff. 246–50v (5 June 1842), quoted at f. 246v.
    [168] 'Christ and the Church', GP 44731, f. 122v (n.d.: 1842?).

from our extremity of misery and guilt'. How do we draw support from that source of life? Only by eating Christ's flesh and drinking his blood—Gladstone quotes John 6: 53—'for by this holy rite it is ordained that we feed upon the Saviour and every other part of divine worship is subordinate to this main and central one'.[169] The twin priorities, doctrinal and liturgical, of incarnation and eucharist have become tightly bonded together.

The fully developed theory was expounded in another sermon on the eucharist three years later. 'If there be', Gladstone told his hearers, 'an idea or doctrine which has a title to rank before all others in the Gospel system . . . it is the doctrine of the incarnation.' Perhaps, he reflected, more properly it was the teaching that drew all others in its train. 'It is the foundation of the whole doctrine of atonement', but that work was confined to the past. In the present, however, the incarnation continues to be 'the medium of our living union with God', because through the communion service we come to share in the life of Christ. 'And now', Gladstone continued, 'we should observe how the Lord connects this doctrine about our feeding upon Him, with the doctrine of His mission from on high in the Incarnation: "as the living Father hath sent me, & I live by the Father: so he that eateth me even he shall live by me." ' This verse, John 6: 56, is repeated in the peroration of the address. Clearly it had made a powerful impression on Gladstone, clinching the unique linkage that he was trying to enforce. 'Hence', he contended, 'the holy Eucharist is indeed the counterpart of the Incarnation.' In the sacrament the living Christ, man as well as God, comes to sustain the community of believers. Through being united with his humanity, they rise to his divinity and so are restored to the fellowship of God.[170] The incarnate Christ continues to wield his mediatorial power. Gladstone's mind now displayed what Owen Chadwick has noted as a characteristic of the Tractarians, a 'greater emphasis upon the Incarnation in its relation to the Atonement'.[171] In company with the eucharist, the incarnation had moved centre stage in his thought.

## III

What were the influences that drew Gladstone towards this conclusion? A wide range of reading was imbuing him with Tractarian convictions and leading him in particular to the bond of eucharist and incarnation. The Oxford movement—and especially Pusey—is known for its patristic learning. Gladstone's debt to the early fathers of the church is evident from a number of specific passages in the politician's manuscripts. On Sunday 1 February 1846, for instance, he read a patristic catena on the gospel passage that he was preparing to expound in his

---

[169] 'The Holy Eucharist', GP 44780, ff. 132, 133v.
[170] 'Holy Eucharist', GP 44780, ff. 249, 249v, 250, 250, 250v.
[171] Owen Chadwick, 'The Mind of the Oxford Movement', in *The Spirit of the Oxford Movement* (Cambridge, 1990), p. 39.

sermon. The point that Christ's sleep in the boat on Galilee was a sign that he had truly taken human nature surely derives, though Gladstone does not say so, from one of the comments by the fathers that he read there.[172] In the following year Gladstone explicitly offers remarks by St Cyril (he does not say which) in explanation of a difficult gospel passage.[173] In 1847, too, he draws on Cyprian, whose life and writings he had absorbed over recent years, in a polemical paper directed against Newman.[174] Not surprisingly in view of Gladstone's extended reading of Augustine in the 1830s, the great Latin father is cited more than once in the sermons and used as the supreme commentator on the Psalms.[175] But more important than individual allusions is the broad correspondence of the central themes of Gladstone's theology of the 1840s with the general pattern of patristic thought. The belief that Christ became man in order, by his obedience, to undo the work of fallen Adam—the work of *recapitulatio*—is there in both. Gladstone's typical idea that the incarnation provides the dynamic for the renewal of human beings is thoroughly patristic. So is his view that the eucharist is the chief means by which renewal is imparted.[176] Gladstone's treatment of the work of Christ is also similar to that in the fathers. Characteristically they did not isolate the death of Christ as the single moment of redemption, but rather considered it, in conjunction with the resurrection, as part of the whole divine drama of the incarnation.[177] Thus Gladstone's evolution away from his early evangelical stress on the cross towards the later twin emphasis on incarnation and eucharist had patristic inspiration. The process can be seen as a harmonization of his theology with the position of the early church.

Many other items in Gladstone's programme of reading bore the distinctive impress of the disciples of the Oxford movement. Taking their Catholicity seriously, they often borrowed from medieval or later Roman sources to provide sustenance for the soul. Thus in 1844 Gladstone read *The Life of our Lord and Saviour Jesus Christ* by the thirteenth-century Franciscan Bonaventura—newly edited by Frederick Oakeley, who was about to go over to Rome.[178] Other medieval reading included the anonymous *Paradisus Animae* (1498), which Gladstone read devotionally in small portions between February and April 1846.[179] Ignatius Loyola taught him 'to reduce all actions to rule';[180] from another Counter-Reformation saint, Francis de Sales, he learned that expressions of self-contempt could in reality represent the essence of pride.[181] *The Spiritual Guide* (1675) by the Spanish quietist Miguel de Molinos at first seemed 'a remarkable

[172] *D*, 1 Feb. 1846. 'Fourth Sunday after Epiphany', GP 44780, ff. 158–62v (1 Feb. 1846), at f. 160.
[173] 'Day of Solemn and Public Humiliation', GP 44780, ff. 193–7v (24 Mar.1847), at f. 193.
[174] GP 44736, f. 331v (8 Aug. 1847). *D*, 11 Apr. 1841, 24 Mar. 1844, 2 Sept., 15, 16, and 18 Dec. 1845.
[175] 'Thirteenth Sunday after Trinity', GP 44780, ff. 121–4v (12 Jan.1845), at f. 123v. '2 S. Epiph.', GP 44781, ff. 146–50v (21 Sept. 1862), at f. 150. GP 44737, ff. 84–98 (n.d., but Oct. 1849).
[176] J. N. D. Kelly, *Early Christian Doctrine*, 4th edn. (London, 1968), pp. 376–7, 450.
[177] H. E. W. Turner, *The Patristic Doctrine of Redemption* (London, 1952), pp. 20, 51.
[178] *D*, 16 June 1844, 12 Jan. 1845.                      [179] *D*, 25 Feb.–17 Apr. 1846.
[180] GP 44736, f. 7 (18 Aug. 1846). *D*, 16 Aug.–6 Sept. 1846.
[181] GP 44732, f. 164 (4 June 1843). *D*, 28 May–4 June 1843.

book' but, like the Roman authorities of the seventeenth century, on further acquaintance Gladstone judged it to contain 'great thoughts, capable of great perversions'.[182] *The Foundations of the Spiritual Life* (1667) by the French Jesuit Jean Joseph Surin, however, was simply 'beautiful'.[183] Surin's book had been edited for Anglicans by Pusey, and this whole body of spiritual reading could have borne his imprimatur. This category of reading may not have contributed substantially to the development of specific ideas, but it certainly pointed the politician to a higher estimate of the eucharist. It brought a wealth of continental devotion, medieval and early modern, to Gladstone's formation.

More decisive for his development, however, were two English divines of the seventeenth century, Lancelot Andrewes and William Laud. Pusey recommended Bishop Andrewes's *Devotions* on the ground, to him supremely persuasive, that they 'entirely express the wants and desires of a mind trained in the teaching of the ancient Church'.[184] Gladstone read both *Tract LXXXVIII*, containing an edition by Newman of Andrewes's Greek *Devotions*, when it appeared in 1838, and the rearranged version that Newman published four years later.[185] Henry Manning's wedding present to Gladstone in 1839 was a copy of the *Devotions*, probably the 1830 edition from which Gladstone quoted a 'noble prayer' in an essay of 1844.[186] In 1841 the politician turned to the sermons for which, in his day, Andrewes was most celebrated.[187] From the bishop Gladstone could derive a spirituality focused on the eucharist and nourished by patristic texts. In particular Andrewes's willingness to believe the doctrine of the real presence without venturing to specify its mode may well have swayed the politician.[188] But Gladstone was also drawn by Archbishop William Laud, who was so close to Andrewes that he published a collection of the bishop's sermons shortly after his death. In 1840 Gladstone read Laud's *Private Devotions*, edited by F. W. Faber who, like Oakeley, would secede to Rome, and two years later Laud's *Autobiography*.[189] The politician admired in Laud not the overbearing man of affairs but the reformer of the University of Oxford as the nursery of the Church of England. Laud, wrote Gladstone in 1848, possessed 'a deep instinct aiding a profound learning and an acute intelligence' that enabled him to adopt a charitable stance towards Roman Catholics without ceasing to protest against their abuses, to check Calvinism within the Church of England, to remain no slave to party, and to die a martyr's death.[190] Laud's prayers appeared alongside those of Andrewes in Gladstone's 'Secreta Eucharistica', the private notebook he carried with him to communion services.[191] Both prelates provided devotions derived

---

[182] *D*, 25 Dec. 1842, 1 Jan.1843.                          [183] *D*, 2 Feb. 1845.

[184] E. B. Pusey, *Preface to the Fourth Edition of the 'Letter to the Right Rev. Father in God, Richard, Lord Bishop of Oxford'* (Oxford, 1840), p. xlii n.

[185] *D*, 3 Dec. 1838; 29 Nov. 1842. These entries are omitted from the *Diaries* index.

[186] GP 44728, f. 259v. W. E. Gladstone, 'Ward's Ideal of a Christian Church', *Gleanings*, 5, p. 84.

[187] *D*, 25 Apr. 1841.                          [188] Dugmore, *Eucharistic Doctrine*, pp. 37–40.

[189] *D*, 2 Feb. 1840, 24 Dec. 1842.

[190] W. E. Gladstone, 'The Duke of Argyll on Presbytery', *Quarterly Review*, 84 (1848), pp. 98, 99, 104.

[191] GP 44831. Unlike the version printed in Lathbury, 2, pp. 421–7, the MS contains attributions.

from ancient liturgies that appealed alike to the seventeenth and nineteenth centuries. Together these two Caroline divines helped form the kernel of Gladstone's piety.

Yet, for all Gladstone's reading of authors from the past, the chief way in which he reached his new phase of faith was through the Tractarians of the present. The sermons of John Henry Newman made a deep impression on Gladstone. The 'noble' sixth volume of Newman's *Parochial Sermons*, Gladstone noted in his diary in 1842, would alone be 'the basis of a high & permanent reputation'.[192] After Newman's secession to Rome in 1845, the politician still read the divine's sermons to his household from time to time. Gladstone was by no means an uncritical disciple. As we have already seen, he had become concerned about Newman's understanding of justification long before the divine left the Church of England;[193] and the politician also entertained serious doubts about Newman's downgrading of reason in order to exalt faith.[194] Nevertheless Newman did much to mould Gladstone's rigorous devotional temper. The annotations of the politician's copies of the *Parochial Sermons* show that he found Newman's probing of subtle sins particularly telling. The sermon on 'Profession without Practice' in volume 1, repeatedly endorsed by Gladstone with favourable signs, clearly hit home; so did another in the same volume on 'The Religion of the Day'. 'Dare not to think', Gladstone marked with approval in the margin, 'you have got to the bottom of your hearts; you do not know what evil lies there.'[195] He also read in Newman, though he did not mark it, that the incarnation was the great doctrine that embraced the two truths of the divinity of Christ and the atonement.[196] Such contentions helped to supplant Gladstone's inherited evangelical views with more characteristic patristic teaching. Furthermore Newman's sustained polemic against the evangelical position had a powerful effect on the politician. A sermon on 1836 on 'Self-Contemplation', wholly directed against evangelicals, condemned their characteristic process of internal scrutiny to discover whether faith was real.[197] Gladstone put a double line in the margin, an unusually strong indication of concurrence. His willingness to criticize the evangelicals freely in his own sermons owed a great deal to Newman's example.

Other figures associated with the Oxford movement also exerted an influence over Gladstone. In 1839 he read a volume of sermons by Frederick Oakeley, finding in it polemic against evangelicals and exhortation to 'an arduous course of self-denial'.[198] Although Gladstone did not become close to John Keble, to whom he sent only a couple of letters during the 1840s, the politician did absorb several

[192] *D*, 24 July 1842.                                            [193] See Ch. 3, p. 53–4.
[194] Newman's sermon on 'The Subjection of the Reason and Feelings to the Revealed Word' attracted Gladstone's censure, as is clear from his annotated copy. Newman, *Parochial Sermons*, 6, esp. p. 282, copy at Hawarden Castle.                    [195] Newman, *Parochial Sermons*, 1, 2nd edn., p. 374.
[196] Ibid., 2, 2nd edn., p. 217.
[197] Ibid., p. 186. Gladstone adds: 'growth with respect to these to be growth with respect to that.'
[198] Frederick Oakeley, *Sermons preached chiefly in the Chapel Royal at Whitehall* (Oxford, 1839), p. xx. *D*, 12 May–16 June 1839. Gladstone read one of Oakeley's sermons aloud to the household: *D*, 2 Aug. 1840.

of his writings and specially delighted in *The Christian Year* (1827).[199] And through Pusey, with whom he corresponded more frequently, Gladstone had access to an immense fund of patristic ideas. The notions of the twofold work of Christ and of participation in his heavenly sacrifice, as we have seen, appeared in the writings of both men.[200] An Easter sermon of Pusey's, 'Christ Risen our Justification', criticized the evangelical custom of attributing all the benefits of Christ's work to his death: 'Close then as the Precious Death and Resurrection are, they have each their own efficacy and distinct gift. That Death paid the Ransom for the whole world, but the world lay, as yet, but in the deeper darkness and sin . . . His death atoned for us; His resurrection justifies us.'[201] Gladstone adopted the same rationale for treating the resurrection as the source of life for the Christian. Pusey extended his anti-evangelical polemic into a letter to Gladstone. The evangelicals could not feel the gravity of heresies about the person of Christ, because they 'never meditate on the Incarnation'.[202] The coming in flesh of the Son of God was the fulcrum of Pusey's theology. In preaching on 'God with us' at Christmas, he pointed to the incarnation as the very centre of the divine mercy. And he went on in the same sermon to stress that God is with us in the sacraments so 'that we, receiving Him, may be partakers of Him'.[203] In Pusey's mind there was a link between the incarnation, the eucharist, and the inward strength of the believer. Although the politician never cites Pusey in the household sermons, Gladstone's thought coincided very closely with that of the Oxford divine.

There are clearer indications of direct dependence on Manning. Nobody was closer to Gladstone during the 1840s, and the two men corresponded extensively.[204] When, in a sermon of 1847, Gladstone catalogued the various forms of fasting, he noted in the margin that the analysis came from 'H.E.M.'.[205] To another sermon, composed in 1849, he subsequently added Manning's definition of faith from the clergyman's volume of sermons that appeared in the following year. And even after Manning, in 1851, had followed Newman into the Church of Rome, Gladstone, when preaching on Zechariah 9: 17, echoed his former friend's teaching in a sermon on the same verse.[206] The two men shared a willingness to criticize the shortcomings they perceived in the evangelicalism of their earlier lives and, as we have seen, the idea of the twofold work of Christ.[207] Manning taught, as did Gladstone, that the crucifixion must not be isolated, since Christ's 'whole life was a part of the one sacrifice'.[208] It is not, of course, to be expected that the

[199] W. E. Gladstone to John Keble, 11 Jan. 1840, 21 Jan. 1845, Package 90, Keble Manuscripts, Keble College Library, Oxford. *D*, 31 May 1829, 8 Apr. 1832, 23, 30 Sept. 1832, 18 Nov. 1832, 16 Dec. 1832, 13 Jan. 1833, 14 Apr. 1833. [200] See above, pp. 92, 95.

[201] E. B. Pusey, *Sermons during the Season from Advent to Whitsuntide*, 2nd edn. (Oxford, 1848), p. 215. There is, however, no mention of this volume in the *Diaries* index.

[202] E. B. Pusey to W. E. Gladstone, [9 Apr.] 1846, f. 226, LBV 38, Pusey House Library, Oxford.

[203] Pusey, *Sermons*, pp. 48, 55. [204] Peter Erb is editing the correspondence for publication.

[205] 'Public Fast', GP 44780, f. 190.

[206] 'Easter Eve', GP 44781, ff. 48–51v (18 Apr. 1852), at f. 51v. Manning, *Sermons*, 4, pp. 228–47.

[207] Manning, *Sermons*, 1, pp. 180, 251. See above, p. 92. [208] Ibid., p. 245.

two men thought identically. There is, in particular, a Platonic strain in Manning's sermons that does not appear in Gladstone's: nothing is real, it seems, except the spiritual life; and we rise to perceive 'the idea of holiness as it exists in the Eternal Mind'.[209] Yet the degree of affinity is striking. Manning urges obedience as the one essential quality in the believer.[210] The power to become new creatures, he explains, flows from the incarnation. 'He took our manhood', writes Manning, 'and made it new in Himself, that we might be made new in Him.'[211] And it is in the sacrament that the work of Christ is brought home to the faithful. There we receive 'our incorporation in His mystical body: His true and substantial union with us: our participation in His divine nature: our perpetual sustenance by His presence, who is the Resurrection and the Life'.[212] Incarnation and eucharist are as bound together in Manning's thought as we have seen them to be in Gladstone's. And there can be no doubt about the primary direction of influence. The clergyman was able to spend time exploring the tradition of Catholic theology, and passed on the fruit of his researches to the politician. Manning must have done more than anyone else to turn Gladstone into a fully fledged Tractarian.

When Gladstone's mature religious position had been worked out, it closely resembled that of Robert Wilberforce, the nearest approach to a systematic theologian thrown up by Tractarianism. Wilberforce's trilogy on the incarnation (1848), baptism (1849), and the eucharist (1853) provided cogent expositions of these central themes. His description of Christ as the 'Pattern Man', a refrain in the early chapters of *The Doctrine of the Incarnation*, crops up in one of Gladstone's later sermons, and variants occur elsewhere in the politician's writings.[213] Although this phrase clearly made an impression on Gladstone, and although he read Wilberforce's annual charges to his archdeaconry from 1841 onwards, the three major works appeared too late to shape most of the politician's theological convictions. Nevertheless the common ground is vast, as a volume of Wilberforce's sermons published in 1850 shows. Wilberforce, like Manning, takes issue with the evangelicalism of his youth, urging that the reality of our union with Christ is just as great a truth of the gospel as the atonement.[214] Like Pusey, he stresses Christ rising for our justification, writes of Christ's 'second work' of renewal, and insists on obedience as the expression of union with Christ.[215] The incarnation, he holds, must be elevated above the cross. 'For that Our Lord should become man, was a far greater descent, than that when He was man he should suffer contempt and death.'[216] And 'The Sacramental System', as he calls one of his most powerful sermons, is the means by which the life won for us is

---

[209] Manning, *Sermons*, 1, pp. 129–45, 234.      [210] Ibid., pp. 117–28, 129–45, 80–3.
[211] Ibid., p. 19.      [212] Ibid., 4, p. 391.
[213] R. I. Wilberforce, *The Doctrine of the Incarnation of Our Lord Jesus Christ in its Relation to Mankind and to the Church* (London, 1848), chs. 1–4. '4 S. Easter', GP 44781, ff. 128–33v (28 Apr. 1861), at f. 132v. 'the Pattern': D, 29 Dec. 1857. 'That higher Pattern': Gladstone, 'Tennyson', p. 149.
[214] R. I. Wilberforce, *Sermons on the New Birth of Man's Nature* (London, 1850), p. 21.
[215] Ibid., pp. 175, 19, 23.      [216] Ibid., p. 138.

passed from Christ to his church.[217] The sacraments, he declares in his book of 1848, are 'the extension of the Incarnation'.[218] There is, once again, the tightest of connections between incarnation and eucharist. Gladstone's respect for Wilberforce was unbounded. The archdeacon had established, Gladstone told him in 1854, 'an association between your own name and the living tradition of the Catholic faith in the Church of England respecting the Incarnation, which I can only compare ... to what the association was between the name of St Augustine and the doctrine of original sin, or the name of St Athanasius and that of the Trinity.'[219] Gladstone was then pleading with the latter-day Athanasius not to abandon his church for Rome, but the appeal fell on deaf ears. Wilberforce, like Newman and Manning before him, passed by the decisive act of secession out of Gladstone's circle. But in his Anglican days Robert Wilberforce was the author of a body of theology that came nearer to expounding the politician's Tractarian convictions than any other.

IV

During the 1840s Gladstone had moved to the heart of the Tractarian ethos. His sermons breathe its spirit. Exhortations to struggle against sin, aided by pious practices such as fasting, form the burden of his message. Worship, he held, must be enriched in order to provide further help for the faithful. The round of the ecclesiastical year, the beautifying of parish churches, and the introduction of chanting would all contribute to the Catholic revival. The poetry of Dante helped to crystallize Gladstone's new spiritual vision. His dogmatic position was now in accordance, he believed, with that of the fathers of the early church. Andrewes and Laud, together with the works of continental spiritual writers, gave fresh substance to his devotion. Newman provided a body of inspiring teaching, Pusey pushed Gladstone towards firmer theological conclusions, and Manning shared in giving expression to many of them. The writings of Robert Wilberforce embodied most fully the doctrinal system that Gladstone came to uphold. It represented a position different—though not worlds apart—from that of the Orthodox churchmen to whom the politician had most approximated down to the writing of *Church Principles* (1840). He still, it is true, read and deferred to divines of that school. In 1849, for instance, when he began a personal commentary on the Psalms, he drew almost as heavily on the late eighteenth-century High Churchman Bishop Horne as on Augustine.[220] By 1844, however, Gladstone was distancing himself from the Orthodox, whom he was willing to label the 'high & dry' party.[221] What had not been lost in the transition, however, was 'a sense of

---

[217] Ibid., sermon XIX.                           [218] Wilberforce, *Incarnation*, p. 410.
[219] W. E. Gladstone to R. I. Wilberforce, 24 Sept. 1854, Sandwith MSS, Harrogate, quoted by Newsome, *Parting of Friends*, p. 382. Newsome discusses Robert Wilberforce's theology at pp. 372–81.
[220] GP 44737, ff. 84–98v (n.d.). *D*, 9–15 Oct. 1849.
[221] W. E. Gladstone to Lord Lyttelton, 14 Mar. 1844, GGM 35, f. 51.

our Christian brotherhood'. The belief that Catholicity was a remedy for selfishness remained and, if anything, was enhanced. The purpose of God, he explained in 1843, was not to deal with separate souls, but to impart to them 'the most inward and vital sentiment of community, and brotherhood, and identity'.[222] Gladstone's new Tractarianism, at least as much as his older ecclesiastical principles, gave him an awareness of the overwhelming importance of the corporate nature of the church.

His new Tractarian position constituted a theological stance very different from that of the evangelicals. Gladstone disagreed with them about matters such as conversion and assurance, but the central contrast was over the place of the atonement in the scheme of things. The cross, for Gladstone, as for his Tractarian mentors, must not be made an excuse for lingering in sin; it must be recognized as giving rise to renewal as well as pardon; and it must be seen in co-ordination with, and in some sense subordinate to, the resurrection. The 1840s did not witness, as Boyd Hilton has suggested, a reappropriation by Gladstone of some of his evangelical roots, leading to a championing of themes associated with the atonement to the end of his career.[223] On the contrary, it was a time when he altered his doctrine of the cross so as to put it in a broader context. Most important was the supersession of the atonement by the incarnation as the central motif in Gladstone's mind. The salvation of humanity, the politician now believed, was to be attributed to the assumption of flesh by the Son of God. Incarnationalism is often taken to be a symptom of a liberalizing trend in nineteenth-century theology. It is true that later on, as the next chapter will show, the more up-to-date version of the stress on the incarnation was to emerge in Gladstone's thinking. That was not, however, the original way in which he approached the centrality of the doctrine. Gladstone adopted the incarnational emphasis not because it was modern but because it harmonized with the teaching of the ancient church. It seemed part of the Catholic package, along with the focus on the eucharist. The real presence in the sacrament was what transmitted the merits of the incarnation to the faithful. The bond of incarnation and eucharist constituted the solid dogmatic core of Gladstone's theology. His Tractarian phase turned Gladstone into an incarnationalist.

[222] Gladstone, 'Present Aspect of the Church', pp. 1, 13.
[223] Boyd Hilton, *The Age of Atonement: The Influence of Evangelicalism on Social and Economic Thought, 1785–1865* (Oxford, 1988), p. 342.

# 5

# The Development of Broad Church Sympathies

GLADSTONE, WITH good reason, is not usually classified as a Broad Churchman. Each of the early phases of his theological pilgrimage—evangelical, Orthodox, and Tractarian—reinforced a commitment to dogma that was alien to the Broad Church temper. Even Colin Matthew, who points to Gladstone's adoption of a Broad Church mode of presentation in the 1870s, justly declares that he 'profoundly mistrusted Broad-Church philosophizing'.[1] But in 1899 G. W. E. Russell asked whether the evangelical and Catholic components of Gladstone's mind were supplemented by Broad Church sympathies and answered in the affirmative.[2] Broad Churchmen, he noted, had received his support. Gladstone twice promoted Charles Kingsley, tried to keep F. D. Maurice at King's College, London, when the divine's advanced views on eternal punishment came under attack, and showed confidence in Frederick Temple, one of the contributors to *Essays and Reviews* (1860), by nominating him to the episcopal bench. Although Kingsley's preferment to a Chester canonry in 1869 owed more to the Queen than to her Prime Minister and although the defence of Maurice in 1853 showed no inclination on Gladstone's part to weaken the dogmatic profession of the church,[3] these episodes do illustrate a certain liberality in his mind. Russell adduced further evidence. Gladstone wrote a highly favourable review of J. R. Seeley's *Ecce Homo* (1865), a book presenting an image of Jesus divested of the supernatural; the statesman disparaged the Athanasian Creed, with its notorious damnatory sections; he was lenient on those he judged to be in schism from the true church; and supremely he came to profess views on immortality that broke with the traditional view of the afterlife. This catalogue will need some qualification, but the list does suggest that Gladstone's leanings towards Broad Churchmanship extended beyond a sense of equity in ecclesiastical appointments. There is a neglected liberal strand in his later theological thinking that calls for analysis.

The emergence of this dimension of Gladstone's mind is the subject of the present chapter. Here attention will concentrate on the period between the 1840s

---

[1] Matthew, p. 260. Cf. pp. 271, 293–5.
[2] G. W. E. Russell, *Mr. Gladstone's Religious Development* (London, 1899), pp. 54–5.
[3] Lathbury, 1, p. 193. Morley, 1, pp. 454–5.

and the 1860s, the subsequent apologetic for his mature position being reserved for consideration in Chapter 8. Already while he was elaborating the Tractarian worldview that was described in the previous chapter, he was developing convictions that pointed in a liberal direction. Indeed there was an organic connection between some of his opinions as a disciple of Pusey and the broader thinking that gradually unfolded. The idea of the incarnation in particular was common ground between the two tendencies, assuming equal prominence in each. The trajectory of Gladstone's thought, however, is harder to trace in the years after 1852. As Colin Matthew has noted, his publications on theological questions dried up at that point.[4] For one thing, he was in office for a great deal of the period; for another, when out of office, he turned away from specifically ecclesiastical topics to classical studies. Homer, the main subject of Chapters 6 and 7, was his new preoccupation. That focus, as will become clear, did not entail a break with Gladstone's broader theological concerns, especially (once more) the doctrine of the incarnation. But the change of emphasis in his studies means that there is much less extended commentary, either published or unpublished, on the evolution of his views about most doctrinal questions. He still composed sermons, right down to 1866, but, as he frequently reused earlier ones, even they provide only a small—though invaluable—body of source material for his religious stance. Nevertheless it is possible to piece together an account of the trends in his theological thinking down to the publication of the review of *Ecce Homo* in 1868. It was in this middle period that the Broad Church sympathies began to emerge.

I

A major precipitant of change was Gladstone's recoil from the state confessionalism of his first book. His theory immediately encountered difficulties. On the very day when he completed the initial text of the first edition in July 1838, he admitted to Philip Pusey, the brother of the Oxford divine and a fellow Conservative MP, that 'I thought my own Church & State principles within one stage of becoming hopeless as regards success in this generation'.[5] The problem was that, especially in the colonies and Ireland, the ecclesiastical policy of the government had perforce to take account of the extent of religious pluralism. It was simply impractical to limit state support to Anglicanism, or even to the faith of the two established churches of Britain. In June 1840 Gladstone himself felt compelled to endorse the Canadian Clergy Reserves Bill that authorized the sale of land previously set aside for the support of the Church of England and the distribution of part of the proceeds among other religious bodies.[6] Later in 1840, while preparing the fourth edition of *The State*, he reflected anxiously that two processes were at

---

[4] Matthew, p. 152.                                                      [5] *D*, 23 July 1838.

[6] Perry Butler, *Gladstone: Church, State and Tractarianism: A Study of his Religious Ideas and Attitudes, 1809–1859* (Oxford, 1982), pp. 98–9.

work simultaneously: a tendency to religious laxity in the state and a contrary reinvigoration of the church. Would the invigoration, he asked himself, be fast enough to check the relaxation?[7] In the month when the new edition appeared he felt more sanguine about specifically political prospects. The Whig government was tottering to its fall, but 'the principle of National Religion' might be saved by 'the united action of the Conservative party' once it came into power.[8] Yet after the Conservative victory of that year and his own appointment to the vice-presidency of the Board of Trade, Gladstone soon abandoned hope in the religious potential of his party. The state, he wrote in March 1842, could not be harmonized with the church. 'We have passed the point at which that was possible.'[9] If even Peel was disinclined to defend the ideal, the principle of exclusive recognition for Anglicanism would founder. As Gladstone memorably put it a quarter of a century later, 'I found myself the last man on the sinking ship'.[10]

The greatest challenge came from the threat to public order in Ireland. The followers of Daniel O'Connell, chafing under the yoke of the Protestant Ascendancy, had to be placated. By 1844 the government determined that the Roman Catholic seminary at Maynooth should be given a permanent and greatly increased grant. Gladstone agonized over the issue, trying to reconcile the proposal with his published views. How far, he asked himself, should an administration support a particular religious body 'when the alternative seems to be the breaking up of all government'? The obligation to support the truth, he had argued, was absolute; but the duty of governors to secure the state, founded in the nature of the political order itself, was logically prior. 'That which is contrary to the law of nature must never be done,' he replied, 'nor that which is contrary to revelation: but that which is according to them may frequently be postponed when its accomplishment is impracticable.'[11] Aristotle, after all, had taught that the safety of the state might entail drastic changes of policy. In critical times there must be concessions so that the state is not subverted. That did not entail the abandonment of the theoretical position expounded in *The State*: 'in a perfect condition of mankind', Gladstone wrote in March 1845, 'the State would be precluded from no part of the law of morality and truth.' Circumstances, however, were against its maintenance: 'we drift with the ebbing tide farther and farther from the normal or ideal State.'[12] As Alec Vidler has argued, Gladstone did not move away from the convictions set out in his first book, but he merely modified them in the light of practical constraints.[13] What can now be added is that he did so in accordance with a preconceived strategy. It was not that his theory was simply overwhelmed by the immediate demands of government, nor that it was

---

[7] GP 44729, f. 55 (17 Nov. 1840).      [8] GP 44819, f. 57 (9 May 1841), in *D*, 9 May 1841.

[9] *D*, 27 Mar. 1842.

[10] W. E. Gladstone, 'A Chapter of Autobiography' [1868], *Gleanings*, 7, p. 115.

[11] GP 44728, f. 337 (n.d.). '39?' has been subsequently added by Gladstone, but the content suggests the memorandum comes from the early 1840s.      [12] GP 44735, p. 13 (14 Mar. 1845).

[13] A. R. Vidler, *The Orb and the Cross: A Normative Study in the Relations of Church and State with Reference to Gladstone's Early Writings* (London, 1945), pp. 137–8, 142.

naturally superseded by the superior wisdom of Sir Robert Peel, but rather that some of its unstated premises had to be invoked in the 1840s. The paternal theory of government worked out in the 1830s had incorporated a technique of concession. Now that method of dealing with popular demands was put into operation. The more flexible element in Gladstone's political thought came into play.

What in these circumstances should be the policy of a loyal churchman in parliament? There was no point in the obdurate reiteration of his ideals. 'To preach the absolute demands of Catholic truth', Gladstone whimsically records in May 1845, 'to a Parliament acting for a nation of all religious colours is as it seems to me like resorting to a gambling house to preach against gaming.'[14] Instead the legislator must urge that the Church of England should be treated fairly. Its rivals, whether Roman Catholic or Dissenting, could receive redress of their grievances from parliament, but Anglican interests must not be forgotten. Gladstone stated his conclusions in 1847 in a published speech on the admission of Jews to the House of Commons: 'as citizens and as members of the Church we should contend manfully for her own principles and constitution, and should ask and press without fear for whatever tends to her own healthy development', but equally they should 'deal amicably and liberally with questions either solely or mainly affecting the civil rights of other portions of the community'. The Church of England should not be backward in making claims on parliament, for example through calling for the legislative endorsement of colonial bishoprics, work in which Gladstone was heavily involved in these years. Similarly, however, Anglicans must give sympathetic attention to the claims of non-established religious bodies. Hence he was willing to urge the admission of Jews to the legislature. The 'ultimate issue' in this case, he urged, was 'social justice, or proportionate dealing as between man and man'.[15] Pusey wrote to express his pain at hearing of Gladstone's endorsement of Jewish emancipation, a further retreat from Christian profession by the state, but the politician replied that, while he was swayed by civil arguments in favour of the Jews, he was influenced even more by apprehension of 'religious dangers' if the church put up continued resistance to Jewish emancipation.[16] He had charted a new policy over church–state relations that diverged from anything that Pusey could envisage.

The dangers that Gladstone feared came chiefly from the state. The Whigs, in office from 1846, were by no means averse to religious questions. Lord John Russell, as Prime Minister, was animated by a warm-hearted version of Broad Churchmanship close to that of Thomas Arnold. Like Arnold, the Whigs in government were unlikely to make a sharp distinction between the roles of the church and of the state. Both institutions, in their view, were designed to raise the

[14] 'Secret', GP 44735, ff. 34–9 (May 1845), quoted at f. 36v. The document is correctly assigned to 11 May in the *Diaries*, though it is also mistakenly attributed to 19 June.

[15] W. E. Gladstone, *Substance of a Speech on the Motion of Lord John Russell for a Committee of the Whole House with a View to the Removal of the Remaining Jewish Disabilities* (London, 1848), pp. 5, 22.

[16] E. B. Pusey to W. E. Gladstone, [13 Dec.] 1847, LBV 85/44, f. 274; W. E. Gladstone to E. B. Pusey, 14 Dec. 1847, LBV 85/45, ff. 283, 284, Pusey House Library, Oxford.

standard of civilization in the mass of the population, especially by means of education. Hence there existed no sacred precinct of church life beyond the legitimate interposition of the state.[17] There was therefore, in the eyes of a vigilant High Churchman such as Gladstone, a constant risk of political interference in ecclesiastical affairs. His church principles dictated that the divinely created Christian community, with its own laws and rulers, should enjoy a large autonomy. He had a horror of what in 1844 he had called 'that system, which absorbs church power into state power, by the name of Erastianism'.[18] The structures of establishment, by binding church and state closely together, actually made erastian forays all the easier. The 'highest and dearest interests', Gladstone told an uncomprehending Pusey in 1847, were 'so mixed up with what is alien to them, as to make it in my view a private duty to strive to extricate or to adjust them'.[19] The aim of the statesman should actually be to dissolve any galling features of establishment, a cause that put him potentially in alliance with Dissent. As early as 1849 Gladstone hailed with satisfaction the rise of opinion in favour of the relief of Dissenting grievances. If Dissenters were granted concessions by the state, Gladstone argued, it would be hard to deny the Church of England the power to regulate its own internal affairs. Hence, Gladstone argued with a touch of paradox, 'the great prize for which the Church has at this day to struggle is *religious equality*'.[20] The slogan recently taken up by the Dissenting campaign for disestablishment was in reality well designed to further the best interests of the Church of England.

The assault on the integrity of the church that Gladstone had anticipated was eventually mounted not by the Whigs but by the courts. The Judicial Committee of the Privy Council determined in March 1850 that the evangelical George Gorham could remain a clergyman while denying baptismal regeneration. A secular court, to the horror of Gladstone and his Anglo-Catholic associates, had pronounced against an article of the faith. Some of us, Gladstone recorded in a memorandum,

are fixed and rooted in the belief that there is still a sacred deposit, a faith once for all committed to the saints, a body of revealed truth which we are free indeed by the constitution of our nature to accept or to deny, but utterly unable to alter in the minutest particular, and of which the remission of sins by the Sacrament of Baptism is defined in the Nicene Creed to be a part.

The struggle between the defenders of the dogmatic principle and the partisans of the Judicial Committee, he added, was nothing less than a battle 'between belief and unbelief'.[21] While his friends Hope and Manning fretted over their position as members of a compromised church, Gladstone crystallized his thoughts in

[17] Richard Brent, *Liberal Anglican Politics: Whiggery, Religion and Reform, 1830–1841* (Oxford, 1987).
[18] W. E. Gladstone, 'The Theses of Erastus and the Scottish Church Establishment' [1844], *Gleanings*, 3, p. 10.          [19] Gladstone to Pusey, 14 Dec. 1847, f. 285.
[20] W. E. Gladstone, 'Clergy Relief Bill', *Quarterly Review*, 86 (1849), p. 63.
[21] 'The Gorham Judgment', GP 44738, ff. 152, 155 (n.d.).

*Remarks on the Royal Supremacy* (1850). The Church of England, he argued, had not been revealed as intrinsically erastian in structure. The arrangements for appeal to the Judicial Committee, only recently created, might be wholly unsatisfactory, but the Reformation settlement had not made the crown the source of authority in the church. The secular power had no more assumed responsibility for the church than for the family, the other God-given human institution. The state might create the army, but it merely regulated the family. In the same way its powers over the church were 'corrective, not directive or motive powers'. Hence the ecclesiastical jurisdiction of the crown did not affect 'the inherent self-governing capacities of the Church'.[22] Gladstone managed to convince himself that there was no reason to desert the Church of England because, in principle, its constitution was not erastian.

The maturer fruit of Gladstone's reflection on the crisis of the Gorham Judgement came in his letter 'On the Functions of Laymen in the Church', written at the end of 1851. In the letter he argues that the Scottish Episcopal Church, whose presiding bishop he addresses, should find a place for the laity in its governing synod. The idea pre-dated the Gorham Judgement: in an article of 1849 Gladstone had contended that the church—in this case the Church of England— should associate with the clergy 'the already vast and rapidly growing body of intelligent laymen'.[23] But in the following year, in the wake of the judgement, Gladstone was even more aware of the danger of what he called 'the greatest of civil calamities': 'the mutilation, under the seal of civil authority, of the Christian religion itself.'[24] Others, such as Samuel Wilberforce, Bishop of Oxford, were canvassing another remedy for the erastian threat, the revival of convocation, the representative body of the clergy that, down to the early eighteenth century, had deliberated in parallel with the Houses of Parliament. If the Church of England had a single collective voice, Wilberforce and his friends believed, it might resist secular inroads more successfully.[25] Although Gladstone spoke on behalf of the scheme in the Commons, he feared that the reinstatement of convocation as a solely clerical body would allow its declarations to be brushed aside by MPs who had no time for the opinions of the cloth. By recommending an alteration in the constitution of the existing synod of the Scottish Episcopal Church, Gladstone was obliquely proposing that the laity should find a place alongside a restored convocation of the Church of England. The idea was anathema to Pusey, who saw it as an unacceptable lay claim to involvement in legislation on matters of faith.[26] But to Gladstone the proposal was a way of mobilizing laymen, 'now a mere fluctuating multitude', as a solid phalanx in support of their church.[27] Although the

---

[22] W. E. Gladstone, 'Remarks on the Royal Supremacy' [1850], *Gleanings*, 5, pp. 192, 223.

[23] Gladstone, 'Clergy Relief Bill', p. 78.

[24] W. E. Gladstone, 'On the Functions of Laymen in the Church' [1851], *Gleanings*, 6, p. 6.

[25] Owen Chadwick, *The Victorian Church*, 2 vols., 2nd edn. (London, 1970), 1, pp. 309–24.

[26] E. B. Pusey to W. E. Gladstone, 19 Jan. 1845, LBV 85/53, f. 351, in H. P. Liddon, *Life of Edward Bouverie Pusey*, 4 vols., 4th edn. (London, 1898), 3, pp. 344–5.

[27] Gladstone, 'Clergy Relief Bill', p. 78.

opposition of those who thought like Pusey meant that when convocation was revived in 1853 it remained a preserve of the clergy, Gladstone had emerged from the discussions as a champion of the laity.

Certain sections of Gladstone's case deserve highlighting. He wrote to assert, against the menace of political interference, 'the principle . . . of a full religious freedom'. The way to guarantee the safety of religious communities was 'the creation of a vigorous and watchful public opinion' in their favour. Laymen in synod would check any threats to religious liberty, but would also learn to uphold it as a principle: 'assuredly the true mode of learning freedom is by its practice.' Their involvement would strengthen the church: 'methodically to enlist the members of a community . . . in the performance of its public duties, is the way to make that community powerful and healthful, to give a firm seat to its rulers, and to engender a warm and intelligent devotion to those beneath their sway.'[28] Here, in 1851, is an exposition of many of the principles of Gladstonian Liberalism. The politician may have learned the practice of economic liberalism from Peel, but the groundwork of his constitutional liberalism was laid in reflection on the best way to structure the church so as to stand up to the state. The value of freedom, the power of public opinion, and the need to extend the principle of participation all emerged from this phase in his thinking—and are said explicitly to apply to 'all systems, whether religious or political'.[29] Parliamentary reform had re-emerged as a subject of discussion in the Commons during 1851, and no doubt Gladstone had been stimulated to reconsider his position on such issues by the political debate.[30] But at this stage he showed no public sympathy whatsoever for the cause of reform. It was in the ecclesiastical sphere that he first publicly espoused many of the constitutional principles he was later to champion as Prime Minister.

The effect of Gladstone's adjustment of his understanding about church–state relations was therefore fundamental. There was no ideological barrier, as he was to explain in his *Chapter of Autobiography* (1868), to prevent him from espousing Irish disestablishment once he had recognized the impracticality of the prescriptions in *The State in its Relations with the Church*.[31] He had adopted the principle of equal treatment of all religious communities in the light of circumstances. That was to align himself with the wish of Broad Churchmen to show greater generosity to non-Anglicans. The high valuation of religious freedom was also common ground with the more liberal school of thought in the Church of England. Where Gladstone differed, and differed sharply, was over erastianism. He rejected Thomas Arnold's theories that made, as Gladstone once put it, 'the whole Church organization a department' of the state.[32] Whereas Broad Churchmen generally approved Arnold's blurring of the boundaries between church and state,

[28] Gladstone, 'Laymen in the Church', pp. 8, 9, 13, 17.       [29] Ibid., p. 17.
[30] F. B. Smith, *The Making of the Second Reform Bill* (Cambridge, 1966), pp. 30–3.
[31] Gladstone, 'Chapter of Autobiography', p. 120.
[32] W. E. Gladstone, 'The Duke of Argyll on Presbytery', *Quarterly Review*, 84 (1848), p. 80.

Gladstone was insistent on the radical distinctiveness of the church. Gladstone did not cease to be a High Churchman as he developed broader sympathies. But he did strike out on a path different from Pusey's: Gladstone believed in making substantial concessions to those outside the Church of England and in entrusting the laity with a part in the central organs of the church. The differences between Pusey and the politician were to widen over Oxford University reform in 1853–4, when Gladstone again advocated giving ground to Dissenters.[33] The politician was following a trajectory that would enable him, as Prime Minister, to act together with Whig-Liberals of Arnoldian opinions. Although Gladstone's colleagues were to find his anti-erastianism hard to accommodate, there was sufficient shared desire to do justice to all confessions for practical solutions to emerge.[34] The dissolution of Gladstone's early ideal of church and state enabled him to assimilate a considerable part of the Broad Church mentality.

II

A second reason for the broadening of his churchmanship lay in his attitude towards the Roman Catholic Church. During the 1840s, as we have seen, Gladstone debated with himself the Roman attitude to the eucharist, reaching a view that, while rejecting transubstantiation, accepted the principle of eucharistic sacrifice.[35] As he moved closer to the Roman Catholic position in doctrine, however, he became more intensely aware of a rivalry with the Roman church for souls. He deeply regretted, he wrote in his 1843 article on the 'Present Aspect of the Church', that a handful of men had been 'perverted' from the English Church and drawn into 'that schismatical communion over which the delegates of the Pope in England, with the name of Vicars Apostolic, preside'. The whole article was designed to rally support for the Catholic cause within the Church of England and so prevent the trickle of converts from turning into a flood. It was 'the absolute duty' of those tempted to secede 'to abide where they are'.[36] Gladstone's case for loyalty, as he explained in a further article of 1844 aiming to consolidate Anglican allegiance, was grounded in his fundamental social theory. To leave for Rome was an expression of selfish caprice, a repudiation of the ordering of the Creator: 'We no more seek in religion to choose according to coincidence with our own personal inclinations, in the innumerable particulars of Christian doctrine, discipline, and ceremonial, than we seek to choose, from among the crowd of parents, a father or a mother for ourselves.'[37] To turn against the national church was an act of disobedience

---

[33] W. R. Ward, *Victorian Oxford* (London, 1965), chs. 9, 10.

[34] J. P. Parry, *Democracy and Religion: Gladstone and the Liberal Party, 1867–1875* (Cambridge, 1986).                                                         [35] See Ch. 4, pp. 94–5.

[36] W. E. Gladstone, 'Present Aspect of the Church' [1843], *Gleanings*, 5, pp. 24, 71.

[37] W. E. Gladstone, 'Ward's Ideal of a Christian Church' [1844], *Gleanings*, 5, p. 159.

to natural law. Members of the English Church must stop their ears against the siren voice of Rome.

The secession of J. H. Newman in 1845, though not unexpected, was therefore a blow that Gladstone felt particularly keenly. The politician's sister Helen had already taken the step three years earlier; the priest at Margaret Chapel, Frederick Oakeley, went over shortly after Newman. Gladstone later accused Newman of conducting a 'constant war against the reason of man', claiming that this fundamental fault ran through his *Essay on the Development of Christian Doctrine* (1845), the theologian's Parthian shot on leaving the Church of England.[38] In that book Newman argued that the beliefs of the Roman Catholic Church, far from being identical with those held in the days of the apostles, had gradually, under the guidance of the Almighty, been unfolded over the centuries. During 1846 and 1847 Gladstone frequently sat down to register his disagreement with various points in the *Essay*.[39] Newman was repudiating the groundwork of Gladstone's church principles, for the divine was denying that Christian truth was what had always been believed by those who enjoyed the apostolic succession. In effect, claimed Gladstone, Newman was setting up private judgement as the arbiter of doctrine.[40] Most seriously, as Gladstone was convinced even before he read the book, Newman was putting the whole Christian cause in jeopardy. If, on traditional Catholic premises, the faith had been safely transmitted from Christ down to the present, then its consistent marks over time could be pointed out to the infidel. Newman was erroneously conceding that there were no such unchanging characteristics testifying to divine revelation.[41] The doctrine of development, Gladstone concluded, 'unfixes the anchors by which the body of faith is held and its permanency and continuous identity guaranteed'.[42] The new Roman apologetic exemplified in Newman's book, potentially undermining Catholic truth, was intellectually repugnant.

The secession of Newman and others were sharp reverses, but they merely redoubled Gladstone's efforts to staunch the outflow. Two years later in his review of *From Oxford to Rome*, a fictional account by Elizabeth Harris of two converts to Rome who subsequently regretted their action, Gladstone commented that many, 'out of this homely England and her homely Church, looked upon the Roman Church as men look upon a warm-toned picture of Claude with its hazy golden distance'. But such diffuse longing, he went on, 'indisposes and unmans for the real work of God appointed to every one of us, the performance of quiet and daily duty'.[43] This was the substance of the case that, over the years between

---

[38] GP 44737, f. 79. This is an undated draft letter to Newman, apparently from the late 1840s. On Newman's doctrine of development, see Owen Chadwick, *From Bossuet to Newman*, 2nd edn. (Cambridge, 1987).

[39] *D*, 20 Sept., 11 Nov. 1846, 10, 24 Jan., 8 Aug. 1847. Nevertheless Gladstone recognized the reality of the development of doctrine: its legitimate form was renovation rather than innovation. See David Nicholls, 'Gladstone and the Anglican Critics of Newman', in J. D. Bastable (ed.), *Newman and Gladstone Centennial Essays* (Dublin, 1978), pp. 121–4.

[40] GP 44736, ff. 265–333 (8 Aug. 1847), at ff. 269, 267.       [41] GP 44735, f. 51 ([5] July 1845).

[42] GP 44736, f. 307.

[43] W. E. Gladstone, 'From Oxford to Rome', *Quarterly Review*, 81 (1847), p. 142.

Newman's departure and the Gorham Judgement, Gladstone was urging on James Hope and Henry Manning, his closest collaborators in the Catholic revival. Neither of them revealed to the politician the extent of his disenchantment with the Church of England. For Hope the result of the Gorham case demonstrated conclusively that the church was a creature of the state; Manning still made efforts to secure a repudiation of the judgement by the church, but in his heart feared that it was a lost cause. Gladstone spent evenings with Manning wrestling for his continued allegiance to the campaign that had bound them together for more than a decade. On 6 April 1851, however, Manning joined Hope in being received into the Roman Catholic Church.[44] Gladstone felt an agony of personal loss. 'On hearing of Manning's secession from the English Church', he later remarked, '. . . I felt as if he had murdered my mother by mistake.'[45] Rome had induced his most intimate friend to commit an act of wanton betrayal. The event was the climax of a long process during which Gladstone came to identify Roman Catholicism as his greatest antagonist.

Gladstone's objections to the Roman Church were manifold. Fundamental was Rome's unchurching of Canterbury. 'The rejection from the fellowship of the Christian covenant', he told Manning in 1850, 'of all who do not receive the authority of the See of Rome is to me an awful innovation on the faith.'[46] But alongside that was the whole gamut of modifications of the apostolic teaching, the developments that Newman had tried to vindicate, whether subtractions or additions. He set out several in a memorandum of 1844:

| Church of Rome_repression, in | 1. | the denial of the Cup |
|---|---|---|
| | 2. | the restraint of Holy Scripture |
| Expansion in_ | 1. | Purgatory |
| | 2. | Indulgences |
| | 3. | Satisfactions & works of superogation |
| | 4. | Saint worship |
| | 5. | Eucharistic sacrifice for the quick & dead.[47] |

Gladstone was soon to delete the final charge in the catalogue, but he returned repeatedly to the others. The refusal of communion wine to the laity constituted 'a mutilated Eucharist'; the limitation of the circulation of the scriptures meant 'a sealed Bible'; 'the purgatorial system' and 'subaltern expiations' (though not emphasized) were unwarranted additions to the faith; and around the invocation of saints and the transfer of their merits there had gathered a cluster of abuses.[48] Although Gladstone was content with prayers for the dead, it was quite another question, he noted in 1846, to decide whether benefits from the deeds of the

[44] Butler, *Gladstone*, ch. 7.
[45] E. S. Purcell, *Life of Cardinal Manning*, 2 vols. (London, 1895), 1, p. 627 n.
[46] W. E. Gladstone to H. E. Manning, 1 June 1850, Lathbury, 2, p. 26.
[47] GP 44734, f. 285 (8 Dec. 1844).             [48] Gladstone, 'From Oxford to Rome', pp. 151, 146.

saintly could be credited to others through intercession with God; and the direct invocation of saints was a further question again.[49] The cult of the Blessed Virgin Mary was particularly offensive. Gladstone had come across a Catholic recension of the Psalms in which 'for the name of the incomprehensible Jehovah was substituted throughout the name of the Blessed Mary'.[50] In Naples he heard sermons offering extravagant praise to the Virgin. And by 1852 he was aware that the pope was about to pronounce in favour of the immaculate conception of the mother of God.[51] In all this there was, as he put it, a 'peril of polytheistic idolatry'.[52] In theory the Roman Church might repudiate such heresies, but in practice it tolerated them.

The Jesuit Order attracted Gladstone's particular disapproval. In 1845, having seen a couple of periodical articles on the Jesuits, the fruit of the anti-Catholic frenzy stirred up by the Maynooth crisis, he embarked on a thorough programme of reading about the order. He did not avoid works of popular prejudice such as Patrick Bull's *A Wolf in Sheep's Clothing: or, an Old Jesuit Unmasked* (1775), but he turned to more serious studies relating especially to the suppression of the order in 1773. Most were substantial histories in French and German.[53] After 1845 he continued his interest more intermittently, but on occasion with real zeal. In 1848, for instance, he read *Il Gesuita Moderno* (1846–7) by the priest turned religious philosopher Vincenzo Gioberti, who had become an outstanding champion of the Risorgimento. So fascinated was Gladstone by this rambling attack on the Jesuits that he took copious notes on the book.[54] In October 1845 he had seized a rare opportunity for a passage of arms with a Jesuit in the flesh. At Baden he encountered a young member of the order named Hasslacher who came to offer advice to Gladstone's sister Helen. The two men disagreed over the nature of the real presence in the eucharist, Gladstone finding that the priest's cast of mind was averse to minimizing differences. The politician told Hasslacher that, as a theologian, he was 'un peu rigoreux'.[55] When, in 1852, Gladstone dipped into the most substantial work of contemporary Jesuit dogmatics, the *Praelectiones Theologicae* (1835–42) of Giovanni Perrone, he was even more repelled. Perrone made a sharp distinction between theology, resting on faith, and philosophy, resting on reason. Gladstone was horrified, seeing no gulf between the disciplines: 'both', he wrote, 'have their origins in the things known, in the handiwork of God.'[56] Perrone was retreating into irrationalism. The Jesuits seemed the advocates of a sinister and obscurantist faith.

Their greatest crime, however, lay in the methods of casuistry with which they had become identified. The Jesuits had urged that in questions of pastoral

---

[49] GP 44736, f. 4v (9 Aug. 1846).　　　　[50] Gladstone, 'Ward's Ideal', p. 122.
[51] W. E. Gladstone, 'Catholic Interests in the Nineteenth Century', *Quarterly Review*, 92 (1852), p. 150.　　　　[52] Gladstone, 'From Oxford to Rome', p. 151.
[53] *D*, 17, 19 Apr., 9 May, 8, 15 June, 10 July, 24 Oct., 5, 14, 15 Nov.
[54] *D*, 4 May 1848. GP 44737, ff. 42–61 (12 Dec. 1848).
[55] *D*, 20 Oct. 1845. GP 44735, f. 92 (24 Oct. 1845).
[56] *D*, 18 July, 12 Sept. 1852. GP 44740, f. 116 (12 Sept. 1852).

theology counsel should never be too severe. If one course of action was only probably allowable, they had taught, then it was legitimate to advise it even if an alternative course of action was more probably right. This was the doctrine of probabilism that in the seventeenth century, as Gladstone was well aware, Pascal had heaped with scorn in his *Provincial Letters*. Probabilism, according to its critics, encouraged the choosing of a dubious agenda that might actually imperil the soul. This was the kernel of 'the morality of the Jesuits' that Gladstone dismissed with contempt. Its refinement in the eighteenth century by Alphonsus Liguori, who was canonized in 1839, seemed if anything more objectionable.[57] Probabilism was no mere theoretical matter. It was the content of the advice given to millions of Catholics in Gladstone's own day. He had discovered a manual for the French clergy recommending that spiritual directors should allow their penitents, in matters of moral conduct, to choose a less probable opinion above a more probable one.[58] The teaching of the Jesuits, Gladstone concluded, had shaped the normal practice of the Roman Catholic Church. It became his settled belief that the church was guilty of a 'pliable morality'.[59] He was as convinced as any popular Protestant demagogue that Jesuitry, in the sense of casuistry and immorality, was part and parcel of the Roman system.

Gladstone set out his case against these abuses in an article of 1845 on 'The Law of Probable Evidence and its relation to Conduct'. It was the substantial intellectual legacy of his reading about the Jesuits during 1845.[60] In the article he admits that probabilism was not the universal teaching of Roman theologians. Even one general of the Jesuits had rejected it, and the alternative principle of probabiliorism, that preference should be given to the course of action likeliest to be right, was sometimes upheld against it. Nevertheless probabilism was the popular doctrine and, on examination, Gladstone found it to 'threaten the very first principles of duty'.[61] Against the teaching of probabilism Gladstone posed the authority of Bishop Butler. The revival of Gladstone's enthusiasm for Butler in 1845, associated, as Boyd Hilton has suggested, with a renewed emphasis on individual conscience, arose from the usefulness of the bishop's works in combating Rome.[62] Butler's *Analogy of Religion* (1736) included the contention that probable evidence, falling far short of demonstration, nevertheless carried with it a duty to follow where it pointed. In his article Gladstone contends that the principle applies not just to intellectual questions but also to daily conduct. Butler's central proposition was that 'probability is the guide of life'.[63] In any moral issue the course of action most likely to be right is obligatory. The idea, as will become

---

[57] GP 44737, f. 77 (n.d.).

[58] W. E. Gladstone, 'The Law of Probable Evidence and its Relation to Conduct' [written 1845, published 1879], *Gleanings*, 7, pp. 157–8.                    [59] Gladstone, 'From Oxford to Rome', p. 145.

[60] *D*, 26 June–1 July 1845.

[61] Gladstone, 'Probable Evidence', p. 192.

[62] Boyd Hilton, *The Age of Atonement: The Influence of Evangelicalism on Social and Economic Thought, 1795–1865* (Oxford, 1988), p. 341–2.

[63] Gladstone, 'Probable Evidence', p. 154.

plain, entered the fibre of Gladstone's thinking.[64] He believed that he had discovered a basic flaw in the fabric of the Roman Church. It was flying in the face of a fundamental axiom in ethics.

Gladstone's disapproval of the content of the spiritual advice given by Catholic priests soon extended to the way in which it was tendered. At first the Roman confessional system had it attractions. In the earlier 1840s, down to 1844, he had pondered the possibility of making his own confession to a priest, but he eventually decided against it.[65] By 1847 he was complaining to Manning about the Roman Catholic rule that confession should be compulsory.[66] The Reformation, he wrote in the following year, by rejecting the notion that auricular confession should be a condition of communion, had achieved 'the restoration of inward personal responsibility and freedom'.[67] Butler, once more, had helped him reach this conclusion. The bishop had taught, in his *Rolls Sermons* (1726), that the conscience was supreme among human faculties. The practice of spiritual direction, however, dethroned the conscience: 'it tampers', Gladstone argued in Butlerian language in an article of 1847, 'with the eternal laws of our reasonable nature, and with the one cardinal principle of our personal responsibility, on which all natural and revealed religion rest.' The French historian Jules Michelet, an anticlerical republican, had shown him that spiritual direction was in fact a recent and significant extension of compulsory confession. The priest no longer offered advice, helping the penitent to probe his own conscience, but exercised dominion, replacing the moral responsibility of the individual with his own authority.[68] Gladstone saw this procedure as an oppressive feature of the Roman Church. Direction, he wrote in 1851, was a 'modern and very remarkable and ominous development in her discipline'.[69] There was a creeping authoritarianism that Gladstone rejected as morally subversive. Rome was branded as a threat to the human conscience.

The tyranny of the Roman Church seemed at its most extreme in its pretensions to infallibility. The pope was not to be defined as being infallible when formally pronouncing on the faith until 1870, but already in 1843 Gladstone was complaining that official documents from the curia were making 'the preposterous claim of infallibility'.[70] The notion seemed to Gladstone another expression of Roman irrationality. Imperfection manifestly pervaded the mental processes of every human being, and 'no combination of fallibles can . . . make up an infallible'.[71] Yet this nonsensical idea was used, Gladstone argued, as 'the very keystone of the system'.[72] It was growingly invoked as the rationale for exalting the power of the papacy. 'To me', Gladstone wrote to the historian Henry Hallam in 1850, 'authority in the Church seems as distinct from infallibility as in a parent or a State: but I constantly find the assumption, which I only name in order to decline

[64] See Ch. 8, p. 23.
[65] Butler, *Gladstone*, p. 163.
[66] W. E. Gladstone to H. E. Manning, 17 Mar. 1847, GP 44247, f. 326.
[67] Gladstone, 'Duke of Argyll', p. 87.
[68] Gladstone, 'From Oxford to Rome', p. 154.
[69] Gladstone, 'Laymen in the Church', p. 18.
[70] Gladstone, 'Present Aspect', p. 55.
[71] Gladstone, 'Probable Evidence', p. 163.
[72] Gladstone, 'From Oxford to Rome', p. 154.

it, that without infallibility there is no authority. Bishop Butler is the fountain of all my conceptions, such as they are, on that subject.'[73] Butler taught that human beings must rest content with probability, doing without the alleged certainty imparted to papal definitions of the faith by infallibility. In 1870 Gladstone was to be outraged when the Vatican Council decided in favour of papal infallibility, and four years later was to assail the doctrine in the Vaticanism controversy.[74] But the foundations of his attitude to the subject had already been laid by 1850.

In that year Gladstone travelled with his family to spend the winter in Naples. One result was the celebrated *Letters to Lord Aberdeen* protesting against misgovernment by the King of Naples, the writings that first and unintentionally brought the politician to the favourable notice of European Liberals;[75] but a more authentic indication of the trend of his thinking was his translation of the newly published treatise on *The Roman State from 1815 to 1850* by Luigi Carlo Farini. The subject was the history of the adjacent Papal States. There the Vatican still ruled over an extensive territory, uniting the spiritual with the civil powers in a theocracy. Farini had held office in the revolutionary government of Rome during 1848, but after the restoration of papal authority had found asylum in Turin. He favoured not a republic and Italian unification but constitutional monarchy and the federation of Italy.[76] The moderation of Farini's analysis commended the book to Gladstone when, during his stay in Naples, he dipped into it in November 1850. There were, it is true, elements to deplore: Farini habitually referred to the need for Italians to combine in a 'holy war' to expel Austria from the peninsula, a measure that, in Gladstone's view, would seriously destabilize the European order.[77] But Gladstone warmed to the Italian's unsparing denunciation of Jesuits in politics: 'you are the Ministers of corruption: you deprave consciences, you dishearten the honest, you outrage virtue, you whitewash vice, cowardice, ambition, and cupidity, with the sacrosanct name of patriotism.'[78] In December Gladstone determined to translate Farini's book into English and within a week of commencing had completed 110 pages.[79] It was a massive undertaking, eventually running to four volumes of about 400 pages each, and, when Gladstone entered the Aberdeen coalition in 1852, the translation of the fourth had to be entrusted to a cousin, Mrs A. R. Bennett.[80] The book did much to mould British public opinion on the Roman question.[81]

Although Farini's history, as Gladstone pointed out, did not draw formal conclusions, its narrative amounted to a formidable indictment of the exercise of secular authority by the pope. Since the restoration of papal government by

---

[73] W. E. Gladstone to Henry Hallam, 15 June 1850, Lathbury, 1, p. 111.

[74] See Ch. 8, pp. 225–6.

[75] D. M. Schreuder, 'Gladstone and Italian Unification: The Making of a Liberal?', *English Historical Review*, 85 (1970).

[76] L. C. Farini, *The Roman State from 1815 to 1850*, 4 vols. (London, 1851–4), 2, p. 429.

[77] W. E. Gladstone, 'Farini's "Stato Romano" ' [1852], *Gleanings*, 4, p. 188.

[78] Farini, *Roman State*, 2, p. 430.                                    [79] *D*, 21, 28 Dec. 1850.

[80] *D*, 27 Nov. 1850, n.

[81] C. T. McIntire, *England against the Papacy, 1858–1861: Tories, Liberals and the Overthrow of Papal Temporal Power During the Italian Risorgimento* (Cambridge, 1982), p. 32.

French troops in 1849, the question, according to Gladstone, was whether 'the temporal power of the Popedom' could reform itself sufficiently to survive.[82] He was sure of the answer. 'The temporal power of the pope,' he told Manning in January 1851, 'that great, wonderful and ancient erection, is <u>gone</u>.'[83] It would collapse if it were not artificially propped up by foreign troops. Gladstone claimed that in the abstract he did not object to clerical government,[84] but in an anonymous review of his own translation of Farini in the *Edinburgh Review* for April 1852 he mounted a critique of precisely this aspect of the Roman Catholic Church. The central theoretical contention was that constitutional government was incompatible with papal sovereignty. If a regular elected assembly were created, it would inevitably clash with the ecclesiastical authorities. Everywhere else in Europe the civil power was in the last resort the arbiter of the limits of its own authority, but any constitutional government in Rome would be told that canon law set limits to its competence. The church would overrule the state, and 'convulsions' would follow. In Rome there was 'the intolerable anomaly of a State obeying in the civil sphere the dictates of the Church'.[85] The Vatican did not recognize the regulative role of the state that, in his *Remarks on the Royal Supremacy* of 1850, Gladstone had identified as legitimate and beneficial in England. That essay was his defence of the existing English constitutional arrangements between church and state. Now he was carrying the war into the enemy camp by arguing that the relations between church and state in Rome itself were inherently faulty. The Papal States stood out, he allowed himself to say, as 'a foul blot upon the face of creation, an offence to Christendom and to mankind'.[86]

Before the end of 1852 Gladstone had opened hostilities against what was long to remain his *bête noire*, ultramontanism. He began to see this principle, the growing disposition to magnify the authority of the pope, as the root of all the abuses in Roman Catholicism. The French liberal Catholic Count Montalembert, whom Gladstone had previously met and corresponded with,[87] had published a new statement of his faith in *Dieu et liberté* in *Des Intérêts catholiques au XIXe siècle* (1852). In a review of the book in the *Quarterly Review* Gladstone applauded his combination 'of Christian belief and of civil freedom'.[88] Montalembert, however, had endorsed the *coup d'état* by Louis Napoleon, praised the vindication of papal absolutism by de Maistre, and defended the continuation of the temporal power of the papacy. When, in 1855, Gladstone sent Montalembert a set of his translated volumes of Farini, the Frenchman acknowledged it as 'a memorial of what is perhaps the only political question on which we disagree'.[89] Gladstone,

---

[82] 'Translator's Preface', Farini, *Roman State*, 1, pp. ix, viii.

[83] W. E. Gladstone to H. E. Manning, 26 Jan. 1851, GP 44248, f. 119.

[84] Gladstone, 'Farini's "Stato Romano" ', p. 10.     [85] Ibid., pp. 150–9, quoted at pp. 152, 158.

[86] Ibid., p. 176.

[87] Louis Allen, 'Gladstone et Montalembert: correspondance inédite', *Revue de littérature comparée*, 30 (1956).     [88] Gladstone, 'Catholic Interests', p. 139.

[89] C. R. F. Montalembert to W. E. Gladstone, 1 June 1855, GP 44384, f. 123, in Allen, 'Gladstone et Montalembert', p. 44.

however, regarded the issue of the temporal power not as a minor debatable topic but as a touchstone of political soundness. By championing the papal claims, the would-be liberal was revealing a 'fundamental antipathy between ultramontanism and freedom'. 'Ultramontanism', wrote the rescuer of prostitutes, 'can never use Liberty, except as vice uses its victim: first to enjoy, and then to spurn her.' Gladstone explained that by ultramontanism he meant not just the assertion of the temporal power or the insistence on the supremacy of the pope in the church. He was describing 'a frame of mind' that exalted 'the hierarchical elements of the Christian system, and the mystical next to them' while depressing the counterbalancing ingredients, 'the doctrine of inward freedom, the rights and responsibilities of individuality, the mixed and tempered organization of ecclesiastical government'. Spiritual direction and extolling the Jesuits were among its symptoms.[90] In the Roman Church the Catholic element had virtually extinguished the liberal tendency.

Gladstone had been gradually moving towards this view over the previous decade. Already in 1843 he had suggested that the Roman Church could give no guarantees for 'spiritual liberty'.[91] In 1847 he deplored the increasing centralization that made the whole church increasingly resemble one of its own religious orders—and no doubt the Jesuits were in his mind. Since the Reformation the Roman Church had contracted the sphere of human freedom so that no Dante could now denounce the vice of the popes, whereas the English mind had moved in the opposite direction. 'Englishmen', he wrote, 'have strong instincts towards loyalty, obedience, order, tradition; but these are effectively balanced by an energetic love of freedom.'[92] It was the Church of England, not the Roman Catholic Church, that exhibited a faith in accord with this combination of values. Authority had to be complemented by liberty. The drift of thought reaches its culmination in a paean to freedom in Gladstone's review of Montalembert: 'Now, in our view, the real lover of freedom is he, and he only, who prizes it as an attribute in which our nature may approximate to its Divine original, and who firmly believes in its efficacy and necessity, as an ordained condition of the highest forms of human thought and action.' Authority might have its place in helping us to discover truth, but truth had to be embraced freely. 'Freedom misused is the path of death: but without the right use of freedom, life can attain but a stinted and sickly development. We therefore love and cherish freedom for its legitimate place in the Divine economy, as a grand determining element of the normal state of man.'[93] Gladstone, though never dismissing traditional English liberties, had begun his political career by denying that freedom possessed any intrinsic merits.[94] Under Peel's tuition he had come to appreciate the pragmatic value of commercial freedom, but it was in antagonism to Roman Catholic claims that Gladstone recognized freedom as essential to human welfare. Here was an

---

[90] Gladstone, 'Catholic Interests', pp. 143, 149, 150.      [91] Gladstone, 'Present Aspect', p. 55.

[92] Gladstone, 'From Oxford to Rome', pp. 151, 152, 155.

[93] Gladstone, 'Catholic Interests', p. 146.      [94] See Ch. 2, pp. 17–18.

ideological shift towards a principled assertion of the importance of liberty, the germ of what was to flower in Gladstonian Liberalism.

More immediately there was an effect on Gladstone's churchmanship. In the polarity that he had constructed, the values of order, truth, and authority, together with the hierarchical and the mystical, were what High Churchmen shared with Roman Catholics. On the other side of the balance, the principles of personal responsibility (entailing the rejection of the confessional), mixed ecclesiastical government (by which he meant lay participation), and, above all, freedom were championed by Broad Churchmen. Gladstone was by no means repudiating the High Church ingredients, but increasingly he was expressing himself in a Broad Church idiom. In 1847, in passing remarks on the relation of Christianity to the intellectual temper of the age, Gladstone urged that both church and Bible should be open 'to historical study, to critical investigation, and to scientific discovery'.[95] By 1852 he had elaborated his ideas. The early church, he argued, had prospered not by elevating the priestly spirit, but

by cultivating and expanding while it sanctified the individual soul—by blending together the reverence for authority and the passion for freedom—by founding itself on the whole nature of man—by joining hands with every influence and every agent that could elevate him as a moral, a social, a responsible being—by marching at the head of art, science, and education, and enlisting into its service every new form of knowledge as it came to light[.]

Christianity should be wholly on the side of intellectual enquiry. The gospel should not be presented as the enemy of culture, but as its complement and crown. Although this policy had once been the programme of Aquinas, it had fallen into disfavour in the Roman Church. It therefore passed to others, 'less equipped in high pretension but better grounded upon homely truth', 'to maintain a true harmony between the Church of Christ and the nations it has swayed so long'. Members of the Church of England—no doubt including Gladstone himself— inherited the commission to reconcile the 'changeful world' with the 'unchanging faith'.[96] Christianity was to be understood as entirely compatible with modern knowledge. The politician had been driven to this moderate Broad Church prescription by reaction against the growing exclusivism of Roman Catholicism.

The Roman Church, however, did not speak with one voice, and Gladstone's relations with the more progressive strands of opinion in its ranks call for consideration. Perry Butler has pointed out that the politician had dealings with two of the French liberal Catholics of the 1830s, François Rio and Montalembert.[97] Meeting the art historian Rio at a breakfast in 1838, Gladstone soon absorbed his *De l'art chrétien* (1836).[98] At several meetings over the next few years the chief

---

[95] Gladstone, 'From Oxford to Rome', p. 165.
[96] Gladstone, 'Catholic Interests', pp. 155, 156.
[97] Butler, *Gladstone*, p. 84 n. Butler does not, however, suggest that Gladstone derived his ideas from this source.
[98] *D*, 11, 18 June 1838. Mary Camille Bowe, *François Rio: sa place dans le renouveau catholique en Europe (1797–1874)* (Paris, [1938]), p. 151.

subject of their conversations was the prospect of Catholic renewal in England and abroad. At their last meeting, in July 1845, for instance, Gladstone lamented that seceders were retarding the Catholic cause within the Church of England.[99] Rio, for his part, urged Gladstone to abandon practical politics for the sake of writing religious philosophy.[100] The Frenchman left no discernible mark on Gladstone's intellectual development, but he did introduce him to the weightier Montalembert. At their first meeting in 1839, according to Rio, Montalembert scored a point against Gladstone by claiming that parliamentary interference in the life of the Church of England was incompatible with the position he had staked out in *The State*.[101] Gladstone had previously appreciated Montalembert's *Life of St Elisabeth of Hungary* (1836), reading which, he assured the author, was so delightful that it resembled his first encounter with Dante's *Paradiso*.[102] Although the *Life* was a hagiography, it was unusual in its genre in indicating sources.[103] The union of piety and scholarship attracted Gladstone, but he felt no strong affinity for a man who attacked the value of nationality in religion for the sake of papal universalism.[104] Montalembert, as we have seen, was far too ultramontane for Gladstone's liking. Yet Montalembert, like Rio, did encourage Gladstone to take a closer interest in the affairs of Catholic Europe, and their words were not wasted.[105]

Of the others in the French liberal Catholic circle, Henri-Dominique Lacordaire seems to have made little impression on Gladstone. The politician read two of his minor books in 1839 and 1843, citing one of them in *Church Principles*, but did not dip into the work that was Lacordaire's chief claim to celebrity, the lecture-sermons delivered at Notre Dame in Paris (1844–51), until 1868—if then, for the identification of the item mentioned in the diary is tentative.[106] Gladstone paid more attention to a book by another in the same set, Olympe Philippe Gerbet, who rose to become Bishop of Perpignan. The politician read Gerbet's *Considérations sur le dogme générateur de la piété catholique* (1829) in English translation in 1845. Gerbet presented the argument that the eucharist functioned as the bond of the primeval social order established by the Creator, a case that Gladstone followed 'with great sympathy'.[107] He read Gerbet again, this time in the original, while travelling to Naples in 1850.[108] Gerbet may have acted

---

[99] 'Notes on certain points in a conversation with Rio July 1845', GP 44735, ff. 45–51 ([5] July 1845).
[100] Rio's journal, 26 Feb. 1839, cited by Bowe, *Rio*, p. 160.
[101] Rio's journal, 4 Mar. 1839, cited by Bowe, *Rio*, p. 153. On Montalembert, see Bernard Reardon, *Liberalism and Tradition: Aspects of Catholic Thought in Nineteenth-Century France* (Cambridge, 1975), pp. 110–12.
[102] *D*, 10 Sept. 1838. W. E. Gladstone to C. R. F. de Montalembert, 4 Aug. 1839, in Allen, 'Gladstone et Montalembert', p. 33.
[103] Jean-René Derré, *Lamennais et ses amis et le mouvement des idées à l'époque romantique* (Paris, 1962), p. 673.
[104] C. R. F. de Montalembert to W. E. Gladstone, 17 Dec. 1842, GP 44359, f. 252, in Allen, 'Gladstone et Montalembert', p. 38.         [105] Allen, 'Gladstone et Montalembert', pp. 29, 31.
[106] *D*, 27–9 Mar. 1839: *Mémoire pour le rétablissement en France de l'ordre des Frères Prêcheurs* (1839), cited in *CPR*, p. 517. *D*, 2 Sept. 1843: *Der Heilige Stuhl* (1843). *D*, 14 June 1868: *Conférences de Notre-Dame de Paris* (1844–51). On Lacordaire, see Reardon, *Liberalism and Tradition*, pp. 107–10.
[107] *D*, 9 Feb.–2 Mar. 1845, quoted at 23 Feb. 1845. On Gerbet, see Derré, *Lamennais et ses amis*, ch. 7.
[108] *D*, 27 Oct.–10 Nov. 1850.

as a stepping-stone to his original master, the Abbé de Lamennais. Gladstone was aware of Lamennais's *Affaires de Rome* (1836–7), which recounted the Frenchman's break with Rome, through a review by Newman, and the book is mentioned as an authority in both *The State* and *Church Principles*.[109] But Lamennais's earlier Roman Catholic apologetic, the *Essai sur l'indifférence* (1817–23), though cited in Palmer's *Treatise on the Church*, did not swim into Gladstone's orbit until 1853.[110] This powerful work was the basis for Gladstone's later estimate that Lamennais was 'the greatest genius of the French clergy of his day'.[111] The politician found much there that was congenial: the claim that private judgement had caused social disintegration; the idea that faith needed to be based on communal convictions; and the assertion of the authority of the visible church. Gladstone was soon to deploy a central part of Lamennais's case as the framework of his Homeric studies, which will be discussed in the next chapter.[112] The immediate effect of absorbing the *Essai*, however, was to reinforce the older communitarianism in Gladstone's thought rather than the emerging motifs of freedom and responsibility. The younger Lamennais, loyal to the papacy, rather than the later free spirit exerted a significant influence over Gladstone. It was the Catholic element rather than the liberal ingredient in Lamennais's liberal Catholicism that left its mark on him.

Peter Erb, however, has suggested that the German version of liberal Catholicism played a part in Gladstone's intellectual formation. In particular, he has shown that Gladstone engaged seriously with the thought of J. A. Möhler, a Roman Catholic apologist at the University of Tübingen.[113] Between 18 October and 2 November 1845, while staying at Baden Baden, Gladstone waded through Möhler's *Symbolism* (1832), a treatise viewing the Catholic–Protestant debate through romantic spectacles.[114] Möhler's supreme aim was to answer Hegel's attack on the Roman Catholic Church as a bastion of unfreedom and a rival to the state.[115] Accordingly Möhler stresses, in liberal fashion, the freedom enjoyed in the church. The tone is irenical, the central theme being the unity of the church as a reflection of the incarnation. Gladstone annotated his copy copiously, wrestling with Möhler on justification and penance while approving much of his teaching on the visibility and unity of the church. He found Möhler's discussion of the pagan desire for community to his taste, and added marginal comments highlighting the 'power of association over the individual' and 'the sociability of

---

[109] Gladstone, 'Ward's Ideal', p. 116 n. *SRC*, 4th, 1, pp. 33 n., 243; *CPR*, p. 367. On Lamennais, see A. R. Vidler, *Prophecy and Papacy: A Study of Lamennais, the Church and the Revolution* (London, 1954); Reardon, *Liberalism and Tradition*, chs. 4 and 5; and W. G. Roe, *Lamennais and England: The Reception of Lamennais's Religious Ideas in England in the Nineteenth Century* (Oxford, 1966).

[110] *D*, 23 Jan.–10 Apr. 1853. William Palmer, *A Treatise on the Church of Christ*, 2 vols. (Oxford, 1842), 1, p. 266.

[111] W. E. Gladstone, 'The Sixteenth Century arraigned before the Nineteenth' [1878], *Gleanings*, 3, p. 255.　　　　　　　　　　　　　　[112] See Ch. 6, pp. 174–5.

[113] P. C. Erb, 'Gladstone and Liberal Catholicism', *Recusant History*, 23 (1997).

[114] *D*, 18 Oct.–2 Nov. 1845.

[115] Alexander Dru, *The Contribution of German Catholicism* (New York, 1963), pp. 60–4.

man'.[116] Once more Gladstone was finding his communitarian preferences confirmed. Later in life Gladstone was to appeal to the German theologian as an authority for the view that diversity is to be expected, and indeed is advantageous, within the unity of the Catholic Church.[117] In the years immediately after reading Möhler, however, Gladstone's concern was to ensure that his Anglican type of Catholicity either met Möhler's criteria or had an answer to them. Manning was swayed by Möhler towards Rome, but Gladstone was not. Although he was not yet aware that Newman was to claim *Symbolism* as the German equivalent of his own *Essay on the Development of Christian Doctrine*, Gladstone treated Möhler as a Roman apologist who was to be handled with care. While Gladstone appreciated aspects of his teaching, it is difficult to discern any liberal influence from Möhler over the course of the politician's thinking. Like Lammennais, Möhler was more a confirmer of Gladstone's existing Catholic preferences than a setter of new directions in his mental evolution.

The same cannot be said, however, of the man who drew Möhler to Gladstone's attention, Ignaz von Döllinger. Before travelling to Baden Baden, Gladstone had visited Munich, a vigorous centre of Catholic intellectual life. He had met, among others, the elderly Johann Joseph von Görres, once a potent force in German resistance to Napoleon, but Gladstone found his loud and guttural vernacular unintelligible.[118] Döllinger, by contrast, was a man of refinement and proficiency in English. On Gladstone's first arrival, unannounced, at Döllinger's door, the German professor immediately enquired whether the visitor was 'the Minister or late Minister', revealing an extraordinary knowledge of English affairs.[119] He was an ardent anglophile, respecting the law of primogeniture and believing English students dressed more smartly than Germans. He shared Gladstone's enthusiasms for Scott and Dante.[120] At the first meeting, which lasted five hours, Gladstone was 'greatly delighted' with him; at the second, Gladstone told his wife, 'I have lost my heart to him'.[121] Döllinger 'seemed to me one of the most liberal and catholic in mind of all the persons of his communion I have known'.[122] Far from setting about converting Gladstone, he showed deep interest in the Church of England. At the third meeting they compared notes on the questions at issue between the churches. Döllinger proved irenical over indulgences, contending that the subject now hardly arose in Germany. Extravagant claims for the Blessed Virgin Mary made in a sermon Gladstone had heard in Naples were pronounced by Döllinger to border on the blasphemous. And the two men found a high degree of approximation on the nature of the consecrated elements at the

---

[116] Erb, 'Gladstone and Liberal Catholicism', pp. 457–62, quoted at p. 462.
[117] See Ch. 8, p. 229.
[118] W. E. Gladstone to Catherine Gladstone, 2 Oct. 1845, in Morley, 1, p. 320.
[119] *Autobiographica*, p. 147.
[120] Louise von Kobell, *Conversations with Dr. Döllinger*, trans. Katharine Gould (London, 1892), pp. 26, 27, 213, 236–7.
[121] *D*, 30 Sept. 1845. W. E. Gladstone to Catherine Gladstone, 2 Oct. 1845, Morley, 1, p. 319.
[122] W. E. Gladstone to Catherine Gladstone, 30 Sept. 1845, Morley, 1, p. 319.

eucharist. 'Well', said Döllinger at the conclusion, 'we are in one Church by water—upon that I shall rest.'[123] The theologian and the politician had formed a mutual regard that was to endure until Döllinger's death in 1890.

While still in Germany Gladstone read a couple of small books by Döllinger,[124] but it was not until the following autumn that he set himself to study a substantial work by the man under whose spell he had fallen. It was Döllinger's two-volume *Lehrbuch der Kirchengeschichte* (1843), providing the staple of Gladstone's Sunday reading for two months.[125] Peter Erb minimizes its impact on the politician, proposing that Görres's *Athanasius* (1838), which Gladstone read in 1847, had the effect on him that in a late memorandum he erroneously attributes to Döllinger's work on church history. But Gladstone, who was always susceptible to the identity of an author when reading his arguments, was unlikely to be swayed by Görres after their encounter in Munich: Döllinger was the man who would probably influence him. And Erb's contention rests on the mistaken belief that Gladstone did not read Döllinger's *Lehrbuch* until 1856, whereas in fact his thorough absorption of the work came in 1846.[126] There is therefore no reason to doubt Gladstone's recollection that Döllinger's book, by showing the divine provision for the defence of orthodoxy in the Arian controversy, strengthened his own allegiance to the Church of England.[127] Presumably it was the absence of papal guidance in the controversy that Gladstone found reassuring. As a citation against infallibility from the German's book in an article of 1847 shows, Gladstone had enrolled him in the band of witnesses against Roman autocracy. Döllinger's strong commitment to critical scholarship in the service of the truth, exposing Felix V as a phantom pope, was now Gladstone's ideal.[128] The politician drew from Döllinger's pages a picture of the mission of the church in the 'young vigour' and 'virgin purity' of its early centuries, nurturing the souls of the faithful through *Bildung*, the cultivation of the individual, rather than by 'propagating anti-social dogmas and winding up to the highest point the spirit of caste'. The effect was the incorporation of the gospel into western civilization. 'Thus', wrote Gladstone, 'it was on man at large, and on society at large, that Christianity fixed its grasp.'[129] The broad strategy of the early church, with its benefits for humanity as a whole, should be copied in the nineteenth century. This was Döllinger's vision of the cultural mission of Christianity, kin to that of some English Broad Churchmen, and it became Gladstone's as well.

III

A further, though closely related, factor tending to broaden Gladstone's outlook was his preoccupation with ecumenical relations. In *Church Principles* 'unity of

---

[123] Memorandum on conversation with Dr Döllinger, 4 Oct. 1845, Lathbury, 2, pp. 383–9, quoted at p. 389.          [124] *D*, 3, 12 Oct. 1845.          [125] *D*, 25 Oct.–20 Dec. 1846.
[126] Erb, 'Gladstone and German Liberal Catholicism', p. 450 and n. 7.
[127] *Autobiographica*, p. 148.          [128] Gladstone, 'From Oxford to Rome', p. 154.
[129] Gladstone, 'Catholic Interests', p. 155.

Christian communion' comes second only to 'the permanence of the faith' in Gladstone's list of the primary needs of the Christian religion. He means in the first place the incorporation of maximum numbers within churches possessing the apostolic succession, but a corollary is the quest for the visible unity of the bodies possessing that privilege. The goal might be well-nigh unattainable, Gladstone admits, but 'when the mind recurs to that most solemn prayer of the Saviour, at that most solemn hour, for the visible unity of his Church, I feel how impossible it is to wrench away the hope of this (however distant and however difficult) achievement from the heart of all true belief in Christ'. The search for unity was therefore a duty. The Church of England, 'like the ancient church between the Arians and the Sabellians', seemed 'to be placed in the very centre of all the conflicting forms of Christianity', whether Protestant, Roman, or Eastern Orthodox. Because she was Reformed as well as Catholic, the Church of England possessed an evident vocation to draw together other Christians.[130] Thus, as we saw in Chapter 3, she need not deny the claims that Dissenters made for their own churches. When duly mollified, they might in the end be attracted back to the communion of the Church of England—a policy reminiscent of that urged by the mentor of the Broad Church party, Thomas Arnold. The method was also Arnoldian, to allow 'the utmost latitude of opinions' within the church. Although Gladstone differed from Arnold's anti-doctrinal stance by adding that the opinions must be 'compatible with the sure integrity of the faith', his irenical approach to other Christians necessarily pulled him in a different direction from Tractarian dogmatism.[131]

In the ecumenical endeavour the Roman Catholic Church presented the greatest obstacles. Her denial of the churchly status of other communions was a grating irritation to Gladstone. 'Her whole scheme', he wrote in 1843, 'is founded upon her exclusive pretensions, and upon the assertion of the illegitimacy of all Churches not under her jurisdiction.' Formal relations with Rome would be 'not a question of communion, but of subjection'.[132] The welcome by Döllinger made much of its impact on him precisely because the German avoided unchurching his visitor from the start. Döllinger represented Gladstone's chief prospect for ecumenical advance on the Roman front. With the theologian's willingness to temper the universal claims of his church by a recognition of the differences between Italian and German Catholicism, he gave substance to Gladstone's idea (already noticed in Chapter 3) that national sections of the Roman Church might break free of papal domination.[133] While in Germany Gladstone took the opportunity to investigate the contemporary Ronge movement that seemed a possible portent of precisely such a denouement, though, from the comment that one of Ronge's books entitled *Catholic Writings* was 'most impudently so called', he appears to have been rapidly disillusioned.[134] In the previous year he had read a

---

[130] *CPR*, pp. 493–4, 507–8.
[132] Gladstone, 'Present Aspect of the Church', p. 55.
[134] *D*, 4, 7, 9, 10, 15 Oct. 1845, quoted at 9 Oct.

[131] Ibid., p. 496. See Ch. 3, pp. 73–4.
[133] See Ch. 3, p. 74.

book commending a combination of national identity and episcopal order, F. B. Gourrier's *National Catholicity: Or the Prospects of the Christian Church in South-Western Europe Considered* (1844).[135] National Catholicity was Gladstone's single gleam of hope for the future of the Roman communion. Perhaps feeling for the various fatherlands of Europe would break it apart, allowing the religious nationality that he championed to take root in its ruins.[136] He gave his support to the Anglo-Continental Society which aspired to encourage exactly that outcome.[137] Any possibility of constructing unity with Rome involved the prior destruction of its international bonds.

'As respects the Eastern Churches', Gladstone wrote in *Church Principles*, 'the barriers are less formidable.'[138] Their abuses were less flagrant, and already they enjoyed a measure of national identity. Russia and Greece, like several other nationalities, each possessed its own church. During the 1840s Gladstone took considerable interest in the Russian Orthodox Church. He absorbed a translation of A. N. Mouravieff's *A History of the Church of Russia* (1842) in the year of its publication; three years later he was introduced to its author by William Palmer (not to be confused with the author of the *Treatise on the Church of Christ*), perhaps the leading Anglican authority on the Russian Church; and in 1846 he read Palmer's new *Harmony of Anglican Doctrine with the Doctrine of the Eastern Church* (1846).[139] In 1845 Gladstone saw the Russian admiral and diplomat E. V. Putyatin 'on religious matters' and examined another book, perhaps a catechism, on the doctrine of the Russian Church.[140] Although he continued to pay attention to Russian Orthodoxy in later years, seeing, for example, the Archpriest Wassilieff, an advocate of Anglo-Orthodox reunion, in 1865, the balance of his interests swung towards Greek Orthodoxy.[141] In 1847 he turned to a classic of the Greek Church, *On the Sacred Liturgy* by the fifteenth-century Simeon of Thessalonica.[142] On his visit to the Ionian Islands in 1858–9 he seized the opportunity to investigate Orthodoxy in practice, admiring the rigour of a monastery on Corfu where in the summer no more than three-and-a-half hours were allocated to sleep.[143] The Greek Church had the attraction that it represented, in a sense, the continuity of the civilization that stemmed from Homer. Already in 1843 he had written that if he were asked how he could justify the suspension of communion between the Eastern Churches and the Church of England, he would

---

[135] *D*, 27 Jan. 1844.

[136] On religious nationality, together with Gladstone's ecumenical concerns, see H. C. G. Matthew, 'Gladstone, Vaticanism and the Question of the East', in Derek Baker (ed.), *Religious Motivation: Biographical and Sociological Problems for the Church Historian*, Studies in Church History, 15 (Oxford, 1978).

[137] *Fifteenth Year's Report of the Anglo-Continental Society for the Year 1868* (London, 1868), p. 87.

[138] *CPR*, p. 509. See Tatiana Soloviova, 'Anglican–Orthodox Dialogue in the Nineteenth Century and Gladstone's Interest in the Reunion of Christendom', in Peter Francis (ed.), *The Gladstone Umbrella* (Hawarden, Flintshire, 2001).

[139] *D*, 22 Oct.–4 Dec. 1842, 8, 13 July 1845, 28 June, 5 July 1846.

[140] *D*, 21 Jan., 9–14 Dec. 1845.        [141] *D*, 15 Feb. 1865.          [142] *D*, 12 Oct. 1847.

[143] *D*, 2 Dec. 1858.

reply that he was 'not aware that it can be justified at all'.[144] Gladstone developed an affinity for Orthodoxy that was later to undergird his protests on behalf of the suffering Christians of the East.

The desire for reunion meant that Gladstone could not be too insular in his Anglicanism. The Church of England, he realized, had much to learn. One aim, as he jotted down in a memorandum of about 1843, could be to appropriate the excellencies of the Protestant communions and of the Roman, Greek, and Russian churches for his own.[145] In a certain way, as he put it in a sermon of 1864, unity was already a reality.

At Rome, at Constantinople, at Jerusalem, in England, & throughout the world, those who are divided in much else yet hold the Head, and teach for the capital article of the faith the doctrine of Jesus Christ come in the flesh, so that notwithstanding all our carnal & foolish divisions we are still in some sense one fold under one shepherd.[146]

But the imperative to realize the spiritual harmony in institutional arrangements was ever pressing so that in the end (as he declared in 1843), 'the children of all Christian Churches should kneel around a common altar'. Hence the Church of England rested under solemn obligations not to aggravate the lacerations of Christendom. It was partly a question of manner. In controversy there should be no 'asperity or rancour'. It was also, however, a question of substance. There must be no following of the awful example of Rome, or equally of the evangelicals, 'by our obtruding matters of opinion into the region sacred to matters of faith'. The great risk was 'setting up standards of orthodoxy more extended or more rigid than those which God has commanded to be used as such'.[147] Gladstone developed an aversion to dogmatism outside a very limited sphere. It fostered within him a preference for seeking common ground in theology. He disliked religious controversy, he told the sympathetic Döllinger in 1862, and the wise course was 'to ascertain and widen all real grounds of concord, and to revere and make the most of the elements of Divine truth wherever they may be found'.[148] The ecumenical enterprise, as it commonly does, nurtured broad-mindedness in Gladstone.

A major reason for seeking reunion of the churches was so that they could present a solid front against infidelity. Here was another preoccupation of Gladstone's that was to lead him not, as might be expected, towards a reactionary dogmatism, but, again, towards a more flexible theological position. He held as early as 1840 that 'the powers and principles of absolute unbelief are spreading more and more widely . . . and indicating symptoms of systematic preparation for the attack upon all belief in Divine revelation'.[149] In retrospect he held that the breakdown of Tractarianism in the 1840s was succeeded by the 'bold development' of a rationalizing movement.[150] One symptom was the appearance of *The*

---

[144] Gladstone, 'Present Aspect', p. 53.          [145] GP 44733, f. 149 (n.d., but bound with 1843 MSS).
[146] 'Whit Tuesday', GP44781, f. 175 (7 Feb. 1864).          [147] Gladstone, 'Present Aspect', pp. 54–5.
[148] W. E. Gladstone to J. J. I. von Döllinger, 22 June 1862, Lathbury, 2, p. 35.          [149] *CPR*, p. 514.
[150] W. E. Gladstone to Sir Stafford Northcote, 9 Aug. 1865, Lathbury, 1, p. 142.

*Life of Jesus* (1835–6), by the Tübingen theologian D. F. Strauss, translated into English by the novelist George Eliot in 1846. The book dismissed the supernatural features in the gospel narratives as accretions of myth, but with none of the scurrility of popular freethinking propaganda. Gladstone read Strauss's *Life*, probably in the original German, in 1848.[151] Although he later thought it less offensive than its French equivalent, *The Life of Jesus* (1863) by Ernest Renan, he found it an ominous work.[152] It was no doubt in his mind when, in 1852, he wrote of the threat from 'the improved tactics of infidelity, the refinement which its tone has acquired, and its specious association with a warm religious phraseology'.[153] In the same year, for the first time, Gladstone sounded a note of alarm on the subject in one of his sermons. Our sins, and especially our heresies and schisms, he contended, had the effect of 'encouraging the infidel and the blasphemer to treat the Gospel as a fable'.[154] By the early 1850s Gladstone was highly sensitive to the challenge to the Christian faith from a resurgent will to disbelieve.

His reaction, however, was not to pull up the drawbridge of the citadel of orthodoxy. In 1853 a received article of faith seemed to be called into question from within the Church of England by Gladstone's former Oxford acquaintance, F. D. Maurice, now the holder of the chair of theology at the Anglican King's College, London. Although Maurice denied being a Broad Churchman, he was widely regarded as the standard-bearer of that emergent school of thought and so was under a cloud of suspicion. When his *Theological Essays* (1853) appeared to cast doubt on the doctrine of the everlasting punishment of the wicked, a storm of criticism broke around him. He believed in eternal punishment, Maurice explained, but he denied that 'eternal' necessarily meant 'everlasting'.[155] Gladstone held no reservations about traditional opinions on this subject. A few years later, in a private memorandum, he set out his view that the problem, such as it was, lay not in the apparent harshness of condemning human beings to suffer agonies forever but in the potential injustice of permitting the wicked to live on and yet not be punished according to their deserts. Maurice ran the risk, on this understanding, of overthrowing the immutable moral law.[156] For Gladstone, then, 'eternal' meant 'everlasting'. Yet when the council of King's College met in October 1853 to discuss the dismissal of Maurice for teaching dangerous doctrine, it was Gladstone who moved an amendment in his favour that a group of theologians should first examine the essays. The amendment failed, but the episode revealed Gladstone as a champion of what in *Church Principles* he had called 'extended liberty of thought'. It demanded that 'differences even upon matters of faith shall only be removed by the persuasive means adopted to the nature of

---

[151] *D*, 15–20 Feb. 1848. He had previously looked at Strauss's book on the subsequent controversy in German: *D*, 24 Mar. 1847.

[152] W. E. Gladstone to E. B. Pusey, 6 Jan. 1868, LBV 85/74, Pusey House Library, Oxford.

[153] Gladstone, 'Catholic Interests', p. 154.     [154] GP 44780, f. 38v (14 March 1852).

[155] Chadwick, *Victorian Church*, 1, pp. 545–9.

[156] GP 44736, f. 209v (n.d.: probably 1861, because similar large blue paper at f. 216 is dated 26 Sept. 1861).

conscientious belief'.[157] Coercion in religion, as Gladstone had maintained against Macaulay, was always wrong. Even though Maurice might be mistaken, he should not be harried from his office. Despite disagreeing with the theologian, Gladstone was prepared to stand up as the advocate of a broader churchmanship.

The ventilation of the issue of future retribution, not only in the Maurice case but also subsequently, led Gladstone to ponder the question for himself. In his earliest note on the subject, probably written in 1861, he decided that the difficulty over eternal punishment was part of the broader problem of evil. In the hereafter, under the government of a good and all-powerful God, either wicked beings should come to an end or their wickedness should be terminated. That they should be punished forever showed, however, that they and their wickedness persisted; and so there was a conflict between evil in the creatures and the attributes of the Creator.[158] In 1864 Gladstone devoted a whole memorandum to the subject. There was a preliminary question, he told himself, before addressing 'questions connected with the administration of the Divine justice in the world to come'. Why should human beings, weak and fallen as they are, be competent judges of the issues? After all, they had an interest in lenient treatment of their sins in the afterlife. 'No civilised nation', Gladstone remarked, 'would allow its criminals to legislate for crime.'[159] Another memorandum of about the same date took up the objections that perpetual suffering was an unfair penalty for finite acts and that divine punishment should be remedial rather than retributory. Experience, Gladstone claims, shows that human beings ripen towards a fixed state of either goodness or the reverse. They are 'unalterable' before death and so must be treated permanently in one way or another in the afterlife. Liberal teachers, however, thought otherwise:

Only the new Gospel as it goes beyond Scripture & the Catholic Faith, so it also goes beyond reason & experience as hitherto understood, & demands a new machinery of cure for dealing with cases that are hopeless under the old one, in order to satisfy its notions as to the manner in which God Almighty ought to govern his universe.[160]

The repudiation of a flaccid theology sanctioned by sentiment is clear enough. But Gladstone, far from being content to reassert traditional dogmatic claims, was ready to think through the newer views; and, as will appear in Chapter 8, he was in due course to allow such arguments to modify his own understanding of life after death.[161]

Gladstone's attitude to the Bible similarly took trends of contemporary opinion into account. Late in life he recalled that the 'first person who pointed out to me that there were some errors of fact in the Gospels was Dr. Pusey'.[162] Butler taught Gladstone that, just as absolutes were not to be expected of other forms of

---

[157] *CPR*, p. 494.                                              [158] GP 44736, f. 210.

[159] GP 44753, ff. 157–60 (13 Nov.1864), quoted at ff. 157, 158v–9; Lathbury, 2, pp. 403–6.

[160] GP 44753, ff. 161–82 (n.d., but similar to previous document).

[161] See Ch. 8, p. 248.

[162] W. E. Gladstone to Sir Richard Owen, 23 Oct. 1885, Lathbury, 2, p. 108.

revelation, so perfection was not to be looked for in the Bible. Thus scripture possessed only a relative perfection, a perfection for its purpose, using imperfect human language.[163] Revelation in scripture might be described as unerring, but it was without error only in the same sense as God's communications through nature or providence. Thus the apostle Paul distinguished his own teaching, which therefore possessed less authority, from that of the Lord.[164] Consequently, as Gladstone showed in a cryptic note of 1863, he faced a number of intellectual issues:

1. Is the <u>Word</u> infallible?
2. Does its infallibility extend to all that it contains?
3. Is there any test by which to separate with absolute certainty what is within the limit of infallibility from what is beyond it?
4. Is this test of immediate & visible operation?
5. By whom can it be applied?[165]

The raising of such questions meant that biblical criticism was in principle welcome. Although Gladstone found much to disapprove in Benjamin Jowett's essay in *Essays and Reviews* (1860) that famously declared the Bible was to be treated like any other book, he had no objection to the axiom.[166] Gladstone judged that Bishop Colenso, with his pedantic criticism of the Pentateuch, had 'passed under the dominion of what may be termed the destructive spirit', but the politician did not regard his enterprise as inadmissible.[167] In 1869 he was willing to endure a tide of protest when he elevated Frederick Temple, one of the other contributors to *Essays and Reviews*, to the episcopal bench.[168] So Gladstone showed no trace of biblical fundamentalism. On the contrary, he was eager for the Bible to be subject to unrestricted academic scrutiny.

The same willingness to respond to contemporary theological developments is evident even in one of Gladstone's sermons. The subject was 'The Christian Miracles'; the date was 1863. After recounting one of the healing miracles of Jesus, Gladstone comments that some people are unable to believe that the Almighty will do at one time and place what he does not do at other times and places. 'These fancies of men have come & gone before, & as they have come so perhaps they will go again.' The Christian miracles, however, were entirely credible. After all they were associated with the compassion of Jesus, a 'sign of goodness and of love'. That was to moralize the traditional vindication of the miracles in a way typical of the age. But how, Gladstone asks, should his hearers deal with 'the efforts of misguided men to overthrow the continuing tradition of the faith'? There should be, in the first place, no coercion of their opponents: 'let us not attempt to call down fire from heaven upon them.' Nor, however, should his audience heed the

---

[163] GP 44736, f. 25 (4 Nov. 1846).          [164] GP 44736, ff. 219–19v (n.d.: probably 1861).
[165] GP 44752, f.319 (7 Aug. 1863), in *D*, 7 Aug. 1863.
[166] Peter Hinchliff, *Frederick Temple, Archbishop of Canterbury: A Life* (Oxford, 1998), p. 67.
[167] W. E. Gladstone, 'Bishop Patteson' [1874], *Gleanings*, 2, p. 239.
[168] Hinchliff, *Temple*, pp. 119–29.

antagonists, 'unless we have such training & such time as would enable us humbly & thoroughly to examine them'. They must not forget 'the glorious gift of reason' which was to guide them. Nor were they to 'fear for the fortress of Divine truth however it be assailed'.[169] Here was Gladstone's prescription for responding to religious sceptics: no enforcement of sanctions against them; careful examination of their arguments; an appeal to reason in their refutation; and a confidence in the permanence of the deposit of faith laid up in the Catholic Church. He was eager to consider traditional dogmatic claims in the forum of public debate. That was a large part of the Broad Church programme in the Victorian era.


IV


A further reason for the growth of a more latitudinarian element in Gladstone's theology lay in the effects of the profound and many-sided crisis through which he passed in 1850–1. His political party was in fragments; he lost one of his daughters and his father by death; his rescue work for prostitutes was leading him into acute temptation; and the Gorham Judgement rocked the Church of England, depriving him of his two religious confidants. In an anguished diary entry for 19 August 1851, written in Italian for greater security, he drifts from Elizabeth Collins, the rescued prostitute whom he found most attractive, to his miserable condition:

These two terrible years have really displaced and uprooted my heart from the Anglican Church, seen as a personal and <u>living</u> Church in the <u>body</u> of its Priests and members; and at the same time the two friends whom I might call the only supports for my intellect have been wrenched away from me, leaving me lacerated, and I may say barely conscious morally: these misfortunes . . . may yet succeed in bringing about my ruin, body and soul.

During 1851 he wrote no fresh sermons. After that year, as he consolidated his faith after the crisis, his preaching took up a number of novel themes. The space given to ecclesiastical intricacies in the sermons narrows; Gladstone concentrates more on what he now regards as the basics.

And what [he wrote in a sermon of 1856] after all is that Christianity of which we hear so much & boast so much, except likeness to Christ? When we talk of repentance & faith, of doctrine & sacraments, of the Word & the Church, we talk of mighty means & instruments which God has appointed for making us like to Christ: but the Christian creed, the holy Sacraments, the infallible Scriptures, the offices & guidance of the Church, are nought and worse than nought for us, except they help us onward in the great work committed to us, of becoming like to Christ.[170]

The spiritual struggle that he had experienced in his own life was the absolute priority, the church merely an auxiliary. It was as though he was emerging from Puseyite constrictions into a freer atmosphere.

---

[169] 'The Christian Miracles', GP 44781, ff. 151–5 (1 Feb. 1863), quoted at ff. 153, 153v, 155.

[170] GP 44781, f. 105 (16 Mar. 1856).

In the new phase Gladstone's faith was pared down to essentials. It was strikingly Christocentric. 'Of the Christian religion', he began a sermon in 1852, 'one object and one only is the beginning the centre and the end: and that object is a living person: and that Person is Christ . . .'[171] It was as though, in the potential shipwreck of his faith, he was clinging to the rudder. Christianity was not about propositions, he declared in 1859, but about Christ.[172] 'Hence', he wrote in 1865, 'all religious teaching is true or untrue, strong or weak, according as it keeps near to, or wanders far from, the person of Jesus Christ.'[173] Likewise the core qualities of the New Testament gained a new prominence. Faith, hope, and charity, he contended in a sermon of 1857 on 1 Corinthians 13: 13, contain within themselves the Christian religion.[174] The third of the triad, Christian love, was particularly stressed. A memorandum of 1852, when Gladstone was still seeking firm spiritual footholds, explains the rationale:

Love is assuredly the first principle of our religion. First ethically: because it is this power which carries us forth from ourselves and fastening our affections upon others is the root & condition of all community of life. And first theologically: for is it not the first action of our faith to believe in God? And when we believe in <u>Him</u>, in <u>what</u> do we believe? I answer we believe in love: for 'God is love'. We do not believe in justice, power, or wisdom: though He in Whom we believe be all-just, all-powerful, all-wise: but we believe in Love because God is Love, and has Himself pointed Love out to us as the innermost (so to speak) & central principle of his Being[.][175]

Gladstone's religion was becoming at once simpler and more profound. Christianity, he still believed, created a selfless community, but the details of its teaching and organization no longer preoccupied him. Jesus and his love were what mattered supremely because of the intense trials the politician had passed through.

The distinctive theological idea that most appealed to him at this stage of his pilgrimage was one that he had already formulated but that now came into its own: the personal struggle of Christ against temptation. It emerged into prominence in a typically convoluted way. Gladstone was eager to vindicate the doctrine of the atonement from the charge that it entailed imposing pain on the innocent Christ. In a paper probably written in 1847, he mounted an elaborate case, using Aristotelian categories, to the effect that pain was not an evil to Christ, but a means of personal growth towards perfection.[176] The line of argument, however, raised a further knotty problem to which Gladstone devoted a lengthy insertion. How could a person who was sinless from birth advance in goodness? The notion

---

[171] GP 44781, f. 56 (21 Nov. 1852: mis-identified by arranger of MSS as 2 Nov.).
[172] GP 44781, f. 127v (23, 24 Oct. 1859).
[173] GP 44781, f. 182 (12 Mar. 1865). 'away' is inserted in pencil after 'far'.
[174] GP 44781, f. 108 (22 Feb. 1857).       [175] GP 44740, f. 165 (3 Oct. 1852).
[176] GP 44728, ff. 175–92. The document, which is headed 'Mediation' and 'Butler' in pencil, is undated, and, because of the 1838 watermark, included with MSS of that year; but it was probably the product of 5 September 1847, when the diary records 'Butler on Mediation—Worked on do'.

seemed to require that Christ started, in some sense, on a lower moral plane. Gladstone ventured the daring suggestion that, apart from 'something extrinsic (so to speak) to itself', Christ's human nature was originally 'capable of falling into sin'.[177] This was the tenet for which the great theological luminary of the 1820s, Edward Irving, had been expelled from the ministry of the Church of Scotland: the notion that the manhood of Christ could lapse into sin was regarded as heretical.[178] Gladstone, however, avoided unorthodoxy by holding that the external force making the human nature of Christ resistant to sin was not the Holy Spirit, as Irving had taught, but the divinity to which Christ's humanity was indissolubly joined. So the person of Christ in its totality was from the first incapable of sin. What changed during the incarnate life of Christ was that the human nature, through the discipline of suffering, became as resistant to sin as the divine nature. The temptations of Christ in particular constituted a real trial that perfected his humanity. There was nothing in principle startling, Gladstone noted, in the assertion 'that His human nature as such was susceptible of change'. Human beings grew from infancy to adulthood, and so, if the incarnation was real, Christ the man must have been capable of change. The state of Christ on earth was therefore 'probationary and progressive'—probationary because he was truly tested, and progressive because his human nature changed for the better as a result.[179]

This apparently recondite speculation proved to be immensely important for Gladstone's subsequent intellectual development. It spoke to his condition, as the document goes on to show when he draws out some of the implications. The temptation of Christ, Gladstone contends, was a deep resource for the Christian. 'For in that He Himself hath suffered being tempted,' according to the Epistle to the Hebrews, 'He is able to succour them that are tempted.'[180] In the midst of the tensions created by his rescue work, Gladstone found this 'wonderful condescension' profoundly reassuring. Again the same book taught that Christ could sympathize with human beings in their struggle against sin: he was 'touched with the feeling of our infirmities'. He possessed, Gladstone inferred, 'that very identical feeling, which we have ourselves in regard to the matter of our temptations'. Christ had passed triumphantly through his time of testing, and so had 'steeled and tempered our common nature'.[181] The aim of mature Tractarian spirituality was, as we have seen, to enter more fully into union with the incarnate Christ through the eucharist.[182] By that process, and by the disciplined life to which it gave rise, the victory over sin that Christ had achieved would be transmitted to the faithful. Their human nature would therefore be strengthened for the combat against unrighteousness. The resulting 'spiritual aid given to the soul in its conflict with sin' was exactly what Gladstone needed in the

---

[177] GP 44728, ff. 186.
[178] M. O. W. Oliphant, *The Life of Edward Irving*, 4th edn. (London, n.d.), pp. 389–96.
[179] GP 44728, ff. 186, 187.                              [180] Heb. 2: 18, quoted in ibid., f. 188.
[181] Ibid., ff. 188v quoting Heb. 4: 15, 189–9v.                    [182] See Ch. 4, p. 93–7.

acute sexual temptation he was suffering.[183] The cluster of ideas surrounding the temptation of Christ therefore made a profound and lasting impression on him.

The theme emerges frequently in the sermons. In one delivered as early as 1844 the idea of Christ perfecting human nature is already present, but there is no dwelling on the struggle against sin.[184] In a Lenten sermon of 1854, however, that element has come to the fore. Entitled 'Our Lord's Temptation', the address portrays Christ as the Second Adam who, by contrast with the first, did not stain his innocent manhood. By submitting to a 'fiery discipline', he placed it beyond the power of the tempter. 'He found it without a flaw like perfect porcelain: but He left it such that however it might be strained or dashed upon the ground it would resist with the strength of well wrought iron.' Consequently the human nature of Christ had become 'a mould in which ours is to be cast'.[185] The same train of thought is evident in an address delivered on Palm Sunday in the following year. Its subject is that in the Garden of Gethsemane Christ prayed that the cup of suffering might pass from him but then accepted the divine will in absolute submission.

Thus even in Him there was a work and a progress. Even He, in His sinless Humanity, was not at first what He became at last: and the Captain of our salvation was perfected through sufferings. His manhood which was to be throughout all time a type & mould to ours, acquired its highest temper & the full strength of its tissue by passing through a furnace of affliction made seven times hotter than its worst.[186]

The repetition of images—the mould, the furnace—illustrates that Gladstone had made a particular perspective on Christ's struggle very much his own. The agony of Christ in the garden, an instance of pain and perseverance leading to final vindication, was a model for his own combat with sin.

Dwelling on this theme had some remarkable intellectual results. They emerge from another sermon given in the same month, April 1855, on the same topic, Christ in Gethsemane, but this time concentrating on the words of Luke that 'He prayed more earnestly'. It is striking, Gladstone comments, that the intensity of Christ's prayer could differ. 'Therefore as to His Manhood He changed, He varied even as we do.'[187] This human passibility was equally evident in Christ's weeping over Lazarus and over Jerusalem. Had he retained 'the high inflexibility of Godhead, that flesh would not have been our flesh, He could not have been either the Victim for us upon the Cross or the mould [the image recurs] in which we are to be cast anew'. It was almost as though the incarnate Christ, in his weakness under testing, had greater moral stature than God in the abstract. The category of humanity was being elevated to an extraordinary degree. The law of variation,

---

[183] GP 44728, f. 188.
[184] 'Palm Sunday', GP 44780, ff. 93–6v (31 Mar. 1844), at ff. 95–6.
[185] 'Our Lord's Temptation', GP 44781, ff. 77–80v (12 Mar. 1854), quoted at ff. 78v, 79.
[186] 'Palm Sunday', GP 44781, ff. 93–6v (1 Apr. 1855), quoted at f. 95.
[187] 'Wedy in Passion Week', GP 44781, ff. 100–3v (22 Apr. 1855), on Luke 22: 44, quoted at f. 100: 'to his Manhood' was changed by Gladstone from 'man' for the sake of theological accuracy.

furthermore, was a law of progress: 'He was ever advancing our Humanity where-with He was clothed, and carrying it upwards higher and higher towards that immutable and supreme perfection in which He now possesses it[.]' So the direction of change in Christ was the equivalent of the contemporary idea of progress. Indeed, that is how Gladstone saw it: he inserted in the sermon the phrase the 'idea of progress & advance as it were applied to our Lord'.[188] This was not simply a theological notion, but the meliorism of the age grafted on to the doctrine of the incarnation.[189] Gladstone's musings were leading him towards a concentration on the potential of humanity.

Another sermon of 1861 provides clues to the background of this dimension of Gladstone's thinking. The text consists of some words of Christ from John's gospel: 'It is expedient for you that I go away.' Gladstone explains that the disciples had previously been spiritual children under tuition. 'This', says the preacher, 'is a very blessed state, but it is not all that man requires in order to the perfection of his nature & to the entire effect of the will of God concerning him.'[190] Here is a hint about one of the influences pushing Gladstone towards a higher estimate of the capacities of humanity. The phrase 'the perfection of his nature' suggests the classical ideal that Matthew Arnold championed in this decade. Gladstone was being drawn by his Homeric studies, to be discussed in the next chapter, into the Greek thought world in which man was the measure of all things. But the Almighty, Gladstone continues, does not want human beings to be mere tools. 'God has appointed one Pattern Man whom we are all to follow, even the Incarnate Son, and as the Incarnate Son Himself underwent a sharper discipline to bring his humanity to a higher excellence, so must his followers.'[191] The title 'Pattern Man', as we have seen, is drawn from Robert Wilberforce, whose book on the incarnation Gladstone greatly admired.[192] The idea of the growth under discipline of Christ's human nature towards perfection appears several times in Wilberforce's sermons.[193] Although Gladstone had already formulated the theme before the publication of the sermons, it is likely that they reinforced his growing appreciation of its importance. In his own sermon Gladstone goes on to describe 'the manhood of religion' to which Christ's followers are called: 'They must walk by faith not by sight: they must face the conflict with their spiritual foes, and come through it: they must learn that they are responsible for the use of the will & faculties which God has given them: good & evil are before them & they must deliberately choose & embrace the good & hold it under difficulty & trial[.]'[194] Here is the programme of Gladstone's new and self-reliant phase of faith. Each individual, in imitation of Christ, must take up the cross of moral struggle. No longer

---

[188] GP 44781, ff. 100v, 101, 100.

[189] J. B. Bury, *The Idea of Progress* (London, 1920), ch. 18.

[190] '4 S. Easter', GP 44781, ff. 128–33v (28 Apr. 1861), on John 16: 7, quoted at f. 132. 'Him' is mistakenly written with an initial capital letter in the MS.                                    [191] Ibid., f. 132v.

[192] See Ch. 4, p. 102.

[193] R. I. Wilberforce, *Sermons on the New Birth of Man's Nature* (London, 1850), pp. 17, 140, 256.

[194] GP 44781, ff. 132v, 133.

under the tutelage of Pusey and his circle, Gladstone was striking out on his own path of spiritual discipline.

The central place of the incarnation in Gladstone's mind was not challenged as this thinking developed. On the contrary, as he declared in a sermon of 1864, the incarnation was 'the masterkey of religion'.[195] But he had expanded his understanding of the doctrine so as to make it a sanction for raising the status of whatever was human. In 1859 he praised Tennyson's poetry as 'human in the largest and deepest sense' and consequently universal in scope; in 1863 he commended the study of history because it puts us in touch with great objects and great thoughts, 'all of them having man for their subject, and therefore all of them commanding the heart of man'.[196] Moreover the belief that Christ made forward strides towards perfection gave a particular slant to his fresh appreciation of humanity. What Christ became, his followers were to become. That was the force of Gladstone's favourite metaphor: Christ's body was to be 'the mould and model of the human race'.[197] Hence human beings were to change over time. Boyd Hilton has pointed out that from the 1850s onwards Gladstone showed signs of appreciating the importance of the passage of time.[198] His new sense, we can now add, was primarily a consequence of his altered understanding of the human condition. He had inherited a cosmology in which human nature was fixed, a constant over time and space, and he did not discard the essentials of that point of view. It remained crucial to his later thinking that human values were permanent and universal. From his fresh insight into the achievement of the incarnate Christ, however, Gladstone had come to see that human beings are also capable of transformation. Christ, though coming into the world without any trace of imperfection, was made perfect over time. Similarly his followers, though possessing unalterable characteristics, could make moral advances. The politician, while retaining a fundamentally static understanding of the human condition, now thought it compatible with more dynamic elements. Gladstone did not, as we shall see, uncritically embrace a full-blooded notion of inevitable progress;[199] but he did come to accept that major improvement was possible. Humanity had immense scope for betterment.

In some measure, furthermore, progress had been realized through Christian history. The gospel, according to Gladstone in a sermon of 1862, possessed a 'leavening power' over the lump of human society. It was intended to bear fruit 'not only in the salvation of the individual soul but also in bettering the common lot of mankind'.

The whole social & political system of these days though it may perhaps be far from what it should be, yet if compared with what it would have been but for the Gospel, is as light compared with darkness. The Gospel has established provision for the poor the sick the

---

[195] 'Whit Tuesday', GP 44781, ff. 172–5v (7 Feb. 1864), quoted at f. 174.
[196] W. E. Gladstone, 'Tennyson' (1859), *Gleanings*, 2, p. 153. GP 44752, f. 332 (18 Sept. 1863).
[197] 'Epiphany', GP 44781, ff. 124–7v (23, 24 Oct. 1859), quoted at f. 124.
[198] Hilton, *Age of Atonement*, p. 343.         [199] See Ch. 6, pp. 171–4.

widow & the orphan: it has abolished slavery, it has made war milder & more rare, it has given us mild laws & kindly relations between man & man, between class & class.[200]

Progress was therefore largely the result of Christian influence permeating social systems and public policies. The work of Christ had exerted a powerful effect on subsequent ages.

The influence which shed itself so gently like a softening dew upon the heart of the converted malefactor has been strong enough to build up empires & to break them down, to master and to mould the greatest intellects of the world, to establish its dominion in every country where the power of man is highest & his civilisation most advanced, and to cast anew the form and features of society.[201]

The cultural sway of Christianity bore witness to its capacity to bring about change. That was not the sole mission of the faith, but it was part of its natural effect. Gladstone was offering something approaching a social gospel.

The broader theological understanding surrounding the potential of human-ity that Gladstone developed during the 1850s and 1860s was largely worked out in the privacy of his own home, but it burst on the world in 1868 in his review of *Ecce Homo* (1865). The anonymous life of Christ, the first in the English language, was in fact written by J. R. Seeley, the young professor of Latin at University College, London.[202] Its prose was attractive, but the book caused dismay by confining itself, as the title implied, to depicting Christ as a man. Lord Shaftesbury famously condemned it as a work vomited forth from from hell; Pusey, as he told Gladstone, judged it 'an infinitely painful book'.

What struck me [Pusey continued] . . . is, the entire humanitarianism of the whole book. It is an ignoring of the operation of God the Holy Ghost or indeed of God at all, such as a Greek or a Mohammedan might believe. And this is, I fear, the secret of the popularity of the book, that it brings down our Lord to our human level and explains what is Divine by our unaided humanity.[203]

These qualities, however, did not deflect Gladstone's admiration. Seeley's book, the politician replied, was totally unlike the 'odious' demythologizing life of Jesus published two years before by Renan. 'In Ecce Homo,' Gladstone explained, 'notwithstanding the jars from time to time, the purpose seemed to me good.'[204] To portray Jesus in his unadorned humanity seemed no crime. Gladstone was less qualified in the evaluation that he passed to the publishers immediately after first reading the book in 1865. He could recollect, he said, 'no production of equal force that recent years can boast of'. It was eminently suited to the present day, he went on, and so 'I hail the entrance into the world of a strong constructive book on the Christian system'. What to Pusey appeared subversive literature was to

---

[200] GP 44781, ff. 142–5v (27 July 1862), quoted at ff. 142v, 145v.
[201] 'Gosp. G. Fri.', GP 44781, ff. 156–60v (3 Apr. 1863), quoted at f. 156v.
[202] For Seeley, see Deborah Wormell, *Sir John Seeley and the Uses of History* (Cambridge, 1980).
[203] E. B. Pusey to W. E. Gladstone, 3 Jan. [1868], GP 44281, ff. 339, 339v.
[204] W. E. Gladstone to E. B. Pusey, 6 Jan. 1868, LBV 46/51, Pusey House, Oxford.

Gladstone 'this noble book'.[205] The difference was a measure of the distance the politician had travelled away from Pusey over the previous two decades.

Gladstone's review, printed in the popular religious periodical *Good Words* to achieve maximum publicity, set out an elaborate vindication of *Ecce Homo*. The synoptic gospels, Gladstone showed at length, concentrated on the human side of Christ, who only gradually revealed the full truth about his own identity. He is presented as 'a Man engaged in the best, and holiest, and tenderest ministries, among all the saddest of human miseries and trials'. The author of *Ecce Homo* was not to be condemned for doing something similar. In England and even more in Scotland, where *Good Words* was published, there was 'a tendency among imperfectly informed Christians practically to merge the humanity in the divinity of our Lord'. Seeley's idea that there was a point at which Christ first became conscious of miraculous powers might disturb such weaker brethren, but their alarm showed an underrating of Christ's humanity. If he grew in wisdom as well as stature, 'and was ever travelling the long stages of the road to a perfection by us inconceivable', then it was reasonable to suppose that, in the crisis of the temptation, he might first become aware of miraculous powers. Behind Gladstone's stalwart defence lay his recent theological evolution. The human Christ, his compassionate ministry, his progress to perfection—these were the themes that now nourished his soul. 'Christianity', he remarked pithily in the review, 'is Christ', echoing a sentence in one of his own sermons.[206] The doctrine of the incarnation had blossomed into a sympathy that readily identified with what Pusey criticized as the humanitarianism of *Ecce Homo*. Gladstone was publicly aligning himself with a classic work of the Broad Church school.

## V

By 1868, the year in which he became Liberal Prime Minister, a more liberal dimension had developed in Gladstone's faith. He did not, during the 1850s and 1860s, turn against the advanced High Churchmanship of the previous decade. He still read to the household his sermons of the 1840s that identified closely with the later trajectory of the Tractarians; and he composed fresh ones elaborating the doctrine of eucharistic sacrifice. It was a period when he championed the traditional High Churchman Archdeacon Denison in his assertion of exalted eucharistic doctrine and the Tractarian Bishop Forbes in his defence of the Scottish Communion Office.[207] Supremely Gladstone still cast himself as an apologist for dogmatic belief against insidious attempts to water it down—a stance that will be

---

[205] W. E. Gladstone to Macmillan & Co., 25 Dec. 1865, Lathbury, 2, p. 88.

[206] W. E. Gladstone, 'On "Ecce Homo" ' [1868], *Gleanings*, 3, pp. 46, 63, 84, 87–8.

[207] W. E. Gladstone to the Earl of Aberdeen, 13 Aug.1856, Lathbury, 1, pp. 372–3; and Lathbury, 1, ch. 9. On the Forbes case, see Rowan Strong, *Alexander Forbes of Brechin: The First Tractarian Bishop* (Oxford, 1995), ch. 4. In both cases, however, Gladstone was on the side of liberty as well as High Churchmanship.

illustrated again in the next chapter.[208] But at the same time he was steadily moving away from Pusey's narrow interpretation of the faith, dismaying his former mentor by his changing attitudes. Essentially Gladstone was adapting the core Tractarian doctrine of the incarnation in new directions. Because his central tenet was common ground between High and Broad Churchmen, the transition involved no repudiation of the past, but it did bring Gladstone much closer to the thinking of the broad school. Despite F. D. Maurice's repudiation of the Broad Church label, his influential brand of loosely defined but generous-minded theology was in many ways its epitome. Gladstone shared with Maurice the belief that the incarnation had transformed the human condition. Baptized men and women must be considered less as fallen descendants of Adam than as incorporated into Christ. Hence human potential was immense.[209] Gladstone did not identify with Maurice's position; nor does he seem to have been influenced by it.[210] Yet the politician's incarnationalism blossomed into a theology that recognizably bears some of the same liberal traits.

Gladstone had not abandoned his conviction that religion was to have a communal basis. He still believed passionately in the centrality of the church in the divine economy. Fresh reading had even reinforced this estimate. Ecclesiastical minutiae, however, were relatively less important to Gladstone from the 1850s onwards than in the 1840s. Against the hierarchical and the mystical elements in religion he explicitly posed the many-sided principle of freedom. There was the metaphysical principle of the freedom of the will, which he had already wholeheartedly embraced.[211] There was the freedom of enquiry for which he admired Döllinger and which he championed in the case of Maurice. It would lead, he was confident, to a rapprochement between the faith and modern culture. There was freedom for the laity to join fully in the life of the church. That induced Gladstone to assert the importance of lay participation in the counsels of the Anglican communion. There was freedom for the church from interference by courts and governments. The regulation of doctrine by the Judicial Committee of the Privy Council in the Gorham affair caused Gladstone immense pain. So, we might add, did Palmerston's bill in 1857 to permit divorce through the secular courts, a legal encroachment on the jurisdiction of the church that Gladstone resisted tooth and nail.[212] Anti-erastianism was to remain a driving force in his later career. Perhaps most deeply felt of all, however, was the need to defend freedom against Roman Catholic domineering. Gladstone hated the despotic international authority of the Vatican that prevented national Catholic bodies from expressing their own genius in the manner of the Orthodox churches of the east.

---

[208] See Ch. 6, pp. 167–71.

[209] On Maurice, see David Young, *F. D. Maurice and Unitarianism* (Oxford, 1992), and B. M. G. Reardon, *Religious Thought in the Victorian Age: A Survey from Coleridge to Gore* (London, 1980), chs. 5 and 6.

[210] W. E. Gladstone to Lord Lyttelton, 18 Mar. 1841, GGM 35, f. 22. *D*, 16 Apr. 1843. Both offer critical comments on Maurice.　　　　　　　　　　　　　　　　　　　　　　　[211] See Ch. 3, pp. 51–2.

[212] W. E. Gladstone, 'The Bill for Divorce' [1857], *Gleanings*, 6, pp. 104–6.

He detested the oppressive and incompetent administration of the Papal States together with its theoretical justification in the claims of the pope to temporal power. And he saw the confessional, with its flawed guidance from spiritual directors, as a device for extinguishing moral responsibility. The whole Roman Catholic system that ensnared his closest friends seemed intent on repressing personal autonomy. Rome was the sworn foe of liberty. During the 1840s Gladstone the politician had learned the practical advantages of ending restrictions on economic freedom, but from the latter part of that decade onwards his general intellectual development led him in a parallel direction. Gladstone was a convinced partisan of liberty long before he was a Liberal.

If Gladstone's anti-Catholicism was deeply felt, so was his personal struggle against temptation in the demanding circumstances of 1850–1. His psychological anguish found comfort, as the household sermons reveal, in a sense that Christ, too, had travelled that road. The furnace of his trials forged in the Redeemer a character of steel. Increasingly the believer could share in the qualities of Christ's humanity. Therefore there was immense scope for personal development, and even for the progress of the human race. Gladstone's experience resembled that of John Stuart Mill, whose mental crisis in the 1820s brought him awareness of the German notion of *Bildung*, self-development. From the static world of Bentham, Mill turned to the evolutionary worldview of the romantics. Gladstone's change of mind was neither so early nor so drastic, but he similarly came to appreciate that human beings were capable of growth over time. Although, unlike Mill, he never abandoned the conviction, derived from Bishop Butler and other thinkers of previous ages, that human nature is essentially constant, Gladstone modified his inherited opinions about human potential. He was no doubt diffusely swayed by many of the same romantic intellectual influences that affected Mill, but the immediate source of his fresh hopes for humanity was wrestling with Christology. By a curious route he emerged from his own period of crisis into a new phase of thought that focused on the person of the incarnate Saviour. Like Seeley, he exalted the human side of Christ. The founder of the Christian religion might be no less than God manifest in the flesh, but Gladstone now wished to insist that the flesh was profoundly real. As a result, on the one hand, the incarnate Christ had imparted a new grandeur to humanity. Henceforward Gladstone made the dignity of the human race a fixed point in his thinking. On the other hand, the exalted Christ still displayed a deep sympathy for the weak in their suffering. A compassionate concern for those in adversity became not just a particular aspect of Christian duty but a central dimension of Gladstone's worldview. The values clustering round the idea of humanity were to undergird the politician's mature thought.

# 6

# The Study of Homer

GLADSTONE'S HOMERIC studies have not fared well with commentators, either past or present. Contemporaries were particularly dismissive of the statesman's apparent obsession with Homer's account of the divinities of Olympus. Sir George Cornewall Lewis, Gladstone's successor as Chancellor of the Exchequer in 1855 and a considerable classical scholar, told a correspondent that Gladstone's estimate of Homer as an exponent of religion was 'fundamentally wrong'.[1] Lord Tennyson thought Gladstone's opinions on the subject 'hobby-horsical'.[2] Even the loyal John Morley was forced to admit that his hero's ideas in this area were 'commonly judged fantastic'.[3] Historians tend to have echoed these judgements and to have assumed that Gladstone's treatment of the poet was an idiosyncratic foible.[4] Sir Philip Magnus is an exception, for he rightly locates Gladstone's preoccupation with Olympian religion within a framework of Christian apologetic.[5] Another exception is the classicist Sir Hugh Lloyd-Jones, who, in a sparkling sketch, brings out the high quality of the statesman's feeling for the heroic society that Homer depicts and the sensitivity of Gladstone's appreciation of the poetry as literature.[6] J. L. Myres, Deryck Schreuder, Agatha Ramm, and Colin Matthew have each offered sympathetic accounts of Gladstone's Homeric scholarship, and Frank M. Turner has given the fullest and most perceptive exposition of his views on the religion and politics of Homer's poems, at the same time stressing Gladstone's desire to vindicate the curriculum of the University of Oxford.[7] What has been neglected, however, is the extent of change in Gladstone's theories. Far from remaining constant, his attitude to Homer, and especially to

---

[1] Sir G. C. Lewis to Henry Reeves, 16 Sept. 1858, in Revd Sir G. F. Lewis, Bart. (ed.), *Letters of the Rt. Hon. Sir George Cornewall Lewis, Bart.* (London, 1870), p. 345.

[2] Asa Briggs (ed.), *Gladstone's Boswell: Late Victorian Conversations by L. A. Tollemache and Other Documents* (Brighton, 1984), p. 16.           [3] Morley, 3, p. 545.

[4] e.g. Roy Jenkins, *Gladstone* (London, 1995), pp. 14–15, 181–3, 392.

[5] Philip Magnus, *Gladstone: A Biography* (London, 1963), pp. 122–5.

[6] Hugh Lloyd-Jones, 'Gladstone on Homer', *Times Literary Supplement*, 3 Jan. 1975, pp. 15–17, repr. in his *Blood for the Ghosts* (London, 1982).

[7] J. L. Myres, 'Gladstone's View of Homer', in *Homer and his Critics* (London, 1958). D. M. Schreuder, 'History and the Utility of Myth: Homer's Greece in Gladstonian Liberalism', in Francis West (ed.), *Myth and Mythology*, Occasional Paper No. 7, Papers from the Australian Academy of the Humanities Symposium 1987 (n.p., n.d.). Agatha Ramm, 'Gladstone as Man of Letters', *Nineteenth-Century Prose*, 17 (1989–90). Matthew, pp. 152–7. F. M. Turner, *The Greek Heritage in Victorian Britain* (New Haven, Conn., 1981), pp. 159–70, 236–44.

the poet's Olympian pantheon, altered considerably over time. Lloyd-Jones does not register the modification; Agatha Ramm has noticed the change, but does not pursue it; Turner comments on two points of detail in Gladstone's view that developed, but does not expound the more substantial transformation in his thinking.[8] The present chapter examines the earlier phase of Gladstone's Homeric project, down to and including his *Studies on Homer and the Homeric Age* of 1858, exploring the reasons for his engagement with the poet. The next chapter, covering the 1860s down to the 1890s, analyses the later shift in the statesman's views. It will become apparent that, though it could sometimes verge on the esoteric, Gladstone's Homeric scholarship was bound up with the evolution of his most fundamental convictions.

The politician's classical interests were not confined to Homer. The study of the ancient philosophers that had occupied so large a portion of his leisure hours in the 1830s was occasionally taken up again in subsequent decades. Plato, Aristotle, and Cicero were each read from time to time. In the autumn of 1860 and again a year later Gladstone actually began preparing an edition of Aristotle's *Politics* designed for undergraduates. The incomplete draft, however, gives few clues to the development of his thought since it concentrates on inculcating a 'thorough familiarity' with the philosopher's scientific terminology in order to give the reader an 'easy mastery' of the work.[9] There were periodic campaigns of broader classical reading. In the summer and autumn of 1852, for instance, he studied in turn Propertius, Tibullus, Longinus, Plautus, and Suetonius, taking careful notes on each.[10] Other authors were compulsive. Once he had taken up Thucydides, as he remarked in correspondence with Lord Acton, he could not bring himself to stop.[11] There were, however, limits to the catholicity of his taste. He held the Greek tragedians to be lacking in 'life-likeness'. He assigned Aeschylus the highest place among them, but does not record reading Sophocles in the original at all after Oxford even though he thought him better than Euripides.[12] In general he preferred Greek to Latin authors, and he despised Virgil as an inferior epic poet who had distorted subsequent generations' appreciation of Homer.[13] Yet Gladstone included passages from Horace in a volume of translations, several of them from Homer, that he issued in 1861 with his brother-in-law Lord Lyttelton.[14] On his final retirement in 1894 Gladstone completed *The Odes of Horace*, a set of translations of his own.[15] But the statesman's publishing output on the classics concentrated overwhelmingly on Homer. Apart from the massive *Studies on Homer and the Homeric Age* in three volumes (containing 576,

---

[8] Turner, *Greek Heritage*, pp. 167, 242.

[9] GP 44750, ff. 35–143 (10–27 Sept. 1860), quoted at f. 41. *D*, 10–27 Sept. 1860, 28 Aug.–25 Sept. 1861.

[10] GP 44740, ff. 70–92 (July–Aug. 1852), 97–110 (1 Sept. 1852), 133–55 (17 Sept. 1852), 156–63 (24 Sept. 1852), 280–312 (n.d., but *D*, 24 Sept.–18 Oct. 1852).

[11] W. E. Gladstone to Lord Acton, 1 Apr. 1888, GP 44094, f. 15v.

[12] W. E. Gladstone, 'On the Place of Homer in Classical Education and in Historical Inquiry', in *Oxford Essays* (London, 1857), p. 10.   [13] *SHHA*, 3, pp. 512–13.

[14] Lord Lyttelton and W. E. Gladstone, *Translations*, 2nd edn. (London, 1863).

[15] W. E. Gladstone, *The Odes of Horace translated into English* (London, 1894).

533, and 616 pages respectively), he composed four smaller books, a programmatic essay, two public lectures, and over two-dozen articles on the poet. There were substantial sections on Homeric themes in other writings. Gladstone possessed a familiarity with the classical texts that was still normal among the educated elite of the nineteenth century, but his scholarly activity was focused to an unusual degree on one author, Homer.

I

Why did Gladstone study the earliest of Greek poets with such enthusiasm? One answer is that the task provided a diversion from politics, a way of spending spare time profitably. In September 1872, after a month of intermittent Homeric study, he noted in his diary that it had been the 'first course of this medicine since 1868'.[16] The therapy, as he pointed out publicly four months later, could rarely be applied while he was Prime Minister. The *Spectator* had reported him as saying that he began every day with his 'old friend Homer'. Gladstone sent off a denial to the editor:

as such a phrase conveys to the world a very untrue impression of the demands of my present office, I think it right to mention that, so far as my memory serves me, I have not read Homer for fifty lines or for a quarter of an hour consecutively during the last four years, and any dealings of mine with Homeric subjects have been confined to a number of days which could readily be counted on the fingers.[17]

Although the earlier diary entries may suggest that Gladstone was exaggerating the degree of his abstinence, it is certainly true that most of his researches on Homer were undertaken when he was not in government. His books were all composed in opposition. He had first turned to the careful examination of the poet in the autumn of 1846 when he was freshly retired from the Colonial Office and actually out of parliament. In the fastness of Fasque, the family home in Kincardineshire, while undertaking his normal vigorous programme of reading, he passed from Virgil's *Aeneid* to Homer's *Iliad* and was surprised by the pleasure it gave him. The description of the shield of Achilles in Book 18, for example, thrilled him: 'how beautiful!', he burst out in his diary.[18] He made copious notes of stray thoughts suggested by the text relating to literary equivalents, biblical parallels, Adam Smith, Coleridge, and much else.[19] One line, he told Lord Lyttelton, gave him a hint that the origin of customs duties might be found in the Book of Genesis. 'I find', he justly remarked to Lyttelton, 'Homer full of interesting matter collateral to the practical purpose . . .'[20] Gladstone moved on to the poet's *Odyssey*, started writing papers on Homeric geography, sacrifice, and other

---

[16] *D*, 16 Sept. 1872.
[17] W. E. Gladstone to the editor, the *Spectator*, 14 Dec. 1872, cutting in GP 44760, f. 212.
[18] *D*, 21 Nov. 1846.          [19] 'Iliad. Notes. 1846', GP 44736, ff. 42–76.
[20] W. E. Gladstone to Lord Lyttelton, 15 Dec. 1846, GGM 35, f. 107v.

themes, and then, in the new year, began exploring the secondary literature. His interest, like that of Lyttelton, was a means of filling vacant leisure hours suited to his station. Although Gladstone pursued the activity with typical intensity, it was essentially the hobby of a gentleman amateur.

Much of Gladstone's preoccupation with Homer was therefore a species of eclectic antiquarianism. Its range expanded when he returned to the study of the poet in 1855, following the fall of the Aberdeen coalition. Among 'the many curious subjects' that Homer's works opened up, Gladstone told Lyttelton on 27 August, was the topography of the plain of Troy.[21] 'The fundamental point of belief', he explained, 'has hitherto been the confluence of the rivers & I am strongly impressed with the idea that there never was any confluence at all.'[22] This topic, alongside such subjects as beauty, number, and colour, was duly covered three years later in *Studies on Homer and the Homeric Age*. Later, as his voluminous manuscripts reveal, Gladstone was to lavish time on the obscurest of Homeric details. In a memorandum 'As to the fastening of doors', for example, he notes that in the first book of the *Odyssey* a bolt is drawn from outside when placed inside a building, adding two illustrations of possible arrangements.[23] The concentration on Homer's actual words was characteristic of Gladstone's project from the 1850s onwards. When considering the resumption of his studies in July 1855, he commented in his diary that he would be 'avoiding Scholarship ... on account of inability'.[24] Ponderous continental works outfaced him. Whereas in the 1840s he had tried to secure the relevant German titles, in 1855 he made do with only two.[25] 'In truth,' he told Lyttelton, 'it is one's duty to look at all the books that are of any note but I work more and more upon the text and the internal evidence.' He analysed the poems, using scissors and paste to extract and collate the examples of Homer's usage, a process he called 'a real decomposition'. The risk, as Gladstone was aware, was of making unjustified connections. 'I am afraid', he confessed to Lyttelton, 'of finding not too little but too much, i.e. of making too much of slight indications.'[26] It was a trap into which many subsequent critics were to accuse him of falling. But the method meant that Gladstone gained an encyclopaedic familiarity with the text that was one of the greatest strengths of his Homeric enterprise.

A second reason for Gladstone's study of Homer, however, and one that transcended mere curiosity, was a desire to vindicate the poet. In part he wanted to support the view that a single individual was the author of both the great poems assigned to him in antiquity. In the previous century the German scholar F. A. Wolf had propounded the view that the *Iliad* and *Odyssey* could be broken down into different blocs by various hands. Some of Gladstone's notes from his first

---

[21] W. E. Gladstone to Lord Lyttelton, 27 Aug. 1855, GGM 35, f. 162v.
[22] W. E. Gladstone to Lord Lyttelton, 31 Aug. 1855, GGM 35, ff. 166–6v.
[23] GP 44752, f. 158 (n.d., but with memoranda of 1862; on *Odyssey* 1: 442).
[24] *D*, 7 July 1855.
[25] W. E. Gladstone to Lord Lyttelton, 22 Jan. 1847, 31 Aug. 1855, GGM 35, ff. 108–8v, 165.
[26] W. E. Gladstone to Lord Lyttelton, 4 Sept. 1855, GGM 35, f. 166v.

period of Homeric study list reasons for believing the two poems to have been composed by a single writer.[27] 'The general structure & arrangement of the Iliad', he remarked in another fragment, 'do not raise those presumptions against the unity of its authorship, which have commonly been supposed.'[28] This message was the burden of Gladstone's first venture into print on a Homeric topic. He rejected the latest version of Wolf's theory, put forward by Karl Lachmann, that the epics were consolidated from as many as eighteen distinct sources.[29] Gladstone continued afterwards to assemble evidence to the same effect.[30] He later included a substantial section in *Studies on Homer* repudiating the more moderate theory of George Grote that the *Iliad* had grown from an original corpus of only thirteen books, and that there was probably more than one author. Gladstone saw consistency in the poem: 'there is no limb of the Iliad', he argues, 'separable from the body without destroying the symmetrical, masculine, and broad development of its general plan.'[31] Yet Gladstone does not insist over-strongly on the unity of authorship. In the last resort the question of a single Homer did not matter: 'even the dissolution of his individuality', Gladstone wrote, 'does not get rid of his authority.'[32] The Homeric works still bore witness to a vanished world near the dawn of time. That was the proposition for which Gladstone was prepared to do battle.

The strongest challenge to the value of Homer as historical testimony came again from Grote. The utilitarian banker whose political views Gladstone had abominated in the 1830s[33] went on to publish a twelve-volume *History of Greece*. Grote had learned from the great German historian of Rome, B. G. Niebuhr, to discern in the misty stories of early times not history but a mass of what was coming to be called myth. Grote concluded that the heroic age purportedly described by Homer was irrecoverable to the historian. All that could be done for the remoter past was to record the tales that subsequently circulated.[34] Gladstone was as alienated by Grote's history as by his politics. 'His ultra sceptical spirit', Gladstone commented in his diary in 1872, 'has made utter havock of all the early ground in Greece.'[35] Grote published the first two volumes of his history in the spring of 1846, the year when, in the autumn, Gladstone first took up Homeric scholarship. Although there is no evidence of his reading Grote before March 1847,[36] he must certainly have been aware of the publishing sensation of the previous year. The issue raised by Grote of the reliability of Homer haunted Gladstone from the beginning of his enterprise. The early poetry of a country, he wrote in an undated memorandum, should be regarded 'as not being wholly fictitious but as clothing facts in a garb of fiction and using them for poetical

---

[27] GP 44736, f. 182 (n.d.).                                    [28] GP 44736, f. 155 (n.d.).
[29] W. E. Gladstone, 'Lachmann's *Essays on Homer*', *Quarterly Review*, 81 (1847).
[30] GP 44684, ff. 48–52 (7 Sept. 1847); f. 54 (10 Sept. 1847).            [31] *SHHA*, 3, pp. 378–9.
[32] Gladstone, 'On the Place of Homer', p. 15.                     [33] See Ch. 2, pp. 38–9.
[34] George Grote, *History of Greece*, 12 vols. (London, 1846–56), 1, pp. xi–xiii. For Grote, see M. L. Clarke, *George Grote: A Biography* (London, 1962).                     [35] *D*, 12 Sept. 1872.
[36] *D*, 19 Mar. 1847.

purposes'.[37] When the legends of other lands had been scrutinized, it had proved possible to distil something of the real past out of them. The same process would be likely to yield similar results for archaic Greece. William Mure's four-volume *Critical History of the Language and Literature of Ancient Greece* (1850–3) seemed to vindicate that approach. Mure, a Peelite colleague of Gladstone's in the Commons as well as a classical scholar, accepted a certain basis of fact in the account of the Trojan War.[38] Grote criticized Mure's views in a pamphlet; Mure replied in another.[39] Gladstone took the side of his fellow-Peelite. He thought Mure's book 'far better' than Grote's and believed, too, that Mure had settled the authorship question in favour of unity.[40] Much of Gladstone's Homeric project was designed to show that it was possible to lay bare the realities of the early Greek world.

Gladstone set out his case in an extended piece of writing 'On the Place of Homer in Classical Education and in Historical Inquiry', published in a volume of *Oxford Essays* in 1857. Why, he asked, was Homer a suitable text for universities? The study of the poet's language was a preliminary task appropriate to public schools, but the inclusion of Homer in higher education could be justified only in terms of his content. That was because Homer intended to illustrate the social history of the heroic age. The main question was 'not whether he has correctly recorded a certain series of transactions, but whether he has truly and faithfully represented manners and characters, feelings and tastes, races and countries, principles and institutions'. The issue could be settled by recognizing that he was 'an original witness' who probably lived no more than forty or fifty years after the siege of Troy. The text of his epics, we could be confident, had been safely transmitted down the generations both because of their celebrity and because of the passionate attachment of the people. Hence the *Iliad* and the *Odyssey* held pride of place as historical sources for archaic Greece. It was a mistake 'to regard and accept all ancient traditions, relating to the periods that precede regular historic annals, as of equal value, or not to discriminate their several values with adequate care'. Instead the rule must be to exalt Homer and 'reduce all other literary testimony, because of later origin, to a subordinate and subsidiary position'. Gladstone's target in this polemic is made explicit, though in typically understated form: 'The name of Mr. Grote must carry great weight in any question of Greek research: but it may be doubted whether the force and aptitude of his powerful mind have been as successfully applied to the Homeric as to the later periods.' 'Historical scepticism' about early Greece was unwarranted.[41] The text of

---

[37] GP 44684, f. 44. Gladstone himself supposed in old age that the batch of papers containing this fragment might date from 1847–8, but its ideas suggest that it is more likely to come from the mid–1850s.

[38] William Mure, *A Critical History of the Language and Literature of Ancient Greece*, 4 vols. (London, 1850–3), 1, p. 32.

[39] William Mure to W. E. Gladstone, 26 Apr. 1857, GP 44387, ff. 242–2v.

[40] W. E. Gladstone to Lord Lyttelton, 31 Aug. 1855, GGM 35, f. 164v. Gladstone, 'On the Place of Homer', p. 3.  [41] Gladstone, 'On the Place of Homer', pp. 23, 44, 49.

Homer allowed the modern student to understand the earliest accessible phase of human history.

What would be learned? It was Gladstone's conviction that 'the Greek mind', best exhibited in Homer, was 'the original mould of the modern European civilization'. What human beings could achieve together was depicted in the pages of the poet. He supplied a full account of 'religion, ethics, policy, history, arts, manners'. His poems enable the reader to understand 'the whole range of our nature, and the entire circle of human action and experience'. Homer, according to Gladstone, possessed two particular advantages as a source for the study of humanity. On the one hand, the poet's world was nearer to the origin of all things than any other recorded society, 'like the form of an infant from the hand of the Creator'. Sin admittedly had intruded, but its worst ravages were yet to come. The Homeric world, as Gladstone put it, 'stands between Paradise and the vices of later heathenism'. The characters in Homer might be fallen, but they had not yet plummeted to the moral depths. So the poet portrayed a closer approximation to human nature as it had been before the Fall than any other writer. On the other hand, Homer laid bare the human condition in isolation from religious truth. The Old Testament concentrated on depicting the relationship between God and human beings. The scriptures contained 'the one invaluable code of Truth and Hope'. But Homer described human affairs undistorted, as it were, by special revelation: 'here we see our kind set to work out for itself, under the lights which common life and experience supplied, the deep problem of its destiny'. That is why the poems could be seen as 'the complement of the earliest portions of the Sacred Records'.[42] In Homer humankind was as free from particular awareness of God as it was from the profounder burdens of sin. There the essence of what it is to be human was distilled.

The study of Homer therefore fulfilled a function of unique importance in Gladstone's intellectual world. During the 1850s the statesman was moving, as the previous chapter has shown, towards the conviction that Puseyism was an inadequate religious outlook. An understanding of God and sin, though continuing to be essential, had to be complemented by a sympathetic appreciation of the circumstances of suffering humanity. Gladstone's version of incarnationalism increasingly drew him to place human potential at the heart of his concerns. In Homer he found a normative account of humanity as it was in itself. If, he wrote, 'among all earthly knowledge, the knowledge of man be that which we should chiefly court', then it was impossible to overvalue Homer's 'primitive representation of the human race in a complete, distinct, and separate form'. Knowledge of human beings, furthermore, must be 'founded on experience'. Homer did not describe human nature in the abstract, like some philosopher, but as it was embodied in real people. In a sense Homer took over the place once occupied by Aristotle among Gladstone's mentors. The poet seemed particularly well qualified to assume that role. According to Gladstone, he analysed the human condition in

---

[42] Gladstone, 'On the Place of Homer', pp. 4, 5.

a form approximating to its original state, 'fresh and true to the standard of its nature', and so, like Aristotle, was not primarily concerned with human beings as fallen. Like Aristotle, Homer was a Gentile and so presented an account of how people lived without the benefit of the particular knowledge of God entrusted to the Jews. And, like Aristotle, the poet depicted not individuals in isolation but human communities: he drew 'a picture of human society, or of our nature drawn at large'.[43] Homer readily took centre stage in a mind immersed in Aristotelian assumptions but increasingly preoccupied, through political practice, with how human beings actually function. The poet had such immense value because he showed affinities with Aristotle as well as with the broadening side of Gladstone's theology.

A third reason for the statesman's Homeric project was a desire to use him as a vehicle for political purposes. The writings of Homer, according to Gladstone, contained 'an admirable school of polity'.[44] Frank M. Turner has well brought out the main features of Gladstone's discussion of the political element in Homer,[45] but they need to be restated at this point. When Gladstone first sketched out the plan of a book on the poet, probably in 1847, one of the six chapters was to analyse 'The Polity of Homer'.[46] When, a decade later, he wrote *Studies on Homer*, the political section occupied roughly a quarter of the third volume. To debate constitutional issues was by no means his chief aim, but it was an integral part of the whole Homeric enterprise. Homer should be studied on such questions, he claimed, because 'the real first foundations of political science were laid in the heroic age'. The principles then set out were capable of contemporary application. The poems were pervaded by an 'intense political spirit'. None should find it so intelligible as the English 'because it is a spirit, that still largely lies and breathes in our own institutions, and, if I mistake not, even in the peculiarities of those institutions'. Gladstone recognized that the parallel could be drawn too closely. 'We must not,' he wrote, 'in connection with the heroic age, think of public life as a profession, of a standing mass of public affairs, of legislation eternally in arrear, of a complex machinery of government.'[47] Yet the pervasive theme of his commentary on the constitutional practice of early Greece is that there are affinities with modern Britain. The chapter concludes with a reminder that in the last book of the *Odyssey*, when the fundamental question of a disputed succession arose, the people of Ithaca did not need to be told what to do. They automatically gathered in the *agore*, the public assembly. The citizens of Homer's poems, on Gladstone's reading, were good parliamentarians.

Why could Gladstone be so confident that there were constitutional lessons for Victorian Britain in ancient Greece? It was primarily because the custom of seeking political guidance from the classical world was still alive. The most influential history of Greece before Grote's had been published between 1784 and 1818 by William Mitford, a Hampshire country gentleman and backbench Pittite MP.

[43] Ibid.          [44] *SHHA*, 3, p. 2.          [45] Turner, *Greek Heritage*, pp. 234–44.
[46] GP 44736, f. 150 (n.d.).          [47] *SHHA*, 3, pp. 3, 8, 143.

Mitford's conservatism induced him to defend tyranny, but he reserved most praise for Phaeacia, which possessed a 'mixture of monarchy, aristocracy and democracy not less marked than in the British constitution'.[48] By contrast Athenian democracy was, in Mitford's view, a dress rehearsal for the mob rule of the French Revolution. Grote's *History* was originally designed to confute Mitford. The earlier historian of Greece, Grote complained, had been 'devoted to kingly government, and to kings, not only with preference but even with passion and bigotry'.[49] The utilitarian was himself a republican, believing that the state should be governed by law rather than by a monarch. Accordingly he described any move away from a single ruler in ancient Greece as an advance. His ideal was 'the collective sovereign, called the City', in which magistrates took turns to hold the reins of power.[50] It was Grote who pioneered the rehabilitation of Athenian democracy as the seedbed of intellectual freedom. So it was natural for Gladstone, the robust champion of monarchy, to try to turn the tables on Grote. He opened his account of political practice in *Studies on Homer* by issuing a protest against Grote's denigration of the institutions of the heroic age. It was 'neither warranted in the way of inference from Homer, nor in any manner consistent with the undeniable facts of the poems'.[51] Gladstone's analysis is conditioned by the imperative to refute Grote.

The task was facilitated, remarkably, by the use to which Gladstone put the novelist Sir Walter Scott. The statesman was a devoted admirer of the Tory romantic. In 1852, on laying down Scott's book set in the Elizabethan age, *Kenilworth*, Gladstone wrote of this 'astonishing novelist' and his 'sublime' book. 'Is Leicester', he asked, 'much below Hamlet?' 'I am not sure', he went on, 'that I know of a novel the perusal of which is so like experience.'[52] Gladstone acknowledged Scott as the master of reproducing a genuine sense of the past and went so far as to put him only third, behind Homer and Shakespeare, as a painter of character in the literature of the world.[53] While preparing *Studies on Homer* in the autumn of 1857, Gladstone devoured four of the Waverley novels in immediate succession to each other.[54] The three volumes on Homer reveal the influence in points of detail: pride of lineage is illustrated by Caleb Balderstone from *The Bride of Lammermoor*; the literary depiction of drunken folly from *Rob Roy*; and error in making the sun set on the east coast of Britain from *The Antiquary*.[55] Far more important, however, is the shaping power of Scott over Gladstone's

[48] William Mitford, *The History of Greece*, 2nd edn., 5 vols. (London, 1789–1818), 1, p. 181, quoted by M. L. Clarke, *Greek Studies in England, 1700–1830* (Cambridge, 1945), p. 108.

[49] George Grote, 'Institutions of Ancient Greece', *Westminster Review*, 5 (1826), p. 282.

[50] Grote, *History of Greece*, 3, p. 23.                                    [51] *SHHA*, 3, p. 6.

[52] GP 44740, ff. 111–14 (4 Sept. 1852), quoted at ff. 112, 111, 113v. There are high appraisals by Gladstone of Scott in Morley, 3, p. 424, and in Briggs (ed.), *Gladstone's Boswell*, pp. 44–7.

[53] *SHHA*, 1, p. 32; 3, p. 556.

[54] *The Fortunes of Nigel* (D, 15–22 Sept. 1857), *Rob Roy* (D, 23–9 Sept. 1857), *Black Dwarf* (D, 2–5 Oct. 1857), *The Heart of Midlothian* (D, 6–30 Oct. 1857). In addition he listened to an extract read from *The Bride of Lammermoor*: 'the sublime catastrophe was resistless' (D, 11 Sept. 1857).

[55] *SHHA*, 1, p. 282; 2, p. 447 n.; 3, p. 313 n.

conceptualization of developments in Homer's day. One of Gladstone's main themes is the fusion of different ethnic groups in ancient Greece, and his mental model, as he makes explicit, is the assimilation of successive waves of conquerors in England.[56] In Greece, he suggests, the relation of the Pelasgian people to the Hellic tribes was much like 'that of the Saxons to the Norman chivalry'.[57] The thought reflects the theme of Scott's *Ivanhoe*, in which the novelist depicts the domination of the Saxon masses by the Norman elite. Sir Walter Scott had evidently fired Gladstone's imagination.

The statesman's greatest debt is to Scott's portrayal of the contrast between the Highlands and the Lowlands in the Scottish past. In *Waverley*, *Rob Roy*, and elsewhere, Scott depicts the passing of the old Highland order of clans, chieftains, and martial spirit before the modern pattern of commercial development and stable government in the Lowlands. Gladstone decided that something like the Scottish Highland form of society had existed in early Greece, since 'the institutions of highlanders in different parts, even at wide intervals of space and time, often present strong mutual resemblances'. The clan chiefs derived their political power from the blood relationship with their dependants. It was a 'patriarchal age of society' in which rights and duties were only gradually being defined.[58] In an extended line of argument all his own, Gladstone contends that the Homeric phrase *anax andron*, 'lord of men', meant the equivalent of a Celtic chieftain.[59] The ruler was like a revered father to his people. This stage of society, however, was beginning to decay. With increasing settlement in the plains, growing wealth, and more trade, some Greek states were turning away from monarchy to forms of plural leadership. There was 'a breaking up of the old monarchical and patriarchal system'.[60] The Trojan War hastened the process since the absence of the kings engaged in the siege led to political disorganization at home such as that depicted in the *Odyssey*. Kings fell into oppressive ways and kingship became detested. But Homer captured an intermediate phase when patriarchy had largely passed away but monarchy still survived. Arbitrary exercise of royal power was no more, but reverence was still paid to royalty. Gladstone concluded that 'it is the very picture before our own eyes in our own time and country, where visible traces of the patriarchal mould still coexist in the national institutions with political liberties of more recent fashion, because they retain their hold upon the general affections'.[61] Homeric Greece was like Victorian Britain in successfully blending the old and the new. The image of the old was derived primarily from Scott; but, armed with this analysis, Gladstone could do battle with Grote.

The republican saw Homeric kings as absolute. Resistance to their authority, according to Grote, seemed odious to the poet; they ruled through 'submission and fear'. But the peoples of Greece, except at Sparta, learned to outgrow the 'personal reverence' that had originally given authority to the king.[62] Gladstone

---

[56] Ibid., 1, p. 435.     [57] Ibid., p. 342.     [58] Ibid., pp. 493, 458.
[59] Ibid., p. 460. W. E. Gladstone to Lord Lyttelton, 11 August 1856, GGM 35, ff. 171v–2.
[60] *SHHA*, 3, p. 14.     [61] Ibid., p. 31.     [62] Grote, *History of Greece*, 2, p. 88; 3, p. 10.

directly challenges this interpretation. A king in archaic Greece, he claims, did not rule by coercion. 'The Homeric King reigns with the free assent of his subjects.' 'Personal reverence' (Gladstone echoes Grote's phrase) still persisted from the patriarchal era. It was wrong to assert, as did Grote, that kingship required personal vigour, so that elderly rulers could be cast aside. The strength of respect for them meant that they either continued to reign or associated their sons with them in authority—or else they entered an honourable retirement. Monarchy commanded general esteem because in the heroic age it was 'always and essentially limited', possessing only 'moderate powers'. The dignity of the ruler was 'founded upon the sure ground of duty, of responsibility, and of toil'. The king, in fact, 'should be emphatically a gentleman'. The later hatred of kingship, on which Grote had dwelt, was a consequence of the degeneration of the office in post-heroic times. The usurper of 'sole and indefinite power' was detested because he had taken away from the people the treasure of 'free government' that they had previously enjoyed under the limited monarchs of the past. The argument amounted to an ingenious rebuttal of Grote's case based on a detailed appeal to the text of the poems. Monarchy in Homer, according to Gladstone, was far from an arbitrary and dangerous force. On the contrary, the *basileus* of the *Iliad* stood for 'a benignant and almost ideal kingship'.[63]

Gladstone bolstered his treatment of monarchy by his account of the other political institutions of heroic times. The *boule*, or council of chiefs, had been described by Grote as 'a purely consultative body' without power to resist the king.[64] Gladstone insists, on the basis of a range of passages, that the members of the council could differ from Agamemnon, the supreme ruler on the Greek side, and even overrule him. The *boule* was

a most important auxiliary instrument of government; sometimes as preparing materials for the more public deliberations of the Assembly, sometimes intrusted, as a kind of executive committee, with its confidence; always as supplying the Assemblies with an intellectual and authoritative element, in a concentrated form, which might give steadiness to its tone, and advise its course with a weight adequate to so important a function.[65]

The council was no puppet; in fact, according to Gladstone, it operated as a type of cabinet. Grote's description of the *agore*, or public assembly, had been even more disparaging. It gathered merely to hear the king's intentions, it took no votes, and it had 'a nullity of positive function'.[66] Gladstone contends that, on the contrary, the narrative of the military assembly in Book 2 of the *Iliad* assumes that 'the army was accustomed to hear the chiefs argue against, and even overthrow, the proposals of Agamemnon'. There was voting in assemblies, though by means of acclamation and silence rather than by an arithmetical count. And the debate and repartee showed that the assembly had a role. There was even a species of party politics: 'those who thought together sat together'. The position of the king

---

[63] *SHHA*, 3, pp. 6, 25, 27, 40–2, 47, 55, 58, 67.     [64] Grote, *History of Greece*, 2, p. 91.
[65] *SHHA*, 3, p. 98.     [66] Grote, *History of Greece*, 2, p. 92.

was therefore circumscribed by the power of a body very like parliament. 'The position of Agamemnon', Gladstone concludes, '. . . bears a near resemblance to that of a political leader under free European, and, perhaps it may be said, especially under British institutions.'[67] The Homeric ruler was bound to accommodate himself to the opinions of others as well as to influence them. Agamemnon was virtually as constitutional a monarch as Queen Victoria and as politically correct as her Prime Minister.

The rebuttal of Grote extended to the question of the social order. The utilitarian had absorbed from James Mill, the Scottish disciple of Jeremy Bentham and father of John Stuart Mill, a stern hatred of the hereditary aristocracy.[68] He favoured a moderate democracy, on the Athenian model, consisting of those citizens possessing an adequate education for rational decision-making. Gladstone, by contrast, still wished to uphold an order in which the elite exercised a beneficent sway over the lower social orders. His vision of contemporary Britain once more moulded his depiction of ancient Greece. Although he pointed to the dignity of the trades and professions in Homer, he insisted that 'society was aristocratically organized'. The concentration of landed property in the hands of the nobles had been safeguarded by the prevalence of primogeniture. Grote had classed free husbandmen with artisans as the superiors of hired labourers and slaves. Gladstone, however, was disposed to lump free husbandmen together with the hired labourers and the slaves, questioning the evidence for the existence of 'a peasant-proprietary class'. Even if there were many petty landowners, they were 'yet not combined, under ordinary circumstances, by any community of interest or of hardship'. The lower agricultural orders were undoubtedly, in Gladstone's view, deferential: the great proprietors 'by superior wealth, energy, and influence, led the remainder of the population'. There was no trace at all in Homer of a clash of interest between different classes in society. Rather, each class found a place within 'the community'.[69] Gladstone projected his continuing conservative social philosophy on to the pages of Homer.

It is true that it is a remarkably progressive version of conservatism. Gladstone suggests that Homer's device of referring to the attitude of *Tis*, or Somebody, is an indication of the existence of 'an intense corporate or public life'. 'The *Tis* of Homer is', he writes, '. . . what in England we now call public opinion.' If the politics of archaic Greece were led by kings and nobles, there was nevertheless a high degree of political awareness. Hence government entailed 'publicity and persuasion'.[70] Compliance could not be assumed, but must be earned by careful explanation of public policy. Together with the high role of the council and assembly, the importance of public opinion was a feature of the Homeric constitutions that looked to the future. The archaic age, Gladstone remarks, 'united reverence with independence, the restraint of discipline with the expansion of freedom', thereby

[67] *SHHA*, 3, pp. 99, 138, 139.
[68] Harriet Grote, *The Personal Life of George Grote* (London, 1873), p. 22.
[69] *SHHA*, 3, pp. 69, 77, 78.                                    [70] Ibid., pp. 7, 140, 141.

achieving 'the mean of wisdom'.[71] With that phrase the mantle of Aristotle's approval was cast over the reconciliation of the conservative with the liberal. It was the political theory of a Peelite, a liberal conservative. Yet the liberalism was still adjectival, the conservatism substantive. Gladstone lays bare his fundamental premises in a revealing passage: 'The relation between ruler and ruled is founded in the laws and condition of our nature. Born in a state of dependence, man, when he attains to freedom and capacity for action, finds himself the debtor both of his parents and of society at large; and is justly liable to discharge his debt by rendering service in return.'[72] These words could have been written in the 1830s. They restate the Aristotelian appeal to what is natural, the traditionalist endorsement of rank, and the Christian obligation to give back in return for what has been received. Notwithstanding his new-found respect for freedom, the foundations of Gladstone's political thinking had not shifted. The commentary on constitutional affairs in Homer reveals a man who was still essentially a conservative.


                                  II


The final reason for Gladstone's engagement with the poet, however, was also the most important. The statesman turned to Homer with a view to apologetic for Christian orthodoxy. Politics might occupy about a quarter of a volume of *Studies on Homer*, but religion occupied the whole of the second volume. In 1864 Gladstone claimed in a letter on Homeric divinities to the German scholar Friedrich Max Müller to have done 'more and harder work upon the text of Homer, with reference to this and similar subjects, than any other person, even in our country, that I am aware of'.[73] Colin Matthew is right to see Gladstone's Homeric studies not as an alternative but as a supplement to his religious works.[74] During the 1850s Gladstone treated writing on Homeric theology as a task specially suited for Sundays.[75] He was intending to defend true religion by enlisting the Greek gods on its side. Unfortunately, however, a misrepresentation of the enterprise has entered circulation. Sir Philip Magnus describes Gladstone as trying 'to analyse the nature of God's Revelation of Himself to the Greeks in Homer, and to relate it to the Revelation which had been vouchsafed to the Jews in the Bible'.[76] Similarly Sir Hugh Lloyd-Jones twice writes of 'a double revelation', through Jews and Greeks.[77] Although Colin Matthew has amended the text in the one-volume version of his biography, the earlier two-volume edition speaks of 'a Divine parallel revelation made to the Greeks as well as to the Jews'.[78]

---

[71] *SHHA*, 2, p. 527 n.                                    [72] Ibid., 3, p. 68.
[73] W. E. Gladstone to F. Max Müller, 28 Sept. 1864, GP 44251(2), f. 273.
[74] Matthew, p. 156.                          [75] e.g. *D*, 26 Aug. 1855, 19 Oct., 7 Dec. 1856.
[76] Magnus, *Gladstone*, p. 123.
[77] Lloyd-Jones, 'Gladstone on Homer', pp. 15, 17. Nevertheless Lloyd-Jones also recognizes that the original divine self-disclosure was universal (p. 16).
[78] H. C. G. Matthew, *Gladstone, 1809–1874* (Oxford, 1986), p. 153.

In reality, however, Gladstone held no such theory of double or parallel revelation. The Greeks, he believed, had inherited elements of a single body of truth given to humanity as a whole in its earliest days. This position is fully appreciated in Frank M. Turner's study of Gladstone on Greek religion, which is as perceptive as his analysis of the statesman on Greek politics.[79] The central contention in Volume 2 of *Studies on Homer* is that certain Greek divinities represented an original illumination by God at the dawn of history.

The kernel of Gladstone's theory of Greek religion was the distinction between tradition and invention. The gods and goddesses in the 'traditive' category bore traces of eternal truth in their characteristics and behaviour whereas those in the 'inventive' category were simply the products of the human imagination. Gladstone did not exclude overlap. On the contrary, all the traditive members of the pantheon showed symptoms of contamination by falsehood. Jupiter in particular was an amalgam of authentic ideas about the true God with qualities generated by fancy. The resulting mixture Gladstone called Homer's 'theo-mythology': the theological element consisted of accurate knowledge derived from tradition while the mythological element was false speculation grafted on to it. There was a 'profound dualism of origin' about the theo-mythology. The two sources, supposed Gladstone, explained why there was so much inconsistency in Homer's portrayal of his divinities. Some were much more superior than others to mortals; the enchantress Circe and the Sirens, though far below the Olympians in rank, could nevertheless exercise greater powers in a particular sphere than Mercury or Vulcan. Hence, he concluded, there must have been different origins and 'imperfect assimilation'.[80] Inclined by his Anglo-Catholic loyalties to see tradition as conveying wisdom from on high, Gladstone was willing to discern in the traditive deities a range of convictions about the Godhead, the redeemer, and the evil one. The theological dimension of the theo-mythology was remarkably similar to some of the cardinal articles of the Christian faith.

How could this be? Gladstone's answer was that humanity had been entrusted at its beginnings with knowledge of the Almighty. The earliest creed was not merely monotheism but a fully orbed faith that embraced acknowledgement of the Holy Trinity and expectation of a messiah. According to the Book of Genesis, Gladstone claimed, this religion was represented 'as brought by our first parents from Paradise, and as delivered by them to their immediate descendants in general'.[81] Adam and Eve, that is to say, had received direct intimations of the truth, which had then been transmitted through their posterity to the first nations of the earth and ultimately to the ancient Greeks. Homer's theology was therefore drawn from a primitive revelation. This conclusion, Gladstone contended, was by no means surprising. There were faint signs in later classical authors—in Aeschylus and Virgil—of awareness of teachings associated with the true God. If

---

[79] Turner, *Greek Heritage*, pp. 163–70.
[80] *SHHA*, 2, p. 333. In *Studies on Homer*, Gladstone refers to deities by their Latin names. Cf. Ch. 7, n. 80.                                                                          [81] Ibid., 2, p. 4.

at that much later stage in history writers had retained an inkling of valid doctrine, then Homer, standing far nearer to the Garden of Eden, was likely to display a closer resemblance to what had been revealed there. Gladstone was assuming, with many of his contemporaries, the substantial reliability of the account in the Book of Genesis and a brief time-span between human origins and the opening of recorded history. On these premises, it was plausible to suppose that the most treasured wisdom possessed by the human race might be retained over the generations down to Homer. Between the original revelation and the Greek poet, he readily conceded, there was quite sufficient time for the stream of tradition to become sullied. Authentic understanding of the divine attributes had fallen into decay while erroneous conjectures had begun to flourish. That, however, was exactly the state of religion portrayed by Homer: 'not strictly a false theology, but a true theology falsified.'[82]

Belief in a tradition going back to a primitive revelation was not as idiosyncratic as it may appear. The idea that ancient mythology reflected the debasement of a universal divine disclosure, maintained in the seventeenth century by the pre-eminent scholars Grotius and Pufendorf, had been frequently repeated during the eighteenth.[83] It was restated in 1815 by the High Church champion, Bishop Samuel Horsley. 'It is obvious', wrote Horsley, 'that the worship of Jehovah was originally universal, without any mixture of idolatry among the sons of Adam for some time after the creation.' It became universal again after the Flood, but then degenerated into superstition. The result was corrupt rather than false religion, 'just as', added Horsley, 'at this day the religion of the church of Rome is more properly corrupt than false'.[84] Gladstone, who must have warmed to the Roman Catholic analogy, paid tribute to the 'clearness and ability' with which Horsley made out the case.[85] Some authors, such as the early eighteenth-century divine Samuel Shuckford, had explicitly avowed seeing traces of the original religion of the world in Homer; and Shuckford's book was reissued in the year that Gladstone published *Studies on Homer*.[86] In the statesman's own day other scholars continued to uphold similar views. William Mure, the historian of Greek literature whom Gladstone greatly respected, supposed that heathen morality and religion derived from the purer tradition recorded in scripture;[87] W. Wigan Harvey, a clergyman who had been Gladstone's contemporary at Eton, believed that 'glimpses of truth' from Paradise

[82] Ibid., p. 9.

[83] There is no evidence of Gladstone having read either Grotius or Pufendorf, an indication of the extent to which their authority had been superseded by the statesman's day.

[84] Samuel Horsley, 'A Dissertation on the Prophecies of the Messiah dispersed among the Heathen', *Nine Sermons on the Nature of the Evidence by which the Fact of our Lord's Resurrection is Established* (London, 1815), pp. 30, 53.

[85] *SHHA*, 2, p. 6. Gladstone, according to the diaries, read Horsley's work on 31 August 1831 and again on 30 August 1857.

[86] Samuel Shuckford, *The Sacred and Profane History of the World Connected* [1728], ed. J. Talboys Wheeler, 2 vols. (London, 1858), 1, p. 154. Gladstone does not record reading Shuckford.

[87] [William Mure], 'Archdeacon Williams's *Homerus*', *Edinburgh Review*, 77 (1843), p. 58. Gladstone read parts of the issue, but does not record reading this article.

were retained by 'the various families of the human race after the deluge';[88] and George Rawlinson, soon to be Camden Professor of Ancient History at Oxford and one of the academics whom Gladstone consulted while preparing *Studies on Homer*, argued in print as late as 1885 that monotheism was the earliest human creed, that it originated in divine revelation, and that the tradition died out only gradually.[89] Perhaps most decisive in moulding Gladstone's opinion was Bishop Butler, whose enduring prestige must have continued to sway others as well. Butler, in a typically roundabout way, argued that 'there can be no peculiar presumption, from the analogy of nature, against supposing a revelation, when man was first placed upon the earth'.[90] So the authority of Butler could be thrown into the scales in favour of primitive revelation. It was not an outlandish theory for Gladstone to propound in the 1850s.

The statesman claimed in later life that he had commenced his study of Homeric religion without any notion that its discrepancies bore witness to sources outside itself.[91] That profession, narrowly construed, may be strictly correct, but the comment should not be taken to mean that the enterprise was undertaken without presuppositions about the derivation of Greek mythology. On the contrary, from the start in 1846–7 Gladstone assumed the view shared by Butler and Horsley. In examining the text of the *Iliad* at that time, he remarked, for example, that Jupiter represented the operation of providence.[92] The head of the Greek pantheon and the Christian idea shared a common origin. Yet there were also contrasts between Homeric theo-mythology and authentic religion. Thus Achilles' reflections on the nature of the gods fell far short of the representation of God as a father. 'How different', exclaims Gladstone, 'is the degenerate from the true!'[93] At about the same period he set out more systematically his understanding of the genesis of Greek religion. First in order of time, he held, 'must come not speculation on the visible world but the remnant be it more or less of patriarchal tradition'.[94] Any explanation of the theo-mythology had to give priority not to natural origins but to wisdom handed down from early times. At that period, according to the scriptures, there was frequent contact between the Almighty and his children. It was therefore a matter of 'necessary inference' that the ancestors of the Greeks carried with them the knowledge of God. As time passed, however, memories of the deposit of faith became blurred. Original attributes of God, especially those connected with beauty, power, and glory, became detached from his personality; because deity was still associated

---

[88] W. Wigan Harvey, 'Preliminary Observations on the Gnostic system', *Sancti Irenaei . . . Libros Quinque adversus Haereses*, 2 vols. (Cambridge, 1857), 1, p. i. Gladstone cites Harvey as concurring with Horsley: *SHHA*, 2, p. 6 n.

[89] George Rawlinson, *The Early Prevalence of Monotheistic Beliefs* (London, [1885]), esp. pp. 50–1. George Rawlinson to W. E. Gladstone, 22 Dec. 1857, GP 44282, ff. 330–1, is Rawlinson's response to Gladstone's etymological enquiry.

[90] Joseph Butler, 'The Analogy of Religion', *WJB*, 1, p. 177. Another passage defends primitive revelation at pp. 126–8.

[91] 'Introduction' [to book on Olympian Religion, *c*.1895], GP 44711, f. 23.

[92] GP 44736, f. 109 (finished 1 Dec. 1846).　　　　　[93] GP 44736, f. 222 (on *Iliad* 24: 525).

[94] GP 44684, f. 128 (n.d., but in batch later marked by Gladstone '1847–8?').

with might, any expression of power was seen as divine; and the idea of God degenerated into polytheism. The veneration of natural forces came in as a late feature. 'So was formed the motley company of Olympus.'[95] Already in the 1840s Gladstone had worked out to his own satisfaction a theory about the blending of the traditive and the invented in the Greek pantheon.

Critics of Gladstone's position often assumed that he was reviving the semi-mystical lore about Homer that had flourished in the seventeenth century. In 1864, for example, Max Müller, the Taylorian Professor of Modern European Languages at Oxford, associated the statesman in a public lecture with the school of interpretation that saw in Greek mythology the shadows of Bible characters.[96] A nettled Gladstone dispatched to the professor a detailed letter of repudiation. So vast was it that Max Müller's servant, having been instructed to forward only letters, failed to send on what seemed to him a parcel.[97] The misunderstanding that afflicted the Oxford professor had to be dispelled. Gladstone took pains in the following year, when delivering an address as rector of the University of Edinburgh, to distinguish his own attitude sharply from the views of those who, like the poet John Milton, derived pagan gods from Jewish sources. The statesman distanced himself from the speculations of scholars such as the Frenchman Samuel Bochart, who, as Max Müller had pointed out, taught in his *Geographia Sacra* (1646–51) that Noah corresponded to Saturn and his three sons to Jupiter, Neptune, and Pluto.[98] The best known of this esoteric school of thought was probably the Dutchman Gerardus Croesius, who asserted in a work of 1704 that the *Iliad* recorded figuratively the conquest of Jericho, equating Helen, for instance, with the prostitute Rahab.[99] Gladstone, however, does not record having read Croesius until March 1858, when *Studies on Homer* was already in the press, and subsequently condemned outright the 'undue and fanciful detail' of this type of 'peculiar learning'.[100] Originally he was not wholly immune to its attractions, for in his first campaign of study of the *Iliad* in 1846 he toyed with the notion that the temptation of Bellerophon by the wife of his master might come from the account in the Book of Genesis of the temptation of Joseph by the wife of his master Potiphar.[101] In 1865, however, he scorned the notion that 'Bellerophon was really Joseph in the house of Potiphar'.[102] He also repudiated the patristic version of the same line of argument, as expressed by Clement of Alexandria, that the Greeks were responsible for the theft of Hebrew ideas.[103] Facets of truth in Homer were

---

[95] GP 44684, ff. 129–30v (n.d., but again '1847–8?'), quoted at ff. 129, 130.

[96] Friedrich Max Müller, *Lectures on the Science of Language*, 2 vols. [1861–4], 2nd edn. (London, 1871), 2, p. 440.

[97] Friedrich Max Müller to W. E. Gladstone, 19 Oct. [1864], GP 44251, f. 275.

[98] W. E. Gladstone, 'Place of Ancient Greece in the Providential Order' [1865], *Gleanings*, 7, pp. 35–7. Max Müller, *Science of Language*, 2, p. 439.

[99] [Mure], 'Archdeacon Williams's *Homerus*', pp. 47, 50.

[100] D, 21 Mar. 1858. Gladstone, 'Ancient Greece', p. 37.

[101] GP 44736, f. 49v (on *Iliad* 6: 178–   ).                    [102] Gladstone, 'Ancient Greece', p. 44.

[103] Ibid., p. 40. Gladstone confirmed his impression of the case mounted by the early Christian writers through correspondence with Pusey: W. E. Gladstone to E. B. Pusey, 13, 21 Sept. 1865; E. B. Pusey to W. E. Gladstone, [? 19 Sept.], 19 Oct. [1865], LBV 46/48, 49, 85/69, 71, Pusey House Library, Oxford.

not to be explained by borrowings from the scriptural narrative. Gladstone insisted that the tap-root of Hellenic mythology was in primeval tradition, not the history of the Jews.

Equally he dismissed the suggestion that he was reviving the theory that the mythology of the Greeks commemorated real figures from their own past. Once again, despite the advocacy of this case by fathers of the early church including Theophilus, Lactantius, and even Gladstone's mentor Augustine, the statesman gave it short shrift.[104] Max Müller's lecture had bracketed Gladstone with the proponents of this point of view, labelling it 'eheumerism', defined as 'that system of mythological interpretation which denies the existence of divine beings, and reduces the gods of old to the level of men'.[105] The philosophical historians of eighteenth-century France had found the explanation attractive since it usefully rationalized what otherwise would have seemed opaque. The interpretation had been elaborated in England by Jacob Bryant, who contended in the 1770s that 'all the rites and mysteries of the Gentiles were only so many memorials of their primitive ancestors; and of great occurrences, to which they had been witnesses'.[106] He undertook to investigate the histories of Saturn, Janus, and so on in order to reveal their latent truths, producing three solid volumes of disorderly but immensely erudite dissertations. Although Bryant's allegorical explanation inspired the views on paganism of G. S. Faber, the Bampton lecturer for 1801, and fired the imagination of William Blake, the apprentice to the engraver of the plates for Bryant's book, the nineteenth century soon realized that his monumental scholarship was virtually worthless.[107] It was therefore a pungent reproach when Sir George Cornewall Lewis privately disdained Gladstone's mythological researches as 'a *réchauffée* of old Jacob Bryant'.[108] Lewis, however, was entirely mistaken. Gladstone's enterprise was of a different order from Bryant's, an attempt to discover traces of eternal verities rather than of contingent events on Homer's Olympus. He assured Max Müller in 1864 that he knew nothing 'about what you term sacred eheumerism'.[109] Gladstone's passion for exploring the recesses of ancient religious systems might appear at first sight to be all too reminiscent of the fruitless efforts of Casaubon, in George Eliot's *Middlemarch*, to discover the key to all mythologies. In reality, however, he was pursuing a much less recondite project than many of his predecessors as students of Greek myth.

One feature of Gladstone's undertaking, however, did attract particular ridicule in his own day and since. He was willing to go further than many of the advocates of the theory of primitive revelation that he espoused by specifying the

---

[104] Gladstone, 'Ancient Greece', p. 41 and n.  [105] Max Müller, *Science of Language*, 2, p. 434.
[106] Jacob Bryant, *A New System, or, An Analysis of Ancient Mythology*, 3 vols. (London, 1774–6), 1, p. xiii.
[107] G. S. Faber, *Horae Mosaicae: or, A View of the Mosaical Records*, 2 vols. (Oxford, 1801), 1, p. iii. Turner, *Greek Heritage*, pp. 78–9.
[108] Sir G. C. Lewis to Sir E. W. Head, 3 May 1858, in Lewis (ed.), *Letters of Lewis*, p. 333.
[109] W. E. Gladstone to F. Max Müller, 28 Sept. 1864, GP 44251, f. 251v (repr. in Max Müller, *Science of Language*, 2, p. 440 n.).

content of the early traditions with some precision. Like many previous commentators, he treated the practice of sacrifice, apparently universal in the ancient world, as a salient feature of the original revealed religion.[110] Similarly, following standard authorities and ultimately the early church historian Eusebius, Gladstone concluded that the sabbath had been observed from the beginning of history.[111] On each point the text of scripture could be construed as endorsing his opinion. In other respects, however, he was prepared to speculate far beyond the letter of the Bible. When first exploring the *Iliad* in 1846, he noted that the three-way division of the world between Jupiter, Neptune, and Pluto is said to have been by lot. That passage suggested to him that, despite being the first-born, Jupiter could not claim superior rights. 'This', he remarked, 'has a bearing traditionally on the doctrine of the Holy Trinity.'[112] He spelt out his case in *Studies on Homer*. The Greek practice of primogeniture would have given Jupiter at least the first chance to choose if the story had been mere invention. The lottery, however, implied 'an essential equality' between the three brothers, a sign that the 'tradition of a Trinity in the Godhead evidently leaves its traces on the Greek mythology'.[113] Gladstone was not alone in discerning a Trinitarian legacy in the poet. J. B. Friedreich, one of the leading contemporary authorities on Homer, believed that Jupiter, Apollo, and Minerva resembled the three persons of the Trinity, and Gladstone was glad to cite the German scholar's general confirmation of his own viewpoint.[114] Yet there is no passage in the Old Testament that explicitly points to the doctrine of the Trinity, and so the natural assumption has to be that the idea does not belong to ancient times. Cornewall Lewis was wryly amused that Gladstone had discovered the Trinity in Homer.[115] Max Müller made a broader point. He criticized 'an eminent writer and statesman of this country' for having yielded to the temptation of finding 'Christian ideas—ideas peculiar to Christianity—in the primitive faith of mankind'.[116] Gladstone appeared to be spinning fanciful webs out of his own imagination.

The technique Max Müller condemns is most evident in Gladstone's treatment of Minerva and Apollo. The statesman believed that in those two figures 'we may best test the amount and quality of the evidence in support of the assertion, that a traditional basis for the religion of the heroic age of Greece is still traceable in the poems of Homer'.[117] Minerva and Apollo, on Gladstone's account, both displayed many of the qualities of Jesus Christ himself. Minerva, as the goddess of wisdom, represented the tradition of the *logos*, identified by John the evangelist with Christ. Furthermore, she shared Jupiter's authority over human affairs. Minerva, as the *Odyssey* relates, does not permit the predatory suitors for the hand of Penelope to avoid the insolence towards Ulysses which seals their eventual destruction at his hands. In this passage Gladstone discerns a

[110] *SHHA*, 1, p. 292; 2, pp. 15, 171.                                    [111] Ibid., 1, p. 172.
[112] GP 44736, f. 60 (on *Iliad* 15: 187–   ).        [113] *SHHA*, 2, pp. 179, 178.        [114] Ibid., p. 138.
[115] Sir G. C. Lewis to Sir E. W. Head, 3 May 1858, in Lewis (ed.), *Letters of Lewis*, p. 333.
[116] Max Müller, *Science of Language*, 2, p. 466.                              [117] *SHHA*, 2, p. 55.

superintendence of events parallel to the scriptural account of the Lord hardening the heart of Pharaoh to refuse permission for the Israelites' departure from Egypt. In each case the deity gives up human beings to their own evil ways. Minerva therefore exercises the providential role of the Almighty.[118] Her persistent care for Ulysses, Gladstone argues, is the nearest thing in Homer to 'spiritual religion ... the tender and intimate relations which have from the first subsisted between the children of faith and their Father in Heaven'.[119] Although the inventive divinities of the poems can assume human form at will, only Minerva can be visible to one person while invisible to others. Here, perhaps, comments Gladstone, is a remnant of 'that inward and personal communication between the Almighty and the individual soul, which constitutes a high distinguishing note of the true religion'.[120] At every turn Gladstone is eager to rake in any scrap of evidence suggesting that Minerva plays the most exalted of parts. The constant aim is to identify features of the Christian faith that are also present in Homer.

The depiction of Apollo is similar. If primitive tradition gave to Minerva, 'one sublime person, distinguishable from the supreme God, and femininely conceived, the attributes of sovereign wisdom, strength, and skill', it gave to Apollo, 'in the form of man, the gifts of knowledge, reaching before and after, and identified in early times with that of Song, as well as that of healing or deliverance from pain and death'.[121] Apollo is a redeemer figure who, as Gladstone points out, is described by Homer as destroying the giants who would otherwise have made war against heaven.[122] The god stands unique as 'an exhibition of entire harmony with the will of Jupiter'.[123] Unlike the other deities, Apollo never takes issue with his father Jupiter, so reflecting the Son of God who was always at one with his Father. Gladstone infers that Apollo must represent recollections of prophecies about the coming messiah that were part of the original deposit of faith. In one of the rare occasions when Gladstone takes issue with a German authority, he will not admit the opinion of Carl Otfried Müller that the veneration of Apollo was originally restricted to the Dorian people. If only a single group worshipped the god, his cult could hardly have been part of the universal tradition descending from the first disclosure of the truth.[124] Gladstone concludes that there is 'a broad line ... almost ... an impassable gulf' between Minerva and Apollo on the one hand and other divinities such as Mars and Venus.[125] Although he concedes that the line is blurred by the existence of traditive elements in some other deities, he claims that there is a stark contrast between these two and the merely inventive members of the pantheon. Apollo represented the tradition of a person, Minerva that of an idea, but both were embodiments of the messianic expectation inherited from the beginnings of human history.

Gladstone's penchant for discovering anticipations of the incarnation in Homer was by no means confined to his treatment of Minerva and Apollo. In his

---

[118] Ibid., pp. 117–19 (on *Odyssey* 18: 346).   [119] Ibid., p. 121.   [120] Ibid., p. 358.
[121] Ibid., p. 64.   [122] Ibid., pp. 72–3.   [123] Ibid., p. 71.
[124] Ibid., pp. 141–2.   [125] Ibid., p. 137.

notes of 1846–7 he draws attention to Latona, a minor goddess who, after sexual relations with Jupiter, became the mother of Apollo the deliverer. Her role seemed a parallel to the promise recorded in Genesis that the seed of the woman would bruise the head of the serpent, customarily seen by Christian commentators as a prophecy of the work of Christ. In this instance, Gladstone commented, Homer's system 'bears a resemblance to its sources quite sufficient for the purposes of identification'.[126] Gladstone takes the goddess's Greek name, Leto, which was associated with night and obscurity, as evidence that her background was shrouded in mystery. The meaning was intelligible if her origins went back before the Olympian system to the ancient traditions of faith. 'What could be more natural', Gladstone asks in *Studies on Homer*, 'than that a name should fasten itself upon her, simply importing that, illustrious as was her motherhood, the fountain-head of her own life and destiny was lost in oblivion?' Such flights of imagination might seem far-fetched, but there was a limit to Gladstone's willingness to speculate: 'I do not presume to enter into the question whether we ought to consider that the Latona of Homer represents the Blessed Virgin, who was divinely elected to be the actual mother of our Lord; or rather our ancient mother Eve, whose seed He was also in a peculiar sense to be.'[127] Two years later Matthew Arnold was to subject this passage to heavy irony. The issue of 'whether the Goddess Latona in any way prefigures the Virgin Mary', he suggested, was one of the Homeric questions attended by the inconvenience 'that there really exist no data for determining them'.[128] For an upholder of the theory that there had been a primitive revelation embracing the doctrine of the incarnation, the suggestions about Latona made perfect sense; for anybody else, they seemed fantastic.

Shortly before the completion of *Studies on Homer*, Gladstone was assailed with doubts about whether his case for the content of the earliest religious traditions would convince his readers. He had illustrated similarities between passages in Homer and distinctively Christian ideas, but he had produced no evidence from the religions of other peoples about the wider circulation of debased remnants of primitive revelation. A couple of paragraphs in his book betray a measure of embarrassment that he had not examined material from Persia, Assyria, or Egypt in order to find resemblances to the supposed earliest truths, though he defended himself with the claim that most of the sources for the beliefs of these lands were later than Homer.[129] But he tried to bolster his argument in another way. In December 1857, when the text of *Studies on Homer* was already being set up in print, Gladstone paid a flying visit to Oxford, en route from London to Hawarden, in order to consult Pusey, the natural intellectual resource for this aspect of his project. The Oxford professor subsequently recommended several books that would help support the theory of primitive revelation, but Gladstone did not have time to track them down. He enquired whether Pusey

---

[126] GP 44736, f. 153 (n.d.).                    [127] *SHHA*, 2, pp. 149, 153.

[128] Matthew Arnold, 'On Translating Homer', in *On the Classical Tradition*, ed. by R. H. Super (Ann Arbor, Mich., 1960), p. 100.                    [129] *SHHA*, 2, pp. 48–9.

would be able to read through his section on the traditive part of Homer's theo-mythology and tell the author if he propounded 'anything that on the ground of ignorance or paradox is beyond the liberty of fair <u>discussion</u> among rational men'.[130] Gladstone felt out of his depth. His directions to the printer, however, were misunderstood, the sheets did not reach Pusey and soon the theologian set off for Paris.[131] Hence Gladstone's treatment of these issues was never subjected to the pre-publication critical scrutiny that he desired. Nevertheless Pusey played a crucial part in the crystallization of Gladstone's case. On Gladstone's visit to Oxford, he borrowed from Pusey a work by Christian Schöttgen, an early eighteenth-century German scholar.[132] At a time when the statesman was seeking intellectual reassurance, he reported to Pusey that 'in the main the valuable Book which you lent me has done enough for my purpose'.[133] Bearing Pusey's imprimatur, Schöttgen supplied the confirmation of his theories that Gladstone required.[134]

Christian Schöttgen had assembled an array of testimonies from Hebrew sources in order to demonstrate to Jewish scholars that their own literature bore witness to Jesus as the messiah. Much of his collection was in fact drawn from John Lightfoot, a moderate Presbyterian at Cambridge during the Commonwealth.[135] Gladstone had already looked at Lightfoot's volumes in 1856, but they had made no detectable impact on him.[136] At the end of 1857, however, Schöttgen seemed to forge the last link in Gladstone's chain of argumentation. The German showed that there was evidence of distinctly Christian belief in the ancient world outside the pages of the Bible. Schöttgen's threefold analysis of orthodox Jewish tradition—Targums, Midrashim, and messianic expositions by rabbis—is reproduced by Gladstone. 'From these sources', he comments, 'may be derived many Messianic ideas and interpretations that were current among the ancient Jews.'[137] The messiah was expected to be no less than God, associated with wisdom, the logos and light, a first-born son, the Lord of Hosts, the mediator, a performer of miracles and a liberator from Satan, death, and hell. Here Gladstone believed he had found indications of the content of the tradition stemming from the earliest revelation. The ancient people of God, more than any other race, would have preserved it with the minimum of dilution. Ignoring the likelihood that much of this messianic speculation had arisen around the beginning of the Christian era, Gladstone assumed that it had been kept relatively intact down the

---

[130] W. E. Gladstone to E. B. Pusey, 24 Dec. 1857, LBV 86/7, f. 50, Pusey House, Oxford.

[131] E. B. Pusey to W. E. Gladstone, 26 Dec. [1857], LBV 86/8, ff. 51–2, Pusey House, Oxford.

[132] The author of the book is identified when Gladstone returned it. W. E. Gladstone to E. B. Pusey, 13 Mar. 1858, LBV 86/9, f. 53, Pusey House, Oxford.

[133] Gladstone to Pusey, 24 Dec. 1857, LBV/7, f. 48.

[134] *D*, 13 Dec. 1857. 'Schöttgen de Messiâ' is mistakenly, though tentatively, identified in the *Diaries* as Schöttgen's *Jesus, der wahre Messias*, but seven days later Gladstone described it as 'Hor. Talm.' (*D*, 20 Dec. 1857). It was therefore Christian Schoettgen, *Horae Hebraicae et Talmudicae . . . De Messia* (Dresden, 1742).

[135] John Lightfoot, *Horae Hebraicae et Talmudicae . . .* (Cambridge, 1658–77).

[136] *D*, 28 Dec. 1856.      [137] *SHHA*, 2, p. 51.

generations. The passage in *Studies on Homer* expounding Schöttgen is clearly an insertion in the text.[138] It was added because it appeared to demonstrate that Homer was not alone in showing traces of the primeval faith of humanity.

Gladstone's whole approach was also undergirded by many of the assumptions of contemporary social anthropology. The dominant school until the 1850s, calling itself 'ethnology', was still heavily indebted to the pioneering work of the Asiatic scholar Sir William Jones, who, in 1784, had argued for an affinity between Indian culture and the classical civilization of the Mediterranean. Although he did not share a belief in primitive revelation, Jones appealed to linguistic and mythological similarities to demonstrate the links between the branches of the Indo-European family of nations.[139] The leading exponent of ethnology in the earlier nineteenth century was J. C. Prichard, a Bristol physician who followed Jones in fitting his researches into a biblical framework based on the dispersion of the descendants of Noah. Culture, on this view, had advanced more by diffusion than by development. Comparative philology enabled the scholar to trace the interplay of races during their migrations. Substantially the same point of view was maintained into the 1850s and beyond by R. G. Latham, director of the ethnological department of the Crystal Palace.[140] Gladstone consulted one of Latham's works while putting the final touches to *Studies on Homer* and one of Prichard's while the book was in the press.[141] The bulk of its first volume, headed 'Ethnology of the Greek Races', was an exemplary instance of their technique. Gladstone carefully sifts Homer's vocabulary in order to establish the characteristics of the two main constituents of the Greek nation, the earlier Pelasgians and the later Hellenes. Gladstone was able to draw on the conclusion of the distinguished German historian B. G. Niebuhr that the Pelasgians were a peaceful agricultural people. The Hellenes, later arrivals in the Greek peninsula, were poorer and less civilized but more energetic. To religion the Pelasgians, who supported priests in their settled communities, contributed the ritual element; the Hellenes added the imaginative dimension.[142] When, conscious of his own amateurism, Gladstone submitted the proofs of his first volume to Connop Thirlwall, Bishop of St David's and a historian of ancient Greece, the reply was reassuring about the statesman's view that the Pelasgian period passed gradually into an era dominated by the Hellenes. 'Nobody', wrote the bishop, 'I think would charge this view of the case with extravagance.'[143] The broad outline of Gladstone's anthropological analysis was in the mainstream of scholarship.

---

[138] The discussion of the traditive deities breaks off on p. 48 and resumes on p. 54 after the section on Schöttgen.

[139] Sir William Jones, 'On the Gods of Greece, Italy and India', in *The Works of Sir William Jones*, 6 vols. (London, 1799), 1, pp. 229–80. G. Cannon, *The Life and Mind of Oriental Jones: Sir William Jones, the Father of Modern Linguistics* (Cambridge, 1990), pp. 296–7.

[140] G. W. Stocking, Jr., *Victorian Anthropology* (New York, 1987), pp. 48–53.

[141] R. G. Latham, *Man and his Migrations* (London, 1851): *D*, 1 Nov. 1857. J. C. Prichard, *The Eastern Origin of the Celtic Nations proved* (Oxford, 1831): *D*, 28–9 Jan. 1858.

[142] *SHHA*, 1, pp. 293–4, 297.

[143] Bishop Connop Thirlwall to W. E. Gladstone, 14 Nov. 1857, GP 44388, f. 252v.

One of its major ramifications, however, was not. On the foundation of his ethnological studies Gladstone tried to erect a theory of the transmission of the earliest religious traditions to Greece. Leading German mythological commentators of the early nineteenth century had commonly maintained that traces of the original faith of humanity spread to peoples such as the Greeks from India. This was the opinion of Joseph Görres, the senior colleague of Döllinger's at Munich whom Gladstone had met in 1845, and of Friedrich Creuzer, whose great work *Symbolik* (1810–23) Gladstone was to consult, apparently for the first time, in 1862.[144] The statesman accepted that Greece received its beliefs from the east, but proposed that they came not from India but from Persia. Did not the very names Perseus, Perse and Persephone, all found in Greek mythology, sound like the word 'Persia'?[145] The Pelasgians, Gladstone claimed, descended from Low Iranian tribes, or Medes; the Hellenes derived from the High Iranians, or Persians. The former originally inhabited the open land enjoying the best climate in the Persian region. The latter, the Persians proper, dwelt, according to Herodotus, in the poorer country that must have been more mountainous. The relationship of the Persians to the Medes was therefore parallel to that of their descendants the Hellenes to the Pelasgians. Sir Walter Scott clearly shapes Gladstone's understanding at this stage of the analysis. 'The needy highlanders come down upon and overpower the richer and more advanced inhabitants of the central valleys.'[146] Gladstone was imposing his vision of the ancient Greek peoples on the land from which they allegedly came. This was to go far beyond the limited evidence of Herodotus, who in any case relied on travellers' tales. Yet Gladstone believed he could recognize affinities between Hellenic and Persian forms of faith. The earliest known Persian religion embraced belief in a single supreme God and the worship of the host of heaven. Such a pattern, Gladstone asserts, reflected the monotheism of primitive revelation together with the beginnings of deviation from it.[147] It was therefore from a Persian source that Greece received its decaying version of the knowledge of God, conveyed by the highland Hellenes as they travelled westwards. The whole picture was highly fanciful.

Gladstone's Persian theory was nevertheless based on several sources. It ignored the leading British authority on the Pelasgians, Bishop Herbert Marsh, who had maintained that this migrant people could be traced back only to their settlement in Thrace.[148] It also contradicted the weighty alternative opinion of the German K. O. Müller that the Pelasgians were aboriginal inhabitants of Greece.[149] Gladstone had read Marsh carefully and had also consulted Müller, but he felt

---

[144] Burton Feldman and R. D. Richardson, *The Rise of Modern Mythology, 1680–1860* (Bloomington, Ind., 1972), pp. 382, 387. *D*, 1 Oct. 1845; 10 Aug. 1862. There is no evidence that Gladstone ever read Görres's *Mythic History of the Asiatic World* (1810), even though, together with Creuzer's book, it was recommended to him by Acton: Sir John Acton to W. E. Gladstone, [June 1860], GP 44093, f. 2.
[145] *SHHA*, 2, pp. 221–2.       [146] Ibid., 1, p. 566.       [147] Ibid., pp. 561–2.
[148] Herbert Marsh, *Horae Pelasgicae, Part the First* (Cambridge, 1815), p. 19.
[149] *SHHA*, 1, pp. 200–1, citing K. O. Müller, *Geschichten Hellenischer Stämm und Städte*, 3 vols., 1, *Orchomenos und die Minyer* (Breslau, 1820), pp. 119–22.

able to repudiate their views on the basis of another work, J. W. Donaldson's *The New Cratylus* (1839).[150] Donaldson, a fellow of Trinity College, Cambridge, provided a breakdown of Indo-European ethnography based on philological evidence. Europe and northern India, he held, had been colonized by peoples from Iran. Low Germans, Hindus, and Pelasgians had a common origin among the Low Iranians; High Germans and Hellenes derived from the High Iranians or Persians proper, the mountaineers of the south. The High Iranians had pressed on the Low Iranians for centuries, propelling them outwards.[151] Gladstone acknowledged his debt to Donaldson for the understanding of human migration that he adopted.[152] Meanwhile his view of Persia itself was derived primarily from Sir John Malcolm, a distinguished servant of the East India Company who had acted several times as envoy to Tehran. Malcolm's *History of Persia* (1815) is the source for an idealized account of the manners of the Persians of his day which, according to Gladstone, shows that they still closely resembled the Greeks of the heroic period—hospitable, courteous, loving poetry recitations and horse races but liable to outbreaks of barbaric violence. Gladstone turns to Malcolm for the specification of the primeval Persian religion, though, for the purposes of his case, dismissing Malcolm's mention of fire-worship as 'a subordinate characteristic'.[153] The statesman's confidence that early Persians were monotheists was probably bolstered by the record in the biblical Book of Ezra that their later King Cyrus believed in one supreme God.[154] So Gladstone was not spinning his intellectual webs out of thin air.

What seems to have clinched his espousal of the Persian theory, however, was a personal contact rather than anything found in books. Another East India Company agent who had served in Persia, Sir Henry Rawlinson, had conducted excavations, deciphered cuneiform inscriptions, and achieved some fame as a specialist on the ancient Middle East. Gladstone met Rawlinson in the spring of 1857, perhaps then noting down for future reference that he drew a contrast between the Medes, wealthy and advanced, and the Persians, highland and poor.[155] Rawlinson had reached the tentative conclusion that the Hellenes were the same people as the Persians and that the Pelasgians were at least related to the Medes.[156] It was part of a grand conjecture about 'a great ethnic conflict both in Asia and Europe' which he expected the inscriptions eventually to confirm.[157]

---

[150] *D*, 23 June–5 Aug. 1856; 4 Aug. 1856: 16 Aug. 1855, 5 Jan. 1856. The text of the diary is wrongly transcribed as 'Gatylus'.

[151] J. W. Donaldson, *The New Cratylus* [1839], 3rd edn. (London, 1859), pp. 123–50.

[152] Ibid., 1, p. 547.

[153] Ibid., pp. 569–72, 561. The primeval Persian religion is mentioned at Sir John Malcolm, *The History of Persia*, 2 vols. (London, 1815), 1, p. 185; the description of the manners is in vol. 2, ch. 25. Gladstone does not record reading Malcolm until *D*, 6 Nov. 1857.

[154] Ezra 1: 2, 3. The text is pointed out in Harvey, *Sancti Irenaei . . . Libros Quinque*, p. viii, which Gladstone had read (*SHHA*, 2, p. 6 n.), though he does not mention it in his diary.

[155] GP 44747, f. 320 (n.d.).

[156] Sir Henry Rawlinson to W. E. Gladstone, 2 May [1857], GP 44387, f. 265v.

[157] Sir Henry Rawlinson to W. E. Gladstone, 6 May 1857, GP 44387, f. 268v.

Gladstone eagerly invited his informant to one of the literary breakfasts that he held during parliamentary sessions. 'Saw Sir H. Rawlinson', he recorded in his diary, 'resp. Achaeans & Pelasgians.'[158] Rawlinson suggested, on the basis of an Assyrian inscription, that a tribe called the Achai in Asia Minor might be the same as Homer's Achaeans.[159] The latest discoveries, it seemed to Gladstone, might illuminate the path taken by the ancestors of the ancient Greeks bearing their precious knowledge of God. He later toyed with the notion that the Achaeans could be linked with Achaemenes, the founder of a dynasty in Persia, so strengthening the bonds between Greece and that country. He was warned off, however, on the grounds that the theory was untenable, by Sir Henry's brother George, the Oxford scholar who was shortly to become Camden Professor of Ancient History.[160] As *Studies on Homer* was going through the press, Gladstone began to worry that the whole Persian proposal might be 'outrageous'. George Rawlinson reassured him that it was not. 'It is my brother's theory rather than mine', he replied to the anxious author, 'but I think it very probable, and he has certainly brought forward <u>some</u> grounds for it, though perhaps scarcely enough to go upon.'[161] Sufficiently fortified by that qualified opinion, Gladstone allowed the contention to appear in print. But it is clear that he was aware of the weakness of his Persian hypothesis even before it was published. He had allowed himself to be unduly excited by Sir Henry Rawlinson's speculations. It was an indication of the importance he attached to buttressing the idea of the transmission of a primitive revelation.


### III


The defence of an initial revelation to humanity loomed so large because Gladstone saw the idea as a bastion of true religion. Although, as we have seen in Chapter 5, the statesman's understanding of the Christian faith was mellowing during the 1850s, he remained as wedded as Pusey to its doctrinal core. He was therefore troubled by the growth of the assumption that little or nothing about it was supernatural. The conviction was to be expected of freethinkers, but now it was making ground even among the clergymen in the University of Oxford that Gladstone represented in parliament. In January 1852, on a visit to his constituency, the statesman heard a university sermon delivered by Benjamin Jowett, then a tutor at Balliol College. At the time he noted that the sermon was 'very remarkable, but unsettling'; decades later this was almost certainly the address of Jowett's that he described as 'epoch-making'.[162] It drew a contrast between the two provinces of faith, the biblical world

[158] *D*, 7 May 1857.
[159] Sir Henry Rawlinson to Gladstone, 2 May [1857], GP 44387, ff. 264–4v.
[160] George Rawlinson to W. E. Gladstone, 22 Dec. 1857, GP 44282, ff. 330–0v.
[161] George Rawlinson to W. E. Gladstone, 11 Mar. 1858, GP 44282, f. 335.
[162] *D*, 25 Jan. 1852. Evelyn Abbott and Lewis Campbell, *The Life and Letters of Benjamin Jowett, M.A.*, 2 vols. (London, 1897), 1, p. 208.

of the supernatural, and experience, the everyday world governed by law, urging that
the former needed to be explained in terms intelligible to the latter. Gladstone saw it
as a sign that what two years later he described to Pusey as 'Germanism and
Arnoldism' had arrived in Oxford.[163] Continental theology, seconded by the influence of Thomas Arnold, was beginning to erode orthodoxy. In June 1855 Jowett, who
became Regius Professor of Greek in the same year and later was to contribute to
*Essays and Reviews*, published a commentary on *Thessalonians, Galatians and
Romans*. It was the first instalment of a scheme concocted with his friend A. P.
Stanley to bring to fruition a project of Arnold's for a critical edition of the letters of
the apostle Paul.[164] Gladstone looked at Jowett's book during a visit to Oxford in the
month of its publication, and must have been troubled. Pusey, whom he visited two
days later, would have confirmed his alarm.[165] Five years on Pusey was to assure
Gladstone that the second edition of Jowett's book was even 'worse than the first'.[166]
A fortnight after his Oxford visit Gladstone lamented in a memorandum that society's hold on the essence of Christianity was growing weaker and weaker. Within
another week he had conceived the idea of recommencing his work on Homer with
a more specific object, the resolve that led to *Studies on Homer*.[167] The Homeric
enterprise was designed as a rebuttal of Jowett.

The notions that Gladstone found most repugnant were published in an essay
on 'Natural Religion' in Jowett's commentary. There Christianity was seen, not as
based on a revelation that made it unique, but, in the manner of the liberal
theologian F. D. Maurice, as the 'perfection and fulfilment' of other religions.
Jowett rejected the traditional contrast between religion as natural, a form of
spontaneous spirituality, and religion as revealed, what was disclosed by the
Almighty. The difference, he claimed, was a matter 'rather of words than of ideas'
because the two ran into each other. The common ground of religion, reverence
for the powers above, sprang from human instinct. Jowett turned to the philosopher Immanuel Kant for the two principles of natural religion, belief in God and
in immortality. Gladstone must have been horrified that this exiguous creed was
commended as sufficient for membership of the church. He cannot have warmed
to Jowett's treatment of Homer either. The poet's conception of the Greek gods
was exonerated from blame on the ground that it was 'natural and adequate to his
age'; and Homer was said to have possessed 'no inner life of morality'. But Jowett
trenched most on Gladstone's favourite convictions when he dismissed the belief
that ancient religions were corruptions of primeval revelation as a 'shallow and
imaginary explanation' and the notion of a primitive tradition as no more than
'the fabric of a vision'.[168] Religion, on Jowett's understanding, came not from

---

[163] W. E. Gladstone to E. B. Pusey, [1854], Morley, 1, p. 505.
[164] Geoffrey Faber, *Jowett: A Portrait with Background* (London, 1957), p. 212.
[165] *D*, 17, 19 June 1855.
[166] E. B. Pusey to W. E. Gladstone, 2 Apr. 1860, LBV 86/16, Pusey House, Oxford.
[167] *D*, 1, 7 July 1855.
[168] Benjamin Jowett, 'Natural Religion', *The Epistles of St. Paul to the Thessalonians, Galatians and
Romans*, 2 vols., 2nd edn. (London, 1859), 2, pp. 432, 437, 438, 456, 461, 469.

above but from below, as a growth of human consciousness. It was not these views that stirred up the storm of criticism that greeted the book, since Jowett's unorthodoxy on the atonement attracted most hostile fire, but they did constitute the polar opposite to Gladstone's theological assumptions. It is no wonder that three years later, when asked for his opinion of Gladstone's *Studies on Homer*, Jowett should have produced a terse reply: 'It's mere nonsense.'[169] Jowett's position on religion was the equivalent of Grote's on politics as a spur to Gladstone's studies of Homer.

Underlying Jowett's interpretation was the rising scholarly claim, buttressed by romantic sensibilities, that awe in the presence of the powers of nature had given birth to the spirit of worship. Such an assumption had become deeply rooted in Germany. There all religions, Acton told Gladstone in 1860, were 'looked upon as things of natural growth, and . . . Revelation was not believed in'.[170] In an age of enduring classical interests, the principle that religion sprang from the veneration of natural forces was applied first and foremost to ancient Greece. Karl Otfried Müller, a professor at Göttingen, long a centre of critical study, and trained by the circle of Niebuhr, the most eminent of German historians, held that the worship of the early inhabitants of Greece formed part of 'a simple elementary religion, which easily represented the various forms produced by the changes of nature in different climates and seasons'.[171] British scholars who admired the achievements of German historiography adopted a similar interpretation of the origins of the Greek pantheon. In the first volume of his *History of Greece* (1835), Connop Thirlwall hypothesized that the Greeks, seeing life in every part of nature, must have associated divinities with each one.[172] As we have seen, Gladstone had Thirlwall read the proofs of *Studies on Homer* while it was in the press with the request that he should point out unjustified conclusions. The gesture was not, as has been suggested, a sign of Gladstone's growing alignment with the liberal-minded bishop,[173] but rather a typical Gladstonian ploy to spike the guns of a potential opponent in advance. Thirlwall did express reservations about the sections of the book on the Persian hypothesis and the idea of primitive revelation, though too late for any modifications to be made.[174] In the text of *Studies on Homer*, however, Gladstone offers no fundamental criticism of Müller, none at all of Thirlwall, and none of Jowett either. Instead he selects a man who could not answer back as an exponent of the naturalistic point of view he is combating. Humphrey Prideaux, Dean of Norwich in the early eighteenth century, held that a cult of the planets turned into the polytheism that was transmitted to Greece.

[169] Briggs (ed.), *Gladstone's Boswell*, p. 12.
[170] Sir John Acton to W. E. Gladstone, [June 1860], GP 44093, f. 1.
[171] C. O. Müller, *The History and Antiquities of the Doric Race*, trans. Henry Tufnell and G. C. Lewis, 2 vols. (Oxford, 1830), 1, p. 16. For Müller, see the memoir prefixed to K. O. Müller, *A History of the Literature of Ancient Greece*, continued by J. W. Donaldson, 3 vols. (London, 1858), 1.
[172] Connop Thirlwall, *A History of Greece*, 8 vols. (London, 1835), 1, pp. 183–90.
[173] Matthew, p. 155.
[174] Bishop Connop Thirlwall to W. E. Gladstone, 19 Feb. 1858, GP 44389, f. 68v.

'The theory', Gladstone observes tartly, 'is not in correspondence with the facts of the heroic age.'[175] He was setting himself to repudiate any supposition that Greek religion derived merely from the worship of natural phenomena.

Gladstone refers to two other advocates of the naturalistic hypothesis, both contemporary Germans. One was Carl Friedrich Nägelsbach, professor at a *Gymnasium* in Nuremberg and the author of a careful study of Homeric theology published in 1840.[176] Gladstone first recorded looking at Nägelsbach's work in January 1857, when he was beginning to formulate the content of Volume 2 of *Studies on Homer*, and used it frequently during the following autumn.[177] Nägelsbach is cited many times in Gladstone's book, but the author expresses dissent from the German's views at least as often as he accepts his opinions.[178] Gladstone is most forthright of all in dismissing Nägelsbach's belief that 'the starting-point of the religion of the heroic age is to be sought only in the facts of the world, in the ideas and experience of man'.[179] That was the essence of the anti-supernatural prejudice that Gladstone wanted to dispel. The other German whom the statesman opposes is, remarkably, his liberal Catholic comrade-in-arms, Ignaz von Döllinger. In the summer of 1857, when Gladstone was preparing for the final campaign of writing *Studies on Homer*, there appeared Döllinger's work on *The Gentile and the Jew*.[180] Gladstone eagerly compared it with the text of the *Iliad*,[181] only to be dismayed by its teaching that the deification of nature was the root of all heathen religion, including that of ancient Greece. Hence, for instance, according to Döllinger, the element of the moral law embodied in Apollo was a later notion grafted on to the god rather than a relic of earlier revealed wisdom.[182] Ever concerned that the Catholic Church should be served by up-to-date historical method, Döllinger agreed on essentials with Karl Otfried Müller. Colin Matthew has suggested that Gladstone's exposition of Homeric theo-mythology was much influenced by Döllinger's work, but in reality the statesman read the book carefully so as to be able to repudiate its point of view.[183] He had been surprised, he told Pusey a few years later, to find that Döllinger agreed with Eusebius that the old mythology had been 'a thing false from the commencement'.[184] Döllinger was aligned with the position that Gladstone was seeking to challenge.

In principle, according to Gladstone, there could have been four ways in which religion appealed to early nations. Apart from genuine fear of the Almighty arising from revelation, there could be worship of human beings, of animals, or of the

---

[175] *SHHA*, 2, p. 11, criticizing Humphrey Prideaux, *The Old and New Testament connected in the History of the Jews and Neighbouring Nations*, 2 vols. (London, 1716–18), 1, p. 198.
[176] Carl Friedrich Naegelsbach, *Die homerische Theologie in ihrem Zusammenhange dargestellt* (Nürberg, 1840).                                   [177] *D*, 5, 8 Jan., 23 Sept.–30 Oct., 30 Nov. 1857.
[178] e.g. *SHHA*, 1, pp. 151 n., 227.                                         [179] Ibid., 2, p. 10.
[180] J. J. I. von Döllinger, *Heidenthum und Judenthum: Vorhalle zur Geschichte Christentums* (Regensburg, 1857), subsequently published in English as *The Gentile and the Jew in the Courts of the Temple of Christ*, trans. N. Darnell, 2 vols. (London, 1862).
[181] *D*, 26 July 1857.                                   [182] Döllinger, *Gentile and the Jew*, pp. 65, 82–4.
[183] *D*, 6 Sept. 1857 n. *SHHA*, 2, pp. 11–12.
[184] W. E. Gladstone to E. B. Pusey, 13 Sept. 1865, LBV 86/68, Pusey House, Oxford.

'elemental powers' of inanimate nature. Gladstone readily accepted that the elevation of human beings to divine rank, what he calls 'anthropophuism', was a main
feature of Hellenic religion.[185] The 'grossness of brute-worship', from which
Gladstone recoiled in disgust, evidently prevailed in ancient Egypt, but he could
discern 'no more than vestiges' of such blatant idolatry among the Greeks.[186] The
question at issue with Müller, Jowett, and their school was the extent of the pene-
tration of Olympian religion by nature worship. Gladstone admitted that it was
possible for a mind untutored in genuine tradition to embrace polytheism
through awe before the power and beauty of natural forces. Systems based on the
veneration of nature had actually been created in the east, but, he insisted, 'from
Homer we are not authorized to believe that such a system of Nature-worship
ever preceded in Greece the Olympian system'. All that he was willing to concede
was that aspects of the oriental schemes had entered Hellenic religion. Those
ingredients, however, were always secondary and 'everywhere surmounted and
circumscribed by developments drawn from tradition or from the principle of
anthropophuism'. Thus although in Homer's pages Apollo had associations with
solar phenomena, in the poet's day he was entirely distinct from the sun. 'The
lesson', according to Gladstone, was 'the repugnance of the Greeks to mere
Nature-worship'. There was little or no relationship between many of Homer's
deities and the powers of the physical universe. Hence the Olympian religion
could not have been created by 'mere human instinct gradually building it up
from the ground'.[187] The origin of Greek religion was not the unaided response of
primitive people to the world around them. There was a supernatural explanation
for the earliest recorded faith of humanity.

Gladstone's profound attachment to the idea of a primitive revelation also
served another purpose, to confute the theory of automatic human progress
down the ages. The statesman, as the previous chapter has shown, was growingly
sympathetic to the idea that human society can change for the better, but he
resolutely believed that improvement, far from being inevitable, depended
entirely on the moral influence of true religion.[188] Grote held on the contrary that
unaided human effort generated progress. The utilitarian had learned from James
Mill that the ancient Greeks could be located on a scale of improvement that had
marked the history of humankind. It was perhaps the most typical expression of
the outlook of the Scottish Enlightenment and had become entrenched in the
pages of the *Edinburgh Review*.[189] Between the heroic age and the flowering of
Athenian civilization in the fifth century, according to Grote, there was a great
advance. The utilitarian insisted that there were no ethics taught in Homer and
that in Homeric society, apart from private ties, there were 'scarcely any other
moralising forces in operation'.[190] The denigration of early Greece cast fresh

---

[185] *SHHA*, 2, p. 174. The word 'anthropophuism' seems to have been coined by Gladstone since the
*Shorter Oxford Dictionary* records no earlier use.     [186] *SHHA*, 2, p. 412.
[187] Ibid., pp. 410, 407, 265, 32.     [188] See Ch. 5, pp. 137–8.
[189] Andrew Skinner, 'Natural History in the Age of Adam Smith', *Political Studies*, 15 (1967).
[190] Grote, *History of Greece*, 2, p. 210.

lustre on the subsequent classical age. Gladstone, by contrast, assumed a very different pattern in the development of human society. When reading the *Iliad* in 1846, he noted that a passage was 'confirmatory of the Scriptural history of mankind as one, apart from Divine interposition, of growing corruption'.[191] He was no doubt thinking particularly of the theme of the Book of Judges, the regular recurrence of a decline in morality following the rescue of the Israelites from oppression by successive God-appointed leaders. So Gladstone expected that human sin would normally ensure the degeneration of society over time. The principle certainly applied to Greece. Grote had canvassed the notion that in heroic times the terminology of the Greeks carried no ethical significance, something that emerged only in the days of Socrates. 'I ask permission', bursts out Gladstone in *Studies on Homer*, 'to protest against whatever savours of the idea that any Socrates whatever was the patentee of that sentiment of right and wrong, which is the most precious part of the patrimony of mankind.' Moral concepts were there from the beginning, not 'an improvement introduced by civilization into the code of barbarism'. Gladstone was taking issue with Grote on a fresh front. 'The movement of Greek morality', he asserts, 'with the lapse of time was chiefly downward, not upward.'[192]

This declaration is consistent with Gladstone's suggestion in the Oxford essay of the previous year that ancient Greece illustrated the 'solemn and melancholy lesson' that, left to itself, humanity pursued a 'continued downward course'.[193] In *Studies on Homer* he set out to substantiate the claim by an examination of the morality of the heroic age. He conceded that, relative to later times, it was weak in its recognition of rights to property and in its toleration of crimes of violence. Security of possessions and persons in the classical period, however, represented less of a moral advance than might be supposed. Both were the natural result of mere self-interest in an age of growing prosperity. In other aspects of life, however, where virtues entailing self-denial came into play, there was a lowering of standards after Homer's day. The poet illustrated the high contemporary regard for the principle of sympathy by the tears of his heroes, for the principle of placability by the character of Achilles, and for the principle of humility by that of Helen.[194] Gladstone devoted a whole chapter to the position of women. Their status, he claimed, was highest under the Christian dispensation, but 'it would be hard to discover any period of history or country of the world, not being Christian, in which they stood so high as with the Greeks of the heroic age'. Gladstone convinced himself that Greek women were allowed to choose their own husbands, a signal sign of 'woman's freedom'. Marriage was lifelong (Gladstone was struggling against divorce legislation while writing the book) and faithfully observed. The concubines in the Greek camp and the eagerness to ravish women on the fall of Troy are explained away as unavoidable features of warfare, not belonging to the age of Homer in particular. In the classical period, Gladstone

[191] GP 44736, f. 57v (on *Iliad* 13: 5, 6).                    [192] *SHHA*, 2, p. 420.
[193] Gladstone, 'On the Place', p. 5.                         [194] *SHHA*, 2, pp. 471–7.

notes by way of contrast, Demosthenes is said to have lumped together prostitutes, concubines, and wives as equal in reputation. The difference between the earlier and the later era, he concludes, is 'a sufficient confutation' of any alleged 'law of continued progress from intellectual darkness into light, and from moral degradation up to virtue'.[195] Gladstone often writes as though, on the contrary, he espoused a law of continued regress.

The worldview he was defending was perhaps shared most fully by Dr John Williams, the elderly Archdeacon of Cardigan. Williams was a Welsh Tory antiquarian, the founder of St David's College, Lampeter, who had been selected by a circle of men including Walter Scott to become the first Rector of Edinburgh Academy. In *Homerus*, a monograph of 1842, Williams argued the rather extravagant case, never favoured by Gladstone, that the *Iliad* illustrated the way in which national sins brought corporate punishment. The thesis rested on the premise that the Trojans, knowing the revealed will of God through inheritance from primeval times, were responsible for rejecting it.[196] When his case was challenged by William Mure in the *Edinburgh Review* for mistakenly supposing that the original revelation contained the distinctive features of the Christian faith, Williams reasserted in *Primitive Tradition* (1843) that Homer did show signs of doctrinal and moral truth but that they had been disguised by a process of corruption.[197] Gladstone almost certainly looked through the proofs of *Homerus* in 1840;[198] he read the book, together with its defence, in 1857;[199] in the same year he corresponded with Williams and spoke to him personally.[200] In *Studies on Homer* Gladstone cites Williams's two works as authoritative expositions of the 'real traditional knowledge' inherited by the Greeks.[201] *Homerus* begins with an attack on the popular belief 'that Man came from the hands of his Creator equally ignorant and helpless, and that, by degrees, he advanced from strength to strength, until he finally reached [a] high degree of civilization'.[202] This supposition, common to the Epicureans and the *Edinburgh Review*, could be refuted, Williams believed, by showing that early times were already marked by high achievement. Homer revealed that the heroic period was not 'a gradually improving age' but one 'in full possession of a moral and intellectual system fully developed'.[203]

---

[195] Ibid., pp. 480, 484, 479.

[196] John Williams, *Homerus*, Part I (London, 1842).

[197] [Mure], 'Archdeacon Williams's *Homerus*', p. 58. John Williams, *Primitive Tradition: A Letter to the Editor of the Edinburgh Review* (Edinburgh, 1843), p. 3.

[198] *D*, 1 Dec. 1840. The 'proofsheets of "Homerus"' are tentatively identified in the *Diaries* as an edition of the *Iliad* by T. S. Brandreth, but on that day Gladstone had attended a meeting in Edinburgh of the Episcopal Church Society where Williams would probably have been present. In 1842 Williams was able to remind him that he had once promised to read *Homerus* when it came out: John Williams to W. E. Gladstone, 3 Mar. 1842, GP 44359, f. 75.

[199] *D*, 26–30 Jan., 28 Aug. 1857. Gladstone's notes on *Homerus* are at GP 44747, ff. 136–7.

[200] John Williams to W. E. Gladstone, 16 May, 8 Aug. 1857, GP 44387, ff. 286–7v, GP 44388, ff. 118–19. *D*, 9 Sept. 1857.

[201] *SHHA*, 2, p. 3 and n. The only other authority cited for the theory is Cesarotti's *Ragionamento Storio-Critico*, a work mentioned in Mure's article in the *Edinburgh Review* but evidently not seen by Gladstone.    [202] Williams, *Homerus*, p. v.    [203] Williams, *Primitive Tradition*, p. 32.

Primitive tradition was wielded by Williams as a weapon for vanquishing the Whig idea of history. Gladstone concurred in the archdeacon's purpose as well as in his methods, as his studies of Homeric morality reveal. Human beings, according to Gladstone, needed to rely on the values that God had disclosed, not on their own innate capacity for improvement. Christianity was not merely a stage 'in the march of human advancement' that could be superseded by another.[204] There was an absolute givenness about the Christian religion. Gladstone was setting out in the name of faith to do no less than overturn the secular idea of progress.

There were implications not only for freethinkers such as Grote but also for Roman Catholics. Newman, as we have seen, adopted a dynamic conception of truth in his *Essay on the Development of Christian Doctrine* (1845).[205] He argued that the church had gradually come to teach a fuller understanding of the original deposit of faith. In a sense Newman was accommodating Catholic doctrine to the idea of progress, though to a version envisaging development not, in the manner of the Enlightenment, as a sequence of stages, but rather, in the romantic fashion, as a process of growth. The theory seemed to give the Roman Church the right to adjudicate on which were legitimate doctrinal extrapolations. It therefore loomed as a serious threat to the intellectual foundations of the Church of England. The hypothesis, remarked Gladstone in a memorandum of July 1845, is 'fatal to us if proved'.[206] Repeatedly during 1846 and 1847, at the very time he was beginning his Homeric studies, Gladstone penned objections to the *Essay on Development*. Among the many points he jotted down was the suggestion that, while it was true that a great public institution such as the Roman Catholic Church was unlikely to have remained unaltered over time, the process of change would probably not be of the kind that Newman envisaged, leading to a firmer grasp of truth. On the contrary, it was likely to be a 'deteriorating process'.[207] Was that not what had happened, as Homer was reminding him, in the early history of humanity, as the original revealed doctrines gradually fell into decay? Gladstone did not fulfil his intention of writing a refutation of the *Essay on Development* at that time, but the seed of a potential critique of Newman had been sown.

In 1853 Gladstone discovered an alternative Roman Catholic doctrine of development. Early in the year, as we have already noticed, he explored the *Essai sur l'indifférence* (1817–23) by the Abbé de Lamennais, who, though later the pioneer of French liberal Catholicism, was very much a traditional defender of the Roman Church at the time he wrote the book.[208] The certitude of faith, according to Lamennais, who owed a great debt to Rousseau, was to be found in a community. The reason to be obeyed was not the mind of the individual but 'la raison générale'. Before the time of Jesus Christ, the true religion was that originally

---

[204] *SHHA*, 2, p. 533.                              [205] See Ch. 5, p. 113.
[206] GP 44735, f. 51 (July 1845). The notes arose from a conversation with A. F. Rio on 5 July, when the theme of Newman's essay, which was not yet published, must have been discussed.
[207] GP 44736, ff. 265–333 (8 Aug. 1847), quoted at f. 299v.
[208] *D*, 23, 30 Jan., 13 Feb., 20 Mar. 1853. See Ch. 5, p. 123.

professed by universal reason, the whole human race. It derived from 'une révéla-
tion primitive'; it was transmitted by 'les traditions primitives'. Mingled with the
fictions of Homer were elements of truth deriving from this source, which
included expectation of the coming of a 'God-man who would be born of a Virgin
mother'. But, crucially, the early traditions gradually fell into decay. 'The further
one goes away from the origin', according to Lamennais, 'the more primitive religion alters.' After the coming of Christ, authority was concentrated in the Roman
Catholic Church, the 'inheritor of all the primitive traditions ... and of all the
truths known from ancient times, of which its doctrine is but the development'.[209] The whole body of thought appealed to Gladstone, but the understanding of development must have particularly struck him. Lamennais, like Newman,
believed in a sacred tradition, but, unlike Newman, he held that it deteriorated
over time. By following Lamennais's understanding of Homer as a quarry of
revealed truths, Gladstone could vindicate a dogmatic, supernatural religion
against those who were undermining it. But he could also do so in a way that
implicitly revealed the inaccuracy of Newman's theory of doctrinal progress. The
tradition of the Catholic Church, if inherited from antiquity, must be subject to
degeneration rather than development. Only if restored to pristine purity by a
process of reform could tradition be faithfully transmitted. The Church of
England, while remaining loyal to Catholic tradition, had been renewed at the
Reformation; the Roman Catholic Church had not. The argument of *Studies on
Homer* should be read as tacit anti-Roman Catholic polemic inspired, in part, by
a Roman Catholic apologist. It was a typically convoluted Gladstonian ploy.

## IV

The whole Homeric project had a variety of aims, but each was concerned with an
aspect of the human condition. Homer, according to Gladstone, had erected 'a
new and distinct standard of humanity'.[210] Part of the resulting estimate of
humankind in *Studies on Homer* was favourable. The human spirit was capable of
creativity. The representation of the gods and goddesses as people, though
destructive of the principle of the unity of God, nevertheless arranged them on the
patterns of a family and a state. 'What is this', asks Gladstone, 'but to bring in the
resources and expedients, which our human state supplied, to repair, after a sort,
the havock which it had made in the Divine Idea?' The inventive quality had
generated some noble and pure characters, as in the cases of Juno and Themis.
The resulting theo-mythological scheme was 'intensely human' in the good sense
that it was the work of the 'human genius' of Homer. Gladstone delights in the
poet's ability to evoke the authentic feelings of men and women. He also approves
Homer's appreciation of 'the value of bodily excellence'. This perception by the

---

[209] Félicité de la Mennais, *Essai sur l'indifférence en matière de religion*, 4 vols. (Paris, 1817–23), 2,
p. lxxxiii; 3, pp. 23, 29, 31, 174, 427.     [210] Gladstone, 'On the Place of Homer', p. 4.

poet was not a pagan as opposed to a Christian view, for it was not true that to elevate the soul necessarily meant to downgrade the body. Homer, according to Gladstone, counteracted 'a somewhat sickly cast of teaching' that denigrated the human body in defiance of the authentic Christian idea that 'the body is part and parcel of the integer denominated man'. The physical was not intrinsically at war with the spiritual. Gladstone was divorcing himself from the ascetic strand of Puseyism that had attracted him a decade previously. Although he is not endorsing the muscular Christianity of Charles Kingsley, Gladstone is revealing the movement of his mind in that direction. And he is also willing to acknowledge the existence of conscience and some 'capacity for good' in human beings.[211] Partly because of his incipient Broad Church tendency, Gladstone's anthropology is by no means uniformly gloomy.

Yet the main thrust of Gladstone's understanding of humanity is distinctly unfavourable. The downward trend of morality over time he sees as the result of innate sinfulness. Human beings are 'the prey of vicious passions' because they suffer from an 'inward disease'. The prevailing influence is not goodness but a spirit of rebellion. The human and the sinful therefore go together. Hence the inventive element in Homeric religion, the 'strictly human' or 'merely human' contribution, is treated primarily as a debasing factor. Anthropophuism, the attribution of human qualities to divinities, injects corruption into the Olympian community. To the character of Jupiter it adds 'earthly, sensual, and appetitive elements'; the chief of the gods is 'human and carnal'.[212] Mercury is far worse, embodying the essence of 'humanism', a word Gladstone claims to be coining:

He represents, so to speak, the utilitarian side of the human mind, which was of small account in the age of Homer, but has since been more esteemed. In the limitation of his faculties and powers, in the low standard of his moral habits, in the abundant activity of his appetites, in his indifference, his ease, his good nature, in the full-blown exhibition of what Christian Theology would call conformity to the world, he is, as strictly as the nature of the case admits, a product of the invention of man.[213]

Gladstone's patent distaste for Mercury—even inducing him to brand the god a utilitarian—leads the statesman to see him as the epitome of the way of life that human beings would adopt if they were free of restraint. What is human is typically associated in *Studies on Homer* with licence and vice. The 'divine life of Olympus', Gladstone concludes, 'wherever it reproduces the human, reproduces it in degraded form'.[214] The legacy of Gladstone's evangelical, Orthodox, and Tractarian formation remains fundamental to his worldview: the defining characteristic of humanity is its sin.

The study of Homer, though conducted partly for relaxation, was an exercise profoundly charged with ideology. Gladstone wished to establish, against Grote,

---

[211] *SHHA*, 2, pp. 36, 37, 332; pp. 408–9; 2, p. 19.     [212] Ibid., 2, pp. 9, 18, 19, 33, 174, 186.
[213] Ibid., pp. 242–3. In fact the word 'humanism' had been used by Coleridge in 1812 to mean belief in the mere humanity of Christ, and its sense had been developed by others since.
[214] Ibid., p. 333.

the reality of Homer's world so that he could demonstrate, against the same author, the compatibility of monarchy with freedom and the tendency of morality to decay over time. The refutation of the idea of self-sustained progress would also undermine Newman. The case against Grote (in part) and Newman (altogether) depended on the theory of a tradition of primeval truth stemming from an original revelation. The chief aim of upholding that position, however, was to discredit the alternative hypothesis of a naturalistic explanation for religious belief. Here Jowett was the immediate target, though with him Gladstone was taking on the rising scholarly orthodoxy that was soon to make his ideas about mythology seem dated and untenable. Yet there were elements of progressive thinking in the Homeric enterprise from its commencement. On the political side, Gladstone was recommending a liberal form of constitutional monarchy that was responsive to public opinion; on the religious side, he was willing to admit that the human element in Homer had value. The preoccupation with the condition of humanity was in itself a symptom of the statesman's evolving incarnationalism. The transition of Gladstone from Conservatism to Liberalism and from Puseyism to broader sympathies was already well under way. Nevertheless there can be no doubt that in *Studies on Homer* he was defending an essentially Tory Christian worldview. His predominant intellectual debts were to Sir Walter Scott, Dr John Williams, the traditional phase of Lamennais, and to Pusey himself. He betrays a continuing sympathy for patriarchalism and a fundamental adherence to social obligations based on Aristotelian premises. Above all, the sinfulness of humanity looms large in his vision, corrupting the Olympian pantheon. It meshed readily with the Augustinian assumption that the state exists to check the unruly behaviour of its charges. *Studies on Homer*, published in the year before Gladstone joined his first Liberal government, should be seen as the climax of his intellectual career as a Conservative.

# 7

# The Olympian Religion

THE EXTENT to which Gladstone changed his views is one of the most remarkable features of his study of Homer. Many contemporaries, like several subsequent commentators,[1] assumed that there was no significant development in his opinions. A decade after the publication of *Studies on Homer* there appeared Gladstone's *Juventus Mundi* (1869). George Cox, an opponent of most of his convictions, complained that after ten years during which the controversy had been wholly transformed, Gladstone had simply repeated 'the confession of his old Homeric faith'.[2] Likewise a reviewer supposed that *Juventus Mundi* was 'only the author's well-known "Studies on Homer", writ smaller'.[3] Gladstone, however, had intended to produce not only *Juventus Mundi*, 'a smaller and simpler book, adapted . . . to schools and young students', but also a second edition of *Studies on Homer*, 'which will involve a good deal of labour'.[4] The second edition was designed to be a full revision of the three-volume work.[5] Because Gladstone gave up the task, concentrating only on the more condensed *Juventus Mundi*, the detail of the alterations is nowhere fully set out. Indeed, the statesman's phraseology in the preface of the smaller book seems calculated to camouflage the degree to which he had changed his mind about the religion of ancient Greece. He remarks merely that he had 'endeavoured to avoid a certain crudity of expression . . . which led to misconceptions of my meaning'. In 1869, the year of Irish disestablishment, he was particularly eager not to supply evidence to political opponents of variableness in his opinions. Yet even then he acknowledges that his results on ethnology and mythology had been 'considerably modified'.[6] Fifteen years on, when there was less reason to avoid the charge of inconsistency, he explained that he was so dissatisfied with the form of his original conclusions on religion that he had determined not to reprint *Studies on Homer*.[7] A careful reading of *Juventus Mundi* and the mass of other later

---

[1] See Ch. 6, p. 143.

[2] G. W. Cox, *The Mythology of the Aryan Nations*, 2 vols. (London, 1870), 1, p. 454.

[3] W. L. Collins, 'Juventus Mundi', *Blackwood's Edinburgh Magazine*, 106 (1869), p. 412. The reviewer, in this case, had evidently not troubled to read the book.

[4] W. E. Gladstone to Robert Scott, 2 Sept. 1867, SCO/1/11/26, Scott Papers, Pusey House, Oxford.

[5] The materials, which afford little evidence of the nature of the changes envisaged, are in GP 44691, ff. 47– .       [6] *JM*, pp. vi, v.

[7] W. E. Gladstone, 'Dawn of Creation and of Worship' [1885], *Later Gleanings*, p. 6. *Studies on Homer* was nevertheless published in a German translation in 1863: D, 2 Jan. 1864.

material on Homer, published and unpublished, reveals that Gladstone had altered some of his fundamental premises.

The transformation was not equally marked in all the various departments of Homeric study. The section on literary criticism and associated questions, he says in the preface, 'I have contracted a great deal, but added and altered little'. There are a few antiquarian additions to *Juventus Mundi*, notably on physics, metals, and measure of value, together with an account of the topography around Troy. Modifications of the political analysis, however, though minor, do possess significance. The sharp criticism of voting by numbers in *Studies on Homer* has disappeared, and instead a single sentence comments with apparent approval that 'the doctrine of majorities' is the result of 'a more advanced social development'. Likewise in the discussion of the place of oratory, the term 'publicity', implying merely the advertisement of government policies, is dropped and in its place there is praise for 'free speech'.[8] The writer has clearly moved beyond Peelism to Liberalism. Yet in other respects his conservatism lives on. The idea of 'reverence', reflecting the Homeric word *aidos*, is said for the first time to be a pervasive value in heroic Greece. Reverence, 'the counter-agent to all meanness and selfishness', is the principle that binds each to each, children to their parents, subjects to their kings.[9] Gladstone, as Frank M. Turner has pointed out, was seeing in reverence a social force that could restrain the masses in the wake of the 1867 Reform Act.[10] But the concept was also rooted in the statesman's early communitarianism. Reverence is the spirit of community, a category that still underlies Gladstone's analysis. 'The separation and conflict of interests', he writes, 'between the different parts of the community had not become a familiar idea; particular classes did not plot against the whole.' In another passage new to *Juventus Mundi* justice and self-restraint, cardinal elements of Aristotelian virtue, are invoked. Aristotle's 'spirit of moderation' is said to lie 'at the root of the Homeric model of the good or the great man'.[11] Notwithstanding its modification, the political analysis in *Juventus Mundi* continues to evoke some of the central themes of Gladstone's reflections during the 1830s.

I

The profoundest changes in the statesman's understanding of the poems arose on the topics of race and myth that filled the first two volumes of *Studies on Homer*. These themes, and particularly the depiction of the Olympian pantheon, were what had attracted most notice when the book appeared. Some periodicals, such as the *Athenaeum*, swallowed Gladstone's theory about the fragments of ancient

[8] *JM*, pp. vi, 431, 434. Nevertheless the term 'publicity' reappears in *Homer* (1878) at p. 113.
[9] *JM*, p. 449. Cf. Ch. 9, pp. 269–70.
[10] F. M. Turner, *The Greek Heritage in Victorian Britain* (New Haven, Conn., 1981), pp. 242–3.
[11] *JM*, pp. 393, 415.

revealed religion in Homer virtually whole.[12] Several ecclesiastical journals, such as the *Guardian* and the *English Churchman*, showed great sympathy for the idea of a division between traditive and inventive deities.[13] Many other reviewers, however, homed in on the contrast between the traditive and the inventive in order to question it. The distinction, according to the *National Review*, was arbitrary: 'We do not at all dogmatically deny that vestiges of patriarchal tradition may survive in the Hellenic mythology; but we do say, that a man cannot identify them by merely sitting down with his Homer on one side, and his Bible on the other.'[14] Gladstone pencilled a line against this sentence, no doubt recognizing a palpable hit. And the *Saturday Review* was roundly dismissive of 'one of the most extraordinary superstructures of religious speculation that our literature has ever produced'. Gladstone was guilty of 'mistaking a natural and universal instinct for a specific historical tradition'.[15] The statesman failed to carry conviction with a large number of his better-qualified readers.

There were two particularly devastating critiques. An anonymous reviewer in *The Times*, whom Gladstone admitted to be 'extremely clever',[16] censured him for the debating-style that made ridiculous theories seem respectable. His theological extravaganza, according to the reviewer, would find favour only with the clergy. The whole hypothesis about patriarchal tradition made very little allowance for the natural workings of the human mind, and it was reasonable to hold that true thoughts about God are possible without divine revelation. Although Gladstone's treatment of plot and character deserved praise, it was regrettable, concluded the reviewer, that on religious issues 'so much fertility should be fertility of words'.[17] *Blackwood's* published a similar line of argument by W. H. Smith—not the newsagent and politician but a leisured man of letters who had written the review of Grote's *History of Greece* that its author most admired.[18] Smith complained that Gladstone neglected Homer the artist for the sake of studying him as theologian. The statesman was revising 'a theory which we thought had passed away from the scholarship of the nineteenth century' that could be disproved by a single fact. The idea of creation was entirely absent from early Greek mythology. Surely so prominent a doctrine could not have been lost in transmission. The messianic element in Gladstone's hypothesis, furthermore, was particularly weak. Why, if Apollo was supposed to represent Christ, should he be just as indifferent as the other Olympian deities to the future destinies of men? The entire enterprise was mistaken because scholars such as Carl Otfried Müller had shown that the pagan gods were based on the phenomena of nature.[19] Like the contributor to *The*

---

[12] *Athenaeum*, 17 Apr. 1858, pp. 489–90, GGM 1636.
[13] *English Churchman*, 1 July 1858, p. 607; *Guardian*, [June 1858?], GGM 1636.
[14] *National Review*, July 1858, p. 54, GGM 1633.
[15] *Saturday Review*, 8 May 1858, pp. 473–4, GGM 1636.
[16] W. E. Gladstone to Lord Lyttelton, 19 Aug. 1858, GGM 35, f. 192v.
[17] *T*, 12 Aug. 1858, p. 7; 13 Aug. 1858, p. 5 (quoted).
[18] Harriet Grote, *The Personal Life of George Grote* (London, 1873), p. 231.
[19] [W. H. Smith], 'Gladstone's Homer', *Blackwood's Edinburgh Magazine*, 84 (1858), pp. 127–48, quoted at pp. 133, 143.

*Times*, Smith had understood Gladstone's intention of challenging the naturalistic interpretation of Greek religion but had found his case entirely unpersuasive. The explanation of Olympus in terms of the veneration of natural forces had become too widely accepted to be dislodged.

Gladstone's initial reaction to the critics was to maintain his position. The review in *The Times*, he told Lord Lyttelton, was 'just in those of its animadversions which may be called personal but I think quite self-contradictory & by no means weighty in its metal on the Homeric <u>question</u>'.[20] Yet over the decade that separated *Studies on Homer* from *Juventus Mundi* Gladstone paid renewed attention to the hypothesis that early religion arose from emotions evoked by the forces of nature. Among the intellectual influences that led him to view this interpretation with greater favour was the rise of the solar theory of ancient myth championed by Friedrick Max Müller, the holder of the Oxford chair of Modern European Languages from 1854. Max Müller's starting point was the demonstration by his mentor Franz Bopp of Berlin that the grammar and vocabulary of all the Indo-European languages had much in common.[21] Max Müller argued that the mythology conveyed by those languages also showed persistent characteristics. The gods and goddesses of each nation were personifications of natural phenomena described in the original Aryan tongue. The separate existence of the divinities was merely a 'disease of language', the decay over time of an appreciation of what their names had originally meant. Their significance, however, could be understood by tracing the divine names back to their linguistic roots. By that technique most features of myth could be explained by the changing appearance of the sun: 'I look upon the sunrise and sunset [he declared], on the daily return of day and night, on the battle between light and darkness, on the whole solar drama in all its details that is acted every day, every month, every year, in heaven and in earth as the principal subject of early mythology.'[22] The theory, which rapidly achieved something close to the status of orthodoxy, offered a sufficient explanation of the Greek pantheon. Zeus, for instance, bore a name resembling the Indo-European root meaning 'sky' and Apollo's epithet 'Delios' was held to signify 'bright one'.[23] The religion of ancient Greece was on this account a disguised species of nature worship.

Gladstone had read Max Müller's hypothesis, as propounded in an essay of 1856, during the preparation of *Studies on Homer*, and had followed it up by turning to Bopp's *Grammar*. He had consulted the professor in person at Oxford on philological points shortly afterwards.[24] When the first series of Max Müller's

[20]  W. E. Gladstone to Lord Lyttelton, 19 Aug. 1858, GGM 35, f. 192v.

[21]  H. H. Wilson, 'Preface', in Franz Bopp, *A Comparative Grammar of the Sanscrit, Zend, Greek, Latin, Lithuanian, Gothic, German and Sclavonic Languages*, trans. Lieut. Eastwick, 3 vols. (London, 1845–50), 1, pp. i–ii.

[22]  Friedrich Max Müller, *Lectures on the Science of Language*, 2 vols. [1861–4], 6th edn. (London, 1871), 2, p. 565.

[23]  Friedrich Max Müller, 'Comparative Mythology', in *Oxford Essays* (London, 1856), p. 45.

[24]  *D*, 22 Nov., 12–16 Dec. 1856; 16 Dec. 1856; 29, 30 Jan. 1857.

*Lectures on the Science of Language* (1861) appeared, Gladstone set them aside for careful summer reading.[25] The solar interpretation of myth was attractive on several scores. Like Gladstone's own approach to the subject, it rested on etymological analysis; it argued that, when left to itself, human spirituality had decayed rather than progressed; and it was stoutly hostile to Grote's dismissal of Greek myths as impenetrable flights of the imagination. Yet Max Müller equally rejected Gladstone's own standpoint: 'it seems blasphemy', wrote the professor, 'to consider these fables of the heathen world as corrupted and misinterpreted fragments of a divine revelation once granted to the whole of mankind.'[26] Gladstone wrestled to come to terms with Max Müller's approach in a memorandum of 1861. The bow and the arrows of Apollo, he mused, certainly seemed to represent the rays of the sun. So much so he was willing to concede to the solar hypothesis. Yet the fact that Apollo, with Artemis, was singled out in the pantheon as the possessor of any weapon at all accorded with 'the primitive and genuine tradition in which the prototype of Apollo was the Lord and saviour of the world'.[27] Apollo was still to be seen as a traditive deity rather than as nothing more than a personification of natural forces. In a lecture of 1865 Gladstone was able to insist, on the authority of Carl Otfried Müller, that in Homer's pages Apollo was not identified with the sun.[28] It was a point to which he returned in *Juventus Mundi* and several subsequent writings, for it was a principle that marked off his position from the solar theory.[29] Gladstone told the professor in a letter of 1864 that he could not 'accept in full the creed of the Dawn'.[30] He never became a disciple of Max Müller.

Nevertheless, remarkably, Gladstone was willing to say in the same letter that the whole of Max Müller's theory was 'in perfect consistency' with his own. That was because he was now willing to admit that 'the materials, out of which the Hellenic mythology grew or was constructed, were in great part supplied by some system or systems of nature worship'.[31] Gladstone had given up the contention that Greek religion did not derive from nature. It was a momentous concession. The rejection of the naturalistic interpretation had been the overriding motive for the whole Homeric enterprise. By establishing that Greek religion took its origin from revelation rather than from nature, from above rather than from below, Gladstone had hoped to defend the supernatural against the insidious subversion of Jowett and his allies. The most that the statesman had been willing to concede was that the worship of the elements had existed in the east; but, he had argued in *Studies on Homer*, the poet did not authorize the belief that 'a system of Nature-worship ever preceded in Greece the Olympian system'. Subsequently, however,

[25] *D*, 18 Feb., 4–19 Aug. 1862.                    [26] Max Müller, 'Comparative Mythology', p. 8.
[27] GP 44751, f. 264 (28 Dec. 1861).
[28] W. E. Gladstone, 'Place of Ancient Greece in the Providential Order' [1865], *Gleanings*, 7, p. 49 and n. C. O. Müller is eager to distinguish Apollo, as a Dorian god, from the deities associated with the elements worshipped by the agricultural races of Greece: C. O. Müller, *The History and Antiquities of the Doric Race*, trans. Henry Tufnell and G. C. Lewis, 2 vols. (Oxford, 1830), 1, pp. 308–13, 329.
[29] *JM*, p. 270.
[30] W. E. Gladstone to F. Max Müller, 28 Sept. 1864, GP 44251(2), f. 267v, in Max Müller, *Science of Language*, 2, p. 440 n.                    [31] Ibid., f. 269.

Gladstone marked this passage in his own copy with a cross, the sign of disagreement.[32] He had come to recognize that, as the weightiest of his reviewers had claimed, his previous position had been untenable. A manuscript jotting from the early 1860s reveals his mind in transition. The personification of the winds in the *Iliad*, he noted, is an instance of what could be called Greek nature worship. But because it consists merely of 'individual personifications not organised into a hierarchy' he still wanted to distinguish it from 'the oriental and orientalising systems which treat nature worship sympathetically'.[33] The veneration of natural forces remained something essentially alien to Greece. But by 1864, as the letter to Max Müller shows, he had reached the reluctant conclusion that the worship of the elements was at one time indigenous to Homer's own land. Pondering the Oxford professor's views seems to have been a contributory factor.

A second influence drawing Gladstone in the same direction was F. G. Welcker's three-volume *Griechische Götterlehre*, a thorough study of the Hellenic pantheon published at Göttingen between 1857 and 1863. Sir John Acton recommended it to Gladstone in a review of scholarly literature on pagan mythology as one of the two 'most comprehensive recent works on Greece'.[34] The hostile reviewer of *Studies on Homer* in *The Times* censured Gladstone for having missed Welcker at that stage.[35] The criticism was not entirely fair, since Volume 1 of the German work had appeared only in the previous year. Gladstone encountered it while revising the proofs of his book and added a note to his third volume explaining that he would have wished to use it had he discovered it earlier.[36] By the time the final volume of Welcker's book was published in 1863, Gladstone realized that to absorb it was a priority. He took it with him on holiday to Penmaenmawr on the north Welsh coast. He launched into the book on his first day of sea-bathing; he was still at work on it after his sixteenth dip; and when called away to be minister in attendance on the Queen at Balmoral he carried it with him.[37] Welcker's coverage is by no means confined to Homer, but his treatment is careful and systematic. He provides evidence that a high proportion of the inhabitants of Olympus were associated with natural phenomena. His first volume contains a section on nature gods in general before going on to catalogue them individually for nearly 400 pages.[38] The conclusion that nature worship once flourished in archaic Greece was virtually impossible to resist. Welcker, Gladstone noted in a memorandum written at Penmaenmawr, assumed a twofold origin for Greek mythology: the idea of God and the worship of nature. Although Gladstone put the emphasis on Welcker's vindication of the existence of an independent conception of God, the statesman offered no argument against the German's case for the pantheon deriving largely from natural

[32] *SHHA*, 2, p. 410, St Deiniol's Library, Hawarden.

[33] GP 44751, f. 267 (n.d., but with other MSS dated 1861).

[34] GP 44093, f. 4. The paper is endorsed by Gladstone: 'Sir John Acton Works on Paganism in its relation to Xty. circ. 1860'.          [35] *T*, 13 Aug. 1858, p. 5.

[36] *D*, 25 Feb. 1858. *SHHA*, 3, p. 5.          [37] *D*, 3–29 Sept. 1863.

[38] F. G. Welcker, *Griechische Götterlehre*, 3 vols. (Göttingen, 1857–63), 1, pp. 214–29, 298–676.

phenomena.[39] Gladstone showed respect for Welcker's opinions when he came to write *Juventus Mundi*. He cites the German as holding that Ares, the god of war, had gone through an earlier phase of evolution 'and that there are traces of him as a Nature-Power'.[40] Gladstone nowhere says as much, but it is clear that Welcker carried weight in persuading him to change his mind about the natural origins of Greek religion.

Another work that seems to have swayed Gladstone was *Albanian Studies* (1854), a treatise in German by Johann Georg von Hahn, who had resided for some time in the Albanian region as an Austrian consul. A learned tome was the result of his investigation of all aspects of the life of the local people. Gladstone selected the book for systematic summer reading before leaving Hawarden in August 1862, began it on the day of his second dip at Penmaenmawr that year and returned to it on the day of his twenty-ninth.[41] The work, he reported to Acton towards the end of his perusal, 'seems to me one of which a <u>good</u> <u>thick</u> account ought to be given in some periodical'.[42] Five years later, to Robert Scott at Oxford, he recalled that he 'learned a great deal from Hahn's Albanesische Studien'.[43] In *Juventus Mundi* Gladstone cites the book only on minor points, but goes out of his way in the preface to acknowledge his debt to Hahn's 'laborious and original treatise'.[44] The crucial principle of Hahn's work was that the modern Albanians represented the original Pelasgians of Greece with their simple rustic ways. The Hellic race had joined the Pelasgians, according to Hahn, and in the resulting creation of the Hellenic nation the Hellic language had prevailed—a point duly noted by Gladstone. The statesman could infer that, by analogy, Pelasgian spirituality could have contributed to the Hellenic faith without dominating it. Hahn had established to his own satisfaction that the Pelasgian religion was earth and nature worship. Probably, mused Gladstone, that would be so.[45] If it was true, then the adoration of natural forces that Gladstone had once excluded from Greece must have existed in archaic times. But subsequently it would have been incorporated in Homer's vision of the Olympian pantheon, though only in a subordinate role. That view, which Gladstone was to expound in his subsequent writings, may well have crystallized while reading Hahn by the sea at Penmaenmawr. Although the Austrian's point is made in an obscure footnote, it may well have been the decisive factor in swinging Gladstone in favour of a naturalistic explanation of religion in archaic Greece.

The chief intellectual stimulus to Gladstone's change of opinion between *Studies on Homer* and *Juventus Mundi*, however, was one that played a different part from Max Müller, Welcker, and Hahn. Whereas each of these works induced

---

[39] GP 44752, f. 327 (14 Sept. 1863).     [40] *JM*, p. 298. See also pp. 303, 327, 330.
[41] *D*, 8 Aug.–12 Sept. 1862.
[42] W. E. Gladstone to Sir John Acton, 9 Sept. 1862, GP 44093, f. 17v.
[43] W. E. Gladstone to Robert Scott, 2 Sept. 1867, SCO/1/11/26, Scott Papers, Pusey House, Oxford.
[44] *JM*, p. vi.
[45] J. G. von Hahn, *Albanesische Studien*, 3 vols. (Jena, 1854), 1, pp. 224, 276 n., 286. GP 44752, f. 132 (n.d.).

him to pay greater attention to the forces of nature as a contributory factor to Greek religion, the other book pointed him to the dimensions of Hellenic faith that kept the nature gods in a subordinate place. The book was *Daedalus*, a study of Greek sculpture by Edward Falkener. It was recommended by Roundell Palmer, a High Church Peelite whom Gladstone had known at Oxford and whom he was later to make his Lord Chancellor. Palmer was right in believing that Gladstone would enjoy the work, which he read carefully over the new year of 1861.[46] The author of *Daedalus* was a scholarly architect who later in the same year was to win a gold medal from the King of Prussia for his research in classical archaeology. Falkener's interests, like Gladstone's, extended to questions of liturgy and theology, embracing the proper mode of antiphonal singing and the Davidic authorship of the Psalms.[47] In *Daedalus* he toyed with establishing 'a Christian standard of ideal beauty', but a much stronger theme was the unfavourable contrast between the decadence of modern art and its excellence among the ancient Greeks. Why, he asked, were their achievements so superior? Falkener reviewed the explanations mentioned by classical writers, giving weight to popular applause for the creations of Greek artists and their powerful desire to do honour to their country. But above all other motives Falkener placed the religious sense. The sculptor 'did not look upon a statue merely as a fine work of art, but he regarded it also as embodying his religion'.[48] Perhaps the photographs of Greek sculpture included in the book, early examples of illustrations derived from the camera, made a particular impression on Gladstone's imagination. Whatever the reason, Falkener's linking of the art of ancient Greece to its mythology roused him to creative thinking.

The passage that most stimulated the statesman was one where the author contrasted ancient with later times. Whereas, wrote Falkener, 'the Greek believed his gods resided in human form, the modern artist is taught by his religion to despise earthly things, and to fix his regard on things of heaven'. Although the author did not dwell on this message, Gladstone marked the sentence with 'NB' in the margin of his copy. He indexed it at the back of the book, linking it with a seminal phrase used by Falkener elsewhere: 'anthropomorphic belief'.[49] The idea that understanding the divinities of Olympus in the shape of human beings was responsible for the finest of artistic attainments appealed powerfully to Gladstone. In his theological development, as Chapter 5 has shown, the doctrine of the incarnation was becoming the foundation for a high view of human potential.[50] Now Falkener seemed to be offering supportive evidence for the notion that the divine becoming human gave impetus to cultural achievement. What the architect

---

[46] W. E. Gladstone to Edward Falkener, 3 Jan. 1861 (copy), GP 44395, f. 16. *D*, 28 Dec. 1860–5 Jan. 1861.

[47] E[dward] F[alkener], *The Book of Psalms of David the King and Prophet* (London, 1875), p. 6; essay 1. *DNB*.

[48] Edward Falkener, *Daedalus: Or the Causes and Principles of the Excellence of Greek Sculpture* (London, 1860), pp. 48, 94 n.

[49] Ibid., pp. 54, 184, St Deiniol's Library, Hawarden.          [50] See Ch. 5, pp. 135–8.

described as the 'anthropomorphic' element in Greek religion was one of the explanations of the quality of Greek sculpture. Gladstone wanted to take the principle further. He dispatched a letter to Falkener, urging what he called a 'vital and central' point. 'I believe', he wrote, 'that the anthropophuism of the Greek religion was not only one among several causes of the extraordinary elevation of Greek Art, but was its characteristic and leading cause.' He explained that by 'anthropophuism' he meant 'the association between the Divine Nature & the human form', an idea over which the Greeks had 'a special custody for the instruction of after y[ea]rs'.[51] Falkener, unsurprisingly, did not grasp the force of Gladstone's last point, an allusion to the Greek preservation of primitive tradition about the incarnation, remarking in his reply that the pagans had striven upwards to depict the divine with qualities of spiritual excellence. But his answer concurred in Gladstone's view that 'the anthropomorphism of the Greeks' was the principal cause of the high attainments of their sculptors.[52] Gladstone's seminal idea was now stamped with the authority of an expert in the field. Although in his letter to Falkener the statesman used the word 'anthropophuism', the term that he had deployed in *Studies on Homer*, on the previous day he had penned a memorandum including, for the first time in his writings, Falkener's own term 'anthropomorphism' to describe the same phenomenon.[53] The adoption of Falkener's usage, which Gladstone was to maintain in *Juventus Mundi* and elsewhere, is an indication of the impact the book made on him.

Gladstone considered some of the implications of *Daedalus* in a densely packed memorandum written while he was reading the book. The ancient Greeks, through the inspiration of Olympian religion for their sculpture, had set a new standard in the representation of the human body. 'What the pattern of the Redeemer's holiness & virtue have [sic] done for the ethical type of man under the Gospel', explains Gladstone, 'that the anthropomorphism of their religion did for his physical type with the Greeks.'[54] This comment marks important developments in Gladstone's thinking. The suggestion that the artistic triumphs of ancient Greece resulted primarily from its system of belief, the proposal that Falkener soon confirmed in correspondence, is new here. In his book of 1858 Gladstone had celebrated 'the worship of beauty in Homer', but he had not connected it to the characteristics of the pantheon.[55] Now he is also willing to speculate whether there may have been a comparable stimulus to the Greek intellect from the anthropomorphic principle. At an earlier stage in his thought, probably while preparing *Studies on Homer*, he had supposed that whereas the influence of Christianity had percolated downwards from the realm of spirit through the intellect to the material sphere of art, in ancient Greece the flow of religious influence was upwards from the material, where it glorified the human body, to the intellect, where its achievements were marvellous but less outstanding, and it hardly penetrated to the spiritual dimension at all. The first

[51] Gladstone to Falkener, 3 Jan. 1861 (copy), ff. 16, 16v.
[52] Edward Falkener to W. E. Gladstone, 22 Jan. 1861, ff. 86, 85v.
[53] GP 44751, f. 260 (2 Jan. 1861).       [54] Ibid.       [55] *SHHA*, 3, pp. 401–9, quoted at p. 407.

pattern was the natural impact on culture of 'the religion of the God-man'; the second was the equally logical outcome of 'the religion of the man-God', that is 'man deified'.[56] The scheme of Greek religiosity, essentially bogus on that understanding, was woefully inadequate in its results. By 1861, however, Gladstone had drastically revised his estimate of the consequences for civilization of Greek religion. Now it brought benefits to the mind as well as to the artistic sphere. Now, furthermore, its genius was not seen as contrasting with the spirit of the Christian faith, but as possessing the same animating principle, the union of the human and divine. Falkener had pointed Gladstone to a stress on the cultural benefits deriving from the legacy of truth in ancient Greek religion.

Likewise Falkener's criticism of the contemporary artist for allowing heavenly things to eclipse earthly things sparked off a fresh train of thought in Gladstone's mind.[57] It reminded him of the world-denying tendencies in Puseyism against which he had been reacting during the 1850s.[58] The Greek legacy, he now realized, was the antidote to undue austerity. It was right that the arrival of the Christian faith in world history had established heavenly principles over human life, but 'some extreme applications of early Christianity' might have led to an unfortunate 'absorption of the other portions of his manifold nature'. The flight to the desert of the first monks, which the statesman no doubt had in mind, was hostile to the artistic and intellectual endeavour that the Creator required from the Christian world. Therefore, Gladstone surmised, it was the purpose of providence to counteract the ascetic developments. 'This was done with extraordinary effect by bringing on the scene of history, and placing at the head of civilisation, that Hellenic race which so far exceeded all others in the fulness & largeness of its map of human nature.' Ancient Greece provided the cultural leaven for the lump of Christian society. The pattern was familiar in the field of philosophy: 'what is this', asked Gladstone, 'but to generalise what we already know of the workings of Aristotle and Plato on Christianised man[?]'[59] A flowering of modern civilization was not to be expected from undiluted religiosity. There must be attention not only to the laws of God but also to the claims of humanity in all its diversity. The religious zeal of Hebraism, as Matthew Arnold was to teach in his essays of the 1860s and 1870s, must be balanced by the reflective temper of Hellenism.[60] The seed of this major theme, so far as Gladstone was concerned, seems to have been sown while the statesman was reading Falkener.

II

The first fruits of the public harvest appeared in Gladstone's closing address to the students as Lord Rector of the University of Edinburgh in 1865. The lecture,

---

[56] GP 44746, ff. 198–8v (n.d., but tentatively dated as possibly 1856 by a librarian).
[57] Falkener, *Daedalus*, p. 184.                    [58] See Ch. 5, pp. 136–7, 138–9.
[59] GP 44751, f. 261.
[60] Supremely in Matthew Arnold, *Culture and Anarchy* (London, 1869), ch. 4.

which, though drastically curtailed in delivery, lasted about two hours, took as its subject the 'Place of Ancient Greece in the Providential Order'. Its undoubted obscurities did not prevent its being 'cheered vociferously for several minutes'.[61] The lecture was a panegyric on the 'anthropomorphic genius of the Hellenic religion'.[62] Gladstone had prepared by means of what he one day called 'very various relative reading', and so the address reflects the material he had been gradually digesting over several years rather than any particular fresh influence.[63] In a footnote to the published text Gladstone calls attention to Grote's testimony to anthropomorphism under the name of the universal 'tendency to personification'. It was less an acknowledgement of intellectual indebtedness than the typical Gladstonian technique of drawing support from an opponent. The statesman also alludes to John Ruskin's 'striking observations' on the same subject.[64] Gladstone is no doubt referring to a passage in the chapter 'Of Classical Landscape' in Ruskin's *Modern Painters*, volume 3, which he had looked at in 1856. Although Ruskin sympathetically defends the conception of 'divine power clothed with human form', there is little distinctive about his position for Gladstone to echo.[65] The true origin of the new prominence of anthropomorphism in his thought is mentioned in another footnote. Falkener's *Daedalus* is quoted as the source for an incidental point about homosexuality. Two references to Greek sculptors in the text reveal the same influence.[66] The reading of *Daedalus* lay behind the Edinburgh lecture.

Its grand theme was the beneficial example of ancient Greek civilization. Its distinction flowed from the '*idée mère* of the Greek religion, the annexation of manhood to deity'. The consequent exaltation of all things human, Gladstone assured his audience, was specially marked in the Homeric period. It generated a reverence for human life and human nature, the *aidos* of the Greeks that embraced 'the highest refinements of feeling which belong to the gentleman'. The inhuman was banished: human sacrifice, incest, polygamy, cannibalism, infant exposure, and homosexual practice. Even caricature, to which the Chancellor of the Exchequer seems to have been particularly sensitive at the time, was unknown to the Greeks. In their place were admiration of personal beauty and respect for the status of women. Divorce, for example, was less acceptable among the Greeks of the heroic age than under the law of Moses. Penelope's patient attachment to her husband in the *Odyssey* and the attractive depiction of Hector and Andromache in the *Iliad*, illustrating 'the moral equality of man and wife', gave further evidence of high esteem for women. Apart from art, philosophy could blossom because the human element was so prominent in the Hellenic mind. Hence Socrates propounded 'as the prime subject for the study of man, the nature, constitution, and destiny of man himself'.[67] The dignity attached to

[61] *Scotsman*, 4 Nov. 1865, p. 7.                    [62] Gladstone, 'Place of Ancient Greece', p. 92.
[63] *D*, 18 Sept. 1865.                               [64] Gladstone, 'Place of Ancient Greece', p. 92.
[65] John Ruskin, *Modern Painters, Volume III* [1856] (London, n.d.), p. 189. *D*, 20 Mar. 1856.
[66] Gladstone, 'Place of Ancient Greece', pp. 57, 72, 95.            [67] Ibid., pp. 59, 65, 73.

human beings as such could be demonstrated from the story in Pausanias of the person in Thasos who, after the death of his enemy, was killed by the fall of his enemy's statue. The sons of the victim prosecuted the statue, it was condemned under a law of Draco and it was thrown into the sea. So sacred, concluded Gladstone, was human life. That principle pervaded the whole of Greek culture.

This feature of Hellenism existed for a purpose. It was designed, according to Gladstone, to operate as a corrective—'I will not say to act as a corrective to Christianity, but to act as a corrective to the narrow views' that might be associated with Christianity.[68] True religion might lapse into a constricting other-worldliness. Remarkably, Gladstone concurs in Rousseau's critique of Christianity as potentially subversive of this-worldly interests: 'I know nothing more opposed to the social spirit.'[69] What Gladstone had in mind was the tendency of 'those various forms of self-restraint and self-conquest . . . to establish the supremacy of the soul, by trampling upon sense, and appetite, and all corporal existence'.[70] The ascetic temper had already invaded the church in New Testament times and, as the freethinker W. E. H. Lecky had just shown in his *Rise and Influence of the Spirit of Rationalism in Europe* (1865), had induced 'thousands upon thousands of anchorites' to renounce the world in the Egyptian desert.[71] Such repression was an exaggeration of the proper Christian attitude. There must instead be a balanced view in which the claims of the body were not ignored. Gladstone's high regard for the physical is striking in this address. Greek education, he declared, recognized 'the right of the body to be cared for'; the Greek heroes recoiled in horror from the thought of the exposure of a corpse. Christian thinkers had often failed to give a proper place to the human body, but the Greeks had found 'a place for the body in the philosophy of human nature'. It was essential to reject any contempt for the physical. Rather, a Christian philosophy must be nourished that did not set the faith apart from embodied existence. There must be no 'Christianity of isolation'. What Gladstone was recalling, as in the memorandum of 1861, was his own Puseyite phase when the battle against sin loomed so large that other concerns had been eclipsed. The type of Christianity required, he now wrote, was one 'filled with human and genial warmth'.[72] The address was the fruit of Gladstone's debate with his old self. The study of Homer had enlarged his mind and freed his spirit. That was why he recommended Hellenism to others.

The Edinburgh lecture of 1865 therefore represents a public statement of a major change in Gladstone's point of view about the significance of ancient Greece. In the lecture, however, he does not announce the other chief alteration in his opinions. He continues to resist the naturalistic interpretation of strands in

---

[68] Ibid., p. 81.

[69] J. J. Rousseau, *The Social Contract*, bk. 4, ch. 8, ed. Maurice Cranston, Harmondsworth, 1968, p. 182. The translation is the version quoted by Gladstone ('Place of Ancient Greece', p. 84).

[70] Gladstone, 'Place of Ancient Greece', p. 84.

[71] W. E. H. Lecky, *History of the Rise and Influence of the Spirit of Rationalism in Europe*, 2 vols. (London, 1865), 2, p. 28, cited in ibid., p. 96.

[72] Gladstone, 'Place of Ancient Greece', pp. 74–5, 75, 88, 89.

Greek religion. He still speaks of the worship of nature contributing only to 'the old religions, outside of Greece and the Greek races'.[73] The open acknowledge-ment of the validity of his opponents' hypothesis did not emerge until the publi-cation of *Juventus Mundi* in 1869. There he admits that the Homeric pantheon, as much as other species of paganism, derived not only from deified men, personi-fied passions, and distorted copies of primitive revelation but also from 'the powers of external nature'. The concession is clearly reluctant. He immediately insists that the Olympian system was 'profoundly adverse to mere Nature-worship'; that the great forces of nature were assigned to leading members of the pantheon rather than to their simple impersonations; and that such worship of the elemental powers as did exist was 'in general local or secondary'.[74] Although he does not wish to advertise the fact, he had shifted his ground. In one respect, however, he frankly avows his change of approach. In *Studies on Homer*, he explains, he had applied the term 'Secondaries' to deities subordinate, even in their own sphere, to Apollo and Athene, the chief bearers of the messianic idea. The description had wrongly implied that gods such as Paieon, a healer less powerful than Apollo, had no independent traditions of their own.[75] Gladstone had previously relegated the 'Secondaries' to the inventive category, but now recognized that the line between that group and the traditive divinities was by no means as sharp as he had supposed. The antithesis between the inventive and the traditive disappears altogether in *Juventus Mundi*. All members of the pantheon are held to have had diverse origins. His previous understanding of Homer's gods and goddesses had been mistaken.

Yet Gladstone was not abandoning his allegiance to the theory of a revelation at the start of human history. In *Juventus Mundi* he airily mentions, as though describing the scholarly consensus, the traditions 'which we are justly wont to refer to a primitive revelation as their fountain-head'.[76] In planning the revision of *Studies on Homer*, he had even intended to present fresh evidence in favour of this notion. He toyed with conjecturing that the divine ancestry of certain mortals in Homer's pages was rooted in 'ideas really pure and primitive' (he originally wrote 'primit. traditions').[77] Gladstone persists in believing that the original divine disclosure contained Christian specifics such as the doctrine of the Trinity. In *Juventus Mundi* Gladstone actually adds the speculation that Poseidon's char-acteristic symbol of the trident is the legacy of 'some tradition of the Trinity'. The trident, he argues, is 'so unsuited to water' that it must possess a more arcane significance—though he ruefully concedes in a footnote that John Ludlow, the barrister and Christian socialist, had reported observing similar iron forks used for harpooning in the Mediterranean.[78] The peculiar treatment of Iris, the messenger-goddess between Olympus and humanity, is also explained by

---

[73] Gladstone, 'Place of Ancient Greece', p. 55.                    [74] *JM*, p. 204.
[75] Ibid., p. 276.                                                  [76] Ibid., p. 209.
[77] GP 44691, f. 62 (n.d., but in material labelled by Gladstone as having been assembled for the revision in 1867).                                          [78] *JM*, pp. 245 n., 250.

Gladstone's continuing commitment to the theory of primitive revelation. Her name, he points out, is also the Greek for rainbow, and in Genesis the rainbow is a sign of the covenant between God and humanity. Homer's goddess and the symbol in Genesis, he triumphantly concludes, both bridge the gulf between heaven and earth and so must be drawn 'from the same early source'. Her dignity as a participant in ancient tradition means, according to Gladstone, that Homer wishes to mark her separation from lesser figures. She declines to feast with the Winds because she has to join a banquet provided for the immortals elsewhere. 'This want of time', Gladstone quaintly explains, 'is evidently an excuse devised by good manners . . .'[79] The reality is that Iris, as a higher deity, will not stoop to the company of mere agents of nature. The whole fanciful interpretation rests not on textual evidence but on Gladstone's supposition that the goddess shows particular marks of authentic religion. Gladstone's literary judgement was entirely subordinated to his apologetic purpose.

As in *Studies on Homer*, the case made out in *Juventus Mundi* for an affinity between the Greek poet and Hebrew tradition rests primarily on the presence of messianic ideas in Homer. Athene (who had been called Minerva in *Studies on Homer*)[80] and Apollo are again discussed together and at length because they embody aspects of the incarnate Son of God who was to come. Both, though they are junior deities, share in the prerogatives of Zeus, the supreme god. Both are regarded by mortals with greater reverence than Zeus, yet both enjoy his special affection: 'These alone he calls by the epithet "dear".' Athene, apparently born of Zeus without a mother, is the only exception in the poems to 'the accustomed method of parentage'.[81] Here, Gladstone suggests, is evidence for the survival among the Greeks of the tradition of the Logos, or Word, of God that emerges in the gospel of John. This was the passage in *Juventus Mundi* that even the sympathetic Robert Scott at Balliol found hardest to accept. 'Are not', he asked Gladstone when the book had come out, 'the words used of "the tradition of the Logos" likely to be understood in a sense inconsistent with the age of Homer?'[82] Scott's sense of anachronism was livelier than Gladstone's because the statesman retained his belief that the central ideas of the New Testament, having been disclosed at the dawn of history, were in circulation in Homer's day. Christian Schöttgen's case about the persistence of Hebrew expectations of the messiah still bolstered Gladstone's view of the valid religious traditions that must have been upheld by Jew and Gentile alike.[83] They included the prediction in Genesis of the Seed of the Woman who would be the saviour of humanity. Since Apollo represented the messianic hope, Gladstone still treats his mother Leto (called Latona in *Studies on Homer*) as equivalent to 'the Woman, of whose seed the Deliverer of

[79]  Ibid., pp. 331, 332. The same interpretation had been offered at *SHHA*, 2, p. 156.

[80]  Whereas in *Studies on Homer* Gladstone retained the traditional custom of referring to Greek deities under their Latin names, in *Juventus Mundi* he went over to the more recent practice of using their Greek names.                                                          [81]  *JM*, pp. 269, 272.

[82]  Robert Scott to W. E. Gladstone, 16 Oct. 1869, GP 44295, f. 381v.

[83]  *JM*, p. 203 n.

mankind was to come'.[84] Gladstone concedes nothing to Matthew Arnold's jibe about his speculations around the goddess. The statesman remains convinced that Homer testifies to the tradition of a coming messiah.

So the transformation of Gladstone's theory did not lie in any weakening of his undergirding belief in a primitive revelation. Rather, it consisted in the admission that the chief alternative view of early religion, the naturalistic hypothesis, applied to Greece after all. If that was so, however, Gladstone had to explain how Olympian religion could bear witness to revealed truth. Why was the stream of supernatural truth not so polluted by refuse from natural sources as to be utterly impure? The answer lay in the power of anthropomorphism, 'that principle which . . . casts the divine life into human forms'.[85] Gladstone had discussed this facet of the poems' theology in *Studies on Homer*, even at one point seeing it as the force that kept the worship of elemental powers in a secondary place.[86] In the older book, however, that function was not emphasized. Instead he claimed that anthropophuism, his earlier term for anthropomorphism, had 'obtruded into the sphere of deity'.[87] The language implied that the human was an alien element, not properly at home in the divine realm. In *Juventus Mundi*, however, 'anthropomorphism' has almost entirely favourable implications. It is the principle that dignifies human life by associating it with the divine, the idea that represents the doctrine of the incarnation. It is what prevented nature worship from ruining the religion of Homer. The 'anthropomorphic force', Gladstone had told Max Müller in 1864, 'left the traditions of the old <u>cultus</u> of nature to take refuge in the recesses of Arcadia'.[88] The depiction of the divine agents as human beings relegated the older nature worship to the margins of the supernatural cosmology. Homer, Gladstone suggests, normally treats nature gods as subterranean; and their veneration was limited to particular localities.[89] The worship of physical phenomena was altogether peripheral. In place of the old antithesis between the inventive and the traditive, Gladstone postulates in *Juventus Mundi* an antithesis between the natural and the anthropomorphic. It was the anthropomorphic element that was the dynamic genius of Homeric religion, keeping the natural in its subordinate place.

The antithesis between the natural and the anthropomorphic corresponded to another, that between the Pelasgian and the Hellenic peoples. It was a familiar ethnic distinction, elaborated by B. G. Niebuhr and deployed extensively in *Studies on Homer*. But in that previous work Gladstone had not admitted that the Pelasgians, the earlier inhabitants of Greece, were worshippers of nature. On the contrary, they were sometimes treated as conveyors of authentic primeval traditions.[90] By the writing of *Juventus Mundi*, however, Gladstone is willing to concede that there existed an 'old Pelasgian Nature-worship'. The Pelasgians, in

---

[84] *JM*, p. 260.      [85] Ibid., p. 232.      [86] *SHHA*, 2, p. 407.      [87] Ibid., p. 174.
[88] W. E. Gladstone to F. Max Müller, 28 Sept. 1864, GP 44251(2), f. 269v; in Max Müller, *Science of Language*, 2, p. 440 n., where 'nature' is given an initial capital.      [89] *JM*, pp. 190–1.
[90] *SHHA*, 1, p. 144.

fact, are specially associated with the adoration of elemental forces while the
Hellenes alone are accorded the honour of transmitting the authentic deposit of
faith from the remote past.[91] Recollections of the promise of the incarnation blossomed among them into the anthropomorphic principle. Consequently in
*Juventus Mundi* there is a revision of the analysis of various gods and goddesses so
as to ensure that the polarity between nature worship and the Pelasgians on the
one hand and anthropomorphism and the Hellenes on the other is sustained. In
*Studies on Homer* Persephone is said to have been originally 'only Hellic';[92] but in
*Juventus Mundi* she is described as partly Pelasgic and not at all Hellic. That is
because, as queen of the underworld, she presided over the realm where, on
Gladstone's new hypothesis, 'all the Pelasgic Nature-Powers had been disposed
of'.[93] Likewise the river Scamander, according to *Studies on Homer*, may have
owed its deification among the Trojans to Hellic influences;[94] but in *Juventus
Mundi* this supposition is roundly excluded. The treatment of the river is called
'an indication, which cannot be mistaken, that a Nature-worship, alien to the
Olympian system, prevailed in Troas'.[95] Gladstone nowhere draws attention to
the difference of approach in the two books, but the details bear witness to a
significant shift of ground. The nature worship of the Pelasgians, though no
longer denied, is consistently deprecated in the later work, and there is a corresponding exaltation of the anthropomorphism of the Hellenes.

The content of Olympian religion is celebrated in *Juventus Mundi* precisely
because the human part in it is so large. In the previous book the human dimension of the pantheon, as we saw in Chapter 6, was normally associated with the
inventive faculty that had sapped the valid inherited traditions.[96] The spirit of
anthropophuism was responsible for debasing the originally pure idea of God
with shameful carnality. In *Juventus Mundi*, by contrast, the anthropomorphic
principle is normally an ennobling force. It is true that Gladstone still believed
that the 'humanitarian element' in the pantheon, since it contained 'the ideas,
passions and appetites known to us all', carried the seeds of 'a profound corruption'. Nevertheless the prevailing note in the later book is respect for the anthropomorphic character of Greek religion that 'associated it so closely with the whole
detail of life'.[97] The treatment of Heré, the consort of Zeus, is a case in point.
Whereas in *Studies on Homer* she had been no more than a nebulous goddess of
motherhood, artificially paired with Zeus for the sake of symmetry, in *Juventus
Mundi* she is presented as a personified version of the all-producing earth, who,
under the influence of the anthropomorphic spirit of Olympian religion, is
'detached from gross matter' to assume 'the queenly prerogative' and become 'the
mother in heaven'.[98] The tone of Gladstone's discussion of Heré is entirely different in the two books. In the first there is said to be a 'want of positive and distinct
attributes in the goddess';[99] in the second she is praised as 'the goddess of all

---

[91] *JM*, pp. 180, 288.      [92] *SHHA*, 2, p. 224.        [93] *JM*, p. 309.        [94] *SHHA*, 3, p. 159.
[95] *JM*, p. 453.        [96] See Ch. 6, p. 176.        [97] *JM*, pp. 181–2, 288.        [98] *JM*, p. 240.
[99] *SHHA*, 2, p. 198. The goddess is called Juno here.

motherhood on earth'.[100] Distaste for an invented deity has given way to a warm appreciation of a character bound up with the everyday life of human beings.

The analysis of Zeus himself reveals a similar contrast between the two books. His character, according to *Studies on Homer*, is 'the most repulsive in the whole circle of Olympian life' because of 'the large intrusion of the human and carnal element into the ethereal sphere'.[101] Fallen humanity so tainted the supreme god as to account for the atheism of the later philosophical school of the Epicureans.[102] Although Gladstone admits that Homer's Zeus reflects the authentic tradition of a personal providence, the supreme god generally exercises that role in a remote fashion very different from that of other divinities who appear in immediate contact with mortal affairs.[103] The picture in *Juventus Mundi* is much more sympathetic. Now Zeus is seen as a merger of an old Pelasgian sky god with an expression of ancient theistic belief. The human element achieves a reconciliation between the nature power and residual traces of the truth about the Almighty and so is no longer a debasing force. Homer's depiction of Zeus has 'grandeur'; the god is 'the moral governor of the world'; his providential role is no longer contrasted unfavourably with that of other divinities.[104] Censure now tends to be understated, even laughably so: 'the individual character of Zeus', remarks Gladstone, 'is of a far lower order than his public capacity would lead us to expect.'[105] The god's pursuit of his own pleasures recalls Shakespeare's Falstaff rather than anything more depraved. Gladstone has come round to approving of joviality, for it is a quality taken from life. The 'humanising or anthropomorphic element', the statesman concludes, makes Zeus 'the masterpiece of the Homeric mythology'.[106] Gladstone has changed his mind about the category of the human, which now earns his benediction.

The alterations surrounding the acknowledgement of natural origins for parts of Greek religion and the enhancement of the human role within the pantheon were not the only substantial modifications of Gladstone's theory in *Juventus Mundi*. A second cluster of changes related to foreign influence on the Greek theo-mythology. The statesman himself, as we have already seen, had qualms about the Persian proposal even before *Studies on Homer* appeared in print.[107] In his own copy of the book, Gladstone put a cross against his theory that Persia was probably the cradle of Achilles' family.[108] In *Juventus Mundi* the Persian hypothesis virtually disappears. Although at one point Gladstone comments that the Persian race may have contributed an element to the formation of the Greek nation, there is no further discussion of the link and at another point he admits that it is impossible to trace the route by which the legacy of original revelation reached the Greeks.[109] Nevertheless he wishes to retain the diffusionist model according to which ideas, rather than springing up independently in various places, spread out gradually from their initial locations to fresh lands. Assuming

[100] *JM*, p. 240.     [101] *SHHA*, 2, p. 186.     [102] Ibid. p. 190.     [103] Ibid. pp. 176–8.
[104] *JM*, p. 223.     [105] Ibid., p. 233.     [106] Ibid., p. 234.     [107] See Ch. 6, p. 167.
[108] *SHHA*, 2, p. 452, St Deiniol's Library, Hawarden.     [109] *JM*, pp. 200, 310.

that the descendants of Noah receiving the primitive revelation dwelt somewhere in the Middle East, Gladstone frequently postulates an eastern origin for aspects of Greek religion. The east, in fact, often figures as a third possible source, alongside the Pelasgians and the Hellenes, for the characteristics of the divinities. Persephone, for example, is associated in *Juventus Mundi* not only with Pelasgian nature powers but also with the east, because in Homer the entrance to her realm of the underworld lay in that direction. She is therefore 'a mixture of Pelasgic and of Eastern traditions'.[110] In the years from the 1860s onwards Gladstone was constantly hunting for indications of sources of eastern cultural influence and channels by which they were transmitted to ancient Greece.

One candidate for attention was India. Ever since, in the late eighteenth century, Sir William Jones had examined the affinities of Hindu with classical mythology, India had appeared a likely origin of Greek beliefs.[111] In Gladstone's day Max Müller's insistence on Vedic origins for western myths kept the question of Indian influence open, Lord Acton cautioning Gladstone about too ready an acquiescence as late as the 1880s.[112] In 1862, while exploring the issue of the early history of priesthood, Gladstone looked at Friedrich Creuzer's *Symbolik* (1810–23), a massive study from the heyday of German romanticism that, like Max Müller's writings, postulated India as the source of Greek religion.[113] Gladstone was not attracted by the German's central hypothesis that pure Indian traditions had been deliberately debased into myths to satisfy the ignorant Greeks, though in *Juventus Mundi* he did consider a suggestion of Creuzer that might cast light on the shadowy deity Aïdoneus.[114] Seven years later Gladstone was more powerfully tempted by the ideas of Louis Jacolliot, a French author who proposed that other religions, including Christianity, were derived from India.[115] Eager to complete *Juventus Mundi* but preoccupied with Irish disestablishment, the statesman accosted Max Müller in a London street to ask why he had not publicized Jacolliot's wonderful discoveries of parallels between the Old Testament and the sacred books of the Brahmins. Max Müller was cutting, both in the street and in a subsequent letter: the book was 'beneath criticism'.[116] Chastened yet diplomatic, Gladstone inserted a footnote in *Juventus Mundi* explaining that 'the general propositions of M. Jacolliot's work are not sufficiently restrained and circumspect

---

[110] Ibid., p. 309.

[111] Garland Cannon, *The Life and Mind of Oriental Jones: Sir William Jones, the Father of Modern Linguistics* (Cambridge, 1990), pp. 296–7.

[112] Lord Acton to W. E. Gladstone, 17 Feb. [1884?], GP 44093, f. 244. Gladstone had sent Acton a work by Max Müller, probably *India: What Can It Teach Us?* (London, 1883), which he had himself read on 20 January 1883.

[113] Friedrich Creuzer, *Symbolik und Mythologie der Alter Völker besonders der Griechen*, 6 vols. (Leipzig, 1810–23). D, 10–11 Aug. 1862. Sir John Acton to W. E. Gladstone, 7 Aug. [1862], GP 44093, f. 10.

[114] Burton Feldman and R. D. Richardson, *The Rise of Modern Mythology, 1680–1860* (Bloomington, Ind., 1972), p. 387. *JM*, p. 255.

[115] Louis Jacolliot, *La bible dans l'Inde* (Paris, 1869). D, 18 Apr. 1869.

[116] F. Max Müller to W. E. Gladstone, 9 July [1869], GP 44251, f. 350 (wrongly identified as 1873). Printed in *The Life and Letters of the Rt. Hon. Friedrich Max Müller*, edited by his wife, 2 vols. (London, 1902), 1, p. 368.

at once to inspire confidence in his judgments'.[117] Gladstone never developed an Indian hypothesis as an alternative to the Persian one that he had discarded, but it is plain that he was willing to be attracted by the possibility.

In *Juventus Mundi*, however, he did develop a hypothesis relating to the Phoenicians. Already in *Studies on Homer* he had postulated that this people, the great seafaring merchants of the Mediterranean world, had transmitted much of the geographical information of the *Odyssey*.[118] He seems to have drawn the germ of the idea from J. W. Blakesley's commentary on Herodotus, published in 1854, which he absorbed in 1857.[119] Subsequently the eloquent pages of Ernest Renan's *Mission de Phénicie* (1864–7) persuaded him that, in a larger sense, the Phoenicians were the schoolmasters of the Greeks.[120] The 'connection of Phoenicia with Greece', he told Acton in 1867, 'I now suppose to be much more considerable in importance than is generally supposed'.[121] Gladstone's exaggeration of the Phoenician role may be excused when it is appreciated that he mistakenly associated the seafarers with the Minoan civilization of Crete, which the twentieth century showed to be a taproot of Hellenic culture. After consulting Max Müller and Henry Liddell, Dean of Christ Church, Gladstone published in January 1868 an article arguing for the strength of the relationship between Phoenicia and Greece. The god Poseidon, he argued, was by no means to be identified with the sea in Homer, but rather represented an imported Phoenician deity; the distinctive mythology of the outer geography of the *Odyssey* reflected the beliefs of the maritime people; and certain families appearing in Homer seemed to be immigrants from Phoenicia.[122] *Juventus Mundi* takes up the theme, pointing out in its preface that the prominence of the Phoenicians is a change since *Studies on Homer*. Engaged as he was in extensive Irish reading as background to his legislative programme, Gladstone ventured the suggestion that the third recorded invasion of Ireland was by a Greek people of Phoenician extraction.[123] Although Gladstone attributed many artistic benefits to the Phoenician influence, the main reason for stressing their achievement is brought out in relation to the links between Hebraic traditions and Homeric theo-mythology. Even though, according to Gladstone, the nature of the connections was uncertain, the Phoenician navigators, in touch at once with Jews and Greeks, offered 'the natural and probable explanation of such phenomena'.[124] In the phase of his thought represented by *Juventus Mundi*, Gladstone credited to the Phoenicians—albeit tentatively—the exalted mission he had once assigned to the Persians.

[117] *JM*, p. 343 n.                                                    [118] *SHHA*, 3, p. 251.

[119] J. W. Blakesley (ed.), *Herodotus with a Commentary*, 2 vols. (London, 1854). *D*, 9 Jan. 1857. W. E. Gladstone to Lord Lyttelton, 2 Sept. 1857, GGM 35, ff. 183–3v.

[120] J. E. Renan, *Mission de Phénicie*, 3 vols. (Paris, 1864–7). *D*, 6 Sept. 1867.

[121] W. E. Gladstone to Sir John Acton, 9 Nov. 1867, GP 44093, f. 64 (copy).

[122] [W. E. Gladstone], 'Phoenicia and Greece', *Quarterly Review*, 124 (1868). *D*, 31 Dec. 1867. F. Max Müller to W. E. Gladstone, 5 Jan. [1868], GP 44251, ff. 284–5.

[123] *JM*, pp. v–vi, 136.                                               [124] Ibid., p. 200.

The new hypothesis raised more problems than it solved. A review of *Juventus Mundi* by James Bryce, the acclaimed author of *The Holy Roman Empire* (1864) who was about to become Regius Professor of Civil Law at Oxford, drew attention to the salience of the Phoenicians in the book. Gladstone, Bryce ambiguously remarked, had 'expended even more than his wonted acumen in detecting the action of a Phoenician influence on the religion and the arts of the Hellenes'.[125] The statesman had been successful in discovering fresh traces of the seafarers' impact, but he seemed inclined to attribute too great a share to the Phoenicians as the moulders of Greek religion. Surely, according to Bryce, Poseidon was a nature power, and not, as Gladstone claimed, a Phoenician import. It was unclear, Bryce justifiably complained, how far the messianic traditions were supposed to derive from the same source. If that was being maintained, the hypothesis faced the difficulty that the Phoenicians were antagonistic to the Jewish religion.[126] Gladstone was himself conscious that the anthropomorphic component of Hebrew traditions sat uneasily with the religion of the Phoenicians.[127] This people seemed to be linked with the worship of Aphrodite, a character 'odious on the side of lawless indulgence', 'Dionusos', a god praised by drunken women, and the Oxen of the Sun, mere brute beasts.[128] Hence the Phoenicians were responsible for blatantly immoral features of the cult together with the veneration of animals, which Gladstone scorned as debased. It appeared incongruous to see the seafaring people as those who transmitted to Greece the substance of divine revelation. To the admission that the forces of nature were worshipped in archaic Greece, Gladstone added the contention that ancient Greek religion contained elements of rampant idolatry derived from Phoenicia. How could he nevertheless argue that the pages of Homer bore witness to revealed truth?

The answer was to exalt the poet himself as the creator of a synthesis that kept the veneration of the natural and animal worlds in their place. Gladstone argued, for instance, that Pelasgian river worship was incorporated into Hellenic religiosity, but in a strictly subordinate role. Homer's 'plastic powers as a poet' had forged a new theo-mythology. He it was who 'acquired a vast command of materials, and by his skilful use of them exercised an immense influence in the construction of the Greek religion'. It is true that Gladstone, in a manner typical of those who had absorbed German romantic thinking, treats the poet's individual role as secondary to the corporate spirit of 'the people', *das Volk*, in generating their thought-world. 'In this process of construction', he writes, 'the actual belief, traditions, and tendencies of the people could not but be the chief determining force.' But immediately the statesman goes on to claim that Homer exerted a greater influence than 'any ever wielded by any other Greek, whether legislator, poet, or philosopher'—which includes even Aristotle.[129] Homer's part was infinitely greater than that of Hesiod, whose later *Theogony* narrated the

---

[125] [James Bryce], 'Mr. Gladstone on Homer', *Macmillan's Magazine*, 21 (1869), p. 31.
[126] Ibid., pp. 33, 34.        [127] *JM*, p. 202.        [128] Ibid., 314–15, 319, 322–3.
[129] Ibid., pp. 176, 179, 192.

genealogy of the gods. Hesiod's poem, announces Gladstone with a sniff of contempt, 'could have no other influence, than a register of births and deaths could have upon the social and political fortunes of a community'. Hesiod is denigrated in order to exalt Homer. The contrast between the two reveals, according to Gladstone, 'the immense power with which the imagination of Homer operated'.[130] The earliest Greek poet, Gladstone told Max Müller in 1864, was, like Aquinas, a maker of theology.[131] By the 1860s Gladstone envisaged Homer as occupying a much higher rank than in the previous decade.

The poet was not only the creator of a religion, for he was also the maker of his nation. Homer lived, according to Gladstone, 'in the midst of an intermixture and fusion of bloods continually proceeding in Greece'.[132] The various elements, Pelasgian, Hellenic, and Phoenician, were slowly being welded into a unity. The Trojan War may have begun the process by giving the Greek tribes a single aim, but Homer supplied the ideological glue. Thus the catalogue of the armies in the second book of the *Iliad* 'implies a purpose with reference to a nation'; and Heré, the most national of the deities, single-mindedly pursues 'the glorification of the Greeks'.[133] Gladstone believed that the poet indulged in elaborate literary subterfuge to achieve his synthesizing purpose. In Book 18 of the *Iliad*, the poet described Thetis as being attended by no fewer than thirty-three named nymphs when she goes to comfort her son Achilles, the hero of the epic. Thetis is the daughter of Nereus, an elemental divinity from the Pelasgian system; but the names of the nymphs are nearly all purely Hellenic. Homer's objective, Gladstone concludes, must have been to graft Hellenic associations on to a Pelasgian root 'in order to <u>nationalise</u> Thetis'.[134] Furthermore in order to avoid compromising the Greek sense of nationality, according to the statesman, the poet scrupulously avoids all reference to the foreign origin of his themes. That is why indebtedness to the Phoenicians is never avowed in the poems. This aspect of the case had all the weaknesses of an argument from silence; and Bryce pointed out in his review that this contention was incompatible with the absence from Homer of the later sharp distinction between Greeks and barbarians.[135] Nevertheless Gladstone's overall doctrine bears some resemblance to the more recent scholarly orthodoxy that Homer's Olympian religion is a symptom of emerging panhellenism.[136] Although Gladstone was depicting the poet as an exponent of his favourite theme of religious nationality, it was entirely reasonable for him to see the Homeric blend of different religious traditions as the foundation of Greek self-awareness. In *Juventus Mundi* Homer is presented as 'the great Bard of the nation'.[137]

---

[130] *JM*, p. 175.     [131] W. E. Gladstone to F. Max Müller, 28 Sept. 1864, GP 44251(2), f. 272v.
[132] *JM*, p. 179.                                            [133] Ibid., pp. 8, 235.
[134] GP 44752, f. 128 (21 Aug. 1862), where the incident is mistakenly attributed to *Iliad* 17. Cf. *JM*, pp. 338–9.                            [135] [Bryce], 'Gladstone on Homer', pp. 31–2.
[136] S. L. Schein, *The Mortal Hero: An Introduction to Homer's 'Iliad'* (Berkeley, Cal., 1984), p. 49. But contemporary scholarly opinion, unlike Gladstone, tends to attribute the poems to the eighth century.
[137] *JM*, p. 181.

Greek identity, according to Gladstone, was reinforced by contrast with Troy. Although the Greek besiegers and the Trojan defenders of the doomed city were part of the same cultural world, Gladstone wants to stress the marks of difference between them. Here there was little or no development in the statesman's thought between 1858 and 1869. In both *Studies on Homer* and *Juventus Mundi*, though Greeks and Trojans are alike portrayed as substantially Pelasgian populations under a Hellenic elite, the Hellenic leaven has worked more thoroughly into the lump of Greek society. The people of Troy are more Pelasgian, more material in their conceptions of religion and less free in their political arrangements. The Trojans are conceived in *Studies on Homer* as showing more similarities to modern Turkey and to 'present Oriental communities'.[138] *Juventus Mundi*, which refers the reader back to the earlier book for fuller treatment of the resemblances and differences between the Greeks and Trojans, depicts Troy as a cultural entrepôt, the meeting point of Greek and Asiatic religious systems.[139] In public life the Asiatic element predominates, extinguishing the spirit of freedom. 'On both sides', writes Gladstone, 'we see the germ of after history: the Trojans bearing in many points the more Asiatic, the Greeks the more European stamp. The one type leans to fraud, where the other inclines to force.' A few pages later he describes the Trojan war as 'the conflict of the Eastern with the Western world' foreshadowing greater conflicts 'down to our own day'.[140] Gladstone is dealing in familiar stereotypes, the cunning Asiatic against the energetic European. In *Studies on Homer* he quotes the literary historian William Mure as drawing exactly the same distinction.[141] There can be little doubt, furthermore, that in Gladstone's case the antithesis had political consequences. If, as he later recalled, he was drawn in 1876 from Homeric studies into the public arena by the growing protest against Turkish repression of the Bulgarians, he carried with him a mindset in which untrustworthy Asiatics were pitched against nobler Europeans. Two years later, while the Eastern Question was raging, he commented on the 'absence of solidity, constancy, and self-command' in Hector that reflected the 'fundamental severance between the Asiatic and the European type'.[142] The polarity between the Trojans and the Greeks seemed to represent a persistent dichotomy in world history.

Nevertheless the contrast between east and west was counterbalanced by another feature of Gladstone's thinking, one that, unlike the last, marks him out from prevailing contemporary trends. During the later nineteenth century the cosmopolitan emphasis of the Enlightenment on the qualities that human beings possess in common was steadily undermined by doctrines asserting racial distinctiveness. In particular it was often contended that there was a great gulf fixed between the Aryan and Semitic peoples. Of this theory the two most prominent popularizers were Max Müller and Ernest Renan, the polymathic French historian

---

[138] *SHHA*, 3, pp. 211, 247.    [139] *JM*, pp. 325, 451.    [140] Ibid., pp. 460, 464.
[141] *SHHA*, 3, p. 207. But for a qualification of Gladstone's 'orientalism', see Ch. 9, p. 293–4.
[142] W. E. Gladstone, 'The Slicing of Hector', *Nineteenth Century*, 4 (1878), p. 760.

of religion.[143] Max Müller claimed the fundamental unity of the Indo-European peoples on the basis of etymology and myth; Renan saw the Jews as inventing monotheism while the Aryans were content with the cult of nature.[144] Gladstone, however, was committed to resisting such speculation. It is true that he sometimes used the terminology of Aryan and Semite, even quoting an authority positing 'a remarkable contrast' between the two.[145] But he was careful not to endorse this judgement and explicitly took issue with Max Müller and Renan on the question. Max Müller, in repudiating any Semitic influence on Greek mythology, once suggested to Gladstone that it was a product of nothing but Aryan myths and the Greek national mind. Gladstone replied that there was another constituent element, what he labelled 'x', the legacy of primeval truth.[146] Equally Gladstone repudiated Renan's theory because the Frenchman ignored divine revelation. The statesman always insisted on the common intellectual stock of the 'Aryan Greeks' and 'Semitic Hebrews'.[147] Furthermore, despite Gladstone's contrast between 'European' Greeks and 'Asiatic' Trojans, his whole analysis was built on the assumption that these peoples were ethnic mixtures. Each of the constituent groups shared in the inheritance of 'one gift, associated with the worship of One God, given at one centre'. The notion of a single revelation bound together 'all the tribes, races, and nations' of the world.[148] Gladstone's vision of human solidarity was not eclipsed on ethnic grounds. His whole approach to ancient history induced him to champion the unity of the human race.

Press coverage of *Juventus Mundi* tended not to weigh up such broader implications of Gladstone's theory, but concentrated instead on his treatment of Olympian religion. The predominant tone was critical. The *Guardian*, whose High Church stance predisposed it in Gladstone's favour, nevertheless remained unconvinced by the theory of indebtedness to messianic tradition. The flaw in the author's argument, the reviewer observed, was that the doctrine of the Word was shaped long afterwards in the history of Israel, far too late to enter Homer.[149] Bryce made the same point, adding the contention that the Greeks, as an inventive people, were entirely capable of transforming nature powers into anthropomorphic figures.[150] This case, that the pantheon could easily be explained as a mixture of nature worship and original imagination, was repeated in other reviews. There was no need to postulate an origin for parts of Greek religion in ancient traditions. The *Scotsman* probably put the point most pungently: 'Because you find that wheelbarrows were used in one place in B.C.900, and in another in

---

[143] Léon Poliakov, *The Aryan Myth: A History of Racist and Nationalist Ideas in Europe* (London, 1974), p. 259.

[144] H. W. Wardman, *Renan: historien philosophe* (Paris, 1979), ch. 8.

[145] George Rawlinson, *The Five Great Monarchies of the Ancient Eastern World*, 4 vols. (London, 1862–7), 4, p. 326, quoted at *JM*, pp. 140–1.

[146] F. Max Müller to W. E. Gladstone, 19 Oct. [1864]; W. E. Gladstone to F. Max Müller, 23 Oct. 1864, GP 44251(2), ff. 276–6v, 279.

[147] Gladstone, 'Olympian System versus the Solar Theory', pp. 750–1, 767.

[148] Ibid., p. 748.                                      [149] *Guardian*, 21 July 1869, GGM 1638.

[150] [Bryce], 'Gladstone on Homer', p. 33.

B.C.1500, must wheelbarrows have been imported from the latter, and was not humanity capable of producing two men able to strike out the idea of a wheelbarrow?'[151] The assumption that cultural forms spread by diffusion was giving way around this time to the notion that they can grow up independently. So Gladstone's main thesis found even less favour than it had in 1858. What the reviews did not generally comment on, however, were the changes in the outworks of the theory made since the appearance of *Studies on Homer*. The *Saturday Review*, picking up Gladstone's avowal of correcting earlier crudities of expression, commented that the modification was achieved 'by disguising the process of argument by which it was sustained, and by the adoption of a lighter touch and slighter treatment of the subject than in the former book'.[152] The charge was substantially accurate: *Juventus Mundi* often tends to the cryptic. But the comment also explains why contemporaries did not notice the alterations of substance in the book. They were too preoccupied with trying to unravel the main thread of Gladstone's argument to compare the details with those of *Studies on Homer*.

## III

In parallel with *Juventus Mundi* Gladstone was contemplating another Homeric work. He intended, he told Acton in 1867, to compile 'a Register of the more significant facts in Homer'.[153] During the 1870s, when out of office, he pushed ahead with the scheme. Three articles in the *Contemporary Review* for 1876 offered five specimen entries from the projected *Thesauros Homerikos*. They dealt fairly exhaustively with all the uses of a given word in the poems.[154] A draft preface for the book in the Gladstone Papers explains that for the study of Homer it is essential to acquire a detailed knowledge of the text. J. B. Friedrich's *Realien* (1851) had been written to publicize the contents of the poems, but it was 'a work more of discussion than of simple presentation'.[155] So Gladstone intended to fill the gap in dictionary form. Meanwhile, however, Eduard Buchholz of Berlin was issuing a far more comprehensive survey of the contents of Homer. Although according to Gladstone its continuous text made it less convenient to consult than a dictionary, the existence of the three-volume German analysis, completed in 1885, may well have contributed to Gladstone's eventual failure to publish his own thesaurus.[156] Probably more important, however, was the sheer vastness of

[151] *Scotsman*, 9 July 1869, GGM 1638.                    [152] *Saturday Review*, 24 July 1869, GGM 1638.
[153] W. E. Gladstone to Sir John Acton, 9 Nov. 1867, GP 44093, f. 63.
[154] W. E. Gladstone, 'Homerology', *Contemporary Review*, 27 (1876), pp. 632–49, 802–20; 28 (1876), pp. 283–309.
[155] 'Preface to Thesauros Homerikos', GP 44762, ff. 45–50 (18 June 1874), quoted at f. 50. A set of entries follows. There are other materials for the thesaurus in GP 44795, ff. 1–88, and in GGM 1458.
[156] Eduard Buchholz, *Die Homerischen Realien*, 3 vols. (Leipzig, 1871–85). Gladstone, 'Homerology', 27 (1876), p. 633. GP 44762, f. 49v. D, 27 Apr. 1874.

an enterprise that demanded too much time as Gladstone was sucked back into the maelstrom of politics. The project was potentially endless, encouraging the exploration of tenuously connected analogies. One of the specimen entries on the poet's use of the work for 'speckled', for instance, allowed the statesman to record the results of his enquiries about the distribution of piebald horses, noting the 'predominance of the chestnut in Shropshire'.[157] But Gladstone's purpose was not simply antiquarian. He wanted, he says in the draft preface, to illuminate 'primitive history' because it 'stands in close association with the bases of religious belief'. Even the thesaurus was designed to help vindicate the idea of an early revelation. By showing that Homer was 'the true mirror of an age', Gladstone hoped to set out the evidence that would reveal similarities with the messianic tradition.[158] It was a prerequisite for that higher apologetic task to demonstrate that the Homeric world was real.

That is why Gladstone was so excited by the archaeological discoveries of Heinrich Schliemann. In a series of excavations beginning in 1871 at Hissarlik near the Dardanelles, the unstable and unscrupulously self-advertising German revealed the remains of a city destroyed by fire. Although his conclusions were far less certain than he alleged, he proclaimed that he had found Priam's Troy.[159] Schliemann sent photographs of his discoveries for the inspection of Gladstone, who was impressed.[160] 'The facts which you appear to have established', the statesman wrote to Schliemann at the start of 1874, 'are of the highest importance to primitive history.'[161] The German directed that the first copy of his findings should be dispatched to Gladstone, who perused them in March.[162] As soon as he was out of office, Gladstone prepared an article for the *Contemporary Review* publicizing Schliemann's achievement.[163] There was, however, a divergence of opinion between the two men. In acknowledging the *Contemporary Review* article, Schliemann explained his position: 'I have long since come to the conclusion that it [Troy] must have been destroyed nearly 2000 years before Christ and the catastrophe must have remained fresh in the memory of the world; it must have been sung by numerous rhapsodes, till—probably 1100 years after the event it was sung by Homer . . .'[164] Gladstone marked the latter part of this passage with a cross for disagreement. It was inconceivable to him that Homer lived so remote in time from the events he described. Likewise when Gladstone sent his article containing the suggestion that the fall of Troy took place between 1286 and 1226 BC, Schliemann told him sharply that this estimate was '<u>not</u> confirmed by the monuments which denote a <u>far remoter antiquity</u>'.[165] The same disagreement

---

[157] Gladstone, 'Homerology', 28 (1876), p. 307.                    [158] GP 44762, ff. 47, 49v.

[159] M. I Finley, 'Schliemann's Troy: One Hundred Years After', *Proceedings of the British Academy*, 60 (1974). On Schliemann, see David Traill, *Schliemann of Troy: Treasure and Deceit* (London, 1995).

[160] *D*, 10, 13 Oct. 1873.

[161] W. E. Gladstone to Heinrich Schliemann, 9 Jan. 1874, in *D*. Schliemann had sent Gladstone an account of his early years, published as *Ithaka, der Peloponnes und Troja* (Leipzig, 1869).

[162] Heinrich Schliemann to W. E. Gladstone, 28 Dec. 1873, GP 44441, f. 243. *D*, 9, 10 Mar. 1874.

[163] W. E. Gladstone, 'Homer's Place in History', *Contemporary Review*, 24 (1874).

[164] Heinrich Schliemann to W. E. Gladstone, 5 June 1874, GP 44444, f. 14.

[165] W. E. Gladstone, 'Homer's Place in History', proofs, p. 14: Schliemann's annotation.

emerged at a meeting of the Society of Antiquaries in London in 1875 when, after a lecture by Schliemann, Gladstone questioned his dating.[166] Schliemann wished to demonstrate his ability to penetrate to the distant past, but Gladstone would not question Homer's capacity for accurate rapportage of the Trojan war.

Nevertheless when Gladstone expanded his article into a book, *Homeric Synchronism* (1876), he expressed continuing admiration for Schliemann's work at Troy. Robert Scott, Master of Balliol College, Oxford, warned Gladstone that some of the views he had expressed were 'heretical', but Schliemann himself descanted on the new book, in reality quite a slight work, as 'the masterpiece of the greatest scholar of all ages'.[167] Astonishingly, Schliemann professed himself persuaded by Gladstone's reasoning about the chronology of the war and the poems, and so recanted his own former position. They were now in agreement even on these issues.[168] Schliemann's change of mind may have been connected with his desire to retain the goodwill of the statesman, who, through the British ambassador in Constantinople, was able to exert pressure on the Turkish authorities to permit further excavations. In a request for help of this kind in June 1875, Schliemann had made the extraordinary promise to Gladstone of a quarter of his finds as a reward.[169] Scott voiced his reservations about Schliemann to Gladstone in a letter of August 1878: 'his mode of dealing with Greece, and his undoubting dogmatism on points where I see he must be wrong, make me feel him an untrustworthy guide for every thing except facts.'[170] Gladstone's continuing sponsorship of Schliemann is remarkable in view of such concerns, which he must have shared. He attended Schliemann's lectures, wrote a preface to the German's account of his fresh excavations at Mycenae, and continued, as Prime Minister in 1881, to recommend him to the ambassador in Constantinople.[171] It was Schliemann, not Gladstone, whose enthusiasm for the other waned. By 1882 the German was patriotically identifying himself with Bismarck's policies and two years later, in his final letter to Gladstone, his tone was hectoring rather than fawning.[172] Gladstone refused to drop Schliemann because he felt that the German had settled the issue of whether Troy was real or mythical: 'it is difficult to suppose', he wrote in *Homeric Synchronism*, 'that the mythical theory, always wofully [sic] devoid of tangible substance, can long survive the results attained by this distinguished explorer.'[173] Ignoring the possibility that the fire whose traces

---

[166] *D*, 24 June 1875 and n.

[167] Robert Scott to W. E. Gladstone, 15 May 1876, GP 44295, f. 399. Heinrich Schliemann to W. E. Gladstone, 8 May 1876, GP 44450, f. 25.

[168] Heinrich Schliemann to W. E. Gladstone, 28 Dec. 1876, GP 44452, f. 283.

[169] Heinrich Schliemann to W. E. Gladstone, 27 June 1875, GP 44447, f. 257.

[170] Robert Scott to W. E. Gladstone, 8 Aug. 1878, GP 44295, f. 406v.

[171] *D*, 22 March, 8 June 1877. W. E. Gladstone, 'Preface', in Heinrich Schliemann, *Mycenae* (London, 1878). Heinrich Schliemann to W. E. Gladstone, 15 Sept. 1881, GP 44467, f. 237.

[172] Leo Duel, *Memoirs of Heinrich Schliemann* (New York, 1977), p. 285. Heinrich Schliemann to W. E. Gladstone, 21 Aug. 1884, GP 44487, f. 180.

[173] W. E. Gladstone, *Homeric Synchronism: An Enquiry into the Time and Place of Homer* (London, 1876), p. 20.

Schliemann had discovered was not caused by conquest, Gladstone believed that
the historicity of Homer had been established by the spade.

The contemporary decipherment of the hieroglyphics on Egyptian monu-
ments seemed to point in the same direction. In the month after his article on
Schliemann, Gladstone published another in the *Contemporary Review* arguing
that the fall of Troy could be approximately located within the chronology of
Egyptian history.[174] Its content was expanded to form Part II of *Homeric
Synchronism*. Gladstone drew heavily on a range of French scholars who had
recently published on ancient Egypt—F. J. Chabas, the Vicomte de Rougé, and
François Lenormant—to fix matters of dating.[175] He also used the philological
evidence adduced by F. J. Lauth of Munich, who sent his *Homer und Aegypten*
(1867) to Gladstone in 1873.[176] Yet Gladstone struck out on paths of his own,
contending, for instance, that the legend of the voyage of Jason and the Argonauts
might represent a concerted Greek expedition to suppress a surviving outpost of
the decaying Egyptian empire on the Black Sea. Some of Gladstone's hypotheses
are frankly fanciful, as when he proposes that the superhuman feats recorded of
Pharaoh Rameses II might have formed the inspiration for the extraordinary
prowess of Achilles or that the 166 children of the same ruler might have induced
Homer to attribute fifty sons, together with more daughters, to Priam of Troy.
Gladstone also explains the paucity of explicit allusions to Egypt in the poems as
the result of a deliberate suppression from patriotic motives—an argument from
silence no more convincing than its equivalent in relation to the Phoenicians in
*Juventus Mundi*.[177] Max Müller, as he told a friend in a private letter, found
*Homeric Synchronism* 'very disappointing':

So great a man, so imperfect a scholar! He has no idea how shaky the ground is on which
he takes his stand. The reading of those ethnic names in the hieroglyphic inscriptions varies
with every year and with every scholar . . . the use which Gladstone makes of their labours
is to me really painful, all the more so because it is cleverly done, and I believe bona fide.[178]

The statesman was over-bold in his use of Egyptian evidence, and the reason is
clear. He was carried away by his eagerness to reinforce the case that the *Iliad* and
its author could be anchored in real history.

Two years after *Homeric Synchronism*, in 1878, Gladstone published a short
primer on the poet. Called simply *Homer*, it was one of a series edited by the
historian J. R. Green, who made a number of corrections in its text that Gladstone

[174] W. E. Gladstone, 'The Place of Homer in History and Egyptian Chronology (Part II)',
*Contemporary Review*, 24 (1874).
[175] F. J. Chabas, *Études sur l'antiquité historique* (Chalon-sur-Saône, 1872). Vicomte Jacques de
Rougé, *Extraits d'un mémoire sur les attaques dirigée contre l'Egypte par les peuples de la Mediterranée
vers le xiv^me^ siècle avant notre éra* (not found). François Lenormant, *Manuel d'histoire ancienne de
l'Orient jusqu'aux guerres médiques*, 2 vols. (Paris, 1868). Gladstone read the first on 4 September 1868
and the last (probably) on 27 April 1874, but does not record reading the second in the *Diaries*.
[176] F. J. Lauth, *Homer und Aegypten* (Munich, 1867). Gladstone, *Homeric Synchronism*, p. 10 n. D, 22
Aug. 1873.          [177] Gladstone, *Homeric Synchronism*, pp. 189–95, 196–7, 198–200.
[178] F. Max Müller to G. W. Cox, n.d., in *Friedrich Max Müller*, 1, p. 417.

adopted.[179] It was not a book, however, that entailed further consultation of other scholars, because it was essentially a digest for students of the various aspects of Homer—his characters, cosmology, ethics, ethnology, geography, and so on. It reiterated many of Gladstone's characteristic messages about the significance of the poet. 'All the first fundamental lessons of political science', he assured his readers, 'may be learned, particularly by Englishmen, in studying the Achaian politics.'[180] The longest chapters were on the Homeric question, which covered the outline of the plots as well as the issue of authorship, and, inevitably, on mythology. A review in the *Spectator* found this section one of those that were 'strong meat for a primer'.[181] Robert Scott, acknowledging Gladstone's gift of a copy, expressed astonishment at the amount of information the book contained, though also noting 'an unfortunate misprint of "<u>nosiest</u>" for "noisiest" '.[182] Praise for the little volume lasted after Gladstone's death. Jane Harrison, a leading early twentieth-century classicist, was surprised in 1904 to find the primer, together with *Juventus Mundi*, 'extraordinarily good', though she wished their author had not 'gone dotty over the Logos and the Divine Wisdom'.[183] There was, in fact, very little change of substance since *Juventus Mundi*. The new book does contain, for the first time, the word 'theanthropism' to describe the principle of the Olympian system, and Gladstone was thereafter to prefer the term to 'anthropomorphism'. But the alteration of usage is not an indicator of a change of standpoint. Gladstone favoured the new word, he explained in an article of the following year, because 'anthropomorphism' had another connotation, of biblical accommoda- tion to human understanding, and also because it might be thought to imply that the Greek divinities resembled human beings only in bodily form and not in 'mental and moral constitution'.[184] So the terminological change was simply to avoid misapprehension. Like *Homeric Synchronism*, the primer on Homer shows no signs of ideological shift.

The same is substantially true of Gladstone's final book on the poet, *Landmarks of Homeric Study* (1890). Although a dozen years had passed since the appearance of the primer, they had been filled in the main with political battles rather than with fresh thinking about Homer. Gladstone published a series of Homeric articles in this period, but they contained little that was new. *Landmarks* offers a taut summary of Gladstone's various earlier perspectives on Homer. His antiquarianism is reflected in a chapter on the geography of the poems; his teaching in *Studies on Homer* persists in the claims that morality decayed after the poet's day and that archaic politics were characterized by

[179] W. E. Gladstone, *Homer* (London, 1878). *D*, 9 June 1878.
[180] Gladstone, *Homer*, pp. 113–14.     [181] *Spectator*, 28 Dec. 1878, GGM 1636.
[182] Robert Scott to W. E. Gladstone, 8 Aug. 1878, GP 44295, ff. 406, 407.
[183] Jane Harrison to Gilbert Murray, 26 Aug. 1904, in Jessie Stewart, *Jane Ellen Harrison: A Portrait from Letters* (London, 1959), p. 66.
[184] W. E. Gladstone, 'The Olympian System versus the Solar Theory', *Nineteenth Century*, 32 (1879), p. 757. *Homer* nevertheless contains (at p. 65) a fresh instance of the term 'anthropophuism' that Gladstone had discarded after *Studies on Homer*.

oratory, collective opinion, and customary rights. The novel emphasis of *Juventus Mundi* on the dignity of humanity recurs in the chapters on the plot of the *Iliad*, which is said to concentrate more than other epics on men rather than things, and on religion, where there is another celebration of 'the theanthropic spirit'.[185] The central contention of the 1870s is repeated in the argument that mining deeper into the texts with the aid of archaeology is the best method of studying the poet. There is, however, a measure of innovation in the chapter on 'Homer as Nation-Maker'. The blending of the ethnic elements into a single Greek people looms large. The patriotic motivation of Jason and the Argonauts is treated far less tentatively than in *Homeric Synchronism*, and an idea originally floated in an article of 1889 is set out for the first time in a book. Odysseus, Gladstone claims, represents the Phoenician element in the Greek ethnic mix, so providing a symmetrical counterpart to Achilles, the Hellenic hero of the *Iliad*.[186] The poet's aim, according to the statesman, was 'before all things national'.[187] The review in *The Times*, which found Gladstone's speculations 'rather ingenious than convincing', calls the notion that Homer fosters the national idea 'strange' and 'unexpected'.[188] Gladstone, in 1890 the champion of the Irish national cause, was inclined to give greater weight to the national identity of ancient Greece. The theme was not new, but it was given greater prominence in *Landmarks*.

The work also contains a fresh consideration of Homer's sources not found in previous books. It concludes with a section 'On the Points of Contact between the Assyrian Tablets and the Homeric Text' that tries to identify legacies from the civilization of the Tigris and Euphrates valleys to ancient Greece. Some, such as the parallel between Aphrodite and Ishtar, the fertility goddess of Syria and the east, were to gain general scholarly acceptance.[189] By contrast with *Homeric Synchronism*, where the connections are primarily with Egypt, Gladstone's publications of the 1890s emphasize the debt to the Assyrians and Babylonians. He made a significant change in the text of *Landmarks*. In the manuscript he wrote that the last generation had shown the acquaintance of Homer with 'Egyptian and Phoenician ideas', but in the published version the phrase has become 'Babylonian and Assyrian ideas'.[190] The influence of Assyrian mythology on Homeric religion was the subject of a seventy-five minute lecture delivered by Gladstone at the Oxford Union early in 1890.[191] Able undergraduates, though initially persuaded while listening to the flowing oratory, soon noticed that the statesman had not shown how the influence had been exerted and so began to doubt.[192] There was even more scepticism about Gladstone's address on 'Archaic Greece and the East', presented to the Oriental Congress at Oxford in 1892, partly because, since the statesman was now in office, it had to be read on his behalf by Max Müller and so lacked Gladstone's personal charisma. The

---

[185] *Landmarks*, p. 64.
[186] Ibid., pp. 33, 54–5. W. E. Gladstone, 'Phoenician Affinities of Ithaca', *Nineteenth Century*, 26 (1889), pp. 289–90.        [187] *Landmarks*, p. 30.        [188] *T*, 16 Oct. 1890, GGM 1636.
[189] *Landmarks*, pp. 142–4.        [190] GP 44795, f. 239. *Landmarks*, p. 84.        [191] *D*, 5 Feb. 1890.
[192] J. L. Myres, 'Gladstone's View of Homer', *Homer and his Critics* (London, 1958), p. 119.

paper still attributed an influence to Egypt: the phrase *anax andron*, which Gladstone had once claimed as a patriarchal epithet, was now said to be the title of Egyptian satraps ruling Greece. Max Müller reported to Gladstone that this idea took the audience by surprise.[193] But the paper also listed fifteen items from the Homeric text that could be assigned an origin among the Assyrians, whom Gladstone did not distinguish sharply from the Babylonians.[194] In his last years he was eager to establish a debt owed by Greece to the civilization of the east.

The sources for this new belief are not hard to discover. Pioneering excavations in the Middle East, including those of A. H. Layard, had brought to light cuneiform tablets which, when translated by George Smith of the British Museum, turned out to show striking parallels to the biblical narrative. There was, most notably, a Chaldaean account of a great flood, subsequently known as *The Epic of Gilgamesh*. To some contemporaries it was alarming that the scripture stories had equivalents in Middle Eastern mythology: perhaps the Bible itself was myth? To Gladstone, however, it was reassuring: the discoveries constituted fresh evidence of the wide diffusion of primitive religious traditions. The 'Assyriological investigations', he told Acton, had 'accredited their substance by producing similar traditions in variant forms inferior to the Mosaic forms and tending to throw these back to a higher antiquity'.[195] Smith's *Assyrian Discoveries* (1875) formed part of Gladstone's Sunday reading in 1890, a hint of its expected apologetic value.[196] Smith argued that classical antiquity borrowed less from Egypt than from Chaldaea, which provided 'the origin and explanation of many of the obscure points in the mythology of Greece and Rome'.[197] In a manuscript fragment of about 1890 Gladstone expresses his agreement with Smith that the Greeks drew more of what was important from Babylonia and Assyria than from Egypt because, he supposes, the Phoenicians were in living contact with these peoples.[198] Alongside George Smith's work Gladstone was indebted to the Hibbert Lectures for 1887 delivered by A. H. Sayce, who was to be Professor of Assyriology at Oxford from 1891. Sayce showed that features of Babylonian religion were close to the thought-world of the Old Testament. Gladstone was impressed with the book, which he annotated favourably and copiously.[199] From it he derived, among much else, the point that the obedience of Merodach to his father in Assyrian mythology paralleled the relationship of Apollo to Zeus, an element, Gladstone believed, of primitive revelation.[200] In such points lay the ultimate value of such Middle

[193] F. Max Müller to W. E. Gladstone, 15 Sept. 1892, GP 44251, f. 384v, printed in *Max Müller*, 2, p. 287.
[194] W. E. Gladstone, *Archaic Greece and the East* (London, 1892), pp. 28–31.
[195] W. E. Gladstone to Lord Acton, 13 May 1888, GP 44094, f. 30v.
[196] *D*, 12 Jan. 1890.
[197] George Smith, *Assyrian Discoveries: An Account of Explorations and Discoveries on the Site of Nineveh, during 1873 and 1874* (London, 1875), p. 451.      [198] GP 44676, f. 17 (n.d., but *c*.1890).
[199] A. H. Sayce, *Lectures on the Origin and Growth of Religion as illustrated by the Religion of the Ancient Babylonians* [1887], 2nd edn. (London, 1888), St Deiniol's Library, Hawarden. *D*, 11–20 Feb. 1887, 12 Feb. 1888, 1 Dec. 1889.
[200] W. E. Gladstone, 'The Greater Gods of Olympos. II. Apollo', *Nineteenth Century*, 21 (1887), p. 751.

Eastern discoveries. They formed a fresh pool of evidence for Gladstone's original theory of an early divine disclosure to humanity.

During the later part of his career Gladstone was forced to defend that position
by the proponents of the solar interpretation of myth. Although he may have been
swayed by its leading exponent, Max Müller, in the early 1860s, Gladstone was
attacked by some of the Oxford professor's disciples in subsequent years. One was
George Cox, the popularizing author of *The Mythology of the Aryan Nations*
(1870) whom Max Müller himself thought a prickly character.[201] Cox was an
advanced Broad Church clergyman who had accompanied Bishop Colenso to
Natal and was to write his biography. He stood closer to Grote than to Gladstone
in his understanding of the ancient Greeks, holding that their moral standard was
constantly rising and that the historical character of the *Iliad* and *Odyssey* had
been 'definitely disproved'. In the fashion of a theological liberal Cox was aston-
ished that the statesman should attribute the origin of the Olympian pantheon,
with all its moral corruption, to an early revelation containing 'the dogmatic
statements of the Athanasian Creed'. The truth about ancient myths, according to
Cox, could be extracted only by the 'strictly scientific' etymological study
pioneered by Max Müller.[202] Gladstone's riposte did not appear until nine years
later, in an article on 'The Olympian System versus the Solar Theory'. While
admitting the existence of nature worship in early Greece, he did not concede that
it was inspired exclusively by the sun. He knew of no systematic attempt to vindicate the allegation that 'the members of the Olympian Court are Nature-Powers
in disguise'. It was just as scientific, he argued, to compare the elements of religious traditions as the composition of divine names in the manner of Max
Müller.[203] Battle was joined over the proper scientific method in the field. Cox
repeated in *Fraser's Magazine* his earlier charge that Gladstone was making
unfounded theological assumptions, though in private urging the statesman,
whom he supported politically and from whom he hoped for preferment, to
ignore the article until pressing national business was over.[204] Gladstone replied
in a further article that the enquiry should be carried on 'with the same cool and
clear impartiality as if we were osteologists who had found a bone and were trying
to fix the animal to whose configuration it belonged'. Applying that technique,
there were at least ten features of Hebrew tradition to be found in Homer: there
must be some common source.[205] Rigorous comparative religion, Gladstone
believed, could only vindicate his underlying convictions about the earliest
human beliefs.

---

[201] F. Max Müller to Charles Kingsley, 16 Apr. 1867, in *Max Müller*, 1, p. 334.

[202] Cox, *Mythology of the Aryan Nations*, 1, pp. 15, 27, 217.

[203] W. E. Gladstone, 'The Olympian System versus the Solar Theory', *Nineteenth Century*, 32 (1879),
quoted at p. 759.

[204] G. W. Cox, 'Homeric Mythology and Religion: A Reply to Mr. Gladstone', *Fraser's Magazine*, 100
(1879). G. W. Cox to W. E. Gladstone, 29 Nov. 1879, GP 44461, f. 190. With great magnanimity,
Gladstone was to give him the preferment he craved: G. W. Cox to W. E. Gladstone, 30 Apr. 1881, 7
May 1881, GP 44469, ff. 209, 236.

[205] W. E. Gladstone, 'Religion, Achaian and Semitic', *Nineteenth Century*, 7 (1880), quoted at p. 717.

There was a similar engagement six years later with another critic from a nearby camp. In 1883 Albert Réville published a series of lectures originally delivered at the Collège de France, and in the following year they were translated as *Prolegomena of the History of Religions* with an introduction by Max Müller. Réville attacked Gladstone's understanding of primitive revelation as conflicting with what was known of the simple early religions of the world. The statesman mistakenly appealed to the Bible, not to science, but in any case the concept of primitive revelation was not to be found in its pages.[206] Gladstone replied in an article on the 'Dawn of Creation and of Worship'. His method, he claimed, made no prior assumptions derived from scripture. He merely showed that the similarities between the Homeric poems and Hebrew poetry required a common origin, 'just as the markings, which are sometimes noticed upon the coats of horses and donkeys, are held to require the admission of their relationship to the zebra'. It was the solar hypothesis that was unscientific. There was inadequate evidence for the origin of many Greek myths in the phenomena of the sun. Etymology was no guide to the subsequent meaning of words: one might as well suppose that 'our dukes were simply generals leading us in war'. And it was improper to assume that all religions were subjective creations, like 'so many answers to the call of a strong human appetite for that kind of food'.[207] Max Müller immediately reacted with a short article upholding the value of etymology: after all, dukes had once actually served as military leaders. But he tried to reduce the distance between himself and Gladstone, pointing out that his own view was only that a part of mythology had a solar origin.[208] Gladstone responded in turn, claiming merely to protest against abuses of etymology and agreeing that his views on solar theory were virtually identical with Max Müller's.[209] It was commonly believed, Gladstone remarked in a late fragment, that ancient religion was the result of the worship of natural objects, or even of the sun alone. Study of the Homeric poems did not exclude either doctrine 'except at the extremest point of fanciful development' if either was used to explain away everything in the Olympian system.[210] Gladstone was eager to minimize his differences with potential allies in the solar school of mythological interpretation.

He did not, however, desire a similar accommodation with the champions of the next theory of myth to gain the public ear. The revolutionary new approach, spearheaded from the 1860s by Edward Tylor, applied to Homer by Andrew Lang, and eventually embodied in James Frazer's *The Golden Bough* (1890), held that tales of gods and heroes were the product of a primitive mentality that revelled in non-rational mystical associations. Tylor, who became Reader in Anthropology at Oxford in 1884, was responsible for turning the study of 'uncivilised' peoples into an academic discipline, social anthropology. The fresh

---

[206] Albert Réville, *Prolegomena of the History of Religions* [1883], trans. A. S. Squire (London, 1884), ch. 3.  [207] Gladstone, 'Dawn of Creation and of Worship', pp. 2, 8, 33.
[208] F. Max Müller, 'Solar Myths', *Nineteenth Century*, 18 (1888), pp. 919–22.
[209] W. E. Gladstone, 'Proem to Genesis: A Plea for a Fair Trial' [1886], *Later Gleanings*, pp. 73–6.
[210] GP 44712, f. 11 (n.d., but 1890s).

perspective was in fundamental conflict with Max Müller's supposition that language had degenerated into myth. Tylor and his colleagues, who were at home in the Darwinian era, believed on the contrary that there had been a progressive evolution in human rationality. Gladstone looked at Tylor's classic statement of his viewpoint, *Primitive Culture* (1871), and took notes on passages in his *Anthropology* (1881) relating to Homer and (no doubt since he was dealing with southern Africa at the time) the Basuto people.[211] The two men met at Oxford in 1890, but the only correspondence between them concerned an intervention by Gladstone later that year on behalf of the University Museum.[212] The statesman examined Lang's general work on *Custom and Myth* (1884), his *Homer and the Epic* (1893), and, most carefully, his *Helen of Troy* (1882).[213] Although he was able to point out a mistranslation in the last,[214] Gladstone did not engage with Lang's theories, either by correspondence or in print. Gladstone does not even record having seen Frazer's *Golden Bough*. Although Max Müller gradually absorbed something of the new point of view,[215] Gladstone did not. In old age he continued to appeal to 'ethnological science', the paradigm of his youth, rather than to social anthropology.[216] He could have little sympathy for Tylor's concepts of 'animism', which posited the origin of all religion in experience of the natural world, or of 'survivals', which suggested the perpetuation of pre-rational motifs in modern civilization. There were hints in Tylor's works, revealing his debt to the sceptical Enlightenment, that Christianity contains much primitive superstition, and Frazer was to follow in his path.[217] The new anthropology must have seemed to Gladstone little more than a clever branch of the rising anti-theistic body of opinion.

Gladstone's affinities were far more with the gentlemen amateurs who pursued antiquarian delvings outside the academy. At least one of their number could be accounted Gladstone's disciple. R. F. Smith, a High Church clergyman at Southwell in Nottinghamshire who was to attain a minor canonry there in 1877, published a piece five years before on 'The Homeric Deities' in *Notes and Queries* 'as subsidiary evidence to the theory so conclusively drawn out from the text of Homer by the author of *Juventus Mundi*'. Smith had unearthed Chaldaean etymological material supporting the identification of the goddess Leto with the Blessed Virgin Mary.[218] Another private scholar, Robert Brown, a solicitor of Barton-on-Humber in Lincolnshire, a Liberal and a Fellow of the Society of

---

[211] E. B. Tylor, *Primitive Culture*, 2 vols. (London, 1871). *D*, 8 Dec. 1871, 24 May 1872. E. B. Tylor, *Anthropology* (London, 1881). GP 44792, f. 291 (n.d., but Gladstone read *Anthropology* on 3 May 1881).

[212] *D*, 4 Feb. 1890. E. B. Tylor to W.E. Gladstone, 31 May 1890, GP 44510, f. 57.

[213] *D*, 16 Nov. 1884, 12, 13 May 1893, 6–10 Oct. 1882.

[214] A[ndrew] Lang to W. E. Gladstone, 15 Oct. [1882], GP 44477, ff. 104v–5.

[215] Gregory Schrempp, 'The Re-Education of Friedrich Max Müller: Intellectual Appropriation and Epistemological Antinomy in Mid-Victorian Evolutionary Thought', *Man*, 18 (1983).

[216] GP 44712, f. 143 (n.d., but with materials of 1890s).

[217] J. W. Burrow, *Evolution and Society: A Study in Victorian Social Theory* (Cambridge, 1966), ch. 7, esp. pp. 256–7. Robert Ackerman, *J. G. Frazer: His Life and Work* (Cambridge, 1987).

[218] R. F. Smith, 'The Homeric Deities', *Notes and Queries*, 4th series, 10 (2 Nov. 1872), p. 345, GGM 1634.

Antiquaries, initiated a correspondence with Gladstone in the same year by sending a copy of his recently published book on *Poseidon*.[219] Gladstone accepted Brown's theory that Poseidon was probably the god of earthquakes and standarly cited Brown as the authority for locating the Cyclops of the *Odyssey* on the north African coast.[220] Gladstone helped Brown secure publication for another of his books and sent a draft of one of his own articles for Brown's opinion of whether pork in the diet could be seen as a symptom of Phoenician influence, a point which duly appeared in the printed version.[221] This was the eclectic intellectual milieu that Gladstone inhabited. Yet such men did not lack a formulated purpose. In 1878 Brown told Gladstone that he had just read the statesman's primer on Homer: 'I greatly rejoice that your learning & influence are so notably exerted on the side of what I do not doubt to be the truth, scientific as well as religious, in such matters, i.e. that man & his belief are not the outcome of Evolution but as the writer of Genesis holds, have degenerated.'[222] Brown saw Max Müller as the champion of this viewpoint and Gladstone confided to Acton that he found Brown 'a little too solar'.[223] But it was true that, ever since his original rebuttal of Grote, Gladstone had shared the conviction that, unaided, human beings do not progressively develop. In that sense he was aligned with Brown and Max Müller against the fundamental evolutionary assumptions of Tylor and social anthropology.

Hence Gladstone's understanding of prehistory in his last years remained unmodified by the developmental ideas of the anthropological school. He still believed firmly in cultural diffusion. He began his address to the Oriental Congress in 1892 by describing how, 'from a central point in Asia, population radiated towards most, if not all, points of the compass'.[224] In private notes he located the original concentration of the races in the plain of the Tigris and Euphrates. From there they spread out, he believed, bringing civilization with them. This ethnological perspective was bound up with Gladstone's view of the early faith of humanity. As they travelled, he wrote, the peoples must have carried traces of their former religion. This understanding of the remote past could be vindicated by demonstrating parallels between Hebrew records and the myths of other lands.

We are not to seek out forced analogies or other resemblances, but if a real relationship is obvious or traceable between any of the classical religions, in particular points, and the traditions of the Hebrews, we are not to be chilled in the prosecution of the search by any idea of a presumptive improbability which places all firmness of footing beyond our hope.[225]

---

[219] Robert Brown junior to W. E. Gladstone, 6 May 1872, GP 44434, f. 106. D, 11 May 1872.
[220] W. E. Gladstone, 'The Greater Gods of Olympos. I. Poseidon', *Nineteenth Century*, 21 (1887), p. 472. Gladstone, *Homer*, p. 61. Gladstone, *Archaic Greece and the East*, p. 21.
[221] Robert Brown junior to W. E. Gladstone, 9 Nov. 1882, GP 44477, f. 224; 2 Dec. 1888, GP 44505, f. 188. Gladstone, 'Phoenician Affinities of Ithaca', p. 286 n.
[222] Robert Brown junior to W. E. Gladstone, 8 May 1878, GP 44456, f. 298.
[223] W. E. Gladstone to Lord Acton, 13 Jan. 1887, GP 44093, f. 282.
[224] Gladstone, *Archaic Greece and the East*, p. 1.
[225] GP 44712, ff. 143–5, quoted at f. 145 (n.d., but with materials for 'Olympian Religion' from 1890s).

Gladstone was clearly conscious that contemporary opinion was against him, but he nevertheless persevered in his exercise in comparative religion. The aim was still to lay bare the common ground of the various religious traditions, which he expected to be 'the leading ideas of what Christians in general take to have been the articles of a primitive revelation from God to man'.[226] The solar and even more the evolutionary school had departed from the proper Christian position by adopting the 'fashionable indisposition ... to acknowledge any relationship between Homeric and Hebraic traditions'. The spirit of the age might be partly a reaction against fanciful interpretations of the seventeenth century, but in part, too, it was 'little more than a momentary fashion, a simple vagary of the human mind'.[227] Gladstone seriously underestimated the extent of intellectual change during the later nineteenth century. As in the Home Rule campaign of the same period, he was unduly sanguine about overcoming entrenched opposition.

He therefore embarked in his final years on 'a long meditated work on The Olympian Religion'.[228] Although the book never appeared, the text in the Gladstone Papers is not far from completion. Out of eight or nine substantial parts, some of them containing several article-length subdivisions, only one is absent from a provisional selection of materials; and a detached manuscript may contain the outline headings of the missing chapter.[229] Much of the book consists of a series of articles on Greek divinities that Gladstone had been printing since 1878 in the *Nineteenth Century,* the *Contemporary Review,* and the *North American Review.*[230] 'Some rudiments of Olympian Religion', he told Acton in 1887, had partially taken shape, but four years later he was complaining to the same correspondent that he could glean too few scraps of time for the project.[231] The underlying premise of the enterprise was that all myth potentially bears evidence of a divine origin. The distinction he had earlier made between traditive and inventive deities, he explains in the draft preface, had been mistaken, but not because, as others claimed, there was no element of authentic tradition in the Greek pantheon. On the contrary, he now claims, all the Olympian deities 'stand upon a basis essentially traditive'.[232] Hints of primeval truth could be traced in each one of them, and that was the task he set himself. His interpretation, he hoped, would challenge the evolutionary understanding of mythology. The signs of monotheism in Homeric religion were supposed by 'some writers today' to be part of a progress towards a simpler, less superstitious faith, but in reality the movement over time was 'adverse to monotheism'.[233] The original authentic worship of humanity was in decay. In the last dated fragment, written less than five months

---

[226] GP 44712, f. 170 (n.d., but 1890s).        [227] GP 44712, f. 316 (n.d., but 1890s).
[228] GP 44713, f. 1 (n.d., but 1890s heading).
[229] Materials for the book form the whole of GP 44711–13. GP 44711 contains all the parts specified in two lists of contents (ff. 2, 3) except part III, which may be summarized in GP 44713, f. 15.
[230] The earliest article that was to be incorporated was 'The Iris of Homer: And her Relation to Genesis IX. 11–17', *Contemporary Review,* 32 (1878).
[231] W. E. Gladstone to Lord Acton, 13 Jan. 1887, GP 44093, f. 284; 26 Mar. 1891, GP 44094, f. 160v.
[232] 'Preface', GP 44713, ff. 124–8, quoted at f. 126 (n.d.).        [233] GP 44711, f. 182 (n.d.).

before his death, Gladstone contrasts two forms of piety, the older and purer, derived from the common stock and founded upon the idea of right, and the newer awe of nature, founded upon the idea of power. The latter conception seems to have entailed a 'progressive moral declension'.[234] At the end of his Homeric studies, as at the beginning, Gladstone was committed to the defence of the idea of primitive revelation. Although the main target had changed from Grote to Tylor and his circle, there was continuity in the statesman's undergirding convictions.

## IV

Nevertheless the degree of change in Gladstone's views about Homer is what deserves stress in any overall evaluation. There was recasting of the nature of the foreign influence with the dropping of the Persian hypothesis, the adoption of the Phoenician theory, and subsequently the treatment of the Assyrians and Babylonians as a source of Hellenic ideas. This cluster of modifications, however, did not affect the underlying purpose of the discussion of overseas influence, which was always to buttress the case for the transmission of early religious traditions. The area where there was greatest ideological shift was in the estimate of humanity. In *Studies on Homer* the human characteristics of the gods and goddesses form a corrupting factor; but from *Juventus Mundi* onwards, as is clear in the analysis of Heré and Zeus, they are an elevating force. As a result of admitting the natural origins of aspects of Greek religion, Gladstone highlighted the contrast between the shallow residual cults of nature and the sublime anthropomorphic image of the deities. In the later writings the combination of the human and the divine in the pantheon is constantly held up for admiration. Homer's achievement, according to a draft introduction to 'Olympian Religion', was to build up 'humanity as a whole' into divinity.[235] The consequences of the admission of anthropomorphism to Olympus, Gladstone believed, had been overwhelmingly good, the planting of the seed that flowered in Hellenic civilization. The eventual results were the celebration of the body in Greek art and the development of the mind in Greek philosophy. There was a major implication for the evolution of Gladstone's thought. The element of the human, which had previously been castigated more than praised, had its valuation transformed. The human was no longer, in Augustinian fashion, associated primarily with sin. Instead it was identified with the good and the ennobling, providing 'a model of beauty, strength, and wisdom'.[236] The category of the human now enjoyed Gladstone's benediction.

The more favourable estimate of humanity did not arise from Homeric scholarship alone. Meditation on the central Christian doctrine of the incarnation, as

---

[234] GP 44713, ff. 80–2 (20 Dec. 1897), quoted at f. 81.     [235] GP 44712, f. 174 (n.d.).
[236] *JM*, p. 376.

Chapter 5 has shown, had led Gladstone to ponder the potential of Christ's human nature. Increasingly, as he was drawn in a Broad Church direction in his theology, the grandeur of the human race figured largely in his thinking. Already in 1860 Gladstone publicly asserted as a 'great truth' that 'man himself is the crowning wonder of creation'.[237] The statesman's growing confidence in humanity was readily transferred to his interpretation of Homer's religion. The examination of ancient Greece was never insulated from Gladstone's broader thought, as he showed by using the Hellenic idealization of the human body as a vehicle for polemic against his former Puseyism. So the theological and the classical strands in his studies converged during the 1860s in a new synthesis that exalted the role of humanity. The resulting position was very similar to that of Matthew Arnold, that broadest of Broad Churchmen, who owed a greater debt to Stoicism and Spinoza than to mainstream theologians. Gladstone was already familiar with Arnold's verse by the time he wrote *Studies on Homer*, where he speaks of the modern poet as close to the Greeks—as 'one of ourselves, who has drunk into their spirit'.[238] Subsequently Gladstone was to absorb many of Arnold's prose writings where he identifies the calm and cultivation of Hellenism as the remedy for the rush and bustle of Victorian Britain. Remarkably, Gladstone, like Arnold, came to see Christianity by itself as an insufficient foundation for modern society. There were two sides to Western civilization, the Christian and the classical, because the Greek mind was 'the secular counterpart of the Gospel'. If Christianity was the salt, Greek culture was the thing salted. It ensured that an exaggerated form of Christian teaching did not cease to value 'every part, and power, and work, of human nature'.[239] The Hellenism of Homer vindicated the dignity of human beings.

The shift towards a higher estimate of things human had affinities with the development of Gladstone's politics. When preparing *Studies on Homer* in the 1850s he was still a Peelite Conservative, and, as we saw in Chapter 6, the book meshes with attitudes that are broadly conservative. It also had a conservative aim in the intellectual world, to resist the naturalistic interpretation of ancient Greek religion. In the early 1860s, however, Gladstone capitulated. He recognized that he could no longer defend the thesis that Hellenic worship had nothing to do with the forces of nature and so, with as little as possible public admission of a change of view, accepted the case of his erstwhile liberal opponents. Nevertheless he still maintained the essence of his former position, believing that Greek life showed a prevailing pattern of degeneration rather than progress and defending the idea of primitive revelation against all comers. Yet his earlier opinions underwent significant change as he gave favourable attention to the human aspects of the Greek pantheon. By the appearance of *Juventus Mundi* the human factor actually enhances the dignity of the gods. The parallel between this process and

---

[237] W. E. Gladstone, 'Inaugural Address: The Work of Universities' [1860], *Gleanings*, 7, p. 8.
[238] *SHHA*, 3, p. 4. *D*, 2 May 1857, 1 Jan. 1858.
[239] Gladstone, 'Place of Ancient Greece', pp. 77, 85.

Gladstone's political evolution is striking. His first membership of a Liberal cabinet, from 1859 to 1865, coincided exactly with the period when his views on Homer underwent the greatest revision. Thereafter he retained much of his earlier Peelite methods and objectives, making the defence of the country's institutions a continuing priority. Yet he did develop as a politician, and in precisely the direction of his thinking about Homer. Just as the poet had created a faith that integrated the natural with the anthropomorphic, so Gladstone believed in adapting the constitution to synthesize the new with the old. In both cases the aim was the forging of national unity. What is more, the rhetoric of humanity studded Gladstone's later speeches, whether in regard to Bulgarians suffering under the Turkish yoke or Irishmen oppressed by English coercion. The humanity that transfigured Olympus and the humanity he demanded of British policy were one and the same, a core value of Gladstonian Liberalism.

# 8

# The Battle of Belief

THE VICTORIAN crisis of faith formed Gladstone's central intellectual preoccupation during the last quarter-century of his life. The tendency of leaders of opinion to indulge in doubt, what he once called 'this strange epidemic',[1] induced him to spend much of his time reading and writing in defence of Christian orthodoxy. Apart from the attempt to vindicate primitive revelation that has been considered in the last two chapters, he frequently entered the lists against the champions of atheism, agnosticism, or any less precise belief in God than he would allow. His thought was therefore expressed in episodic literary jousts rather than in any systematic form. He crossed swords with the growingly sceptical English lawyer James Fitzjames Stephen and his resolutely secularist American co-professional Robert G. Ingersoll, with the mildly theistic novelist Mary Ward and—most frequently—with the archetypal agnostic scientist Thomas Huxley. His one monograph in the field, *The Impregnable Rock of Holy Scripture* (1890), was a collection of magazine articles written for a popular audience. The solidest contribution was the major work of his retirement, an edition of *The Works of Joseph Butler, D.C.L.* (1896), together with *Studies Subsidiary to the Works of Bishop Butler* (1896), consisting respectively of sparse annotations on the text of the eighteenth-century bishop and an apparently heterogeneous assemblage of essays. Gladstone's intermittent part in the debate over belief has merely been noticed in passing, whether by writers about the statesman or by specialists in his opponents, rather than subjected to careful scrutiny. Scholars interested primarily in his antagonists usually depict him as a discredited defender of hopelessly outmoded points of view. Thus Adrian Desmond, the biographer of Huxley, can call the chapter describing his hero's efforts against Gladstone 'Polishing off the G.O.M.'.[2] Those with Gladstonian sympathies, however, have held barely a higher estimate of his apologetic enterprise. Even D. C. Lathbury, while eulogizing Gladstone's role as a church leader within a decade of his death, believed that the statesman's amateurishness marred his share in the agnostic controversy. 'In this field', Lathbury concedes, 'Mr. Gladstone is not seen at his best.'[3] The statesman's body of writing in this field, extensive though it is, has therefore not

[1] W. E. Gladstone to the Duke of Argyll, 28 Dec. 1872, Lathbury, 2, p. 90.
[2] Adrian Desmond, *Huxley: From Devil's Disciple to Evolution's High Priest* (London, 1997), ch. 27. The phrase was Huxley's own.
[3] D. C. Lathbury, *Mr Gladstone* (London, 1907), p. 209.

attracted evaluation. Gladstone the Christian apologist has fallen into a limbo of neglect.

For the statesman himself, however, the rebuttal of unbelief was the chief task of the age. Men of letters and popular scientists, he noted in an undated memorandum, were denying the reality or even the possibility of miracle, prophecy, and revelation. The dismissal of the supernatural was 'not so much the conclusion as the assumption' of their approach to questions of religious belief. 'In other times [he went on], those who thought a religion untenable, likewise thought they were bound to do battle seriously with it. In our day . . . judgement seems to be passed upon the Christian dogma by default.' Although the reluctance of the sceptics to state the grounds of their supposition might be a result of respect for sacred feelings, they were failing to set out their case 'with due care and method' so that others might examine it. Questions of the proper status of human knowledge were not being discussed as they ought to be. If such epistemological issues were pursued, Gladstone believed, the orthodox would carry the day. But at present the anti-supernaturalists were simply presuming that the observable world was all that there was to know. Gladstone viewed 'with great alarm the modes of thought and reasoning which extensively prevail in the present day with respect to questions bearing on religious belief'.[4] As early as 1840, as we have seen, Gladstone was perceiving infidelity as a threat; and by the mid-1850s he had inklings that the hold of society on the essence of Christianity was growing weaker.[5] Two decades later, however, the spectre haunted his mind. 'I am convinced', he told his wife in 1874, 'that the welfare of mankind does not now depend on the State or the world of politics: the real battle is being fought in the world of thought, where a deadly attack is made with great tenacity of purpose and over a wide field upon the greatest treasure of mankind, the belief in God, and the Gospel of Christ.'[6] The assault was so bold—and so misconceived—that Gladstone felt bound to take up arms in order to repel it.

I

Gladstone's first blow in the campaign (apart from the Homeric enterprise) was struck while he was Prime Minister in 1872. At the start of the year his former Peelite cabinet colleague the Duke of Somerset published *Christian Theology and Modern Scepticism*. Recognizing some of the difficulties in upholding traditional Christianity, the duke fell back on a severely pared down belief in God. Gladstone does not record in his diary the occasion when he read the book, though he kept a newspaper cutting that noted its destructive tone

---

[4] GP 44744, ff. 151–2 (n.d.). Although this short note is bound with papers from 1854, the handwriting appears to be of a later date.     [5] See Ch. 5, p. 128. GP 44745, f. 253 (1 July 1855).
[6] W. E. Gladstone to Catherine Gladstone, 6 Apr. 1874, in A. Tilney Bassett (ed.), *Gladstone to his Wife* (London, 1936), pp. 201–2.

and years later he referred to it as a 'poor, thin, ineffectual production'.[7] But it was a sign of the times. On 1 December, just after Friedrich Max Müller had mentioned the book to him,[8] Gladstone began reading D. F. Strauss's rejection of a personal God and a future state in *The Old and the New Faith*, which had recently appeared in Germany. Three days later he started *The Martyrdom of Man*, also newly published, a freethinking indictment of religion by Winwood Reade, an eloquent writer who had travelled in Africa. The unholy tide seemed to be sweeping onwards. Gladstone alternated the two books in his reading over the next few days,[9] and on 21 December, when delivering the prize-day address at Liverpool College, warned his young hearers about 'the extraordinary and boastful manifestations in this age of ours, and especially in this year which is about to close, of the extremest forms of unbelief'. Choosing the foreigner among the sceptics for particular censure, he attacked Strauss, 'a man of far wider fame than any British writer who marches under the same banner'.[10] Gladstone had absorbed Strauss's classic *Life of Jesus* in 1848; and twenty years later he had condemned a modified version for offering the 'staggering proposition' that Christ was the subject of fable and poetry, not history.[11] Now the best that he could say about Strauss was that he was superior to Auguste Comte, whose catechism of a strange 'positive religion' that celebrated the advance of natural knowledge the statesman re-examined before delivering the speech.[12] Gladstone forebore any attempt to reason away Strauss's point of view, but hoped that bringing the German's latest opinions to public notice would cause 'a shock and a reaction'.[13]

I have been touching upon deep and dangerous subjects at Liverpool [he told the Duke of Argyll shortly afterwards]. Whether I went beyond my province many may doubt. But of the extent of the mischief I do not doubt more than of its virulence . . . we politicians are children playing with toys in comparison to that great work of and for mankind which has to be done and will yet be done in restoring belief.[14]

In that cause Gladstone wanted to exert his full influence.

His diagnosis of the contagion of unbelief was threefold. In the first place, as he often remarked, the negative opinions represented by Strauss or Comte constituted a mere fashion. In all its varieties—whether scepticism or atheism, agnosticism or secularism, pantheism or positivism, revived paganism or practical materialism—the rejection of belief in a transcendent God was a shallow phenomenon. None of these systems, which Gladstone catalogued in an article of 1876, could satisfy whole communities, sufficing only for 'a few intellectual and

---

   [7] 'The Duke of Somerset's Scepticism', *Exeter Gazette*, 26 Jan. 1872, GGM 1631. W. E. Gladstone to Lord Acton, 1 Apr. 1888, Lathbury, 1, p. 110.
   [8] Friedrich Max Müller to W. E. Gladstone, 27 Nov. [1872], GP 44251, f. 336v.
   [9] *D*, 1–16 Dec. 1872.                        [10] *T*, 23 Dec. 1872, p. 8.
   [11] See Ch. 5, p. 129. W. E. Gladstone, ' On "Ecce Homo" ' [1888], *Gleanings*, 3, p. 43.
   [12] *D*, 7 July 1867, 16, 17 Dec. 1872.               [13] *T*, 23 Dec. 1872, p. 8.
   [14] Gladstone to Argyll, 28 Dec. 1872, Lathbury, 2, p. 90.

cultivated men'.[15] Such individuals often supposed that the progress of science had undermined the claims of traditional religion. Their allegations, however, were nugatory, because unfounded on careful reasoning. The malaise was not 'worthy of being a rational or scientific process'.[16] Rather it was a passing fad. Gladstone adhered to this conviction down to the end of his life. 'Schemes of negation', he wrote in 1896, 'may each for a while fret and fume upon the stage of human affairs.' It was therefore mistaken to suppose, with Matthew Arnold in his poem 'Dover Beach', that the age was marked by a once-for-all retreat of the sea of faith. There might be a 'melancholy, long, withdrawing roar',[17] but the tide would turn. In a private memorandum of 1881 Gladstone deployed a similar image.

The sea ever weltering on our coasts from time to time gains here and loses there. And even so it might seem as though the restless human intellect, moving onwards at periods so much and widely & in many things were nevertheless insensibly and simultaneously losing ground in others on which it had relaxed its hold: and as if this mixture of progress and recession were for our wayward race almost a law.[18]

The secularization of the European mind might be developing apace, but the process could be halted and, in the course of time, would undoubtedly be reversed.

A second explanation of the doubts about Christianity, according to Gladstone, lay in the errors of its defenders. We members of the church, he admitted in an article of 1888, 'alike by our exaggerations and our shortcomings in belief, no less than by faults of conduct, have contributed to bring about this fashionable hostility to religious faith'.[19] In the same year he listed the contribution of religion towards scepticism under five headings:

1. Exaggerations of statement and belief
2. Sins
3. Persecution & intolerance
4. Offensive assumption of moral superiority
5. Overvalue of position as compared with moral commands.[20]

The mistakes of the orthodox were clearly not only intellectual, but extended deep into the realm of behaviour. Yet the inflated assertions were serious enough. They included, as a fuller list of 1881 headed 'Idola Templi' shows, some distinctive positions of the Roman Catholic Church such as the excommunication of all beyond her borders and the assertion of papal infallibility. Others were evangelical weaknesses, identified long before, such as turning the atonement into the

---

[15] W. E. Gladstone, 'The Courses of Religious Thought' [1876], *Gleanings*, 3, pp. 125–35, quoted at p. 127.    [16] Gladstone to Argyll, 28 Dec. 1872, Lathbury, 2, p. 90.
[17] Matthew Arnold, 'Dover Beach' [written 1851, published 1867], in *Poems: Lyric and Elegiac* (London, 1885), p. 64.
[18] GP 44765, f. 132 (24 Sept. 1881), printed with variations at *D*, 24 Sept. 1881.
[19] W. E. Gladstone, 'Ingersoll on Christianity' [1888], *Later Gleanings*, p. 120.
[20] GP 44773, f. 68 (May 1888).

payment of a debt or the separation of divine pardon from moral transformation. A further class consisted of traditional claims that contemporary debate seemed to be revealing as worthless. 'Assumption of a title to rule the decision of questions lying within the domain of natural science' was one.[21] The churches, Gladstone was realizing, had ventured too far from their own ground in pulling together the strands of scientific knowledge and theological teaching. The skein was now unravelling, casting doubt on the theological threads. The renunciation of such untenable positions was essential for the successful rebuttal of sceptical arguments.

The third reason for the prevalence of unbelief, in Gladstone's view, was the advance of prosperity. In classifying the various forms of negative belief in 1876, he identified one as materialism. He meant primarily philosophical materialism, the idea that matter alone exists, but he suggested that in common use the term indicated the practical elimination of God from human life. 'Such a materialism', he suggested, 'is the special danger of comfortable and money-making times.'[22] In an article of the following year he generalized the point, declaring that material progress was one of the causes of the disintegration of belief and admitting that, ironically, his own public work had contributed to advancing the process.[23] By 1890 he had decided that the growth of wealth was not just a single explanation among several others but the main one. Wealth promoted leisure, travel, and opportunities for enjoyment: 'we have before us an increased power of things seen, and ... this increased power implies ... a diminishing hold upon us of things unseen.'[24] To the role of entertainment and mobility he added in a memorandum of 1893 the increase of available knowledge and the wider distribution of political power (for both of which, again, he had a large measure of responsibility) as forces distracting the mind from the immaterial to the material.[25] The implication of this sustained analysis was that the decay of faith was not ultimately due to the intellectual stance of its opponents ('either real or pretended science') or of its defenders ('the errors and excesses of believers'). 'It is the increased force within us', he argued, 'of all which is sensuous and worldly that furnishes every sceptical argument, good, bad, or indifferent, with an unseen ally, and that recruits many and many a disciple of the negative teaching.'[26] It was economic change that was behind the crisis of faith. This quasi-Marxist approach to understanding ideological developments may at first seem surprising, but for Gladstone this line of thought afforded some comfort. The issue, on this interpretation, was at root not intellectual, a question of agnostics having made good their case with the public; rather it was moral, a matter of the people being led astray by the will-o'-the-wisp of affluence. It was difficult, he recognized, to contend against the environment created by modern prosperity, but it could be done. The churches

---

[21] 'Idola Templi', GP 44765, ff. 169–70 (19 Dec. 1881), in *D*.
[22] Gladstone, 'Courses of Religious Thought', pp. 131–2.
[23] W. E. Gladstone, 'Rejoinder on Authority in Matters of Opinion' [1877], *Gleanings*, 3, p. 213.
[24] *IRHS*, p. 288.                    [25] GP 44775, ff. 246–51 (19 Nov. 1893), spec. f. 249.
[26] *IRHS*, p. 292.

could return to the debate in the confidence that they had not already lost the struggle in the world of ideas. The battle of belief could be won.

How should the campaign be conducted? The received answer in the English-speaking world was that the best apologetic consisted of Christian evidences. Belief could be vindicated by appealing to stock arguments for the existence of God and for the specifics of the Christian religion. The strongest tradition was that of 'natural theology', associated supremely with William Paley, whose book with that title Gladstone had read in 1828.[27] The design evident in the natural world, it was held, revealed that it must have had a Designer. Gladstone, though disliking Paley's version because of its shallowness and its association with his utilitarianism,[28] embraced the argument from design in the more sophisticated form popularized by Thomas Chalmers.[29] The constitution of the world, Gladstone believed, provided evidence for a God of justice and mercy. Its disruption by sin and pain (here was the Chalmers element) suggested the likelihood that there would be 'exceptional provisions for good, meant to supply the defect of nature'. That remedy was indeed available through revelation.[30] Gladstone upheld this rationale in a memorandum of 1882 and repeated it, though with rather more questions about the problem of evil, in 1893.[31] Yet the statesman already knew by the 1860s that this case was less convincing than it had seemed earlier in the century. The argument from design, he admitted in a note of 1863, even if valid, did not demonstrate that the Designer was infinite, a doctrine that had to be accepted on other grounds.[32] By that time Charles Darwin's *Origin of Species* (1859) had set a question-mark against the whole contention by suggesting that organisms could adapt to the environment of their own accord. The case for a Designer was seriously undermined. Gladstone admitted in print in 1868 that 'the evidences purely traditional have lost their command (among others) over those large classes of minds which, in other times . . . would perhaps most steadily and even blindly have received them'.[33] There was no going back to the argument from design if the threat of unbelief was to be met.

Yet Gladstone did not retreat from the task of defending the faith by means of argument. On the contrary, he constantly insisted that religion was intrinsically reasonable. 'Belief in God', he asserted at the opening of a memorandum of 1881, 'is required by reason.'[34] The heading of this document, 'A Grammar of Assent', echoed the title of J. H. Newman's book of 1870 vindicating the reasonableness of Christian—and Catholic—belief. Despite earlier reservations about Newman's low estimate of the powers of human reason, the statesman's apologetic was now bolstered by the case mounted in the book: he turned to it in 1879, when revising

---

[27] *D*, 10 Sept. 1828. On the broad tradition, see J. H. Brooke, *Science and Religion: Some Historical Perspectives* (Cambridge, 1991). [28] Cf. Ch. 2, pp. 25–6.
[29] D. W. Bebbington, 'Science and Evangelical Theology in Britain from Wesley to Orr', in D. N. Livingstone et al. (eds), *Evangelicals and Science in Historical Perspective* (New York, 1999), pp. 126–9.
[30] GP 44766, ff. 118–18v (14 Aug. 1882), in *D*.
[31] 'Theism' (3 Sept. 1893), Lathbury, 2, pp. 406–8. [32] GP 44752, ff. 324–4v (12 Sept. 1863).
[33] Gladstone, 'On "Ecce Homo" ', p. 90. [34] GP 44765, f. 166 (4 and 6 Dec. 1881), in *D*.

an essay on Butler for publication, and again in 1888, when devising a riposte to a freethinker.[35] Newman's discussion of an 'illative sense' that clinches certitude on the basis of disparate evidence is assumed by a reference to 'the illative faculty' in the second article.[36] Gladstone's notion of the powers of reason, however, is much less sophisticated than Newman's. It is simply the faculty that examines evidence in order to reach a considered judgement. Religion is firmly within its province. Gladstone did not treat intuition as a distinct mode of apprehending God. 'I cannot', he once remarked, 'assert any method of knowing Him otherwise than by operations in strict conformity with the general laws of our nature.'[37] All religious claims are therefore to be tested by reason. In *The Impregnable Rock* Gladstone rejected what he saw as a trap laid by the eighteenth-century philosopher David Hume of exempting the grounds of faith from debate by treating 'our "holy religion" as a matter in no way amenable to the view of reason'. The appeal to reason runs like a refrain through the book: its case is said to be made out 'on general grounds of reason'; there can be 'no rational objection' against one point; a 'spirit of reason' should prevail in the discussion; his readers should all be 'rational investigators'.[38] It was part of the enduring appeal of Bishop Butler that he had no time for any disharmony between faith and reason.[39] In Gladstone's view human rationality provided the common ground on which the battle of belief could be fought out.

Near the heart of his case for orthodox Christianity was an appeal to history. Part of Gladstone's apologetic strategy was to show the way in which the Christian faith had contributed to the progress of society. Together with the study of Butler, he remarked in 1875 to William Stubbs, Regius Professor of Modern History at Oxford and a future bishop, it was 'the truly historical treatment of Christianity, and of all the religious experience of mankind' that would supply 'effectual bulwarks against the rash and violent unbelief . . . rushing in upon us'.[40] The quest for evidence of a primitive revelation clearly fitted into this scheme, but equally prominent in Gladstone's mind was the need to set out the benefits that had accrued to humanity from the religion of the incarnation. To compensate for the weakening of the argument from miracles, he noted in his edition of Butler, 'the evidential force of the existence of the Church, and its operation on the world and on society, has grown progressively'.[41] By the 1860s, as we have seen, Gladstone was stressing in his household sermons the social benefits generated by the Christian faith,[42] and in the following decade he developed the theme in his

---

[35] *D*, 12 Mar. 1879, 1 Jan. 1888. Gladstone also read *A Grammar of Assent* on 27 March 1870, 25 August 1878, and 9 December 1883: the diaries' index reference to 28 September 1873 seems to be mistaken.

[36] Gladstone, 'Ingersoll on Christianity', p. 153.

[37] Gladstone, 'Rejoinder on Authority', p. 213.                    [38] *IRHS*, pp. 5, 44, 170, 230, 266.

[39] *Studies Subsidiary*, pp. 42–3, 90.

[40] W. E. Gladstone to William Stubbs, 27 Dec. 1875, in W. H. Hutton (ed.), *Letters of William Stubbs, Bishop of Oxford, 1825–1901* (London, 1904), pp. 147–8.                    [41] *WJB*, 1, p. 247 n.

[42] See Ch. 5, pp. 137–8.

public writings. The religion of Christ, he asserted in 'The Courses of Religious Thought' (1876), had elevated women, restrained violence, enforced mutual love, relieved the poor, and reined in pride.[43] The faith, Gladstone contended in a remarkably utilitarian manner, was justified by its results. He was equally eager to rebut the challenges that social advance had been independent of revelation. Gladstone's old freethinking antagonist George Grote, for example, had seen the flowering of Athens as the fruit of philosophy. Gladstone's answer to such claims was that classical Greece, though advanced in civilization, had not raised moral standards in the mass of the population. The case of Athens in the time of Socrates, he declared in a letter of 1873, was 'of immense importance with regard to the controversy of belief'. Athenian society, he held, was afflicted by 'vice, and even foul vice', and so could not claim the first rank in morality.[44] Christianity, by contrast, had abolished gladiatorial shows, human sacrifice, polygamy, exposure of children, slavery, and cannibalism.[45] Orthodox teaching could be vindicated by pointing out the moral improvements it had conferred on humanity.

## II

Gladstone was particularly concerned that the churches should avoid less attractive strategies. Before an examination of his own engagement with non-Christian writers, it is worthwhile considering his attitude to alternative apologetic methods, especially those of the Roman Catholic Church. He realized, to his dismay, that Rome was abandoning the twin appeal to reason and history in favour of a blatant assertion of authority. The growing ascendancy of the ultramontane party within the church meant that by the 1860s it was becoming axiomatic that whatever the pope promulgated was to be accepted without question. A contrary point of view within the Roman communion was still being championed in that decade by Gladstone's friend, the Munich theologian Ignaz von Döllinger. It had been Döllinger's thorough account of church history that had encouraged Gladstone to see, as early as the 1840s, the Christian faith as the motor of moral improvement in society.[46] In 1863, at a conference in Munich, Döllinger tried to rally the theologians of Germany to defend the faith by means of scholarly history and modern philosophy rather than by the neo-scholasticism increasingly dominant at Rome. It was a call to assert the 'freedom of science'.[47] In the following year his dream of intellectual independence within the church was shattered by Pius IX's Syllabus of Errors. The Syllabus defined a range of modern opinions that were contrary to the faith, famously anathematizing the proposition that the pope should adjust to

[43] Gladstone, 'Courses of Religious Thought', p. 127.
[44] W. E. Gladstone to J. B. Mozley, 22 Oct. 1873, Lathbury, 2, p. 97.
[45] W. E. Gladstone to Sir Anthony Panizzi, 8 Feb. 1874, Lathbury, 2, p. 99.
[46] See Ch. 5, p. 125.
[47] Roger Aubert et al., *The Church in the Age of Liberalism* (London, 1981), p. 228; Alexander Dru, *The Contribution of German Catholicism* (New York, 1963), p. 87 (quoted).

'progress, liberalism and modern civilization'. Döllinger was incensed that his whole project of deploying historical research, as it had been refined in nineteenth-century Germany, in the service of the church was being dismissed out of hand by the Vatican.[48] Gladstone viewed these developments with growing alarm. He shared with Döllinger a desire to halt the apparent slide into obscurantism by Catholic theologians.[49] By contrast with the Syllabus, they both wanted the churches to adjust to progress, liberalism, and modern civilization. 'I know no one', Gladstone told his wife while visiting Döllinger in Munich in 1874, 'with whose mode of viewing and handling religious matters I more cordially agree.'[50] Döllinger was Gladstone's *beau ideal* of the noble champion of the faith.

In 1870, however, came the triumph of ultramontanism at the first Vatican Council. To the discomfiture of Döllinger, who was eventually excommunicated for his refusal to accept the Vatican decrees, the council defined the pope's pronouncements *ex cathedra* as infallible. Döllinger's former pupil Lord Acton, resident in Rome for the council, warned Gladstone of the scheme to press through papal infallibility. Gladstone knew that the measure would seriously complicate government policies towards the Catholic Irish, but, as he explained to Acton, his fundamental reason for deploring the development was that it would advance the cause of secularism. 'Ultramontanism', he continued, '& secularism are enemies in theory and intention, but the result of the former will be to increase the force, & better the chances of the latter.'[51] His analysis was that the overweening claims of papal authority would only alienate people from Christian allegiance. Acton concurred, telling Gladstone of a paper circulating at the council denying that scholarly disciplines possessed any certainty without endorsement by the church.[52] The bearings of 'this insane enterprise' were incalculable, according to Acton, both in its impact on the Prime Minister's policies and especially in 'its consequences for the conflict against sin and unbelief'.[53] Gladstone marked this phrase with two lines in the margin, warmly agreeing with its prophecy. Acton appealed to Gladstone to sound the alarm before it was too late. The Prime Minister responded by trying to persuade the cabinet to issue a note of protest, but failed to secure the support of Lord Clarendon, his Foreign Secretary.[54] The Vatican decrees were duly issued without effective remonstrance from Britain or any public statement by Gladstone. But the new departure by the Roman Catholic Church deeply troubled him. The decrees, he declared in a speech at King's College, London, in May 1872, 'seemed much to resemble the proclamation of a perpetual war against the progress and the movement of the

---

[48] Robrecht Boudens (ed.), *Alfred Plummer: Conversations with Dr. Döllinger, 1870–1890* (Leuven, 1985), p. xviii.

[49] W. E. Gladstone to J. J. I. von Döllinger, 22 June 1862, Lathbury, 2, p. 35.

[50] Morley, 2, p. 513.

[51] W. E. Gladstone to Lord Acton, 1 Dec. 1869, GP 44093, f. 97v, Lathbury, 2, p. 49.

[52] Lord Acton to W. E. Gladstone, 1 Jan. 1870, GP 44093, f. 103v.

[53] Lord Acton to W. E. Gladstone, 10 Mar. 1870, GP 44093, f. 125v.

[54] Matthew, pp. 184–5.

human mind'.[55] The appeal for abject and irrational submission could not but imperil the credibility of Christianity.

Gladstone's detestation of ultramontanism burst out in the most widely circulated of all his writings, *The Vatican Decrees*, in November 1874. The pamphlet was very much an *ad hominem* riposte to Henry Manning, the former comrade-in-arms who was now Roman Catholic Archbishop of Westminster and the leading English exponent of the system Gladstone deplored. *The Vatican Decrees* should be seen as a rebuttal of Manning's *Caesarism and Ultramontanism* (1874), an exposition, occasioned by the *Kulturkampf* in Germany, of the right of the church not to submit to the state.[56] Gladstone's book was primarily an appeal to his Roman Catholic fellow-subjects to declare that their political loyalty was to the crown and not, as Manning appeared to have suggested, ultimately at the disposal of the Vatican.[57] Underlying the statesman's argument, however, was his consternation that the ultramontanes had abdicated the proper ground on which to substantiate the faith of Christendom. In May 1872 Manning had delivered to the Metaphysical Society, a forum for debating questions of belief to which we shall return, a paper urging 'That Legitimate Authority is an Evidence of Truth'. Although Gladstone had not been present, he marked a copy of the lecture he had received with signs of dissent. He objected to the paper's basic contention, that in matters of debate a magisterium could decide the issue.[58] Instead of authority, the age needed to hear the testimony of history. But, as Gladstone made explicit in *The Vatican Decrees*, the Roman Church had repudiated the appeal to history by accepting the notion that the pope possessed the power to define novel doctrines. No longer did it claim to hold the same teaching as the apostles. This was a serious matter 'for those who think that against all forms, both of superstition and unbelief, one main preservative is to be found in maintaining the truth and authority of history, and the inestimable value of the historic spirit'.[59] This line of argument, a theological topic, was not pursued in a book that concentrated on the political issue, but it was part of the reason for Gladstone's vehemence in *The Vatican Decrees*. Ultramontanism seemed to have sold the pass in the most fundamental controversy of all.

Gladstone's book provoked a host of replies, including a temperate and therefore powerful riposte by Newman, who saw no inconsistency in being 'at once a good Catholic and a good Englishman'.[60] There can be little doubt that Newman showed Gladstone's fears about the loyalties of the Catholic community to be

[55] *Guardian*, 22 May 1872, quoted by Morley, 2, pp. 523–4.

[56] Jeffrey P. von Arx, 'Archbishop Manning and the *Kulturkampf*', *Recusant History*, 21 (1992).

[57] W. E. Gladstone, 'The Vatican Decrees in their Bearing on Civil Allegiance: A Political Expostulation'[1874], *Rome and the Newest Fashions in Religion* (London, 1875), pp. xix, lxiii–lxvi. On the Vaticanism controversy, see Damian McElrath, *The Syllabus of Pius IX: Some Reactions in England* (Louvain, 1964).

[58] Archbishop Manning, 'That Legitimate Authority is an Evidence of Truth', GGM 1628.

[59] Gladstone, 'Vatican Decrees', p. xxv.

[60] J. H. Newman, *A Letter addressed to His Grace the Duke of Norfolk on occasion of Mr. Gladstone's Recent Expostulation* (London, 1875), p. 4.

alarmist fantasies. But Gladstone restated his position in February 1875 with *Vaticanism*, receding hardly at all from his previously expressed views. Towards the conclusion he approaches the ultimate issues at stake. Vaticanism, he contends, is 'dangerous to the foundations of civil order', but it is also 'not less dangerous . . . to the foundations of . . . Christian belief, which it loads with false excrescences, and strains even to bursting'. The additions to the burdens of the faithful, supremely the doctrine of papal infallibility, were mistaken and indefensible. The new style of Roman teaching, furthermore, elevated authority to the disparagement of reason and liberty. Such a stance, he explains on the final page of *Vaticanism*, was vulnerable to opponents who are 'making war, some upon Revelation, some upon dogma, some upon Theism itself'.[61] Neither side, the ultramontanes or their critics, was in the right: there must be a synthesis of the gospel of the church with the liberty of the freethinkers. Likewise in 'Courses of Religious Thought', published in the following year, Gladstone raised a series of objections to ultramontanism. They included 'its hostility to mental freedom at large' and 'its incompatibility with the thought and movement of modern civilisation'. The result was summed up as 'the *de facto* alienation of the educated mind of the countries in which it prevails'.[62] The Roman Church in its post-Vatican Council phase was incapable of effective defence of the faith.

The revolt from reason by Rome meant that other churches occupied the strategic ground in the struggle. Against the ultramontanes on the one hand, who believed too much, and the Protestant evangelicals on the other, who believed too little, Gladstone posed what he called the Historical school of opinion. Its adherents included, alongside Anglicans, all who conformed to the apostolic insistence on a visible church, appealing to tradition as their warrant but without ultramontane modifications. The category embraced the continental Old Catholics who left the Roman Church because they could not embrace papal infallibility and the Liberal Catholics who, while remaining within the Latin communion, hoped for some relaxation of the Vatican Decrees. The former group agreed with Döllinger, though he never joined their ranks; the latter included Acton. The Historical school also included the Orthodox Churches of the East. Although, Gladstone admitted, these Eastern Churches had their abuses, they were commonly judged too harshly for, unlike the Latin Church, they knew nothing of a conflict with the state, the scriptures, the family, the individual mind, or 'modern culture, science, and civilisation'.[63] Eastern Orthodoxy was therefore no foe to human welfare. The hallmark of the school as a whole was that 'it regards the general consent of Christendom, honestly examined and sufficiently ascertained, as a leading auxiliary, at the least, to the individual reason in the search for religious truth'.[64] Its respect for research and for reason set it apart from current

---

[61] W. E. Gladstone, 'Vaticanism: An Answer to Reproofs & Replies' [1875], *Rome and the Newest Fashions*, pp. 117, 120.

[62] Gladstone, 'Courses of Religious Thought', p. 105.               [63] Ibid., p. 108.

[64] Ibid., p. 106.

Roman teaching. Gladstone entertained hopes that the Historical school had sufficient in common to consolidate. His old ecumenical aspirations focused in the 1870s on the Bonn conferences, organized by Döllinger to bring together representatives of Orthodoxy and the Western Churches.[65] Gladstone became fired with enthusiasm for the reunion of East and West, even expressing a willingness to concede the perennial Orthodox demand that the *Filioque* clause, added to the Nicene Creed by the Western Church, should be dropped.[66] The new-found unity—a dream soon shattered by the suspension of the Bonn conferences in 1876—would light a beacon of truth. Those tempted to ignore the claims of historic Christianity would have to take notice.

With the failure of the broader scheme for a rapprochement with the Eastern Churches, Gladstone fell back in the following decade on bolstering the claims of the Church of England as the citadel of 'Historical' religion. In a series of three articles during 1888–9 he argued for the continuity of the church, preserving the episcopal succession through the upheavals of the sixteenth century. His case dwelt on the historical contention that the changes of the period were voluntary acts of the church rather than impositions by the state.[67] Inevitably he provoked Roman Catholics. His first article was answered by the Jesuit John Morris, once Manning's secretary, who claimed that 'it scarcely contains a single historical statement that is not inaccurate' and reasserted that 'the royal supremacy was forced by Henry VIII on an unwilling clergy'.[68] Fortified by correspondence with the historian Bishop Stubbs, Gladstone rebutted Morris's points one by one. The controversy descended into many fine points of detail, but Gladstone's overriding complaint against Roman Catholic writers on the English Reformation was their concentration on the conflict between pope and king to the neglect of 'the National Church in itself'.[69] It was his original assertion that England was different from other European countries in the sixteenth century because 'the instinct of national unity was throughout more powerful than the disintegrating tendencies of religious controversy'.[70] Acton, who commented on Gladstone's article and Stubbs's remarks about it, suggested that the author was exaggerating English exceptionalism.[71] But Gladstone was making less of a sober historical analysis than a deeply felt combative point. The Church of England, in his eyes, was strongly identified with the nation. Already before the Reformation the English church had resented interference by the pope. All that Henry VIII and subsequently Queen Elizabeth had done was to give expression to a pre-existing desire for

[65] On the context, see H. C. G. Matthew, 'Gladstone, Vaticanism and the Question of the East', in Derek Baker (ed.), *Religious Motivation: Biographical and Sociological Problems for the Church Historian*, Studies in Church History, 15 (Oxford, 1978) , pp. 417–42.

[66] W. E. Gladstone to J. J. I. von Döllinger, 29 Aug. 1875, Lathbury, 2, p. 63.

[67] W. E. Gladstone, 'The Elizabethan Settlement of Religion' [1888], *Later Gleanings*, p. 165.

[68] John Morris, 'Mr. Gladstone on the Elizabethan Settlement of Religion', *Dublin Review*, 20 (1888), pp. 243, 258. Gladstone's annotated copy of the article is in GGM 1632.

[69] W. E. Gladstone, 'The Church under Henry VIII' [1889], *Later Gleanings*, pp. 221–8, quoted at p. 226. *D*, 26 Sept. 1889. Morley, 2, p. 535.

[70] Gladstone, 'Elizabethan Settlement', p. 159.          [71] GP 44094, f. 41.

national freedom from external meddling. Church and nation intertwined with each other and had their character fixed as a result. It was a deeply cherished part of Gladstone's appeal to history that the national church was the natural home for any Englishman.

Gladstone's final exchange with the Roman Catholic Church took place very near the close of his life. Lord Halifax, the lay leader of the Anglo-Catholic party, hoped to advance the cause of eventual reunion between Canterbury and Rome by securing Vatican confirmation of the validity of Anglican orders of ministry. It was largely a question of obtaining agreement that the episcopal succession in England had not been interrupted by the Reformation. Cardinal Vaughan, now heading the Roman Catholics of the land, however, resisted what he interpreted as a threat to his church. While in May 1896 the question was under investigation in Rome, Gladstone issued an open letter, favourably received in the Vatican, designed to strengthen the will of the pope to exercise a 'paternal' magnanimity.[72] Nevertheless the venture failed. Vaughan's opposition triumphed, and in September Anglican orders were condemned as 'absolutely null and utterly void'.[73] In a postscript on the episode written in the following year Gladstone gave vent to his indignation. The pronouncements of the Roman see had never, he complained, acknowledged the value of efforts to reunite Eastern and Western Christendom, but instead the Vatican Council had widened the schism; and 'now has come this damnatory bull against English orders'. Rome was fostering division, not unity.

I write [he explained] entirely from one defined and immovable point of view. According to my mind, the whole interests of the human race eventually depend upon one question, the question of belief; as, again, belief is summed up in Christianity, and Christianity in Christ . . . every measure, and every movement, in matters of religion, without any exception, ought to be ultimately tried by its tendency to bring mankind nearer to Christ, or to remove them further from Him.[74]

Gladstone's ambivalence towards the Roman Catholic Church, like his sympathy for Eastern Orthodoxy and his unwavering attachment to the Church of England, was conditioned by his ultimate commitment to upholding the faith.

The inspiration for his thinking in this late stage of his career was rarely new reading. Rather it was the enduring effect on him of writers who had made the greatest impression long before. Two must be singled out. One was William Palmer, whose defence of the Anglican position had underpinned his own original articulation of a high ecclesiology. Palmer is cited, for instance, in the first of Gladstone's articles of 1888–9 vindicating the Church of England against Rome.[75] In 1885 Gladstone unsuccessfully tried to have Palmer's *Treatise on the Church* (1838) republished.[76] In Palmer's view the Church of England, alongside the

---

[72] W. E. Gladstone, 'Soliloquium' [1896], *Later Gleanings*, p. 393.
[73] J. J. Hughes, *Absolutely Null and Utterly Void* (London, 1968).
[74] W. E. Gladstone, 'Postscript' [1897], *Later Gleanings*, pp. 396, 405.
[75] Gladstone, 'Elizabethan Settlement', p. 178. On Palmer, see Ch. 3, pp. 67–9.
[76] 'Palmer on the Church, 1838', GP 44769, ff. 77–9 (12 Apr. 1885).

Roman and Eastern communions, was one of the branches of the universal church. Although the statesman was concerned, as he had been nearly half-a-century earlier, to disavow the book's severity towards Presbyterians and Nonconformists, he continued to endorse Palmer's principles of catholicity. The second book to leave an indelible mark on the statesman's mind, however, was one that refined those principles. Peter Erb has shown that J. A. Möhler's *Symbolism* (1832) was a continuing influence on Gladstone's later years.[77] Möhler, though a Roman Catholic, showed none of the neo-scholastic rigidity that provided the rationale for ultramontanism, but instead favoured engagement with modern philosophy and the use of historical method. Gladstone continued to refer to his pages during the 1870s.[78] *Symbolism* taught that Christ himself through the incarnation supplied the basis for the unity of the church. Despite all the differences of Christendom, the common mind of the church persisted in its understanding of the person of Christ. The Nicene Creed—as Gladstone, citing Möhler, delighted to point out—had remained undisturbed through the shocks of the Reformation.[79] The statesman cherished the idea of catholic consent, the idea beloved of Augustine that what the whole church believed must be true. It provided a basis for ecumenical endeavour. Why should Christians who thought almost identically not aspire to be organically one? Meanwhile, as Möhler argued, the agreement of different branches of the church in the central doctrines of the faith provided additional evidence of their veracity: 'will not', Gladstone demanded in 1896, 'the candid unbeliever be disposed freely to admit, that this unity amidst diversity is a great confirmation of the faith ...?'[80] What the humble faithful of all communions believed in common rose, on Möhler's authority, to become a central category in Gladstone's thought. The concurrence of virtually the whole of Christendom seemed a powerful apologetic tool.

### III

How did Gladstone himself go about the apologetic task? His closest encounters with the assailants of Christianity took place in the arena of the Metaphysical Society, a metropolitan discussion club founded in 1869 to which James Knowles, architect and soon editor of the *Contemporary Review*, invited representatives of all schools of educated opinion, ultramontane and positivist, Anglican and free-thinking.[81] After laying down the premiership, Gladstone accepted the presidency

---

[77] P. C. Erb, 'Gladstone and German Liberal Catholicism', *Recusant History*, 23 (1997). For Möhler, see also J. A. Möhler, *Symbolism: Exposition of the Doctrinal Differences between Catholics and Protestants as Evidenced by their Symbolical Writings*, introd. M. J. Himes (New York, 1997), pp. xi–xxi. See Ch. 5, pp. 123–4.

[78] *D*, 27 Sept. 1874, 1 Sept. 1878 (though the second item is not indexed).

[79] W. E. Gladstone, ' "Robert Elsmere": The Battle of Belief' [1888], *Later Gleanings*, p.103.

[80] Gladstone, 'Soliloquium', p. 392.

[81] A. W. Brown, *The Metaphysical Society: Victorian Minds in Crisis, 1869–1880* (New York, 1947).

of the society for 1875. The first meeting at which he took the chair, on 12 January, was addressed by the lawyer James Fitzjames Stephen, the society's most frequent speaker and most pugnacious critic of revealed religion.[82] Stephen's paper was a sustained assault on Newman. 'Discussion on Mysteries as defined by Newman until after 10.30', noted Gladstone in his diary. The statesman was again in the chair in November, when Fitzjames Stephen returned to the fray with a paper on miracles. It would be practically impossible, argued the speaker, to show that any alleged miracle could not have been caused in a non-supernatural way. Drawing on his experience of the law, Stephen asserted that 'I find it hard to imagine reasonable grounds for undoubting belief of any matter of fact which cannot even be proved by legal evidence'. Gladstone was unconvinced by the precirculated paper: 'e.g. Julius Caesar—glacial period—The Norman Conquest', he noted in the margin against Stephen's observation. Could events of the past be subjected to such tight requirements of proof?[83] Gladstone must have been restrained on the evening by the etiquette of chairmanship, but it was agreed that the subject should be resumed in the new year.[84] This time the statesman would personally take up the cudgels against Stephen.

Gladstone's notes for his presentation in February 1876 are preserved in his papers. There are two strands in the reply that he develops. One was based on his long-standing allegiance to the method of Bishop Butler. Probability, not certainty, was the guide of life:

Ought not <u>moral action to follow</u> upon <u>a balance of probability</u>?
    Which may leave <u>much doubt</u>
    The question is do miracles have a balance of probability in their favour upon a view of the whole circumstances.[85]

Fitzjames Stephen, who had once published a critique of Butler's ethics,[86] was not treating the bishop's teaching with the respect that it demanded. 'Argument for the obligation of probable evidences of religious truth is needless', contends Gladstone, '<u>until Bishop Butler has been overthrown</u> . . .' Fitzjames Stephen had demanded absolute proof, but that was too stringent a stipulation for religious matters. 'This distinction of proof absolute and proof probable', Gladstone holds, 'goes to the root of the whole reasoning of the paper.' His second line of argument takes the battle into the enemy's camp. His opponent had dwelt on the need for miracles to measure up to the criteria of proof governing the courts. But it was a mistake to expect legal norms to apply to a broader field. Judicial proof, Gladstone proposes, is '<u>isolated</u>', concerned only with matters of fact. Religious

---

[82] J. A. Colaiaco, *James Fitzjames Stephen and the Crisis of Victorian Thought* (London, 1983).

[83] 'Remarks on the Proof of Miracles', GP 44763, f. 6 (= p. 9).

[84] *D*, 9 Nov. 1875. The subsequent meeting on 15 February 1876 is usually considered to have continued the discussion of Huxley's paper on the evidence for the miracle of the resurrection from 11 January, an occasion when Gladstone was absent (Brown, *Metaphysical Society*, p. 330). But Gladstone's diary reveals that the true purpose was to return to the broader subject of Fitzjames Stephen's paper.                    [85] GP 44763, ff. 10v–17v (n.d.), quoted at f. 10v.

[86] E. C. Mossner, *Bishop Butler and the Age of Reason* (New York, 1936), p. 222.

proof, on the other hand, is '<u>compound</u>', including not only miracles but also prophecy, history (embracing scripture, church, Christian civilization and its fruits), and personal experience. The evidence in favour of religion—here Gladstone draws on Butler again, and on Newman's case, influenced by Butler, in *A Grammar of Assent*—is a matter of converging probabilities. So the case for miracles has collateral support from other sources. 'This compound character of religious proof', remarks Gladstone in an admission that betrays a certain discomfort with the ethos of the Metaphysical Society, 'makes the Evidences hard to deal with in conversational discussion . . .'[87] Fitzjames Stephen, perhaps seeing his advantage, claimed in response that he had not confined himself to criminal charges and that, though there might be a duty to act, there was no duty, on the basis of probable evidence, to believe. Nevertheless Gladstone's diary verdict on the evening was 'long debate, all <u>verifying</u> Butler'.[88] He had bearded the lion of the negative school in his own den.

When, a year later, James Knowles invited Gladstone to contribute to the first issue of the new *Contemporary Review*, he was happy to accept. Gladstone determined to raise the fundamental issue underlying the Metaphysical Society's debates: why was Christianity to be believed? He needed an intellectual ally, preferably one no longer able to speak for himself, who would commend his case to the sceptical. His choice fell on Sir George Cornewall Lewis, his former rival for the Chancellorship and opponent on Homeric questions, who had died in 1863. The ploy may well have been suggested by a passage in *A Grammar of Assent* where Newman indicates that Lewis's dismissal of early Greek history as myth, like George Grote's, was a result of his presuppositions rather than of the evidence.[89] Gladstone knew from previous research that he could turn the classical scholar's rigorous doubt to advantage. In September 1871 Gladstone had read with great care a copy of Lewis's rare work *An Essay on the Influence of Authority in Matters of Opinion* (1849), a programmatic essay on intellectual method.[90] His notes at the time show that he disagreed with many of Lewis's views inherited from the sceptical Enlightenment such as that the formation of opinion by authority could never produce an increase of knowledge. Gladstone held on the contrary that authority, as an abridgement of the accumulated wisdom of mankind, acted as a springboard for intellectual progress. Most of all he dissented, as a marginal cross in his notes indicates, from Lewis's assertion that the principle of authority does not apply to religion.[91] Gladstone was as attached to the teaching authority of the church as he had been when he wrote *Church Principles*

---

[87] GP 44763, ff. 12, 13, 15, 17.                                    [88] *D*, 15 Feb. 1876.

[89] J. H. Newman, *An Essay in Aid of a Grammar of Assent* [1870] (London, 1892), pp. 364–71. Newman's idea in the book that matters of faith have the certainty of spiritual sight was in Gladstone's mind as he read Lewis: GP 44763, f. 100. *D*, 27 Mar. 1870. On Grote, see Ch. 6, p. 146.

[90] *D*, 11–23 Sept. 1871.

[91] GP 44763, ff. 102–2v, 113. The notes on Lewis, described as untraced in the diary, are to be found under the heading 'Authority. Opinion. Controversy with Sir J. Stephen. 1877' at GP 44763, ff. 98–118, some of them dated September 1871.

in 1840. Yet he also held, as he had then done, that there is no antithesis between authority and reason. One of the functions of reason, he told his son Stephen in 1868, was 'to comprehend the nature and limits, and to recognize the office, of authority'.[92] Gladstone was delighted to discover Lewis providing unexpected support for that position. Lewis declared, as Gladstone noted down, that the opposition between authority and reason rested on a confusion of thought.[93] Much of Lewis's case, Gladstone concluded, could be exploited in support of authority, even in the field of religion he disavowed. It was to his notes on *The Influence of Authority* that Gladstone turned when Knowles requested an article.

The purpose of the resulting essay, 'The Influence of Authority in Matters of Opinion', was, then, to vindicate Christianity on the basis of critical methodological principles. The starting point of the central argument is an axiom of Lewis's: 'In general, it may be said that the authority of the professors of any science is trustworthy in proportion as the points of agreement among them are numerous and important, and the points of difference few and unimportant.'[94] Gladstone surmounts Lewis's refusal to apply the maxim to religion by suggesting that, on the author's own principles, the common opinion of Christendom, which Lewis himself equates with the civilized world, should provide the basis of belief. Here Gladstone brings Möhler's favourite argument into play.[95] The various denominations, the statesman points out, were overwhelmingly agreed on the duties of morality and the tenets of the creed. Hence orthodox Christianity was as entitled to our concurrence as any other body of knowledge. Revolt against its legitimate authority, Gladstone concludes, was 'a childish or anile superstition'. He was performing a delicate balancing act. Whereas in the Vaticanism controversy he had been endorsing intellectual freedom, now he was urging the claims of its polar opposite. He therefore takes pains to distinguish his position from that of Rome by denying obedience in religion to be a matter of dragooned discipline. Rather than offering any support to an ultramontane view of authority, he was pointing to the need, as he explains at the opening of the article, not to accept the customary opposition between authority and truth: 'For the fashion is to call in question, and to reject as needlessly irksome, all such rules of mental discipline as, within the sphere of opinion, require from us a circumspect consideration, according to the subject-matter, of the several kinds as well as degrees of evidence.'[96] It was the atmosphere of the Metaphysical Society, and perhaps especially the sweeping pronouncements of Fitzjames Stephen, that occupied his mind. Lewis, whose ideas were not so very different from Stephen's, might provide the remedy.

---

[92] W. E. Gladstone to S. E. Gladstone, 26 May 1868, Lathbury, 2, p. 179. Cf. Ch. 3, pp. 72–3.

[93] GP 44763, f. 112.

[94] Sir G. C. Lewis, *An Essay on the Influence of Authority in Matters of Opinion* (London, 1849), p. 50, quoted by W. E. Gladstone, 'The Influence of Authority in Matters of Religion' [1877], *Gleanings*, 3, p. 145.

[95] GP 44763, f. 112. W. E. Gladstone, 'Universitas Hominum; Or the Unity of History', *North American Review*, 145 (1887), p. 601 n.     [96] Gladstone, 'Influence of Authority', pp. 137, 169.

It is hardly surprising that Gladstone's article provoked a rebuttal by Fitzjames Stephen himself. The response, first delivered as a paper to the Metaphysical Society, appeared in the next issue of the *Nineteenth Century*. 'Great religious problems', Stephen observed pungently, 'cannot be solved by voting upon them.'[97] General consent did not demonstrate validity; and Gladstone had distorted Lewis in order to suggest that it did. The statesman was induced to write a rejoinder, making a 'feeble beginning' on 14 June 1877.[98] In truth the result was not a powerful piece. Gladstone deals with a range of detailed points such as Stephen's ridicule of his own comparison of authority to a crutch. But a significant theme emerges. In noticing Stephen's contrast between the habits of mind of Lewis and his own, he observes, on the authority of Burke, that no profession is more liable to 'peculiarities of mental habit' than the bar. Gladstone objects to the use of evidence as though it were 'merely legal', made 'in a witness-box'. There are questions, he insists, 'larger than a trial in court'. The law, he is implying, is a poor training for the discussion of ultimate issues. Stephen, furthermore, appealed to the few who had devoted much study to questions of belief. According to Gladstone, however, the subject of the being of God is a question for the whole human race, not for a coterie of individuals. In some fields such as pure mathematics or philology, the experts reigned; but in others, especially politics, morals, and religion, light was given to all. On the question of belief Augustine was a safe guide: *securus judicat orbis terrarum*—'the whole world judges rightly'.[99] Gladstone was branding Fitzjames Stephen's over-confidence in the judgement of an educated elite a form of cultured arrogance. Lawyers possessed no monopoly of reasoning skills; nor did the agnostics have a privileged avenue to truth. As in the national debate over the Eastern Question that was raging at the time, the mass of the people rather than the knot of so-called specialists seemed to Gladstone to have right on their side. The general consent of civilized humanity was preferable to the sectional opinion of an intellectual aristocracy.

IV

An even more formidable foe than Fitzjames Stephen attended the Metaphysical Society. The biologist T. H. Huxley, the champion of Darwinism, had delivered the paper when Gladstone first attended in 1869.[100] Huxley spent the evening in February 1876 when Gladstone submitted his critique of Stephen examining the statesman's head: its 'curious breadth of parietals, & flatness' combined with its feline shape, he surmised, might explain Gladstone's eccentricities.[101] Huxley was impatient with what seemed to him the statesman's obscurantism. The biologist

---

[97] J. F. Stephen, 'Mr. Gladstone and Sir George Lewis on Authority', *Nineteenth Century*, 1 (1877), p. 292.                                                                  [98] *D*, 14 June 1877.
[99] W. E. Gladstone, 'Rejoinder on Authority in Matters of Opinion' [1877], *Gleanings*, 3, pp. 178, 180, 189, 190, 210, 211.                    [100] Brown, *Metaphysical Society*, pp. 53, 318–19. *D*, 17 Nov. 1869.
[101] Desmond, *Huxley*, p. 466.

cast himself as the champion of what Frank M. Turner has called 'Victorian scientific naturalism'.[102] This school of opinion identified the scientific with the rational and the rational with the secular. Christianity was dismissed as unscientific and irrational, a branch of metaphysics that was incapable of investigation by legitimate techniques. Only the tangible world could yield true data. As Huxley declared in 1866, 'there is but one kind of knowledge and but one method of acquiring it'.[103] Here was a version of positivism unencumbered by the speculations of Comte. The supernatural was ruled out of court as territory that was necessarily unknowable. Hence Huxley could describe his intellectual position simply as 'agnosticism'. Those who did claim to know the beyond, supremely the clergy, were on this understanding at best mistaken and at worst charlatans. They needed to be replaced as the arbiters of culture by the advocates of science. Gladstone objected to their appropriation of the title 'scientific men'. All knowledge, divine as well as human, was in his view a form of science so long as it was set out systematically. Men such as Huxley, however, Gladstone complained in 1874, were guilty 'of first unduly narrowing the definition of Science, and then as unduly extending it to all the opinions which those persons think fit to hold, and all the theories they erect on the subjects they term scientific.'[104] The militant demand of Huxley and his friends that the old natural philosophy should become a new queen of the sciences was anathema.

It is usually supposed that Gladstone took little interest in natural science. Morley judged that 'from any full or serious examination of the details of the scientific movement he stood aside'.[105] His biographer was reflecting the widespread contemporary estimate that Gladstone was immune to science. His cabinet colleague the Duke of Argyll, who took a deep though amateurish interest in the progress of geology, remarked that Gladstone never seemed to care for the natural sciences.[106] A reviewer of Gladstone's edition of Butler commented in 1896 that 'the tendency—or rather the settled attitude—of scientific opinion is simply invisible to him'.[107] But on occasion the statesman repudiated such charges. When, as early as 1871, Herbert Spencer, the theorist of the social sciences, referred to him as holding 'the anti-scientific view', Gladstone successfully demanded that he should withdraw the passage.[108] In reality the statesman had never shared the prejudice against scientific endeavour that had prevailed, for example, among the Tractarians.[109] In his later years, as in the rejoinder to

[102] F. M. Turner, *Between Science and Religion: The Reaction to Scientific Naturalism in Late Victorian England* (New Haven, Conn., 1974).

[103] T. H. Huxley, *Collected Essays* (London, 1893–4), 1, p. 41, quoted by Turner, *Between Science and Religion*, p. 17.

[104] W. E. Gladstone to Herbert Spencer, 12 Jan. 1874, Lathbury, 2, p. 98.

[105] Morley, 1, p. 209.

[106] George Douglas, Eighth Duke of Argyll, *Autobiography and Memoirs*, ed. Dowager Duchess of Argyll, 2 vols. (London, 1906), 2, p. 2.        [107] *Athenaeum*, 1 Feb. 1896, p. 142.

[108] David Duncan, *The Life and Letters of Herbert Spencer* (London, 1908), pp. 162–4.

[109] N. A. Rupke, *The Great Chain of History: William Buckland and the English School of Geology, 1814–1849* (Oxford, 1983), ch. 20.

Fitzjames Stephen, he insisted that it was a duty to learn more about the physical world, 'as when we inquire about the results obtained by the "Challenger" '.[110] He practised what he preached, for example, by spending a fortnight while Prime Minister in 1883 absorbing the new life of James Clerk Maxwell, the first Professor of Experimental Physics at Cambridge.[111] Between 1859 and 1877 he read no fewer than fifty-three different titles relating to human evolution alone.[112] And he even published an article on a scientific subject, though it was simply an offshoot of his studies of archaic Greece. In 'The Colour-Sense' (1877) he largely concurred with the findings of Hugo Magnus, a Breslau ophthalmologist, that early literary sources suggested a gradual growth in human awareness of colour. Gladstone confirmed that senses of only light, dark, and red were clearly evident in Homer, though the limitations of the statesman's scientific credentials were apparent in a preference for Goethe over Newton as a theorist of colour.[113] Unlike Lord Salisbury, who set up a laboratory at Hatfield House,[114] Gladstone was no scientist himself. Yet he followed scientific thinking with close attention, especially when it had a bearing on his own special concerns.

He set out the main elements of his engagement with science in a series of memoranda written in December 1881. They were the fruit of reflection on a new book, *The Creed of Science*, by William Graham, a polymath who then lectured in mathematics at St Bartholomew's Hospital. Graham applauded the advances of science, broadly accepting the positivist assumption that human beings cannot grasp a reality beyond the phenomenal world. Yet Graham by no means conceded everything to scientific naturalism, asserting his belief in an attenuated version of God.[115] In thanking Graham for sending a copy of his book, Gladstone proclaimed himself 'a determined rebel' against the dogmatism of science.[116] Privately he took exception to the positivist claim 'that we have only to do with phenomena, that Science is truly & only [sic] method applied to these phenomena, that there is no philosophy beyond'. Experience showed that there were entities behind the material things accessible to the senses. Lord Salisbury's recently installed telephone, he believed (though in fact it was wiring for arc lights), had just killed a man who had touched its electric wire.[117] Again the existence of thought was a serious problem for anyone proposing that there was nothing in the world except material objects.[118]

---

[110] Gladstone, 'Rejoinder on Authority', p. 175.

[111] Lewis Campbell and William Garnett, *The Life of James Clerk Maxwell* (London, 1882). *D*, 27 Jan.–10 Feb. 1883. GP 44767, f. 8.

[112] E. H. Bellmer, 'The Statesman and the Ophthalmologist: Gladstone and Magnus on the Evolution of Human Colour Vision, One Small Episode of the Nineteenth-Century Darwinian Debate', *Annals of Science*, 56 (1999), pp. 28–9.

[113] W. E. Gladstone, 'The Colour-Sense', *Nineteenth Century*, 2 (1877), pp. 366–88. Cf. Bellmer's article (n. 112).

[114] Andrew Roberts, *Salisbury: Victorian Titan* (London, 1999), pp. 111–13.

[115] William Graham, *The Creed of Science: Religious, Moral and Social* (London, 1881). *D*, 5–18 Dec. 1881.       [116] W. E. Gladstone to William Graham, 5 Dec. 1881 (copy), GP 44545, ff. 66v–7, in *D*.

[117] GP 44766, ff. 178–81 (14, 15, 16 Dec. 1881), quoted at f. 178.

[118] GP 44766, f. 188 (16 Dec. 1881).

The sum of the matter, in my mind, is this. 'Science' on her own ground is valuable, nay invaluable. But where Scientism trespasses on the ground belonging to Theology and Philosophy—as in other days Theology domineered over the territory of Science—it becomes no better than an impudent impostor and must expect like other impostors to be detected & chastised[.]'[119]

The contrast between science and scientism conditioned Gladstone's thinking about such questions. Science must be fostered, but the inflated claims of certain scientists must be resisted.

The difficulty lay in drawing the line between science and scientism. What hypotheses called for acceptance by any thinking observer? In Gladstone's day the issue loomed largest over evolution. Did Darwin's theory of the transformation of species, announced to the world in 1859, deserve credence? Gladstone displayed a mixture of an open mind with cautious reserve. Darwin had been preceded in postulating evolutionary development by Robert Chambers's *Vestiges of the Natural History of Creation*. Gladstone read it in 1847, three years after its publication, and faced its teaching, which alarmed many of the orthodox because of its implicit denial of design, with surprising aplomb: 'there is nothing', he wrote in a private memorandum, 'in his account of the production of man which ought in the slightest degree to shake the faith of the Christian.' Its errors lay rather in its materialist and necessitarian assumptions. The idea that 'the higher forms ... were evolved out of the lower', though improbable, posed no problem to one who believed that humanity was created from dust.[120] In the early 1870s Gladstone examined the literature on evolution sufficiently to conclude that, 'if it be true', it enhanced his appreciation of the greatness of a God who masterminded the whole process.[121] By 1881, in his memoranda arising from Graham's book, Gladstone was centrally concerned with scientistic inferences from Darwinism. Those who advocated the principle of natural selection not as a physical law but as 'part of the creed of evolutional morality' were wrong to suggest that the future lay with enlarged human sympathy; instead, on their own principles, there was the prospect of 'the dropping of the weak and inferior specimens'.[122] In any case Darwin's teachings did not overthrow the argument from design, but enlarged it: 'The old argument from design resting only on the thing produced claimed at once for it a producer without any intermediate wonder. But now the method of production even apart from the thing produced is a thing so constructed as to supply a new chapter of argument to prove the existence of its Maker.'[123] Gladstone was resisting the implications drawn from Darwinian evolution by those unfriendly to the faith. In no sense, he held privately, did the new scientific school subvert a theistic worldview.

[119] GP 44766, f. 184 (16 Dec. 1881).
[120] 'On "Vestiges of Natural Creation" in relation to Butler', GP 44731, ff. 74–82 (n.d.), quoted at f. 75v. D, 12–17 July 1847, including a note of writing the MS on 17 July. Butler is not in fact mentioned in the text.          [121] W. E. Gladstone to W. S. Jevons, 10 May 1874, Lathbury, 2, pp. 100–1.
[122] GP 44766, f. 193 (18 Dec. 1881).
[123] 'Darwinism', GP 44766, ff. 189–90 (17 Dec. 1881), quoted at f. 190; in D, though 'producer' is mistranscribed 'produce'.

Gladstone took a similar line when, in 1885, he allowed his opinions on evolution to appear before the public. He concedes in one article that physical evolution 'may be true', though he still ranks the hypothesis no higher in the scale of credibility than Max Müller's solar theory of myth. But it must not, with its focus on the material creation, be allowed to provide a sanction for the dethronement of mind and spirit. Furthermore, he claims, evolution was no novelty, for anticipations of the idea can be traced in the apostle Paul, in Eusebius, and in Augustine. It must not be supposed that it had shaken 'the old foundations', for it was wrong 'to substitute a blind mechanism for the hand of God'.[124] In a second article Gladstone sustains his ambivalence. On the one hand he was surprised at how rapidly 'the Darwinian hypothesis' had been received by scientific opinion. 'To the eye of a looker-on their pace and method seem rather too much like a steeple-chase.' On the other hand, he was sympathetic to the idea of evolution because of its support for the design argument. Connecting the whole of creation in a single series, the new theory made each link in the chain a witness to what preceded it and a prophecy of what was to follow. Evolution could be understood as providence in operation. Gladstone cites in support the leading American defender of Darwinism, the Harvard evangelical Calvinist Asa Gray. For Gray, whose *Natural Science and Religion* (1880) Gladstone read at the time he was producing the article, the idea of evolution might decrease the weight given to divine intervention in the universe but provided compensation by underlining divine fore-ordination. The degree of integration between Christianity and evolutionism in Gray's lectures made them 'very remarkable'.[125] Gladstone was inclined to favour Gray's Christian Darwinism, but he still kept his distance from any full endorsement of evolution.

By *Studies Subsidiary* (1896), however, the idea is treated as received fact rather than tentative theory. There Gladstone reassures his readers that evolution should properly be called 'Devolution' because it is merely the way in which the Almighty chose to run his universe.[126] In the same year, in the introduction to *The People's Bible History*, while still speaking rather pejoratively of evolution as 'the darling of our age', he goes a step further. He supposes a series of future discoveries by science. One might be that 'the first and lowest forms of life had been evolved from lifeless matter'; another could be that 'man sprang, by a countless multitude of indefinitely small variations, from a lower and even from the lowest ancestry'; a third might be of means for establishing that the human remains unearthed by geologists had 'the spiritual, as well as the animal and intelligent life'.[127] None of

---

[124] W. E. Gladstone, 'Dawn of Creation and of Worship' [1885], *Later Gleanings*, pp. 37, 38.

[125] W. E. Gladstone, 'Poem to Genesis' [1886, though given as 1885], *Later Gleanings*, pp. 69–70, quoted at p. 69 and n. *D*, 20 Dec. 1885. Gladstone must have previously looked at the lectures in order to be able to cite them in the article. For Gray, see J. R. Moore, *The Post-Darwinian Controversies: A Study of the Protestant Struggle to Come to Terms with Darwinism in Great Britain and America, 1870–1900* (Cambridge, 1979), pp. 269–80.      [126] *Studies Subsidiary*, pp. 306–10.

[127] W. E. Gladstone, 'General Introduction', in G. C. Lorimer (ed.), *The People's Bible History* (London, 1896), pp. 10, 11, 12.

these scientific advances, he claims, would undermine Christian belief. This, Gladstone's final public statement on evolution, is a remarkable declaration. For many Christian thinkers of his day, there could be no question of a transition between the inorganic and the organic or between humanity and the rest of the evolutionary series. God alone had the power to implant life and the soul in the created order. Gladstone, however, did not flinch from accepting that these transitions could be achieved by secondary causes, undoubtedly under the control of God but not as the result of his direct intervention. Characteristically, these surmises are stated only hypothetically. Yet Gladstone had advanced, albeit slowly, a long way along the path towards the full reception of the most influential scientific ideas of his day, despite their apparent questioning of Christian teaching. There was evolution in his understanding of evolution.

Although the most celebrated public debate over science in which Gladstone joined touched on evolution, its focus was on the relation between the fossil record and the early chapters of Genesis. Huxley, his antagonist, was a self-conscious aggressor. Pained by what he considered Gladstone's atavistic stance at the Metaphysical Society, disgusted by his failure as premier to provide adequate funding for science, and increasingly alienated by his appeal to the masses, in 1885 Huxley launched an attack on the 'intrusion of an utter ignoramus into scientific questions'.[128] Gladstone had published an article, 'Dawn of Creation and of Worship', in the November issue of the *Nineteenth Century* that alluded to palaeontology and cosmology. The main purpose, however, had nothing to do with science, for Gladstone was responding to a denial of his favourite doctrine of primitive revelation by Albert Réville.[129] The Book of Genesis, Réville had alleged, contained scientific errors. Gladstone repudiated his specific charges, going on to claim that in reality the record of creation in Genesis corresponded closely with modern discoveries. The sequence of the creation of living organisms—water-population, air-population, land-population, man—had been 'so affirmed in our time by natural science, that it may be taken as a demonstrated conclusion, and established fact'.[130] Huxley could not abide so blatant a misrepresentation of palaeontology. He rushed into print in the next issue of the *Nineteenth Century* with a sustained assault on Gladstone's claim. The true sequence, on the contrary, was that land creatures had roamed the earth before birds flew in the air. The statesman's attempt to square scripture with the fossils fell to the ground, and so Réville's observations retained exactly the value they possessed before Gladstone attacked them.[131] The statesman's argument, Huxley told Max Müller, was 'utter bosh'.[132] It was a powerful demolition job.

Gladstone recognised his discomfiture. He had 'too hastily assumed', he explained to a correspondent, that 'there was a general acceptance of the fourfold

---

[128] T. H. Huxley to Friedrich Max Müller, 1 Nov. 1885, quoted by Desmond, *Huxley*, p. 544.
[129] See Ch. 7, p. 209.                    [130] Gladstone, 'Dawn of Creation and of Worship', p. 21.
[131] T. H. Huxley, 'The Interpreters of Genesis and the Interpreters of Nature', *Nineteenth Century*, 18 (1885), pp. 849–60.
[132] Huxley to Max Müller, 1 Nov. 1885, quoted by Desmond, *Huxley*, p. 64.

succession of fishes, birds, beasts and men'.[133] The assumption had not been made blindly. Gladstone had sent the proofs of the article to Sir Richard Owen, the Superintendent of the Natural History Museum and a leading palaeontologist with orthodox theological credentials. Although Owen had supplied some comments and Gladstone had accordingly modified the article, his correspondent had not challenged the claim about the fourfold order.[134] Gladstone's typical effort to guard his flank had on this occasion proved ineffectual. But, despite heavy involvement in the gestation of Home Rule, it was now possible to make further consultations, adopt more circumspect views, and return to the combat. Sir Richard Owen, on being approached again, offered some rather Delphic encouragement.[135] H. W. Acland, the Regius Professor of Medicine at Oxford, replied to Gladstone's enquiries with a caution about the rapidity of biological developments, but also provided proofs of a new work by Joseph Prestwich, Professor of Geology, that might help his argument.[136] Gladstone duly drew on Owen's *Palaeontology* (1861), a manual of geology Owen recommended, and Prestwich's text in order to mount a defence to the effect that previously he had not been so very far wrong. His case appeared as 'Proem to Genesis' in the January 1886 issue of the *Nineteenth Century*. Before he finally dispatched it, as his private notes show, he was aware that a recent American work recommended by Acland recognized that reptiles had emerged before birds.[137] Reptiles, he frankly concedes in the article, existed at an early date, but they were treated 'in a loose manner' by the author of Genesis because they were not one of the main features of the picture.[138] Huxley pounced on the admission. In his February reply, the final discharge in the debate, he insisted that the issue was simply whether reptiles were among the creeping things assigned by Genesis to the day of creation after the flying creatures. It was clear from Hebrew usage that they were; hence Genesis recorded wrongly that birds preceded all land animals. Gladstone's 'plea for a revelation of truth from God' was based on 'an error as to matter of fact'.[139] Huxley undoubtedly had the better of the encounter.

A subsidiary issue in the controversy concerned cosmology. In 'Dawn of Creation and of Worship' Gladstone urged that the nebular hypothesis gave additional support to the depiction of the universe in Genesis. This hypothesis, propounded by the French physicist Laplace at the turn of the century, explained

[133] W. E. Gladstone to Professor H. W. Acland, 11 Dec. 1885, in *D*.

[134] Sir Richard Owen to W. E. Gladstone, 21 Oct. 1885, GP 44492, ff. 205–12. W. E. Gladstone to Sir Richard Owen, 23 Oct. 1885 (copy), GP 44492, ff. 217–20v, Lathbury, 2, pp. 107–9. *D*, 23 Oct. 1885. Sir Richard Owen to W. E. Gladstone, 25 Oct. 1885, GP 44442, ff. 236–7v.

[135] Sir Richard Owen to W. E. Gladstone, 14 Dec. 1885, GP 44493, ff. 223–4v.

[136] Professor H. W. Acland to W. E. Gladstone, 13 Dec. 1885, GP 44091, ff. 141–4v, summarized inaccurately in *D*, 11 Dec. 1885, n.

[137] GP 44770, f. 18 (24 Dec. 1885). Professor H. W. Acland to W. E. Gladstone, 21 Dec. 1885, GP 44091, f. 154. The book was Marsh's *Ornithodontes* (Washington, DC, 1884). The last addition to the article and its despatch took place on 26 December (*D*).

[138] Gladstone, 'Proem to Genesis', p. 62.

[139] T. H. Huxley, 'Mr. Gladstone and Genesis', *Nineteenth Century*, 19 (1886), p. 192.

the universe as the result of the coming together of shapeless nebulae. The nebular theory seemed, in Gladstone's estimation, to show that there was a correspondence between the grand vistas of science and the Bible. 'It appears', Gladstone declares in the article, 'on the whole to be in the possession of the field.'[140] Gladstone complained in his subsequent article that Huxley entirely ignored the subject, together with the authoritative names of men who endorsed it—Georges Cuvier, Sir William Herschel, and William Whewell.[141] All these figures, however, belonged to previous generations. Huxley had been able to brush the hypothesis aside as now carrying no weight with scientific practitioners, and in the final article in the exchange argued very reasonably that the nebular theory offered no more support to the doctrine of creation than to the belief that matter has existed from eternity. The problem was that Gladstone could not pretend to be up-to-date in specialist reading. Huxley made the point when he cheekily suggested that Gladstone could have put his case for the harmony of science with the Bible much more forcefully if he had consulted the standard work of the American geologist James D. Dana.[142] Although the statesman was afterwards able to send a letter in support of his own position from Dana to the *Nineteenth Century*, Gladstone had not managed to draw on this crucial resource until the day he returned the proofs of his second article to the printers.[143] Despite his vigilance in the scientific world, he made no pretensions to familiarity with the latest developments in its various burgeoning departments. He could hardly hope to avoid being worsted by a nimble opponent such as Huxley when suddenly thrust into controversy.

Nevertheless Gladstone made out a stronger case in this debate than is usually supposed. As in the exchanges with Fitzjames Stephen—and as in his private memoranda of the 1830s[144]—the statesman was constantly raising underlying issues. Was the outlook of a scientist the correct way to approach broader questions? 'Proem to Genesis' opens with an extended challenge to Huxley's method: the scientist assumes, Gladstone claims, expertise outside his legitimate province; he exaggerates; he ignores appropriate authorities; and he takes a part of the subject at issue for the whole. Huxley is wrong, Gladstone goes on, to assert the scientific worthlessness of the biblical text if it 'will not stand the test of a strict construction'. Huxley mistakenly treats it as if it were a legal document or an arithmetical problem. Above all, he is hasty to assert that 'outside the province of science . . . we have only imagination, hope, and ignorance'. Scientific discourse possessed no monopoly of concrete truth, for there were 'vast fields of knowledge only probable' beyond its bounds.[145] The word 'probable' is a key to Gladstone's

---

[140] Gladstone, 'Dawn of Creation and of Worship', p. 24.

[141] Gladstone, 'Proem to Genesis', pp. 45–6.

[142] Huxley, 'Interpreters of Nature and the Interpreters of Genesis', p. 858; 'Mr. Gladstone and Genesis', pp. 202, 204.

[143] W. E. Gladstone, 'Note on Genesis and Science', *Nineteenth Century*, 20 (1886), p. 304 (reprinted in *Later Gleanings*, p. 39). D, 26 Dec. 1885. The annotated article by Dana, republished as *Creation: or the Biblical Cosmogony in the Light of Modern Science* (Oberlin, 1885), is in GGM 1632.

[144] See Ch. 2.                              [145] Gladstone, 'Proem to Genesis', pp. 51, 65, 70.

meaning: Butler is being invoked as a methodological mentor. Gladstone's article, he told Acland, contained 'a Butlerian argument'.[146] Accordingly he writes of 'probable evidence', of 'reasonable and probable interpretation', and of 'the most probable, and therefore the rational guide'. The central question at issue is 'essentially one for the disciples of Bishop Butler'.[147] Against the assumption of Huxley that science alone is capable of generating hard facts, Gladstone is positing that most knowledge is of varying degrees of solidity. It is for the mind to evaluate the relative weight of the various considerations bearing on any subject in order to reach a judicious conclusion. When in the 1890s he was reading Huxley's reply to 'Proem' in his collected essays, Gladstone marked as specially noteworthy an admission of Huxley's about the epistemological status of science: 'If nothing is to be called science but what is exactly true from beginning to end, I am afraid there is very little science in the world outside mathematics.'[148] Gladstone applauded Huxley's recognition that scientific knowledge was much softer than it is usually assumed to be—and softer than Huxley himself usually took it to be. The statesman was challenging the positivistic notion that assured wisdom for all human affairs is available to the methods of science.

## V

The first controversy with Huxley raised only tangentially the issue that was to be the focus of the second a few years later: the reliability of the Bible. Gladstone, as we have seen, was no fundamentalist.[149] 'The gift of revelation in holy Scripture', he wrote in a fragment of 1882, 'is a divine light struggling . . . through the clouds of human thought and language . . .'[150] Accordingly the rise of higher criticism posed no fundamental difficulty for him. Gladstone endorsed the demonstration by Samuel Driver, Pusey's successor as Regius Professor of Hebrew at Oxford and the leading Anglican biblical scholar of his generation, that the basis of the critical enterprise was sound.[151] Much of the biblical criticism of the day, however, seemed highly doubtful. In particular Gladstone singled out for censure Edouard Reuss, a theologian at Strasbourg who had inaugurated the modern phase of Old Testament study in the 1830s.[152] When Gladstone tried to absorb his major work in 1884–5, he found the German scholar 'wordy, oracular, dogmatic to a degree'.[153] Gladstone's alienation must have been completed when

---

[146]  W. E. Gladstone to Professor H. W. Acland, 16 Dec. 1885, in *D*.

[147]  Gladstone, 'Proem to Genesis', pp. 45, 49, 54, 66.

[148]  T. H. Huxley, 'Mr. Gladstone and Genesis', *Essays upon some Controverted Questions* (London, 1892), p. 125, St Deiniol's Library, Hawarden.                          [149]  See Ch. 5, pp. 130–1.

[150]  GP 44766, f. 74 (13 May 1882).

[151]  *IRHS*, pp. 6, 10.

[152]  Ibid., p. 174. For Reuss, see John Rogerson, *Old Testament Criticism in the Nineteenth Century: England and Germany* (London, 1984), p. 259 n.

[153]  E. W. E. Reuss, *Die Geschichte der heiligen Schriften Alten Testaments* (Braunschweig, 1881). W. E. Gladstone to Lord Acton, 27 Jan. 1885, in *D* (quoted). *D*, 9–12 Dec. 1884, 27 Jan. 1885.

Huxley treated the opinion of Reuss as decisive.[154] The central contention of Reuss was that the law of the Jews, though ostensibly given at the start of their history, had in fact emerged much later, during the period of the prophets. This was the principle subsequently elaborated by Julius Wellhausen, the most influential of nineteenth-century German critics. Examining Wellhausen in 1889–90, Gladstone found him capricious and unconvincing.[155] 'My thoughts', Gladstone told Acton in 1889, 'are always swimming back to the parallel question about Homer.'[156] The critics of the Homeric text, 'a soulless lot', had suggested that the poems were late compilations of diverse material, but their shallow proposals no longer had the public ear. Credence for 'the Old Testament destructives' would similarly pass away.[157] Gladstone was still jotting down unfavourable comments on higher criticism within six months of his death.[158] 'Inwardly', he had explained to Acton in 1890, 'I am but a half-believer in it.'[159]

In any case Gladstone found that scholarly opinion in his day was deeply divided on questions of biblical criticism. In 1888 he was asked to write a series of articles for the popular Christian journal *Good Words* on the 'claims of the Holy Scriptures for the working man'.[160] He set about examining the relevant academic literature in the autumn. For nearly a month he absorbed the Congregationalist Alfred Cave's *The Inspiration of the Old Testament Inductively Considered* (1888), which set out to demolish the whole edifice erected by Wellhausen, arguing that it was full of implausibilities.[161] The author undoubtedly swayed Gladstone, who went on to publicize an article by Cave challenging the higher critics on similar grounds.[162] In the following year Gladstone's unfavourable estimate of recent criticism was bolstered by his study of E. W. Hengstenberg and Franz Delitzsch, older German scholars of a more conservative viewpoint who had retarded the advance of the new analytical methods.[163] Early in 1890 the statesman determined to canvass opinion in Oxford. Only a few months before, Charles Gore, the head of

---

[154] Huxley, 'Mr. Gladstone and Genesis', *Essays upon some Controverted Questions*, p. 123 n. Gladstone wrote 'NB' against Reuss's name in his copy, now at St Deiniol's Library.

[155] *D*, 25 Aug. 1889, 17 Nov. 1889, 8 May 1890. On the second consultation, the entry in the diary should be 'Bleek–Wellhausen', not 'Bleck–Wellhausen' as printed, and refers to Wellhausen's edition of Friedrich Bleek, *Einleitung in das Alte Testament* (5th edn., Berlin, 1886). Cf. *IRHS*, p. 13 n. The first consultation is probably, as the editor of the diaries suggests, of Julius Wellhausen, *Geschichte Israels* (Berlin, 1878) and the second is of his *Die Composition des Hexateuchs und der historischen Bücher des Alten Testaments* (Berlin, 1889), the latter being cited at *IRHS*, p. 177.

[156] W. E. Gladstone to Lord Acton, 23 Jan. 1889, GP 44094, f. 48, Lathbury, 2, p. 116.

[157] W. E. Gladstone to Lord Acton, 4 Aug. 1889, GP 44094, f. 63v, Lathbury, 2, p. 119.

[158] 'O.T.', GP 44776, f. 190 (13 Dec. 1897).

[159] W. E. Gladstone to Lord Acton, 21 [but in fact 4 according to *D*] Mar. 1890, GP 44094, f. 78.

[160] W. E. Gladstone to Lord Acton, 28 Apr. 1889, GP 44094, f. 53v, in J. N. Figgis and R. V. Laurence (eds.), *Selections from the Correspondence of the First Lord Acton*, 1 (London, 1917), p. 220.

[161] *D*, 16 Sept.–14 Oct. 1888. Cf. W. B. Glover, *Evangelical Nonconformists and Higher Criticism in the Nineteenth Century* (London, 1954), pp. 186–93.

[162] Alfred Cave, 'The Old Testament and the Critics', *Contemporary Review* (1890), pp. 537–51, cited in *IRHS*, p. 173.

[163] *D*, 10, 17 Mar. 1889; 6, 13, 20 Oct. 1889, 28 Jan., 16, 23 Feb., 2, 3 Mar. 1890. Gladstone to Acton, 21 [but 4] Mar. 1890, ff. 87–8v. Cf. Rogerson, *Old Testament Criticism*, ch. 5, pp. 111–20.

Pusey House in Oxford, had announced his acceptance of higher critical methods in the epoch-making *Lux Mundi*. H. P. Liddon, Pusey's biographer, was deeply perturbed that the great man's legacy was being betrayed. The value of higher criticism was the talk of the senior common rooms. On arriving in Oxford Gladstone immediately read Gore's essay on inspiration and soon afterwards turned to Liddon's sermon denouncing his teaching. Gladstone spent part of his time in intensive discussion with specialists in and about the field. He saw Samuel Driver for a 'long conversation on Genesis I. &c' and consulted the other leading Oxford Old Testament critic G. K. Cheyne.[164] Neither entirely persuaded him, so that he lingered in opinion somewhere between Gore and Liddon. In theory the critical enterprise might be entirely legitimate, but in practice it was far too arbitrary. In the following year he was to criticize Cheyne in print for making the assumption, entirely unwarranted as he believed, that the idea of immortality emerged only late in ancient Israel.[165] Even the competent authorities of Oxford failed to convince him that current scholarship could shed much light on the text.

Accordingly he decided to circumvent most of the issues of biblical criticism in his articles for *Good Words*, subsequently republished in book form as *The Impregnable Rock of Holy Scripture*. Criticism, he claimed, concerned itself with the literary form of the Bible, not its substance. Its practitioners considered questions of age, text, and authorship, but the message of revelation stood firm. Even if the most destructive theories were to be established as true, they would not impair the basic facts of history about the role of the Jews in the world. Yet it was Gladstone's aim to show that 'there are grave reasons for questioning every really destructive proposition'. The Old Testament as a whole enforces the themes of sin and redemption; the Psalms, for which Gladstone shows deep affection, nurture the soul; and the Pentateuch (against the more extreme critics such as Wellhausen) can be associated with the historical figure of Moses. Gladstone took up again the themes of his 1885 articles, arguing that although the Book of Genesis was 'to convey moral and spiritual training', its early chapters harmonized with natural science. He was content to call himself a reconciler of science and the Bible, even repeating his claim that the nebular hypothesis fitted the creation story. It was the account of creation which, in Gladstone's estimate, presented the most distinct evidence for revelation, but the rest of his book provided the sort of cumulative corroboration that he had commended to the Metaphysical Society. The assembling of probabilities was the method of Bishop Butler, to whom Gladstone twice appeals.[166] He saw *The Impregnable Rock* as an exercise in Butlerian apologetic.

Gladstone had a specific target in view, again Thomas Huxley. Since their debate of 1885–6, Huxley had written a string of articles attacking the clergy, the church, and the faith. The latest polemic by 'the Achilles of the opposing army',

---

[164] *D*, 31 Jan., 19, 2, 5 Feb. 1890.
[165] W. E. Gladstone, 'On the Ancient Beliefs in a Future State' [1891], *Later Gleanings*, pp. 352–83.
[166] *IRHS*, pp. 9, 24, 54, 259.

as Gladstone calls him, appeared as the statesman was finishing his series for *Good Words*.[167] Huxley had seized the opportunity of the controversy over Gore's contribution to *Lux Mundi* to mount a two-pronged assault. Old Testament stories, according to Gore, need not be historical. But the real question, in Huxley's eyes, was this: are the Bible's statements true or false? Liddon affirmed that they were true; Huxley denied it. The intermediate position of *Lux Mundi*, Huxley concluded, was raked alike by 'the old-fashioned artillery of the Churches' and 'the fatal weapons of precision ... of the advancing forces of science'.[168] Huxley having thrown down the gauntlet, Gladstone immediately picked it up. 'I deny', he wrote in *Good Words*, 'that the weapons of belief are antiquated: I pause even before admitting that those of scientific men are always, except in their own particular sciences, weapons of precision.'[169] Gladstone could cite an instance of Huxley trespassing far beyond his proper sphere of expertise. In another recent article, his opponent had pronounced on the episode of the Gadarene swine in the gospels. Jesus was recorded as having cast out evil spirits from a possessed man near Gadara and having allowed them to enter a herd of pigs, which rushed to their deaths in the Sea of Galilee. How could anyone, Huxley asked, believe in 'unclean spirits'? Either Jesus did, which shakes his authority; or the gospel writers were mistaken, which shakes theirs. Huxley had the temerity to appeal to Butler's axiom of probability, surely a sly dig at Gladstone.[170] In any case the statesman was provoked. The destruction of the Gadarene swine could be explained, he argued in the final contribution to *Good Words*, by the fact that they were being kept by Jews, not Gentiles, despite the prohibition on eating pork in the Jewish law. Their loss was legitimate because their possession was unlawful. Was Huxley, then, using 'weapons of precision'? Once more Gladstone was wanting 'to challenge the methods pursued by some critics of the Holy Scriptures'.[171] The scientist seemed to stand convicted of methodological inexactitude.

Inevitably Huxley rose to the challenge. Gadara, he argued in the *Nineteenth Century* for December 1890, was Greek, as the ancient historian Josephus asserted and the modern German authority Schürer confirmed. Gladstone's scholarship was dubious and his language intemperate. Huxley professed himself 'a student trained in the use of weapons of precision, rather than in that of rhetorical toma- hawks'.[172] Gladstone, however, was by no means abashed, replying with 'Professor Huxley and the Swine-Miracle' in February 1891. Josephus, argues the statesman, did not prove the case for a Gentile population of the area, and Schürer was unre- liable. A range of other evidence pointed to the population having been Jewish.[173]

[167] *IRHS*, p. 264.
[168] T. H. Huxley, 'The Lights of the Church and the Lights of Science', *Nineteenth Century*, 28 (1890), p. 22.                                                          [169] *IRHS*, p. 266.
[170] T. H. Huxley, 'Agnosticism', *Nineteenth Century*, 25 (1889), pp. 172–7.
[171] *IRHS*, pp. 274–80, quoted at p. 280.
[172] T. H. Huxley, 'The Keepers of the Herd of Swine', *Nineteenth Century*, 28 (1890), p. 975.
[173] W. E. Gladstone, 'Professor Huxley and the Swine-Miracle' [1891], *Later Gleanings*, pp. 246–79.

Gladstone thought that his article overturned all Huxley's contentions,[174] but the irrepressible professor re-entered the lists in March. Gladstone, he claimed, was missing the point: the law of Moses condemned only eating pork and touching carcases, not, as the statesman assumed, possessing pigs. Whatever their race, the owners of the swine were defrauded of their property. But the issue was really whether 'the men of the nineteenth century are to adopt the demonology of the men of the first century as divinely revealed truth'.[175] The church said yes, but science said no. The debate had a particularly sharp edge because the two combatants were divided over the Irish Question in politics. Huxley quoted the Conservative Chief Secretary for Ireland as condemning Gladstone's 'grossest exaggerations'; whereas Gladstone speculated that Gadara might have been enjoying Home Rule.[176] But even more than politics was at stake. Each believed that on the dispute about the Gadarene swine hung the issue of the general reliability of scripture, and each held that the other's method of approaching the question was erroneous. For Huxley, Gladstone's techniques were antiquated and verbose; for Gladstone, Huxley's were pretentious and narrow. The statesman's aim was to show that his opponent's 'boast' about the precise weapons of 'the adepts in natural science' was ill founded.[177] The discussion, which terminated inconclusively, was as much about the applicability of scientific method as about the legitimacy of pig-keeping on the shores of Lake Galilee.

The same attempt to raise methodological considerations is evident in another controversy between Gladstone and an opponent of Christian belief. In 1888 he intervened in a debate in the *North American Review* between Henry M. Field, the Presbyterian editor of the *New York Evangelist*, and Robert G. Ingersoll, the leading popular lecturer against religion in the United States. Field had tried to persuade Ingersoll that Christianity offered the highest moral ideals; Ingersoll replied in the interest of free thought; and Field responded in an issue of the magazine that also contained an unrelated article by Gladstone. It was therefore natural for the statesman to read, in January 1888, Ingersoll's rejoinder, and, even though Gladstone was on holiday in Florence, he was so incensed by what he saw as its sophistries that he composed a reply.[178] He complains that the American assumes that the sacrifice of Jephthah's daughter was to be approved by the reader of the Bible; and he throws out Ingersoll's claim that Darwin had discredited religion. Most tellingly, Gladstone takes exception to the idea put forward by Ingersoll that nobody is responsible for what goes on in the mind. How then, demanded the statesman, could Americans argue for the superiority of their

---

[174] W. E. Gladstone to Lord Acton, 9 Jan. 1891, GP 44094, f. 147v.

[175] T. H. Huxley, 'Illustrations of Mr. Gladstone's Controversial Method', *Nineteenth Century*, 29 (1891), p. 465.    [176] Huxley, 'Keepers', p. 979. Gladstone, 'Professor Huxley', p. 253.

[177] Gladstone, 'Professor Huxley', p. 246.

[178] Henry M. Field, 'An Open Letter to Robert G. Ingersoll'; Robert G. Ingersoll, 'A Reply to the Rev. Henry M. Field, D.D.'; Henry M. Field, 'A Last Word to Robert G. Ingersoll'; Robert G. Ingersoll, 'Letter to Dr. Field', *North American Review*, 145 (1887), pp. 128–39, 473–505, 616–28, and 146 (1888), pp. 31–46. D, 18 Jan. 1888. For Ingersoll, see D. D. Anderson, *Robert Ingersoll* (New York, 1972).

constitution? On Ingersoll's principles the preference of others for monarchy was unavoidable. But Gladstone's underlying preoccupation is once more with method. He objects to the 'tumultuous' manner of his opponent's article. 'Instead of arguing, it pelts.'[179] Gladstone, who turned to Butler and Newman for aid while writing his response, calls on his readers to appreciate that, since 'demonstrative proofs' are not to be expected, the being of God is to be established on the basis of evidence that guides us in everyday life.[180] Ingersoll failed to appreciate the limitations on human knowledge recognized by Newman and Butler alike; and he would do well to turn to Bishop Butler for the elucidation of future retribution. The brashness of the American orator would be reined in by the moderation of the English bishop.

The defence of the faith, however, had to be sustained on more than one front. In 'Courses of Religious Thought' (1876) Gladstone had distinguished from the negative school, which included agnosticism, what he called 'the Theistic school'. This was the varied body of opinion that accepted belief in God but rejected expressions of dogma. His chief public critique of what he privately described to Acton as 'among the least defensible of the positions alternative to Christianity'[181] came in 1888, immediately after the completion of the article against Ingersoll. The new opponent was altogether more subtle, the writer Mary Ward, the grand-daughter of Thomas Arnold. Her novel *Robert Elsmere* narrated the loss of ortho-dox faith by its hero, his surrender of holy orders in the Church of England, and his creation of a 'New Christian Brotherhood' for the uplift of the working people of the East End of London. Gladstone read the book during the second half of March 1888, finding its central character shallow but its theme gripping.[182] Knowles persuaded him to review the novel, but first, while staying at Keble College, Oxford, he had two encounters with the author, who carefully recorded their discussions. Gladstone explained that he now found 'the evidence of Christian history' the most compelling; and at one point talked of 'trumpery objections' in what Mary Ward called 'his most House of Commons manner'.[183] In the review, which was to ensure that sales of *Robert Elsmere* rocketed, Gladstone contends that it was mistaken to expect the moral and spiritual results of Christianity without its dogmas and miracles. The fundamental problem of theism shorn of the incarnation, on his diagnosis, is that it ignored the power of sin and therefore neglected the need for a remedy. Mary Ward had not argued

---

[179] W. E. Gladstone, 'Ingersoll on Christianity', *Later Gleanings* [originally *North American Review*, 146 (1888), pp. 481–509], pp. 122, 132.                                    [180] Ibid., p. 141. *D*, 1 Jan. 1888.

[181] Gladstone to Acton, 1 Apr. 1888, Lathbury, 2, p. 110.

[182] *D*, 16–30 Mar. 1888. On the novel's significance, see Bernard Lightman, '*Robert Elsmere* and the Agnostic Crisis of Faith', in R. J. Helmstadter and Bernard Lightman (eds.), *Victorian Crisis of Faith: Essays on Continuity and Change in Nineteenth-Century Religious Belief* (Houndmills, Basingstoke, 1990).

[183] Janet P. Trevelyan, *The Life of Mrs. Humphry Ward* (London, 1923), p. 60. [Mary A.] Ward, *A Writer's Recollections* (London, 1918), p. 238. For Mary Ward, see also John Sutherland, *Mrs Humphry Ward: Eminent Historian, Pre-eminent Edwardian* (Oxford, 1990); and on the debate, see P. C. Erb, 'Politics and Theological Liberalism: William Gladstone and Mrs Humphry Ward', *Journal of Religious History*, 25 (2001).

through these issues in the novel, where the intellectual difficulties of miracles are presented as insuperable. Orthodoxy, 'the ancient and continuous creed of Christendom', however, was not in reality played out.[184] The novel unjustly gave all the reasoning to the new scheme of religion, but only emotion to the old. In face-to-face debate with Mary Ward Gladstone attempted, in a way she found wholly unsatisfactory, to meet her objections with arguments from Bishop Butler.[185] It was the reasoning power of which the bishop was a master, Gladstone believed, that would settle the issue. An impoverished theism must concede the palm to historic Christianity if only there were a fair statement of the questions under debate.

## VI

It was Gladstone's ambition, in the years after his final retirement from the premiership in 1894, to offer a deeper analysis of the issues involved in the debate over belief than was possible in periodic passages of arms. His chief method was to use as a vehicle the thought of Bishop Butler. Gladstone had frequently recurred to Butler's teaching in the years since, during the 1840s, he had discovered in *The Analogy of Religion* an arsenal of arguments against Rome.[186] In controversy with Ingersoll and Mary Ward, as much as with Fitzjames Stephen and Huxley, he frequently had recourse to Butlerian principles of probability. When perusing the prologue to Huxley's collected essays, published in 1892, Gladstone pencilled against one of the author's more egregious claims the terse comment 'NB Butler'.[187] The eighteenth-century bishop supplied the ammunition needed for the war between faith and scepticism. Shortly after publishing, in 1896, his edition of Butler's works, Gladstone also issued a volume of *Studies Subsidiary to the Works of Bishop Butler* in which he explained his understanding of the contemporary value of the bishop's teaching. The statesman brought out some of its salient features such as the analysis of human nature, the doctrine of habits, and the claims of conscience, adding a number of tangentially connected essays on such themes as teleology and miracle. Gladstone did not avoid criticizing the bishop, at one point listing ten 'questionable theses' and raising the still debated issue of the relationship between conscience and self-love in Butler's scheme.[188] But the overwhelming impression conveyed is of an author who must continue to be heard in Gladstone's own day. The statesman treated Butler as 'the guide through the perplexities of thought and conduct in modern life'.[189]

[184] Gladstone, ' "Robert Elsmere": The Battle of Belief', p. 117.
[185] Ward, *Writer's Recollections*, p. 238.    [186] See Ch. 5, p. 116.
[187] T. H. Huxley, 'Prologue', *Essays upon some Controverted Questions* (London, 1892), p. 49, St Deiniol's Library, Hawarden. There is no diary mention of this volume.
[188] *Studies Subsidiary*, pp. 91–3. Cf. R. G. Frey, 'Butler on Self-Love and Benevolence', in Christopher Cunliffe (ed.), *Joseph Butler's Moral and Religious Thought: Tercentenary Essays* (Oxford, 1992).
[189] Asa Briggs (ed.), *Gladstone's Boswell: Late Victorian Conversations by L. A. Tollemache and Other Documents* (Brighton, 1984), p. 42.

Supremely Butler is presented by Gladstone as a master of methodology, an exemplar in the conduct of debate. It was not so much Butler's content as his manner that was instructive. Hence the first chapter in *Studies Subsidiary* was entitled 'The Method of Butler'. Gladstone had been indignant at the self-confidence displayed by his agnostic opponents in setting aside the long centuries of Christian tradition. Butler, by contrast with Huxley's crisp flippancy, had shown 'a reverential sentiment'.[190] The bishop possessed a deep-seated quality of moderation, commending a middle way and often (as Gladstone points out in the notes of his edition) revealing affinities with Aristotle. In another note Gladstone calls attention to 'the rare fairness of Butler's mind'.[191] The bishop was hostile to exaggeration, willing to make concessions to his opponents and even prepared to set out objections to his own case with as much force as any adversary. 'If there are over-statements in Butler', according to Gladstone, 'they are commonly against himself.'[192] The bishop's cautious technique therefore contrasted not only with the style of negative writers such as Huxley but also with the approach of many later Christian defenders of the faith. That is why five essays on a future life are included in *Studies Subsidiary* even though most of their content is remote from Bishop Butler. Their purpose, obscured by a rambling structure that betrays Gladstone's failing powers in his mid-eighties, was to show that a belief in natural immortality was not essential to Christianity. The early church, according to the statesman, had deliberately avoided defining whether the soul was imperishable, but the spread of the philosophical opinion that it was had led to the acceptance of the severe doctrine of everlasting punishment and, by reaction, to the lax dismissal of any expectation of future retribution for sin. Christians had incautiously indulged in exaggeration, consequently entangling the faith in unnecessary difficulties.[193] In a parallel way Gladstone argued in an article of 1894 on the atonement that false conceptions of the doctrine had misled many into rejecting it altogether.[194] Butler's 'singularly circumspect' technique would have averted such dangers.[195] The bishop's method of argumentation deserved imitation by both sides if Christian belief was to be assessed with adequate care.

Butler's manner of reasoning, according to Gladstone, was the inductive method of science. It was idle for Huxley to pretend that scientists possessed weapons of superior accuracy when there was no fundamental difference between his research technique and the great apologist's mode of enquiry. 'Butler', according to Gladstone, 'was a collector of facts, and a reasoner upon them.' Unlike most of the thinkers of his day, Butler did not undertake the 'speculative castle-building' of a priori argumentation. Gladstone was keen to stress the bishop's allegiance to induction. Against the claim of Sara Hennell, a freethinker of George Eliot's circle, that Butler's method is of a 'metaphysical kind', the statesman

---

[190] *Studies Subsidiary*, p. 8.        [191] *WJB*, 2, p. 85.        [192] *Studies Subsidiary*, p. 86.
[193] Ibid., part II, chs. 1–5. These essays were also published in *North American Review*, 162, between January and June 1896.
[194] W. E. Gladstone, 'True and False Conceptions of the Atonement' [1894], *Later Gleanings*.
[195] *Studies Subsidiary*, p. 86.

asserts that it is 'purely experimental throughout'; and against Leslie Stephen's similar contention in a review of Gladstone's edition of Butler, he repeats that the bishop draws exclusively from 'the facts of experience'. Although Butler did touch on metaphysical points, to which Gladstone allocates a short chapter in *Studies Subsidiary*, the apologist was disinclined, according to his editor, to explore such questions.[196] It is clear that the statesman actually went beyond the evidence in dwelling on this case, for there are substantial non-empiricist elements in Butler's epistemology.[197] Gladstone chose to ignore them. He did not take Acton's advice to look for affinities with Kant, whose writings might have alerted him to the a priori in Butler.[198] By contrast with the version of Butler's works published in 1900 by J. H. Bernard, subsequently Archbishop of Dublin, there is no allusion in Gladstone's edition to Kant, whom he never read.[199] Nor can Gladstone's neglect be explained by intellectual fashion. Whereas earlier commentators on Butler had stressed the similarity of his method to Bacon's empiricism, Gladstone's contemporaries acknowledged the bishop's awareness of the deficiencies of induction.[200] The reason for the statesman's insistence on Butler's use of inductive technique was polemical. Butler, Gladstone wanted to insist, was just as open to persuasion by rational evidence as any practitioner of natural history. Indeed, what the bishop offered was 'a scientific treatise'.[201] There was no question of ruling Butler out of court on the ground that he made unjustifiable assumptions. Agnostics were not to be permitted to lay exclusive claim to the methods of science.

Butler could be deployed, on the other hand, to reveal the limitations of scientific reasoning. In most questions of importance, Gladstone argues, certainty is not to be expected. Human beings have to be content with various degrees of evidence that fall short of the absolutely persuasive. Butler taught that 'probable evidence is the guide of life'. Naturally Gladstone seized the opportunity to deal out blows against the ultramontane claim that dogmas defined by the Roman Church were certain. The statement of this position by his former friend Manning, according to Gladstone, 'never could have been written by a follower of Butler'.[202] But the main thrust of his discussion was directed against the agnostic threat. 'In matters of the intellect', Huxley had written in 1889, 'do not pretend that conclusions are certain which are not demonstrated or demonstrable.'[203] Huxley clearly believed that probabilities could be transcended by firmly assured knowledge. Gladstone pointed out, however, that Butler had demonstrated the wide extent of human ignorance. Freshly acquired knowledge, according to the bishop, merely served to illuminate the vast areas about which we know little or nothing.

[196] Ibid., pp. 1, 2, 42, 56, 121.
[197] Anders Jeffner, 'Our Knowledge of Ourselves', in Cunliffe (ed.), *Butler's Thought*, p. 191.
[198] Lord Acton to W. E. Gladstone, 28 Jan. 1895, GP 44094, f. 264v. Acton believed Kant's idea of conscience derived from Butler.
[199] J. H. Bernard (ed.), *The Works of Bishop Butler*, 2 vols. (London, 1900), 2, p. 29.
[200] Jane Garnett, 'Bishop Butler and the *Zeitgeist*: Butler and the Development of Christian Moral Philosophy in Victorian Britain', in Cunliffe (ed.), *Butler's Thought*, p. 77.
[201] *Studies Subsidiary*, p. 112.   [202] Ibid., pp. 4, 12.   [203] Huxley, 'Agnosticism', p. 187.

There is no part of his teaching [wrote Gladstone] more urgently required at the present day, when not only are the large recent accessions to human knowledge apt to be over-valued by some of those who have laboured hard to learn and perhaps to add to them; but many who are totally ignorant of what they are, vaingloriously boast of them as if sciolism approximated to omniscience.[204]

Ingersoll as well as Huxley was in Gladstone's sights. All who appealed to science as an engine for overturning the edifice of faith needed to appreciate, with Butler, that human powers of understanding are severely circumscribed. It was a point very similar to that made by the future Prime Minister A. J. Balfour, in *A Defence of Philosophic Doubt* (1879): science cannot be used as a test of religious truth because its powers are limited. Whereas, however, Balfour stressed that the premises of scientific endeavour were unproved,[205] it was Gladstone's case that its province was extremely restricted. In most aspects of human life we have to rely on a mode of reasoning that produces only provisional knowledge. The Butlerian contention that probability is the guide of life was a battle-cry against the assumptions of scientific naturalism.

It has been common to treat Gladstone's oeuvre on Butler as a dated and ineffectual exercise. Reviewers of the *Works* often suggested that the bishop did not address the issues of the hour;[206] and E. C. Mossner, writing in 1936, dismissed Gladstone's efforts as 'pathetic and anachronistic'.[207] Jane Garnett shows that the statesman, drawing on a lifetime's study of Butler, was defending the bishop against criticisms mounted in an earlier period, from the 1850s to the 1870s.[208] It is true that Gladstone was stating in public views that had been germinating in his mind since the 1840s and in some cases earlier. It is also true that his edition failed to stimulate a new wave of Butlerian scholarship.[209] Yet because Gladstone was engaging with a figure who still attracted widespread interest, the statesman's writings about Butler did achieve some contemporary resonance. The severest judgements on Gladstone's work came either from 'the champions of negation'[210] or those liberal Christian spokesmen who felt he had taken too little account of recent developments in natural science and biblical criticism. Thus a rationalist reviewer sweepingly claimed that he ignored the 'scholarship and the scientific achievements of the last one hundred and fifty years'.[211] R. A. Armstrong, the author of the most trenchant review, was an authority on Butler, but he was also a Unitarian minister. When he condemned Gladstone for disregarding new approaches, Armstrong was expressing his sympathy for recent critical works that gave support to his own anti-confessional position.[212] Although some

[204] *Studies Subsidiary*, p. 105.

[205] J. C. Greene, *Debating Darwin: Adventures of a Scholar* (Claremont, Cal., 1999), pp. 56–66.

[206] *Pall Mall Gazette*, 6 Jan. 1896. *Daily Telegraph*, 15 Jan. 1896. *Eastern Daily Press*, 18 Jan. 1896. All in GGM 1644.                               [207] Mossner, *Butler and the Age of Reason*, p. 228.

[208] Garnett, 'Bishop Butler and the *Zeitgeist*', p. 74.

[209] H. S. Holland, *The Optimism of Butler's 'Analogy'* (Oxford, 1908), p. 4.

[210] *Studies Subsidiary*, p. 293.

[211] *The Literary Guide: A Rationalist Review*, 1 Aug. 1896, GGM 1644.

[212] Garnett, 'Bishop Butler and the *Zeitgeist*', p. 75. Herbert McLachlan, *The Unitarian Movement in the Religious Life of England* (London, 1934), p. 201.

well-disposed reviewers could not endorse Gladstone's treatment of the bishop, others showed far more appreciation of the statesman's work. Both *The Times* and the *Manchester Guardian* carried wholly favourable notices of the edition of Butler.[213] The *Standard*, echoing words of Gladstone, approved the 'mental tissue' of Butler; the *Glasgow Herald* grasped the editor's main point by lauding 'the *temper*' of the bishop's writing—clear thinking, fairness in attack and defence, scrupulous statement.[214] The *Athenaeum*, which had criticized the edition of Butler for neglecting science, was much better disposed towards *Studies Subsidiary*. Although the journal criticized the omission of Kant and Darwin from the discussion, it actually wished that more space had been given to probability because Butler's method was so useful.[215] Gladstone evidently managed to convey his message to some of his readers.

The statesman was, in fact, expounding a point of view that enjoyed, in certain quarters, considerable and growing support in his day. His opinions harmonized with prevailing currents of Anglican opinion. The *Church Quarterly Review*, though not particularly perceptive about *Studies Subsidiary*, praised its more original chapters as 'Christian common sense'.[216] Although Gladstone's edition of Butler has sometimes been compared unfavourably with that of J. H. Bernard, who inserted a larger number of explanatory notes, there was a remarkable degree of overlap between their understandings of the bishop. Bernard comments approvingly on several of Gladstone's observations and criticizes none of them. Like Gladstone, he lingers over Butler's doctrine of probability, he reinforces the statesman's case about natural immortality, and he deploys the bishop (though in a different way from Gladstone) to engage with agnosticism.[217] Furthermore, as Jane Garnett shows, the study of Butler made a significant contribution to the development of incarnationalist social philosophy in the Church of England during the late Victorian years. Charles Gore, one of its leading exponents and the moving spirit of *Lux Mundi*, insisted, like Gladstone, that Butler employed inductive method and that there was no gulf between faith and reason.[218] Henry Scott Holland, another contributor to *Lux Mundi*, though disliking Butler's use of 'probability', nevertheless emphasized that the bishop was not a metaphysician but a man who, like scientists, constantly appealed to experience. Butler, according to Scott Holland, repudiates the agnostic argument that we cannot gain knowledge of the supernatural and yet shows that, where we can come to know, the comprehension cannot be total.[219] Scott Holland's concern, like Gladstone's, was with method, and his purpose was the defence of Anglican orthodoxy,

[213] *T*, 17 Jan. 1896. *Manchester Guardian*, 16 Jan. 1896. Both in GGM 1644.

[214] *Standard*, 16 Jan. 1896; *Glasgow Herald*, 24 Jan. 1896; both in GGM 1644.

[215] *Athenaeum*, 1 Feb. 1886; 8 Aug. 1896, GGM 1644.

[216] 'Mr. Gladstone's Studies on Butler', *Church Quarterly Review*, 43 (1896), p. 27.

[217] Bernard (ed.), *Works of Butler*, 2, pp. 10–12, 29–31, 33, 96 n, 118. Bernard claims that Butler recognized the truth in agnosticism by appreciating that knowledge, though trustworthy, is only partial.

[218] Garnett, 'Bishop Butler and the *Zeitgeist*', pp. 89–90.

[219] Holland, *Optimism of Butler's 'Analogy'*, pp. 16–23.

broadly conceived. In his understanding of Butler, Gladstone was not out on a limb. He was aligned with the rising school of intellectual High Churchmen who produced *Lux Mundi*.

In an essay on Gladstone's apologetics written shortly after his death, William Tuckwell, an admiring clergyman but also a self-conscious modern, suggested that Gladstone failed to grasp the significance of scientific and biblical criticism because 'like his old friend Liddon, he had never been educated to understand it'.[220] That was a mistaken estimate because in his last decades Gladstone did not identify with Liddon, the biographer and champion of Pusey, but with the younger clergy who, though inheriting the legacy of the Oxford movement, were open to contemporary influences in the world of ideas. As we have seen, Gladstone had broken free from Pusey's dominion at an earlier stage in his development,[221] and he looked on the Puseyite stance, like that of the ultramontanes, as an unwarrantable rejection of modern knowledge. His affinities were rather with what Gore called 'Liberal Catholicism', a version of High Churchmanship that frankly accepted biblical criticism, scientific discovery, philosophical analysis, and social engagement.[222] Its manifesto, *Lux Mundi*, presented a theology founded (like Gladstone's personal faith) on the incarnation and drew from the doctrine a confidence that the divine could be understood in the everyday world. Gladstone was close to several of the eleven contributors. Already in 1885 he discerned great promise in Gore.[223] By 1893 the statesman was hoping that the young clergyman would move on from Pusey House because he was 'a much broader man than Dr. Pusey . . . and the association with the name does him some injustice'.[224] Of the other *Lux Mundi* authors, Scott Holland was frequently at Hawarden from 1876 onwards, J. R. Illingworth also stayed there, and Francis Paget owed the Regius Professorship of Divinity at Oxford to Gladstone's nomination.[225] Two contributors to the volume were actually members of the family: Arthur Lyttelton, Master of Selwyn College, Cambridge, was Catherine Gladstone's nephew, and E. S. Talbot, Warden of Keble College, Oxford, had married her niece. Gladstone was a welcome visitor in both lodges.[226] These were the men with whom Gladstone most enjoyed conversation, often on long walks at Hawarden. They were providing one of the two great apologetic desiderata about which Gladstone had written to William Stubbs in 1875, a 'truly historical treatment of Christianity'. Gladstone's complementary aim was to draw attention to what he had described to Stubbs as the other great need of the hour, 'a rational philosophical method such as that of Butler'.[227] The *Lux Mundi* writers could

---

[220] William Tuckwell, 'Mr. Gladstone as Critic', in Sir Wemyss Reid (ed.), *The Life of William Ewart Gladstone* (London, 1899), p. 472.                          [221] See Ch. 5, pp. 136–7, 138–9.

[222] James Carpenter, *Gore: A Study in Liberal Catholic Thought* (London, 1960).

[223] *D*, 12 Jan. 1885; 10, 12 Nov. 1888. G. L. Prestige, *The Life of Charles Gore: A Great Englishman* (London, 1935), p. 79.                          [224] W. E. Gladstone to S. E. Gladstone, 20 Mar. 1893, in *D*.

[225] *D*, 9 Aug. 1876, 16 Jan. 1879. Stephen Paget and J. M. C. Crum, *Francis Paget* (London, 1912), p. 88.

[226] *D*, 1 Feb. 1887, 13 Nov. 1872, etc. Gladstone also corresponded with Aubrey Moore and met Walter Lock at Keble (*D*, 27 Nov. 1883).

[227] Gladstone to Stubbs, 27 Dec. 1885, in Hutton (ed.), *Letters of William Stubbs*, pp. 147–8.

build some of the defensive bulwarks against unbelief; Gladstone could show how Butler had already erected others. They were engaged in a common enterprise.

It was the cultural authority of such men that Huxley and his associates most wanted to break. Frank M. Turner has drawn attention to the social dimension of their intellectual struggle to supplant a supernatural understanding of the world with a natural one. The scientific naturalists aspired to replace the Anglican clergy as the arbiters of knowledge and the educators of society. Traditional amateurism must be banished, especially from science itself, if their aims were to be realized.[228] Gladstone recognized and deplored the ambition of the scientists to achieve a new social hegemony. The 'present scientific spirit', he told Acton in 1887, was not going to produce great men because it was marred by 'specialising tendencies & necessities'.[229] Huxley and his friends perforce had narrow concerns that restricted their outlook. Since his first administration, for instance, Gladstone had been painfully conscious of their calls for the public funding of science, demands which, with Gladstone's backing, the Treasury had resisted.[230] The scientists formed a pressure group in pursuit of their own interests; they did not look to the common concerns of society. They were suffering from a habit of mind incidental to their profession. Butler, by contrast, had possessed a broader vision. 'He does not write like a person addicted to any profession or pursuit', according to Gladstone; 'his mind is essentially free.' Butler stood for the values of a liberal education. Hence he 'was not a man indifferent, as some are, to knowledge outside his profession'.[231] Members of the Huxley circle, insisting that science was the one path to authentic knowledge, tried to impose their own intellectual straitjacket on society at large. We 'need to inquire pretty strictly', wrote Gladstone, 'whether the professors of science are sometimes apt to push their legitimate authority beyond their own bounds into provinces where it becomes an usurpation'.[232] Their arrogant campaign to replace the clergy as the guides of the people had to be resisted.

The assumptions of the agnostics, whether scientists or not, needed to be turned on their heads. They took it for granted, Gladstone complained, that they held the intellectual ascendancy over the multitude. The statesman characterized Fitzjames Stephen's case as the assertion of the claims of the 'very select few' to judge in religion, but Gladstone argued instead for the 'competency of the race'.[233] Likewise he put a cross of dissent against a contrast drawn by Huxley between 'instructed people' and 'ignorant people'.[234] The reality, Gladstone believed, was that the population at large has the capacity to decide on questions of religion and

---

[228] F. M. Turner, *Contesting Cultural Authority: Essays in Victorian Intellectual Life* (Cambridge, 1993), ch. 7.

[229] W. E. Gladstone to Lord Acton, 26 June 1887 (copy), GP 44093, f. 291v.

[230] Jonathan Parry, 'Gladstone, Liberalism and the Government of 1868–1874', in David Bebbington and Roger Swift (eds.), *Gladstone Centenary Essays* (Liverpool, 2000), p. 107. Desmond, *Huxley*, p. 422.

[231] *Studies Subsidiary*, pp. 3, 105.                                    [232] *IRHS*, p. 270.

[233] Gladstone, 'Rejoinder', pp. 189–90.

[234] Huxley, 'Mr. Gladstone and Genesis', *Essays upon some Controverted Questions*, p. 114, St Deiniol's Library, Hawarden.

morality. 'Science is made for few men', he observed; 'but duty is the mistress of all men.'[235] It was the testimony of the rank and file of Christendom to which he constantly appealed. What Christians held in common, the beliefs centred on the Trinity and the incarnation that formed 'the undenominational religion of heaven', carried its own credentials.[236] It was not an elite, puffed up by its own intellectual pretensions, that should set the tone of opinion: its members would soon find themselves the mental slaves of newspapers and clubs. Rather it was 'the testimony of the ages, the tradition of their race'.[237] The bulk of the population retained a firm grasp on Christian conviction such as belief in life beyond the grave; the exceptions were to be found only among 'a small fraction of educated and civilized mankind'.[238] It was the self-confident agnostics who were lapsing into error. During his later years, as we shall see, Gladstone developed a political analysis according to which the superior 'classes', swayed by privilege, had banded together against the 'masses', whose judgement was uncorrupted by sectional interests.[239] The same contrast between the classes and the masses undergirded his understanding of the agnostic controversy. Far from possessing a monopoly of wisdom, his opponents ignored the best guide to true opinions, the sound Christian instincts of the people.


## VII


A review of Gladstone's part in the debates arising from the Victorian crisis of faith reveals that he was a willing participant, eager to meet the doubters on their own ground. He had no time for the tendency of the Roman Catholic Church to retreat into the citadel of authority. The ultramontane rejection of dialogue with the modern world, in Gladstone's view, was tactically mistaken and intellectually suicidal. Instead there must be a free and open exchange of ideas. Nevertheless, as Gladstone insisted against Fitzjames Stephen, there was a legitimate role for authority in religion so long as it was seen as a complement to free enquiry and not as its antagonist. There must be a balance between a reverential deference to the wisdom of the Christian centuries and an unflinching commitment to the use of reason. Unbelief, the statesman supposed, drew its strength from irrational factors—intellectual fashion, unwarranted pleas for the faith, and the decadence induced by prosperity. Christianity, by contrast, could readily be defended by rational debate. In that spirit Gladstone took up the challenge from any assailant of religious orthodoxy, whether doubter, freethinker, or plain theist. The most formidable assault in Gladstone's day came from Huxley, the champion of agnosticism who could pose as the representative of dispassionate science. Gladstone was a friend of scientific endeavour, but

[235] Gladstone, 'Rejoinder', p. 198.    [236] Gladstone, 'Heresy and Schism', p. 300.
[237] Gladstone, 'Influence of Authority', p. 170.    [238] *Studies Subsidiary*, p. 170.
[239] See Ch. 9, p. 287.

he could not abide the taunts of Huxley that the progress of knowledge had shown Christianity to be hopelessly outmoded. Gladstone wished to mount a methodological counter-revolution against the agnostics. A return to the techniques of Bishop Butler was the sovereign prescription for the spiritual ills of the time. Like the scientists, Gladstone claimed, Butler used inductive method, but, unlike them, he recognized the limitations of the human intellect. The bishop showed how religious knowledge did not depend on the kind of certainty that Huxley demanded but on an accumulation of probabilities. Adoption of Butlerian method would restore the fortunes of the Christian faith. The inflated claims of scientific naturalism would be punctured and the supernatural once more accorded its due.

Gladstone's part in these debates sheds light on the groundwork of the final stage of his religious thought. It was essentially a blend of Broad with High Churchmanship, a species of liberal Catholicism. Although, as Boyd Hilton has pointed out, Gladstone showed a fresh appreciation of the evangelicals in his later years, the statesman never went back on his repudiation of their distinctive point of view.[240] When in 1894 Gladstone published an article on the atonement, he was criticized by the reviewer in the leading evangelical periodical, the *Churchman*, but approved by Unitarians. It was a sign of the times, remarked one of the latter, 'that so conservative a theologian has made such a good journey to the rationalists' Promised Land'.[241] It was true that he married the conservative theology of a High Churchman to the rationalist sympathies of a Broad Churchman. There were many enduring Anglo-Catholic features in his thought: his high esteem for Palmer's church principles, his strong desire for a rapprochement with Eastern Orthodoxy, and his constant adherence to dogma. Yet the trend in a Broad Church direction that had set in as he moved away from Pusey continued in the later years of his life. He was open-minded towards evolution, he denied that natural immortality was an essential belief, and he asserted that Christianity was vindicated by its part in achieving social progress. He was therefore closely aligned with the men of his day who also synthesized the legacy of the Oxford movement with the broader thinking of the age, the younger liberal Catholics who contributed to *Lux Mundi*. Gladstone preserved his intellectual independence, allowing his reservations as a classicist to restrain him from endorsing biblical criticism. Yet he believed, as did the writers of *Lux Mundi*, in the centrality of the incarnation, an emphasis deriving equally from the high and the broad traditions. Like them, he saw the doctrine of the incarnation as a dogma to be guarded and a sanction for engagement with everything that was human. The resulting combination of churchliness with modern knowledge was a stance that was to dominate the Church of England during the earlier

[240] Boyd Hilton, *The Age of Atonement: The Influence of Evangelicalism on Social and Economic Thought, 1785–1865* (Oxford, 1988), pp. 357–8. See above, Ch. 3, pp. 44–54.
[241] *Churchman*, 29 Dec. 1894, pp. 879–81. A[lexander] G[ordon] in *Christian Life and Unitarian Herald*, 8 Sept. 1894, pp. 427–8. J. Page Hopps in *Coming Day*, Oct. 1894, pp. 145–8, quoted at p. 148.

twentieth century.[242] For all his respect for the past, many of Gladstone's theological affinities were with the future.

Above all, Gladstone upheld the validity of the beliefs of the common people. The ordinary folk in the pews, whether outwardly of the ultramontane, the evangelical, or the 'Historical' school, were united in 'the great central dogmas of the Christian system, the Trinity and the Incarnation'.[243] The faith of the rank and file of all communions, as Möhler had taught the statesman, bore its own testimony. What Christendom as a whole, east and west, had maintained down the centuries was at the very least likely to be true. The creed of the masses possessed legitimate authority in matters of opinion. Here, Gladstone explained, was an instance of 'the law of human interdependence'.[244] The believing community on a global scale had a central place in Gladstone's thinking. The freethinkers, the theists, and the agnostics formed only tiny coteries of thinkers; believers in the incarnation stood for the common mind of the church. The unsound, in religion as in politics, constituted mere sections of opinion; the sound-minded represented the whole. The views of the scientific naturalists must therefore be rejected as a species of arrogant elitism. The faith that united so many, furthermore, had been responsible for the improvement of the world since the coming of Christ. Orthodox Christianity had banished from the earth 'many of the foulest monsters that laid waste humanity'.[245] The wellbeing of the human race, the purpose of the incarnation, loomed large in Gladstone's mind. Christian influence had achieved social progress, the replacement of pride and coercion by law and love. The continuation of that development, however, depended entirely on dismissing the denials of the faith. Only if orthodoxy prevailed in the battle of belief would the future welfare of humanity, temporal as well as eternal, be secure.

[242] A. M. Ramsey, *From Gore to Temple: The Development of Anglican Theology Between* Lux Mundi *and the Second World War, 1889–1939* (London, 1960).
[243] Gladstone, 'Courses of Religious Thought', p. 101.
[244] Gladstone, 'Influence of Authority', p. 169.
[245] Gladstone, 'Courses of Religious Thought', p. 124.

# 9

# The Nature of Gladstonian Liberalism

GLADSTONE WAS the spokesman of British Liberalism for more than a quarter of a century. There had been other authoritative representatives before him. Between 1834 and 1855, as Jonathan Parry has put it, Lord John Russell had been 'the most effective interpreter of the Liberal frame of mind'; in the 1850s and early 1860s, David Steele has argued, Lord Palmerston was the authentic Liberal voice of the country; during those very years, but even more after Palmerston's death in 1865 opened the floodgates for parliamentary reform, John Bright eloquently articulated the radical aspirations of the people; and at the same epoch John Stuart Mill expounded a classic set of Liberal opinions with due philosophical undergirding.[1] But in the years from the late 1860s to the mid-1890s Gladstone was the unrivalled definer of the nature of Liberalism. T. H. Green might recast its theoretical foundations and Joseph Chamberlain might (for a while) claim to represent the next stage of its onward march, but, even during Gladstone's temporary retirement from the party leadership in the later 1870s, it was to him that the people of the United Kingdom, and increasingly of the wider world, looked to know what Liberal convictions might be. For that reason Gladstone's political opinions in his later years possess an importance that far transcends the bounds of personal intellectual biography. The present chapter tries to indicate some of the main contours of the statesman's monumental contribution to discussion of the groundwork of politics. It does not address his engagement with particular issues, but instead concentrates on his more theoretical statements about public affairs. It concerns itself with premises rather than with policies. In part Gladstone was no doubt offering retrospective justifications for actual policy decisions, a stance that was explicit in his *Chapter of Autobiography* of 1868. Yet such rationalizations could delve down to the foundations of his thinking. The resulting public expositions of Liberalism, however angled towards self-vindication, are almost as revealing of his

---

[1] J. P. Parry, *The Rise and Fall of Liberal Government in Victorian Britain* (New Haven, Conn., 1993), p. 132. E. D. Steele, *Palmerston and Liberalism, 1855–1865* (Cambridge, 1991). John Bright, *Speeches on Questions of Public Policy*, ed. J. E. T. Rogers (London, 1869), most recently reinterpreted by Patrick Joyce, *Democratic Subjects: The Self and the Social in Nineteenth-Century England* (Cambridge, 1994). William Stafford, *John Stuart Mill* (Basingstoke, 1998), offers a concise guide to the voluminous literature on its subject.

mind as the private statements of his early Conservatism. What they display is a remarkable congruence with what has previously been shown about his evolving beliefs in other fields. Gladstonian Liberalism turns out to have been cognate with the statesman's attitudes as Christian believer and Homeric scholar.

I

The sources for Gladstone's later thinking about public affairs are less yielding than might be wished. Gladstone published no sustained work of political theory in his Liberal years. The books he did write are not particularly useful. Even *Studies Subsidiary to the Works of Bishop Butler* contains only a sentence or two recommending Butler's intellectual method to 'the intending politician, if of masculine and serious mind'.[2] The successive volumes on Homer do have a measure of value because each, apart from *Landmarks of Homeric Study*, contains a section on the social and political practices of the poems. Yet, not surprisingly, explicit allusions to the Victorian state in Gladstone's accounts of Agamemnon's campaigns and Ulysses' wanderings, though present (as we have seen), are relatively few.[3] More instructive are the statesman's articles, published almost every month during periods of opposition. Well over half of them concern public affairs, but their limitation is that they usually relate to specific contemporary questions rather than to broader questions of political philosophy. Even more helpful, therefore, are Gladstone's speeches. As rhetorical exercises they reflect the audience almost as much as the speaker, and so allowance has to be made for time and place. But Gladstone's methods of preparation, which involved jotting down the main intended heads of a speech shortly before delivery rather than any long gestation or deployment of speech-writers, ensured that the content faithfully reflected his own mind. Parliamentary deliverances, however, were normally concerned with particular issues of policy and were standardly addressed primarily to opponents or potential waverers rather than to supporters. Hence they did not rehearse the authentic Gladstonian reasons for a course of action as much as the addresses out of doors. It is therefore in the public oratory of the statesman that much of the most illuminating evidence is to be found. The Midlothian addresses of 1879–80 come closest to laying out the fundamental principles of Liberalism, though even there the statements are often incidental to diatribes against Tory misgovernment. But in the public speeches as a whole there are frequent appeals to the values that underpin the orator's political philosophy.[4] In fact Gladstone's social assumptions often appear most clearly in the non-partisan addresses delivered at the opening of a library or the prize-giving of a horticultural society. Peter Stansky has written a successful biography of the statesman

---

[2] *Studies Subsidiary*, p. 6.          [3] See Ch. 7, pp. 179, 205.
[4] On Gladstone's rhetoric, see J. E. Meisel, *Public Speech and the Culture of Public Life in the Age of Gladstone* (New York, 2001).

around a selection of his speeches.[5] In the present chapter, however, the rather different aim is to use the oratory, together with the various other sources, in order to set out the main parameters of Gladstone's mature political thought.

What can be established, first of all, is that a body of thinking exists in this area waiting to be recovered. At times, it is true, Gladstone could show impatience with theorists of the state. He remarked when Acton sent him J. A. Froude's new study of Machiavelli that 'all these bigwigs' made out political life to be worse than it was.[6] On another occasion Gladstone conceded that 'we of this island are not great political philosophers'.[7] The ancients, he mused in a fragment that has been published in the diaries, were more concerned than the moderns with the business of government 'as an art and as a science', and it was Christianity that had dethroned it in favour of a preoccupation with individual ethics.[8] Yet, he believed, reflection on government was still a worthy pursuit. The first criterion of statesmanship, he suggested in an article of 1889 on Daniel O'Connell, was 'the capacity to embrace broad principles and to hold them fast'.[9] Gladstone advocated more than a practical concern with policy objectives, for he commended the normative study of public life. This is how he put the point two years later:

> Political philosophy, taking for its point of departure the constitution of human nature, and the conditions appointed for its action in communities, has to determine or to inquire, with these data before it, concerning the proper laws applicable to the conduct of those human affairs which concern the public weal. Within this sphere, its business is to show what ought to be.[10]

The task was analogous to Butler's reasoning in his sermons from human nature to personal obligations; and Aristotle had undertaken much of the enquiry about how human beings behaved in communities. These two masters pointed the way to a systematic ('proper laws') understanding of political theory. Even if Gladstone composed no mature treatise on the science of government, he possessed structured convictions about 'the public weal'.

The most obvious feature of Gladstone's political thought from the time of his assuming the Liberal leadership was a sublime faith in freedom. 'I did not learn when I was at Oxford', he told the university Palmerston Club in 1878, 'that which I have learned since—namely, to set a due value on the imperishable and inestimable principles of human liberty.'[11] He frequently insisted, as on the platform in Midlothian in 1890 and in private to John Morley a year later, that the fundamental alteration in his opinions over the years was his embracing of liberty.[12] Acton once chided him for not taking the process far enough. Gladstone, he

---

[5] Peter Stansky, *Gladstone: A Progress in Politics* (New York, 1979).
[6] W. E. Gladstone to Lord Acton, 16 Aug. 1891, GP 44094, f. 181v.
[7] W. E. Gladstone, 'Kin beyond Sea', *Gleanings*, 1, p. 247.
[8] GP 44773, f. 51, in *D*, 11 June 1888.
[9] W. E. Gladstone, 'Daniel O'Connell', *Nineteenth Century*, 25 (1889), p. 162.
[10] W. E. Gladstone, 'Electoral Facts No. III', *Nineteenth Century*, 30 (1891), p. 328.
[11] *T*, 31 Jan. 1878, p. 10.          [12] *T*, 24 Oct. 1890, p. 4; Morley, 3, pp. 474–5.

claimed, did not appeal to freedom, 'the principle of liberalism', but rather to the lesser principles of democracy, nationality, and progress.[13] Acton, however, was discussing Gladstone's treatment of the role of Christianity in history, and the charge was never applicable to the statesman's estimate of freedom as a political tenet. Although Gladstone readily conceded that, like everything good, freedom was capable of abuse, it possessed 'a value I cannot describe ... without liberty there is nothing sound'.[14] Its attainment was the glory of English history. Its origins might, as he occasionally suggested, go back a millennium to the forests of Anglo-Saxon England; it certainly took a leap forward with the creation of the medieval parliament; then national freedom emerged decisively under Elizabeth I and individual freedom followed under the early Stuarts.[15] This catalogue, based on a rudimentary Whig understanding of history, meant that Tories as much as Liberals were the beneficiaries of constitutional evolution. The whole nation should stand for liberty against despotism.[16] To the English, he asserted after his retirement from parliament, 'the air of freedom is the very breath of their nostrils'.[17] Almost any public address was an opportunity for a paean to liberty.

The freedom that Gladstone had in mind was primarily an uncomplicated ability to live without oppression, whether physical or mental. It encompassed free speech, freedom of assembly, freedom of the press, freedom to worship, and freedom of the person.[18] It also included liberty for subject races struggling against repressive authorities. Gladstone took his adulation of freedom in this context to remarkable lengths. A war for liberty, he asserted in 1880, was the only type of conflict that did not contain elements of corruption.[19] Although he would not countenance revolution in general, disapproving, for example, of the Irish rebellion of 1798,[20] he readily gave his blessing to the revolt of the Bulgarians against the Turks in the late 1870s. 'It is the business of every oppressed people', he wrote in 1878, 'to rise upon every reasonable opportunity against the oppressor.'[21] The liberty he championed so forthrightly, overriding the right of government to expect obedience, was essentially negative, the privilege of each individual and nation to go unmolested. Yet there are signs that Gladstone saw it as something more. The legislation of the last half-century, he declared in 1891, had been 'setting men free, removing artificial obstacles to the full development of their powers'.[22] Could they be free if their powers were not fully developed? There may be a hint here of the positive conception of liberty that had recently been expounded by T. H. Green. And freedom was undoubtedly in Gladstone's

[13] Lord Acton to W. E. Gladstone, 2 May 1888, GP 44094, f. 29v, Morley, 3, p. 361.

[14] *T*, 24 Oct. 1890, p. 4.

[15] *T*, 28 Oct. 1889, p. 8. GP 44765, f. 131 (24 Sept. 1881), in *D*.

[16] GP 44776, f. 114 (n.d.: 1894?).

[17] W. E. Gladstone, *The Eastern Crisis: A Letter to the Duke of Westminster, K.G.* (London, 1897), p. 16.

[18] W. E. Gladstone, 'Italy in 1888–89', *Nineteenth Century*, 25 (1889), pp. 763, 770–1. *T*, 8 Nov. 1888, p. 10.

[19] W. E. Gladstone, *Political Speeches in Scotland, March and April 1880* (Edinburgh, 1880), p. 30.

[20] *T*, 4 July 1892, p. 4.

[21] W. E. Gladstone, 'The Peace to Come', *Nineteenth Century*, 3 (1878), p. 221.

[22] *T*, 10 Dec. 1891, p. 10.

estimation a creative force. Those who were emancipated from tyranny and developed free institutions learned to enjoy freedom, to work their institutions, and to defend their liberties against invasion. 'Fortresses may be levelled with the ground', intoned Gladstone in Midlothian in 1880; 'treaties may be trodden underfoot—the true barrier against despotism is in the human heart and in the human mind.'[23] An esteem for freedom guaranteed its permanence. 'We say', Gladstone announced during the 1892 general election campaign, 'that the possession of liberty increases the appreciation of liberty.'[24] It was a principle that, once planted, would not fail to blossom. Freedom, like the rose, had an innate capacity for self-propagation.

The exaltation of freedom implied the diminution of the state. Gladstone, as Colin Matthew stresses in the epilogue of his study of the statesman, was associated with the achievement of 'the minimal state', its withdrawal from economy and society so that each could operate freely.[25] The statesman expounded his view of the matter particularly clearly when, as Prime Minister, he delivered his first planned public speech since the general election of 1868 to his working-class electors at Greenwich in the shadow of the Paris Commune. The working people, he commented, were being told to look to the legislature for social remedies. That was a fundamental error. Those who promised town-dwellers an airy garden or markets selling retail quantities at wholesale prices were quacks. The state could provide no panacea. 'It is the individual mind and conscience, it is the individual character, on which mainly human happiness or misery depends.'[26] Human beings must rely on themselves, the orator concluded, not on an outside agency. Gladstone's apostolate of self-help induced him, in 1877, to praise the work of the friendly societies. Groups such as the Oddfellows and Foresters displayed the virtues of self-reliance as opposed to dependence on the state:

the best thing the Government can do for the people is to help them to help themselves— that is, to remove the obstacles which are in the way of their so helping themselves. I have no faith in any system of Government which strikes at the root of human freedom; and if any Government pretends that it teaches men how to live, that it will undertake the finding for them of what as citizens and fathers of families they ought to find for themselves, the Government, be its intention good or bad, is not conferring a benefit, but inflicting an injury on that people.[27]

So much for the nanny state. Hence Gladstone repudiated the aim of the prohibition movement, contending that the remedy for intemperance lay 'within the individual breast'; and he insisted, even to a predominantly mining audience in 1890, that on labour questions, unless absolutely unavoidable, it was infinitely preferable not to resort to 'the coercive and rigid operation of public authority'.[28] Gladstone constantly seemed to be reining in the sections of opinion that wanted the state to do more.

---

[23] Gladstone, *Speeches, 1880*, p. 219.
[24] *T*, 20 June 1892, p. 12.
[25] Matthew, pp. 640–1.
[26] *T*, 30 Oct. 1871, p. 3.
[27] *T*, 5 Feb. 1877, p. 10.
[28] *T*, 19 Dec. 1867, p. 8; 24 Oct. 1890, p. 4.

His own aim, he often declared, was to cause it to do less. He repeatedly endorsed Lord Grey's watchword from the 1830s of peace, retrenchment, and reform.[29] At the 1892 general election he pointed out that, while his administrations had not been pacifist, they had been pacific; that, though retrenchment was at present out of fashion, it would be enforced again whenever the people demanded it; and that, despite the electorate having been enlarged to 6 millions, there was still more to do by way of parliamentary reform.[30] The goal of peace entailed less military expenditure, the issue on which Gladstone chose to retire from the premiership in 1894. Retrenchment meant the reduction of the machinery of the state and its capacity to interfere in the life of the people. Reform enlarged the number of electors on whose vigilance the limitation of public authority depended. But the supreme agency transferring powers from the state to the people was always, in Gladstone's mind, free trade. He reminded his Greenwich audience in 1871 that the greatest of boons had been the initiation of the free entry into the ports of everything the working people could want.[31] Free trade, he claimed twenty years later, rested on the principle of 'setting free both the physical and mental powers of every man, without interference of the law, to do the best he can in industrial directions'.[32] He remained a stalwart champion of Cobdenism to the end of his days.[33] Underpinning his position was a commitment to the axioms of political economy. On that ground he denounced strikes in 1867 as 'a very great evil'; and seven years later he appealed to liberty for non-trade unionists as the reason for rejecting strike action by union members who were his own tenants at Hawarden.[34] Freedom of contract was a sacred principle with which the government should tamper as little as possible. Gladstone's desire to circumscribe the powers of the state rested on premises which can legitimately be associated with economic individualism.

There were other features of Gladstone's political thought that seemed shaped by a cognate mould. In the reform debates of the 1860s he was prepared, to the dismay of less advanced Liberals, to deploy the language of 'rights'.[35] His usage of the term, however, oscillated between a more fixed and a more fluid conception. In two of the most famous passages from the Midlothian campaign he spoke of 'the rights of the savage' in Afghanistan as though they were enjoyed universally and of 'the equal rights of all nations' as though they were absolute.[36] He seemed to be assuming some notion of natural rights inherent in individuals and nations. Yet at other times he talked of *establishing* the rights of individuals and wrote of *securing* rights as the aim

---

[29] *T*, 20 Dec. 1867, p. 5; 2 Feb. 1874, p. 5; 1 Nov. 1878, p. 8.          [30] *T*, 6 July 1892, p. 11.

[31] *T*, 30 Oct. 1871, p. 3.          [32] *T*, 5 Oct. 1891, p. 12.

[33] Anthony Howe, 'Gladstone and Cobden', in David Bebbington and Roger Swift (eds.), *Gladstone Centenary Essays* (Liverpool, 2000), pp. 121–7.

[34] *T*, 19 Dec. 1867, p. 8; 10 June 1874, p. 12.

[35] J. W. Burrow, *Whigs and Liberals: Continuity and Change in English Political Thought* (Oxford, 1988), p. 46.

[36] W. E. Gladstone, *Political Speeches in Scotland, November and December 1879* (Edinburgh, 1879), pp. 94, 116.

of Christian civilization.[37] Rights, in Gladstone's mind, appear to be contingent, in some Burkean sense, on circumstances. They ought, perhaps, to be recognized, but their actual consolidation is an achievement. They were, in fact, the fruit of progress. The consequence of self-help, in Gladstone's view, was social amelioration. He had come to believe, as we have seen, that human progress was possible.[38] Those who had improved their own gifts, he told a working-class audience at the opening of a reading room in 1889, could do some good to their fellow creatures and 'labour a little to diminish sin and sorrow in the world'.[39] Patrick Joyce has seen the improvement of the people, supremely in the moral sphere, as the grand political narrative purveyed by Gladstone in the later 1860s. It qualified them for participation in the institutions of the country.[40] The statesman subsequently invoked progress as a cause to which Liberalism was committed and often rehearsed the advances of the Queen's reign— parliamentary reform, mitigation of the criminal law, reduction in the price of food, elementary education, machinery, transport, and communication.[41] Society was moving in the right direction. The idea of progress, like the notion of rights, had a powerful resonance for audiences steeped in the legacy of the Enlightenment, and so allowance must be made for the statesman's desire to echo the assumptions of his hearers. But both concepts sprang readily to Gladstone's lips because they formed part of his own mental stock. They blended with the cluster of doctrines surrounding freedom, self-help, and suspicion of the state to give his political thinking a strand of classic individualism that some commentators have not been slow to identify as the whole of Gladstonian Liberalism.

On the other hand, however, there are many indications that Gladstone's personal political theory retained a strongly conservative cast. His disposition in all things was to cherish tradition. He loved the forms of the House of Commons, on one occasion having the speaker send a serjeant-at-arms to rebuke a new member who had the temerity to put his feet up on a bench.[42] In 1885 he paid for the replacement of Edinburgh's market cross, which, he regretted, had been swept away in the previous century.

It is in my judgement [he declared on that occasion] a great misfortune to any country when it finds itself or thinks itself under the necessity of breaking the ancient traditions. It is a degradation to men to be reduced to the life of the present; and never will he cast forth his hopes, and his views, and his efforts towards the future with due effect and energy, unless at the same time he prizes and holds fondly clasped to his heart the recollections of the past.[43]

The respect for tradition had affinities with Gladstone's Anglo-Catholic love for the historic church, but it applied equally to politics. He had always felt, he told

---

[37] T, 5 Oct. 1891, p. 12. W. E. Gladstone, 'Vaticanism', Rome and the Newest Fashions in Religion (London, 1875), p. 95.                                        [38] See Ch. 5, pp. 137–8.
[39] T, 28 Oct. 1889, p. 8.                          [40] Joyce, Democratic Subjects, pp. 197–9.
[41] A. W. Hutton and H. J. Cohen (eds.), The Speeches and Public Addresses of the Right Hon. W. E. Gladstone, M. P.: 1886–1888 (London, 1892), pp. 275–7 (30 Aug. 1887). T, 28 Oct. 1889, p. 8.
[42] W. C. Lubenow, Parliamentary Politics and the Home Rule Crisis: The British House of Commons in 1886 (Oxford, 1988), p. 331.                          [43] Daily News, 24 Nov. 1885, S & P, XXXII, p. 112.

an audience of Midlothian working-class electors in 1890, a veneration for things ancient. 'I dislike,' he went on, 'I may almost say I detest, gratuitous change.'[44] Any proposed alteration must be fully justified. Although he was a Liberal, he had remarked earlier in the same year, he was not an innovator. One of his great complaints against the members of the Tory majority was their neglect of precedent and usage, their refusal 'to be guided by the experience of former times'.[45] In the campaign of 1879–80 he condemned the Tories for their 'dangerous novelties'; the true threat to the constitution, he claimed, came from the Conservatives, not from the radicals.[46] When visiting Romsey in Hampshire shortly after the erection of memorials to Lord Palmerston in 1868, Gladstone was eager to annex the Palmerstonian tradition. The deceased peer and his supporters, he claimed, were Liberals without epithet, but they were nevertheless 'the best Conservatives'.[47] Gladstone's mature political thinking was hardly less wedded to the traditional than its earlier phase.

His stance can be illustrated by closer scrutiny of his attitude to freedom. When he spoke of having come to uphold liberty, he was eager to insist that this was the chief—or even the only—shift in his thinking. He had not changed, he used to comment, in *all* his political opinions.[48] Freedom had simply been added to his pre-existing fundamental values. Already in the later 1840s, when his Conservative assumptions still predominated, he was recognizing that freedom needed to be yoked with loyalty, obedience, order, and tradition. A 'mixture of loyalty and freedom, of deference to authority with the sense of individual responsibility', he wrote in the *Quarterly Review* in 1847, was 'the peculiar characteristic of our political system'.[49] By the time Gladstone held the Liberal leadership he was performing exactly the same balancing act, but, knowing the expectations of his followers, he was taking freedom as the given. His government's aim, he told the Lord Mayor's Banquet in 1871, was 'to extend and confirm as far as we can that union of freedom and order, of attachment to ancient institutions with the lively desire for improvement, which we believe to be in some degree at least characteristic of this country'.[50] It was his constant message. He called a rally of more than 20,000 working men during the first Midlothian campaign 'a festival of freedom', but, he told them, they celebrated a 'rational freedom . . . allied with order and loyalty'.[51] The recipe for personal excellence and national greatness, he explained in 1888, was love of liberty together with respect for law and order.[52] It was equally the package that Britain had for export. British (and French) influence had traditionally been exerted, he wrote in 1880, on behalf of 'ordered freedom'.[53] The final principle of foreign policy, he declared in the

---

[44] *T*, 24 Oct. 1890, p. 4.

[45] W. E. Gladstone, *The Parnell Commission and the Vote of Censure upon the Irish Members* (London, [1890]), p. 15.                    [46] Gladstone, *Speeches, 1879*, p. 20; *Speeches, 1880*, p. 65.

[47] *T*, 23 July 1868, p. 10.                    [48] *T*, 31 Jan. 1878, p. 10; 24 Oct. 1890, p. 4.

[49] W. E. Gladstone, 'From Oxford to Rome', *Quarterly Review*, 81 (1847), pp. 151, 164.

[50] *T*, 31 July 1871, p. 6.          [51] Gladstone, *Speeches, 1879*, p. 163.          [52] *T*, 28 Oct. 1889, p. 8.

[53] W. E. Gladstone, 'Russia and England', *Nineteenth Century*, 7 (1880), p. 551.

third Midlothian speech, was 'a sympathy with freedom', but not freedom in the abstract, for the sympathy was based on a conviction that 'in freedom you lay the firmest foundations both of loyalty and order'.[54] Freedom was, as we have seen, creative; but what it generated provided a check on itself. Despite its prominence in the statesman's hierarchy of values, liberty did not stand in splendid isolation at the top of the scale. Rather Gladstone habitually balanced liberty against principles that can properly be seen as conservative—or at least conserving—attributes of the state.

The continuing legacy of Gladstone's own Conservative past is at its most obvious in his attitude towards equality. It is true that at Hawarden he was noted for mingling with his tenants, free from the traditional hauteur of the landed classes. At the opening of the Hawarden Institute in 1893 he laid it down that wage-earners were not distinct from their superiors and that it had been wrong in the past to treat them as outsiders. They could confer benefits on others just as much as others could confer benefits on them.[55] Yet this form of social rapprochement did not spring from any species of egalitarianism. In archaic Greece, Gladstone noted with evident approval, while liberty was highly prized, equality was not even dreamt of.[56] The same was true of modern England. Unlike the French, he asserted at the time of the Commune, the English had no affection for naked political equality. 'England', he declared, 'is a great lover of liberty, but of equality she has never been so much enamoured.'[57] In this respect there was also a fundamental contrast with the United States. The English people believed in the reverse of the proposition that all men were born equal.[58] For the political expression of social egalitarianism, democracy, Gladstone had little time. The franchise was a trust, not a right. As late as 1879 he was equating democrats with agitators as much as no-rent doctrinaires with social subversives.[59] In 1892 the London Liberal and Radical Union called for one man one vote. Gladstone would have none of it: 'if I am told that there are men of different capacity, and that they ought to exercise different degrees of influence upon the Legislature of the country, I admit it . . . and I say the people of England are the proper judges of those claims to superior influence . . .'[60] A further broadening of the franchise was called for, but it was not on the basis of any right to its possession. Once while staying at Hawarden, John Ruskin accused Gladstone of being a leveller. The statesman sharply denied it, professing himself instead 'an out-and-out *inequalitarian*'.[61] He remained an exponent of the theory of social rank he had espoused when he was young.

Hence Gladstone remained a stout champion of the landed aristocracy. On occasion, it is true, he was willing to put himself at the head of an agitation to make the will of the House of Commons prevail over the House of Lords. In

---

[54] Gladstone, *Speeches, 1879*, p. 117.    [55] *T*, 23 May 1893, p. 10.    [56] *JM*, p. 447.
[57] *T*, 30 Oct. 1871, p. 3.    [58] Gladstone, 'Kin beyond Sea', p. 234.
[59] Gladstone, *Speeches, 1879*, p. 210    [60] *T*, 1 June 1892, p. 7.
[61] Lisle March-Phillipps and Bertram Christian (eds.), *Some Hawarden Letters, 1878–1913* (London, 1917), p. 37.

1860–1 over the paper duties (successfully) and in 1894 over blocking Liberal legislation in general (abortively) he cast himself as the leader of the people in what he retrospectively called the 'great controversy between Lords and Commons'.[62] But these efforts were designed to limit what he regarded as an abuse of privilege rather than to assert any novel constitutional principle. In 1871, with the French republic abolishing inherited legislative powers, Gladstone rallied to the defence of the House of Lords. The general opinion of the nation, he claimed, was that the descendants of men ennobled for public service should take part in framing the laws.[63] With Burke, he declared in 1885, he believed that only knowledge and virtue possessed an intrinsic right to govern, and so in theory the second chamber might be reconstructed on that basis alone. Yet in practice, he held, it was a sound principle that wealth and birth must also be taken into account.[64] When, in 1890, the fabulously successful American entrepreneur Andrew Carnegie argued that the wealthy should disperse their property during their lifetimes, Gladstone insisted that, on the contrary, family acquisitions should be kept together so that responsibility for social leadership should be transmitted down the generations. It was a good thing that Lord Salisbury's ancestors had been taking a similar part in public affairs ten generations before. Landlords, furthermore, potentially played a critical integrative role in their localities as well as in politics: 'the office of landed proprietor binds together the whole structure of rural society.'[65] Bad landlords might neglect their duties by absenteeism, but good landlords excited gratitude among the masses by their philanthropy. They recognized that 'the possession of landed property entails great social duties' and so could be relied on to confer benefits on their tenants and humbler neighbours.[66] Great proprietors continued to have a place in the Liberal party. It was characteristic of British history, Gladstone believed, that 'the cause of the people' had enjoyed leadership 'among the highest families in the country'.[67] That aspect of the British experience, in his view, helped explain stability in the state as much as cohesion in society. Down to the end of his life Gladstone maintained social assumptions that were derived from a traditional paternalism.

At the apex of the justly unequal society was the monarchy. As Liberal leader Gladstone showed a conspicuous but notoriously unreciprocated attachment to Queen Victoria. It was rooted in his continuing conviction that the constitutional monarchy that had evolved in Britain was a bulwark of order. He now rejected the Burkean supposition that the Glorious Revolution had reaffirmed the principle of absolute hereditary succession for the future. Since the Revolution, on the contrary, the authority of the crown had been 'expressly founded upon contract'. Any breach of the contract on the part of the sovereign dissolved the obligation of the subject to obey. But there was no provision to meet that eventuality other than

---

[62] *Autobiographica*, pp. 116–17 (13 Feb. 1897).                          [63] *T*, 30 Oct. 1871, p. 3.
[64] W. E. Gladstone, *Political Speeches in Scotland, November 1885*, rev. edn. (Edinburgh, 1886), p. 16.
[65] W. E. Gladstone, 'Mr. Carnegie's "Gospel of Wealth": A Review and a Recommendation', *Nineteenth Century*, 28 (1890), p. 684.
[66] *T*, 13 Feb. 1891, p. 12.                          [67] Gladstone, *Speeches, 1885*, p. 110.

the broader 'general rule' of hereditary succession. Constitutional monarchy might be 'a scientific abortion' in the eyes of Plato or Aristotle, but it was a great advantage to have 'the object of all our political veneration ... rather in a person, than in an abstract entity, like the State'.[68] Gladstone exerted himself to nurture the veneration, especially during his first administration, in order to counteract the rise of republican sentiment feeding on the Queen's withdrawal from public duties.[69] At Windsor in December 1871 he persuaded a reluctant Victoria to hold a thanksgiving service to mark the recovery of the Prince of Wales from serious illness. He admitted to the Queen, he noted down afterwards, that the religious importance of the event was symbolic, but it was not therefore slight. 'Royalty was in one point of view a symbol,' he told her, 'and one of great consequence'.[70] Like members of the aristocracy in their particular spheres, the monarchy was an integrating factor in the nation at large. It was therefore indispensable. The vindication of the crown was often the ultimate item in the peroration of Gladstone's speeches, as when, in 1891, he urged his hearers in a final sentence to advance 'to the union of classes, to the domination of the law, to promote the stability of the Throne'.[71] So it was extremely painful to receive no word of gratitude from Victoria at his final resignation as Prime Minister: two years afterwards he was still dreaming about 'the unsatisfactory ending of my over half a century of service'.[72] The upholding of the monarchy was a primary task imposed by enduring personal conviction.

Gladstone's conservative sensibilities are particularly evident in one of the areas usually associated with his individualism, the doctrine of progress. Although, as we have seen, he was willing to invoke the idea, he hedged it about with a range of qualifications. The rapid progress of the Victorian era, he affirmed in 1879, might have been a good in itself, but it was also a threat to national equilibrium.[73] If civilization was to advance, he remarked six years before, there must equally be reverence for the past.[74] Progress was certainly not inevitable, as contemporaries tended to believe. At best the advance of mankind was 'a chequered and an interrupted progress'.[75] When Acton challenged him to allow more room in an article for upward progress, Gladstone announced, while grudgingly making a modification, that 'I do not much believe in it'—as a moral, as opposed to an intellectual, phenomenon.[76] All his convictions about the decay of a primitive revelation militated against a simplistic acceptance of progress.[77] A further revelation, the founding of Christianity, he believed, was a necessary condition for human advance. The development of Christian civilization might

---

[68] Gladstone, 'Kin beyond Sea', pp. 227, 228, 229.

[69] Freda Harcourt, 'Gladstone, Monarchism and the "New" Imperialism', *Journal of Imperial and Commonwealth History*, 14 (1985).     [70] GP 44760, ff. 129–34 (21 Dec. 1871), quoted at f. 134v.

[71] *T*, 18 Mar. 1891, p. 11.                          [72] *Autobiographica*, p. 169 (2 Jan. 1896).

[73] Gladstone, *Speeches, 1879*, p. 234.               [74] *T*, 20 Aug. 1873, p. 5.

[75] W. E. Gladstone, 'Inaugural Address: The Work of Universities', *Gleanings*, 7, p. 3.

[76] W. E. Gladstone to Lord Acton, 26 June 1887 (copy), GP 44093, f. 292.

[77] See Ch. 6, pp. 171–4.

have no limits, but that was because of its Christian, not its civilized, component.[78] The implications for politics, as Gladstone explained in Dublin in 1877,
were chastening: 'I am not a man very sanguine about what is called political
progress; that is to say, I labour for it, I thankfully accept its results, but I am
convinced that we are very far indeed from the day when . . . the actual state of
political and social circumstances will so much approximate to anything like our
ideal standard.' In a metaphor similar to the image of the ship of state in the writings of the twentieth-century conservative political philosopher Michael
Oakeshott, Gladstone went on to comment that 'while we are stopping one leak
in the vessel' sin and decay were opening 'a great many other leaks in other quarters'.[79] The achievement, as Oakeshott stressed, was not to reach a harbour but to
keep the ship afloat.[80] Gladstone might have conceded the same. His mind was
tinctured as little by utopianism as that of any conservative philosopher.

Consequently Gladstone's mature political thought appears to have been
deeply ambiguous. On the one hand it showed signs of classical liberalism in the
vein of the Manchester school. It was individualist, asserting human rights and
the value of self-help, while aiming to limit the state through decreasing public
expenditure. It was associated with free trade, political economy, and, at times,
laissez-faire. On the other hand it appeared to be imbued with a species of conservatism, endorsing tradition against those who decried it. It was anti-egalitarian,
upholding royalty and the peerage as matters of priority. The eulogies of freedom
stirred Liberal audiences, and yet freedom was carefully balanced by order. There
was celebration of progress, and yet progress was doubtful and contingent.
Gladstone seemed to have turned away from his previous ideas to embrace an
authentic Liberalism but nevertheless to have maintained the substance of his
earlier Conservatism with untiring tenacity. How is the apparent contradiction to
be explained? A key (though not, as will be seen, the only one) lies in recognizing
that for Gladstone the individual was always to be seen in a social context. In
*Landmarks in Homeric Study*, published in 1890 while the statesman was at the
height of his ascendancy over the Liberal party, he pointed to the exemplary sentiments uttered in the *Iliad* by Phoenix, the tutor of Achilles. Tempted to patricide,
Phoenix had found his anger checked by a god: 'he warned me', according to
Phoenix, 'of what the whole realm would say.'[81] This remark, according to
Gladstone, embodied one of the most favourable ethical characteristics of the
ancient Greeks in the heroic age. It represented a 'marked deference in the individual to the moral judgements of the community . . . ascribed to a divine infusion'.[82] The individual did not stand alone. If respectful towards divine guidance,

---

[78] W. E. Gladstone, 'Universitas Hominum: Or the Unity of History', *North American Review*, 145
(1887), p. 601; id., ' "Robert Elsmere": The Battle of Belief' [1888], *Later Gleanings*, pp. 110–11.

[79] *Daily News*, 8 Nov. 1877, S & P, XXIII, p. 119.

[80] Michael Oakeshott, 'Political Education', *Rationalism in Politics and Other Essays*, new edn.
(Indianapolis, Ind., 1991), p. 60.

[81] Homer, *The Iliad*, 9: 460, trans. Robert Fagles (London, 1990), p. 267.

[82] *Landmarks*, p. 94.

any human being would submit to the traditional values of the social unit. That conviction lay at the core of Gladstone's understanding of human life. His version of individualism could coexist with traditionalism because it was always compatible with the idea of community.

## II

The language of community ran through the whole of Gladstone's discourse as Liberal leader. It applied to corporate life of all kinds, whether in small groups or in large, at home or abroad. 'The sense of a common life', Gladstone declared as a guest of the Lord Provost of Dundee in 1890, '—parochial, municipal, county, national—is an ennobling qualification to civilized man ...'[83] The concert of Europe, he argued in his Midlothian definition of the principles of foreign policy, was to unite the powers in 'common action' to promote 'the common good of them all'.[84] Sometimes he elaborated the idea. In 1891, when receiving the freedom of Newcastle-upon-Tyne, he contrasted his visit with a former one in 1862 to make a partisan speech. 'I am not now placing myself in contact with any section, any party, any portion of the community', he told his audience, 'but with the entire community of this great city.'[85] The 'community' represented the whole of a human group as opposed to any subdivision. And the word usually carried with it not just social but also political overtones. This was clear, for instance, when he wrote about the Irish Question in an article of 1889. Unionists were arguing, he noted, that the people of Ireland could not claim Home Rule because they were only a portion of the community of the United Kingdom. The whole must decide for the part. That case, Gladstone contended, was erected on a false premise. 'The people of Ireland were once a community, just as much as the people of England or of Scotland ever were.'[86] They ceased to be so in law only because of the Act of Union. A community, in this usage, is a nation with distinct political standing: Ireland constituted one, at least in the full sense, only while she possessed her own parliament. The ideal form of the community, for Gladstone, was the *polis*, the ancient Greek city that was also a state. The term 'community' still fitted cities such as Newcastle, but it also suited much larger entities, whether whole nations or even the entire international arena. The concept, though diverse in its applications, was fundamental to Gladstone's political thought.

The community was animated by common values. Supreme among them was 'reverence', which Gladstone called 'one of the firmest and surest bonds of human society'.[87] Reverence was a respect for the customary, the traditional, the established ways of the group. It was directed particularly towards the leaders, to the

---

[83] *T*, 30 Oct. 1890, p. 4.   [84] Gladstone, *Speeches, 1879*, p. 116.   [85] *T*, 5 Oct. 1891, p. 12.
[86] W. E. Gladstone, 'Plain Speaking on the Irish Union' [1889], *Special Aspects of the Irish Question* (London, 1912), p. 97.   [87] Gladstone, 'Carnegie's "Gospel of Wealth" ', p. 683.

landowners and the crown. The word had the religious overtones of the hushed awe in church introduced by the Oxford movement. It also had roots in Gladstone's classical studies.[88] In *Studies on Homer* the statesman cites the great German historian Theodor Mommsen as claiming that the inspiration for collective human life came from ancient Rome and the inspiration for individual human life from historic Greece. In Gladstone's estimation, however, archaic Greece combined the virtues of both: 'it united reverence with independence.'[89] Reverence is the principle of living together, the quintessence of civic virtue. It appears in the same guise in *Juventus Mundi* (1869), where it is associated with order as a balancing factor against freedom.[90] Liberty and reverence, according to a detached memorandum of 1890, are the twin poles of a sound political creed, the one specially associated with the Liberals, the other with the Conservatives.[91] Accordingly the Conservatives were particularly blameworthy for its decay alike in the House of Commons and in the country at large. Toryism, Gladstone noted down in December 1885, once stood on two legs, the lame leg of class interest and the sound leg of reverence. But Toryism now stumped along on class interest alone, no longer leaning on its sound leg.[92] 'Reverence', Gladstone told a dinner party the following month, 'is a barrier, a check upon licence.'[93] His high regard for the quality is a symptom of his lasting conservative leanings, but it is more. As the sentiment of mutuality, reverence was an expression of Gladstone's belief in the essential gatheredness of human existence.

The 'primary element of society', as Gladstone remarked in a Midlothian address, was the family.[94] As much as the rising young Tory author of *The State in its Relations with the Church*, the Grand Old Man at the head of the Liberal party took the family to be the building-block of larger communities. The 'union of families' was 'the basis of . . . national felicity'.[95] Alongside the state, the family was one of the two organic units that constituted human society, and, when compared with the state, it was 'yet more fundamental and more sacred'.[96] Its high esteem in the modern world was one of the greatest achievements of Christianity. Respect for family life, according to Gladstone, went hand in hand with the dignity of women. He believed that it was generally admitted, even by freethinking critics of the faith, that the position of women was higher under the Christian dispensation than in ancient Greece.[97] This was one of the very few

---

[88] F. M. Turner, *The Greek Heritage in Victorian Britain* (New Haven, Conn., 1981), pp. 242–3. Turner, however, does not note the appearance of the term in *Studies on Homer*. Cf. Ch. 7, p. 179.

[89] *SHHA*, 2, p. 527 n. Reverence for rank and station is also approved at 3, p. 87.

[90] *JM*, p. 413.                                    [91] GP 44773, f. 195 (15 Aug. 1890), in *D*.

[92] GP 44770, f. 4 (10 Dec. 1885), in *D*.

[93] Lady Dorothy Stanley's Diary, 18 Jan. 1886, Joseph Chamberlain Papers, University of Birmingham Library, JC8/2/2, quoted in Lubenow, *Parliamentary Politics*, p. 330.

[94] Gladstone, *Speeches, 1879*, p. 84.                    [95] *T*, 28 Oct. 1889, p. 8.

[96] W. E. Gladstone, 'The Place of Heresy and Schism in the Modern Christian Church' [1894], *Later Gleanings*, p. 303. *Female Suffrage: A Letter from the Right Honourable W. E. Gladstone, M.P., to Samuel Smith, M.P.* (London, 1892), p. 7.

[97] W. E. Gladstone, 'Place of Ancient Greece in the Providential Order' [1865], *Gleanings*, 7, p. 65.

areas in which Gladstone was willing to challenge the authority of Aristotle. In his unfinished edition of the *Politics*, the statesman noted that in the philosopher's discussion of the household, the woman was allotted a sadly depressed status. 'The mother', complained Gladstone, 'forms no central part of the family but exists relatively to her husband ...'[98] Homer's estimate of the role of women, according to the statesman, was much superior—higher, in fact, than any outside the bounds of Christendom.[99] With the arrival of the Christian faith, however, women actually achieved a status of moral and social equality.[100] From that point on the foundations of healthy family life were well and truly laid.

Gladstone never suggested that the equality of the sexes should extend to the franchise. He was not known as a friend of the suffrage cause, although Martin Pugh has pointed out that by the early 1890s he may have been preparing the ground for concessions to its aims.[101] Even then, however, he publicly voiced fears that voting might do harm to a woman, trespassing on 'the delicacy, the purity, the refinement, the elevation of her own nature', and so dislocate domestic life.[102] The statesman's resistance to female enfranchisement was founded on a theory of the distinction between the sexes that underlay all his discourse. He habitually praised the 'manly' and the 'masculine' and, though he lauded the 'feminine', he regularly deprecated the 'effeminate' and the 'womanish'.[103] Women were markedly different from men. There is no indication that he subsequently altered the view that he took in *Studies on Homer*: 'To the very highest range of intellectual strength known among the children of Adam, woman seems never to have ascended, but in every or almost every case to have fallen short of it. But when we look to the virtues, it seems probable both that her average is higher, and that she also attains in the highest instances to loftier summits.' When intellectual inferiority was weighed against moral superiority, the net result was a fair distribution of qualities between the sexes.[104] So in the mini-community of the family the relationship between man and woman was one of complementarity. Unlike many of his contemporaries, Gladstone does not dwell on the authority of the male head of household. Instead he writes with admiration of the 'reciprocal deference' between husband and wife that he discerned in the Homeric world.[105] Anything that threatened the relationship was anathema. Gladstone castigated John Milton for tolerating polygamy, and so striking at the heart of the Christian value-system.[106] But the greatest threat was divorce, against which Gladstone had raged in 1857. He remained to the end its vehement opponent, seeing it as the harbinger of revolutionary social change.[107] The question of marriage, he assured a correspondent in

---

[98] GP 44750, f. 58 (on *Politics*, I. iii. 1).          [99] *JM*, p. 405.

[100] W. E. Gladstone to Sir Anthony Panizzi, 8 Feb. 1874, Lathbury, 2, p. 99.

[101] Martin Pugh, *The March of the Women: A Revisionist Analysis of the Campaign for Women's Suffrage, 1866–1914* (Oxford, 2000), pp. 134–5.      [102] *Female Suffrage*, p. 7.

[103] For the first, second, and fourth, see *JM*: pp. 459, 511; 134, 460; 511, 513. For the third and fifth, see W. E. Gladstone, 'Journal de Marie Bashkirtseff', *Nineteenth Century*, 26 (1889), p. 605.

[104] *SHHA*, 2, pp. 479–80.                  [105] *JM*, p. 410.

[106] W. E. Gladstone, 'Macaulay' [1876], *Gleanings*, 2, p. 304.

[107] W. E. Gladstone, ' "Divorce"—A Novel', *Nineteenth Century*, 25 (1889), p. 214.

1888, was 'the one cardinal test of Christian civilization'.[108] The stability of society rested on the permanence of the family.

A second form of community that Gladstone always had in view was the church. It remained his assumption, in the 1890s as much as in the 1830s, that 'our Lord founded the Church as a visible and organised society'.[109] A place had to be found for the church in any developed theory of political relations. The most fundamental point was that the state should not interfere in ecclesiastical life, doctrine, or discipline. One of the achievements of Elizabeth I, in Gladstone's High Church perspective on the Tudor age, had been to make provision against 'the system of governing the Church by the direct agency of the State' that had operated under Thomas Cromwell and Edward VI.[110] Although during Gladstone's career the erastian threat to the church had receded, in his Liberal years there was still danger to the religious training of the young. The state, under Gladstone's own premiership, assumed responsibility for elementary education and, he feared, might subsequently be tempted to impose undenominational teaching on schools erected by the Church of England. The remedy was to 'let Christianity keep its own acts to its own agents'.[111] In this area lay one of the sharpest areas of divergence between Gladstone and many of his colleagues in the Liberal party, ever prepared to blur the boundaries between church and state.[112] Gladstone knew that threats also remained abroad: colonial churches (as in southern Africa) might still face state interference with their understanding of the creeds; and colonial authorities (as in Malta) might be inclined to make arrangements with the Vatican over the appointment of Catholic bishops.[113] The Roman Catholic communion, like her Anglican sister, should enjoy the privilege of freedom from domination by the civil power. The ever-present problem in church–state relations was that, since each was composed of the same human beings, a clash between rival authorities was almost inevitable. But Gladstone was clear in his own mind that there was a way of avoiding conflict. It lay in 'the separation of the two jurisdictions'.[114] Notwithstanding his endorsement of the royal supremacy, he had never doubted the fundamental contrast between the spiritual and the secular communities.[115] All would be well if the state recognized the distinct life of the churches as autonomous bodies, resisting the constant temptation to intervene in them.

The danger to the delicate relationship, however, came not only from the state but also from the church—at least, Gladstone supposed, when the ecclesiastical body concerned was under the thumb of the pope. The Vatican had been lured not into the erastian trap but into the opposite snare, the assertion of the theocratic supremacy of the church. Instead of the state controlling the church, the

---

[108] W. E. Gladstone to W. G. F. Phillimore, 27 Nov. 1888, Lathbury, 1, p. 138.

[109] Gladstone, 'Heresy and Schism', p. 280.          [110] Gladstone, 'Queen Elizabeth', p. 192.

[111] Gladstone, 'Heresy and Schism', p. 304.

[112] J. P. Parry, *Democracy and Religion: Gladstone and the Liberal Party, 1867–1875* (Cambridge, 1986), pp. 164–7.          [113] *T*, 20 June 1891, p. 14; 31 July 1890, p. 4.

[114] Gladstone, *Rome*, p. lii.          [115] See Ch. 5, pp. 108–10.

authority of the church was exalted over that of the state. There were, on Gladstone's analysis, four dimensions of the problem. First, the ultramontane claims of the papacy reduced its adherents to abject submission. Freedom and conscience were extinguished in ordinary members of the church. Roman Catholicism was turning into an Asian monarchy: 'nothing but one giddy height of despotism, and one dead level of religious subserviency.'[116] Secondly, the Vatican trespassed on the grounds of the civil power. Its claims to regulate the behaviour of the subjects of Christian states undermined their obligations to their rulers. It was the central contention of Gladstone's *Vatican Decrees* (1874) that the papacy was subverting political order by transgressing its own spiritual province. Thirdly, the Vatican unwarrantably asserted the right to define the boundary between that province and the province of the state. Henry Manning as a cardinal argued that his church possessed the supreme power to declare what was the extent of the authority entrusted to it by its divine founder.[117] Gladstone was scandalized by the claim of his former friend. It was outrageous, he fulminated, for 'the venomous ambition of Curialism' to assert such a supremacy,[118] which in England had properly been exercised by the crown since the sixteenth century. And finally, the Vatican was willing to exert force, not just persuasion, in pursuit of its aims. That was to deploy the methods peculiar to civil government. 'Our Saviour', wrote Gladstone in 1874, 'had recognised as distinct the two provinces of the civil rule and the Church ...' The ultramontane error, in this respect like its erastian converse, was to confuse the two. Gladstone's fundamental premise was that what he called 'civil communities' and 'Christian communities' were different entities.[119]

A third form of self-regulating community that loomed large in Gladstone's perspective was the municipality, the nearest modern equivalent of the ancient *polis*. Whenever he received the freedom of a city he would praise 'the principles of self-government of this country'.[120] Similarly, the achievement of Italy since the Risorgimento was to replace 'the stagnant uniformity of despotism' with 'a vigorous municipal life'.[121] Even tiny Hawarden, when enriched by a village institute, should enjoy a quickened corporate life, 'a sense of unity in this community'.[122] Gladstone, as he told his Dublin audience in 1877, was a foe to centralization. Municipal government in England had been weakened by dealing out public money and transferring power from local to central authorities.[123] The great desideratum—and the germ of his later Home Rule policy—was, as he explained in an article of the following year, to relieve the overworked legislature by 'judicious devolution'.[124] Municipalities were capable of decisive initiative—as when

---

[116] Gladstone, *Rome*, p. 9.
[117] J. P. von Arx, 'Archbishop Manning and the *Kulturkampf*', *Recusant History*, 21 (1992), p. 261.
[118] W. E. Gladstone, 'Italy and her Church' [1875], *Gleanings*, 6, p. 261.
[119] Gladstone, *Rome*, p. lii.                          [120] *T*, 5 Oct. 1891, p. 12.
[121] Gladstone, 'Italy in 1888–89', p. 763.             [122] *T*, 23 May 1893, p. 10.
[123] *Daily News*, 8 Nov. 1877, S & P, XXIII, p. 109.
[124] Gladstone, 'Kin beyond Sea', p. 216.

Newcastle undertook river improvements, Aberdeen halted the cattle plague, and Glasgow provided artisans' dwellings.[125] They could be entrusted with large powers, even extending to the limitation of freedom. On this point Gladstone differed from Lord Hartington, his nominal party leader, during the run-up to the 1880 election, when the option to prohibit alcohol by local referendum was being urged by temperance activists. Hartington could not contemplate local option because it would constitute a majority dictating to a minority and consequently interfere with 'the principles of perfect individual freedom'.[126] Gladstone, however, accepted local option as legitimate in principle, having supported an abortive Liverpool bill to introduce it. It was opinion in the locality that was to be decisive.[127] Likewise he was willing in 1892 to treat the miners' eight-hours issue on the same basis as the temperance question. If 'a community—a mining community—is unanimous', the opposition of the employer should not be allowed to stand in the way of limiting hours down the mine.[128] Freedom of contract must bow before the corporate will. Gladstone took a very elevated view of the opinion of a united community.

He also thought highly of participation in municipal affairs. Through local government, he declared in 1885, 'an immense number of individuals of almost all classes in this country are called upon to step out of merely selfish considerations, and to embrace the noble idea of doing something for their fellow-creatures'.[129] Municipal service was good for the soul, inculcating a corporate spirit and acting as a school for higher things. The 1835 Municipal Corporations Act, by introducing popular representation, had created a training ground for legislators.[130] Experience in Europe, Gladstone argued in 1890, proved that giving human beings power over their own destinies brought benefits to them and their countries. It had been so in Bulgaria and, he trusted, would be so in Ireland.[131] The same principle applied equally on a smaller scale. Co-operation in industry gave working men a form of practice in self-government that benefited their class.[132] Local collectivities, Gladstone argued, were admirable: joining friendly societies, for example, did not separate the members from their local community but bound them into it.[133] Any institution that promoted civic involvement was desirable. That was why Gladstone set himself to extend local government, his last bill as Prime Minister being for the creation of councils in the parishes.[134] Participation in the public life of the locality was a good in its own right.

The broader collectivity of the nation, the fourth type of community envisaged by Gladstone, properly commanded an even stronger loyalty. The spirit of nationality or patriotism (in his usage the two were interchangeable) was among the greatest of virtues. Homer and the Church of England, two of Gladstone's

---

[125] *T*, 5 Oct. 1891, p. 12; 27 Sept. 1871, p. 69. Gladstone, *Speeches, 1879*, p. 224.

[126] Marquis of Hartington, *Election Speeches in 1879 and 1880* (London, 1880), p. 126 (24 Mar. 1880).

[127] Gladstone, *Speeches, 1879*, pp. 75–6.                    [128] *T*, 8 July 1892, p. 5.

[129] Gladstone, *Speeches, 1885*, p. 111.                    [130] *T*, 5 Oct. 1891, p. 12.

[131] W. E. Gladstone, *Speeches delivered in Scotland in 1890* (Edinburgh, [1890]), p. 70 (27 Oct. 1890).

[132] *T*, 24 Oct. 1890, p. 4.            [133] *T*, 5 Feb. 1877, p. 10.            [134] Matthew, p. 607.

strongest affections, gained fresh lustre in his eyes because they had fostered nationality.[135] In the modern world nationalism, according to Gladstone, was normally a force for good. It had conquered the bigotry of the Irish Protestant ascendancy in the eighteenth century; and it had stimulated industrious activity wherever it had come into play.[136] Gladstone admitted that nationalism had its dangers, as when it encouraged the Irish rebellion of 1798[137] or the jingoism that he resisted in the late 1870s. Patriotism was close to selfishness and 'national pride' could blind eyes to the dictates of justice.[138] But in general the sense of solidarity with one's compatriots was an ennobling quality. Gladstone's speeches are studded with encomia to the nation, though there is some ambiguity about which nation he intends. Like nearly all his contemporaries, he usually used 'England' when referring to his country as a whole, though on one occasion during the 1880 election campaign he pulled himself up, remembering he was in Scotland. 'I said England', he confessed, '—do not be shocked; it is the shortest word,—Great Britain or United Kingdom is what I ought to say.' But a few minutes later he had reverted to 'England'.[139] Nevertheless he professed a strong feeling for Scotland on account of his parentage and for Wales on account of his residence.[140] There was a definite shift over time in his conceptualization of the nationhood of the British Isles. Down to the 1870s he would speak of 'the British nation' and in Dublin in 1877 declared that 'these three kingdoms should be one nation in the races of the world'.[141] From the mid-1880s, having pondered the claims of Irish nationality more deeply, he preferred to talk of Scottish and Welsh nationality, of three or four nations in the British Isles.[142] He now explicitly acknowledged that people had a twin allegiance, as British subjects and as those born in England, Scotland, Wales, or Ireland. He was increasingly allowing for the internal diversity of the islands, distinguishing nation from state, though always holding that patriotism was due at least as much to the United Kingdom as to its component parts. As he insisted against his opponents, he too was a Unionist.

What, then, was a nation? Gladstone several times listed the contributory elements—most exhaustively in 1888 as 'race, religion, language, history, sympathy or antipathy in character, geographical proximity, internal conformation of the country, material wants and interests, relief from internal difficulties, relations to the outer world', and supremely the 'sentiment of nationality'.[143] He sometimes, as in 1878, pinned on the first four in this list as the most formative factors.[144] In Wales he would dwell on history—the castles, the saints, the

---

[135] See Chs. 7 and 8, pp. 198, 206 and 227–8.
[136] W. E. Gladstone, 'Lessons of Irish History in the Eighteenth Century' [1887], *Special Aspects*, p. 29. Hutton and Cohen (ed.), *Speeches, 1888–1891*, p. 58.  [137] *T*, 4 July 1892, p. 4.
[138] Gladstone, 'Lessons of Irish History', p. 11; id., *Speeches, 1879*, p. 94.
[139] Gladstone, *Speeches, 1880*, pp. 31, 37.
[140] Gladstone, *Speeches, 1879*, p. 89. Hutton and Cohen (eds.), *Speeches, 1886–1888*, p. 228.
[141] *T*, 31 July 1871, p. 6. *Daily News*, 8 Nov. 1877, S & P, XXIII, p. 110.
[142] Hutton and Cohen (eds.), *Speeches 1886–1888*, p. 228. Gladstone, *Speeches, 1885*, p. 167. *T*, 8 Nov. 1888, p. 10.
[143] W. E. Gladstone, 'Further Notes and Queries on the Irish Demand' [1888], *Special Aspects*, p. 197.
[144] W. E. Gladstone, 'Liberty in the East and West', *Nineteenth Century*, 3 (1878), p. 1163.

Tudors—and language. He celebrated the Welsh tongue, that 'venerable relic of the past', at eisteddfods in 1873 and 1888.[145] He also protested against an apparent initiative by the authorities on Malta to replace the Italian language with English.[146] But he linked nationality to religion much more frequently than to language. Sometimes faith and nation were treated as parallel mainsprings of corporate behaviour. 'What', he asked, 'are the two most powerful motives that act upon nations? The one of them is religion, the other is patriotism.'[147] More often, however, he blended the two together to form the amalgam of 'religious nationality'.[148] There were precedents in antiquity, where Homer had welded a 'national unity in religion',[149] but since the Reformation the Church of England was the pioneer of the successful integration of the two. The 'spirit of nationalism' arose powerfully under Henry VIII, was eclipsed by partisan polemics under his two successors, but then triumphed under Elizabeth, 'its 'restorer' and 'champion'.[150] Gladstone applauded, as he had in the 1840s, any sign of a disposition within the Roman Catholic communion to assert separate national identities and so move closer to the Anglican model.[151] Yet nationhood was not, in Gladstone's estimate, a phenomenon unique to Christendom. The Muslims of Afghanistan had also forged a nation.[152] Religion, of whatever kind, was a powerful agent of nation-building.

The foundations of nationhood, however, were usually laid in race. Gladstone supposed from his Greek researches that belief was normally an expression of ethnic identity. 'Religion and race', he wrote in *Juventus Mundi*, 'have ever run much together.' But the two were independent, since religion had created the unity of the Greeks out of their original 'intermixture and fusion of bloods'.[153] Race was itself a major determinant of national characteristics. Agrarian crime in Ireland, he once suggested to the House of Commons, could not be attributed to the Celtic identity of the people. Since crime was higher in Ulster than Connaught (the year was 1870), resistance to oppression was evidently the result of 'the infusion both of English and Scottish blood' pouring in 'a spirit of pride and of ready self-defence' absent from the original Irish.[154] Although the argument was shaped by the occasion, its form was also moulded by underlying racial stereotypes. Gladstone often celebrated 'the British race', 'the great Anglo-Saxon race', and the blood relationship with the Americans, 'our own kith and kin'.[155] This race was spirited, courageous, and energetic, giving an essential character to the nations it generated. Furthermore Gladstone had learned by experience in the Ionian Isles, whose retention by Britain he had recommended but which had successfully

---

[145] *T*, 20 Aug. 1873, p. 5. Hutton and Cohen (eds.), *Speeches, 1886–1888*, pp. 226–7.
[146] *T*, 31 July 1890, p. 4.                     [147] Gladstone, *Speeches, 1880*, p. 291. Cf. *IRHS*, p. 218.
[148] See Ch. 3, pp. 60–1.      [149] *Landmarks*, p. 56.      [150] Gladstone, 'Queen Elizabeth', p. 187.
[151] Gladstone, 'Italy and her Church', pp. 230–42. Cf. Chs. 3 and 5, pp. 74 and 126.
[152] Gladstone, *Speeches, 1880*, p. 25.                          [153] *JM*, pp. 179, 210.
[154] *A Correct Report of the Speech of the Right Honourable W. E. Gladstone, on proposing the Irish Land Bill, February 15 1870* (London, 1870), p. 8.
[155] Gladstone, *Speeches, 1880*, pp. 69, 321. *T*, 29 Mar. 1889, p. 101 (Anglo-Saxon race).

demanded union with Greece, that 'it is natural, legitimate, and right for people of a given race to be associated with their brethren of that race'. He identified these aspirations as 'national affinities', 'a good and an honourable part of our nature'.[156] Conversely it was unnatural for one nation to rule over another that was distinct in blood (this factor came first), language, history, and religion. Therefore, although he was prepared to talk of the British in India as a 'superior race', he had no enthusiasm for British authority in the Subcontinent, which he called exceptional and perhaps provisional.[157] Race was not the sole, or even an absolutely essential, component of national loyalties, but, together with an ambition to be free from oppression, it was, he held, the normal basis for the 'collective or corporate identity' that qualified a group to be a nation.[158] Gladstone was fully aware of the complexity of the phenomenon of national allegiance in the modern world.

He had no doubt, however, of its extremely high place in the scheme of things. In an article on the Irish Question of 1888, Gladstone described the 'sentiment of nationality' as almost assuming 'in and for the nation, the office which conscience discharges for the individual, as the tribunal of ultimate appeal'.[159] Acton, to whom he sent the article in draft, objected to the passage. Nationality, Acton argued, was a vehicle for the customary forces that quench individuality, whereas conscience allowed people to rise above them. Furthermore, nationality could be dangerous where, as in the Slav territories, its boundaries did not coincide with those of the state. If the end of politics was liberty, he concluded, it was perilous to erect anything else in its place as a court of final appeal.[160] Gladstone inserted some extra qualifications in the text of the article, but did not shift his ground. He reaffirmed that in his view nationality was 'one of those permanent and ultimate principles which in the last resort become inappellable'.[161] In response Acton explained that he feared the implication of Gladstone's position. There could not be two courts of final appeal; and Gladstone would be driven to admit 'the priority of national Independence before individual liberty—the figurative conscience before the real'.[162] Acton, the prophet of liberty, recognized a significant difference between his own deepest convictions and those of his correspondent. For Acton, the advancement of the freedom of the individual was the supreme value, the aim of liberalism and the very purpose of God in history. For Gladstone, despite his attachment to individual freedom, the destiny of the nation was of equivalent importance. By associating the sense of nationality with conscience, Butler's governing faculty, he was claiming a place for it alongside liberty. He was willing to disagree with Acton by asserting the right of a people to be guided by its corporate sentiment even at some risk to personal freedom. The sense of

---

[156] Gladstone, *Speeches, 1880*, p. 288.
[157] W. E. Gladstone, 'Liberty in the East and West', p. 1163. Gladstone, *Speeches, 1879*, p. 200 (superior race).          [158] Gladstone, 'Further Notes and Queries', pp. 197–8.
[159] Ibid., p. 197.          [160] Lord Acton to W. E. Gladstone, 18 Feb. 1888, GP 44094, ff. 6–6v.
[161] W. E. Gladstone to Lord Acton, 24 Feb. 1888, GP 44094, f. 9v.
[162] Lord Acton to W. E. Gladstone, [26 Feb. 1888], GP 44094, f. 13.

278 The Nature of Gladstonian Liberalism

nationality, Gladstone wrote in the article, might almost be described as 'immortal':[163] it virtually shared in the attributes of God. The community of the nation should exercise ultimate claims over the individual.

Yet nations themselves were part of a wider aggregation of peoples, a fifth expression of the principle of community. Acton's mentor Ignaz von Döllinger, as a Roman Catholic theologian, was able to posit that the various nationalities were bound together by the church of Christ.[164] Gladstone rejected any such ecclesiastical internationalism, but he did believe in a supranational bonding between different peoples. His third Midlothian principle of foreign policy was the maintenance of the concert of Europe. If the European powers operated together, he argued, the effect was to 'neutralize and fetter and bind up the selfish aims of each' because 'common action is fatal to selfish aims'. Their ambition must be to achieve 'the common good of them all'.[165] The members of Beaconsfield's government had been casting themselves as champions of British interests, but national concerns could be pursued in excess to the detriment of the wider welfare.[166] What was needed was a 'United Europe', prepared to act against any recalcitrant member of the international community that threw over the traces.[167] Action could ultimately mean coercion, but normally remonstrance would suffice. 'I have a great faith', wrote Gladstone in relation to the Bulgarian horrors, 'in the power of opinion, of the opinion of civilised and Christian Europe.'[168] His international ideal, in fact, was highly pacific, drawing considerable inspiration from Richard Cobden's hopes for a world in which a network of commercial exchange would render war so contrary to the interests of the various states that it would wither away.[169] The teachings of their science, Gladstone told the Political Economy Club in 1876, repressed the human passions that were the great cause of war.[170] The preservation of peace was itself one of the Midlothian principles. It could be achieved by avoiding 'needless and entangling engagements' (another principle) that threatened collision with other powers. All was predicated on the vision set by Gladstone before the electorate in 1879 that 'Christendom is formed of a band of nations who are united to each other in the bond of right'.[171] The countries of Europe themselves constituted a community.

Nor was this comity of nations confined to the great powers. The European nations, Gladstone went on in 1879, are 'without distinction of great and small; there is an absolute equality between them,—the same sacredness defends the

---

[163] Gladstone, 'Further Notes and Queries', p. 198.
[164] Ignaz von Döllinger, The Church and the Churches, trans. W. B. MacCabe (London, 1862), p. 33.
[165] Gladstone, Speeches, 1879, pp. 115–16. Cf. Carl Holbraad, The Concert of Europe: A Study in German and British International Theory, 1815–1914 (London, 1970), pp. 144–7, 165–9.
[166] W. E. Gladstone, 'The Friends and Foes of Russia', Nineteenth Century, 5 (1879), p. 192.
[167] W. E. Gladstone, Bulgarian Horrors and the Question of the East (London, 1876), p. 60.
[168] W. E. Gladstone, Lessons in Massacre (London, 1877), p. 5.
[169] Howe, 'Gladstone and Cobden', pp. 117–21.
[170] Revised Report of the Proceedings on the 31st May, 1876, held in Celebration of the Hundredth Year of the Publication of the 'Wealth of Nations' (London, 1876), pp. 42–3.
[171] Gladstone, Speeches, 1879, pp. 115–16, 129.

narrow limits of Belgium, as attaches to the extended frontiers of Russia, or Germany, or France'. The equal rights of all nations constituted Gladstone's fifth Midlothian principle, and the one he claimed as the greatest. Only if each country were regarded as possessing the same privileges as any other could the triumph of might over right be averted. Beaconsfield had spoken of the ideal of 'Imperium et Libertas'; but Rome, the origin of the watchword, had denied the equal rights of other nations, trampling their independence underfoot.[172] The implication was that Britain had to be vigilant on behalf of the rights of other nations. Although British policy should be designed to avoid joining in any continental quarrel, Gladstone said in a speech of 1887, he was not urging a policy of indifference to others. Britain should sympathize with the advance of liberty abroad (a further Midlothian principle) and should pay special regard to the interests of smaller powers that might need defending.[173] The country was marked out, he wrote in 1880, 'by tradition, by honour, and by feeling, as the one independent champion of the smaller free States of Europe'.[174] The rights of small nations formed an insistent Gladstonian theme during the 1880 general election. Britain, he declared, had successfully defended the integrity of Belgium during the Franco-Prussian War. If the British people had taken up arms, it would have been for freedom, for public right, and to save human happiness from a tyrannous and lawless power. It remained the country's duty 'to have a tender and kindly feeling for the small States of Europe, because it is in the smaller States of Europe that liberty had most flourished'.[175] At the same time Gladstone was standing for the rights of emergent peoples struggling to be free, most notably the Bulgarians. Rising nationalities also deserved a place in the circle of countries that were treated equally. The nation may have been the primary group above the family to which an individual owed allegiance, but every nation in turn had rights and responsibilities within a wider international community.

Just as the interests of the various nations of Europe diverged within the continental arena, so the interests of the various sections of the public diverged within the domestic arena. The community, whether international or national, was internally differentiated. It had not always been so. In the world of Homer, Gladstone noted, the people under one government were bound together by religious reverence and reciprocal duty. 'The separation and conflict of interests', he went on, 'between the different parts of the community had not become a familiar idea . . .'[176] But separation and conflict formed the staple of political experience in the modern era. In Ireland, for example, as Gladstone contended during the 1868 election campaign, the church establishment had separated 'man from man, class from class, kingdom from kingdom . . . exhibiting us to the world as a divided country'.[177] Classes in particular possessed permanently divergent interests. By 'class' Gladstone meant roughly the same as Marx, even if he allowed for

[172] Ibid., pp. 116, 123, 127, 129.  
[173] *T*, 28 Dec. 1887, p. 4.  
[174] Gladstone, 'Russia and England', p. 550.  
[175] Gladstone, *Speeches, 1880*, pp. 32, 352.  
[176] *JM*, p. 415.  
[177] *Daily News*, 16 Nov. 1868, S & P, XVIII, p. 223.

greater internal variety: the landed upper classes, the mercantile bourgeoisie (though he usually differentiated the professions), and the labour proletariat. He recognized that self-interest induced them to call for different policies and as Chancellor of the Exchequer he had shaped his fiscal policies accordingly. Unlike Marx, however, he believed that the different classes could be accommodated by wise statesmanship. The Liberal bill of fare at the 1885 general election, he declared in Midlothian, did not appeal to 'the cupidity of any class' but was fair to 'every class of the community'. That was possible because the programme aimed at 'the general benefit of the whole mass of the people'.[178] There was a community interest transcending the particular interest of any individual, section, or class. Perhaps the greatest peril arose when the contending groups were not just in rivalry with each other but also in antagonism to the welfare of the whole. It was worse than any class struggle when 'the interests of persons or classes . . . compete with those of the public'.[179] In those circumstances it was the task of the statesman to stand for the whole against the part, for the general against the sectional interest. It was a vision of the political process that gave pride of place to communal welfare.

Gladstone's analysis of political strife was therefore cast in terms of threats to the public good from sectional interests. The disruption of community equilibrium could potentially come, as many feared, from revolutionary action by the working classes. From his celebrated speech of 1864 arguing for artisans to come within the pale of the constitution onwards, however, Gladstone displayed confidence in the attachment of the labouring people to constitutional ways. They were more likely, he believed, to disturb the body politic by their economic claims, looking for an undesirable regulation of trade. Yet Gladstone maintained that they were less culpable than other groups. Their mistaken pursuit of restrictions damaged chiefly themselves, not society at large, 'whereas the sins of other classes are almost entirely in the interests of their class against the rest of the entire community'.[180] More serious sectionalism, he pointed out in 1891, arose from the advocates of protection—whether farmers or paper-makers in the past or the shale oil industry in the present. Protectionists preferred 'their own particular interest' to 'the public good'.[181] Even aristocrats and squires, for all Gladstone's esteem for landed property, could form a sectional group: 'we decline to recognise any class whatever', he declared in 1880, 'be they peers or be they gentry . . . as entitled to direct the destinies of this nation against the will of the nation'. It was the great crime of the Conservatives in office between 1874 and 1880 to put themselves at the disposal of the various sections. They made themselves the tools of licensed victuallers, clergymen, church establishments, and farmers; they constituted 'a landlords' Government'.[182] They had discarded Peel's policy of introducing 'great measures of legislation addressed to the national benefit' and replaced it with 'a careful regard to interest and class, from Bishops down to

[178] Gladstone, *Speeches, 1885*, p. 124.          [179] Gladstone, 'Kin beyond Sea', pp. 217–18.
[180] *Proceedings on 31st May, 1876*, p. 47.                      [181] *T*, 5 Oct. 1891, p. 12.
[182] Gladstone, *Speeches, 1880*, pp. 106, 114, 268.

beershops'.[183] For all its bombast about pursuing national interests abroad, in its domestic policies the Beaconsfield administration was ignoring the welfare of the nation as a whole.

Gladstone identified several sectional groups as particularly liable to resist measures designed—chiefly by himself or his administrations—for the general good. 'The present Government', he declared in 1871, 'had not hesitated when it thought the public interest required it to make proposals which had been highly offensive to powerful classes in this country.' On this occasion he was referring particularly to the well-connected circles who stood to lose by the recent abolition of army purchase. The London, but not the provincial, press had taken up the cry against the government, reflecting 'the opinions of the Clubs, rather than the opinion of this great nation'.[184] In other lands there were even stronger cliques of the privileged who obstructed the broader welfare. In contemporary Russia, for instance, the oligarchic, diplomatic, and military classes imposed an aggressive policy on emperor and people alike.[185] There were similar tendencies, Gladstone averred, at home, where he always saw the naval and military pressure for greater armaments expenditure as one of the most sinister forces in public life. But it was in Ireland that sectionalism had done its worst. The ascendancy party, at the union and ever since, had preferred its own interests to those of the nation. Before the 1885 general election the Irish constituency was so small that what was heard at Westminster was not 'the voice of the nation' but 'the voice . . . of a class'.[186] With the proposal of Home Rule in 1886, the self-interested groups consolidated their resistance—dukes, squires, established clergy, military officers, any highly privileged or publicly endowed profession. Barristers and doctors, more open professions, were exceptions.[187] Arrayed against what Gladstone conceived as a measure supremely in the interest of the whole United Kingdom were 'station, title, wealth, social influence . . . in a word, the spirit and power of Class'. There was, however, the heartening reminder that on other great issues the classes had been beaten by 'the upright sense of the nation'.[188] In the enduring struggle of class against nation, it was the whole and not the part that would prevail once more.

Gladstone's explanation of the reason for sectional assertiveness was highly moral, even moralistic. It was legitimate, he conceded in a speech of 1877, for us to pursue our own interests, but a man should 'test his interests by his duties' rather than 'test his duties by his interests'. 'I hope the day will never come', he declared, 'when the idea of duty will not take precedence over every other idea.'[189] The culture of altruism, 'an obsessive antipathy to selfishness', Stefan Collini has pointed out, was deep-seated among the mid-Victorians. Gladstone, whose career, according to Collini, was parasitic on the growth of this mood, participated fully

---

[183] W. E. Gladstone, *England's Mission* (London, 1878), p. 4.
[184] *T*, 4 Sept. 1871, p. 12.     [185] Gladstone, 'Friends and Foes of Russia', p. 171.
[186] Gladstone, *Speeches, 1885*, p. 35.     [187] Gladstone, *Speeches, 1886*, p. 292.
[188] Ibid., pp. 176, 177.     [189] *T*, 14 July 1877, p. 13.

in its flowering.[190] He found the frank Georgian avowal of the importance of human self-love in Bishop Butler's writings embarrassing: it may seem, he commented in *Studies Subsidiary*, 'to grate a little upon the ear'. He wished the bishop had taken greater pains to mark off legitimate self-love from selfishness, 'which, of course, he nowhere commends'.[191] Selfishness, however, was the attitude that underlay sectional behaviour, whether by great powers in international affairs or by particular groups in domestic politics. Nations, Gladstone wrote, were commonly lured by 'self-love and pride'; but Britain was to play a part 'far lifted above all selfish aims and objects'.[192] Likewise in home affairs the people must get rid of 'all selfish and narrow ends'. The narrow was virtually synonymous with the selfish because it represented a contracted vision, not conforming to the 'general sense of the community'.[193] The high moral tone of Gladstone's rhetoric was valuable because it motivated audiences (on this occasion Nonconformist ministers), but it also faithfully mirrored the mind of the orator. The mortification of selfishness was at the core of sanctification as he conceived it.[194] It is consequently not surprising that the exhortation to selflessness was cast in gospel phraseology: 'let us recollect that golden law of doing to others, in political no less than in private life, as we would be done by.'[195] The dictum was at once part of his theology and part of his analysis of public affairs.

The selfishness endemic in human society was reinforced in his own day, Gladstone believed, because of the material circumstances of the times. 'You are threatened, gentlemen', he gold a City livery company in 1876, 'in the foundations of national character by the rapid creation and extension of wealth in this country.' The danger was not to the bulk of the population but to the prosperous classes who had gained disproportionately from the economic advances of the century. There was a resulting change of habits among them, a greater willingness to pursue enjoyment at the expense of 'the inward health, the manhood, the vigour' of the country.[196] Gladstone returned to the same social diagnosis in his address to the University of Glasgow as Lord Rector during the Midlothian campaign. The 'incitements to gain, the avenues of excitement, the solicitations to pleasure' had been multiplied for the governing classes, some of whom were giving themselves to disreputable speculative ventures.[197] Wealth, Gladstone had assumed in *Studies on Homer*, tends to corrupt simplicity of manners.[198] During the nineteenth century it had generated, the statesman complained in 1880, an 'age of sham', symbolized by the arrival of a butter substitute called 'Oleo-Margarine'.[199] It was responsible, he supposed for the scale of the revolt in the educated elite against Home Rule. John Tyndall, T. H. Huxley's scientific

---

[190] Stefan Collini, *Public Moralists: Political Thought and Intellectual Life in Britain* (Oxford, 1991), ch. 2, quoted at p. 65.   [191] *Studies Subsidiary*, p. 102.

[192] Gladstone, *England's Mission*, p. 7; id., *Speeches, 1880*, p. 222.

[193] *T*, 4 Sept. 1871, p. 12; 10 May 1888, p. 7.   [194] See Ch. 3, pp. 47–8.

[195] *T*, 4 Sept. 1871, p. 12.   [196] *T*, 17 Feb. 1876, p. 10.

[197] Gladstone, *Speeches, 1879*, pp. 239–40.   [198] *SHHA*, 3, p. 80.

[199] Gladstone, *Speeches, 1880*, p. 352.

colleague in arms and a fellow-Unionist, had remarked that there was a 'consensus of intellect' arrayed against Gladstone on the Irish Question. It was less intellectual causes, Gladstone mused on paper, than moral causes that were operative. Recent advances meant that 'the myriad forms of human self regard ... impart a hopeless bias to character in the wrong direction'. Tyndall and his like were the victims of 'darkening moral influences'.[200] As we saw in the last chapter, Gladstone had assigned an identical explanation to the rise of agnosticism in precisely the same circles. Affluence, leisure, and 'worldly attachment', in Gladstone's view, had generated the twin evils of unbelief and Unionism.[201] A profound decay was at work, undermining reverence for the Almighty and the sound political altruism that would bring justice to Ireland.

Gladstone, however, gave at least as much attention to cure as to diagnosis. The remedy lay in achieving an equilibrium between the competing sectional interests in the state. 'It is upon a just balance of forces', Gladstone remarked in *Juventus Mundi*, 'that good government now mainly depends.'[202] The aim was 'to bind together the whole of the country in harmony and concord'.[203] The integrity of the community was restored by neutralizing the ambitions of self-interested sub-groups. Appeal to a theory of balance was, of course, widespread among Gladstone's contemporaries. Lord Salisbury, for example, wanted to implement a multitude of balancing acts—between class and class, town and country, majority and minority, and so on.[204] The primary intellectual lineage of most such analyses derived from the eighteenth-century ideal of a balanced constitution, carefully poised between crown, Lords, and Commons. Gladstone, however, found such old theories of a combination of three elements inadequate. They were abstract notions, he wrote in 1876, deriving from the age of Cicero and not doing justice to the British system in operation. Crucially, they omitted the need for 'a reconciling power, what may be called a clearing house of politics'.[205] In one sense Members of Parliament adjusted the competing interests of different classes; and representative local government, in its own sphere, performed a similar function.[206] But in his chief effort to analyse the British constitution, 'Kin beyond Sea', a comparison with American institutions, Gladstone argued from experience that the cabinet was the main setting for the resolution of forces. The cabinet, 'the three-fold hinge' between crown, Lords, and Commons, also provided a mechanism for adjusting all the other claims on government. 'Like a stout buffer-spring', he wrote, 'it receives all shocks ...'[207] The cabinet was the arbiter that turned the chaos of rival sectional interests into a harmonious whole.

---

[200] GP 44773, ff. 46–7 (undated but assigned to June 1887).
[201] *IRHS*, pp. 285–91, quoted at p. 291. Cf. Ch. 8, p. 220–1.   [202] *JM*, p. 415.
[203] *Speeches of the Right Honourable William Ewart Gladstone, M.A., in South-West Lancashire, October, 1868* (Liverpool, n.d.), p. 27.
[204] Michael Pinto-Duschinsky, *The Political Thought of Lord Salisbury, 1854–1868* (London, 1967), ch. 5.
[205] Gladstone, 'Kin beyond Sea', p. 238.   [206] Gladstone, *Speeches, 1880*, pp. 202, 253.
[207] Gladstone, 'Kin beyond Sea', pp. 224, 239.

The grand aim in politics, then, was the reconciliation of divergent interests. Colin Matthew has shown how Gladstone worked for this goal in his fiscal policy. Budgets were designed to alter the burdens on the different classes so as to achieve an equitable settlement that would command consensus support.[208] Dealing with the income tax, as Gladstone put it in his great budget speech of 1853, meant adjusting 'the relations of classes brought into the nicest competition one with another'.[209] Thus when, in the late 1870s, the Conservative government reduced the local rates on landlords, it was fair, according to Gladstone, that the same class should bear 'some moderate equivalent burden'.[210] Direct taxation, falling disproportionately on the wealthy, needed to be balanced by indirect taxation, falling disproportionately on the working classes. The contributions of capital and labour should be kept in something like equilibrium.[211] Anything that promoted class conciliation was to be encouraged. In 1868 he applauded a co-operative mill at Oldham because it turned working men into capitalists as well as labourers, supplying a link between the two classes.[212] Co-operation, he declared over twenty years later, 'tends . . . to the harmony of the classes and the union and the solidity of the whole community'.[213] Likewise he commended profit-sharing as a beneficial means of creating common interests.[214] In the countryside as well as the towns the same objectives were to be pursued. Despite tensions between landlords and tenant farmers arising from the agricultural depression, Gladstone declared that he wanted to see 'the relations of those classes to one another harmonious and sound, their interests never brought into conflict'.[215] The result would be 'one rural community, joined together and assisting one another in the discharge of every good office'.[216] Classes tended to pull society apart, but Gladstone aspired to consolidate its cohesion. Accordingly his hope was ever to check the centrifugal tendencies of classes by means of the bonding power of community.

The criterion by which conflicting interests were to be harmonized was the principle of justice. This quality, Gladstone remarked in *Juventus Mundi*, is 'to political society as its vital spark'.[217] Although it was a heathen rather than a Christian virtue, he commented in a book review of 1889, 'it forms part of the bed of nature, on which Christianity itself is built'.[218] He sometimes took a less exalted view of the principle, as when, in 1880, he identified it with the market mechanisms that would settle relations between landlord and tenant.[219] But frequently his eulogies were unmeasured. Justice was 'the rarest of all virtues, the most precious'; 'the sanctuary of pure justice . . . is a Holy of Holies'; there existed

---

[208] H. C. G. Matthew, 'Disraeli, Gladstone, and the Politics of Mid-Victorian Budgets', *Historical Journal*, 22 (1979), p. 616.

[209] G. M. Young and W. D. Handcock (eds.), *English Historical Documents, 1833–1874* (London, 1956), p. 480.          [210] Gladstone, *Speeches, 1880*, p. 152.

[211] Gladstone, *Speeches, 1885*, pp. 108, 117.          [212] *T*, 19 Dec. 1867, p. 8.

[213] *T*, 5 July 1892, p. 12.          [214] Gladstone, *Speeches, 1868*, p. 39.

[215] Gladstone, *Speeches, 1879*, p. 106.          [216] Gladstone, *Speeches, 1880*, p. 89.

[217] *JM*, p. 391.

[218] W. E. Gladstone, ' "For the Right" ', *Nineteenth Century*, 25 (1889), p. 617.

[219] Gladstone, *Speeches, 1880*, p. 79.

'sacred principles of justice'.[220] All this was not merely a riot of rhetorical flourishes. Gladstone held a very specific view of the role of justice. Its fundamental function, as Aristotle had taught, was to assign to every class of the community what was its due. Justice had to be done, no matter what protests might be mounted by the aggrieved. Resentments were in the final account outbalanced by greater advantages, as Gladstone assured Dublin Corporation in 1877: 'by the establishment of political justice, even when it may seem to press hard upon a part, such is its value in knitting together the hearts and minds of men, that you confer, even in the most extreme cases, a far greater benefit on the particular class that thinks itself injured than you can possibly be aware of.'[221] What was just pointed the way, in the longer perspective, to social harmony. Accordingly Gladstone made the appeal to justice central to the Liberal philosophy he expounded at the hustings. 'Be just and fear not' was his slogan at the 1868 general election and, with Irish disestablishment in view, his speeches were peppered during the campaign with calls to do justice.[222] The election has rightly gone down to posterity as one in which Gladstone demanded justice for Ireland. On occasion he would also rage against what seemed palpable instances of injustice,[223] but the idea of distributive justice usually predominated in his mind. The essential Gladstonian notion was of 'perfect justice to every class of the community'.[224]

Law, as Gladstone conceived it, was to be an embodiment of justice. English and Scottish law, by and large, had already achieved this standard of impartiality, but Irish law had not. It was his ambition, wrote Gladstone in 1868, to create an attachment to law in Ireland by making it 'the friend of every class, but especially of those classes which have the greatest need of its protection'.[225] It was one of his most serious charges against Balfour's administration of Ireland in the later 1880s that the authorities were giving countenance to lawlessness perpetrated by their agents. The government was making odious the principles of law and order, 'which are sacred principles, and which involve the vitality of every well-ordered community'.[226] It was relying on coercion rather than 'legality', the spirit of voluntary submission to the law.[227] The replacement of conciliation by force was equally abhorrent to Gladstone in the international field. There, as he saw it, the law of nations was gradually growing up from the germ of the idea of political justice.[228] He punctuated his speeches on overseas questions with appeals to 'public law', by which he meant documents such as the Treaty of Paris concluding the Crimean War that formalized relations between the powers.[229] Increasingly, abstract notions were being crystallized in written form. The Treaty of Washington concluded in 1871 by Gladstone's administration to settle the

---

[220] *Daily News*, 8 Nov. 1877, S & P, XXIII, p. 110. Gladstone, ' "For the Right" ', p. 617. *Daily News*, 22 Dec. 1868, S & P, XVIII, p. 235.    [221] *Daily News*, 8 Nov. 1877, S & P, XXIII, p. 110.
[222] Gladstone, *Speeches, 1868*, pp. 15, 27, 37, 61, 64.
[223] e.g. Gladstone, 'Liberty in the East and West', p. 1165.
[224] Gladstone, *Speeches, 1885*, p. 124.    [225] Gladstone, *Speeches, 1868*, p. iv.
[226] *T*, 8 Nov. 1888, p. 10.    [227] *T*, 10 May 1888, p. 7.    [228] *SHHA*, 3, p. 4.
[229] Gladstone, *Speeches, 1879*, pp. 128, 193.

*Alabama* claims of the United States was, he urged later in the year, an instance of a way of ending quarrels 'better than the brutal arbitrament of the sword'.[230] The establishment of public right was a symptom of the advance of Christian civilization superseding the reign of violence.[231] Gladstone avowed the belief that 'true civilisation largely consists in, and may be absolutely tested and measured by, the substitution of moral for physical forces'.[232] No power in the international arena, no section of the domestic community, should impose its will on others by deploying superior strength. It was law that best brought down the mighty from their seats.

Nevertheless government sometimes had to resort to force in order to ensure the triumph of justice. The Manchester school, Gladstone told the electors of Midlothian in 1880, was guilty of a noble error in supposing that war could be banished from human relations. No government could avoid finding that 'that dream of a Paradise upon earth was rudely dispelled by the shock of experience'. Wars might be deplorable, but 'there are times when justice, when faith, when the welfare of mankind, require a man not to shrink from the responsibility of undertaking them'.[233] The use of force always had to be justified by presenting reasons to the public, but it was part of the essential role of government (as Romans 13 taught) to bear the sword.[234] As Deryck Schreuder has shown, Gladstone could be a zealous interventionist, far more willing to risk war than his cabinet colleagues.[235] Equally in domestic affairs intervention could be called for in the interest of protecting the weak. In general Gladstone upheld freedom of contract, as he reaffirmed in 1880; it should be real freedom, however, based on the equality of the parties concerned. 'But where the parties do not meet on a footing of equality,' he went on, 'there the question of interference with the freedom of contract is one of pure policy and expediency.'[236] He was fettered by no fundamental theoretical objections against state intervention for the benefit of the disadvantaged. He presided, after all, over an administration in 1868–74 that legislated extensively for social improvement.[237] The Irish Land Act of 1870 even provided, by the so-called Bright clauses, for public loans so that tenants could acquire their holdings from their landlords. Gladstone may have been reluctant to impose an additional burden on the taxpayer, but he supported the measure, even drafting the detail of the clauses himself.[238] The legislature was perfectly entitled to buy out landed proprietors, Gladstone declared in 1880, 'if it is known to be for the welfare of the community at large'.[239] Encapsulated there was a main thread

---

[230] *T*, 31 July 1871, p. 6.     [231] Gladstone, *Speeches, 1879*, p. 123.

[232] Gladstone, 'Italy in 1888–89', p. 770.     [233] Gladstone, *Speeches, 1880*, pp. 30–1.

[234] Gladstone, 'Kin beyond Sea', p. 207.

[235] D. M. Schreuder, 'Gladstone as "Trouble Maker": Liberal Foreign Policy and the German Annexation of Alsace-Lorraine, 1870–1871', *Journal of British Studies*, 17 (1978).

[236] Gladstone, *Speeches, 1880*, p. 86.

[237] Jonathan Parry, 'Gladstone, Liberalism and the Government of 1868–1874', in Bebbington and Swift (eds.), *Gladstone Centenary Essays*, p. 95.

[238] E. D. Steele, *Irish Land and British Politics: Tenant-Right and Nationality, 1865–1870* (Cambridge, 1874), pp. 280, 289.     [239] Gladstone, *Speeches, 1880*, p. 102.

in his thinking: if a weaker section of the community needed to be defended against a stronger section, then government intervention was as justified at home as it was abroad.

The community as a whole, as Gladstone famously put it in the wake of his introduction of Home Rule, contained the masses (who were virtuous) and the classes (who were not). This idea, though less forthrightly expressed, had long been central to his analysis. In the ethnological section of *Juventus Mundi* he contrasted 'the mass' of a people, where its vitality lay, with 'mere class', which was liable to exhaustion.[240] In a political speech of 1867 he had already drawn a distinction between 'the people' and 'a narrow class',[241] and in 1875 he returned to this antithesis. 'The people are the trunk of the tree', he declared, 'and the classes are the branch of the tree.'[242] The characteristic disparagement of the classes, already in place, gained fresh intensity in 1877: 'On one side commonly stand the public, and on the other side in this country stands what are called classes. The public very seldom thinks seriously about its own interests; classes always do. The public goes to sleep; classes, even if they go to sleep at night, keep one eye open.'[243] The classes had turned into a baleful monster, sinister in its eternal vigilance. So the theme had a long prehistory before, in 1886, Gladstone alarmed respectable opinion by calling for 'a combination of the masses against the classes'.[244] He enumerated ten topics from the abolition of slavery onwards on which the masses had been right and the classes wrong. It seemed little short of a declaration of class war. That, however, was to misconceive Gladstone's meaning. By 'the classes' he certainly intended the social elite; but by 'the masses' he was not indicating the working people alone. His earlier antitheses provide the explanation. The masses were the public, the people at large, the solid trunk that could do without the branches because, in a sense, it was the whole tree. Gladstone conceptualized the masses as the true political nation. In 1880 he had contrasted the groups he called the classes with 'the entire community', 'the nation itself'.[245] Six years later he was not summoning the masses to class struggle but distinguishing, as so often, between sectional interests and the community at large.

Yet the masses, after the 1884 Reform Act, did consist predominantly of working men. Gladstone, as he told Acton in the following year, believed 'the sense of justice . . . abides tenaciously in the masses'.[246] Working men had, after all, taken the initiative in the moral indignation against the Bulgarian horrors.[247] Their judgement, he assured a working-class audience in 1890, had always been 'more just, equitable, and enlightened' than that of the educated classes.[248] From 1887 onwards Gladstone was a willing advocate of the party policy of one man one vote.[249] But he went further. During the 1892 election campaign he announced

[240] *JM*, p. 92.   [241] *T*, 19 Dec. 1867, p. 7.   [242] *T*, 12 Nov. 1875, p. 10.
[243] *T*, 21 Aug. 1877, p. 4.   [244] Gladstone, *Speeches, 1886*, p. 292.
[245] Gladstone, *Speeches, 1880*, pp. 354, 355.
[246] W. E. Gladstone to Lord Acton, 11 Feb. 1885, GP 44093, f. 261.
[247] W. E. Gladstone, *A Speech delivered at Blackheath* (London, 1876), p. 9.
[248] *T*, 24 Oct. 1890, p. 4.
[249] W. E. Gladstone, *The Liberal Programme for Great Britain & Ireland* (London, 1887), p. 5.

that 'it was high time for labour to bestir itself' and press for legislation in its favour.[250] There must be more labour representatives in parliament, and to that end he urged that election expenses should be paid from public funds. He even spoke in favour of giving MPs independence of financial difficulties, something close to public payment of members.[251] It seemed very much like a slice of the Labour party programme of the Edwardian years. Certainly Gladstone envisaged 'the labouring people of this country' turning into the dominant force in politics. They would soon, he told a working-class audience in his constituency in 1890, 'become supreme to such a degree that there is no other power to balance and counteract the power which you possess'. Would they follow the leisured and wealthy class in allowing their judgement to be corrupted by power? Or would they pass the deep moral trial awaiting them and 'continue to be just'?[252] The freighting of the final word was far more than Gladstone's hearers can have imagined, for they were being challenged to act fairly on behalf of the whole community, giving all interests their due. The statesman returned to the theme in 1895, when in retirement he addressed a delegation of Yorkshire Liberals visiting Hawarden. Power, he pointed out, had been in the hands of the people for a decade. Would they use it for 'the general and rational interest' or for their 'interests which are sectional'?[253] The choice before the working classes was whether to act on behalf of the nation as a whole or instead to pursue exclusively working-class concerns. Gladstone was speaking with remarkable prescience; but he was doing so on the basis of his long-standing analysis of the dynamics of the political community.

III

The concept of community, however, was not the sole organizing principle of Gladstone's mature political philosophy. Alongside it was the idea of humanity. The dignity of human beings, as we have seen, was the chief intellectual fruit of the liberal tendency in Gladstone's theology; and the value of the human element in the Greek pantheon was the most important legacy to his wider thought of his Homeric studies.[254] By 1860 he had reached the conclusion that human nature was to be the focus of study, and human improvement the object of all effort.[255] A preoccupation with the human inevitably flowed into Gladstone's statements in the public arena. During the years surrounding the first administration, it is true, it played only a relatively minor part. He referred in 1868 to humanity as one of the Christian objects of the Liberal programme, in 1870 he deplored the Franco-Prussian War 'in the name of wounded humanity', and in the following year he described non-political legislation on questions of public health as actuated by

---

[250] *T*, 1 June 1892, p. 7.     [251] *T*, 5 July 1892, p. 12.     [252] *T*, 24 Oct. 1890, p. 4.
[253] *T*, 16 Apr. 1895, p. 10.     [254] See Chs. 5 and 7, pp. 141 and 213–15.
[255] W. E. Gladstone, 'Inaugural Address: The Work of Universities' [1860], *Gleanings*, 7, p. 8.

'considerations of humanity and philanthropy'.[256] From the mid-1870s, however, the theme was promoted to a more central place in Gladstone's speeches. It loomed large in his discussion of the Eastern Question and of the Irish Question alike. In the Midlothian campaign he declared that he had taken 'the wider interests of mankind' as 'the pole-star of my life'.[257] By 1890 he was contrasting Lord Melbourne's record unfavourably with that of Lord John Russell because of a weaker sense of the needs of humanity at large.[258] He had reached the point where he was using the idea as a gauge of Liberalism.

Gladstone, however, was no sentimental optimist about the human condition. He continued to the end of his days to acknowledge the dire corruption of mankind. 'The most terrible and conspicuous fact of human observation', he jotted down in 1894, 'is the universal prevalence of sin.'[259] He discerned the idea of sin in Homer, though not in his successors in classical Greece, and saw it as deeply ingrained among the ancient Jews.[260] It was an awful reality, permeating all the peoples of the world. Nevertheless, as Gladstone pointed out, the ruin of humanity had not prevented Bishop Butler from adopting a high estimate of human nature.[261] In an article of 1887 called 'Universitas Hominum', designed as his intellectual testament to American readers, Gladstone explained his own conviction: 'Torn and defaced as is the ideal of our race, yet have there not been, and are there not, things in man, in his frame, and in his soul and intellect, which, taken at their height, are so beautiful, so good, so great, as to suggest an inward questioning, how far creative power itself can go beyond what, in these elect specimens, it has exhibited?' There was a grandeur about the spectacle of human achievement that commanded Gladstone's awed admiration: 'humanity itself, deeply considered, touches the bounds of the superhuman.'[262] Unlike Friedrich Nietzsche, who in the same decade was speculating about the superman, Gladstone did not draw from antiquity a contempt for the mass of humanity, the non-elect specimens who failed to attain the highest standard. On the contrary, he regretted the trivialization of human life evident in the slaughter recounted by Homer, though noting favourably the regard there for the suppliant, the stranger, and the poor.[263] In Gladstone's mind there was a nexus between the dignity of humanity and the quality of compassion for the weak, the suffering, and the oppressed. The human was bound up with the humane.

This was the dimension of the theme of humanity that emerged most powerfully in Gladstone's speeches on the Eastern Question. Colin Matthew has isolated the idea of 'common humanity' as providing a rationale for Gladstone's grand alliance against the brutal oppression of the Bulgarians from 1876.[264] Initially, in

---

[256] *Speeches, 1868*, p. 220. *Observer*, 31 July 1870, S & P, XIX, p. 272. *T*, 30 Oct. 1871, p. 123.
[257] Gladstone, *Speeches, 1879*, p. 221.
[258] W. E. Gladstone, 'The Melbourne Government: Its Acts and Persons', *Nineteenth Century*, 27 (1890), pp. 43, 54.     [259] GP 44776, f. 78 (22 June 1894).
[260] *Landmarks*, pp. 90–2; Gladstone, 'Universitas Hominum', p. 596.
[261] *Studies Subsidiary*, p. 102.     [262] Gladstone, 'Universitas Hominum', p. 590.
[263] *IRHS*, p. 127; *Landmarks*, p. 93.     [264] Matthew, p. 294.

fact, the phrase was designed, when used in the statesman's speech at Blackheath in September 1876, to rally support from Conservatives as well as Liberals. The reiterated allusions to the 'humane and merciful', to 'humanity and justice' and to 'the happiness of mankind' were calculated to suggest that the cause was intrinsically non-partisan, deserving the endorsement of all who loved compassion.[265] Humanity was also, however, being posited against government appeals to British interests and Turkish territorial integrity as a superior object of policy.[266] It became the warp and woof in Gladstone's continuing crusade. He docketed an extract from an American article on the misery in the Balkans simply 'Antihumanism'.[267] He constantly drew parallels between the upsurge of moral outrage over the Bulgarians and the anti-slavery campaign that had triumphed in another humanitarian cause.[268] Gradually, however, as the Conservatives refused to alter their policy in any way that might endanger the security of Turkey and as Gladstone continued his shrill denunciations, the relief of the victims came to be associated exclusively with the Liberal opposition. Humanity became a key element in the party creed as articulated by its former and future leader. He voiced the sentiment memorably in his appeal for the hill tribes of Afghanistan during the Midlothian campaign. 'Remember', he declared, 'that He who has united you together as human beings in the same flesh and blood, has bound you by the law of mutual love.'[269] Sympathy for suffering fellow-human beings was again the ground of his call for protection for the Jews of Russia in 1889 and for the Armenians of Turkey in subsequent years.[270] Intervention on their behalf, he wrote in 1896, would be 'humane', 'humanitarian', and 'agreeable to humanity'.[271] Gladstone turned his sense of the importance of the human into the main sanction for British championing of oppressed peoples abroad.

Likewise during the Home Rule campaign he minted arguments on behalf of the Irish people out of the metal of their humanity. Like the Bulgarians, they were presented as downtrodden victims: 'Believe in the Irish people to this extent [he told a Swansea audience in 1887], that they are human beings—full of noble qualities—and that if they have defects . . . in my belief there is no country on the face of the earth in which you can so clearly trace those defects to the misgovernment and oppression from which they have been suffering for centuries.'[272] By contrast with the previous Liberal administration of Lord Spencer, under whom penal policy, for instance, showed 'great leniency, decency, and humanity',[273] Balfour's regime in Ireland, according to Gladstone, treated the people badly. Observers of Irish affairs, he maintained, were struck with 'the small respect for their feelings, the slight consideration apparently entertained of them either as human beings or as citizens'. Gladstone returned to the watchword of his crusade on the Eastern

---

[265] Gladstone, *Speech at Blackheath*, pp. 11, 24, 32.       [266] Gladstone, *Bulgarian Horrors*, p. 51.
[267] GP 44763, f. 79.                  [268] *T*, 17 Jan. 1877, p. 10; 29 Jan. 1877, p. 10; 14 July 1877, p. 10.
[269] Gladstone, *Speeches, 1879*, p. 94.                  [270] Gladstone, *Speeches, 1890*, pp. 88, 89.
[271] W. E. Gladstone, 'The Massacres in Turkey', *Nineteenth Century*, 40 (1896), p. 678.
[272] Hutton and Cohen (eds.), *Speeches: 1886–1888*, p. 236 (4 June 1887).
[273] *T*, 6 Nov. 1888, p. 7.

Question, 'justice and humanity'.[274] The reiterated appeal to our 'common humanity', as before, was partly designed to attract Tory support,[275] but it also expressed Gladstone's impassioned sense that a fundamental value of civilization was being flouted. He frequently recounted detailed anecdotes about the treatment of particular individuals. He complained that under the Conservatives' Coercion Act poor newspaper vendors in the street, 'the weak and helpless', were being thrown into prison merely because their papers carried reports of banned organizations.[276] An Irishman named Dunn, suffering from a bronchial complaint and unable to find his rent money, had begged not to be turned out of his home, but he was evicted by the heartless authorities and died shortly afterwards. Above all, there was the shameful episode at Mitchelstown, when troops fired on a nationalist crowd, killing three people, but the government failed to investigate.[277] Ireland was being administered by methods of barbarism. 'Is this the way', he demanded of a later incident, 'in which human life ought to be treated, or in which people ought to be governed?'[278] The Irish were being relegated to the category of the sub-human.

More remarkably, Gladstone applied his concept of humanity to the condition of the working people. His theological development had led him to put a high estimate on the human body, the flesh taken by the Son of God at the incarnation.[279] The idea was carried over into his broader thought. He took the opportunity of the opening of a free public library at St Martin's-in-the-Fields in 1891 to express approval for promoting 'the corporeal health' of the people. 'Let us never forget', he adjured his hearers, 'that we cannot separate the properties of a man's body from those of his soul.'[280] There must be a harmonious development of body, soul, and spirit. Accordingly in his final years in the public arena Gladstone increasingly endorsed policies favouring the physical welfare of the population even though they carried the radical whiff of government interference. Michael Barker has noticed that in the late 1880s and early 1890s he spoke for the limitation of the hours of railway employees ('a <u>duty</u> from the humanity point of view'), for leasehold enfranchisement (because leaseholds conflicted with 'every other human interest'), and even for the principle of old age pensions (one of society's 'duties to its poorest members').[281] Gladstone also endorsed the principle of the restriction of miners' work to eight hours a day. This policy tack was of course doubly advantageous: it calmed the restiveness of the miners at a time when their hotter spirits were contemplating independent labour action; and it kept up working-class enthusiasm for the Irish cause. Gladstone was careful to balance his provisional support for the eight-hour day with a eulogy of freedom as a preferable to legislative action. Yet there was a note of sincerity about his declaration at West Calder in 1890 that all who had been down a mine, as he had done several

[274] W. E. Gladstone, *The Present Mode of Governing Ireland* (London, 1887), pp. 10, 23–4.
[275] *T*, 28 Dec. 1887, p. 4.   [276] *T*, 10 May 1888, p. 7.   [277] *T*, 8 Nov. 1888, p. 10.
[278] *T*, 22 Oct. 1890, p. 6.   [279] See Ch. 7, p. 189.   [280] *T*, 13 Feb. 1891, p. 12.
[281] Michael Barker, *Gladstone and Radicalism: The Reconstruction of Liberal Policy in Britain, 1885–1894* (Brighton, 1975), pp. 196–8.

times, must believe 'that eight hours out of every 24 are quite enough for any human being to labour under such conditions'.[282] He echoed the same sentiment during the 1892 general election. There would be delay before the subject could become ripe for legislation, but eight hours underground (he repeated) were 'enough for a human being'.[283] The physical circumstances of labour properly fell within the purview of the politician.

Working people, furthermore, possessed their own dignity. In presenting prizes for the science and art classes at Greenwich, in 1875, Gladstone celebrated the achievement of all who worked with their hands. His esteem for the skill of the craftsman led him, remarkably, to deprecate the quest for upward social mobility. 'Be not eager', he told his audience, 'to raise your children out of the working class but be desirous that they should remain in that class and elevate the work of it.' Their aim (and here there is probably a debt to Thomas Carlyle) should be 'to ennoble labour'.[284] Gladstone certainly shared with Carlyle a deep regret that the cash payment was becoming the sole nexus between employer and workman, a dehumanizing process.[285] Carlyle may also have been an inspiration for Gladstone's tree-felling, an activity that became regular only in 1867, as the states-man assumed the leadership of the Liberal party. 'The Hero as Wood-Chopper' was a section of *On Heroes and Hero Worship* that Gladstone had read on the book's publication in 1841.[286] In any case the practice gave him a way of identify-ing with the working man that he carefully exploited. He had long wielded the woodman's axe, he told the Turners' Company, whose emblem it was, on receiv-ing their honorary freedom in 1876.[287] He was eager to be acknowledged as 'a comrade' of the workers; he hoped he was 'a labouring man myself'.[288] The result-ing sense of identification with the working people enabled Gladstone to speak convincingly, as he often did, of brotherhood. There should not only be restored brotherhood between Britain and Ireland but also a fresh fraternal spirit between the classes that would solve difficulties in labour relations. 'Establish', he told the workforce at Lever Brothers' soapworks at Port Sunlight in 1891, 'some kind of brotherhood between man and man.'[289] The idea was not just, as in the rising socialist rhetoric of the period, that working men should enjoy a strong solidarity among themselves. Rather it was a broader sense of shared interest between capi-talist and labourer, the two sides being united by their common nature. Workers were as much part of the human family as their social superiors.

A final dimension of humanity in Gladstone's rhetoric was the theme of sympathy, the bond of human feeling between different groups. The principle was prominent in his discussion of colonial affairs. His involvement in the process of giving responsible government to the colonies in the 1840s meant that he was

---

[282] *T*, 24 Oct. 1890, p. 4.          [283] *T*, 5 July 1892, p. 12.          [284] *T*, 12 Nov. 1875, p. 10.
[285] Gladstone, 'Carnegie's "Gospel of Wealth" ', p. 681.
[286] *D*, 6, 21, 22, 27, 28, 30 Sept., 1, 4–6 Oct. 1841.          [287] *T*, 17 Feb. 1876, p. 10.
[288] *T*, 12 Nov. 1875, p. 10; 24 Oct. 1890, p. 4.
[289] *Daily Telegraph*, 30 Nov. 1891, S & P, XXXVII, p. 28. Cf. Gladstone, 'Lessons of Irish History', p. 30; *T*, 4 July 1892, p. 4; 23 May 1893, p. 10.

deeply convinced that they could be retained only by voluntary allegiance. 'The substance of the relationship lies', he wrote in 1878, 'not in dispatches from Downing Street, but in the mutual affection ... which can only flourish between adult communities...'[290] The sole alternative, he declared in 1880, to retaining colonies by the threat of force was to hold them 'in the silken ties of love and affection'.[291] In the same way, the settlement of the *Alabama* claim had allowed goodwill to cement the relations of Britain to the United States.[292] But the most famous context in which Gladstone deployed the language of sympathy was over the Irish Question. At present, he told an audience in 1868, Ireland was estranged, but his ambition in office would be that 'the hearts of the people shall be united together'.[293] After 1886 this vocabulary became pervasive. Conservative coercion of Irish unrest had to be replaced by 'a measure which will really unite the hearts of the whole people throughout the United Kingdom'.[294] What, Gladstone asked in 1890, is a Unionist? 'In my opinion a Unionist is in the first place a man to whom if you talk about unity in the hearts of the people, of unity in the wills of the people, of unity in the intelligence of the people, he looks upon you as a dreamer and a fool ... There is no such thing in human kind [says the Unionist] as heart as well as intelligence.'[295] For Gladstone, on the contrary, an awareness of affinity, emotional as well as rational, was the tightest bond between social groups. By 1892, he pointed out, an Irish crowd would greet the cry of 'God save England' with enthusiasm, manifesting 'real union, something more solid and more durable than paper or than parchment'.[296] Human sympathy had greater significance than any Act of Union.

The underlying premise of all Gladstone's thinking about the human condition was that people in every land were fundamentally the same. They shared skills and flaws, the experience of suffering and the capacity for sympathy. There were, it is true, elements of cultural relativism in his attitudes that led him to emphasize what distinguished nation from nation. Ireland, and particularly its code of land law, had to be treated differently from England or Scotland.[297] Again India could not be accorded unbounded freedoms. 'I do not say', he remarked in this context, 'that the vast and miscellaneous Asiatic population is suited for the highly developed institutions that belong to a country such as this...'[298] Yet, as Eugenio Biagini has argued, it would be wrong to suppose, with Edward Said, that Gladstone was a straightforward proponent of 'orientalism', attributing to the East the deficiencies that were the mirror-image of the achievements of the West. He believed, on the contrary, in exporting British institutions as far as possible to other lands.[299] 'What is good for human nature in the East', he contended in 1890,

---

[290] Gladstone, *England's Mission*, p. 9.     [291] Gladstone, *Speeches, 1880*, pp. 97–8.
[292] Gladstone, *Speeches, 1879*, p. 135.     [293] *T*, 23 July 1868, p. 10.
[294] *T*, 8 Nov. 1888, p. 10.     [295] *T*, 24 Oct. 1890, p. 4.     [296] *T*, 4 July 1892, p. 4.
[297] C. J. Dewey, 'Celtic Agrarian Legislation and the Celtic Revival: Historicist Implications of Gladstone's Irish and Scottish Land Acts, 1870–86', *Past & Present*, 64 (1974).
[298] Gladstone, *Speeches, 1880*, p. 96.
[299] Eugenio Biagini, ' "Western & Beneficent Institutions": Gladstone and Empire, 1880–1885', in Bebbington and Swift (eds.), *Gladstone Centenary Essays*. Edward Said's *Orientalism* (London, 1978), though citing Disraeli, does not mention Gladstone.

'is good for it in the West.'[300] Gladstone never doubted that human beings were constituted alike by their Creator. There was a 'common nature which runs through us all'. That was why, in urging concern for the hill villagers of Afghanistan on the women of Midlothian in 1879, he could appeal to 'mutual love': 'that mutual love is not limited by the shores of this island, is not limited by the boundaries of Christian civilisation . . . it passes over the whole surface of the earth, and embraces the meanest along with the greatest in its unmeasured scope.'[301] From the start of the Bulgarian campaign Gladstone insisted that the basic reason for sympathy for the victims was not that they were fellow-Christians (that might be a secondary motive) but that they were fellow-human beings.[302] He made the same point about agitation on behalf of the Armenians in 1890 and 1895.[303] Suffering men and women throughout the world deserved relief simply in virtue of their flesh and blood. Just as he rejected the ethnic discrimination of Friedrich Max Müller and Ernest Renan,[304] so Gladstone resisted any suggestion that there should be favour for one nation rather than another on grounds of special affinity. The solidarity of the human race transcended all other differences.

IV

What were the sources of the twin themes of community and humanity in Gladstone's version of Liberalism? The idea of community, in the first place, was the bedrock because it had remained so ever since the 1830s. In his early political thought Gladstone had drawn on Christian and classical resources, and in his years as Liberal leader the defender of the faith and Homeric scholar found inspiration in the same traditions. His notes to the edition of Butler show that he treated New Testament corporatism as normative: 'Our nature as a whole proves that each part of a body has a function for itself and has also an office to discharge on behalf of the body to which it belongs, so every member of a society or incorporation has to discharge in it duties to himself and other duties to the association.'[305] Human beings belonged as naturally to each other as (in the apostle Paul's expression) the hand or foot belonged to the body. The parts of the community had to seek the common good and not just their own sectional interests. The power of the metaphor had grown in Gladstone's imagination over the decades as his appreciation of the corporate dimension of the Christian faith had expanded. His vision of the Church of England, reinvigorated on Puseyite lines but tolerating internal diversity, deepened his veneration for the religious community to which he belonged. His ideal of a European fellowship of national churches, Catholic but not Roman Catholic, was (as commentators have recognized) a model for his view of the concert of nations.[306] The last phase of his

---

[300] Gladstone, *Speeches, 1890*, p. 90.          [301] Gladstone, *Speeches, 1879*, pp. 89, 94.

[302] *T*, 25 Sept. 1876, p. 6.          [303] Gladstone, *Speeches, 1890*, p. 89. *T*, 7 Aug. 1895, p. 4.

[304] See Ch. 7, pp. 199–200.          [305] *WJB*, 2, p. 29 n.

[306] J. L. Hammond, 'Gladstone and the League of Nations Mind', in J. A. K. Thomson and A. J. Toynbee (eds.), *Essays in Honour of Gilbert Murray* (London, 1936). Matthew, pp. 271–5.

religious thought envisaged the consensus of orthodox Christians, transcending their separate allegiances, as powerful corporate testimony to the nature of truth.[307] Both within the national church and among Christians internationally there were therefore apt analogies for the notion of a community subsuming partial groups in a larger whole. These ecclesiastical theories, based ultimately on scripture, continued to underpin the cast of mind he brought to understanding politics.

Antiquity provided further sanctions for Gladstone's mature analysis of public affairs. There was a germ of inspiration in Homer. One of the ways in which, according to the statesman, Homeric and British political ideas were similar was that both included 'a practical belief in right as relative, and in duty as reciprocal'. But there must be more than a suspicion that Gladstone was reading a greater amount into Homer than he was taking from his pages; and in any case, as Gladstone admits, the relevance of Homer to modern society in this respect was limited because archaic Greece was not marked by sectional conflict.[308] Yet classical sources other than Homer were crucial to Gladstone's understanding of community. 'The common life of man', he wrote, 'is strongly dwelt on by the ancients.'[309] The Stoic school, as represented by Cicero, was one source. But overwhelmingly important was Aristotle. Gladstone's speeches for mass consumption were still shot through with Aristotelian themes more familiar to the elite. They included a dislike of extremes, a love of the mean, a reference to a 'true polity', and the remark that instability was the reproach of popular governments.[310] Unsurprisingly therefore, Gladstone refers readers of Butler for an authoritative account of the common life to the *Nicomachean Ethics*.[311] Aristotle provided what Homer did not, a discussion of how to ensure a balance of interests in different constitutions.[312] The Aristotelian opposition between the many and the few lay squarely behind the Gladstonian antithesis between the masses and the classes. And, most of all, the capstone of Gladstone's political structure is hewn from Aristotle. Occasionally, as when the statesman asserted on Blackheath in 1876 that prudence must always be a part of justice, there are particular echoes of the Greek philosopher.[313] But the pervasive notion that disputes within the political community must be resolved by the criterion of justice was also pure Aristotelianism. During his long political life, Gladstone told a Birmingham audience in 1877, he had had much to learn and unlearn, but 'one firm conviction from the beginning to the end has been that justice should prevail'.[314] The thread of continuity derived above all from Aristotle.

Although Gladstone had lavished detailed attention on the Aristotelian texts himself, he also owed a debt to those who had previously built on the philosopher.

[307] See Ch. 8, p. 2560.    [308] *JM*, pp. 413, 415.    [309] *WJB*, 2, p. 29 n.
[310] *T*, 20 Dec. 1867, p. 5. Gladstone, *Speeches, 1879*, p. 237. Gladstone, *Bulgarian Horrors*, p. 14. W. E. Gladstone, 'Electoral Facts of 1887', *Nineteenth Century*, 22 (1887), p. 435.
[311] *WJB*, 2, p. 29 n.    [312] *JM*, p. 415.
[313] Gladstone, *Speech at Blackheath*, p. 29. Cf. Ernest Barker (ed.), *The Politics of Aristotle* (Oxford, 1946), p. 103 (III. iv. 7).    [314] *T*, 2 June 1877, p. 12.

Dante, another of Gladstone's four doctors, had revered Aristotle and had lived in the tight-knit city state of Florence, but his political thought was too bound up with the universal claims of the medieval empire to generate useful analysis of community politics. Gladstone treated Dante's *De Monarchia* as unduly abstract, complaining to Acton that the poet was far too rigid in separating church and state.[315] The subsequent popularization of Aristotle among the intellectuals of Florence, however, gave rise to a major tradition of political reflection that did affect Gladstone's way of thinking. This was the style of commentary embodied in Machiavelli's *Discourses* (1531) that J. G. A. Pocock, following Hans Baron, has called 'civic humanism'. Its aim was to elaborate on Aristotle's account in the *Politics* of how to preserve constitutions. Perceiving a cycle in the course of human affairs whereby once-flourishing states fell into decay, Machiavelli and his imitators down to James Harrington in *Oceana* (1656) and beyond looked for the conditions that would arrest the natural tendency to declension. A mobilized citizenry, well informed about issues and active in public life, could alone guarantee the security of the state. Participation by the people in public affairs was essential; so in turn was leisure, as a condition of participation. The great peril to the state was the spread of luxury. In its train moneymaking and entertainment would occupy people's leisure time with personal concerns, distracting them from promoting the general good. The nurture of 'public virtue' was therefore a constant imperative if the state was to survive in freedom.[316] Because civic humanism was often a militantly republican creed, its influence over the arch-monarchist Gladstone is at first sight surprising. But, as his vocabulary shows, its legacy was undoubtedly present in his mind. In 1876, for example, Gladstone admitted that even Turkey had produced men exhibiting 'the true civic virtues'. If there had been a true polity round them they would have been proper 'citizens'.[317] The republican term 'citizens', like the characterization of their qualities, suggests the derivation of Gladstone's comments. The persistence of civic humanist themes into the nineteenth century—in J. S. Mill, for instance—is increasingly being recognized.[318] Gladstone was also among those swayed by the tradition.

Civic humanist motifs therefore helped to construct his idea of community. This is apparent, for example, in his speech to the City livery company when receiving its honorary freedom in 1876. Local self-government should be extended, he argued, so that the people would be trained in the 'habits which befit the free citizens of a free State'. Their attention needed to be turned to public duties so that the existing structure of society could endure. But danger, warned

---

[315] Gladstone, 'Universitas Hominum', pp. 593–4. W. E. Gladstone to Lord Acton, 26 June 1887 (copy), GP 44093, f. 291.

[316] J. G. A. Pocock, *The Machiavellian Moment: Florentine Political Thought and the Atlantic Republican Tradition* (Princeton, 1975), stressing the Aristotelian component at pp. 66–74.

[317] Gladstone, *Bulgarian Horrors*, p. 14.

[318] Burrow, *Whigs and Liberals*, ch. 5. E. F. Biagini, 'Liberalism and Direct Democracy: John Stuart Mill and the Model of Ancient Athens', in E. F. Biagini (ed.), *Citizenship and Community: Liberals, Radicals and Collective Identities in the British Isles, 1865–1931* (Cambridge, 1966).

the statesman, was afoot. The threat came from sectional selfishness, what Gladstone on this occasion called the advance of 'luxury and enjoyment' among 'the wealthier and leisured classes'.[319] They were putting private indulgence before their public responsibilities and so endangering national welfare. The cycle feared by civic humanists was about to take a downward turn. The remedy lay in a renewed call to participation in public affairs, which, independent of its results, had a value of its own: 'the conscientious exercise of important duties', Gladstone told a working-class audience in 1890, 'is a function that tends to elevate a man'. An active political role was itself, as the civic humanists taught, an ennobling experience. His hearers must cultivate 'public spirit'; the result, as he often said, would be the nurturing of 'public virtue'.[320] The language of 'virtue' would have been comprehensible in the Renaissance Florence of Machiavelli. Gladstone was immersed in the terminology of the civic humanist tradition.

The version of the tradition that he articulated was chiefly what had become current in the eighteenth century. John Morley suggests that in his later career Gladstone raised 'a partially Rousseauite structure' of thought, pointing particularly to his feeling for simplicity.[321] Although there may be a touch of Rousseau in Gladstone's dislike of luxury, for the statesman had absorbed *Émile*, the *Confessions*, and *La Nouvelle Héloïse*,[322] there is no trace of the teaching of the *Social Contract* in his political thinking. The sharp internal differentiation of Gladstone's community is sufficient to mark off his understanding from Rousseau's. Gladstone's aversion to corruption came much more directly from writers of the eighteenth century in England, where the civic humanist tradition had made an uneasy peace with monarchism in the ideology of the country Whigs. Stressing the need for the defenders of the people's liberties to be free of court influence, country Whigs insisted that civic virtue could survive only if its champions enjoyed the independence of landed proprietors.[323] Many of these assumptions formed the mind of Edmund Burke, who continued to cast a spell over the mature Gladstone. It was less, however, the conservative Burke of the *Reflections* that now appealed to him, than the progressive Burke who defended the liberties of America and Ireland. On the French Revolution, Gladstone told Matthew Arnold in 1881, Burke was 'largely wrong', but on other political subjects he was 'splendidly right'.[324] Burke's defence of aristocracy was originally designed, in country Whig style, to vindicate those who would stand up for the people against the pretensions of the crown. Gladstone's views about the responsibilities of the landed elite are closely allied to Burke's way of thinking. 'The natural condition of a healthy society', wrote Gladstone in 1887, 'is, that governing functions

---

[319] *T*, 17 Feb. 1876, p. 10.       [320] *T*, 5 Oct. 1891, p. 12; 19 Dec. 1867, p. 7; 4 July 1892, p. 4.
[321] Morley, 1, pp. 203–4.       [322] *D*, 8–11, 17–21, 23–6 Aug. 1858, 23–8 Sept., 1, 2 Oct. 1861.
[323] H. T. Dickinson, *Liberty and Property: Political Ideology in Eighteenth-Century Britain* (London, 1977), pp. 102–18, 169–75.
[324] W. E. Gladstone to Matthew Arnold, 8 July 1881, GP 44544, f. 383, quoted in W. H. G. Armytage, 'Matthew Arnold and W. E. Gladstone: Some New Letters', *University of Toronto Quarterly*, 18 (1949), p. 225.

should be discharged in the main by the leisured class.'³²⁵ They alone had the freedom from financial cares that allowed them to concentrate on public service. The exalted role of the landed proprietors in Gladstone's way of thinking, though a truly conservative trait, was also a symptom of his debt to the progressive Whiggery of the previous century.

Civic humanist assumptions, living on in country Whig ideology, had helped to create the United States. Gladstone took a particular interest in America during his later years, hoping to atone for his unguarded endorsement of Southern separatism during the Civil War.³²⁶ He lost no opportunity to speak of 'our natural relations in America' and even expressed the hope for 'moral and social union' with the United States.³²⁷ In an article of 1878 written for publication in America he lavished praise on the constitution of the United States, though puzzling over why it permitted the disturbance of presidential elections, the subsequent clean sweep of the civil service, and, most of all, the absence of checks on executive authority once a president was elected. He claimed, however, that the underlying political values of the United States were shared with Britain—with the single exception of the egalitarianism of America. Gladstone endorsed the American revolution because, like Britain's Glorious Revolution, it was in the main 'a vindication of liberties inherited and possessed' and so 'a Conservative revolution'.³²⁸ He specially recommended to working men the study of the American revolutionary period, which had thrown up an incomparable group of statesmen.³²⁹ Among them he quoted Benjamin Franklin with approval,³³⁰ but the thinker with whom he shows most affinity was James Madison. In the tenth *Federalist* paper Madison condemns the factions operating against 'the permanent and aggregate interests of the community'; sees the regulation of the sectional interests as the great objective; and wants to establish 'the public good' according to the criterion of justice.³³¹ There is no record of Gladstone having read the *Federalist* essay, but he was almost certainly familiar with Madison's stance. Conversation with James Bryce, Regius Professor of Civil Law at Oxford on Gladstone's nomination and MP from 1880, must have enhanced the Liberal leader's awareness of the original ideals of the United States. Bryce's *American Commonwealth* (1888), a classic study of American institutions, owed much to Gladstone's encouragement.³³² So the American founding fathers, with their exhortations to public virtue, were part of Gladstone's intellectual world.

³²⁵ W. E. Gladstone, 'Notes and Queries on the Irish Demands' [1887], *Special Aspects of the Irish Question* (London, 1912), p. 145.

³²⁶ P. J. Parish, 'Gladstone and America', in P. J. Jagger (ed.), *Gladstone* (London, 1998), ch. 5. Murney Gerlach, *British Liberalism and the United States: Political and Social Thought in the Late Victorian Age* (Houndmills, Basingstoke, 2001), pp. 48–57.

³²⁷ Gladstone, *Speeches, 1879*, p. 183; id., 'An Olive Branch from America', *Nineteenth Century*, 22 (1887), p. 611.        ³²⁸ Gladstone, 'Kin beyond Sea', pp. 208–9, 210, 213, 220–1.

³²⁹ *T*, 28 Oct. 1889, p. 8.        ³³⁰ Gladstone, *Special Aspects*, p. 100.

³³¹ Alexander Hamilton, James Madison, and John Jay, *The Federalist: Or, the New Constitution* (Oxford, 1948), pp. 41–3.

³³² H. A. L. Fisher, *James Bryce (Viscount Bryce of Dechmont, O.M.)*, 2 vols. (London, 1927), 1, pp. 188–9.

The most instructive feature of the American experience in Gladstone's estimation, however, was something that Alexis de Tocqueville had highlighted in his *Democracy in America* (1835). Gladstone, as we have seen, had studied the book in detail on its first appearance.[333] In 1884 he read de Tocqueville's *Memoirs*, concluding that its subject had been 'A man of real note'.[334] In *Democracy in America* de Tocqueville dwelt on the lowest tier of popular institutions, the townships that gave the Americans a sense of 'communal liberty' that was so markedly missing in continental Europe: 'the strength of free peoples', he observed, 'resides in the local community.'[335] This practice of local self-government, as opposed to central government, was what Gladstone singled out as exemplary when commending the American model to working men. It was the very motor of civic virtue, tending 'to bring home to the mind of every father of a family a sense of public duty'. 'That', he concluded, 'is the secret of the strength of America.'[336] He had already pointed out during the Midlothian campaign that the energy and expansion of the United States were due to its self-government in local institutions.[337] De Tocqueville had driven home the same lesson in a later work. His case in *The Ancien Régime and the Revolution* (1856), which Gladstone looked at in 1861, was that French history provided a counterfactual equivalent to America.[338] The over-centralization of France under Louis XIV and his successors had ground down local institutions and so prepared the way for the outburst of repressed forces at the Revolution.[339] Gladstone adopted the same analysis. When recommending reading about the American revolution, he also urged his hearers to study the history of France in the seventeenth and eighteenth centuries. There misgovernment had effaced 'the true idea of law and public rights', substituting 'arbitrary will and unlimited and vicious intolerance'.[340] France still suffered, he believed, from 'her want of municipal, provincial, and generally local life'.[341] Acton disagreed with Gladstone's view of centralization in France before the Revolution,[342] but the statesman refused to unlearn what he had been taught by de Tocqueville. The French commentator, he wrote, was 'the Burke of his age'.[343] The prominent place of municipal participation in Gladstone's thinking owed a great deal to de Tocqueville.

Gladstone was by no means unusual among Victorian intellectuals in regarding public service through local government as a priority. It lay, for example, near the heart of the Liberalism of T. H. Green, who made a stir by practising what he preached as a town representative on Oxford council.[344] But Gladstone owed no debt to Green, whose posthumous lectures he did not record reading, and in any

---

[333] See Ch. 2, pp. 29–30.  [334] *D*, 8–24 Dec. 1884.
[335] Alexis de Tocqueville, *Democracy in America*, ed. J. P. Mayer and Max Lerner, 2 vols. (New York, 1966), 1, p. 55.  [336] *T*, 28 Oct. 1889, p. 8.
[337] Gladstone, *Speeches, 1879*, p. 220.  [338] *D*, 28 Oct. 1861.
[339] Larry Siedentop, *Tocqueville* (Oxford, 1994), ch. 6.  [340] *T*, 28 Oct. 1889, p. 8.
[341] Gladstone, 'Further Notes and Queries', p. 203.
[342] Lord Acton to W. E. Gladstone, 18 Feb. 1888, GP 44094, f. 5.
[343] Gladstone, 'Kin beyond Sea', p. 203.
[344] Melvin Richter, *The Politics of Conscience: T. H. Green and his Age* (London, 1964), p. 346.

case the statesman had formulated his thinking long before the Oxford philosopher. Others, however, probably did supplement de Tocqueville's encouragement
to see local communal liberties as the guarantee of broader national freedoms. A
group of historians was responsible for perceiving the root of constitutional
government in the communalism of the remote past. One of them, E. A. Freeman,
celebrated civic independence on the continent as a perpetuation of ancient Greek
ideals, and, though Gladstone does not record reading his main book on the
history of federal government, he did examine several of the historian's other
works. Freeman's friend J. R. Green traced the lineage of constitutional development back to the 'tiny moots' of pre-Conquest England.[345] To Green's *Short
History of the English People* (1874) and his subsequent *History of the English People*
(1877) Gladstone repeatedly turned as standard authorities. He also read *The
Constitutional History of England* (1866) by William Stubbs, the third member of
the trio of historians who saw local participation as the key to national greatness.[346] To Stubbs, whom he recommended to a bishopric in 1884, Gladstone
showed 'deferential respect'.[347] The statesman gave credit to the national myth
that parliamentary liberties came down from Anglo-Saxon times even before
reading these historians,[348] but they helped to reinforce his belief that the localities were the training ground for public service. English history confirmed what
he had learned from Aristotle and the civic humanist tradition, from the country
Whigs and the Americans, that politics was built on communities.

The origins of the other main motif of Gladstone's later political thinking, the
theme of humanity, are not surprising in view of what has already been set out in
earlier chapters. The centrality of the incarnation in his theology, both in its
Tractarian and in its more liberal dimensions, ensured that the worth of human
beings would loom large in his mind. His 'theanthropic' account of the divinities
of Olympus pointed him towards the same conclusion. It was essential, in
Gladstone's view, that the human race should be seen as a single entity. The article designed to expound his deepest assumptions for posterity, 'Universitas
Hominum' (1887), dwells on 'collective man, as an unity'.[349] Activities might be
diverse, as they were depicted on Homer's shield of Achilles, but each was part of
the single human condition. In the article Gladstone relates the unity of mankind
to the intentions of providence, but there were more fundamental reasons for his
conviction. It was one of the greatest lessons of Bishop Butler, he believed, to
teach that all men and women possess a single human nature.[350] The variations of
human behaviour over time and place reflected only minor oscillations, for the
structure of rationality was always and everywhere the same. Although Gladstone

[345] J. W. Burrow, *A Liberal Descent: Victorian Historians and the English Past* (Cambridge, 1981), ch.
7, p. 125.
[346] *D*, 1–8 Dec. 1875, 19 Feb. 1878, 15 Aug. 1880, 1 July 1883, 14 Aug. 1884, 2 Sept. 1887; 22–5, 29 Nov.
1875, 14 Aug. 1884.
[347] W. H. Hutton (ed.), *Letters of William Stubbs* (London, 1904), p. 204. Cf. Ch. 8, p. 222.
[348] Christopher Hill, 'The Norman Yoke', *Puritanism and Revolution* (London, 1958), pp. 115–16.
[349] Gladstone, 'Universitas Hominum', p. 590.          [350] *Studies Subsidiary*, pp. 100–3.

had modified Butler's anthropology by recognizing the place of emotional and spiritual growth, he still agreed with him that reason and conscience were unchanging human attributes. He retained the pre-historicist doctrine, upheld by Christian scholasticism and the mainstream Enlightenment alike, that human nature is a fixed datum. The principle of the constancy of human nature, as German historicists complained, was rooted in belief in natural law. There was one standard of morality that applied to all. Gladstone, as we have seen, had imbibed the idea of natural law as a young man from the ancients,[351] and it still undergirded his later thinking. There was such a thing as 'natural justice', he wrote in his notes on Aristotle's *Politics* in 1860, an 'unwritten law of relative right, ingrained in our nature'.[352] Hence people of every nation belonged to a single race with mutual obligations. There was a universal sweep to Gladstone's conception of humanity that derived primarily from classical sources together with the Christianized Aristotelianism that had dominated European thought from the time of Dante to that of Butler.

## V

How, then, does the evidence of Gladstone's mature convictions locate him as a political thinker? It is clear that he displayed characteristics of a classic form of liberalism alongside traits of an enduring conservative cast of mind. His Janus-like views were often the despair of contemporaries, who could not know whether the progressive or the traditionalist would predominate on any given issue. But the tension can be understood, if not wholly resolved, by an appreciation of the true foundations of his thinking. Accepting the legitimacy of political philosophy, he frequently expressed his own beliefs about public affairs at a level of abstraction that rose above everyday questions of policy. It is true, of course, that typical liberal themes such as self-help, free trade, and the restriction of the state did appear prominently in Gladstone's speeches; and liberty was undoubtedly something he treasured. Yet his subject was rarely the individual in isolation, and he was at the furthest possible remove from supposing there was no such thing as society. On the contrary, individuals were always conceived as members of families, churches, cities, and nations and even as responsible participants in the international order. There was merit in joining in the life of the local community, which could give individuals their fulfilment. Their freedom, in fact, was enhanced by involvement in groups that united them with others. On the other hand there are indications of a commitment to order and tradition that balanced Gladstone's love of freedom. Progress, he held, was by no means assured, equality was a foolish chimera, and the established structure of society (especially the aristocracy) and government (especially the monarchy) were to be stoutly defended. Yet certain features of his thinking that it is easy to label conservative

---

[351] See Ch. 2, pp. 23–4.     [352] GP 44750, f. 108 (on III. ix. 1).

(and in many ways were so) were not merely designed to preserve the existing order. The quality of reverence was certainly, he believed, a conservative virtue, but it was also a question of mutual regard, a part of what was entailed by communal living. And the insistence on the role of the landed aristocracy as an independent constitutional force owes a great deal to the country Whig version of civic humanism. So elements in his mind that might seem straightforwardly traditionalist can turn out to be the fruit of another orientation. It is clear that he owed an immense continuing debt to the holistic pattern of thought stemming from the ancient *polis*.

In truth, Gladstone was very much an upholder of community as the undergirding principle of public affairs. Colin Matthew has pointed out that, during negotiations over the 1884 Reform Act, the statesman adopted 'a communitarian theory of representative government'.[353] His preference on this occasion for giving small boroughs the vote rather than breaking regions down into areas of class or sectional interest was symptomatic of the fundamental premises of his thinking. The integrity of municipalities was as sacred to him as the inviolability of national territories. Cities and nations, like families or churches, must not be dissolved into warring sections. The different internal interests, insofar as they enter into competition with each other, must be reconciled by the application of just remedies for their grievances. The same principle needed to be injected into international affairs, so that countries great and small could coexist in harmony. Sectional selfishness, at whatever level, must give way to the common good. 'That mankind is a community,' wrote Bishop Butler in his sermons, 'that we all stand in a relation to each other, that there is a public end and interest of society which each particular is obliged to promote, is the sum of morals.' Gladstone actually dissented from this observation in a footnote to his edition, but his objection was only to Butler's suggestion that ethics had no other branches. He agreed with Butler that this dictum was the sum of morals 'in that department of the science which contemplates the public good, or relative right and duty'.[354] Gladstone was happy to follow the bishop in affirming a communitarian understanding of politics.

Gladstone's theory therefore approximates to the one put forward by the school of thought that has been labelled 'communitarian'. The theorists of this loose grouping, writing in the 1970s and 1980s, submitted an indictment of the assumptions underpinning the political life of the United States as practised at the time. The critique was focused on John Rawls's justification, in his *A Theory of Justice* (1971), of political arrangements giving an absolute priority to liberty. Such a liberal polity, according to Rawls, would be chosen in the abstract by any rational agent. The communitarians, however, denied that human beings can be so conceived. Men and women are, on the contrary, bound up with a particular community possessing a distinct territory, shared activities, and a common set of values. The deficiency of a Rawlsian version of political theory, according to these critics, was that it deprived human beings of the benefits of community, especially

---

[353] Matthew, p. 432.     [354] *WJB*, 2, p. 131 and n.

the mutual encouragement to pursue the good life.[355] In the writings of Charles Taylor, one of the leading representatives of the communitarian school, the prototype for the sense of corporate solidarity is the 'ethical life' attributed to the state by Hegel.[356] In Alasdair MacIntyre's *After Virtue* (1981), probably the most influential statement of the communitarian case, however, the great exemplar is Aristotle. The ideal political society is the *polis* about which Aristotle wrote. Although, according to MacIntyre, the Greek philosopher had an inadequate appreciation of the tragic element of conflict in society, the virtues nurtured by community are Aristotelian in character.[357] Here was an exposition of a point of view with deep roots in antiquity but applied directly to the condition of the modern state. The communitarians claimed to be offering an analysis of the rationale for contemporary political arrangements that was at once more accurate and more moral than that of their liberal individualist opponents.

The outlines of Gladstone's position closely resemble those of the modern communitarians. The liberal creed of personal autonomy is rejected by Charles Taylor, Alasdair MacIntyre, and their allies on the ground that individuals can be understood only in the social context of the relationships into which they are born. The community, since it confers benefits on individuals, has claims on their allegiance beyond any calculation of personal advantage they may make. Involvement in public life is a responsibility, as are respect for family and nation. Patriotism, based on a sense of shared values, territory, and history, is a virtue. The principle of justice can be embodied in a community.[358] All these attitudes, more or less articulated by the various communitarian theorists, were upheld by Gladstone. He also concurred in their judgement that the values associated with the ideal of the community were in decay. The assertion of private interests against the public good was in his estimation as sinister a development as the loss of the sense of community appeared to its champions a century or so later. Roughly their standpoint, rather than any version of liberal individualism, was the starting place of his later political theory as much as of his lifelong ecclesiastical theory. The explanation is not far to seek. MacIntyre went direct to Aristotle for his inspiration; Taylor went to Hegel, who in turn had gone to the classical *polis* for his. Likewise the primary source for Gladstone's theoretical understanding of politics was antiquity. In his early thinking Gladstone had shown surprising parallels with Hegel;[359] the whole of his intellectual career rested on Aristotelian foundations. Gladstone and the communitarians shared an immense debt to classical ideas. Furthermore, enthusiasm for early American republicanism constitutes additional common ground between the statesman and thinkers

---

[355] Shlomo Avineri and Avner de-Shalit (eds.), *Communitarianism and Individualism* (Oxford, 1992), provides a useful overview. For critical evaluation, see David Conway, *Classical Liberalism: The Unvanquished Ideal* (Basingstoke, 1995), ch. 4, and D. L. Phillips, *Looking Backward: A Critical Appraisal of Communitarian Thought* (Princeton, 1993).

[356] Charles Taylor, *Hegel and Modern Society* (Cambridge, 1979).

[357] Alasdair MacIntyre, *After Virtue: A Study in Moral Theory* (London, 1981), esp. ch. 12.

[358] See works cited in n. 353.                              [359] See Ch. 3, pp. 66–7.

associated with the communitarian school.[360] Both saw the ideals of the youthful United States, themselves reflecting classical sources, as a reaffirmation of the need for active participation in the public sphere. Consequently the leader of the late Victorian Liberal party was, in terms of recent debate, far more of a communitarian than a liberal. The repudiation of modern liberalism by communitarian theorists must not blind us to the extent of the affinity between their viewpoint and Gladstonian Liberalism.

Yet the affinity does not constitute an identity. Gladstone showed little of the reluctance to use the language of rights sometimes found among recent communitarians;[361] and he was more inclined to minimize the powers of the state than any late twentieth-century thinker of this school could be. There is also no sense in Gladstone, as there is in MacIntyre, that conflict is ineradicable. Indeed, according to the Liberal leader, the aim of the statesman in domestic matters is to establish consensus and in foreign affairs to reduce collisions by the promotion of international law. But the most significant qualification of Gladstone's communitarianism lies elsewhere. The contemporary school upholding this principle is often criticized for restricting the scope of sympathy to those sharing the same cultural identity, the rest of humanity being beyond the frontiers of the group to whom any obligation is owed.[362] Gladstone, however, did not make this limitation. On the contrary, he insisted that concern for the suffering knew no boundaries of nationality or religion. In the agitation against Turkish massacres of Armenians after his retirement he maintained that the case set out by the protestors was not based on British objectives, European interests, or even concern for fellow-Christians. 'Nothing narrower than humanity could pretend for a moment justly to represent it.'[363] With his powerful awareness of the solidarity of the human race, Gladstone believed that values were universal in application. Sympathy must extend to all, whether European or Asian, Christian or Muslim. His mature political thought, though it can legitimately be seen as a species of communitarianism, was tempered by his humanitarianism.

Gladstone's blend of these principles constituted the core of the Liberalism that he commended to his devoted audiences. It was natural that he should speak in terms familiar to him from the other fields to which he devoted his attention. He could impose no sharp demarcation between his political theorizing on the one hand and the preoccupations of his leisure hours on the other. His mature thought about the groundwork of public affairs was affected by the basic assumptions that also conditioned his stance on issues in religion and the study of Homer. Hence it is not surprising that the notion of community was one lodestar.

---

[360] Phillips, *Looking Backward*, p. 5–6. The particular thinkers are Michael J. Sandel (though he is uneasy with the label 'communitarian') and Robert Bellah (though he is not always ranked with communitarians).

[361] e.g. Michael J. Sandel (ed.), *Liberalism and its Critics* (New York, 1984), p. 6. Charles Taylor, 'Atomism', in Avineri and De-Shalit (eds.), *Communitarianism and Individualism*, pp. 30–1.

[362] e.g. Stephen Holmes, *Passions and Constraint: On the Theory of Liberal Democracy* (Chicago, 1995), pp. 39–40.                    [363] *T*, 25 Sept. 1896, p. 5.

Human beings, he believed, needed to live in groups and every subordinate section was required to serve the common good. By no means all the loose ends were tied up. Gladstone offered little by way of answer to the question, for instance, of when a community, legitimately claiming the allegiance of its members, should draw back from asserting its claims against other communities. Yet, notwithstanding such unresolved tensions, the central conviction that an obligation was owed to a larger grouping by any smaller constituent element formed a perennial axiom of Gladstone's thought. Likewise the ideas clustering around humanity were constantly on his lips. Anything human, he explained in his article of 1887 called 'Universitas Hominum', was commendable. There was an underlying unity in all the affairs of men and women that called, at whatever level, for sympathetic interest in the concerns of others. Under the guidance of providence, human beings were moving towards a greater sense of universal solidarity. The greatest evidence of the tendency so far was the emergence of 'a common judgment among civilized mankind under the name of the Law of Nations'.[364] That was a profoundly welcome embodiment of collaboration in the widest of all groupings, the international arena. Politics, in Gladstone's mature view, was about the realization of human values in the setting of communities. The complex whole of Gladstonian Liberalism contained a synthesis of community and humanity at its heart.

[364] Gladstone, 'Universitas Hominum', pp. 592, 600.

# 10

# Conclusion

GLADSTONE WAS an heir to eighteen centuries of the intertwining of theological discussion with the literary legacy of antiquity. He was moulded by the interaction of Christianity and the classics. Religion was a constant preoccupation, regulating his daily life through worship, devotion, and self-examination, but it is important to insist that it formed his mind as well as his behaviour. Theology often took the lion's share of his reading. Consequently it is crucial in the case of Gladstone to heed the call of Frank M. Turner to integrate religion into the study of the Victorian intellectual world.[1] Christianity, in Gladstone's mature view, should blend into the other concerns of life: 'It must be filled full with human and genial warmth, in close sympathy with every true instinct and need of man, regardful of the just titles of every faculty of his nature, apt to associate with and make its own all, under whatever name, which goes to enrich the patrimony of the race.'[2] There must be no impassable barrier, in Gladstone's view, between religion and thought, or religion and society, or religion and politics. The classical inheritance, furthermore, remained normative for the statesman. Using it as a gauge for estimating the value of subsequent developments in western civilization, he expected it to teach weighty lessons about every aspect of life. Gladstone stood at an early stage in the process whereby the classics changed 'from culture to discipline', from the common stock of the social elite to the professional pursuit of specialist scholars. In his last years he was said to be the only man who ventured to quote Greek in the House of Commons.[3] Many of the commonplaces of antiquity remained his assumptions. So these twin influences, Christian and classical, shaped Gladstone's conceptualization of the public sphere. The two conditioning factors are inescapable in any scrutiny of the manuscripts that embody his early political thought. Likewise themes from religion and antiquity are interwoven in the public speeches of his final years. It would be as artificial to divorce Gladstone's political thought from his Christian faith and his classical studies as to put asunder these other two components of his mind.

---

[1] F. M. Turner, *Contesting Cultural Authority: Essays in Victorian Intellectual Life* (Cambridge, 1993), ch. 1.
[2] W. E. Gladstone, 'Place of Ancient Greece in the Providential Order' [1865], *Gleanings*, 7, p. 89.
[3] Christopher Stray, *Classics Transformed: Schools, Universities, and Society in England, 1830–1960* (Oxford, 1998), pp. 11, 66 n.

In each of these fields there was development in his thinking. Although never tempted to betray his allegiance to the Church of England, Gladstone several times altered his relationship to its constituent parts. The first move, as other commentators have already recognized, brought him away from evangelicalism to the species of High Churchmanship avowed in *Church Principles* (1840). This was an irenical and non-partisan version of the Orthodox position in the church. His theological stance became substantially that of Augustine, as it remained until the end of his life. The subsequent transitions, however, have been identified much less clearly. There was initially a discernible raising of the temperature of his churchmanship as, during the 1840s, in company with Henry Manning, he was swept into Tractarianism. His spirituality was quickened by a flush of enthusiasm for eucharistic devotion and the theology of Edward Pusey. Any further heightening of his churchmanship, however, was checked by a revulsion against the authoritarianism he perceived in the Roman Catholic Church. In the wake of the psychological crisis of 1850–1 he turned away from the narrowness of Puseyism to a sense of affinity with the incarnate Christ. The result was a tendency towards Broad Churchmanship that eventually bore fruit in the favourable review of *Ecce Homo* published in 1868. It is important to appreciate that Gladstone's theological development did not halt either in 1840 or in the later 1840s. While remaining committed to the Catholic inheritance of the Church of England, he added an appreciation of more liberal teaching. There was little that could legitimately be branded obscurantist about the position that he defended in the controversies of the 1870s to the 1890s. His apologetic was a product of a trend of thought just beginning to gather force at that time among younger clergymen, the liberal Catholicism of Charles Gore and his *Lux Mundi* circle that blended high ecclesiastical claims with wide intellectual and social sympathies. This was the grouping that was to go on to dominate the Church of England into the middle years of the twentieth century. By the end of his life Gladstone was religiously aligned with the future.

The statesman's classical studies also passed through different phases, though, in ploughing the lonely furrow of scholarship, he was far less identified with specific trends of thought in the wider world. During the 1830s he laid the philosophical foundations for his career by examining Plato, Cicero, and especially Aristotle in depth. As late as 1860 an edition of Aristotle's *Politics* remained a pet project. By that date, however, he had become immersed in the study of Homer. Gladstone's research was always self-consciously that of a gentleman amateur, often pursuing antiquarian detail for its own sake. Yet the choice of Homer was not simply the result of seeking an author to give him pleasure during leisure hours. Homer stood at the headwaters of western civilization, and by expounding the poet Gladstone hoped to turn the currents that flowed downwards from him into more salubrious channels. *Studies on Homer* (1858) was designed to bolster a conservative case in religion and politics alike. The grand purpose of one volume was to vindicate the idea of divine revelation against its detractors while the account of political institutions in another aimed to confute those who saw monarchy as an evil. By the time of *Juventus Mundi* (1869), however, Gladstone's approach to Homer had changed. Although the statesman did not wish to advertise his concessions, he tacitly admitted that the ground he had taken for the defence of revelation was in several respects mistaken. The case about constitutional matters was modified only slightly, but the analysis of ethnology and mythology was transformed. Gladstone showed in his altered account of the Olympian divinities a much more favourable view of humanity. There were to be lesser developments in his appreciation of Homer in later years, but the exaltation of humanity was the most significant of his shifts of opinion. Yet there was continuity in his classical scholarship, for the Greek gods and goddesses still seemed, in his very last months, to provide evidence that revelation had been delivered to the human race in its earliest days. Gladstone championed Hellenism, and especially Homerology, for its own sake, but at the same time he believed that the classics constituted a field on which the ideological battles of the nineteenth century could be fought and won.

Nobody has ever doubted that there was evolution in Gladstone's political opinions. He is a standing refutation of the adage that the older people grow the more conservative they become, for the convinced participant in Peel's revival of the Conservative party in the wake of the first Reform Act turned into the demagogic leader of the Liberal masses after the third. At first he believed deeply in tradition, rejoicing in 1841 in the deference of an old Hawarden cottager as 'one of the best forms of feudalism, still thank God! extremely common among us'.[4] He learned from Edmund Burke a passionately felt set of anti-revolutionary principles. Yet even his early Toryism included a theoretical commitment to concession that antedated his tutoring in pragmatism by Peel. Gladstone developed during the 1840s a commitment to liberty that was derived not just from the implementation of commercial freedom but also from aversion to the spiritual and political domineering of Rome. That is not to propose that the study of theology (or of Homer) was responsible for turning Gladstone into a Liberal: political experience had far more to do with the change than anything derived from his reading. But he emerged as Liberal leader with a formulated body of theory mingling some of his earliest convictions with ideas derived from more recent influences in other fields. The result was a complex amalgam that contained classic liberal individualist traits alongside some very different opinions. Morley could quote the statesman as saying in his last years that 'I am for the individual as against the state'. Yet in the same breath Gladstone announced that 'I am for old customs and traditions against needless change'.[5] Conservative characteristics could coexist with obviously liberal views because both found their place within a broader philosophy. Gladstone's mature political thought was a remarkably coherent system that was closely integrated into the wider body of his ideas.

Gladstonianism was, in reality, a version of communitarian political theory. The statesman's insistent sense of the priority of the community over the individual

---

[4] *D*, 10 July 1841.     [5] Morley, 1, p. 204.

derived chiefly from classical sources. It was the presumption of antiquity that human beings would inhabit a city-state in which face-to-face relations would prevail. Like many another in the early nineteenth century, Gladstone was also sharing in the romantic reaction against Enlightenment atomism. One of the chief early influences over him was Coleridge; and some of the themes in his youthful writing are paralleled in Hegel. Gladstone's rising vision of the Catholic church also affected his political thought, 'uplifting the ideas of the community in which we live'.[6] The result was the argument for corporate personality that forms the core of *The State in its Relations with the Church*, more implicitly in the first edition but, in answer to Macaulay, entirely explicitly in the subsequent revision. Belief in the common life as the antidote to self-ish wilfulness remained Gladstone's lodestar ever afterwards. His view was that sectional interests and whole classes would inevitably pursue their own goals, coming into conflict with each other and, if not checked, ultimately destabilizing the state. The task of the statesman was to discover a just balance between their self-interested points of view and so to reconcile each to each and each to all. This pattern applied to the internal affairs of the nation, but equally to the relations between different countries that were regulated by the concert of Europe. It also had implications for lesser communities. The integrity of the family, the primary community, must be respected by the state. Likewise the autonomy of the church must be guarded, just as, on the other hand, the state must not be allowed to fall into the clutches of an authoritarian church. Admiration for the municipality, the closest modern equivalent of the ancient *polis*, led Gladstone to emphasize the value of local self-government as a school of civic virtue. The civic humanist tradition, in its country Whig and American expressions, fostered in him a high view of participation in local institutions, as did de Tocqueville and the English historians. But Aristotelianism, seconded by a High Church ecclesiology, still provided the fertile soil for Gladstone's theory. Its fruit was the communitarianism that differentiated him so markedly from any stereotype of liberal individualism.

Gladstone's social analysis took further the intertwining of his classical and religious sources. It was one of the purposes of *Studies on Homer* to confute the idea of progress in any secular form that might threaten reliance on providence. The battle-ground for deciding the issue was ancient Greece. George Grote held the field with his assertion that civilized moral standards had emerged only as the result of rational enquiry in the classical period. Gladstone replied that, on the contrary, morality had generally declined between archaic and classical times, a standpoint he was still maintaining in his last published book on Homer in 1890. In his later years he held an ambivalent attitude towards progress. On the one hand, progress was certainly possible, as national wealth and constitutional reform bore witness; on the other, it was not assured. It depended on the continued acceptance of the Christian faith, the essential motor of progress. Without

---

[6] *Autobiographica*, p. 143.

'the doctrines of Christianity', its 'moral and spiritual fruits' were unobtainable.[7] Gladstone therefore saw peril in the contemporary situation. There was a decay of reverence, the mutual respect that was the bond of society, as a consequence of growing prosperity. The social elite was failing in its responsibilities of political leadership. Public virtue, as it was described in the civic humanist paradigm, was falling into abeyance, at least among the so-called 'classes', who revealed their decadence by ignoring the moral claims of Home Rule. But the potential remedy for their dereliction of duty was also under threat. It was religion that might prompt the privileged to action in an altruistic cause, but the Christian faith itself was at risk. Wealth had bred worldliness, a materialism that tempted those who enjoyed affluence and leisure to disbelief. Gladstone poured the vials of his wrath on T. H. Huxley so freely because he saw the scientist (and Unionist) as an agent of the forces that were undermining the one hope for the future. The statesman came forward to argue that holy scripture was an impregnable rock not only because he believed passionately in divine revelation but also because he supposed the profession of Christianity to be a necessary condition for the further progress of western civilization. His religious and socio-political diagnoses of contemporary ills meshed closely together.

The welfare of society, Gladstone assumed throughout his life, depended on the soundness of its religious beliefs. *The State in its Relations with the Church* was an early version of this conviction, contending that only if there was public confession of Anglicanism could government be conducted in a manner pleasing to the Almighty. When circumstances caused the disintegration of this state confessionalism, Gladstone retreated to the view that has just been discussed, the idea that the advance of civilization depended on the Christian faith. For this formative notion of cultural mission he was indebted to Ignaz von Döllinger, whom the statesman regarded as the foremost exemplar of wrestling with the intellectual and social implications of belief. Gladstone became convinced that it was folly for the church to retire into a spiritual ghetto, preoccupied introspectively with issues of ecclesiastical policy. By 1865 it was Gladstone's charge that Pusey was guilty of advocating 'a Christianity of isolation'.[8] Similarly it was one of his repeated charges against official Roman Catholic teaching that increasingly it put itself outside the mainstream of European thought. Nevertheless Gladstone owed a great intellectual debt to two other Catholics. The German J. A. Möhler gave him the idea that the consensus of all orthodox Christians in central doctrines bore witness to their correctness, a favoured weapon in his apologetic armoury; and J. H. Newman, though propounding a doctrine of development that Gladstone vigorously assailed, had helped form his devotional temper and gave him further arguments in defence of the faith. But the master to whom Gladstone turned again and again in such matters was Bishop Butler. It was Butler whose doctrine of probability roused Gladstone decisively against

---

[7] W. E. Gladstone, ' "Robert Elsmere": The Battle of Belief' [1888], *Later Gleanings*, p. 111.

[8] W. E. Gladstone, 'Place of Ancient Greece', p. 88.

Catholic teaching in the 1840s, and it was Butler whose method seemed the ultimate remedy for Huxley's agnosticism four decades later. Gladstone's last published work was on Butler because the bishop provided the tools for vindicating Christianity and thus saving civilization.

The influence of Butler has been associated by Boyd Hilton with persistent evangelical traits in Gladstone's later career. The statesman, on this account, was keenly conscious of sin, eager to deal with it by measures of atonement, and pleased to forge an alliance with evangelical Nonconformists.[9] There is much truth in this analysis. Gladstone could write of the need for a Conservative government to repent of its abominations in Ireland, could call for sanctions against Turkey 'until atonement has been made', and in 1879 composed an appreciative article on the rise of the evangelical movement.[10] Yet it has been shown here that during the 1830s he turned decisively against the content of his early evangelicalism. It was not just that he embraced baptismal regeneration, higher eucharistic beliefs, and the doctrine of apostolic succession, adding, as it were, to his juvenile deposit of faith. Rather he repudiated much of its content. He rejected the evangelical idea of assurance and he dismissed the Calvinistic notion that predestination was bound up with justification. He criticized the evangelicals' understanding of conversion, one of the shibboleths of the movement, and censured their version of the doctrine of the atonement, which was the kernel of their faith. Nor was this a passing phase. As late as 1894 he published an article on the atonement that was received by its evangelical reviewers as an onslaught on their position.[11] Any proper understanding of the atonement, Gladstone wrote in this article, is 'part and parcel of the Incarnation'.[12] The subordination of the atonement to the incarnation was near the heart of Gladstone's worldview. He was far from denying the idea of redemption through sacrifice, which was why associated themes found a place in his rhetoric, but the notion was not central, as it was among the evangelicals. The idea of incarnation had taken its place.

The reasons why the incarnation moved to the heart of Gladstone's intellectual system are not far to seek. The Tractarians, Gladstone's friend Henry Manning among them, bound the doctrine to eucharistic devotion, making it the theological principle that nurtured the spiritual life. Under their influence, the statesman came to see the Son of God as, in the words of Robert Wilberforce, the 'Pattern Man'. The subsequent transition to a broader theological position did not threaten the prominence of the incarnation in Gladstone's scheme. On the contrary, Christ as God incarnate was a model for the suffering, struggling,

[9] Boyd Hilton, *The Age of Atonement: The Influence of Evangelicalism on Social and Economic Thought, 1785–1865* (Oxford, 1988), pp. 340–61.

[10] W. E. Gladstone, 'Plain Speaking on the Irish Union', *Nineteenth Century*, 26 (1889), p. 6; id., *A Speech delivered at Blackheath, on Saturday, September 9th, 1876* (London, 1876), p. 24; id., 'The Evangelical Movement: Its Parentage, Progress, and Issue', *Gleanings*, 7, pp. 201–41.

[11] T. S. Childs in *Churchman*, 29 Dec. 1894, pp. 879–81. *British Weekly* quoted by A[lexander] G[ordon] in *Christian Life and Unitarian Herald*, 8 Sept. 1894, p. 427. GGM 1643.

[12] W. E. Gladstone, 'True and False Conceptions of the Atonement' [1894], *Later Gleanings*, p. 320.

tempted human beings such as Gladstone knew himself to be. Notwithstanding the varieties of human frailty, the Almighty had stamped his approval on the dignity of the race. Shortly afterwards the statesman began to recognize in the Greek cultural achievement, and especially its depiction of the body, a parallel appreciation of the worth of all things human. It was the providential role of ancient Greece to prepare the way for the incarnation. As Gladstone's opinions on Homer altered, so he came to see the same high estimate of humanity enshrined in the divinities of Olympus. He emerged sharing with the Greeks 'a profound reverence for human life and human nature'.[13] From the late 1860s onwards, during his years as Liberal leader, Gladstone's most animating principle was the transcendent value of men and women. All of them, throughout the world, shared a common set of noble qualities. Anybody was capable of a profound altruism; everybody deserved unmeasured sympathy in suffering. The result was the universal humanitarianism that marked Gladstone's later rhetoric. The campaigns on behalf of the Bulgarians and the Irish were rooted in the states-man's belief in a 'common humanity'. His style of compassionate Liberalism was an expression of an incarnational theology.

Consequently the legacy bequeathed by Gladstone to posterity blended the twin values of humanity and community. Whereas in Gladstone's thought the communitarianism came first and the importance of humanity was grafted into it, those who came after him tended to give the priority to the humanitarian approach. Yet the relevance of the community ideal was unquestionable in an urban age. A thinker who exemplifies the transmission of Gladstonianism to subsequent generations was Canon Henry Scott Holland, a frequent visitor to Hawarden during the statesman's lifetime and from 1911 Regius Professor of Divinity at Oxford. Scott Holland, as we have seen, shared Gladstone's liberal Catholicism, but he was also, from 1889, the leading spirit behind the Christian Social Union, the Anglican movement for the study of the problems of society. Although Scott Holland regretted Gladstone's lack of sympathy for the tenden-cies making towards socialism,[14] much of the canon's writing echoes Gladstonian themes. In the handbook he wrote for the Christian Social Union in 1911, Scott Holland presented the humanity of Christ (grounded in the incar-nation) as the rationale for a compassionate sense of social solidarity. Human betterment could be achieved only 'by the united action of the Community', whether the municipality or the state.[15] Humanity and community are almost as prominent as in Gladstone's thinking, but with the novel twist that turned the end into social reform and the means into collectivism. Scott Holland drew inspiration from F. D. Maurice, T. H. Green, and many others,[16] but the affin-ity with Gladstone is palpable. The continuities between Gladstonian Liberalism

---

[13] Gladstone, 'Place of Ancient Greece', p. 59.

[14] Henry Scott Holland, *Personal Studies* (London, 1905), p. 41.

[15] Henry Scott Holland, *Our Neighbours: A Handbook for the C.S.U.* (London, 1911), chs. 4, 9, p. 5, chs. 6, 7.

[16] Alan Wilkinson, *Christian Socialism: Scott Holland to Tony Blair* (London, 1998), ch. 2.

and the Edwardian progressivism that united New Liberals and the infant Labour party are increasingly coming into view, though the emphasis has hitherto been on the current of radicalism flowing at a popular level.[17] It needs to be added that among theorists of politics, especially those with a strong church allegiance in and about the Christian Social Union, there were powerful links as well. If Gladstone is seen as something very different from a liberal individualist, the similarities of his thinking to what came afterwards become much more obvious.

Scott Holland is by no means the only instance that can be cited in support of this case. The British idealist philosophers were generally Liberals in their politics. The reaction against individualism that they championed becomes more explicable when it is appreciated that their political leader was himself an opponent of its cruder expressions. Bernard Bosanquet, for instance, was in quest of a communal identity 'that links together all humanity'. The aspiration was thoroughly Gladstonian. Similarly Sidney Webb could write in 1908 that at the opening of the twentieth century everybody was 'thinking in communities'.[18] The strong humanitarian thread that runs through R. H. Tawney's *Equality* (1931) reflects the same theme in Gladstone's rhetoric; Tawney's idea of fellowship contains elements of Gladstone's notion of community; and even Tawney's opening chapter title, 'The Religion of Inequality', is a quotation from Gladstone.[19] William Temple's *Christianity and Social Order* (1942) upholds the same ideal of fellowship on the basis of an incarnational theology, contributing to the swelling tide of opinion that founded the welfare state.[20] Down to the time of Temple, Anglican theology was dominated by the motif of incarnation that had reigned since *Lux Mundi*, regularly stimulating fresh thought on the worth of humanity in a Christian community.[21] Nor was the Gladstonian legacy limited to the British Isles. In the United States the youthful Woodrow Wilson hung Gladstone's portrait over his desk, adopted his internationalism, and went on to propose the idea of a League of Nations.[22] Alan Bullock and Maurice Shock have pointed to the League and the United Nations that followed it as delayed expressions of Gladstone's beliefs.[23] His vision of a community of nations lived on in the century of Hitler and Stalin. Gladstone's political theory may have been the

[17] E. F. Biagini and A. J. Reid (eds.), *Currents of Radicalism: Popular Radicalism, Organised Labour and Party Politics in Britain, 1850–1914* (Cambridge, 1991), pp. 17–19.

[18] Bernard Bosanquet, *Essays and Reviews* (London, 1889), p. 195, and Sidney Webb, 'Twentieth Century Politics', in *The Basis and Policy of Socialism* (London, 1908), p. 78, both quoted by Sandra I. den Otter, *British Idealism and Social Explanation: A Study in Late Victorian Thought* (Oxford, 1996), p. 150.

[19] R. H. Tawney, *Equality* (London, 1931). Thomas Jones, 'Marginal Notes by Mr. Gladstone', *National Library of Wales Journal*, 4 (1945–6), p. 52.

[20] William Temple, *Christianity and Social Order* (Harmondsworth, 1942).

[21] A. M. Ramsey, *From Gore to Temple: The Development of Anglican Theology between 'Lux Mundi' and the Second World War, 1889–1939* (London, 1960).

[22] R. S. Baker, *Woodrow Wilson: Life and Letters*, 2 vols. (New York, 1927), 1, pp. 71, 87.

[23] Alan Bullock and Maurice Shock (eds.), *The Liberal Tradition from Fox to Keynes* (London, 1956), p. xl.

product of a classical learning and a Christian faith that both faded in Britain over the years after his death, but its themes long continued to leaven thinking about public affairs. He should be seen as an influential thinker of an age of incarnation that moulded minds long into the twentieth century.

# Bibliography

PRIMARY

*Manuscripts*

Gladstone of Fasque Papers, Fasque, Kincardineshire
Gladstone Papers, British Library, London
Glynne–Gladstone Manuscripts, Flintshire County Record Office, Hawarden
Hope-Scott Manuscripts, National Library of Scotland, Edinburgh
Keble Manuscripts, Keble College Library, Oxford
Pusey Papers, Pusey House Library, Oxford
Scott Papers, Pusey House Library, Oxford

*Published Works by W. E. Gladstone*

*Archaic Greece and the East* (London, 1892).
*Arthur Henry Hallam* (Boston, Mass., 1898).
*Bulgarian Horrors and the Question of the East* (London, 1876).
*The Church of England and Ritualism* (London, 1875).
*Church Principles considered in their Results* (London, 1840).
*The Eastern Crisis: A Letter to the Duke of Westminster, K.G.* (London, 1897).
*England's Mission* (London, 1878).
*Female Suffrage: A Letter from the Right Honourable W. E. Gladstone, M.P., to Samuel Smith, M.P.* (London, 1892).
'General Introduction', in G. C. Lorimer (ed.), *The People's Bible History* (London, 1896).
*Gleanings of Past Years, 1843-79,* 7 vols. (London, 1879).
*Homer* (London, 1878).
*Homeric Synchronism: An Enquiry into the Time and Place of Homer* (London, 1876).
*The Impregnable Rock of Holy Scripture,* revised and enlarged edn. (London, 1890).
*Juventus Mundi: The Gods and Men of the Heroic Age* (London, 1869).
*Landmarks of Homeric Study* (London, 1890).
*Later Gleanings* (London, 1897).
*Lessons in Massacre* (London, 1877).
*The Liberal Programme for Great Britain and Ireland* (London, 1887).
*A Manual of Prayers from the Liturgy arranged for Family Use* (London, 1845).
*The Odes of Horace translated into English* (London, 1894).
'On the Place of Homer in Classical Education and in Historical Inquiry', in *Oxford Essays* (London, 1857).
*The Parnell Commission and the Vote of Censure upon the Irish Members* (London, [1890]).
*Political Speeches in Scotland, March and April 1880* (Edinburgh, 1880).
*Political Speeches in Scotland, November and December 1879* (Edinburgh, 1879).
*Political Speeches in Scotland, November 1885,* revised edn. (London, 1886).

'Preface', in Heinrich Schliemann, *Mycenae* (London, 1878).

*The Present Mode of Governing Ireland* (London, 1887).

*The Psalter with a Concordance and Other Auxiliary Matter* (London, 1895).

(trans.) L. C. Farini, *The Roman State from 1815 to 1850*, 4 vols. (1851–54).

*Rome and the Newest Fashions in Religion* (London, 1875).

*A Speech delivered at Blackheath* (London, 1876).

*Speeches delivered in Scotland in 1890* (Edinburgh, [1890]).

*The Speeches and Public Addresses of the Right Hon. W. E. Gladstone*, ed. A. W. Hutton and H. J. Cohen, 2 vols. (London, 1892).

*Speeches of the Right Honourable William Ewart Gladstone, M.A., in South-West Lancashire, October, 1868* (Liverpool, n.d.).

*The State in its Relations with the Church*, 1st edn. (London, 1838); 2nd edn. (London, 1839); 3rd edn. (London, 1839); 4th edn., 2 vols. (London, 1841).

*Studies on Homer and the Homeric Age*, 3 vols. (Oxford, 1858).

*Studies Subsidiary to the Works of Bishop Butler* (Oxford, 1896).

*Substance of a Speech on the Motion of Lord John Russell for a Committee of the Whole House with a View to the Removal of the Remaining Jewish Disabilities* (London, 1848).

(ed.) *The Works of Joseph Butler, D.C.L.*, 2 vols. (Oxford, 1896).

(with Lord Lyttleton), *Translations*, 2nd edn. (London, 1863).

*Subsequently Published Writings by W. E. Gladstone*

*Correspondence on Church and Religion of William Ewart Gladstone*, ed. D. C. Lathbury, 2 vols. (London, 1910).

*The Gladstone Diaries*, ed. M. R. D. Foot and H. C. G. Matthew, 14 vols. (Oxford, 1968–94).

*Gladstone to his Wife*, ed. A. Tilney Bassett (London, 1936).

*Gladstone's Speeches: Descriptive Index and Bibliography*, ed. A. Tilney Bassett (London, 1916).

*The Prime Ministers' Papers: W. E. Gladstone: I: Autobiographica*, ed. John Brooke and Mary Sorensen (London, 1971).

*Special Aspects of the Irish Question* (London, 1912).

'Speeches and Pamphlets', St Deiniol's Library, Hawarden.

*Periodicals*

*Note*: Journal articles by Gladstone and his contemporaries are not itemized separately here. A full list of articles by Gladstone will be found under 'Publications' in the subject index to volume 14 of *The Gladstone Diaries*.

*The Contemporary Review*
*The Edinburgh Review*
*The English Review*
*The Eton Miscellany*
*Good Words*
*The Nineteenth Century*
*The North American Review*
*The Quarterly Review*
*The Times*

*Other Published Works*

ABBOTT, EVELYN, and LEWIS CAMPBELL, *The Life and Letters of Benjamin Jowett, M.A.*, 2 vols. (London, 1897).

ARNOLD, MATTHEW, *Culture and Anarchy* (London, 1869).

—— 'Dover Beach', *Poems: Lyric and Elegiac* (London, 1885).

—— 'On Translating Homer', *On the Classical Tradition*, ed. R. H. Super (Ann Arbor, Mich., 1960).

BAIN, ALEXANDER (ed.), *The Minor Works of George Grote* (London, 1875).

ARISTOTLE, *The Ethics of Aristotle*, trans. J. A. K. Thomson (Harmondsworth, 1955).

—— *The Politics*, trans. T. A. Sinclair (Harmondsworth, 1962).

BENTHAM, JEREMY, *A Fragment on Government*, ed. Wilfrid Harrison (Oxford, 1948).

BERNARD, J. H. (ed.), *The Works of Bishop Butler*, 2 vols. (London, 1900).

BLACKSTONE, WILLIAM, *Commentaries on the Laws of England*, 8th edn., 4 vols. (Oxford, 1778).

BURKE, EDMUND, *Reflections on the Revolution in France*, ed. C. C. O'Brien (Harmondsworth, 1968).

COLERIDGE, S. T., *Aids to Reflection* (London, 1825).

—— *On the Constitution of the Church and the State*, ed. John Colmer, *The Collected Works of Samuel Taylor Coleridge*, vol. 10 (London, 1976).

COX, G. W., *The Mythology of the Aryan Nations*, 2 vols. (London, 1870).

DENISON, S. C., *Is the Ballot a Mistake?* (London, 1838).

DE TOCQUEVILLE, ALEXIS, *Democracy in America*, ed. J. P. Mayer and Max Lerner (New York, 1966).

FALKENER, EDWARD, *Daedalus: Or the Causes and Principles of the Excellence of Greek Sculpture* (London, 1860).

FIGGIS, J. N., and R. V. LAURENCE (eds.), *Selections from the Correspondence of the First Lord Acton*, 1 (London, 1917).

GRAHAM, WILLIAM, *The Creed of Science: Religious, Moral and Social* (London, 1881).

GROTE, GEORGE, *History of Greece*, 12 vols. (London, 1846–56).

GROTE, HARRIET, *The Personal Life of George Grote* (London, 1873).

[HALLAM, A. H.], *Remains in Verse and Prose of Arthur Henry Hallam* (London, 1863).

HEGEL, G. W. F., *The Philosophy of Right*, ed. A. W. Wood (Cambridge, 1991).

HOLLAND, H. S., *Personal Studies* (London, 1905).

—— *The Optimism of Butler's 'Analogy'* (Oxford, 1908).

—— *Our Neighbours: A Handbook for the C.S.U.* (London, 1911).

HORSLEY, SAMUEL, 'A Dissertation on the Prophecies of the Messiah dispersed among the Heathen', in *Nine Sermons on the Nature of the Evidence by which the Fact of Our Lord's Resurrection is Established* (London, 1815).

HUTTON, W. H., (ed.) *Letters of William Stubbs, Bishop of Oxford, 1825–1901* (London, 1904).

HUXLEY, T. H., 'Mr. Gladstone and Genesis', in *Essays upon some Controverted Questions* (London, 1892).

JOHNSTON, J. O., *Life and Letters of Henry Parry Liddon, D.D., D.C.L., LL. D.* (London, 1904).

JOWETT, BENJAMIN, 'Natural Religion', in *The Epistles of St. Paul to the Thessalonians, Galatians and Romans*, 2 vols, 2nd edn. (London, 1859).

[KEBLE, JOHN], 'Gladstone—The State in its Relations with the Church', *British Critic and Quarterly Review*, 26 (1839).

KNOX, ALEXANDER, *Remains of Alexander Knox, Esq.*, 2 vols. (London, 1834).

LAING, S[AMUEL], *Modern Science and Modern Thought* (London, 1886).

——— *Problems of the Future and Essays* (London, 1889)

LA MENNAIS, FÉLICITÉ DE, *Essai sur l'indifférence en matière de religion*, 4 vols. (Paris, 1817–23).

LATHBURY, D. C., *Mr Gladstone* (London, 1907).

LECKY, W. E. H., *History of the Rise and Influence of the Spirit of Rationalism in Europe*, 2 vols. (London, 1865).

LEWIS, Sir G. C., *An Essay on the Influence of Authority in Matters of Opinion* (London, 1849).

LEWIS, Revd. Sir G. F., BART (ed.), *Letters of the Rt. Hon. Sir George Cornewall Lewis, Bart* (London, 1870).

LIDDON, H. P., *Forty Sermons on Various Subjects preached in the Cathedral Church of St. Paul, London* (London, 1886).

——— *Life of Edward Bouverie Pusey*, 4 vols., 4th edn. (London, 1898).

MANNING, H. E., *Sermons*, 4 vols. (London, 1842–50).

——— *The Unity of the Church* (London, 1842).

MANT, RICHARD, *An Appeal to the Gospel* (Oxford, 1812).

MARCH-PHILLIPPS, LISLE, and BERTRAM CHRISTIAN (eds.), *Some Hawarden Letters, 1878–1913* (London, 1917).

MAURICE, FREDERICK (ed.), *The Life of Frederick Denison Maurice*, 2 vols., 2nd edn. (London, 1884).

[MAX MÜLLER, FRIEDRICH], *The Life and Letters of the Rt. Hon. Friedrich Max Müller*, edited by his wife, 2 vols. (London, 1902).

MAX MÜLLER, FRIEDRICH, 'Comparative Mythology', in *Oxford Essays* (London, 1856).

——— *Lectures on the Science of Language*, 2 vols. [1861–4], 2nd edn. (London, 1871).

MILL, J. S., *On Liberty*, ed. Stefan Collini (Cambridge, 1989).

MORLEY, JOHN, *The Life of William Ewart Gladstone*, 3 vols. (London, 1903).

MUIR, WILLIAM, *A Critical History of the Language and Literature of Ancient Greece*, 4 vols. (London, 1850–53).

MÜLLER, C. O., *The History and Antiquities of the Doric Race*, trans. Henry Tufnell and G. C. Lewis, 2 vols. (Oxford, 1830).

NEWMAN, J. H., *Parochial Sermons*, 6 vols. (1835–42).

——— *A Letter addressed to His Grace the Duke of Norfolk on occasion of Mr. Gladstone's Recent Expostulation* (London, 1875).

——— *An Essay in Aid of a Grammar of Assent* [1870] (London, 1892).

OAKELEY, FREDERICK, *Sermons preached chiefly in the Chapel Royal at Whitehall* (Oxford, 1839).

ORNSBY, ROBERT, *Memories of James Robert Hope-Scott*, 2 vols. (London, 1884).

PALMER, WILLIAM, *A Treatise on the Church of Christ*, 2 vols., 3rd edn. (London, 1842).

*Plain Sermons by Contributors to 'Tracts for the Times'*, 10 vols. (London, 1839–48).

PURCELL, E. S., *Life of Cardinal Manning*, 2 vols. (London, 1895).

PUSEY, E. B., *Preface to the Fourth Edition of the 'Letter to the Right Rev. Father in God, Richard, Lord Bishop of Oxford'* (Oxford, 1840).

——— *Sermons during the Season from Advent to Whitsuntide*, 2nd edn. (Oxford, 1848).

RÉVILLE, ALBERT, *Prolegomena of the History of Religions* [1883], trans. A. S. Squire (London, 1884).

*Revised Report of the Proceedings on the 31st May, 1876, held in Celebration of the Hundredth Year of the Publication of the 'Wealth of Nations'* (London, 1876).

ROBBINS, A. F., *The Early Public Life of W. E. Gladstone* (London, 1894)

RUSKIN, JOHN, *Modern Painters, Volume III* [1856] (London, n. d.).

RUSSELL, G. W. E., *Mr. Gladstone's Religious Development* (London, 1899).

SHOETTGEN, CHRISTIAN, *Horae Hebraicae et Talmudicae . . . De Messia* (Dresden 1742).

STANLEY, A. P., *The Life and Correspondence of Thomas Arnold, D.D.*, 2 vols., 2nd edn. (London, 1844).

*Tracts for the Times*, 1, new edn. (London, 1838).

TUCKWELL, WILLIAM, 'Mr. Gladstone as Critic', in Sir Wemyss Reid (ed.), *The Life of William Ewart Gladstone* (London, 1899).

VON DÖLLINGER, J. J. I., *The Gentile and the Jew in the Courts of the Temple of Christ*, trans. N. Darnell, 2 vols. (London, 1862).

VON KOBELL, LOUISE, *Conversations with Dr. Dollinger*, trans. Katharine Gould (London, 1892).

WARD, [MARY A.], *A Writer's Recollections* (London, 1918).

WILBERFORCE, R. I., *The Doctrine of the Incarnation of Our Lord Jesus Christ in its Relation to Mankind and to the Church* (London, 1848).

—— *Sermons on the New Birth of Man's Nature* (London, 1850).

WILLIAMS, JOHN, *Homerus*, Part I (London, 1842).

—— *Primitive Tradition: A Letter to the Editor of the Edinburgh Review* (Edinburgh, 1843).

## SECONDARY SOURCES

*Note*: This list is highly selective, not even including all the items cited in the notes to the text.

*Books*

AVINERI, SHLOMO, and AVNER DE-SHALIT (eds.) *Communitarianism and Individualism* (Oxford, 1992).

BARKER, MICHAEL, *Gladstone and Radicalism: The Reconstruction of Liberal Policy in Britain, 1885–1894* (Brighton, 1975).

BEBBINGTON, DAVID, *Evangelicalism in Modern Britain: A History from the 1730s to the 1980s* (London, 1988).

—— *William Ewart Gladstone: Faith and Politics in Victorian Britain* (Grand Rapids, Mich., 1993).

—— and Roger Swift (eds.), *Gladstone Centenary Essays* (Liverpool, 2000).

BIAGINI, E. F., *Liberty, Retrenchment and Reform: Popular Liberalism in the Age of Gladstone* (Cambridge, 1992).

—— *Gladstone* (Houndmills, Basingstoke, 2000).

—— and A. J. REID (eds.), *Currents of Radicalism: Popular Radicalism, Organised Labour and Party Politics in Britain, 1850–1914* (Cambridge, 1991).

BOWE, MARIE CAMILLE, *Francis Rio: sa place dans le renouveau catholique en Europe (1797–1874)* (Paris, [1938]).

BRENT, RICHARD, *Liberal Anglican Politics: Whiggery, Religion and Reform, 1830–1841* (Oxford, 1987).

BRIGGS, ASA (ed.), *Gladstone's Boswell: Late Victorian Conversations by L. A. Tollemache and Other Documents* (Brighton, 1984).

BROWN, A. W., *The Metaphysical Society: Victorian Minds in Crisis, 1869–1880* (New York, 1947).

BURROW, J. W., *A Liberal Descent: Victorian Historians and the English Past* (Cambridge, 1981).

—— *Whigs and Liberals: Continuity and Change in English Political Thought* (Oxford, 1988).

BUTLER, PERRY, *Gladstone: Church, State and Tractarianism: A Study of his Religious Ideas and Attitudes, 1809–1859* (Oxford, 1982).

CANNON, GARLAND, *The Life and Mind of Oriental Jones: Sir William Jones, the Father of Modern Linguistics* (Cambridge, 1990).

CARPENTER, JAMES, *Gore: A Study in Liberal Catholic Thought* (London, 1960).

CHADWICK, OWEN, *From Bossuet to Newman*, 2nd edn. (Cambridge, 1987).

—— 'The Mind of the Oxford Movement', in *The Spirit of the Oxford Movement* (Cambridge, 1990).

—— *The Victorian Church*, 2 vols. (London, 1970).

CHECKLAND, S. G., *The Gladstones: A Family Biography, 1764–1851* (Cambridge, 1971).

CLARK, J. C. D., *English Society, 1688–1832* (Cambridge, 1985).

CLARKE, M. L., *Greek Studies in England, 1700–1830* (Cambridge, 1945).

—— *George Grote: A Biography* (London, 1962).

COLAIACO, J. A., *James Fitzjames Stephen and the Crisis of Victorian Thought* (London, 1983).

COLLINI, STEFAN, *Public Moralists: Political Thought and Intellectual Life in Britain* (Oxford, 1991).

CROSBY, T. L., *The Two Mr Gladstones: A Study in Psychology and History* (New Haven, Conn., 1997).

DEN OTTER, SANDRA I., *British Idealism and Social Explanation: A Study in Late Victorian Thought* (Oxford, 1996).

DERRÉ, JEAN-RENÉ, *Lamennais et ses amis et le mouvement des idées à l'époque romantique* (Paris, 1962).

DESMOND, ADRIAN, *Huxley: From Devil's Disciple to Evolution's High Priest* (London, 1997).

DICKINSON, H. T., *Liberty and Property: Political Ideology in Eighteenth-Century Britain* (London, 1977)

DRU, ALEXANDER, *The Contribution of German Catholicism* (New York, 1963).

DUGMORE, C. W., *Eucharistic Doctrine in England from Hooker to Waterland* (London, 1942).

FABER, GEOFFREY, *Jowett: A Portrait with Background* (London, 1957).

FELDMAN, BURTON, and R. D. RICHARDSON, *The Rise of Modern Mythology, 1680–1860* (Bloomington, Ind., 1972).

FORBES, DUNCAN, *The Liberal Anglican Idea of History* (Cambridge, 1952).

FRANCIS, PETER (ed.), *The Gladstone Umbrella* (Hawarden, Flintshire, 2001).

GARNETT, JANE, 'Bishop Butler and the *Zeitgeist*: Butler and the Development of Christian Moral Philosophy in Victorian Britain', in Christopher Cunliffe (ed.), *Joseph Butler's Moral and Religious Thought: Tercentenary Essays* (Oxford, 1992).

HÄRDELIN, ALF, *The Tractarian Understanding of the Eucharist* (Uppsala, 1965).

HELMSTADTER, R. J., 'Conscience and Politics: Gladstone's First Book', in B. L. Kinzer (ed.), *The Gladstonian Turn of Mind: Essays Presented to J. B. Conacher* (Toronto, 1985).

HILTON, BOYD, 'Gladstone's Theological Politics', in Michael Bentley and John Stevenson (eds.), *High and Low Politics in Modern Britain* (Oxford, 1981).

—— *The Age of Atonement: The Influence of Evangelicalism on Social and Economic Thought, 1785–1865* (Oxford, 1988).

HINCHLIFF, PETER, *Frederick Temple, Archbishop of Canterbury: A Life* (Oxford, 1998).

JAGGER, P. J., *Gladstone: The Making of a Christian Politician: The Personal Religious Life and Development of William Ewart Gladstone, 1809–1832* (Allison Park, Penn., 1991).

—— (ed.) *Gladstone, Politics and Religion* (London, 1985).

—— (ed.) *Gladstone* (London, 1998).

JENKINS, ROY, *Gladstone* (London, 1995).

JENKINS, T. A., *Gladstone, Whiggery and the Liberal Party, 1874–1886* (Oxford, 1988).

KOLB, JACK (ed.), *The Letters of Arthur Henry Hallam* (Columbus, Ohio, 1981).

LUBENOW, W. C., *Parliamentary Politics and the Home Rule Crisis: The British House of Commons in 1886* (Oxford, 1988).

MACINTIRE, C. T., *England Against the Papacy, 1858-1861: Tories, Liberals and the Overthrow of Papal Temporal Power During the Italian Risorgimento* (Cambridge, 1982).

MACINTYRE, ALASDAIR, *After Virtue: A Study in Moral Theory* (London, 1981).

MAGNUS, PHILIP, *Gladstone: A Biography* (London, 1963).

MATHER, F. C., *High Church Prophet: Bishop Samuel Horsley (1733–1836) and the Caroline Tradition in the Later Georgian Church* (Oxford, 1992).

MATTHEW, H. C. G., Gladstone, Vaticanism and the Question of the East', in Derek Baker (ed.), *Religious Motivation: Biographical and Sociological Problems for the Church Historian*, Studies in Church History, 15 (Oxford, 1978).

—— 'Gladstone, Evangelicalism and "The Engagement" ', in Jane Garnett and Colin Matthew (eds.), *Revival and Religion Since 1700: Essays for John Walsh* (London, 1993).

—— *Gladstone, 1809–1898* (Oxford, 1997).

MOSSNER, E. C., *Bishop Butler and the Age of Reason* (New York, 1936).

MYRES, J. L., 'Gladstone's View of Homer', in *Homer and his Critics* (London, 1958).

NEWSOME, DAVID, *The Parting of Friends* (London, 1966).

—— *Two Classes of Men: Platonism and English Romantic Thought* (London, 1964).

NICHOLLS, DAVID, 'Gladstone and the Anglican Critics of Newman', in J. D. Bastable (ed.), *Newman and Gladstone Centennial Essays* (Dublin, 1978).

NOCKLES, P. B., *The Oxford Movement in Context: Anglican High Churchmanship, 1760–1857* (Cambridge, 1994).

PARRY, J. P., *Democracy and Religion: Gladstone and the Liberal Party, 1867–1875* (Cambridge, 1986).

RAMSEY, A. M., *From Gore to Temple: The Development of Anglican Theology Between* Lux Mundi *and the Second World War* (London, 1960).

REARDON, BERNARD, *Liberalism and Tradition: Aspects of Catholic Thought in Nineteenth-Century France* (Cambridge, 1975).

—— *Religious Thought in the Victorian Age: A Survey from Coleridge to Gore* (London, 1980).

ROE, W. G., *Lamennais and England: The Reception of Lamennais's Religious Ideas in England in the Nineteenth Century* (Oxford, 1966).

ROGERSON, JOHN, *Old Testament Criticism in the Nineteenth Century: England and Germany* (London, 1984).

SCHREUDER, D. M., 'Gladstone and the Conscience of the State', in P. T. Marsh (ed.), *The Conscience of the Victorian State* (Hassocks, Sussex, 1979).

—— 'History and the Utility of Myth: Homer's Greece in Gladstonian Liberalism', in Francis West (ed.), *Myth & Mythology*, Occasional Paper No. 7, Papers from the Australian Academy of the Humanities Symposium 1987 (n.p., n.d.).

SHANNON, RICHARD, *Gladstone*, 2 vols. (London, 1982, 1999).

SMITH, F. B., *The Making of the Second Reform Bill* (Cambridge, 1966).

SOLOVIOVA, TATIA, 'Anglican–Orthodox Dialogue in the Nineteenth Century and Gladstone's Interest in the Reunion of Christendom', in Peter Francis (ed.), *The Gladstone Umbrella* (Hawarden, Flintshire, 2001).

STEELE, E. D., *Palmerston and Liberalism, 1855–1965* (Cambridge, 1991).

STOCKING, G. W., JR, *Victorian Anthropology* (New York, 1987).

STRAY, CHRISTOPHER, *Classics Transformed: Schools, Universities and Society in England, 1830-1960* (Oxford, 1998).

STRONG, ROWAN, *Alexander Forbes of Brechin: The First Tractarian Bishop* (Oxford, 1995).

TAYLOR, CHARLES, *Hegel and Modern Society* (Cambridge, 1979).

TURNER, F. M., *Between Science and Religion: The Reaction to Scientific Naturalism in Late Victorian England* (New Haven, Conn., 1974).

—— *The Greek Heritage in Victorian Britain* (New Haven, Conn., 1981).

—— *Contesting Cultural Authority: Essays in Victorian Intellectual Life* (Cambridge, 1993).

VIDLER, A. R., *The Orb and the Cross: A Normative Study in the Relations of Church and State with Reference to Gladstone's Early Writings* (London, 1945).

—— *Prophecy and Papacy: A Study of Lamennais, the Church and the Revolution* (London, 1954).

VINCENT, JOHN, *The Formation of the British Liberal Party, 1859-1868* (London, 1966).

—— *Disraeli* (Oxford, 1990).

WARD, W. R., *Victorian Oxford* (London, 1965).

WARDMAN, H. W., *Renan: historien philosophe* (Paris, 1979).

WORMELL, DEBORAH, *Sir John Seeley and the Uses of History* (Cambridge, 1980).

### Articles

ALLEN, LOUIS, 'Gladstone et Montalembert: correspondance inédite', *Revue de Littérature Comparée*, 30 (1956).

BELLMER, E. H., 'The Statesman and the Opthalmologist: Gladstone and Magnus on the Evolution of Human Colour Vision, One Small Episode of the Nineteenth-Century Darwinian Debate', *Annals of Science*, 56 (1999).

BEST, G. F. A., 'The Evangelicals and the Established Church in the Early Nineteenth Century', *Journal of Theological Studies*, NS, 10 (1959).

CHADWICK, OWEN, 'Young Gladstone and Italy', *Journal of Ecclesiastical History*, 30 (1979).

CLAYTON, RUTH, 'W. E. Gladstone: An Annotation Key', *Notes and Queries*, 246 (2001).

DEWEY, C. J., 'Celtic Agrarian Legislation and the Celtic Revival: Historicist Implications of Gladstone's Irish and Scottish Land Acts, 1870–86', *Past & Present*, 64 (1974).

ERB, P. C., 'Gladstone and German Liberal Catholicism', *Recusant History*, 23 (1997).

LLOYD-JONES, HUGH, 'Gladstone on Homer', *Times Literary Supplement*, 3 Jan. 1975, pp. 15–17, repr. in Lloyd-Jones, *Blood for the Ghosts* (London, 1982).

LYNCH, M. J., 'Was Gladstone a Tractarian? W. E. Gladstone and the Oxford Movement, 1833–45', *Journal of Religious History*, 8 (1975).

MATTHEW, H. C. G., 'Disraeli, Gladstone, and the Politics of Mid-Victorian Budgets', *Historical Journal*, 22 (1979).

POINTON, MARCIA, 'W. E. Gladstone as an Art Patron and Collector', *Victorian Studies*, 19 (1975).

POWELL, JOHN, 'Small Marks and Instinctual Responses: A Study in the Use of Gladstone's Marginalia', *Nineteenth-Century Prose*, 19 (n.d.).

RAMM, AGATHA, 'Gladstone's Religion', *Historical Journal*, 28 (1985).

—— 'Gladstone as Man of Letters', *Nineteenth-Century Prose*, 17 (1989–90).

SCHREUDER, D. M., 'Gladstone and Italian Unification: The Making of a Liberal?', *English Historical Review*, 85 (1970).

—— 'Gladstone as "Trouble Maker": Liberal Foreign Policy and the German Annexation of Alsace-Lorraine, 1870–1871', *Journal of British Studies*, 17 (1978).

VON ARX, J. P., 'Archbishop Manning and the *Kulturkampf*', *Recusant History*, 21 (1992).

# Index

9 780199 267651